RHC

Handbook of Soviet and East European Films and Filmmakers

Handbook of Soviet and East European Films and Filmmakers

Edited by Thomas J. Slater

Greenwood Press
NEW YORK • WESTPORT, CONNECTICUT • LONDON

Library of Congress Cataloging-in-Publication Data

Handbook of Soviet and East European films and filmmakers / edited by Thomas J. Slater.
     p. cm.
  Includes bibliographical references and index.
  ISBN 0-313-26239-X (alk. paper)
  1. Motion pictures—Soviet Union—History. 2. Motion pictures—Europe, Eastern—History. 3. Motion picture producers and directors—Soviet Union—Biography. 4. Motion picture producers and directors—Europe, Eastern—Biography. I. Slater, Thomas J.
PN1993.5.R9H28   1992
791.43′0947—dc20   91-9255

British Library Cataloguing in Publication Data is available.

Copyright © 1992 by Thomas J. Slater

All rights reserved. No portion of this book may be reproduced, by any process or technique, without the express written consent of the publisher.

Library of Congress Catalog Card Number: 91-9255
ISBN: 0-313-26239-X

First published in 1992

Greenwood Press, 88 Post Road West, Westport, CT 06881
An imprint of Greenwood Publishing Group, Inc.

Printed in the United States of America

The paper used in this book complies with the Permanent Paper Standard issued by the National Information Standards Organization (Z39.48-1984).

10 9 8 7 6 5 4 3 2 1

CONTENTS

	Preface	vii
	Introduction	xi
CHAPTER 1	The Soviet Union *Thomas J. Slater*	1
CHAPTER 2	Poland *Bruce R. S. Litte*	69
CHAPTER 3	Czechoslovakia *Thomas J. Slater*	129
CHAPTER 4	Yugoslavia *Daniel J. Goulding*	185
CHAPTER 5	Hungary *Tomasz Warchoł*	229
CHAPTER 6	East Germany *Judith Roof*	275
CHAPTER 7	Romania *Judith Roof*	309
CHAPTER 8	Bulgaria *Bruce R. S. Litte*	343

APPENDIX	*A Chronology of Major Historical, Cultural and Film Events in the Soviet Union and Eastern Europe, 1890–1990*	377
	Subject Index	389
	Film Index	405
	About the Contributors	445

PREFACE

The idea for this project occurred in approximately late 1986 while I was working on the reference book *Milos Forman: A Bio-Bibliography* (also published by Greenwood Press, 1987). It wasn't difficult to notice that anyone wanting to do research in the area of Soviet and Eastern European film would have to do a lot of scrambling around to find the basic, necessary resources. Therefore, my goal was to fill this gap in cinema scholarship, and I believe this volume goes a long way towards doing so. With it, students and professional scholars should be able to quickly identify sources and films for studying major figures, genres, and eras in any of the countries included. In addition, the historical essays for each country provide some initial considerations on the significance of various figures and films. Finally, the historical chronology at the end of the volume provides a blending of the political and cultural developments important to film throughout the region.

Prior to 1986, only a few volumes provided comprehensive and focused discussions of Soviet and Eastern European film history. These included Antonín and Mira Liehm's *The Most Important Art: Eastern European Film After 1945* (1977), Michael Jon Stoil's *Cinema Beyond the Danube: The Camera and Its Politics* (1974), and *Politics, Art and Commitment in the East European Cinema*, edited by David W. Paul (1983). In 1989, *Post New Wave Cinema in the Soviet Union and Eastern Europe*, edited by Daniel J. Goulding, was added to this brief list. Therefore, it is not surprising that many of the writers in this volume have continued to use those works.

However, even aside from the dramatic changes in the political and economic structures of these formerly Communist countries that occurred during 1989–1990, a continual updating of developments in their film industries would be necessary. For the truth is that the film artists of the Soviet Union and Eastern Europe have a long, rich history of quality productions. Even under the oppressive political and cultural policies of Josef Stalin, these nations were producing far more accomplished works than were ever given appropriate recognition in the West. Unfortunately, even this book can give such acknowledgment to only a limited extent. For some periods in some countries, there were simply too many noteworthy accomplishments to be commented on adequately within the space available, and this consideration involves only fiction films. Great achievements in documentaries, animation, and shorts have also received only brief mention or none at all in this volume. That is why this effort can only be considered a starting point; the works cited in the bibliographies must serve as an addendum, and even those lists had to be selective. But this book still constitutes a very necessary starting point. None of the other volumes in this area, being presented entirely in essay form, were intended to be reference works and therefore could not have been as comprehensive. While providing excellent analysis, they are less useful for scholars wishing to do more research in this area.

All of these works, however, can offer only a glimpse of the quality achieved by the often courageous and always committed film artists from these lands. As indicated earlier, it is possible to say that even as early as the end of Stalin's reign (1953), film art had progressed so far in the Soviet Union and Eastern Europe that it would have been impossible for it ever to have retreated permanently. At a December 1990 symposium on Soviet film in the thirties, for example, David Bordwell summarized the meeting's lessons by observing that it is perhaps more important to begin focusing on the continuities between Soviet film in the twenties and thirties than to keep re-emphasizing the traditional split between the avant-garde and socialist realism. Unquestionably, films made before the strict imposition of Party cultural doctrines in the mid-thirties were far more accomplished works. Yet they established the genres, characterizations, plot structures, and ideological framework that continued during the more authoritarian times. Furthermore, without more thorough studies of Soviet films and directors under Stalin, gauging the achievements and struggles of the artists in concert with or contrary to the regime's doctrines remains impossible. A similar situation exists in other countries. A case in point is Czechoslovakia, where directors like Otakar Vávra and Martin Frič would repeatedly claim their allegiance to each new regime (including the Nazis) in order to keep working. Surely, their goals were more artistic than ideological and their efforts, regardless of quality, raise important questions about art and morality under totalitarian regimes. For filmmakers are in a unique situation. Without access to the technology and materials needed, their work will never exist, and when those items are completely controlled by the state, their choices are reduced to the very basic level of whether or not to continue working. Therefore, even their constant production of works deemed "acceptable" by the regimes in power cannot be understood simply as works that supported those regimes.

That is another reason why this book was necessary. For the achievements realized under Stalinism and its successors were not merely cinematic successes, but also triumphs of the human spirit that have received too little recognition. For decades, as America strutted its freedom in peacock fashion before the Communist countries, it still paid scant attention in either its theaters or its universities to what the filmmakers from those nations were producing. Such hypocrisy could only have the effect of discouraging dictators from allowing free expression and limiting Americans' understanding of others. How much more useful it would have been to let Stalin, Brezhnev, and their puppets know loudly and clearly that their efforts were doing nothing to squelch the voices of freedom.

Therefore, although some would argue that since these films represent a now-completed historical era, they no longer require attention, I would respond that they have still not received the attention they deserve. Also, since I believe that Soviet and Eastern European film would have continued to progress regardless of the political systems in power, it will be impossible to understand where these national cinemas go in the future without having knowledge of their historical context. Certainly, as a people changes, so does its art, and thus film is one of the most accessible means for understanding a nation's character. Scholars who wish to continue keeping up to date with developments in these areas can do so through such journals as *Soviet Film, Hungarofilm,* and *Czechoslovak Film,* all of which have so far been available free of charge. Addresses for these journals are available in the back of the annual *International Film Guide,* which is also cited by several of the contributing authors here. Readers who scan the bibliographies provided with each national chapter will also notice that several American and British journals also provide information on important developments on a more irregular basis. By looking at the films from these countries, it is easy to conclude that Americans have spent the twentieth century understanding too little about the sufferings and triumphs of the Soviet and Eastern European peoples. In this era of radical change, as those people search for ways to deal with economic hardships and ethnic conflicts, it is even more important to develop an understanding of what is going on and how the West should respond. The West should also be looking at itself in search of ways for making these films more accessible to millions and instilling a popular desire to see them.

At this same time, I would like to make a personal appeal for a greater openness on the part of the U.S. immigration services as well. A major delay in completing this work resulted because officials barred my colleague, Gautum Kundu, an excellent film scholar, from completing the chapters he was to have contributed after more than a year of research. During this time, it seems that Dr. Kundu's only offense was to have all his required paperwork completed on time while also coping with significant health problems for some of his family members. East or West, bureaucracy always causes ridiculous and unnecessary hardships.

These problems were far more troublesome to Dr. Kundu than myself, since I was fortunate enough to have Daniel J. Goulding and Tomasz Warchol take over his chapters. Both came in on very short notice, simply asked what was needed, and produced excellent contributions. Similarly, my other contributors, Judith Roof and Bruce R. S. Litte, dedicated great amounts of time and talent to producing quality work. All of the writers also responded positively to all suggested changes, though it sometimes gave them an extra burden that they could hardly afford to take on. For all their work, they have my deepest thanks.

Following a brief introductory survey, the eight chapters of this volume cover film in the Soviet Union, Poland, Czechoslovakia, Yugoslavia, Hungary, East Germany, Romania, and Bulgaria. Each chapter begins with a historical and analytical survey of the film industry and artistry, with reference to filmmakers and films of particular significance. A bibliography of sources cited completes this narrative section. Because of the difficulties in obtaining research materials from some Eastern European countries, some contributors were less able than others to utilize journal and review sources from the relevant countries. Biographical notes on major figures and chronologies of major films follow each chapter. For some countries these materials were necessarily restricted to the post-World War II period. Directors figure most prominently in the biographical entries, but there are also entries for actors and actresses, writers, cinematographers, designers, producers and administrators, and theorists and critics.

The Biographical Sketches and Selective Filmographies are mutually cross-indexed employing a system of asterisks largely devised by Bruce R. S. Litte, to whom I give extra thanks. Abbreviations utilized in the filmographies are as follows: d = director; a.d. = assistant director; sw = screenwriter; au = author of original literary source; c = cinematographer; m = music composed by; with = with the following actors. Other credits occasionally noted, such as costume or set designers, are clearly indicated as such. For each film, we have tried to include as much information as possible, including the production studio and length, though this information was infrequently available. Sometimes the length is stated in meters and sometimes in minutes.

Finally, I would like to give heartfelt thanks to Dr. Steven P. Hill of the University of Illinois for his proofreading and suggestions in relation to my chapters on the Soviet Union and Czechoslovakia and to Pavel Kvetko at the University of Pittsburgh for adding diacritical markings to the Czechoslovakia chapter and valuable suggestions for emphasizing the contributions of Slovak filmmakers. Unfortunately, there was, once again, not enough room to incorporate all of his suggestions. I also need to thank Marilyn Brownstein of Greenwood Press for her enormous patience, assistance, and friendliness throughout the long work on this project. I believe it is time now to send it out to begin the work it needs to do.

Thomas J. Slater
Indiana, Pennsylvania

INTRODUCTION

Now that the Soviet Union and the Eastern European nations are no longer under complete Communist control, it is a good time to begin summarizing what was achieved by the filmmakers working under these regimes. Neither this introduction nor this book is intended to provide a complete or final summary, but rather to suggest some basic ideas and materials as starting points for more intensive investigations. The outcome, somewhere down the road, will, it is hoped, be a wider understanding of what can be learned from this now bygone era of socialist film, a basis for comprehending the evolution of these national cinemas, and new insights on American cinema through comparisons.

The role of art as a servant of state goals was always a staple of social policy in Soviet Bloc countries. Vladimir Lenin stated that for the Communists film was the most important art, and Soviet directors such as the great Sergei Eisenstein sought to use their art for the state. Soviet film historian Jay Leyda writes, "The purposive direction of the spectator's emotion is a social responsibility— in time of peace as well as of war. This social function . . . underlines every word of Eisenstein's film theory" (Eisenstein, *Sense,* viii). Under state socialism, contemporary East European filmmakers appeared to share Eisenstein's beliefs. Writing about two excellent productions from the early eighties, David W. Paul states that they both possess "a profound commitment to the proposition that film, as an art, has a vital sociopolitical function to perform" ("Introduction," 1). Paul further comments, "In the Hungary of the early 1980s, the artist is substantially freer than he was thirty years earlier, but he is by no means independent of his patron, the socialist state. This is the subtle implication underlying the universality of [István Szabó's] *Mephisto,* and it is this allusive subtlety that marks the film as East European" ("Introduction," 2). Thus, in *Mephisto,* Szabó presents a story with which he can identify, about an artist who has paid the price of freedom in order to be able to create.

But for East European filmmakers, this trade had to occur. Czech émigré director Miloš Forman put the case very clearly:

All you need is a pencil and paper and you can write a book. And if it's published today or tomorrow or in ten years or fifty years or a hundred years, it's still the book which you wrote and made. But if you write an opera, and you don't have means to hire singers, rent a theatre, hire an orchestra, director, build the sets, it will never be done. The same is with film. You can have a script, but if you don't find the millions of dollars to hire a cameraman, buy raw stock, hire actors, find locations, and pay everybody, and shoot the film and edit it, it doesn't exist. Your effort doesn't exist. So, especially in these areas, you are very much depending on the wide open mindedness of those who control the money, those who are willing and capable to finance your artistic effort. (Slater, "Part I," 8–9)

Yet, during the past four decades, great films have been consistently coming out of East Europe. Paul's statement that Soviet Bloc artists were freer in the eighties than ever before is certainly true. But this development represented not a change in the artists' relationship to the state, but only an evolution in the way socialism controlled artists.

Under Josef Stalin, the Soviet Union adopted the theory of "socialist realism" as the official state formula for works of art. The Cultural Expert to the Soviet Central Committee, Andrei A. Zhdanov, outlined the policy at the First Congress of Soviet Writers in 1934 when he said, "the truthfulness and historical concreteness of the artistic portrayal should be combined with the ideological remolding and education of the laboring people in the spirit of socialism" (Liehm and Liehm, 433). Stalin supported this philosophy when he stated, "The writer is the engineer of the soul" (Haraszti, 129), a compliment which he used to define the artist as someone meant to shape public consciousness along party lines while also limiting him or her to the status of just another organized professional. The result in the Soviet Union from the early thirties to the late fifties was the production of boring films that adhered strictly to Party lines and stereotypical portrayals.

In the eighties, East European films were far more interesting, but the states' commitment to socialist realism had not diminished. Early in that decade, Hungarian cultural spokesperson Gyorgy Aczel stated, "Such responsible intellectual action derived from sizing up the situation with a sense of realism, such a creation of values, shaping people and their thinking, is needed more than ever" (Haraszti 124–25). Haraszti explains how the dictates of modern socialist realism allowed for greater artistic freedom:

Progressive censorship does not demand from us a vision of the perfect society, or even evidence of ideological fealty, but rather proof of sincere participation. Its chief wish is that social unity be preserved. Its tolerance, although not unlimited, is considerable. Its scope is determined not by autocratic fiat but by the flexibility of minds that are willing to cooperate. Its slogan is: "He who is not against us is with us." It is like an empty sack that artists with a secure existence fill with anything that will not burst it. (79)

Thus it is possible to conclude that the majority of East European films, regardless of their complexity, quality, or view of socialist life, still served the state. As

Haraszti says, "Art, by its very existence, can only affirm the system—whether capitalist or socialist—that guarantees its survival" (81). Throughout this century, Soviet and East European filmmakers simply exchanged freedom for security. Like the lead character in *Mephisto,* he or she was willing to sacrifice to maintain the right to create.

But despite this "tyranny," great films kept emerging from Soviet Bloc countries, films that are often far more challenging in every way than the majority of pictures produced in the West and, almost always, if only by requirement, show far more social consciousness. Additionally, at times, circumstances worked out in such a way that a nation's films could go beyond what the state really wished to allow. Miloš Forman says of Czech filmmakers in the sixties, "As is true in socialist societies, you don't feel any commercial pressure, and now we were really excited that we would get rid of the ideological pressure. ... For a while it was that way. It was actually an ideal situation for a filmmaker" (Slater, "Part II," 9). Antonín J. and Mira Liehm state that the relationship between politics and art in a nationalized film industry is sometimes the industry's bane and sometimes its boon (2).

But now it will be neither, since this relationship no longer exists. Therefore, commentators must remember Haraszti's statement that *all* art implicitly supports the system that helps produce it, whether capitalist or socialist, and is similarly limited by that system. Thus the editor of *Soviet Film* has complained,

Soviet film-makers have recently abrogated Socialist Realism. In words, that is. But in reality, Socialist Realism continues to produce its crop of canned "educating" art. [Our best films] are swamped by the flood of "commercialized," stupid, incoherent films pandering to primitive tastes. What is worse, they are far from innocuous in terms of the ecology of our souls, our culture. ("From the Editor's")

In this respect, perhaps Soviet Bloc films challenged their limits even more frequently, and in more meaningful ways, than did those from other nations in recent years.

But if the filmmaker does not draw on the resources of the social system, he or she will cease to be an artist. Unlike the writer, the filmmaker must depend on outside support. Therefore, whatever system they live in, conscientious filmmakers, as Miloš Forman states, have only one real choice: "you have to fight for your own vision. And you have to fight people whose vision is often very limited because they are not artists. And it doesn't make any difference if it's an emperor or if it's a state-run film studio or a state-run theatre or if it's a president of a major studio in Hollywood" (Slater, "Part I," 10). Thus, for Soviet and East European filmmakers, the fight has not ended, it's merely changed, and they will certainly continue producing great films. There will still be more lessons to learn from them, for these are artists who know how to fight.

WORKS CITED

Eisenstein, Sergei. *The Film Sense*. Jay Leyda, ed. New York: Harcourt Brace Jovanovich, 1975.

"From the Editor's Point of View." *Soviet Film* 10 (1989):8.

Haraszti, Miklos. *The Velvet Prison: Artists Under State Socialism*. New York: Basic Books, 1987.

Liehm, Antonín J., and Mira Liehm. *The Most Important Art: Eastern European Film After 1945*. Berkeley: University of California Press, 1977.

Paul, David W., ed. *Politics, Art, and Commitment in the East European Cinema*. New York: St. Martin's, 1983.

Slater, Thomas J. "Miloš Forman: An Interview, Part I." *Post Script* 4.3 (Spring–Summer 1985):1–15.

———. "Miloš Forman: An Interview, Part II." *Post Script* 5.1 (Fall 1985):2–16.

Handbook of Soviet and East European Films and Filmmakers

1

Thomas J. Slater

THE SOVIET UNION

The history of Soviet film is one of a struggle for truth—for the right of the individual filmmaker to create a work that presents reality honestly according to his or her own vision. The same struggle, of course, has taken place in all of the Soviet Bloc countries, and at various times filmmakers in each of these countries have won temporary victories. Soviet filmmakers have also enjoyed such periods of success, however brief, but until recently their hopes had always been crushed. The reason was that a struggle naturally has two sides, and the filmmakers' opponent had the power to enforce its views since the artists had to depend upon this adversary for their very existence. Not only did they depend upon it, the great directors of sixty years ago actually created it in calling for state control and voluntarily giving themselves over to it. They "dug their own graves. They themselves asked for the Party to take complete control of their artistic work, the result of which was eventually suicide" (Marshall, 37). Thus the state was the source of both the artists' sustenance and their despair. Most importantly, it believed that it had the force of history on its side and it cared nothing for art.

What the artists gained for their forfeiture of artistic control was freedom from box-office pressures and access to all the materials and technology necessary for cinema. That was the idea in theory. In reality, tight ideological controls kept film production down, falling to as low as ten films a year in the final years of Josef Stalin's reign (1927–1953) and also kept Soviet technology lagging behind the West's. In return for this "freedom," the state merely expected to receive films that would serve its purposes. That almost sounds like a fair exchange, especially since the state's basic interest was the welfare of the entire population, which included the filmmakers themselves. The state could argue that in attempting to control filmmakers, it was ultimately trying to help them, just as a loving parent does when correcting a child. But children always reach a point when they must have the right to assert their own visions of reality, to define themselves no longer as children but as individual men and women. In fact, the truly loving parent realizes that children must receive the encouragement and confidence right from the beginning to make their way through the world on their own. They must have the right to fail without the fear of humiliation or punishment.

Thus the basic problem for Soviet filmmakers is that for over fifty years the state insisted on acting like a bad parent. Whenever a filmmaker asserted a vision of reality that differed from the official view, the state would use whatever pressure it could to alter, restrict, or condemn that vision. It refused to acknowledge alternative visions which could establish the boundaries for a dialogue about the nature of reality and a set of commonly agreed-upon goals. For example, in 1932 the Party criticized Vsevolod Pudovkin's *Prostoi sluchai* (*A Simple Case*), not for ideological reasons, but for artistic ones: "Terrified of the abstract, they always wanted things prosaic, they were afraid of the poetic" (Marshall, 27). Thus, by restricting both content and style, the Party unnaturally attempted to enforce a permanent state of infancy. To do so was not only to deny freedom of expression, but also to deny the artists their humanity. This factor is what made being a film artist in the Soviet Union or any Soviet Bloc country an existence full of pain and anxiety.

By denying the artists' humanity and making the practice of their art and love of their country fit narrow definitions, the state created unnecessary emptiness in the lives of many film artists. Such was the case for three directorial giants of Soviet film history, Sergei M. Eisenstein, Vsevolod Pudovkin, and Alexander Dovzhenko. In the beginning, all three shared the vision of the leaders of the Bolshevik Revolution of October 1917 that established the Communist government of the Soviet Union. They believed that the cooperative ideals of Karl Marx could lead their poor, backward country out of the poverty and oppression of the past and into the twentieth century and beyond, with jobs, food, shelter, and culture for everyone. It was a grand dream, and most importantly the artists possessed the time and freedom to develop their talents and express their own visions, going beyond what had ever been achieved in art anywhere in the world before. They did so not only in service to themselves but also in service to their country, for the Bolshevik vision of the future inspired their own. Ironically, it was the very chaos and lack of organization existing in the immediate post-Revolution years that enabled these filmmakers to reach their greatest achievements. Once the government centralized its power and began establishing the shared dream of a Communist state, the artists had to fight for any measure of independence they could get.

In the pre-war years, Russian film was only a commercial enterprise dominated by foreign companies and just good enough artistically to be considered a pale imitation of what existed in the West. Companies such as Pathé or Lumière or Scandinavia's Nordisk dominated the market. Gerald Mast states, "No film was shot in Russia by a Russian company until some ten years after the invention of the moving picture" (*A Short History of the Movies*, 181). Even after that, "costume films, horror films, and melodramas . . . were the staples of the pre–1917 Russian film diet" (Mast, 181). Nevertheless, once Russia did begin producing its own films, the cinema quickly became an integral part of the national culture. Alexander Drankov founded the first Russian film studio in 1908, and by 1917 the country had produced over 1,200 films (Liehm and Liehm, 8). Although most of these were naturally shown in urban areas, films spread throughout the countryside by means of traveling companies using portable generators. Lenin was well aware of this practice when he later gave film a central role in educating the people about the country's new government and social systems. The Bolsheviks began a program of sending "agit-trains" deep into the countryside to present lectures, skits, and films. While the practice had its problems, it also achieved much. Films were particularly popular, especially with children: "The *Lenin* train, for example, attracted an audience of 22,800 children in the period January to March 1919" (Taylor, *The Politics*, 49). Not only were they entertaining and a curiosity to many peasants, but silent films had the added advantage of being able to break through all language barriers. All of which made them a particularly valuable propaganda tool.

The short newsreels and *agitki* shown on the trains, produced by the great director and theorist Dziga Vertov, also represented an artistic advance over early Russian films. They were popular not only with the peasants, but in the cities as well. But the early Russian cinema had not been totally void of artistic efforts, either. In fact, a recent retrospective of pre-Revolutionary Russian film revealed both a high degree of artistic achievement and the mastery of director Evgeni Bauer, whose name might also now be used to identify that entire era of the nation's cinema (Robinson, "Evgeni Bauer"). Also notable were the animated puppet films of the Polish immigrant Wladyslaw Starewicz (Starevich). These included *Beautiful Leukanida, The Cameraman's Revenge,* and *The Dragonfly and the Ant.* Though his films received little distribution in the West, Starewicz was a true artist who later "began to combine live film with animation, using film techniques, as Melies did, to create dreamlike poetic sequences and a romantic unreality." He also made significant experiments with "multiple exposures, fade-outs and fade-ins, and montage" (Liehm and Liehm, 8). Additionally, in 1915 and 1916, theatrical innovator Vsevolod Meyerhold applied some of his original methods in the films *Portret Doriana Greya* (*The Picture of Dorian Gray,* 1915) and *Silnyi chelovek* (*Strong Man,* 1917). Also at that time, Yakov Protazanov made two noteworthy adaptations, *Pickovaya dama* (*Queen of Spades,* 1916) and Tolstoi's *Otets Sergii* (*Father Sergius,* 1917).

Father Sergius is easily identifiable as a pre-Revolutionary film because of the absence of *montage,* the method of suggesting ideas through editing exploited fully by the great Soviet directors of the twenties. Protazanov mainly keeps his characters in the foreground and occasionally will use a close-up, but there are certainly no montage effects. Instead, the cutting is mainly to keep the camera in front of the actors, and Protazanov often fills the rest of the frame with action as well, part of his attempt to disrupt the static quality of the film.

He doesn't fully succeed, but *Father Sergius* is still an appealing piece of work in terms of the acting, Protazanov's artistic attempts, and the theme. Father

Sergius is a hollow man, lacking all convictions except for the knowledge that he has none. Appropriately, Protazanov constantly shows him leaning on railings, an altar, or a cane. When he cannot lean, he can only grovel on the floor. Psychologically, Sergius is always leaning on someone as well. His life is constantly guided by someone else. He never looks inwards and therefore always feels inferior.

Paradoxically, Sergius still manages to do much good. For a while, his fame continues to grow to the same proportion that he seeks seclusion. People feel redeemed by him because they believe in his goodness, representing a powerful anti-religious statement. People can receive spiritual fulfillment from belief in something completely hollow. Feeling unworthy, Sergius continues retreating. Ultimately, he becomes a convict in Siberia for illegal teaching. Finally controlled by the state, he has now reached his professed goal of anonymity. *Father Sergius* provides a fine example of pre-Revolutionary film in that it not only reveals an obvious effort to develop cinematic art, but also it does not carry with it the burden of political meanings. Completed and released in 1917, the film does present an indictment of bourgeois callousness and political oppression. In the end, Sergius is arrested for no important reason, and it is a double irony that the tsar to whom he had earlier pledged his devotion eventually fulfills his desire for freedom from temptation by sending him to a Siberian prison. But the anti-religious theme, though daring for a Russian film at that time, could also be interpreted as strongly anti-Bolshevik, since it warns against blind faith. Yet it does not deny that people also benefit from their faith, even if its object is hollow. This view is more complex than Lenin's proclamation that "religion is the opiate of the people" and its later damnation as an empty endeavor in such films as Eisenstein's *October* (1928) and Vertov's *Entuziazm (Enthusiasm/The Donbass Symphony,* 1931). Additionally, those directors had to wait at least eleven years before they felt comfortable about making an all-out attack on religion. Eisenstein handled the topic very carefully in his masterpiece *Bronenosets 'Potyomkin'* (*Battleship Potemkin,* 1925–1926).

With directors like Bauer and Protazanov, there's no telling how Russian film might have developed under its original structure. At the end of 1916, "the Russian cinema showed all the outward signs of a flourishing economic concern. As a political force, it was virtually non-existent, but intellectually and artistically it was beginning to gain recognition" (Taylor, *The Politics,* 15). Nevertheless, Soviet film would never have achieved the heights that it reached in the 1920s had not the Bolshevik Revolution of October 1917 wiped away all that existed before, providing the avant-garde with an opportunity to take control of its artistic direction. The coalition "provisional" Government established by the February 1917 revolution was unable to do anything more for the film industry than relax censorship, to which the studios responded with exploitative films aimed at gaining big profits. Important issues long suppressed by the tsars were still not addressed (Taylor, *The Politics,* 21–22).

This situation was completely reversed under the Bolsheviks. On August 27,

1919, Lenin signed the second decree for nationalization of the film industry, setting in motion the apparatus for both the heights and depths that Soviet film would reach during its subsequent history. For, with this decree, Lenin took his support away from the entrepreneur film producers of the pre-Revolutionary days who were still guiding the fate of Soviet cinema and gave his blessing to the young avant-gardists who could take the medium in new directions. But at the same time, Lenin felt that the impact of a film could be predicted by a review panel of Marxists and literary men. When he named film the Soviets' "most important art," he was not primarily concerned with art but with propaganda, giving no consideration to the fact that the most predictable works of art are only the most uninteresting and that eventually this entire system would fall prey to the particular tastes of just one man. Yet in the beginning, the benefits of his pronouncements fell to the artists (Liehm and Liehm, 34).

This outcome was due to the fact that no one had any idea of where film should go. The artists and authorities only knew that to accomplish their goals, film, like their society, had to go in new directions. Moreover, because of the continuing civil strife and a blockade against any negative film stock entering the country, supplies of film and films available for viewing were low. What was available were often bits and pieces that required creative minds to make useful. One such group of minds was the Cinema Arts Workshop of Lev Kuleshov (Mast, 182).

What the Kuleshov group discovered was that the secret of film art is not in the individual shot, but in the editing, or cutting, of a film. A primary source for their discoveries was the great American director D. W. Griffith. Somehow, the group managed to obtain a copy of Griffith's monumental work *Intolerance* (1918) in which the director blends four loosely related stories from different periods of history. Kuleshov and his students watched the film endlessly to learn how Griffith had created powerful effects through editing. They "re-cut" the film several times to study the effects that a different organization of shots would have. They played it until the print finally disintegrated, learning all that Griffith had to teach about narrative film editing. Kuleshov's efforts eventually produced not only two landmark films of the twenties, *Neobychainye prikliucheniya Mistera Vesta v stranye bolshevikov* (*The Extraordinary Adventures of Mr. West in the Land of the Bolsheviks*, 1924) and *Po zakonu* (*By the Law*, 1926), but also the theory of montage that was to be crucial to the great Soviet directors of the twenties and filmmakers everywhere ever since (Mast, 182–197).

Dziga Vertov was another young director and theorist making important discoveries in the early twenties. Vertov began by taking his camera out to the Civil War battlefronts and using whatever film he could find to record the action. He then combined his bits and pieces of film to make the accounts dramatic and sent them back to the cinemas to be shown in support of the Revolution. Vertov's *Kino-glaz* (Kino-Eye) films enjoyed such demand for their content that they reinforced the avant-garde's theories about film form as well. If the new films could really excite audiences, the young directors had probably found a means for advancing socialism and art simultaneously. Through the art of montage, the piecing together of shots for narrative, intellectual, and emotional purposes, the new Soviet filmmakers could present a more complex and accurate picture of reality than film had ever done before. They could look at the world around them and present it in exciting new ways.

In his masterpiece documentary, *Chelovek s kinoapparatom (Man with a Movie Camera*, 1929), Vertov emphasized the key element of the art of montage, an editor working with individual shots. Even though much of the editing is made obvious through stop action, tremendously quick cutting, multi-image screens, making images "magically" appear, and showing the editor at work, Vertov still creates the great illusion that a single cameraman could wander far and wide across a modern city capturing a large amount of its life on film in a single day. Three cities, Moscow, Kiev, and Riga were actually used in the filming. But the man in the film also keeps viewers oriented, functioning as a structural device linking all the various scenes together into a story about a day of Soviet life. Through following this man as he films in coal mines, from the tops of towers, buildings, and bridges, in the middle of traffic, or on the beach and through all of the editing devices and tricks employed, Vertov reveals many of the ways that film can capture reality. Yet the very variety of means employed also reveals how each one, and even the combination of all of them, is still limited. The film supports this interpretation because Vertov is dealing with only the urban setting. *Man with a Movie Camera* presents modern, technological Russia moving at a brisk pace into the future while still allowing time for contemplation and slower intellectual activities. But, for Vertov, this perspective is authentic and cannot be dismissed as simply following the Party line. His film is too honest in revealing all that can be accomplished and the limitations at the same time. The future looks exciting, so why shouldn't the mood be upbeat? Yet the Soviet film needed to find ways of dealing with tragedy, failure, and sorrow because those are also parts of reality. But instead of the multiplicity of perspectives needed, the nation's cinema became limited to just one.

Ironically, the great achievements of Soviet directors in the 1920s, creating what could be called "propaganda for the artist's sake," helped develop an intellectual basis for Stalinism, the force that would eventually entrap them. The directors' devotion to their cause in the 1920s created a mythic vision of the Soviet Union that had some very specific aspects. These included capitalists and tsarist or Provisional Government representatives who were always oppressive, foolish, and had some kind of physical deformity. Often the directors would use camera angles or double exposures to emphasize these deformities. Religion, in these films, was always as Lenin had described it, "the opiate of the people." In contrast, the workers and peasants, though sometimes reluctant at first, were always able eventually to see facts clearly. And when they did, they inevitably joined the Bolsheviks. From then on, they possessed a spirit that simply could not be defeated. This point was emphasized through scenes in many films in which workers survive firing squads or certain execution. Structural characteristics such as Eisenstein's consistent use of downward and upward movement and Pudovkin's regular use of death-to-life transitions also emphasized this point. With all of these common aspects, the great revolutionary films of Eisenstein, Pudovkin, and Dovzhenko combined created a mythic world not unlike that of American westerns in which the good forces of Bolshevism always triumphed over their evil enemies and won over skeptics and neutrals.

With this basic plot idea, established by the Revolution, and the common goal of rallying the public to the Bolshevik cause, the filmmakers simply took off from the *agitki* and newsreels of Dziga Vertov to create imaginative works that would embed socialist myths in the minds of the people. Since the people already knew the outcome of the Revolution, there was no need to keep repeating the facts. Therefore the filmmakers could focus on exhorting the glorious righteousness of the Soviet cause and finding powerful new ways for communicating their message. Taking the audience's knowledge of events for granted gave Eisenstein, Pudovkin, and Dovzhenko the freedom to put their film theories into practice by experimenting with symbolism, structure, and editing. Thus, though the audience had a simple myth to grasp, the filmmakers did not talk down to them, but instead kept challenging them with exciting new ways of presenting their ideas. They were not merely entertaining and propagandizing, but also teaching their audiences new ways of seeing. Unfortunately, Soviet audiences (like most) preferred basic entertainment, and Josef Stalin preferred that nobody present ideas that were not his own.

Though Dziga Vertov had proclaimed that Soviet film should look to "capture life unawares," his work formed the basis for his countrymen's subsequent departures from documentary realism. "The film drama is the opium of the people," Vertov declared, continuing, "The film drama and religion are a fatal weapon in the hands of the capitalists. The screenplay is a fairy-tale thought out by literature for us. . . . Down with bourgeois screenplay fairy-tales! Long live life as it is!" (Taylor, 129).

Yet Vertov was not merely trying to present what the camera recorded without alteration. In fact, alteration was the very essence of cinematic art for him. Vertov believed that "because of montage the cinema could also go beyond reality and create, in a sense, a *new reality*" (Taylor, *The Politics,* 126). Vertov was not even adverse to altering the reality the camera recorded before the footage ever got to the editing room. Herbert Marshall reports one example of Vertov actually acting out a scene himself to include in one of his early newsreels (*Masters,* 73). These elements in Vertov's work took him away from "life as it is," but "had a decisive influence on the stylistic development of the Soviet film" (Taylor, *The Politics,* 56). Other directors not only developed their own theories of montage, but also produced their own distinct socialist reality. As Marshall states, "They gave an artistic image of a socialist revolution that had never really taken place. The cinema of fact became the cinema of non-fact" (96).

The reasons for the importance of Segei Eisenstein's *Battleship Potemkin* to the development of Soviet film are both artistic and political. In both senses, it is flawless (at least, its political aspect was flawless originally). *Potemkin* is not only a perfect and impressive display of all of Eisenstein's ideas up to that point, but also an emotionally effective presentation of the Soviet view of history during the 1920s and 1930s and the Bolshevik hopes for the future. *Potemkin* thus contains one of the great paradoxes of much great art, which is that despite the complexity of its composition the message is simple and clear. For example, Eisenstein's contrast of the socialist sailors and their sympathizers ashore with their enemies, in this case, the tsarist commanders, is simplistic. The commanders are clearly a pampered, well-dressed lot who are ruthless in their treatment of the sailors. Yet they create their own downfall by stupidly expecting the men to accept as truth what all of them know are lies. Thus when the men can see maggots in their meat but the ship doctor pronounces it edible, the officers clearly have no support for their authority. Nevertheless they continue to believe that the men will just blindly follow them. By these simple means, Eisenstein presented the important historical fact that the tsarist forces always underestimated the intelligence of the proletariat. Oppressors are particularly ignorant when they do not believe that people will recognize their own oppression.

Eisenstein's creation of a mass hero in the film was welcomed because "although the 1905 Revolution was later depicted by the Communist party as the brainchild of an omnipotent Lenin, the propaganda of the pre-Stalin era depicted both the 1905 and 1917 revolutions as spontaneous movements of the enraged Russian prolitariat. Thus, Eisenstein's interpretation of the 'Potemkin' mutiny fit that of the Party" (Stoil, 24). Eisenstein skillfully creates the mass hero by first getting his audience to sympathize with a sailor whipped by an evil boatswain for no apparent reason. The audience's sympathies later move to a larger group of men who complain about the maggoty meat, and then to all the sailors when the captain orders a mass execution. This structure continues throughout the film. Thus, by presenting the rebellion as a spontaneous uprising, Eisenstein transfers his audience's sympathies to the ideals of the Bolshevik Revolution.

The starting point for the collective socialist myth developed by Eisenstein, Vsevolod Pudovkin, and Alexander Dovzhenko was the unaltering evil and foolishness of capitalists, tsarists, and Provisional Government figures: in other words, anyone who opposed the Bolsheviks. To present these broad characterizations effectively, Eisenstein developed his theory of "typage" in choosing actors for his first feature, *Stachka* (*Strike*, 1925). In that film, all of the company spies have animal names and physical characteristics that Eisenstein emphasizes by superimposing the animal face over the human's and then lifting it to show the similarity. Their personalities match as well, since the spies delight in tricking and preying upon the workers. The factory shareholders in the film are pompous fat men who lean back in their chairs, smoking their cigars and getting drunk while using the workers' list of demands to wipe their shoes. Additionally, the plant manager is an intellectual wimp and his chief stool-pigeon a comic dullard. When they finally get dumped into a river, it is a fitting comic punishment,

reminiscent of hundreds of American slapstick films. Similarly, in *October*, Eisenstein employs the simple yet powerful means of associating Provisional Government leader Alexander Kerensky with objects such as crown-shaped bottle caps, wooden soldiers, a Rolls-Royce, and an American flag in order to reveal his hollowness. Eisenstein continued such caricatures through their culmination in *Staroe i novoe* (*Old and New/The General Line*, 1929), in which he uses a wide-angle lens to present an absolutely huge wealthy farmer staring down scornfully at the peasant farmer, Martha, who has come to beg from him.

Pudovkin was generally more subtle in presenting "the enemies of the people," but the effect was still the same. For example, in *Mat* (*The Mother*, 1926), the association he makes between the "bad" characters and animals is not specifically pointed out. In an early scene, the factory's "black guards" are devouring fish as they talk about destroying the workers. To them, the two are obviously the same. Later, before the revolutionary Pavel's trial, one judge is praising the picture of another's horse. During the trial the proud owner draws a picture of his pet beast. They obviously care more about horses than workers or justice. A final example involves the police chief, whose dog lies comfortably nearby while he gives orders to "spare no bullets" in putting down a march.

Dovzhenko resorted to the totally bizarre in his presentation of these characters. In *Zvenigora* (1928), the anti-revolutionary Pavlo raises money by promising to shoot himself in front of an audience of wealthy Europeans. His sophisticated listeners wait anxiously for him to complete his show, but he gets away with all their money. In *Arsenal* (1929), a World War I battle sequence includes a bald, bespectacled German soldier who cannot stop laughing because of all the gas being used. He howls with laughter and enjoys himself as he witnesses such horrors as the hand and grinning face of a dead soldier sticking out of the dirt. The viewer's knowledge that such ridiculous scenes never occur in war proves Dovzhenko's point that war is not glamorous and soldiers do not enjoy fighting and dying.

Contrasted to the tsarists and capitalists are, naturally, the proletarians, and these characters are always presented as more human because they always grow. Oppressors might sometimes see their errors, but they will refuse to change. But once workers see the light, they always take action. In *The Mother* and *Potomok Chingis-khana* (*The Heir to Genghis-Khan/Storm Over Asia*, 1928), Pudovkin gives his proletarian characters mythic strength by associating them with the land and the forces of history. When the mother of the first film dies, she helps give birth to a whole new era. On her way to the people's march at the end of the film, she meets a woman breastfeeding her newborn son. As the march proceeds, Pudovkin intercuts shots of the ice on the river breaking up and the water rushing downstream. Similarly, it is springtime for the people as they break out of the ice age of capitalist rule and into the new life of a workers' state. When the mother is shot down by the police, the flag she was carrying is seen finally raised in triumph over Russia.

In *Storm Over Asia*, the main character is an Asian trapper barely managing to scratch out a living in a barren landscape. Added to this association with the landscape is a document that his British oppressors and captors believe associates him with Genghis Khan. When they try to install him as a puppet ruler, he plays along for a while until he witnesses their execution of one of his countrymen. Then, suddenly regaining his ancient warrior strength, he almost single-handedly, like Samson, tears down their false temple. When he charges his enemy on horseback, two thousand warriors suddenly appear behind him and the storm over Asia arises. The isolated trees seen throughout the film and the British Army are blown back by the wind as the land itself rises against them to support its oppressed people. Of course, the trapper's earlier association with a socialist resistance group has helped him regain his connection with the land and his historic dignity.

Dovzhenko's *Zvenigora* begins three hundred years ago and then jumps quickly to the modern era after revealing the mystery of the land. A grandfather figure, intent on extracting the land's treasures, appears in both ages as well as within a fantasy sequence set during the Viking invasion of Russia. Similarly, a female character appears as Oksana in modern Russia and Roksana during the Viking invasion. The artifacts from this battle are the physical treasures buried in the land. But, more important, the land also contains mineral resources that can only be extracted by science and the spirit of the people. The two grandsons in the film each pursue a separate idea of the land's treasures, using different methods. Pavlo (Paul) accepts his grandfather's legends, but his attempts to extract the artifacts only lead to his suicide. Timoshka (Tim) has a better idea of "working with science and chemistry to unlock the treasures of his land." As a result, industry and prosperity begin to grow. Dovzhenko makes this connection with a few brief shots, spending more time detailing Pavlo's downfall than Timoshka's rise. Thus he presents the new socialist myth and the Ukrainian legends side by side. The audience is entertained and free to choose which path to follow.

In *Arsenal*, the Bolsheviks possess a strength of character that overwhelms their enemies. They have created the myth that Dovzhenko's camera is struggling to record and piece together. But the change comes so fast that the camera can only record bits and pieces, placing symbols here and there. The narrative structure is very sketchy, but the viewer does not need more. Bolshevism is the force of movement and change, a greater force than the camera itself. It enlivens the oppressed peasants from the beginning, leaving the old bourgeoisie frozen in positions as if figures from impressionist paintings. It transforms war from grotesque to glorious. At the end, the main character faces three anti-Communist soldiers whose bullets cannot kill him. Baring his chest to them, he cries, "There's a spirit here that you just can't kill." It is the ultimate image of the superworker.

Nevertheless, Soviet critics demanded a more politically specific cinema, one that focused on current reality and made it more exciting than fiction ("Symposium," 35). Sergei Tretiakov proclaimed that it was time to begin waging a campaign against the arbitrary placement of cameras, and scenarist Victor Shklovski concluded that the Party could and should give form to Soviet film ("Symposium," 31, 34). To a certain extent, these critics had a point. None of the early masters of Soviet film could argue with the idea that their work should serve the socialist cause. That philosophy had provided their inspiration and purpose from the beginning, and they had willingly helped create the very system that would now control them, one which was far more interested in serving socialism than in creating great art. So if the art did not adequately fit the cause, as defined by the Party, it could be rejected. The only problem with this system, and it is a major one, is that it leaves no room for mistakes. Thus the critics could find a way to attack *October* for revealing Eisenstein's genius more than the benefits of socialism (Brik/Shklovski). But in doing so, they had to reject all of its artistic qualities. The result of this approach was that artists would tend to aim for only the safest, plainest presentations, a practice that is not conducive to creating great art. Art means the restructuring of the world according to the artist's personal vision, and whether or not that vision is admirable should be debated. But the vision must be allowed. Denying it produced the sterile Soviet art of Stalin's reign.

The tragic aspect of these developments is that, from the beginning, the artists asked for them and fully cooperated in bringing them about. Miklos Haraszti states,

The anti-authoritarian rebel wanted to salvage freedom and individualism, those unfulfilled promises of the bourgeoisie, from the wreckage of capitalism. Once in power, he wanted to enjoy the privileges of socialism while behaving as though he were intellectually independent. But he was quickly reminded: "Within the Revolution, complete freedom; against the Revolution, none." He liquidated himself. (120–121)

In 1929 a group of cinema directors including Eisenstein, Pudovkin, Mikhail Romm, Grigori Kozintsev, Leonid Trauberg, Sergei Yutkevich, and Alexei Popov called for a special organ to carry out Party politics for cinema. Their plea resulted in the creation of the Committee for Cinematography under the Council of Peoples' Commissars (Cabinet) of the USSR, chaired by Party statesman Y. A. Rudziutak (Marshall, 37). Also at this time, the highly doctrinaire, generally conservative Russian Association of Proletarian Writers (RAPP), which usually opposed leftist artists like Eisenstein, Meyerhold, and Mayakovsky, became the cultural mouthpiece for the Party. Their sectarianism created so much strife and name-calling among arts groups that when, in 1932, the Party moved to establish a single Union of Writers and dissolve all other such organizations, RAPP was the only voice of opposition (Liehm and Liehm, 37).

A further problem for the avant-garde was that during the twenties it had tough competition from America. Soviet audiences preferred Chaplin, Keaton, and Fairbanks to accounts of their own history: "In other words, they preferred escapism to realism, however unreal that realism might in fact have been"

(Taylor, 98). Herbert Marshall states that in the Soviet Union, "hardly any of the classics were widely shown successes" (188). Of course, this fact makes the Soviet public no different from the American. But it had a devastating effect on the intellectual content of Soviet cinema. Given the choice between great art and ideological correctness, Stalin definitely preferred the latter. A filmmaker could still experiment, as long as he or she produced a film "which was accessible and comprehensible to the millions in the form of its conception" (Taylor, 119). This formula, of course, is a guarantee for killing all experimentation, and filmmakers soon learned that the only way to keep working was to take the safest and simplest route possible. The audiences could fall asleep, but at least they would receive the correct message, over and over again.

To paraphrase Herbert Marcuse, Stalinism wanted art that was not art, and it got what it wanted (Liehm and Liehm, 435). Several factors which have been mentioned contributed to this rise of Party control over the cinema. But one more factor was still needed. The crucial element for cementing the Party's hold was the coincidental development of sound film. This potentially exciting new technology put an added restriction on directors by requiring that they work from a script, and scripts could be reviewed prior to shooting (Stoil, 7). Thus an elaborate system grew up for the approval of all films to be produced, and the Soviet film output plummeted in both quality and quantity. In 1938, Dziga Vertov complained, "now for one violinist there are a hundred conductors" (Marshall, 93). Quite contrary to Vertov's goal of "catching life unawares," an admirable ambition no matter how impossible, all Soviet film would now be minutely planned before the cameras ever started. As a result, all evidence of spontaneity and vitality disappeared.

But these Stalinist restrictions failed to fulfill the Party's propaganda aims for the cinema. Films were also needed that the critics could praise and the Party could hold up as models. Producing such films required a theory setting forth the elements they would contain. The theory that emerged was socialist realism, and its chief spokesperson was the Central Committee's official "expert" on cultural affairs, Andrei A. Zhdanov. At the First Congress of Soviet Writers in 1934, Zhdanov interpreted Stalin's dictate for writers to be "engineers of human souls" to mean

knowing life so as to be able to depict it truthfully in works of art, not to depict it in a dead, scholastic way, not simply as "objective reality," but to depict reality in its revolutionary development.

In addition to this, the truthfulness and historical concreteness of the artistic portrayal should be combined with the ideological remolding and education of the laboring people in the spirit of socialism. This method . . . is what we call the method of socialist realism. (Liehm and Liehm, 433)

What this decree meant, as Marcuse later explained, was that "the established social reality [became] the final framework for the artistic content transcending it neither in style nor in substance" (Liehm and Liehm, 435). For despite Zhdanov's claims that Soviet art should not be lifeless, Soviet artists were, in fact, prevented from presenting "reality" in an ambiguous manner. All works had to conform to the socialist/Stalinist vision of history as proceeding inevitably towards its own goals. All conflicts were clear-cut and the characters, who were supposed to be living, multi-dimensional human beings, sometimes emerged almost as stereotypically as the crude stereotypes of Eisenstein et al. in the 1920s.

The results were predictable (which is exactly what Stalin desired), and have by now become well known. All of the great works of the twenties fell into official disfavor, and their creators suffered along with them. Eisenstein was able to complete only three more films during his life, *Alexander Nevsky* in 1938, and *Ivan Grozny* (*Ivan the Terrible, Pts. I and II*) in 1944–1946. In the mid-thirties, he worked long and hard on *Bezhin Meadow,* incorporating several "requests" for changes, but eventually was not able to complete it. In the meantime, all of his proposals were rejected. In response, he retreated to teaching and writing, producing a great volume of theoretical work.

Vertov, Pudovkin, and Dovzhenko each began the thirties well, but also suffered the same fate as Eisenstein, leading Herbert Marshall to comment that "these great artists died of broken hearts, because the works that they created were no longer their works and they were no longer able to create them. They had to make them according to the instructions of Stalin and the Party" (221).

Vertov's brilliance is still evident in *Enthusiasm* and *Tri pesni o Lenine* (*The Three Songs of Lenin,* 1934), but after that he simply became a neglected artist. Pudovkin moved to a quietly personal tone in his last two artistic successes, *A Simple Case* (1932) and *Dezertir* (*Deserter,* 1933). *Deserter* contained a creative use of sound in counterpoint to the image, and *A Simple Case* possessed perhaps the last example of intellectual montage between 1928 and the beginning of the Khrushchev era (Marshall, 33, 38). But neither film was clear enough for Stalin, and Pudovkin reacted to his censure by becoming a loyal defender of the regime. For the rest of the decade, he turned out mainly insipid biographical tales, returning only to a complex presentation in his final film, *Vozvrashchenie Vasili Bortnikova* (*The Return of Vasily Bortnikov,* 1952). Dovzhenko also tried adhering to the Party line, but it only hurt his work. The opening of *Shchors* (1939) still reveals his poetic skill, and he did produce some noteworthy but neglected war documentaries (Marshall, 149, 156). But never again did he approach the brilliance of his great trilogy.

Despite the Zhdanov line, there are still a number of noteworthy Soviet films from the thirties and forties. Yet the majority were burdensome, and one of the major weaknesses with socialist realist films in general is evident in the portrayals of their most stereotyped character, Stalin himself. While the myth established by Soviet films in the twenties centered on the uprising of the people and their promising future under socialism, the myths of socialist realism often focused on just one man. In these films, Stalin did not appear as "a particularly intelligent man or 'genius' leader, but rather a familiar god or incarnated transcendence'' (Bazin, 36). At the beginning of Mikhail Chiaureli's *Kliatva (The Vow,* 1946), Stalin is divinely anointed as Lenin's successor. Wandering alone following Lenin's funeral, Stalin stops by a river where he hears the late leader's voice and, looking up, is struck on the forehead by a ray of light. When he returns to his friends, "he will be distinguished from them, set apart—not only because of his wisdom and genius, but because of the presence in him of History" (Bazin, 38). Later in the same film, strolling through Red Square with some colleagues Stalin encounters a frustrated mechanic struggling with one of the first Soviet-built tractors. Stalin taps the engine a few times and quickly pronounces the correct diagnosis, "It's the spark plugs." Similarly, Soviet films would also show the great leader winning World War II almost single-handedly. In the films *Stalingradskaya bitva (The Battle of Stalingrad,* 1949) and *Tretiy udar (The Third Blow,* 1948), Stalin wins crucial military victories by calmly making the key decisions in complete solitude. All the action correlates to his point of view and he is never wrong. Therefore all of Soviet film, like Soviet history, was leading to a dead end, "or at least the end of the dialectical process at the heart of the socialist world" (Bazin, 37). With all the answers known, what possibility was there for drama or growth? A final example of Stalin's image in socialist realist films appears in Mikhail Romm's *Lenin v Oktiabre (Lenin in October,* 1937), in which Lenin's first request is always to talk with Stalin every time he arrives at a conference. The film ends with Lenin preparing to speak to a cheering crowd of Bolshevik supporters. In the final shot, Stalin moves into the frame directly behind him, the obvious next in line.

Nevertheless, despite their obscurity and extremely limited artistic boundaries, there were some qualified successes within the socialist realist canon. Perhaps its most successful practitioner was the director Friedrich Ermler, a commited Stalinist who possessed considerable talent. In 1929, working in Leningrad within his Workshop for Experimental Film, he produced *Oblomok imperii (Fragment of an Empire,* 1929), "one of the classics of silent film" (Liehm and Liehm, 41). Ermler's *Vstrechnyi (Counterplan,* 1932) became a work that the Stalinists would use against the avant-garde for years. Finally, in 1938–1939, he produced the two-part *Veliki grazhdanin (A Great Citizen)* about which the Liehms write:

Just as Leni Riefenstahl served the consolidation of the myth of Adolf Hitler without allowing this propagandistic goal to weaken the artistic quality of her work, so in the late thirties, Ermler served—with lesser talent—the creation of the myth of justified purges and terrorism with a motion picture that belongs artistically (mainly its first part) among the better ones made during that period. (41)

Other notable socialist realist productions include Efim Dzigan's *My iz Kronstadta (We Are from Kronstadt,* 1936), Alexander Medvedkin's *Happiness,* Vladimir Legoshin's *Lone White Sail,* and Boris Barnet's *Okraina (Outskirts)* (Liehm and Liehm, 40). Additionally, Nikolai Ekk's *Putëvka v zhizn (The Road to Life,*

1931) was "the first great success of the Soviet sound film" (Mast, 216). However, the limited nature of the style is evident in that none of these directors was able to achieve more than one notable work.

The same is true for the creators of socialist realism's most famous production, *Chapaev* (1934), by Georgi and Sergei Vasiliev. After his private screening of the film (a common practice for the insomniac dictator), Stalin himself pronounced it a masterpiece that should be the new model for all Soviet productions and ordered that it receive numerous prizes (Stoil, 68). *Chapaev* is able to hold the viewer's attention because its main character is not an omnipotent hero incapable of containing any dramatic interest. Instead, Chapaev has believable human weaknesses, which allowed the Vasilievs to inject a good deal of humor and enables viewers to sympathize with their main character despite his overwhelming arrogance. Throughout the film the flawless Party commissar, Furmanov, offers gentle advice and lets events take their course until Chapaev sees the light. Thus Chapaev has room to grow as a character.

Clearly, placing the wise Party adviser in the background enabled the Vasilievs to produce whatever entertainment value *Chapaev* has. The film is really no less tolerable than a great number of Hollywood productions from the same decade and possesses even better qualities than a good deal more. Yet, for the so-called peak of an art form to be merely tolerable does not bode well for its followers. *Chapaev* should have been considered as stock entertainment. If so, it would have been fairly harmless. But when Stalin made it the model to shoot for, he condemned Soviet film to existing on its low level.

During the period of socialist realist dominance (early thirties to mid-fifties), the themes sometimes varied but the quality did so only rarely. The thirties were dominated by civil war films until 1937. These stories gave filmmakers a chance to please Stalin by depicting events he had experienced, and provided young people a vicarious revolution. But the constant repetition of superior Soviet forces always winning easy victories over hopelessly inept opponents (and thus trivializing the whole struggle) drove a large part of the audience away. In 1937, Stalin needed new films to explain the political purges then taking place and, a year later, ones that would rally the people against the threat of foreign invasion. Thus, anti-Nazi films surfaced briefly, disappeared after the signing of the Hitler-Stalin pact, and then resurfaced in 1941 when the two nations became antagonists. Following the war, anti-Americanism and support for Stalin's unpopular fourth five-year plan became dominant themes (Stoil, 79–97).

But with socialist realism, directors were saddled with a theory that made all propaganda goals unobtainable. Aesthetically indefinable, the theory was mainly meant to enforce whatever the Party wanted, but it did possess some definitive characteristics. These were a heavy emphasis on the role of the Party, more emphasis on heroes than on historic events, an obvious falsification of history, a need for long speeches to explain political messages, and simplistic technical aspects (Stoil, 76). In *Alexander Nevsky* and *Ivan Grozny* (*Ivan the Terrible, Part I*), Eisenstein proved he could still create art even within these tight restrictions, and Dovshenko achieved some quality in the opening of *Shchors*. But both directors were very disappointed with their films (Stoil, 83–86). During the relaxed standards of the war era, Abram Room created a believable portrait of an alienated soldier in *Nashestvie* (*Invasion*, 1945). But other examples of quality were very rare. Finally, probably out of frustration with the limitations, Eisentein openly challenged Stalin's wishes with *Ivan the Terrible, Part II*, which he completed shortly before his death in 1948 (Stoil, 92–94).

In this second part of his projected trilogy, Ivan saves Russia but at the cost of his soul. The great leader is really a lonely orphan with homosexual inclinations, a portrait which in itself would be enough to draw Stalin's condemnation as an inadequate depiction of a Russian hero. But Eisenstein went even further in drawing parallels to contemporary events and between Ivan and Stalin himself. For Ivan also conducts his purges, just as Stalin had in 1936–1938, ruthlessly executing victims whose only crime was to have the wrong political associations at the wrong time.

Stylistically, the film departs from socialist realism in a manner that heaps further condemnation on its protagonist. Eisenstein combines grotesque costuming, close-ups, and physical characteristics with a constant use of songs and theatrical performances to emphasize the similarities between the characters and the performers they watch. In other words, the art within the film mirrors the characters' lives too accurately. Everyone plays a public role while their inner confusion, suspicion, and emptiness keeps growing.

The sets also contribute to and parallel the characters' psychological conditions. The architecture either produces low ceilings that hang heavily over the characters or cavernous rooms that dwarf them. At the end, Ivan is alone in his throne room, claiming that he will allow no one to hurt Russian unity. But he has built his own hell.

After his personal screening of the film, Stalin responded with a single word: "Smyt!" (Wash it off!). He also ordered all the work completed on Part III destroyed. Eisenstein, already in poor health, was unable to fight back any longer and died of a heart attack on February 10, 1948. With his passing, Stalin might also have hoped to have vanquished the final remnants of the avant-garde (Liehm and Liehm, 50). Dovzhenko and Pudovkin struggled to please the authorities while also maintaining some artistic integrity, but produced a total of only three films after the war and died in 1956 and 1953 respectively (Hecht, 560). Stalin's reimposition of tight controls drove production levels down to a total of only five feature films in 1952 (Stoil, 94). Popular themes from 1946 to 1953 included glorifying Stalin, anti-Americanism, and historical biographies (Hecht, 561). Seemingly, the situation could not have looked more dismal. But hidden below the surface, as always, change was in the works.

Late in 1948, Zhdanov mysteriously disappeared. He was reported as dying of a heart attack, but it is also very likely that Stalin feared his growing power and had him removed (Liehm and Liehm, 65). In 1953, Stalin died. But change did not come quickly. The best directors were either old or dead, and the young ones had not yet learned to be innovative. With the political climate uncertain, directors were also wisely choosing to remain cautious. They knew that work which might be acceptable in the immediate post-Stalin years might get them into deep trouble when either Nikita Khrushchev, Georgi Malenkov, or someone else finally solidified control (Stoil, 109–110).

In the meantime, some filmmakers turned to adaptations of literary classics as an alternative. Thus began a genre of Soviet film that has continued to the present, with some noteworthy results. Sergei Yutkevich's *Othello* (1955) employed the distinctly Russian theme of misplaced trust. Grigori Kozintsev's *Don Quixote* (1957) sought contemporary relevance in the classic text, and Alexei Batalov's *The Overcoat* (1959) was also an excellent production. Although it fails to capture the humor of Gogol's story, it does feature a wonderful performance by Rolan Bykov. Iosef Heifitz's *The Lady with the Little Dog* (1960) continued the style of unresolved dilemmas that had entered Soviet films in the late fifties. The story presents a man and woman, unhappy in their separate marriages, who meet on their solitary vacations in Yalta and fall in love. Though living a great distance from each other, they eventually agree to begin occasional clandestine meetings which they plan to continue indefinitely. Though constantly struggling to escape upwards (shown through repeated character movement), each is unable to shake the past because of their commitments to their families. Other successful works in this genre have included Kozintsev's *Hamlet* (1965), comments on the fleeting and corrupt nature of power and the effects on those who possess it as they suffer through isolation and distorted senses of time, place, and relationships. The eternally submissive presence of the peasantry is also a factor. They will always be there, even longer than the solid walls that dominate the settings. Other important works were Kozintsev's masterful *King Lear* (1970), and Andrei Mikhalkov-Konchalovski's *Uncle Vanya* (1970 to 1971), which the Liehms refer to as "easily the best film version of the Chekhov play" (*Most Important*, 309). (Material in this paragraph comes from Stoil, 111–112; Liehm, *Most Important*, 205, 217; and personal analysis.)

In 1956, Nikita Khrushchev's speech to the 20th Congress of the Soviet Communist Party revealed Josef Stalin's crimes to the nation and the world. The impact on cinema was not one of complete liberation, since directors were still reluctant to address contemporary issues and policies. But they did gain the ability to attack Stalin and present complex characters and relationships. Within these narrow confines, they found a great amount of room for artistic innovation.

Mikhail Kalatozov's *Letiat zhuravli* (*The Cranes Are Flying*, 1957) provided the first major thematic and stylistic breakthrough. Unlike Stalin's preferred version of the war, Kalatozov's film shows suffering everywhere, in the midst of which, official pronouncements state only basic facts that either ignore or contradict personal feelings. But the film's real theme is of a renewal of life, appropriately emphasized through Kalatozov's stylistic breaks with socialist realism. For the film celebrated both rising out of the war's destruction and breathing new life into Soviet film. In one notable sequence, Kalatozov intercuts a wedding montage with the fall of a dying soldier. In another, the main character runs up to her parents' bombed-out apartment and finds a clock, half destroyed but still ticking. It slows down for a few beats, the same as life seems to when death comes to loved ones, but then it keeps on going. The brief shot forms an appropriate metaphor for the Soviet Union surviving Stalin's reign. At the same time, these scenes also serve as a warning. Both the soldier and the girl's parents die when they believe they are most secure. The conclusion, in which the soldier does not return though that possibility has remained open, also seems sufficient to refute charges that the film was overly optimistic.

Grigori Chukhrai's *Ballada o soldate* (*Ballad of a Soldier*, 1959) presented another tale of suffering and loss through which people sustain themselves with hopes, dreams, and illusions. A voice-over narrator calls the main character a hero, but the film's opening shows him running from two tanks. He happens to find an anti-tank gun and surprises himself by getting it to work against his pursuers. His commander grants him a ten-day pass, saying, "The army could use more cowards like you." The pass allows him four days to travel home, two to visit his mother, and four to get back. But the trip home takes an extra day and a half, so the soldier is only able to greet his mother on the road and then head back. Along his journey, he finds immense suffering, crowded conditions, and people struggling with broken families and marriages. These aspects reveal a reality that the Soviet people need to face. They cannot live on dreams and heroism forever. But, through its somber tone, episodic structure based on the narration of a memory, presentation of human characters, and use of upside-down camera angles and montage, *Ballad of a Soldier* reveals how a poetic memory can be more valuable and accurate than anything presented as socialist realism.

World War II is still a popular theme for Soviet filmmakers, perhaps because many of their lives were formed by the events of that time and they have waited long to be able to say what they want about it. In the early sixties, it was the basis for a film, *Ivanovo detstvo* (*Ivan's Childhood*, 1962), that secured the reputation and career of the man whom many consider the greatest modern Soviet director, Andrei Tarkovski. In his film, Tarkovski set off not artificially to capture "reality," but to produce his own poetic vision that would keep audiences involved. He felt that as long as he maintained a strong moral basis for his work, audiences would not get lost and the honesty of his vision would be maintained. Authorities fought his deviations from a strictly structured rendering of the script every step of the way. But when he was finished, Tarkovski had created a film that took top honors at the Venice and San Francisco film festivals of 1962 and bought him a degree of independence.

What Tarkovski achieved was a film that went stylistically beyond any previous Soviet productions and captured the dull and grisly reality of war, all through being set inside the head of Lieutenant Galtsev, one of the main characters. The setting is full of mud, ruined buildings, dead trees, stuck trucks, dripping water, occasional gunshots, and complete weariness. Yet, as one character tells Galtsev,

"Everything in life is sudden." Life is constant change, and Tarkovski's approach takes in life completely, including dreams, a part of life and consciousness that most people ignore. The film begins with what appears to be Ivan's dream of a pleasant afternoon spent running through the countryside with his mother. But the final scene continues this dream, triggered by Galtsev's discovery that Ivan was captured and executed by the Gestapo shortly after they had last seen each other. Obviously, then, the entire film has been Galtsev's memories.

Galtsev imagines Ivan's dreams at two other times as well, and Ivan is young and fresh in each one, much the opposite of the way he actually was during the war. Tarkovski wants to engender an appreciation for life itself, which he does by almost strictly dividing life and death. The war is associated completely with death, while all the dream sequences are brimming over with life. The war was not glorious, and Galtsev's final reaction is to choose life. Recognizing the reality of war, it is the choice that must be made.

Tarkovski's portrait of the fifteenth-century icon painter Andre Rublev, in his film of the same title (1966), provides another powerful example of his style. The film's biblical structure, in which its sections are simply linked together rather than being interwoven by following various characters or plot developments, confronts the viewer with an archaic form of storytelling, complex because of its very simplicity. Similarly, the camera often simply stares at this world as broadly as possible, as if it might miss something by getting too close. At times, in fact, when we are focusing on one character, something happens with another that the camera shifts to, but too late to catch the cause of the action. So everything is laid out in an orderly fashion, but the camera still denies an ability to present a coherently organized picture of this world in twentieth-century terms.

Throughout the rest of his career, despite attacks in the Soviet press for being " 'difficult' and self-indulgent," Tarkovski continued to pursue his poetic style and explorations of the subconscious in *Soliaris* (1972), *Zerkalo* (*Mirror,* 1975), *Stalker* (1980), and *Nostalgia* (1983).

Though he obviously received state funding for these projects, Tarkovski did not actually get state support. His films obtained limited distribution and advertising, and eventually, even his international reputation could not protect him from the authorities. In 1982, Tarkovski went to Italy to complete work on *Nostalgia.* But he was stripped of his citizenship when he decided to extend his stay in 1984, and he died in Paris in December 1986, of cancer (Lawton, 48). Tarkovski completed one film while in exile, *The Sacrifice* (1986).

Following Tarkovski into the poetic realm was the Armenian director Sergei Parajanov, who produced two beautiful films in the 1960s, *Teni zabytykh predkov* (*Shadows of Forgotten Ancestors,* 1964) and *Tsvety granata* (*The Colors of the Pomegraniate,* 1969). Recently, he also completed *Legenda o Suramskoi kreposti* (*The Legend of the Surami Fortress,* 1984, released 1986) and *The Demon* (1989), based on an original work by Lermentov. In *Shadows of Forgotten Ancestors,* the camera occupies the spiritual realm of nature, shooting through the shadows at the characters trapped in the temporal world, and constantly circling them in amazing shots from both high and low angles. The characters, in their attempts to identify with this natural cycle of life, are also regularly performing rituals that involve forming circles. But the main character, Ivan, has death as a constant companion. His entire family and his lover all die, and a scene of Ivan digging a grave late one night shows that he views death as his natural home. Shortly after, he marries but always ignores his wife. Eventually, she takes a lover, and Ivan goes to the woods to die. Ivan is a tragic fool, but the camera supports his view of reality. In his own way, he transcends the physical barriers that entrap his agrarian society, eventually reuniting with his true love after death. This was a film worthy of Dovzhenko's legacy. But it does not give any narrow political solutions, and it even denies our ability to define right and wrong. In the end, it argues that we must go beyond all such determinations.

Nevertheless the Party had other ideas, and Leonid Brezhnev's rise to power in the mid-sixties signaled the beginning of another long, hard period for Soviet artists. In September 1965 the first writers were jailed since Khrushchev's 1956 speech. The next month, the Central Committee informed the First Congress of Film Workers of the Soviet Union that artists were expected to follow an ideological line (Liehm and Liehm, 306). In addition to the ideological pressures, the studios became more consumer oriented and less demanding (Lawton, 2). This situation produced obvious hardships for directors, and many had films that were either never made or never shown even if they were (Liehm and Liehm, 311–312). In the seventies, the State Committee for Cinematography (Goskino) experienced great bureaucratic growth, and scripts that strayed too far from the Party line were crushed. Several filmmakers who demonstrated either great promise or great talent had their films either officially suppressed or condemned. These included Aleksander Askoldov, Gleb Panfilov, Alexei German, Larisa Shepitko, Vladimir Naumov and Alexander Amov (a team), Vasili Shukshin, and Mikhail Kalik. Sergei Parajanov was arrested in 1973 and 1982.

But film had advanced too far to retreat permanently. Audiences demanded good products, and film had its own ways of proceeding. In the non-Russian provinces of the Soviet Union in particular, directors avoided socialist realism by making use of nationalist folklore, history, and culture to develop truly autonomous film cultures (Liehm and Liehm, 324). Directors also worked within specific genres to gain notable achievements.

Eldar Riazanov directed a pair of *"byt,"* slice-of-life, comedies that became very popular: *Ironia sud'by, ili s legkim parom* (*Irony of Fate, or Have a Good Sauna*, 1975) and *Sluzhebnyi romans* (*An Office Romance*, 1978). Both appeared very "safe." But his next film, *Garazh* (*Garage*, 1980), contained stinging satire that earned rebuke from the authorities. In it, a committee working on garage construction is locked in a meeting room for a night, during which the papers establishing their authority are destroyed, relieving them of their official duties. The dialogue then turns to a number of confessions and revelations. In the morning they leave the building to start a new day, but the events have indicated that they will most likely return to their old routines (Lawton, 10–11). Other directors working in this genre include Georgi Danelia, who produced *Afonia* (1975), *Mimino* (1977), and the highly praised *Osennii marafon* (*Autumn Marathon*, 1980); Nikita Mikhalkov with *Piat' vecherov* (*Five Evenings*, 1979) and *Rodnia* (*Kinfolk*, 1982); and Gleb Panfilov, who began his career with *V ogne broda net* (*No Ford in the Fire*, 1968) and *Nachalo* (*Debut*, 1970). His next films, *Proshu slova* (*May I Have the Floor*, 1977) and *Tema* (*Theme*, 1979), encountered great difficulties. *Tema* was shelved for seven years, but then achieved international acclaim when finally released in 1986. Panfilov's films focus on the problems of artistic creativity. Two women directors working in the "*byt*" genre are Dinara Asanova, whose *Ne bolit golova u diatla* (*Woodpeckers Don't Get Headaches*, 1975) and *Kliuch bez prava peredachi* (*The Restricted Key*, 1977) focus on youth, and Lana Gogoberidze, who addressed problems of Soviet women in *Perepolokh* (*Commotion*, 1977) and *Neskolko interviu po lichnym voprosam* (*Some Interviews on Personal Matters*, 1979) (Lawton, 6–17).

Other important genres included historical dramas and adaptations of literary classics, with the major figure working in this area being Nikita Mikhalkov. A former actor, Mikhalkov began his directorial career with a "Western" *Svoi sredi chuzhikh, chuzhoi sredi svoikh* (*At Home among Strangers, Stranger at Home*, 1975) and *Raba liubvi* (*A Slave of Love*, 1976). Both were set during the Russian Revolution and Civil War of 1920–1921. *Raba liubvi* involved a silent film crew and achieved international popularity. Mikhalkov created a pair of successful literary adaptations with *Neskolko dnei iz zhizni I. I. Oblomova* (*Some Days in the Life of I. I. Oblomov*, 1982), based on the novel *Oblomov* by Ivan Goncharov, and *Neokonchennaia p'esa dlia mekhanicheskogo pianino* (*Unfinished Piece for Player Piano*, 1977), based on the Chekov play *Platonov* (Lawton, 18). In this film, a group of isolated characters who have lost all senses of love, meaning, and idealism attempt to cope with the emptiness of their lives by continually celebrating nothing and isolating themselves even further from each other. Their daily lives have killed all their youthful senses of purpose, but they fail to realize how many others they touch through all the routine activities they dread. In the end, however, there is hope because the piece remains unfinished, so there is always more to do.

Another director working in this area was Mikhalkov's older brother, Andrei Mikhalkov-Konchalovski, who produced the epic historical drama *Sibiriada* (*Sibiriana/The Siberiade*, 1979). The film did very well at the box office but was then withdrawn when Konchalovski emigrated to the West (Lawton, 19). Elem Klimov also contributed to this genre with *Agoniia* (*Rasputin*, 1975), which was unfortunately drastically altered through editing (Lawton, 19).

The major genre of World War II films was dominated in the seventies by Alexei German, whose works include *Proverka na dorogakh* (*Trial on the Road*, 1971, released in 1986), *Dvadtsat' dnei bez voiny* (*Twenty Days Without War*, 1976), and his latest masterpiece, *Moi drug Ivan Lapshin* (*My Friend Ivan Lapshin*, 1983, released in 1985). In addition, Elem Klimov contributed the powerful *Idi i smotri* (*Come and See,* 1985), which, "while portraying the war ... wants to spread a peace message. In line with the Soviet policy of arms control, the film with its apocalyptic title warns the viewer about the possibility of a nuclear holocaust" (Lawton, 42). Finally, there was also the late Vasili Shukshin, whose films of country life based on his own short stories, *Strannye liudi* (*Strange People,* 1971), *Pechki-lavochki* (*Shop Crumbs,* 1973), and *Kalina krasnaia* (*The Red Guelder Rose,* 1974), earned him a large popular following.

Thus, despite its reputation as an era of cultural stagnation, the seventies saw the production of a number of excellent films, many more than can be adequately noted here. In fact, documentary director Herz Frank remembers the decade as a very productive time, which, he says, only proves that developments in politics and art are not always parallel.

Despite these accomplishments, the outlook for Soviet cinema at the beginning of the eighties was bleak, due to trends that had developed in the previous decade. Both the public and the film industry (including government officials) turned their backs on the most innovative works, and several talented ethnic directors such as Parajanov, Panfilov, Tengiz Abuladze, Yuri Ilenko, Khodzhikuli Narliev, Bolotbek Shamshiev, and Tolomush Okeev were persecuted and thus reduced either to complete silence or the production of very bland pictures. Filmmaking became centralized in Moscow, and as a result no young directors or significant trends emerged. The cinema lacked any guiding spiritual leader. At the same time, attendance began dropping as television's popularity increased and audiences became bored with the standard repertoire. In response, the film industry adopted a policy of concentrating on mass genres. Spearheaded by the theoretical concepts of director Andrei Mikhalkov-Konchalovski, now living in the West, this trend resulted in the heavy promotion of the enormously popular *Moskva slezam ne verit* (*Moscow Does Not Believe in Tears,* Vladimir Menshov, 1980), which won an American Academy Award for best foreign film. The film offered little room for future artistic development because of its concentration on an ordinary romantic plot (not unlike any Hollywood soap opera) to the exclusion of any stylistic or formal complexity.

Nevertheless, films of this nature dominated Soviet production at the beginning of the eighties. An example of such a production would be Nikolai Gubenko's *Podranki* (*The Orphans,* 1983). Even though it won a Special Jury Prize at the Cannes Film Festival, Gubenko's portrait of a man remembering his childhood at a boy's military school after being orphaned during the war makes a very tame statement about not being able to judge the past. The film presents life under Stalin as not being all bad. The boys' problems were mainly caused by the war, and the main character develops a love of poetry and becomes a famous writer, though how these interests developed is never explained. The state cares for the boys well, and the school administrators preach a lack of hatred towards the Germans and reprimand an instructor who strikes the main character. The child's witnessing of this teacher's heartfelt grief appears to lead directly to his conclusion that the past cannot be judged.

This message would not seem to be the most urgent one for a society which still needed to face the reality of Stalinism in order to discover its identity and move forward both culturally and economically. With the rise to power in 1985 of Mikhail S. Gorbachev, it is no longer the message that dominates Soviet films. A comparison of Rolan Bykov's *Chuchelo* (*Scarecrow*, 1984) with *The Orphans*, for example, reveals a world of difference. In *Scarecrow* the schoolchildren are caught between cultures, with no sense of tradition and only a gross sense of materialism picked up from the West. Thus the rock music blasting from their radios is often completely inappropriate to the action taking place. But the local brass band plays on a concrete slab out in the woods, and the only protector of the town's heritage is an old man who has filled his small house with art works. With no sense of values, the children adopt a fascist group mentality and persecute this man's granddaughter into leaving for another home. *Scarecrow*, therefore, presents a poignant statement about the lack of values in contemporary society.

Under Gorbachev's policy of *glasnost*, Soviet films began displaying a new openness in examining both the past and contemporary society and the entire film industry has been reorganized. In the late eighties, two productions that dealt with the past in an intensely honest fashion, Tengiz Abuladze's *Pokaianie* (*Repentance*) and Alexander Askoldov's *Komissar* (*Commissar*), were taken off the shelves and given international distribution. *Repentance* focuses on the destruction and evil behind the smiling face of Stalinism, its lingering aftereffects, and the search for a spiritual connection with deeper, sturdier values. It continually challenges audiences by providing surrealistic episodes while also keeping them involved through its horrific account of Stalinism at work in a small town. Its existence and the reasons that some continue to defend it become understandable. But a powerful sense of spiritual emptiness and the need to replace it are also present. The film ends with an old lady asking, "What good is a road that doesn't lead to a church?"

Commissar was mainly controversial in the Soviet Union because of its Jewish theme. But it still upholds the Red Army over the Whites and concludes with the need to fight for ideals. A better world will not come about if people just sit around waiting for it. By contrasting the cold and practical world of a female commissar with that of a poor Jewish family, Askoldov argues that we must not lose our humanity or forget the inhumanity of war. Nor must we abstain from the fight. Before the commissar enters the Jewish home, she is in danger of losing all her compassion, having hypocritically ordered the execution of a comrade for his sexual indiscretion. But the international kindness dreamed of by Yefim, the man of the house, is only a fairy tale. He is unable to keep even his children from terrorizing each other. Therefore the film ends with the commissar leaving her baby at the house in order to rejoin the fight against the White Army. Askoldov tells parts of this simple story with great simplicity. But he also shows how human, complex, and hypocritical all his characters can be, and he does so with such powerful dreamlike images that the viewer must search for the meanings, which remain haunting.

Two other progressive developments have been the release of previously banned films by Alexander Sokurov and the emergence of the Kazakhstan "New Wave." Sokurov's work might be described as taking Tarkovski's methods one step further, challenging the ways in which audiences see, think, and understand narration. According to Amos Vogel, Sokurov's work is "permeated by despair and flashes of hope. It is difficult, slow, disjointed and requires concentration. Discordant montage, sudden intrusion of documentary materials, non-realist use of color, varying film speeds and a shockingly atonal, expressionist soundtrack validate Sokurov's stylistic fragmentation" (Vogel, 64). The young Kazakhstan filmmakers have distinguished themselves by not latching onto the major trends from the largest studios. Instead, such directors as Sergei Solovyov, Rashid Nugmanov, Serik Aprimov, Abai Karpikov, Ardak Amirkulov, Naana Chankova, and the team of Bakhyt Kilibaev and Alexander Baranov (among others) have focused on a wide range of subjects to produce films that have gained significant critical attention (Ciesol).

Structural changes within the film industry itself began at the fifth Congress of the Filmmakers' Union in May 1986, when controversial director Elem Klimov became First Secrectary of the Union in an election that ousted the superconservative Lev Kulijanov, who had maintained control since 1965. Six months later, Brezhnev's Goskino chairman, Filipp Ermash, was replaced by Alexander Kamshalov, a man who represents the new Party attitudes towards the film industry. As Anna Lawton states, "He is expected to establish a viable relationship with the Filmmakers Union and to foster a policy that favors artistic expression" (36–37).

To produce greater artistic freedom, Klimov's administration, which lasted two years, began the process of dismantling the film industry, a process which is now almost complete (Horton, personal letter). One of the immediate results of decentralization was the rise of new independent studios and the promotion of young filmmakers. Their films, such as *Malenkaia Vera (Little Vera)*, by twenty-eight-year-old Vasili Pichul, are showing honest pictures of a Soviet life that appears very bleak and young people who respond to the situation by breaking all the rules of sexual and social propriety. Other films showing young people attempting to forge their own culture in defiance of the state and the past include *Vzlomshchik (The Burglar,* Valeri Ogorodnikov, 1987), *Legko li byt' molodym? (Is It Easy to be Young?,* Iuris Podnieks, 1987), and *Kurier (The Courier,* Karen Shakhnazarov, 1987). Films that promise further revelations include the titles *The Black Monk, Solovetsky Power, Confession,* and *The Fountain* (Williamson, "Rubles," 26). Clearly, the current era is the most exciting period in Soviet film since the early sixties.

But there are a number of problems involved with these changes. Though studios are attempting to establish funds to support the most artistically avantgarde productions, they first need to develop some profits, which is no easy task and poses further dangers towards the alternate goal of an aesthetically innovative cinema. Commercialization now seems to be the only new ogre, no longer sharing the role with ideological restrictions. Directors are consciously turning away from artistic challenges to try to fulfill audience desires. At the same time, audiences are shrinking because of competition from television, VCRs, and other sources of entertainment developing parallel to the cinema (Williamson, "Rubles," 26). Robert Kolker believes that television has, in fact, opened great new opportunities for Soviet directors and some fascinating new works, both documentary and fiction, are appearing there. However, most filmmakers have a bias against the medium and instead harbor illusions of American co-productions and international successes. Thrilled with their new freedom to explore sex and violence, they are creating films that aim only for shock value, sometimes in ludicrous style.

In contrast, Andrew Horton, who has worked with and studied East European filmmakers, is cautiously optimistic about the future. While agreeing with Kolker that Soviet filmmakers are now producing much more "trash," spilling over more and more into pornography, Horton sees this development as natural and good. Soviet filmmakers now have the freedom to produce more trash, and "as in the United States, this industry will find its level" (personal letter). He believes that artistic filmmakers such as Sokurov will always find a way to keep producing, which sounds logical. If Tarkovski could work under Brezhnev, Sokurov should be able to work under Gorbachev. But the true path forward for Soviet film, Horton believes, will be through what he refers to as "crossover" productions: films that have a large audience appeal, but still have significant aesthetic quality. He finds several examples of such films in the recent Kazakhstan releases and in productions like *Little Vera, Intergirl, The Needle,* Alexander Proshkin's *The Cold Summer of '53, Where to Find Nophelet, The Day Lasts More Than a Hundred Years, Freedom is Paradise* (awarded "Best Film" at the 1989 Montreal World Film Festival), and *Utoli pechali (Assuage My Sorrow)*. Such productions are coming from conscientious filmmakers who are simply recognizing the necessity of needing to reach a larger audience. The heightened commercialization of Soviet film is now a fact, but it is presenting great opportunities amidst all the confusion to aggressive filmmakers while wiping away what Horton refers to as " 'spoiled socialist artists' who simply thought up an idea, got approval, shot and had no problem" (personal letter).

The greater possibilities for individual expression under *glasnost* are both the cause and product of the decentralization of the film industry. The Soviet Filmmakers' Union is now a very loose organization made up of representatives of the republics and a few officers. In response, there has been a growing number of independent producers, from five or ten in April of 1989 to over thirty-five a year later, and these had already formed their own organization (Horton, personal letter). As a result, the Soviet film industry is now beginning to resemble Yugoslavia's, which Horton sees as a positive development:

The Yugoslav film industry is a highly diversified collection of production companies which primarily work on a cost effective basis, sharing production costs between distribution, box office income, Cultural Committee funding, and other sources such as television (a large number of co-productions) and foreign co-investment funds.

Such a decentralized self management model which emphasizes the importance of the artist in the artistic process is truly in between a rigid Stalinist system and an open market Hollywood structure. If the Soviet cinema after *glasnost* does evolve more clearly in this direction, filmmakers . . . will have moved that much closer to becoming semi-independent "freelance" artists like their counterparts in the non-socialist world. (Horton and Brashinsky ms., 25)

Television and international co-productions are also offering new opportunities. Horton sees the interplay between TV and film as good, natural, and increasing in the future, part of the overall current need for filmmakers to reach larger audiences. An example of the positive potential for co-productions is the film *Swan Lake: The Zone,* a Ukranian-Swedish-Canadian-Mosfilm joint venture that held the interest of all age groups, though it included no words for the first half-hour (personal letter). But Horton, like Kolker, warns against Soviet filmmakers banking on super co-productions such as Mikhalkov's *Dark Eyes* (1987), shot in Italy and the Soviet Union and starring Marcello Mastroianni. Such films, in his view, tend to replace nationally based substance with internationally based style in their attempts to reach global audiences (Horton and Brashinsky ms., 32–33). Finally, as in the twenties, Soviet documentaries seem to be leading the way into this new era, with filmmakers again taking up Vertov's call to go out and capture reality. These are films that are challenging the fiction filmmakers through their intensity and quality. They are also still further proof that serious content can hold an audience (Horton, "Six Hundred," 32). The result of all these changes is that Soviet filmmakers have now a greater potential than ever before for telling the truth. The struggle is never over, but the new situation is offering some fascinating possibilities.

BIBLIOGRAPHY

Books

Arossev, Alexander. *Soviet Cinema*. Moscow: Voks Publishing, 1935.

Babitsky, Paul, and John Rimberg. *The Soviet Film Industry*. New York: Praeger for Research Program on the USSR, 1955.

Bakshy, Alexander. *The Path of the Modern Russian Stage and Other Essays*. London: C. Palmer & Hayward, 1916.

Baskakov, V. E. "The Revolutionary Cinema." *Marxist-Leninist Aesthetics and the Arts*. Vladimir Eryomin, ed. Moscow: Progress, 1980: 310–20.

Bazin, Andre. "The Stalin Myth in Soviet Cinema (with an Introduction by Dudley Andrew)." *Movies and Methods, Volume II*. Bill Nichols, ed. Berkeley: University of California Press, 1985: 29–40.

Berest, Boris. *History of the Ukrainian Cinema*. New York: Shevchenko Scientific Society, 1962.

Birkos, Alexander S. *Soviet Cinema: Directors and Films.* Hamden, Conn.: Archon Books, 1976.
Bryher, Annie Winifred Ellerman. *Film Problems of Soviet Russia.* Territet, Switzerland: Riant, 1929.
Carter, Huntly. *The New Spirit in the Russian Theatre.* New York: B. Blom. 1970. Reprint of the 1929 ed.
———. *The New Theatre and Cinema of Soviet Russia.* London: Chapman and Dodd, 1924.
Cohen, Louis H. *The Cultural-Political Traditions and Developments of the Soviet Cinema 1917–72.* New York: Arno, 1974.
Cowie, Peter, ed. *International Film Guide.* New York: A. S. Barnes & Co., 1963-present (annual). See in particular, "IFG Dossier: Soviet Film Now." 1989: 22–69.
Christensen, Peter G. "*Aelita,* Individual Psychology, and the Soviet State." *Holding the Vision: Essays on Film.* Kent, Ohio: International Film Society, Kent State University, 1983: 95–101.
Dickinson, Thorold, and Catherine de la Roche. *Soviet Cinema.* New York: Arno Press. 1972.
Eagle, Herbert. *Russian Formalist Film Theory.* Ann Arbor: University of Michigan Press. 1981.
———. "Visual Patterning and Meaning in Eisenstein's Early Films." *Russian Literature and American Critics: In Honor of Deming B. Brown.* Kenneth N. Brostrom, ed. Ann Arbor: University of Michigan Press, 331–46.
Eisenstein, Sergei M. *Film Form: Essays in Film Theory.* New York: Harcourt Brace Jovanovich, 1949.
———. *The Film Sense.* Jay Leyda, trans. & ed. New York: Harcourt Brace Jovanovich, 1942, 1970, 1975.
———. *Ivan the Terrible.* London: Lorrimer Publishing Ltd., 1970.
———. *The Soviet Screen.* Moscow: Foreign Languages Publishing House, 1939.
Farnsworth, Rodney. "Eisenstein's Conversion to the Herocentric Narrative as Seen in the Context of Russian Criticism." *Purdue University Seventh Annual Conference on Film.* West Lafayette, Ind.: Department of English, Purdue University, 1983: 27–32.
Fifty Years of Soviet Cinema: 1917–67. London: British Film Institute, 1967.
Golovskoy, Val S., with John Rimberg. *Behind the Soviet Screen: The Motion-Picture Industry in the USSR, 1972–1982.* Ann Arbor, Mich.: Ardis, 1986.
Haraszti, Miklos. *The Velvet Prison: Artists Under State Socialism.* New York: Basic Books, 1987.
Hecht, Leo. "Union of Soviet Socialist Republics." *World Cinema Since 1945.* William Luhr, ed. New York: Ungar Publishing Co., 1987: 558–86.
Hecht, Leo., ed. *NEWSNOTES on Soviet and East European Drama and Theatre* (periodical), Fairfax, Va.: George Mason University.
Hibbin, Nina. *Eastern Europe: An Illustrated Guide.* Screen Series. New York: A. S. Barnes, 1969.
Hildreth, Lee, Constance Penley, and Andrew Ross, trans. *Montage Eisenstein.* Bloomington: Indiana University Press, 1979.
Horton, Andrew, and Michael Brashinsky. *Soviet Cinema Under Glasnost: Our Hearts Demand Change* (MS. copy). Princeton, N.J.: Princeton University Press, 1991.

Huaco, George A. *The Sociology of Film Art*. New York: Basic Books, 1965.
Kepley, Vance. *In the Service of the State: The Cinema of Alexander Dovzhenko*. Madison: University of Wisconsin Press, 1986.
Knight, Arthur. *The Liveliest Art: A Panoramic History of the Movies*. New York: Macmillan, 1957.
Kuleshov, Lev. *Fifty Years in Films: Selected Works*. Ekaterina Khokhlova, comp. Moscow: Raduga, 1987.
——. *Kuleshov on Film*. Ron Levaco, ed. Berkeley: University of California Press, 1974.
Lary, N. M. *Dostoevsky and Soviet Film*. Ithaca, N.Y.: Cornell University Press, 1986.
Lawton, Anna. "Toward a New Openness in Soviet Cinema, 1976–87." *Post New Wave Cinema in the Soviet Union and Eastern Europe*. Daniel J. Goulding, ed. Bloomington: Indiana University Press, 1989: 1–50.
LeFanu, Mark. *The Cinema of Andrei Tarkovsky*. Champaign: University of Illinois Press, 1988.
Leighton, Lauren G., ed. *Studies in Honor of Xenia Gasiorowska*. Columbus, Ohio: Slavica Publishers, 1983.
Leyda, Jay. *Kino: A History of the Russian and Soviet Film*. London: Allen & Unwin, 1960.
Liehm, Antonín J., and Mira Liehm. *The Most Important Art: Eastern European Film After 1945*. Berkeley: University of California Press, 1977.
Lovgren, Hakan, and Lars Kleberg, eds. *Eisenstein Revisited: A Collection of Essays*. Stockholm: Almqvist & Wiksell, 1987.
Macdonald, Dwight. *Dwight Macdonald on Movies*. Englewood Cliffs, N.J.: Prentice-Hall, 1969.
Manvell, Roger. *Films and The Second World War*. New York: A. S. Barnes & Co., 1974.
Manvell, Roger, and Lewis Jacobs, eds. *International Encyclopedia of Film*. New York: Crown, 1972.
Marshall, Herbert. *Masters of the Soviet Cinema: Crippled Creative Biographies*. London: Routledge and Kegan Paul, 1983.
Mast, Gerald. *A Short History of the Movies*. 2nd ed. Indianapolis: The Bobbs-Merrill Co., 1976.
Michelson, Annette, ed. Kevin O'Brien, trans. *Kino-Eye: The Writings of Dziga Vertov*. Berkeley: University of California Press, 1984.
Pisarevskii, Dmitrii Sergeivich. *100 Soviet Films*. Moscow: Progress. 1967.
Pronay, Nicholas, and D. W. Spring, eds. *Propaganda, Politics, and Film, 1918–45*. London: Macmillan Press, 1982.
Reddaway, Peter. "Literature, the Arts and the Personality of Lenin." *Lenin: The Man, the Theorist, the Leader*. Leonard Schapiro and Reddaway, eds. New York: Praeger, 1967.
Rimberg, John David. *The Motion Picture in the Soviet Union: 1918–1952: A Sociological Analysis*. New York: Arno Press, 1973.
Robinson, David. *The History of World Cinema*. New York: Stein and Day, 1973.
Salisbury, Harrison E., ed. *The Soviet Union: The Fifty Years*. New York: Harcourt Brace & World, 1967.
Schnitzer, Luda, Jean Schnitzer, and Martin Marcel. *Cinema in Revolution: The Heroic Era of the Soviet Film*. London: Secker & Warburg, 1973.

Seton, Marie. *Sergei M. Eisenstein*. New York: Grove Press, 1960.
Slide, Anthony. *The International Film Industry: A Historical Dictionary*. Westport, Conn.: Greenwood Press, 1989.
Solmatovskaya, Galina, and Irina Shilova. *Who Is Who in the Soviet Cinema*. Moscow: Progress. 1979.
Soviet Cinematography. Bombay: People's Publishing House, Ltd., 1950.
Stoil, Michael Jon. *Cinema Beyond the Danube: The Camera and Its Politics*. Metuchen, N.J.: The Scarecrow Press, 1974.
"Symposium on Soviet Documentary: S. Tretyakov, V. Shklovsky, E. Shub, and O. Brik." *The Documentary Tradition: From Nanook to Woodstock*. Lewis Jacobs, ed. New York: W. W. Norton, 1971:29–36.
Tarkovsky, Andrei. *Sculpting in Time: Reflections on the Cinema*. New York: Alfred A. Knopf, 1987.
Taylor, Richard. *The Politics of the Soviet Cinema, 1917–1929*. Cambridge: Cambridge University Press, 1979.
──────. *Film Propaganda: Soviet Russia and Nazi Germany*. London: Croom Helm; New York: Barnes & Noble Books. 1979.
Taylor, Richard, ed. *S. M. Eisenstein: Selected Works, Volume 1, Writings, 1922–34*. Bloomington: Indiana University Press, 1988.
Taylor, Richard, and Ian Christie, eds. *The Film Factory: Russian and Soviet Cinema in Documents 1896–1939*. Cambridge, Mass.: Harvard University Press, 1988.
Thompson, Kristin. *Eisenstein's Ivan the Terrible: A Neoformalist Analysis*. Princeton, N.J.: Princeton University Press, 1981.
Usai, Paolo Cherchi, and Yuri Tsivian, eds. *Silent Witnesses: Russian Films 1908–1919*. London: British Film Institute, 1989.
Vaughan, Dai. *"The Man With the Movie Camera." The Documentary Tradition: From Nanook to Woodstock*. Lewis Jacobs, ed. New York: W. W. Norton, 1971:53–59.
Vorontsov, Yuri, and Igor Rachuk. *The Phenomenon of the Soviet Cinema*. Moscow: Progress Publishers. 1980.
Vronskaya, Jeanne. *Young Soviet Film Makers*. London: Allen and Unwin. 1972.
Wollen, Peter. *Signs and Meaning in the Cinema*. 3rd ed. Bloomington: Indiana University Press, 1972.
Youngblood, Denise J. *Soviet Cinema in the Silent Era, 1919–1934*. Ann Arbor: University of Michigan Research Press, 1985.
──────. *Young Soviet Film Makers*. London: Allen and Unwin, 1972.
Zorkaia, Markovna. *The Illustrated History of the Soviet Cinema*. Bryn Mawr, Pa.: Hippocrene Books, 1989.

Articles

Abdrashitov, A. "Georgian Cinema: A Glorious Tradition." *Soviet Film* 10 (October 1983):37–39.
"Biographical Notes and Acronyms." *Screen* 15.3 (Autumn 1974):112–18.
Bollag, Brenda. "Klimov & Co." *Film Comment* May–June 1987:40–43.
Bordwell, David. "The Idea of Montage in Soviet Art and Film." *Cinema Journal* 11.2 (Spring 1972):9–17.

Bortnikov, I. "Georgian Cinema: 'Enchanting Evenings.' " *Soviet Film* 7 (July 1985):22–23.

Brewster, Ben, ed. "Documents from 'Novy Lef.' " *Screen* 12.4 (Winter 1971–72):59–100.

Burch, Noel. "Film's Institutional Mode of Representation and the Soviet Response." *October* 11 (1979):77–96.

Burlaiev, N. "Face the Audience." *Soviet Film* 4 (April 1985):23–24.

Burns, Paul E. "Cultural Revolution, Collectivization and Soviet Cinema." *Film & History* 11.4 (December 1981):84–96.

———. "Linkage: Pudovkin's Classics Revisited." *Journal of Popular Film and Television* 9.2 (Summer 1981):70–77.

Carduner, A. "The Tyranny of the Marketplace and the Tyranny of the Commissar, or Fools Russian Where Critics Fear to Tread." *Film Critic* 1.1 (September–October 1972):42–49.

Carroll, Noel. "For God and Country." *Artforum* 11.5 (January 1973):56–60.

Christie, Ian. "Russians." *Sight & Sound* 52.3 (Summer 1983):174–180.

———. "Soviet Cinema: Making Sense of Sound." *Screen* 23.2 (July–August 1982):34–49.

Ciesol, Forrest S. "Kazakhstan Wave." *Sight and Sound*, Winter 1989–90:56–58.

Collum, D. Duncan. "Opening Stalin's Tomb: A Soviet Film That Refused To Die." *Sojourners*, May 1989:39–41.

Corliss, Richard. "Censors' Day Off." *Time*, 10 April 1989:127–28.

Crofts, Stephen. "Ideology and Form: *Chapayev* and Soviet Socialist Realism." *Film Forum* 1.1 (Spring 1976):65–77.

Denkin, H. "Linguistic Models in Early Soviet Cinema." *Cinema Journal* 17.1 (Fall 1977):1–13.

Dyomin, Victor, and Alexander Batchen. "Mad Russian." *Film Comment*, May–June 1987:48–51.

Feldman, S. "*Cinema Weekly* and *Cinema Truth:* Dziga Vertov and the Leninist Proportion." *Sight & Sound* 43.1 (Winter 1973–74):75–78.

Fisher, William. "Gorbachev's Cinema." *Sight & Sound*, Autumn 1987:238–43.

Fomin, V. "From the 70s to the 80s: Quirks of Style." *Soviet Film* 2 (February 1983):18–19.

"From the Editor's Point of View." *Soviet Film* 10 (1989):8.

Georgakas, D. "Soviet Cinema Today." *Cineaste* 7.2 (1976):30–32.

Hill, Steven P. "Jay Leyda's *Kino*." *Film Culture* 63–64 (1976):164–77.

———. "Kuleshov—Prophet Without Honor." *Film Culture* 44 (1967):1–40.

———. "A Quantitative View of Soviet Cinema." *Cinema Journal* 11.2 (Spring 1972):18–25.

———. "Russian Film Terminology." *Slavic and East European Journal* 12 (1968):171–77.

Horton, Andrew. "Laughing Matter: American Comedy and Soviet Satire Today." *Soviet Film* 5 (1990):30–31.

———. "Six Hundred Film-Makers in Search of the Subject Matter." *Soviet Film* 2 (1989):32–33.

Istomina, M. "Meetings in Jordan." *Soviet Film* 9 (September 1984):17–18.

Karajaev, K. "Years and Films." *Soviet Film* 10 (October 1984):8–11.

Kennedy, Harlan. "Soviet Spring." *Film Comment* (May–June 1987):34–36.

———. "Tarkovsky: A Thought in Nine Parts." *Film Comment*, May–June 1987:44–46.
Kepley, Vance, Jr. "Building a National Cinema: Soviet Film Education, 1918–1934." *Wide Angle* 9.3 (1987):4–20.
———. "*Intolerance* and the Soviets: A Historical Investigation." *Wide Angle* 3.1 (1979):22–27.
———. "The Origins of the Soviet Cinema: A Study in Industry Development." *Quarterly Review of Film Studies* Winter 1985:22–39.
———. "Strike Him in the Eye: Dovzhenko's *Aerograd* and the Stalinist Terror." *Post Script* 2.2 (Winter 1983):37–54.
———. "The Workers' International Relief and the Cinema of the Left 1921–1935." *Cinema Journal* 23.1 (Fall 1983):7–23.
Kepley, Vance, Jr., and B. Kepley. "Foreign Films on Soviet Screens: 1923–1931." *Quarterly Review of Film Studies* 4.4 (Fall 1979):429–442.
Kimball, G. R. "A Brief Stay in the Sun." *Film and History* (April 1984):16.
Klimov, Elem. "Back in the USSR." *American Film*, March 1988:45–48, 58.
Kostikov, P. "The Noble Mission of Cinema Art." *Soviet Film* 9 (September 1984):18.
Krol, Jack. "Soviet Films: A Sharp Focus." *Newsweek*, 11 January 1988:56.
Lane, J. F. "Moscow-Rome Package." *Sight & Sound* 47.4 (Autumn 1978):221–22.
Lightman, H. A. "Filmmaking in the Soviet Union." *American Cinematographer* 55.8 (August 1974):918–22, 948–51, 982–84.
Marshall, Herbert, and B. Goldberg. "The Fuse." *Sight & Sound* 47.2 (Spring 1978):119–20.
Mayne, Judith. "On the Edge of the Dialectic: Women's Space in the Soviet Film Narrative." *Jump Cut* 23 (October 1980):26–29.
———. "Soviet Film Montage and the Woman Question." *Camera Obscura* 19 (January 1987):25–52.
Mead, G. "Ideology." *Sight and Sound* 53.4 (Autumn 1984):235–36.
Menashe, Louis. "Glasnost in the Soviet Cinema." *Cinéaste* 16.1&2 (1987–88):28–33.
———. Review of *Behind The Soviet Screen. The Motion Picture Industry in the USSR, 1972–1982*, and *In The Service Of The State: The Cinema of Alexander Dovzhenko*. *Film Quarterly* 40.4 (1987):36–40.
Montagu, Ivor. "When We Were Very Young." *Sight & Sound* 43.1 (Winter 1973–74):32–33.
Murray-Brown, Jeremy. "False Cinema: Dziga Vertov and Early Soviet Film." *The New Criterion* 8.3 (November 1989):21–33.
Pann, F. "The Role of Soviet Cinema in the 20s." *Films in Review* 28.2 (February 1977):83–88.
Robinson, David. "Evgeni Bauer and the Cinema of Nikolai II." *Sight and Sound*, Winter 1989–90:51–55.
Sancton, Thomas A., and John Kohan. "A Tragic Phantasmagoria." *Time* (14 December 1987):54.
Scmidt, Paul. "First Speculations: Russian Formalist Film Theory." *Texas Studies in Literature and Language* 17 (1975):326–36.
Sherwood, R., ed. "Documents from 'Lef.' " *Screen* 12.4 (Winter 1971–72):25–28.
Shumakov, S. "For Life's Sake, For the Future's Sake." *Soviet Film* 2 (February 1985):3–6.

Smith, D. "Soviet Film in the Sixties." *Russian Literature Tri-quarterly* 7 (1973):321–41.
Strasser, Steven, and Joyce Barnathan. " 'Glasnost': Moscow's New Rallying Cry." *Newsweek* (5 January 1987):21–23.
Strauss, Bob. "Cinema Summit." *Film Comment*, May–June 1987:37–38.
Thompson, Kristin. "Eisenstein, Marshall and Soviet Cinema." *Millennium Film Journal* 14.15 (Fall–Winter 1984–85):15–21.
Turner, George. "Powerful Images from the Soviet." *American Cinematographer* (May 1987):42–50.
Van Leeuwen, T. "A Return to Dialectics." *Lumière* 22 (April 1973):4–7.
Vogel, Amos. "Sokurov's 'Lonely Voice.' " *Film Comment*, May–June 1989:64–66.
Williams, Alan. "The Camera-Eye and the Film: Notes on Vertov's 'Formalism.' " *Wide Angle* 3.3 (1979):12–17.
Williamson, Anne. "Prisoner: The Essential Paradjanov." *Film Comment*, May–June 1989:57–63.
———. "Rubles of the Game." *Film Comment*, January–February 1989:23–26.
Willis, D. " 'A Singing Blackbird' and Georgian Cinema." *Film Quarterly*. 31.3 (Spring 1978):11–14.
Woll, Josephine. "Daring Voices in Soviet Films." *Dissent* 34.2 (Spring 1987):159–62.

Personal Letters and Interviews

Horton, Andrew, 17 July 1990.
Kolker, Robert, June 1990.

BIOGRAPHICAL SKETCHES

ABULADZE, TENGIZ (1924–), director. Abuladze started as an acting student in 1943–1946 in Tbilisi, but moved on to the Moscow State Institute of Cinematography with his friend Revaz Chkheidze, where both studied under Sergei Yutkevich. After Abuladze had made a few short documentaries alone, the two teamed up for *Lurdzha Magdany (Magdana's Donkey)*, 1954,* a film that revitalized Georgian and Soviet film. His first independent success came in 1959 with *Chuzhie deti (Other People's Children)*,* which was followed by the poetic *Ya, babushka, Iliko i Illarion (Grandma, Iliko, Illarion, and Me)*, 1962, and *Molba (The Appeal)*, 1968. All previous accomplishments, however, were far outstripped by *Pokaianie (Repentance)*,* the film that returned Soviet cinema to world prominence.

ALEXANDROV, GRIGORI (1903–1983), actor, director. Beginning his acting career with Eisenstein, Alexandrov also grew as a director under his tutelege. Their last work together was on *Que Viva Mexico!*, 1933. Alexandrov then proceeded to establish musical comedies as a Soviet genre. His films included *Veselye rebiata (Jazz Comedy)*, 1934; *Tsirk (Circus)*, 1936; *Volga-Volga*, 1938; and *Kompozitor Glinka (The Composer Glinka)*, 1952. Many of these starred his wife, the very popular Liubov Orlova (1902–1974). During World War II he succeeded Eisenstein as director of Mosfilm Studios and served on the editorial boards of the *Fighting Film Albums* series and of the Art Council of the Committee for Cinema Affairs.

BARNET, BORIS (1902–1965), actor, director. While appearing in several films including Kuleshov's *Neobychainye prikliuchenia Mistera Vesta v strane bolshevikov (The Extraordinary Adventures of Mr. West in the Land of the Bolsheviks)*, 1924,* and Fyodor Otsep's *Zhivoi trup (The Living Corpse)*, 1929, Barnet also became known as a directorial master of satire and tragicomedy. His successful satires included *Devushka s korobkoi (Girl With a Hatbox)*, 1927, and *Dom na Trubnoi (The House on Trubnaya Square)*, 1928. His most successful tragicomedy was *Okraina (Outskirts)*, 1933.

BATALOV, ALEXEI (1928–   ), actor, director. Nephew of Nikolai Batalov, he appeared in numerous major films of the fifties and early sixties, the most significant being Heifitz's *Bolshaya semya (Big Family)*; *Dama s sobachkoi (The Lady with the Little Dog)*, 1960;* and *Day of Happiness*. He also directed some fine literary adaptations such as *Shinel (The Overcoat)*, 1959, and *Igrok (The Gambler)*, 1972.*

BATALOV, NIKOLAI V. (1899–1937), actor. Trained in the Moscow Art Theater's Studio of Young Actors, Batalov became the cinema's "leading man" from the mid-twenties until his early death from lung disease. Like other popular performers, he was boosted to popularity by the top "actor's director," Protazanov, for whom he starred in *Aelita*, 1924.* His other important films included Pudovkin's *Mat (The Mother)*, 1926;* Room's *Tretia meshchanskaia (Bed and Sofa)*, 1927;* and Ekk's *Putevka v zhizn (A Pass to Life/Road to Life)*, 1931.*

BAUER, EVGENI F. (1865–1917), director. One of the foremost figures of the pre-Revolutionary cinema, Bauer did not direct his first film until the age of forty-eight, but then created more than eighty from 1913 to 1917. He was also a key influence on Soviet film, particularly through his work with Ivan Perestiani and Lev Kuleshov. With a recent retrospective of pre-Revolutionary films bringing much of his work back to light, the years of his activity are now becoming known as "the age of Bauer." Some of his works now being acclaimed are *Ditia bolshovo goroda (Child of the Big City)** and *Zhizn v smerti (Life in Death)*, both 1914;* *Zhizn za zhizn (A Life for a Life)*, 1916;* and *Revolutsioner (The Revolutionist)*,* *Nabat (The Alarm)*,* and *Korol Parizha (The King of Paris)*, all 1917.*

BONDARCHUK, SERGEI (1920–   ), actor, director. A favorite with the authorities throughout the sixties, seventies, and eighties, he has nevertheless achieved respectability through his prolific, honest, and often challenging work as both actor and director. In 1959 he worked in both capacities on *Sudba cheloveka (Destiny of a Man)*,* presenting a subject that would have been unthinkable during the Stalin years. In the sixties he directed the superproductions *Voina i mir (War and Peace)*, 1966, and *Waterloo*, 1970, both based on the Napoleonic wars.

BYKOV, ROLAN (1929–   ), actor, director. As a director, Bykov has gained international recognition by creating excellent films about young people throughout his career. Foremost among these have been *Vnimanie, cherepakha! (Careful, a Turtle!)*, 1970; *Telegramma (Telegram)*, 1973; and *Chuchelo (Scarecrow)*, 1984.* His performances have included roles in the powerful films *Proverka na* *dorogakh (Trial on the Road)*, 1971,* by Alexei German and *Pis'ma mertvogo cheloveka (Letters from a Dead Man)*, 1986,* by Konstantin Lopushansky.

CHERKASOV, NIKOLAI (1903–1966), actor. One of the Soviet film's most powerful performers. He first gained international fame in Zarkhi and Heifitz's *Deputat Baltiki (Baltic Deputy)*, 1937.* He also appeared in Yutkevich's *Chelovek s ruzhem (The Man with the Gun)*, 1938, and starred in Eisenstein's *Alexander Nevsky*, 1938;* *Ivan Grozny (Ivan the Terrible, Pts. I and II)*, 1944, 1946;* and Kozintsev's *Don Quixote*, 1957.*

CHIAURELI, MIKHAIL (1894–1974), actor, director. Known primarily as the foremost idolizer of Stalin in films such as *Kliatva (The Vow)*, 1946, and the two-part *Padenie Berlina (The Fall of Berlin)*, 1950, Chiaureli is considered by some to be a technically excellent director with a fine sense of drama. His later works, *Otarova vdova (Otar's Widow)*, 1957, and *Povest ob odnoi devushke (Story of a Girl)*, 1960, received more respect. After 1960, he largely disappeared.

CHUKHRAI, GRIGORI (1921–   ), director. Best known as director of the excellent *Ballada o soldate (Ballad of a Soldier)*, 1959,* he was perhaps understandably unable to recapture its moving qualities in the somewhat heavyhanded *Chistoe nebo (Clear Sky)*, 1961, but then produced the touching contemporary fairy tale *Zhili byli starik so starukhoi (There Was an Old Man and an Old Woman)* in 1965. Tragically, however, he was unable to make any films of his own liking thereafter.

DANELIA, GEORGI (1930–198?), director. Specializing in light, socially relevant humor, Danelia has made several excellent films. Among them are *Serezha (A Summer to Remember)*, 1960, co-directed with Igor Talankin; *Ya shagayu po Moskve (I Walk About Moscow)*, 1963; *Ne goryui (Cheer Up!)*, 1969; *Afonia*, 1975; *Mimino*, 1977; and *Osennii marafon (Autumn Marathon)*, 1980.*

DONSKOI, MARK SEMYONOVICH (1901–1981), director. A true Renaissance man, Donskoi was talented as a youth in the arts and sciences, and even considered a career for a while as a boxer. He served in the Red Army, was a prisoner of the Whites for a time, and published a book of stories about his experiences. After getting into film, he worked for a time with Eisenstein and then co-directed some silent films with M. Averbakh, of which *The Value of Man*, 1928, and *In the Big City*, 1929, achieved critical success. He also co-directed the highly acclaimed *Pesnia o schaste (Song About Happiness)*, 1934, before moving on to his greatest personal triumph, *The Gorki Trilogy*, 1938–1940: *Detstvo Gorkovo (Childhood of Gorki)*, 1938;* *V liudiakh (Out in the World), 1939;* and *Moi universitety (My Universities)*, 1940.* His other critical successes include *Kak zakalyalas stal (How the Steel Was Tempered)*, 1942;

Raduga (The Rainbow), 1944; *Mat (Mother)*, 1956; *Serdtse materi (Heart of a Mother)*, 1966; *Vernost materi (A Mother's Devotion)*, 1967; and *Nadezhda*, 1973.

DOVZHENKO, ALEXANDER PETROVICH (1894–1956), theorist, director. One of the giants of Soviet and world cinema, Dovzhenko served in the Red Army, taught school, worked as an artist, and finally entered the film industry as a screenwriter. In the late twenties, he created a trilogy whose astonishing and complex symbolism, energetic cutting, and emotional power have rarely been equaled anywhere. These films were *Zvenigora*, 1928;* *Arsenal*, 1929;* and *Zemlia (Earth)*, 1930.* After that, he came under increasing political pressure and made the noteworthy *Ivan** in 1932, but only achieved moments of quality in *Aerograd*, 1935;* *Shchors*, 1939;* and *Michurin*, 1947.*

DRANKOV, ALEXANDER O. (1880– ?), producer. One of two major producers in the early Russian film industry, Drankov produced the first Russian dramatic film, *Stenka Razin*, 1908,* and achieved success through flamboyance and sensationalism.

DUNAEVSKI, ISAAK (1900–1955), composer. The Soviet Union's greatest composer of popular musicals, he contributed scores to Eisenstein's *Que Viva Mexico!*, 1933; several of Alexandrov's musicals, including *Veselye rebiata (Jazz Comedy)*, 1934; and several of Pyriev's, including *Bogataya nevesta (The Rich Bride)*, 1938; *Traktoristy (Tractor Drivers)*, 1939; and *Kubanskiye kazaki (Cossacks of the Kuban)*, 1950.

EISENSTEIN, SERGEI MIKHAILOVICH (1898–1948), director and film theoretician. Prominent figure in world cinema for both his achievements as a director and his deep, comprehensive explorations of film theory, which began with the essay stating his most famous contribution to the field, the "Montage of Attractions." Eisenstein's brilliance and dedication were fueled by the Bolshevik Revolution, but, like many of his colleagues, his career after Stalin's rise to power was marked mainly by persecution. Many of his projects were either censored, rejected, or destroyed for political reasons. Two others, *Alexander Nevsky*, 1938,* and *Ivan Grozny (Ivan the Terrible, Pt. I)*, 1944,* were severely hampered by political restrictions. His most famous and studied film is *Bronenosets Potyomkin (Battleship Potemkin)*, 1925–1926,* but various scholars will also argue for *Stachka (Strike)*, 1925;* *October*, 1928;* *Staroe i novoe (Old and New)*, 1929;* or *Ivan Grozny (Ivan the Terrible, Pt. II)*, 1946,* as his most impressive work. The unfinished but recently restored *Que Viva Mexico* (1932, 1979) is also a truly brilliant work.

ERMASH, FILIPP (1923–), administrator. Chief of Goskino, 1972–1986, mainly as a result of high connections in the Politburo. Under his tenure, the industry moved towards satisfying popular tastes with films that also upheld orthodox ideology and socialist morality, a philosophy that reached its pinnacle with the domestic and international success of *Moskva slezam ne verit* (*Moscow Does Not Believe in Tears*), 1980.*

ERMLER, FRIEDRICH MARKOVICH (1898–1967), director. Strongly devoted to the Communist Party throughout his career, Ermler was taken prisoner and tortured by the Whites in the Civil War. He later produced films that focused on moral rejuvenation through social interaction. Though heavily ideological, his work also contained complex characters. His best work was done in the twenties: *Katka—bumazhnyi ranet* (*Katka's Reinette Apples*), 1926;* *Dom v sugrobakh* (*House in the Snow-Drifts*), 1928; *Parizhski sapozhnik* (*Parisian Cobbler*), 1928;* and *Oblomok imperii* (*Fragment of an Empire*), 1929.* After suffering some deep personal doubts, he successfully returned to co-direct *Vstrechnyi* (*Counterplan*), 1932,* with Sergei Yutkevich. His most notable achievements after that were *Veliki grazhdanin* (*A Great Citizen, Pts. I and II*), 1938–1939,* and *Veliki perelom* (*The Great Turning Point*), 1946.*

ERMOLEV, OSIP (1889–1962), producer. Second leading pre-Revolutionary producer, who worked his way up from office boy to build his own large studio, at which luminaries like Protazanov and Mozhukhin made several of their greatest films. He emigrated to France in 1919.

GARDIN, VLADIMIR (1877–1965), actor, director. One of the most popular pre-Revolutionary directors, Gardin contributed *agitki* to the new government in 1918, proposed the idea of a state film school, and became its first director. His films *Zheleznaya piata* (*The Iron Heel*), 1919, and *Golod—golod—golod* (*Hunger—Hunger—Hunger*), 1921,* were important steps towards feature filmmaking, but his work was soon overshadowed by the greater directors of the twenties. As an actor, he became well known for his performances in Ermler's *Vstrechnyi* (*Counterplan*), 1932,* and Donskoi and Legoshin's *Pesnia o schaste* (*Song About Happiness*), 1934.

GERASIMOV, SERGEI APOLLINARIEVICH (1906–1985), actor and director. Began as an actor with the avant-garde FEKS group in the late twenties, where he was influenced by American films. During the thirties he made two notable films on the problems of youth, *Do I Love You?*, 1934, and *Uchitel* (*Teacher*), 1939. He also received high praise for *Semero smelykh* (*The Brave Seven*), 1936. In the forties he supervised the making of World War II documentaries, and in the fifties he made one of the best films of that decade, *Tikhi Don* (*The Quiet Don, Pts. I, II, and III*), 1957.* In his final film, he both directed and starred in a drama about the final years of Tolstoi.

GERMAN, ALEXEI, director. One of the most brilliant and innovative directors of his generation, whose World War II films *Proverka na dorogakh* (*Trial on *the Road*), 1971, released in 1986,* and *Dvadtsat' dnei bez voiny* (*Twenty Days Without War*), 1976,* are boldly conceived works that apply the traditional style of the Soviet war film to unconventional characters and situations. However, his masterpiece has been acclaimed to be *Moi drug Ivan Lapshin* (*My Friend Ivan Lapshin*), 1983, released in 1985.*

GOGOBERIDZE, LANA, director. Has received high praise for her feminist films *Perepolokh* (*Commotion*), 1977;* *Neskol'ko interv'iu po lichnym voprosam* (*Some Interviews on Personal Matters*), 1979;* and *Den' dlinnee nochi* (*The Day Is Longer Than the Night*), 1984.*

GURCHENKO, LUDMILA (1935–), actress. While studying acting with Gerasimov and Tamara Makarova, Gurchenko achieved immense popularity through the title role in Riazanov's *Karnavalnaia noch* (*Carnival Night*), 1956. However, in the sixties her fame diminished until she made a successful comeback with her first serious role as the director of a textile factory in Tregubovich's *Starye steny* (*The Old Walls*), 1973. Since then, she has made significant contributions to some of the most powerful Soviet films of the last two decades, including German's *Dvadtsat' dnei bez voiny* (*Twenty Days Without War*), 1976;* Mikhalkov's *Piat' vecherov* (*Five Evenings*)* and Mikhalkov-Konchalovski's *Sibiriada* (*Siberiana/The Siberiad*), 1979;* and Riazanov's *Vokzal dlia dvoikh* (*Train Station for Two*), 1983.*

HEIFITZ, IOSIF (1905–), director. Graduated from film school in 1927 along with Alexander Zarkhi, with whom he collaborated until 1950. Heifitz's greatest work is his adaptation of Chekhov's *Dama s sobachkoi* (*The Lady with the Little Dog*), 1960,* although *Deputat Baltiki* (*Baltic Deputy*), 1937,* has been acclaimed as one of the top Soviet films of that decade. His other admirable works with Zarkhi included *Chlen pravitelstva* (*Member of the Government*), 1940, and the documentary *Defeat of Japan*, 1945.

ILINSKI, IGOR (1901–1987), actor. The most popular Soviet comic actor ever. His films include Protazanov's *Aelita,* 1924;* *Zakroishchik iz Tozhka* (*The Tailor from Torzhok*), 1925; and *Protsess o trekh millionakh* (*The Three Million Case*), 1926; Yuri Zheliabuzhsky's *Papirosnitsa ot Mosselproma* (*Cigarette-Girl from Mosselprom*), 1924; Barnet and Fyodor Otsep's *Miss Mend,* 1926; Sergei Komarov's *Kukla s millionami* (*The Doll With Millions*), 1928; Alexandrov's *Volga-Volga,* 1938; and Riazanov's *Karnavalnaia noch* (*Carnival Night*), 1957.

ILENKO, YURI (1936–), cinematographer, director. Best known for his brilliant award-winning camera work on Parajanov's *Teni zabytykh predkov* (*Shadows of Forgotten Ancestors*), 1964,* he later directed one of the best Soviet films of the early seventies, *Belaia ptitsa s chernoi otmetinoi* (*White Bird with a Black Spot*), 1971.* His other solo features, *Vecher nakanune Ivana Kupaly*

(*The Eve of Ivan Kupala Day*/[Halloween Night]), 1967, and *Naperekor vsemu* (*In Spite of Everything*), 1972, were also in the poetic Parajanov mode. His latest, *Straw Bells*, 1989,* was about Soviet collaborators during World War II.

KALATOZOV, MIKHAIL (1903–1973), director. If he had only made *Letiat zhuravli* (*The Cranes are Flying*), 1957,* Soviet cinema would still be forever indebted to Kalatozov. He began as a documentarist and worked with Kuleshov, Shub, and Vertov in the twenties, finally achieving his own success with *Sol Svanetii* (*Salt for Svanetia*), 1930. For the next thirty years, he stayed along the edges of official grace, keeping active enough to please the authorities but always striving for his own artistic goals. In the sixties he made *Ya Kuba* (*I Am Cuba*), 1963,* and the international production *Krasnaia palatka* (*The Red Tent*), 1969, starring Sean Connery.

KHANZHONKOV, ALEXANDER (1877–1945), producer. An early major figure in establishing the Russian film industry. In his commercial duel with Drankov, he sought victory through promoting art, style, and variety. He entered the industry in 1908 and sometimes directed. After the Revolution, he served as an adviser to Goskino and director of production for Proletkino.

KHOLODNAIA, VERA (1893–1919), actress. The leading actress of pre-Revolutionary Russian cinema in terms of talent, popularity, and salary. Discovered by Bauer, she first starred in his *Pesn torzhestvuyushchei liubvi* (*Song of Triumphant Love*), 1915.* Her other films included Vyacheslav Viskovsky's *Zhenshchina, kotoraya izobrela liubov* (*The Woman Who Invented Love*) and Cheslav Sabinsky's *Zhivoi trup* (*A Living Corpse*), both 1918.

KLIMOV, ELEM (1935–   ), director. Serving as First Secretary of the Soviet Filmmakers' Union from 1986 to 1988, after winning the position in a surprise election, Klimov helped guide the Soviet film industry into the era of *glasnost* during those difficult years. Having felt the sting of censorship (his own *Agoniia* (*Rasputin*),* made in 1975, was not released until 1984), Klimov immediately began a policy of releasing other suppressed films while battling criticism from both the left and the right. Other works of his that have made powerful impacts include *Dobro pozhalovat!* (*Welcome!*), 1964;* *Proshchanie* (*Farewell*), 1982;* and *Idi i smotri* (*Come and See*), 1985.*

KOZINTSEV, GRIGORI MIKHAILOVICH (1905–1973), director. Beginning work on the Soviet agit-trains during the Civil War, Kozintsev there met Leonid Trauberg in 1921, with whom he collaborated until 1946. In December of 1921 the two, along with Sergei Yutkevich, formed the Factory of Eccentric Actors (FEKS) workshop and issued a fifteen-page manifesto on their circus- and vaudeville-influenced theatrical style. After creating two popular shorts, they proceeded to make a number of silent classics: *Chertovo koleso* (*The Devil's*

Wheel), 1926;* Shinel (The Cloak), 1926;* S.V.D., 1927;* Novyi Vavilon (New Babylon), 1929;* and Odna (Alone), 1931. Their Maxim Trilogy—Yunost Maksima (The Youth of Maxim), 1935;* Vozvrashchenie Maksima (The Return of Maxim), 1937;* and Vyborgskaia storona (The Vyborg Side), 1939—is also still a great work. But, following Stalin's death, Kozintsev would show his brilliance to an even greater degree in his superb adaptations of Don Quixote, 1957;* Hamlet, 1964;* and King Lear, 1971.*

KRIUCHKOV, NIKOLAI (1909–   ), actor. Coming straight from a worker's background into acting, he gained his first starring role in Boris Barnet's Okraina (Outskirts), 1933. Throughout the thirties and forties, he played the cheerful, energetic, young socialist with energy and skill, also appearing in Kozintsev and Trauberg's Vozvrashchenie Maksima, 1937,* as well as in many others. In the fifties his work began to take on new psychological depth, and the remainder of his career was highlighted by three films with Chukhrai: Sorok pervyi (The Forty-First), 1956;* Ballada o soldate (Ballad of a Soldier), 1959;* and Zhili byli starik so starukhoi (There Was an Old Man and an Old Woman), 1965.

KULESHOV, LEV VLADIMIROVICH (1899–1970), director and film theoretician. A giant of Soviet film who influenced all the other giants, including Eisenstein, it was Kuleshov who first developed a theory of montage and the idea of blending documentary and fictional elements. Many others learned through his production of a number of short agitki and his workshops. In 1920 he produced the documentary Na krasnom fronte (On the Red Front)* and followed that with three notable works: Neobychainye prikliuchenia Mistera Vesta v strane bolshevikov (The Extraordinary Adventures of Mr. West in the Land of the Bolsheviks), 1924;* Luch smerti (The Death Ray), 1925;* and the powerful Po zakonu (By the Law), 1926.* His major films all starred his wife, Alexandra Khokhlova (1897–1985). After that, his life became an endless series of political and artistic problems, but he did leave behind an important pair of theoretical books in Russian, translated in part by Ron Levaco: The Art of the Cinema (1926) and Fundamentals of Film Directing (1941).

KULIJANOV, LEV (1924–   ), director. Most notable as superconservative head of the Union of Soviet Filmmakers from 1965 to 1986, he also made a strong adaptation of Prestuplenie i nakaznie (Crime and Punishment), 1970,* and his first film, Dom, v kotorom ya zhivu (The House I Live In), 1956,* still packs a punch.

LEVITSKI, ALEXANDER ANDREEVICH (1885–1965), cinematographer. Beginning in 1910, Levitski shot some of the most famous pre-Revolutionary films, including Meyerhold's Portret Doriana Greya (The Picture of Dorian Gray), 1915.* Possibly entitled to rank as founder of the Russian school of cinematography, he co-created Soviet newsreel cinema with Tisse. Films included Kuleshov's *Neobychainye prikliuchenia Mistera Vesta v strane bolshevikov* (*The Extraordinary Adventures of Mr. West in the Land of the Bolsheviks*), 1924,* and *Luch smerti* (*The Death Ray*), 1925.*

MEDVEDKIN, ALEXANDER I. (1900–   ), director, scriptwriter. In charge of the Soviet propaganda train, 1931–1932, he used the opportunity to develop a comic style blending folktales, Mack Sennett, and Dada. This produced works such as *Stiazhateli* (*Snatchers*), 1935, but the film industry did not encourage or pursue his ideas.

MIKHALKOV, NIKITA (1946?), actor, director. Younger brother of Andrei Mikhalkov-Konchalovski, he has received acclaim as an actor in his own *Svoi sredi chuzhikh, chuzhoi sredi svoikh* (*At Home among Strangers, Stranger at Home*), 1975,* and Riazanov's *Vokzal dlia dvoikh* (*Train Station for Two*), 1983,* and *Zhestoki romans* (*A Ruthless Romance*), 1984.* His own films are not only beautiful, but also significant commentaries on alienation caused by separation from nature and mixtures of melodrama and history. His other films have included *Raba liubvi* (*A Slave of Love*), 1976;* *Neokonchennaia p'esa dlia mekhanicheskogo pianino* (*Unfinished Piece for Player Piano*), 1977;* *Piat' vecherov* (*Five Evenings*), 1979; *Neskol'ko dnei iz zhizni I. I. Oblomova* (*Some Days in the Life of I. I. Oblomov*), 1982;* *Rodnia* (*Kinfolk*) 1982; *Bez svidetelei* (*Without Witnesses*), 1983; and *Dark Eyes,* 1988, an international production starring Marcello Mastroianni.

MIKHALKOV-KONCHALOVSKI, ANDREI (1937–   ), director, scenarist. One of the modern masters, he became associated with Andrei Tarkovski at the State Institute of Cinematography, from which he graduated in 1961. He had previously studied piano. He first gained acclaim for *Pervyi uchitel* (*The First Teacher*), 1965,* and then contributed the impressive *Asino schaste* (*Asya's Happiness*), 1966, released 1989;* *Dvorianskoye gnezdo* (*A Nest of Gentry*), 1969; *Diadia Vania* (*Uncle Vanya*), 1971;* and *Sibiriada* (*Siberiana/The Siberiad*), 1979,* before moving his career to America, where he has directed films as diverse as *Runaway Train,* 198?, and *Shy People,* 1989.

MOZHUKHIN, IVAN I. (1888–1939), actor. The most popular pre-Revolutionary Russian actor, who gained an avid following because of his " 'magnetic' eyes, clear features, and noble carriage" (Leyda, *Kino,* 66), he has recently attracted an increasing amount of scholarly attention in the United States. His films included Petr Chardynin's *Kreitzerova sonata* (*The Kreutzer Sonata*), 1911, and Protazanov's *Nikolai Stavrogin,* 1915; *Pikovaia dama* (*The Queen of Spades*), 1916; and *Otets Sergii* (*Father Sergius*), 1917.*

PANFILOV, GLEB (1934–   ), director. Highly regarded for his sensitive studies on the problems of artistic creation, usually starring his wife, Inna Churikova, who plays strong and positive characters, sources of spirituality. Panfilov's films include *V ogne broda net* (*No Ford in the Fire*), 1968;* *Nachalo* (*Debut*), 1970;* *Proshu slova* (*May I Have the Floor*), 1977;* *Tema* (*Theme*), 1979, released in 1986; and *Vassa*, 1983.*

PARAJANOV, SERGEI (1924–1990), director. Studied at the State Institute of Cinematography under Igor Savchenko and Lev Kuleshov, graduating in 1951. He showed an early interest in rural legends and folk traditions, and his brilliant *Teni zabytykh predkov* (*Shadows of Forgotten Ancestors*), 1964,* proved him a more than worthy heir to Dovzhenko. He also created *Tsvet granata* (*The Colors of the Pomegranate*), 1968,* before running into problems with the authorities. Over the next decade he was jailed twice, returning in 1984 with *Legenda o Suramskoi kreposti* (*The Legend of the Surami Fortress*), released in 1986,* and *Ashik Kerib* (*The Demon*), 1989.*

PROTAZANOV, YAKOV ALEXANDROVICH (1881–1945), director. An artist who might almost be called the Russian Cukor, since he strove for high artistic quality while making real commercial successes featuring popular performers. Though many consider his masterpiece to be *Otets Sergii* (*Father Sergius*), 1917,* a powerful film, his works during the twenties are also considered significant for their innovations and humanitarian portraits. These included *Aelita*, 1924;* *Ego prizyv* (*His Call*), 1925; *Sorok pervyi* (*The Forty-First*), 1927;* *Belyi orel* (*The White Eagle*), 1928;* *Chelovek iz retorana* (*The Man From the Restaurant*), 1929; and several comedies starring Igor Ilinski and Anatoli Ktorov such as *Prazdnik svyatogo Iorgena* (*The Holiday of St. Jorgen*), 1930.

PUDOVKIN, VSEVOLOD ILLARIONOVICH (1893–1953), actor, director, theoretician. Pudovkin's background was in painting, music, and chemistry, and he also spent three years as a prisoner during World War I. Although he did not begin studying film until the age of twenty-seven, he was to become one of the most important directors and theoreticians in all of cinema history. His most widely admired film is certainly the powerful *Mat* (*The Mother*), 1926,* but *Konets Sankt-Peterburga* (*The End of St. Petersburg*), 1927,* and *Potomok Chingis-khana* (*The Heir to Genghis-Khan/Storm Over Asia*), 1928,* are equally impressive. His hilarious short, *Shakhmatnaia goriachka* (*Chess Fever*), 1925,* also deserves mention. However, with Stalin's rise to power, his artistic independence was already being curtailed, and from then on, he sought to curb his talents in line with the Party doctrines. Thus, although *Prostoi sluchai* (*A Simple Case*), 1932;* *Minin i Pozharski* (*Minin and Pozharski*), 1939; and *Suvorov*, 1941,* showed glimpses of his old brilliance, the remainder of his work was fairly banal. Only with his last film, *Vozvrashchenie Vasilia Bortnikova* (*The Return of Vasili Bortnikov*), 1953,* did he finally show signs of beginning to return to his old form.

PYRIEV, IVAN (1901–1968), director. A popular director who enjoyed a long, successful career, usually choosing themes that fit Party policies. In the twenties he studied directing at the Moscow dramatic arts institute and worked in Meyerhold's avant-garde theater. Beginning his cinematic career with a witty satire, *The Other Woman*, 1929, he also made musicals, dramas, including *V shest chasov vechera posle voiny* (*At 6 p.m. After the War*), 1944, and some critically acclaimed adaptations of Dostoevsky late in his career: *The Idiot*, 1957; *Belye nochi* (*White Nights*), 1959; and *Bratya Karamazovy* (*The Brothers Karamazov*), 1969, completed by the two lead actors after his death.

RAIZMAN, YULI (1903–   ), director. Thought by some to be one of the most gifted Soviet directors, he has certainly been neglected in the West. Nevertheless, his career has been marked by working around and through official restrictions in order to present the most humanistic portraits possible, often from scripts by Evgeni Gabrilovich. His long struggle has paid off in the latter part of his career with films such as *Strannaia zhenshchina* (*A Strange Woman*), 1978;* *Chastnaia zhizn'* (*Private Life*), 1983;* and *Vremia zhelanii* (*Time of Desires*), 1984,* that present accomplished, complex character studies. His earlier works include *Kartorga* (*Penal Servitude*), 1928; *Zemlia zhazhdet* (*The Earth Thirsts*), 1930; *Posledniaia noch* (*The Last Night*), 1937; *Mashenka*, 1942; *Kommunist* (*The Communist*), 1958;* *A esli eto liubov?* (*And What If It's Love?*), 1962; and *Tvoi sovremennik* (*Your Contemporary*), 1967.

RIAZANOV, ELDAR ALEXANDROVICH (1927–   ), director. Studied under Kozintsev at the State Institute of Cinematography, graduated in 1950, and joined Mosfilm Studios in 1955. He is a master of light comedy and social satire, often attacking the bureaucracy in works that have consistently found favor with both the critics and the public. Some of the best have been *Karnavalnaia noch* (*Carnival Night*), 1957; *Devushka bez adresa* (*Girl Without an Address*), 1957; *Beregis avtomobilia* (*Look Out for Cars*), 1966; *Ironiia sud'by, ili S legkim parom* (*Irony of Fate, or Have a Good Sauna*), 1975; *Garazh* (*Garage*), 1980; *Vokzal dlia dvoikh* (*Train Station for Two*), 1983* (co-directed with Emil Braginsky); and *Zhestoki romans* (*A Ruthless Romance*), 1984.* His latest was *A Forgotten Tune for the Flute*, 1989*, a satiric look at *glasnost* and *perestroika*.

ROMM, MIKHAIL ILICH (1901–1971), director. Though he met with early success in *Trinadtsat* (*The Thirteen*), 1937, Romm was basically an adherent to socialist-realist guidelines in such burdensome efforts as *Lenin v Oktiabre* (*Lenin in October*), 1937.* However, in the sixties he suddenly captured international acclaim with the poignant and provocative *Deviat dnei odnogo goda* (*Nine Days in a Year*), 1961, and *Obyknovennyi fashizm* (*Ordinary Fascism*), 1965.*

ROOM, ABRAM (1894–1976), director. His masterpiece is the excellent *Tretia meshchanskaia* (*Bed and Sofa*), 1927,* but Room also created notable achievements with *Bukhta smerti* (*Death Bay*), 1926;* *Prividenie, kotoroe ne vozvrashchaetsia* (*The Ghost that Never Returns*), 1930; *Plan velikikh rabot* (*Plan of Great Works*), 1930; *Strogii yunosha* (*A Severe Young Man*), 1934 (banned); and *Nashestvie* (*Invasion*), 1945.* However, his career went into artistic decline thereafter.

SHEPITKO, LARISA (1939–1979), director. Shepitko won considerable attention for her portraits of psychological intensity in such films as *Znoi* (*Heat*), 1962; *Krylia* (*Wings*), 1968;* and *Ty i ya* (*You and I*), 1971.* Later she turned to anti-war themes in such films as *Voskhozhdenie* (*The Ascent*), 1977,* and *Proshchanie* (*Farewell*), 1982,* which was completed by her husband, Elem Klimov, following her death in an automobile accident.

SHKLOVSKI, VICTOR BORISOVICH (1893–1984), writer, scenarist, literary and film historian. Contributed to some of the most significant films of the twenties: Room's *Bukhta smerti* (*Death Bay*), 1926,* and *Tretia meshchanskaia* (*Bed and Sofa*), 1927;* Kuleshov's *Po zakonu* (*By the Law*), 1926;* and Boris Barnet's *Dom na Trubnoi* (*The House on Trubnaya Square*), 1928. He continued writing screenplays and books about film to the end of his life.

SHOSTAKOVICH, DMITRI (1906–1975), composer. Contributed great musical scores for almost all the major Lenfilm Studio productions, many for Kozintsev and Trauberg, including their *Novyi Vavilon* (*New Babylon*), 1929,* and the *Maxim Trilogy*, 1934–1939, and continuing through Kozintsev's *Hamlet*, 1964,* and *Korol Lir* (*King Lear*), 1971.*

SHUB, ESTHER (1894–1959), editor, director. Shub made her mark with historical compilation films, doing diligent work throughout the 1920s in gathering film footage (and thus providing great motivation towards the establishment of the Soviet film archives), which she later wove into masterful historical dramas. Her trilogy of the Russian Empire's fall and the Soviet Union's rise won her her greatest acclaim. These films included *Padenie dinastii Romanovykh* (*Fall of the Romanov Dynasty*), 1927;* *Veliki put* (*The Great Road*), 1927;* and *Rossiia Nikolaia II i Lev Tolstoi* (*The Russia of Nikolai II and Lev Tolstoy*), 1928.

SHUKSHIN, VASILI (1929–1974), writer, actor, director. He gained acclaim in the sixties for both the comedy and honesty in his works. His final film, however, *Kalina krasnaya* (*The Red Snowball Bush*), 1974,* which has been acclaimed as his greatest, was a tragedy of the Soviet underworld. His other works were *Zhivet takoi paren* (*There's a Certain Fellow*), 1964;* *Vash syn i brat* (*Your Son and Brother*), 1966; *Strannye liudi* (*Strange People*), 1971; and *Pechki lavochki* (*Shop Crumbs*), 1973.

SHUMIATSKY, BORIS (1886–1938), Party activist and administrator. According to the Schnitzers and Marcel, "Head of Soviet film industry [Soyuzkino, State Directorate for the Cinema and Photographic Industry] from 1930 to 1937, dismissed when his grandiose plans to step up film production and create a Soviet Hollywood foundered miserably. Apparently both philistine and anti-Semitic, he was generally unpopular in the industry, and the sworn enemy of Eisenstein whose career he effectively and completely thwarted during the years of his power'' (p. 200).

SMOKTUNOVSKI, INNOKENTI (1925–   ), actor. After fighting in World War II while still a teen-ager and spending several years in the theater, Smoktunovski began moving into films and discovering himself as an actor in the late fifties. In some of his greatest roles, such as *Hamlet* (Kozintsev, 1964)* and Diadia Vania *(Uncle Vanya)* (Mikhalkov-Konchalovski, 1971),* he has discovered new depths in both himself and the character. The winner of several important state prizes, he feels his other most important roles were in Alexander Ivanov's *Soldaty (The Soldiers)*, 1957; Romm's *Deviat dnei odnogo goda (Nine Days in a Year)*, 1962;* and Riazanov's *Beregis avtomobilia (Look Out for the Cars)*, 1966. His latest appearance was in Rodion Nakhapetov's *At the Close of the Night,* 1989.*

SOKUROV, ALEXANDER (1951–   ), director. The Soviet director following most closely in Andrei Tarkovski's footsteps. Sokurov creates films that break every rule of narrative structure and cinematic composition, challenging the viewer's concentration through unconventional uses of color, sound, camera stability, and mise-en-scène. What results are mystifying, alternately political and metaphysical works. These have included *Odinokii golos cheloveka (A Man's Lonely Voice)*, 1978, released 1987;* *Skorbnoe beschuvstvie (Solemn Heartlessness)*, 1987;* and *Days of the Eclipse,* 1988.*

TARKOVSKI, ANDREI (1932–1986), director. Widely acknowledged as the greatest contemporary Soviet filmmaker, he possessed a cinematic imagination and artistic style that enabled him to produce truly unique works, taking cinematic language far beyond where it had been before. He has been followed in the eighties most closely by Alexander Sokurov. But, for most filmmakers and audiences, he left a great challenge to follow the direction in which he led. Tarkovski first gained international attention when his student film (made in collaboration with Mikhalkov-Konchalovski), *Katok i skripka (The Steamroller and the Violin)*, 1960,* took first prize at the New York Student Film Competition. Two years later, *Ivanovo detstvo (Ivan's Childhood)*,* won the Grand Prizes at the San Francisco and Venice Film Festivals. This was followed by what most consider his masterpiece, *Andrei Rublev (Andrei Rublev)*, 1966.* Tarkovski's other Soviet films were *Soliaris (Solaris)*, 1972;* *Zerkalo (Mirror)*, 1975;* *Stalker,* 1980;* and *Nostalgia,* 1983.* His final film, *The Sacrifice,* 1986, was made in West European exile.

TISSE, EDUARD (1897–1961), cinematographer. Eisenstein's cameraman, who started in newsreels and documentaries in World War I and the Russian Civil War. To be successful, the great director needed a cameraman whose innovations were equal to his own artistic ideas, and he had one in Tisse.

TRAUBERG, LEONID (1902–), director. See Kozintsev.

URUSEVSKI, SERGEI (1908–1975), cinematographer, director. One of the two greatest Soviet cinematographers ever, he was a pupil of avant-garde photographer Alexander Rodchenko and helped Kalatozov revive Soviet cinema in 1957 with his work on *Letiat zhuravli* (*The Cranes Are Flying*).* They also collaborated on *Neotpravlennoye pismo* (*The Letter That Wasn't Sent*), 1959, and *Ya Kuba* (*I Am Cuba*), 1963*. In 1968, he had a controversial directorial debut with *Beg inokhodtsa* (*The Trotter's Gait*). His second and last film as director was a biography of Sergei Yesenin, *Poi pesniu, poet* (*Sing Your Song, Poet*), 1973.

VERTOV, DZIGA (real name: Denis Arkadievich Kaufman) (1896–1954), director. Another major figure of Soviet silent and world cinema, Vertov began working on the Soviet agit-trains, promoted the aesthetic philosophy that film should "capture life unaware," and organized a group of documentarists known as Kino-Eye. The *cinéma-vérité* film movement to which he gave birth still has devoted followers and a significant influence in contemporary films. Along with producing dozens of newsreels from 1918 to 1925, notably the *Kino pravda* series, 1922–1925, he also produced feature-length documentaries, his masterpiece being *Chelovek s kinoapparatom* (*Man with a Movie Camera*), 1929.* His other highly regarded works include *Leninskaia kinopravda* (*Leninist Film-truth*), 1925;* *Shagai, Soviet!* (*Stride, Soviet!*), 1926;* *Shestaia chast mira* (*A Sixth of the World*), 1926;* *Odinnadtsatyi* (*Number Eleven*), 1928;* *Entuziazm* (*Enthusiasm/The Donbass Symphony*), 1931;* and *Tri pesni o Lenine* (*Three Songs of Lenin*), 1934.* Although he kept working on documentaries until his death, Vertov also had to fight Stalinist restrictions and suffered artistically following 1934.

YUTKEVICH, SERGEI IOSIPOVICH (1904–1985), director, teacher, film historian. Co-founder of FEKS with Trauberg and Yutkevich's childhood friend Kozintsev, he first began gaining critical attention with *Cherni parus* (*The Black Sail*), 1929.* In the thirties he achieved success with *Vstrechnyi* (*Counterplan*), 1932,* co-directed with Ermler, and *Chelovek s ruzhem* (*The Man with the Gun*), 1938.* His later triumphs included *Othello*, 1955,* and *Lenin v Polshe* (*Lenin in Poland*), 1965.* But perhaps his greatest contributions to Soviet film came through influencing several other filmmakers as a teacher at the State Institute of Cinematography, which he joined in 1938, and through personally keeping Donskoi and Ermler active.

SELECTED FILMOGRAPHY

1907

Boris Godunov. d. I. Shuvalov; au. Alexander Pushkin; c. Alexander & L. Drankov;* with G. Martini, Z. Loranskaya, Khovansky. Drankov. 285 m.

1908

Stenka Razin. d. Vladimir Romashkov; sw. Vasili Goncharov; c. Drankov* & Nikolai Kozlovsky; with Evgeni Petrov-Kraevsky. Drankov. 224 m.

1914

Ditia bolshovo goroda (Child of the Big City). d. Bauer;* c. Boris Zavelyov; with Y. Smirnova, M. Salarov, A. Bibikov, Emma Bauer, & L. Tridenskaya. Khanzhonkov. 1,135 m.

Zhizn v smerti (Life in Death). d. Bauer;* sw. Valeri Briusov; c. Boris Zavelyov; with Mozhukhin,* I. Lashchinilina, & P. Biriukov. Khanzhonkov. 1,300 m.

1915

Pesn torzhestvuyushchei liubvi (Song of Triumphant Love). d. & sw. Bauer;* au. Ivan Turgenev; c. K. Bauer & Boris Zavelyov; with Kholodnaia,* Osip Runich, & Vitold Polonsky. Khanzhonkov. 1,433 m.

Portret Doriana Greya (The Picture of Dorian Gray). d. & sw. Meyerhold;* au. Oscar Wilde; c. Levitski;* with Varvara Yanova, Meyerhold, G. Enriton, P. Belova, Doronin, Y. Uvarova, & Alexander Volkov. Russian Golden Series. 2,124 m.

1916

Zhizn za zhizn (A Life for a Life). d. & sw. Bauer;* au. Georges Ohnet; c. Boris Zavelyov; with Olga Rakhmanova, Lidia Koreneva, Kholodnaia,* & Vitold Polonsky. Khanzhonkov. 2,175 m.

1917

Korol Parizha (The King of Paris). d. Bauer;* au. Georges Ohnet; c. Boris Zavelyov; with Nikolai Radin, Vera Coralli, Lidia Koreneva, & M. Boldyrev. Khanzhonkov.

Nabat (The Alarm). d. & sw. Bauer;* c. Boris Zavelyov; with Nikolai Radin, Vera Coralli, M. Narokov, V. Svoboda, Zoya Barantsevich, Vladimir Strizhevsky, Konstantin Khokhlov, & Nikolai Tseretelli. Khanzhonkov. 7 reels.

Otets Sergii (Father Sergius). d. Protazanov;* sw. Alexander Volkov; au. Leo Tolstoi; c. Fedor Burgasov & N. Rudakov; with Mozhukhin,* V. Jeneeva, Vladimir Gaidarov, Natalia Lisenko, Vera Orlova, Pyotr Baksheyev, & Nikolai Panov. Yermoliev. 1,920 m.

Revolutsioner (The Revolutionist). d. Bauer;* sw. Ivan Perestiani; with Perestiani, Vladimir Strizhevsky, & Z. Bogdanova. Khanzhonkov. 4 reels.

1919

Za krasnoye znamia (For the Red Banner). d. Vladimir Kasianov; sw. A. Smoldovsky; c. S. Zebel; with V. Ostrovsky, Oleg Froelich, V. Vasiliev, & A. Kasianov. Neptune & Mos-Kino-Committee. 316 m.

1920

Na krasnom fronte (On the Red Front). d. & sw. Kuleshov;* c. Pyotr Yermolov; with Leonid Obolensky, Y. Reich, & Alexandra Khokhlova. Kino-Section, Moscow Soviet & VFKO. 700 m.

1921

Golod-golod-golod (Hunger-Hunger-Hunger). d. & sw. Gardin* & Pudovkin;* c. Tisse;* with N. Vishniak & A. Gromov. Gos-Kino-School & VFKO. 500 m.

Istoriia grazhdanskoi voiny (History of the Civil War). d. Vertov.* All-Russian Kino Committee (of Narkompros).

1922

Kino-pravda (Film-Truth). d. Vertov;* c. Mikhail Kaufman, I. Beliakov, & A. Lemberg. Newsreel series.

1923

Krasnye diavolata (Red Imps). d. Ivan Perestiani; sw. Perestiani & Pavel Blyakhin; c. Alexander Digmelov; with Pyotr Yesikovsky, Sofia Jozeffi, Kador Ben-Selim, V. Sutyrin. Kino Section of Georgian Commissariat of Education. 3,800 m.

1924

Neobychainye prikliuchenia Mistera Vesta v strane bolshevikov (The Extraordinary Adventures of Mr West in the Land of the Bolsheviks). d. Kuleshov;* sw. Nikolai Aseev & Pudovkin;* c. Levitski;* with Profiri Podobed, Valya Lopatina, Barnet,* Pudovkin,* Khokhlova, Pyotr Galadzhev, Sergei Komarov, Leonid Obolensky, & Vladimir Fogel. Goskino. 2,680 m.

Aelita. d. Protazanov;* sw. Fyodor Otsep & Alexei Faiko; au. Alexei Tolstoy; c. Yuri Zheliabuzhsky, E. Schoneman; with Valentina Kuinzhi, Nikolai Tseretelli, Konstantin Eggert, Yulia Solnterva, Yuri Zavadsky, Igor Ilinsky, & Nikolai Batalov. Mezhrabpom-Russ. 1,841 m.

Kino-glaz (Film-Eye). d. & sw. Vertov;* c. Mikhail Kaufman. Goskino. 1,627 m.

Pokhozdenia Oktyabriny (Adventures of Oktyabrina). d. & sw. Kozintsev* & Trauberg;* c. F. Verigo-Darovsky & Ivan Frolov; with Zinaida Tarkhovskaya & Sergei Martinson. Sevzapkino & FEX. 970 m.

1925

Bronenosets 'Potyomkin' (Battleship Potemkin). d. Eisenstein;* sw. Nina Agadzhanova-Shutko; c. Tisse;* with Antonov, Alexandrov, Vladimir Barsky, Levshin, Gomarov, Strauch. Goskino. 1,740 m.

Leninskaia kinopravda (Leninist Film-truth). d. Vertov;* c. Mikhail Kaufman. Kultkino. 755 m.

Luch smerti (The Death Ray). d. Kuleshov;* sw. Pudovkin;* c. Levitski;* with Komarov, Porfiri Podobed, Vladimir Fogel, Khokhlova, Pyotr Galadzhev, Leonid Obolensky, & Pudovkin.* Goskino. 2,995 m.

Stachka (Strike). d. Eisenstein;* sw. Proletkult collective (Valeri Pletnyov, Eisenstein, I. Kravchunovsky, Grigori Alexandrov); c. Tisse* & Vasili Khvatov; with Alexandrov, Maxim Strauch, Mikhail Gomarov, Judith Glizer, Boris Yurtsev, & Alexander Antonov. Goskino & Proletkult. 1.969 m.

Shakhmatnaia goriachka (Chess Fever). d. Pudovkin* & Nikolai Shpikovsky; sw. Shpikovsky; c. Anatoli Golovnia; with Vladimir Fogel, Anna Zemtsova, Jose Raoul Capablanca, Anatoli Ktorov, Ivan Koval-Samborsky, Yakov Protazanov, Yuri Raizman, & Mikhail Zharov. Mezhrabpom-Russ. 400 m.

1926

Bukhta smerti (Death Bay). d. Room;* sw. Boris Leonidov; au. Alexei Novikov-Priboi; c. Evgeni Slavinsky; with V. Yaroslavtsev, N. Saltikov, Kartashova, L. Yurenev, & Nikolai Okhlopkov. Goskino. 2,284 m.

Chertovo koleso (The Devil's Wheel). d. Kozintsev,* Trauberg;* sw. Adrian Piotrovsky; au. Veniamin Kaverin; c. Andrei Moskvin; with Ludmila Semyonova, N. Foregger, Pyotr Sobolevsky, Sergei Gerasimov, & Emil Gal. Leningradkino. 2,650 m.

Katka—bumazhnyi ranet (Katka's Reinette Apples). d. Eduard Johanson & Ermler;* sw. M. Borisoglebsky & Boris Leonidov; c. Evgeni Mikhailov & Andrei Moskvin; with Veronica Buzhinskaya, B. Chernova, Valeri Solovtsov, & Vakov Gudkin. Sovkino (Leningrad). 2,084 m.

Mat (The Mother). d. Pudovkin;* sw. Nathan Zarkhi; au. Maxim Gorky; c. Anatoli Golovnya; with Vera Baranovskaya, Nikolai Batalov, Alexander Chistiakov, & Ivan Koval-Samborsky. Mezhrabpom-Russ. 1,800 m.

Meekhanikha golovnovo mozga (Mechanics of the Brain). d. & sw. Pudovkin;* c. Anatoli Golovnya. Mezhrabpom-Russ. 1,850 m.

Po zakonu (By the Law). d. Kuleshov;* sw. Shklovski* & Kuleshov;* au. Jack London; c. Konstantin Kuznetsov; with Alexandra Khokhlova, Sergei Komarov, Vladimir Fogel, Pyotr Galadzhev, Porfiri Podobed. Goskino. 1,673 m.

Predatel (Traitor). d. Room;* sw. Lev Nikulin & Shkolvski;* c. Evgeni Slavinsky; with

Nikolai Panov, P. Korizno, David Gutman, Nikolai Okholpkov, & Naum Rogozhin. Goskino. 2,100 m.
Protsess o trekh millionakh (The Three Million Case). d. Protazanov;* sw. Oleg Leonidov & Protazanov; c. Pyotr Yermolov; with Igor Ilinsky, Mikhail Klimov, Anatoli Ktorov, & Olga Zhizneva. Mezhrabpom-Russ. 1,931 m.
Shagai, Soviet! (Stride, Soviet!). d. & sw. Vertov;* c. I. Beliakov. Goskino (Kultkino). 1,650 m.
Shestaia chast mira (A Sixth of the World). d. Vertov;* c. Mikhail Kaufman, with I. Beliakov, Samuel Bendersky, P. Zotov, N. Konstantinov, A. Lemberg, N. Strukov, & Yakov Tolchan. Goskino. 1,767 m.
Shinel (The Cloak). d. Kozintsev;* & Trauberg;* sw. Yuri Tynianov; au. Nikolai Gogol; c. Andrei Moskvin & Evgeni Mikhailov; with Andrei Kostrichkin, Sergei Gerasimov, & Anna Zheimo. Leningradkino. 1,921 m.

1927

Konets Sankt-Peterburga (The End of St Petersburg). d. Pudovkin;* sw. Nathan Zarkhi; c. Anatoli Golovnia; with Alexander Chistiakov, Vera Baranovskaya, Ivan Chuvelev, & A. Obolensky. Mezhrabpom-Russ. 2,500 m.
Padenie dinastii Romanovykh (Fall of the Romanov Dynasty). sw. & ed. Shub.* Sovkino. 1,850 m.
Sorok pervyi (The Forty-First). d. Protazanov;* sw. Boris Lavrenev & Boris Leonidov; au. Lavrenev; c. Pyotr Yermolov; with Ada Voitsik, Ivan Koval-Samborsky, & I. Strauch. Mezhrabpom-Russ. 1,855 m.
S.V.D. (The Club of the Big Deed). d. Kozintsev* & Trauberg;* sw. Yuri Tynianov & Yuri Oxman; c. Andrei Moskvin; with Pyotr Sobolevsky, Sergei Gerasimov, Sophie Magarill, & Andrei Kostrichkin. Sovkino (Leningrad). 2,100 m.
Tretia meshchanskaia (Bed and Sofa). d. Room;* sw. Shklovski* & Room; c. Grigori Giber; with Nikolai Batalov, Ludmila Semyonova, Vladimir Fogel. Sovkino (Moscow). 2,025 m.
Vasha znakomaia (Your Acquaintance). d. Kuleshov;* sw. Alexander Kurs, Vitold Ashmarin, & Kuleshov; au. Kurs; c. Konstantin Kuznetsov; with Alexandra Khokhlova, Boris Ferdinandov, Vasilchikov, & A. Chekulaeva. Sovkino (Moscow). 1,800 m.
Veliki put (The Great Road). sw. & ed. Shub.* Sovkino (Moscow). 2,350 m.

1928

Belyi orel (The White Eagle). d. Protazanov;* sw. Protazanov, Oleg Leonidov, & Y. Urinov; au. Andreyev; c. Pyotr Yermolov & B. Filshin; with Vasili Kachalov, Vsevolod Meyerhold, Anna Sten, & Ivan Chuvelev. Mezhrabpomfilm. 1,850 m.
Kruzheva (Lace). d. Yutkevich;* sw. Yutkevich, Yuri Gromov, & Vladimir Legoshin; au. M. Kolosov; c. Evgeni Schneider; with Nina Shaternikova, Boris Poslavsky, K. Gradopolov, & Boris Tenin. Sovkino. 2,100 m.
October. d. Eisenstein;* sw. Eisenstein & Grigori Alexandrov; c. Tisse;* with Nikandrov & N. Popov. Sovkino (Moscow & Leningrad). 2,800 m.
Odinnadtsatyi (Number Eleven). d. & sw. Vertov;* c. Mikhail Kaufman. VUFKU. 1,600 m.

Parizhsky sapozhnik (*Parisian Cobbler*). d. Ermler;* sw. N. Nikitin & Boris Leonidov; c. Evgeni Mikhailov & G. Bushtuev; with Veronica Buzhinskaya, Fyodor Nikitin, Valeri Solovtsov, Yakov Gudkin, Varvara Miasnikova. Sovkino (Leningrad). 2,065 m.

Potomok Chingis-khana (*The Heir to Genghis-Khan/Storm Over Asia*). d. Pudovkin;* sw. Osip Brik; au. Ivan Novokshonov; c. Anatoli Golovnia; with Valeri Inkizhinov, A. Dedintsev, Anna Sudakevich, V. Tsoppi, Boris Barnet, Alexander Chistiakov, & Leionid Obolenski. Mezhrabpomfilm. 3,082 m.

Zvenigora. d. Dovzhenko;* sw. Mikhail Johansen & Yuri Yurtik; c. Boris Zavelyov; with Semyov Svashenko, Mikola Nademsky, & Alexander Podorozhny. VUFKU. 1,799 m.

1929

Arsenal. d. & sw. Dovzhenko;* c. Danylo Demutsky; with Semyon Svashenko, Mikola Nademsky, Ambrosi Buchma, Pyotr Masokha. VUFKU. 1,830 m.

Chelovek s kinoapparatom (*Man with a Movie Camera*). d. & sw. Vertov;* c. Mikhail Kaufman. VUFKU. 1,830 m.

Chërnyi parus (*The Black Sail*). d. Yutkevich;* sw. K. Feldman, G. Zelondzhev-Shipov; c. Z. Martov; with Nina Shaternikova & Poslavsky. Sovkino (Leningrad). 1,952 m.

Novyi Vavilon (*The New Babylon*). d. & sw. Kozintsev* & Trauberg;* c. Andrei Moskvin & Evgeni Mikhailov; m. Shostakovich;* with Yelena Kuzmina, Pyotr Sobolevsky, D. Gutman, Sophie Magarill, Gerasimov, Andrei Kostrichkin. Sovkino (Leningrad). 2,200 m.

Staroe i novoe (*Old and New/The General Line*). d. Eisenstein;* sw. Eisenstein & Grigori Alexandrov; c. Tisse;* with Marfa Lapkina, Vasya Buzenkov, & Kostya Vasiliev. 2,469 m.

Turksib. d. & sw. Victor Turin; c. Evgeni Slavinsky & Boris Frantzisson. Vostok-kino. 1,666 m.

1930

Zemlia (*Earth*). d. & sw. Dovzhenko;* c. Danylo Demutsky; with Semyon Svashenko, Stepan Shkurat, Mikola Nademsky, Yelena Maximova, & Pyotr Masokha. VUFKU. 1,704 m.

1931

Entuziazm (*Enthusiasm/The Donbass Symphony*). d. & sw. Vertov;* c. Zeitlin. Kiev Film Studio, Ukrainfilm. 96 min.

Putëvka v zhizn (*A Pass to Life/The Road to Life*). d. Nikolai Ekk; sw. Ekk, Alexander Stolper, & Regina Yanushkevich; with Ivan Kyrla, Nikolai Batalov, Mikhail Zharov, & Yanushkevich. Mezhrabpomfilm. 3,300 m.

1932

Ivan. d. & sw. Dovzhenko;* c. Danylo Demutsky, Yuri Ekelchik, & Mikhail Glider; with Pytor Mashokha, Semyon Shagaida, D. Golubinsky, Stepan Shkurat, & Gnat Yura. Kiev Film Studio. 85 min.

Mërtvyi dom (The House of the Dead). d. Vasili Fedorov; sw. Shklovski* & Fedorov; au. Fedor Dostoevsky; c. Vasili Pronin; with Nikolai Khmelyov, Nikita Podgorny, N. Vitovtov, N. Radin, Vasili Kovrigin, & Shklovsky. Mezhrabpomfilm. 2,500 m.

Prostoi sluchai (A Simple Case). d. Pudovkin;* sw. Alexander Rzheshevsky; c. G. Kabalov & G. Bobrov; with A. Baturin, Evgeniya Rogulina, Alexander Chistiakov, & A. Belov. Mezhrabpomfilm. 2,633 m.

Vstrechnyi (Counterplan). d. Ermler* & Yutkevich;* sw. Leo Arnstam, D. Del, Ermler, & Yutkevich; c. I Martov, Alexander Ginsburg, & Wulf Rappoport; with Vladimir Gardin, Maria Blumenthal-Tamarina, T. Guretskaya, Andrei Abrikosov, Boris Tenin, & Poslavsky. Rosfilm (Leningrad). 3,170 m.

1933

Dezertir (Deserter). d. Pudovkin;* sw. Nina Agadzhanova, M. Krasnostavsky, & A. Lazebnikov; c. Anatoli Golovnkin & Yuli Fogelman; with Boris Livanov, Tamara Makarova, Vasili Kovrigin, Judith Glizer, & A. Chistiakov. Mezhrabpomfilm. 2,661 m.

Velikii uteshitel (Great Comforter). d. Kuleshov;* sw. Alexander Kurs & Kuleshov; au. O. Henry; c. Konstantin Kuznetsov and G. Kabalov; m. Zinovi Feldman; with Konstantin Khokhlov, Ivan Novoseltsev, Alexandra Khokhlova, Andrei Fait, & Weyland Rudd. Mezhrabpomfilm. 97 min.

1934

Chapaev. d. & sw. Sergei & Georgi Vasiliev; au. Dmitry Furmanov and A. Furmanova; c. Alexander Sigaev & A. Xenofontov; with Boris Babochkin, Boris Blinov, Leonid Kmit, Varvara Miasnikova, Illarion Pevtsov, Stepan Shkurat, & Boris Chirkov. Lenfilm. 2,600 m.

Tri pesni o Lenine (Three Songs of Lenin). d. & sw. Vertov;* c. Surensky, Mark Magidson, & Bentsion Monastirsky. Mezhrabpomfilm. 1,873 m.

1935

Aerograd. d & sw. Dovzhenko;* c. Tisse* & Mikhail Gindin; with Semyon Shagaida, Stepan Shkurat, Boris Dobronravov, & Sergei Stoliarov. Mosfilm & Ukrainfilm. 2,296 m.

Krestiane (Peasants). d. Ermler;* sw. Ermler, Mikhail Bolshintsov, & V. Portnov; c. Alexander Gintzburg; with A. Petrov, Ekaterina Korchagina-Alexandrovskaia, Nikolai Bogoliubov, Yelena Yunger, Boris Poslavsky, Gardin,* Ivan Chuvelev, V. Lukin, B. Sladkopevtsev, & Pyotr Aleinikov. Lenfilm. 120 min.

Yunost Maksim (The Youth of Maxim). d. & sw. Kozintsev* & Trauberg;* c. Andrei Moskvin; m. Shostakovich;* with Boris Chirkov, Stepan Kayukov, Valentina Kibardina, & Mikhail Tarkhanov. Lenfilm. 2,678 m.

1936

Beleet parus odinoky (Lone White Sail). d. Vladimir Legoshin; sw. & au. Valentin Kataev; c. Bentsion Monastirsky & G. Garibian; with Igor But, Boris Runge, A. Melnikov,

Ivan Peltser, A. Chekaevsky, Fedor Nikitin, & Nikolai Plotnikov. Soyuzdetfilm [Mezhrabpomfilm]. 92 min.
My iz Kronstadta (We Are From Kronstadt). d. Efim Dzigan; sw. Vsevolod Vishnevsky; c. N. Naumov-Strazh; with Vasili Zaichikov, Grigori Bushtuev, Oleg Zhakov, Raisa Esipova, & Peter Kirillov. Mosfilm. 2,655 m.

1937

Bespridannitsa (Without Dowry). d. Protazanov;* sw. Vladimir Schweitzer & Protazanov; c. Mark Magidson; with Nina Alisova, Mikhail Klimov, Anatoli Ktorov, Boris Tenin, & Olga Pyzhova. Mezhrabpomfilm. 2,392 m.
Deputat Baltiki (Baltic Deputy). d. Alexander Zarkhi & Heifitz;* sw. D. Del, Zarkhi, Leonid Rakhmanov, & Heifitz; c. M. Kaplan; with Nikolai Cherkasov, M. Domasheva, Boris Livanov, Oleg Zhakov, & A. Melnikov. Lenfilm. 2,628 m.
Lenin v Oktiabre (Lenin in October). d. Romm;* sw. Alexei Kapler. c. Boris Volchok; with Boris Shchukin, Nikilai Okhlopkov, Vasili Vanin, & I. Golshtab. Mosfilm. 3,034 m.
Vozvrashchenie Maksima (The Return of Maxim). d. Kozintsev* & Trauberg;* sw. Kozintsev, Lev Slavin, & Trauberg; c. Andrei Moskvin; m. Shostakovich;* with Boris Chirkov, Valentina Kibardina, Alexander Zrazhevsky, Al Kuznetsov, Mikhail Zharov, Vasili Vanin, Alexander Chistiakov, & Kriuchkov.* Lenfilm. 3,082 m.

1938

Alexander Nevsky. d. Eisenstein;* sw. Pyotr Pavlenko & Eisenstein; c. Tisse;* m. Sergei Prokofiev; with Nikolai Cherkasov, Nikolai Okhlopkov, Andrei Abrikosov, Valentina Ivashova, Dmitri Orlov, Vladimir Yershov, & Varvara Massalitinova. Mosfilm. 3,044 m.
Detstvo Gorkovo (Childhood of Gorky). d. Mark Donskoi; sw. I. Gruzdev & Donskoi; c. Pyotr Yermolov; with Alexei Liarsky, Varvara Massalitinova, M. Troyanovsky, & Daniel Sagal. Soyuzdetfilm. 2,753 m.
Komsomolsk. d. Gerasimov;* sw. Z. Markina, M. Vitukhnovsky, & Gerasimov; c. Alexander Ginsburg; with Ivan Novoseltsev, Tamara Makarova, Kriuchkov,* & S. Krylov. Lenfilm. 2,954 m.
Pobeda (Victory). d. Pudovkin* & Mikhail Doller; sw. Nathan Zarkhi (revised by Vsevolod Vishnevsky); c. Anatoli Golovnia; with V. Solovyov, A. Zubov, & Elena Korchagina-Alexandrovskaya. Mezhrabpomfilm & Mosfilm. 2,325 m.
Veliki grazhdanin (A Great Citizen, Pt. I). d. Ermler*; sw. Mikhail Bleiman, Mikhail Bolshintsov, & Ermler; c. Arkadi Kaltsati; with Nikolai Bogoliubov, Ivan Bersenev, Oleg Zhakov, & Alexander Zrazhevsky. Lenfilm.

1939

Lenin v 1918 godu (Lenin in 1918). d. Romm;* sw. Alexei Kapler & Tatian Zlatogorova; c. Boris Volchock; with Boris Shchukin, Mikhail Gelovani, Nikolai Cherkasov, Nikolai Bogoliubov, Nikolai Okhlopkov, & Vasili Vanin. Mosfilm. 3,677 m.
Petr Pervyi (Peter the First). d. Vladimir Petrov; sw. Alexei Tolstoi, Petrov, & N. Leshchenko; c. Vladimir Yakovlev; with Nikolai Simonov, Alla Tarsova, Nikolai

Cherkasov, Mikhail Zharov, Mikhail Tarkhanov, & Irina Zarubina. Lenfilm. 3,423 m.

Shchors. d & sw. Dovzhenko;* c. Yuri Ekelchik; with Evgeni Samoilov, Ivan Skuratov, & Hans Klering. Kiev Studio. 3,850 m.

Veliki grazhdanin (A Great Citizen, Pt. II). d. Ermler;* sw. Mikhail Bleiman, Mikhail Bolshintsov, & Ermler; c. Arkadin Kaltsati; with Nikolai Bogoliubov, Oleg Zhakov, Ivan Bersenev, Boris Poslavsky, & Yuri Tolubeev. Lenfilm. 3,640 m.

1941

Suvorov. d. Pudovkin* & Mikhail Doller; sw. Georgi Grebner & H. Ravich; c. Anatoli Golovnia & Tamara Lobova; with Nikolai Cherkasov-Sergeev, A. Yachnitsky, Alexander Khanov, Vsevolod Aksyonov, Mikhail Astangov. Mosfilm. 2,984 m.

1942

Kak zakalyalas stal (How the Steel was Tempered). d. & sw. Mark Donskoi; au. Nikolai Ostrovsky; c. Bentsion Monastirsky; with V. Perest-Petrenko, Daniel Sagal, & I. Fedotova. Kiev & Ashkhabad Studios. 2,529 m.

1943

Ona zashchishchaet rodinu (She Defends Her Country). d. Ermler;* sw. Mikhail Bleiman & I. Bondin; c. Wulf Rapoport; with Vera Maretskaya, L. Smirnova, Pyotr Aleinikov, & Nikolai Bogoliubov. Combined Studio. 2,189 m.

Vo imia rodiny (In the Name of the Fatherland). d. Pudovkin* & Dmitri Vasiliev; au. & sw. Konstantin Simonov; c. Boris Volchok & E. Zavelyova; with Nikolai Kriuchkov, Mikhail Zharov, V. Gribkov, Olga Zhizneva, & Pyotr Aleinikov. Combined Studio. 2,626 m.

1944

Chelovek No. 217 (Girl No. 217). d. Romm;* sw. Evgeni Gabrilovich & Romm; c. Boris Volchok & E. Zavelyova; with Elena Kuzmina, Anna Lisyanskaya, & Vasili Zaichikov. Mosfilm & Tashkent Studio. 2,776 m.

Ivan Grozny (Ivan the Terrible, Pt. I). d. & sw. Eisenstein;* c. Tisse* (exteriors) & Andrei Moskvin (interiors); m. Sergei Prokofiev; with Nikolai Cherkasov, Ludmila Tselikovskaya, Serafima Birman, Pavel Kadochnikov, Mikhiail Nazvanov, Andrei Abrikosov, Mikhail Zharov, Ambrosi Buchma, & Pudovkin.* Combined Studio. 2,745 m.

1945

Nashestvie (Invasion). d. Room;* sw. Boris Chirkov; au. Leonid Leonov; c. S. Ivanov; with Zhakov, Olga Zhhizneva, Vasili Vanin, & V. Gremin. Combined Studio, Alma-Ata. 2,745 m.

1946

Admiral Nakhimov. d. Pudovkin;* sw. Igor Lukovsky; c. Anatoli Golovna & Tamara Lobova; with Alexei Diki, Evgeni Samoilov, Reuben Simonov, & Pudovkin.* Mosfilm. 2,541 m.

Ivan Grozny (Ivan the Terrible, Part Two). d. & sw. Eisenstein;* c. Andrei Moskvin; with Nikolai Cherkasov, Serafima Birman, Pavel Kadochnikov, Andrei Abrikosov, Mikhail Zharov, & Ambrosi Buchma. Mosfilm (released in 1958).

Kliatva (The Vow). d. Mikhail Chiaureli; sw. Chiaureli & Pyotr Pavlenko; c. Leonid Kosmatov; with Mikhail Gelovani, Sophia Giatsintova, Nikolai Bogoliubov, Alexei Gribov, Tamara Makarova, & Nikolai Plotnikov. Tbilisi Studio. 14 reels.

Veliki perelom (The Great Turning Point). d. Ermler;* sw. Boris Chirkov; c. Abram Kalsati; with Mikhail Derzhavin, P. Andrievsky, Andrei Abrikosov, Alexander Zrazhevsky, & Mark Bernes. Lenfilm. 11 reels.

1947

Michurin. d. & sw. Dovzhenko;* c. Leonid Kosmatov & Yuli Kun; m. Dmitri Shostakovich; with G. Belov, A. Vasilieva, & F. Grigoriev. Mosfilm. 2,830 m.

1948

Russkii vopros (The Russian Question). d & sw. Romm;* au. Konstantin Simonov; c. Boris Volchok; with Vsevolod Aksyonov, Boris Tenin, Mikhail Astangov, Mikhail Nazvanov, Elena Kuzmina, & Boris Poslavsky. Mosfilm. 9 reels.

1951

Taras Shevchenko. d & sw. Igor Savchenko; c. Abram Kaltsati & Danylo Demutsky; with Bondarchuk,* Natalia Uzhvi, Evgeni Samoilov, & Alexei Konsovsky. Kiev Studio. 11 reels.

1952

Nezabyvaemyi 1919 god (The Unforgettable Year 1919). d. Mikhail Chiaureli; sw. Vsevolod Vishnevsky, Chiaureli, & A. Filimonov; au. Vishnevsky; c. Leonid Kosmatoov & V. Nikolaev; m. Dmitri Shostakovich; with I. Moschanov (Lenin), Mikhail Gelovani, Boris Andreev, M. Kovaleva, Evgeni Samoilov, Sergei Lukianov, Victor Stanitsin (Churchill), V. Koltsov (Lloyd George), Gnat Yura (Clemenceau), & L. Korsakov (Wilson). Mosfilm. 11 reels.

1953

Vozvrashchenie Vasilia Bortnikova (The Return of Vasili Bortnikov). d. Pudovkin;* sw. Galina Nikolaeva & Evgeni Gabrilovich; au. Nikolaeva; c. Sergei Urusevski;* with Sergei Lukyanov, Natalia Medvedeva, N. Timofeyev, & Vsevolod Sanayev. Mosfilm. 11 reels.

1954

Vernye druzia (True Friends) d. Kalatozov;* sw. Alexander Galich & Konstantin Isaev; c. Mark Magidson; with Vasili Merkuriev, Boris Chirkov, & A. Borisov. Mosfilm.

1955

Lurdzha Magdany (Magdana's Donkey). d. Abuladze* & Revaz Chkheidze; sw. K. Gogodze; au. Gabashvili; c. L. Sukhov & Alexander Digmelov; with D. Tserodze & Akaki Vasasdze. Georgia Films. 7 reels.

Neokonchennaya povest (Unfinished Story). d. Ermler;* sw. Kilsaev; c. Anatoli Nazarov; with Elina Bystritskaya, Bondarchuk,* Evgeni Samoilov, & Sophia Giatsintova. Lenfilm. 2,712 m.

1956

Dom, v kotorom ya zhivu (The House I Live In). d. Kulijanov* & Yakov Segel; sw. Olshanski; with Mikhail Ulianov & Zhanna Bolotova.

Othello. d. & sw. Yutkevich;* au. William Shakespeare; c. Yevgeni Andrikanis; with Bondarchuk,* Irina Skobtseva, Andrei Popov, & Vladimir Soshalsky. Mosfilm. 11 reels.

Pervyi eshelon (The First Echelon). d. & sw. Kalatozov;* c. Yuri Ekelchik & Urusevski;* m. Shostakovich;* with V. Sanaev, S. Romodanov, N. Annenkov, O. Yefremov, & Izolda Izvitskaya. Mosfilm. 11 reels.

Sorok pervyi (The Forty-first). d. Chukhrai;* sw. G. Koltunov; au. Boris Lavrenev; c. Urusevski;* with Oleg Strizhenov, Izolda Izvitskaia, & Kriuchkov.*

1957

Don Quixote. d. Kozintsev;* sw. Evgeni Schvartz (from Cervantes' novel); c. Andrei Moskvin & Apollinari Dudko; with Nikolai Cherkasov, Yuri Tolubeev, & Serafima Birman. Lenfilm. 11 reels.

Letiat zhuravli (The Cranes Are Flying). d. Kalatozov;* au. & sw. Victor Rozov; c. Urusevski;* m. M. Veinberg; with Tatiana Samoilova, Alexei Batalov,* & Vasili Merkuriev. Mosfilm. 10 reels.

Tikhi Don (The Quiet Don, Pts. I, II, and III). d. & sw. Gerasimov;* au. Sholokhov; c. Wulf Rapoport; with Daniel Ilchenko, Pyotr Glebov, Elina Bystritskaya, & Zinaida Kirienko. Gorky Studio. 11, 12, 12 reels.

1958

Dorogoi moi chelovek! (My Dear Fellow!). d. Heifitz;* sw. Yuri German & Heifitz; au. German; c. M. Magid & L. Sokolovsky; with Alexei Batalov,* Inna Makarova, & P. Konstantinov. Lenfilm. 2,958 m.

Kommunist (The Communist). d. Yuli Raizman; sw. Evgeni Gabrilovich; c. Alexander Shelenkov & Chen Yu-lan; with Evgeni Urbansky, Sophia Pavlova, Evgeni Shutov, & Sergei Yakovlev. Mosfilm. 3,045 m.

Pervyi den' (The First Day). d. Ermler;* sw. Konstantin Isaev; c. Anatoli Nazarov; with Olga Petrenko, Eduard Bredun, G. Yuchenkov, & Smoktunovski.* Lenfilm. 2,498 m.

Rasskazy o Lenine (*Stories about Lenin*). d. Yutkevich;* sw. Mikhail Volpin, Nikolai Erdman, & Yevgeni Gabrilovich; c. Yevgeni Andrikanis & Andrei Moskvin; with Maxim Strauch (Lenin), Marina Pastukhova (Krupskaia), A. Lisyanskaya, & Vsevolod Sanaev. Mosfilm. 3,147 m.

1959

Ballada o soldate (*Ballad of a Soldier*). d. Grigori Chukhrai; sw. Valentin Ezhov & Chukhrai; c. Vladimir Nikolaev & Era Saveleva; with Vladimir Ivashov, Zhanna Prokhorenko, Antonina Maximova, Kriuchkov,* & Evgeni Urbansky. Mosfilm. 2,452 m.
Otchii dom (*My Father's House*). d. Kulijanov;* sw. Budimir Metalnikov; c. Pyotr Kataev; with V. Kuznetsova, Valentin Zubkov, Noyabrina (Nonna) Mordiukova, & Pyotr Aleinikov. Gorky Studio. 2,729 m.
Sudba cheloveka (*Destiny of a Man*). d. Bondarchuk;* sw. Yuri Lukin & Fyodor Shakhmagonov; au. Sholokhov; c. Vladimir Monakhov; with Bondarchuk, Zinaida Kirienko, & Pavlik Boriskin. Mosfilm. 2,807 m.

1960

Dama s sobachkoi (*Lady with the Little Dog*). d. & sw. Heifitz;* au. Anton Chekhov; c. Andrei Moskvin & Dmitri Meskhiev; with Iya Savvina & Alexei Batalov. Mosfilm. 2,450 m.
Katok i skripka (*The Steamroller and the Violin*). d. Tarkovski;* sw. Mikhalkov-Konchalovski* & Tarkovski; c. Vadim Yusov; m. Viacheslav Ovchinnikov; with Igor Fomchenko, Vladimir Zamansky, & N. Arkhangelskaia. Mosfilm Children's Film Unit. 50 min.
Neotpravlennoe pismo (*The Letter That Wasn't Sent*). d. Kalatozov;* sw. Grigori Koltunov, Valeri Osipov, & Victor Rozov; au. Osipov; c. Sergei Urusevski; with Smoktunovski,* Tatyana Samoilova, Boris Livanov, & Evgeni Urbansky. Mosfilm. 2,668 m.
Serezha (*A Summer to Remember*). d. Georgi Danelia & Igor Talankin; sw. Vera Panova, Danelia, & Talankin; c. A. Nitochkin; with Boris Barkhatov, Bondarchuk,* & Irina Skobtseva. Mosfilm.

1961

Chistoe nebo (*Clear Sky*). d. Chukhrai;* sw. Daniel Khrabrovitsky; c. Sergei Poluyanov; with Nina Drobysheva, Evgeni Urbansky, Vitali Koniaev, N. Kuzmina, L. Kniazev, G. Georgiu, Oleg Tabakov, Alik Krylov, Vitalik Bondarev, & Georgi Kulikov. Mosfilm. 109 min.

1962

Bania (*The Bath*). d. Yutkevich;* sw. Yutkevich & Anatoli Karanovich; au. Vladimir Mayakovsky; c. Mikhail Kamenetsky. Soyuzmultifilm. 1,458 m.
Deviat dnei odnogo goda (*Nine Days in a Year*). d. Romm;* sw. Romm & Danil Khrabrovitsky; c. German Lavrov; with Aleksei Batalov,* Smoktunovski,* Tamara Lavrova, Nikolay Plotnikov, & Nikolai Sergeev. Mosfilm. 110 mins.

Ivanovo detstvo (*Ivan's Childhood*). d. Tarkovski;* au. Vladimir Bogomolov; sw. Bogomolov & Mikhail Papava; c. Vadim Yusov; m. Vyacheslav Ovchinnikov; with Kolia Burlaev, Irina Tarkovskaya, Valentin Zubkov, Evgeni Zharikov, Valentina Maliavina, D. Milyutenko, S. Krylov, & Nikolai Grinko. Mosfilm. 95 min.

1963

Ya Kuba (*I Am Cuba*). d. Kalatozov;* sw. Evgeni Evtushenko & Enrico Barnet; c. Urusevski.* Mosfilm.

1964

Dobro pozhalovat! (*Welcome!*). d. Klimov;* sw. S. Lungin & I. Nusinov; c. A. Kuznetsov; with Evgeni Evstigneev, A. Aleinikova, I. Rutberg, L. Smirnova, & V. Kosykh. Mosfilm.

Hamlet. d. & sw. Kozintsev;* au. William Shakespeare; c. Jonas Gricius; m. Shostakovich;* with Smoktunovski,* Mikhail Nazvanov, E. Radzinya, Yuri Tolubeev, & Anastasia Vertinskaa. Lenfilm. 16 reels.

Mne dvadtsat let (*I'm Twenty [or, Lenin's Sentries]*). d. Marlen Khutsiev; sw. Khutsiev & Gennadi Shpalikov; c. Margarita Pilikhina; with V. Popov, Nikolai Gubenko, Stanislav Liubshin, & Marianna Vertinskaya. Gorky Studio. 18 reels.

Teni zabytykh predkov (*Shadows of Forgotten Ancestors*). d. Parajanov;* sw. Parajanov & Ivan Chendei; au. Michael Kotsiubinsky; c. Yuri Ilyenko; with Ivan Mikolaichuk, Larisa Kadochnikova, Spartak Bagashvili, & Nikolai Grinko. Dovzhenko Studio. 10 reels.

Zhivet takoi paren (*There's a Certain Fellow*). d. & sw. Vasili Shukshin; c. Valeri Ginzburg; with Leonid Kuravlev, L. Alexandrova, & L. Burkova. Gorky Studio. 10 reels.

1965

Lenin v Polshe (*Lenin in Poland*). d. Yutkevich;* sw. Yevgeni Gabrilovich & Yutkevich; c. Jan Liaskowski; with Maxim Strauch, A. Lisianskaya, & A. Pavlycheva. Mosfilm. 10 reels.

Obyknovennyi fashizm (*Ordinary Fascism*). d. Romm;* sw. Romm, Maya Turovskya, & Yuri Khaniutin. I. 7 reels, II. 7 reels.

Pervyi uchitel (*The First Teacher*). d. Mikhalkov-Konchalovski;* sw. Chingiz Aitmatov, Boris Dobrodeyev & Mikhalkov-Konchalovski; au. Aitmatov; c. Georgi Rerberg; with Bolot Beishenaliev, Natalia Arinbasarova, & Darkul Kuyukova. Kirghizfilm & Mosfilm. 10 reels.

1966

Andrei Rublev. d. Tarkovski;* sw. Tarkovski & Mikhalkov-Konchalovski;* c. Vadim Yusov; m. Viacheslav Ovchinnikov; with Anatoli Solonitsyn, Ivan Lapikov, Nikolai Grinko, Nikolai Sergeev, Irma Raukh, Nikolai Burliaev, Yuri Nikulin, Yuri Nazarov, Nikolai Grabbe, S. Krylov, Bykov,* Bolot Beishenaliev, B. Matisik, A. Obukhov, & Volodia Titov. Mosfilm. 185 min.

Asino schastie (*Asya's Happiness*). d. Mikhalkov-Konchalovski;* sw. Yuri Klepikov; c.

G. Rerberg; with Iya Savina, Aleksandr Surin, Lubov Sokolova, Gennadi Egoryschev, & Ivan Petrov. Mosfilm. 90 min.

Voina i mir (*War and Peace*). d. Bondarchuk;* sw. Bondarchuk & Vasili Solovev (from Tolstoi's novel); c. Alexander Shelenkov, Chen Yu-lan, & Anatoli Petritsky; with Ludmilla Saveleva, Bondarchuk, Vyacheslav Tikhonov, Victor Stanitsin, Oleg Tabakov, Anatoli Ktorov, Anastasia Vertinskaya, Irina Skobtseva, & Vasili Lanovoi. Mosfilm. I: 16 reels, II: 12 reels, III: 10 reels, IV: 10 reels.

1967

Molba (*Prayer*). d. Abuladze;* sw. Abuladze & Anzor Salukvadze; c. Alexander Antipenko. Gruzia-film (Georgia-film).

Pokhozhdenia zubnogo vracha (*Adventures of a Dentist*). d. Klimov;* sw. Alexander Volodin; c. S. Rubashkin; with A. Miagkov, B. Vasileva, A. Freindlikh, P. Krymov, & Igor Kvasha. Mosfilm.

1968

Anna Karenina. d. Alexander Zarkhi; sw. Zarkhi & Vasili Katanin; au. Leo Tolstoi; c. Leonid Kalashnikov; with Tatiana Samoilova, Nicolai Gritsenko, Vasili Lanovoi, Iya Savvina, Anastasia Vertinshaya, & Maya Plisetskaya.

Krylia (*Wings*). d. Shepitko;* sw. Valentin Yezhov & Nataliya Riantseva; c. Igor Slabnevich; with Maya Bulgakova, P. Krumov, Zhanna Bolotova, & Nikolai Grabbe. Mosfilm.

Tsvet granata (*The Colors of Pomegranate*). d. & sw. Parajanov;* c. A. Samvelian; m. Tigran Mansurian; with Sofiko Chaurieli, M. Alekian, V. Galestian, G. Gegechkori, & O. Minasian. Armenfilm. 73 min.

V ogne broda net (*No Ford in the Fire*). d. Panfilov;* sw. Evgeni Gabrilovich & Panfilov; c. D. Dolinin; with Inna Churikova, Maia Bulgakova, Michael Kononov, & Anatoli Solonitsyn. Lenfilm.

1969

Belorussky vokzal (*Belorussian Station*). d. Andrei Smirnov; sw. Vadim Trunin; c. Pavel Lebeshev; with Anatoli Papanov, Evgeni Leonov, Vsevolod Safonov, & Alexei Glazyrin. Mosfilm. 10 reels.

Dvorianskoye gnezdo (*A Nest of Gentry*). d. Mikhalkov-Konchalovski;* sw. Valentin Yezhov & Mikhalkov-Konchalovski; au. Turgenev; c. Georgi Rerberg; with Leonid Kulagin, Beata Tyszkiewicz, Irina Kupchenko, Mikhalkov,* & Nikolai Gubenko. Mosfilm.

1970

Nachalo (*Debut*). d. Panfilov;* sw. Panfilov & Evgeni Gabrilovich; c. Dmitri Dolinin; with Inna Churikova, Valentina Telichkina, T. Stekanova, Leonid Kuravlev, Michael Kononov, N. Skomorokhova, Tamara Bedova, Y. Klepikov, & G. Belov. Lenfilm. 95 min.

Ne goriui! (*Don't Grieve!*) d. Georgi Danelia; sw. R. Gabriadze; c. Vadim Yusov; with

Buba Kikabidze, S. Zakariadze, Anastasia Vertinskaya, S. Filippov, G. Kavtaradze, Sofia Chaurieli, & Evgeni Leonov. Gruzia Film (Georgia-film).

Prestuplenie i nakazanie (Crime and Punishment). d. Kulijanov;* sw. Nikolai Figurovski & Kulijanov; au. Fedor Dostoevski; c. Vyachaslav Shumski; with Georgi Tartorkin, Smoktunovski,* Tatiana Bedova, Efin Kopelian, Maya Bulgakova, & Viktoria Fedorova.

U ozera (By the Lake). d. & sw. Gerasimov;* c. Vladimir Rappoport & Vladimir Arkhangelsky; with Natalia Belokhvostikova, Oleg Zhakov, Vasili Shukshin, & Valentina Telichkina. Gorky Studio. I: 2,782 m., II: 2,252 m.

1971

Diadia Vania (Uncle Vanya). d. & sw. Mikhalkov-Konchalovski; au. Anton Chekov; c. Georgi Rerberg & E. Guslinsky; with Smoktunovski,* Bondarchuk,* Irina Miroshnichenko, & Irina Kupchenko. Mosfilm. 10 reels.

Korol Lir (King Lear). d. & sw. Kozintsev* (from Shakespeare's play); c. Jonas Gricius; m. Shostakovich;* with Yuri Yarvet, Elza Radzinya, Galina Volchek, Valentina Shendrikova, Donatas Banionis, Oleg Dal, Regimantas Adomaitis, Karl Cebric, Vladimir Emelyanov, Aleksandr Vakach, A. Petrenko, I. Budraitis, & Leonard Merzin. Lenfilm. 140 min.

Pirosmani. d. Georgi Shengelaya; sw. Shengelaya & Erlom Akhvlediani; c. Konstantin Apryatin; with Avtandil Varazi, David Abashidze, & Zurab Kapianidze. Gruziafilm. 85 min.

1972

Igrok (The Gambler). d. A. Batalov;* sw. M. Ol'shevsky (from Dostoevski's story); c. D. Meskhiev; with Nikolai Burliaev, Tatiana Ivanova, Liubov' Dobrozhanskaia, Vsevolod Kuznetsov, Itka Zelenegorska, Vasili Livanov, & Alexander Kaidanovsky. Lenfilm & Barrandov, Czechoslovakia.

Soliaris (Solaris). d. Tarkovski;* sw. Tarkovski & Friedrikh Gorenstein; au. Stanislaw Lem; c. Vadim Yusov; m. J. S. Bach & Eduard Artemiev; with Natalia Bondarchuk, Donatas Banionis, Yuri Jarvet, Anatoli Solonitsyn, Vladislav Dvorzhetski, Nikolai Grinko, Sos Sarkissian, & Parajanov.* Mosfilm. 165 min.

1973

Liutyi (The Ferocious One). d. Tolomush Okeev; sw. Mikhalkov-Konchalovski* & E. Tropinin; au. Mukhtar Auezov; c. K. Kydyraliev; with K. Valiev, S. Chokmorov, A. Dzhangorotova, K. Sataev, & N. Ikhtimbaev. Kazhakhfilm. 90 min.

Sovsem propavshii (Hopelessly Lost). d. Danelia;* sw. Danelia & Victoria Tokareva; au. Mark Twain; c. Vadim Yusov; with Vakhtang Kikabidze, Feliks Imokoude, & Evgeni Leonov. Mosfilm. 95 min.

1975

Ne bolit golova u diatla (Woodpeckers Don't Get Headaches). d. Dinara Asanova; au. Yuri Klepikov.

Zerkalo (Mirror). d. Tarkovski;* sw. Tarkovski & Alexandr Mishurin; c. Georgi Rerberg;

m. Eduard Artemiev, J. S. Bach, Giovanni Battista Pergolesi, & Henry Purcell; with Margarita Terekhova, Filip Yankovsky, Ignat Daniltsev, Oleg Yankovsky, Nikolai Grinko, Alla Demidova, Yuri Nazarov, Anatoli Solonitsyn, Innokenti Smoktunovski, L. Tarkovskaya, Tamara Ogorodnikova, Y. Sventikov, T. Reshetnikova, E. del Bosque, L. Correcher, A. Gutierres, D. Garcia, Ta. Pames, Teresa del Bosque, & Tatiana del Bosque. Mosfilm Unit 4. 106 min.

1976

Dvadtsat' dnei bez voiny (Twenty Days Without War). d. German;* sw. & au. Konstantin Simonov; with Yuri Nikulin, Gurchenko,* Alexei Petrenko, & Mikhail Kononov. Lenfilm. 102 min.
Raba liubvi (A Slave of Love). d. Mikhalkov;* sw. Friedrikh Gorenstein & Mikhalkov-Konchalovski;* c. Pavel Lebeshev; with Elena Solovey, Rodion Nakhapetov, Aleksandr Kaliagin, & Konstantin Grigorev. Mosfilm. 94 min.
Til Eulenspiegel. d. Aleksandr Alov and Vladimir Naumov.

1977

Assya. d. & sw. Heifitz;* au. Ivan Turgenev; c. Henrikh Matadzhan; m. Oleg Karavaychuk; with Elena Koreneva, Viacheslav Vezerov, & Igor Kostolevsky.
Kliuch bez prava peredachi (The Restricted Key). d. Dinara Asanova; sw. Georgi Polonsky; c. Yuri Veksler & Dmitri Dolinin; m. Evgeni Krylatov; with Aleksei Petrenko, Elena Proklova, Marina Levtova, & Lidia Fedoseeva-Shukshina.
Mayakovsky smeetsia (Mayakovsky Laughs). d. & sw. Yutkevich* and Anatoli Karanovich; au. Vladimir Mayakovsky; c. Yuri Neiman & T. Bunimkovich; m. V. Dashkevich & A. Kremer; with Yuri Chernov, Iya Savvina, Leonid Bronevoi, & Galina Volchek. Mosfilm. 85 min.
Mimino d. Danelia;* sw. Danelia, Revaz Gabriadze, & Viktoria Tokareva; c. Anatoli Petritsky; m. Georgi Kancheli; with Vaktang Kikavidze, Frunzik Mkrchian, Elena Proklova, & Evgeni Leonov. Mosfilm.
Neokonchennaia p'esa dlia mekhanicheskogo pianino (Unfinished Piece for Player Piano). d. Mikhalkov;* sw. Mikhalkov & Alexandr Adabashian; au. Anton Chekov; c. Pavel Lebeshev; with Alexander Kaliagin, Elena Solovei, Evgenia Glushenko, Antonia Shuranova, Yuri Bogatyrev, Mikhalkov, Oleg Tabakov, & Pavel Kadochinikov. Mosfilm. 100 min.
Perepolokh (Commotion). d. Gogoberidze;* sw. Gogoberidze & Zaira Arsenaschvili; c. Erlom Akhvlediani; with Nadezda Haradze & Sofiko Chaurieli. Gruzia Film. 85 min.
Proshu slova (May I Have the Floor). d. & sw. Panfilov;* c. Alexander Antipenko; with Inna Churikova, Nikolei Gubenko, Leonid Bronevoi, & Vasili Shukshin. Lenfilm. 136 min.
Slovo dlia zashchity (Speech for the Defense). d. Vadim Abdrashitov; sw. Alexander Mindadze; c. Antonin Zabolotsky; with Marina Neyolova, Galina Yatskina, Oleg Yankovsky, Stanislav Liubshin, Viktor Shulgin, & Elena Kebul. Mosfilm. 90 min.
Step (The Steppe). d. & sw. Bondarchuk;* au. Anton Chekhov; c. Leonid Kalashnikov; m. Viacheslav Ovchinnikov; with Stanislav Liubshin, Ivan Lapikov, Innokenti

Smoktunovski, Igor Kvasha, Mikhail Gluzski, Nikolai Trofimov, Irina Skobtseva, & Oleg Kuznetsov. Mosfilm. 135 min.

Voskhozhdenie (The Ascent). d. Shepitko; sw. Shepitko & Yuri Klepikov; c. V. Chuhknov; with Boris Plotnikov, Vladimir Gostiukhin, Sergei Yakovlev, Anatoli Solonitsyn, & Ludmila Poliakova. Mosfilm. 105 min.

1978

Otets Sergii (Father Sergius). d. & sw. Igor Talankin; au. Leo Tolstoi; c. Georgi Rerberg & Anatoli Nikolaev; with Bondarchuk,* Valentina Titova, Vladislav Strzhelchik, Ludmila Maksakova, Alla Demidova, & Irina Skobtseva. Mosfilm. 99 min.

Sluzhebnyi romans (An Office Romance). d. Riazanov;* sw. Emil Braginsky; c. Vladimir Nakhabtsev; with Andrei Miagkov, Alisa Freindlikh, Svetlana Nemolyaeva, Oleg Basilashvili, Liya Akhejakova, and Liudmila Ivanova.

Strannaia zhenshchina (A Strange Woman). d. Yuli Raizman; sw. Raizman & Evgeni Gabrilovich; c. Naum Ardashnikov; with Irina Kupchnko, Svetlan Korkoshko, & Vasili Lanovoi. Mosfilm.

1979

Neskolko interv'iu po lichnym voprosam (Some Interviews on Personal Matters). d. Gogoberidze;* sw. Gogoberidze, Zair Arsenishvili, & Erlom Akhvlediani; c. Nugzar Erkomaishvili; m. Ghia Kancheli; with Sofiko Chaurieli, Ghia Badridze, Ketevan Orakhelashvili, Zhanri Lolashvili, Salome Kancheli, & Ketevan Bocharishvili. Gruzia Film Studio, Tbilisi. 90 min.

Piat' vecherov (Five Evenings). d. Mikhalkov;* s. Alexandr Adabashian; c. Pavel Lebeshev; m. Yuri Mikhalkov; with Stanislav Liubshin, Gurchenko,* Valentina Telechkina, Larisa Kuznetsova, Igor Nefedov, & Adabashian. Mosfilm. 100 min.

Povorot (The Turning Point). d. Vadim Abdrashitov; sw. Alexander Mindadze. c. Elizbar Karavayev. with Irina Kupchenko, Oleg Yankovsky, Yuri Nazarov, Anatoli Solonitsyn, & Oleg Anufriev. Mosfilm.

Sibiriada (Siberiana/The Siberiad). d. Mikhalkov-Konchalovski; s. Valentin Ezhov & Mikhalkov-Konchalovski; c. Levan Paatashvili & Nikolai Lichmanov; with Vladimir Samoilov, Misha Babukov, Vitali Solomin, Natalia Andreichenko, Evgeni Petrov, Mikhail Krononov, Maxim Manshuk, Sergei Shakurov, Volodia Levitan, Mikhalkov,* Gurchenko,* Ruslan Mikaberidze, & Vsevolod Rodionov. Mosfilm. 210 min.

Stalker. d. Tarkovski;* au. & sw. Arkadi Strugatsky & Boris Strugatsky; c. Alexandr Kniazhinsky; m. Eduard Artemiev; with Alexander Kaidanovsky, Anaatoli Solonitsyn, Nikolai Grinko, Alisa Freindlikh, Natasha Abramova, R. Yurna, E. Kostin, & R. Rendi. Mosfilm Unit 2. 161 min.

1980

Osennii marafon (Autumn Marathon). d. Danelia;* sw. Aleksandr Volodin; c. Sergei Vronsky; with Oleg Basilashvili, Natalia Gundareva, Marina Neyelova, & Evgeni Leonov. Mosfilm. 90 min.

Valentina. d. & sw. Panfilov;* au. Alexander Vampilov; c. Leonid Kalashnikov; with

Rodion Nakhapetov, Inna Churikova, Yuri Grebenshikov, & Daria Mikhailova. Mosfilm.

1981

Legkie dengi (Easy Money). d. & sw. Evgeni Matveev; c. Leonid Kalashnikov; with Liudmila Nilskaya, Elena Solovei, Aleksandr Mikhailov, Yuri Yakovlev, Pavel Kadochnikov, & Leonid Kuravlev. Mosfilm.

Moskva slezam ne verit (Moscow Does Not Believe in Tears). d. Vladimir Menshov; sw. Valentin Chernykh; c. Igor Slabnevich; m. Sergei Nikitin; with Vera Alentova, Irina Muraveva, Raisa Riazanova, Yuri Vasiliev, Alexei Batalov, & Natalia Vavilova. Mosfilm (Second Artistic Unit). 130 min.

26 dnei v zhizni Dostoevskogo (26 Days in the Life of Dostoevsky). d. Aleksandr Zarkhi; sw. V. Vladimirov & Pavel Finn; c. Vladimir Klimov; m. Irakei Gabeli; with Anatoli Solonitsyn, Evgenia Simonova, & Eva Shikulska. Mosfilm. 87 min.

Vasilii i Vasilisa (Vasili and Vasilisa). d. Irina Poplavskaia; sw. Vasili Solovev; au. Valentin Rasputin; c. Kadyrian Kydyraliev; with Olga Ostroumova, Mikhail Kononov, & Natalia Bondarchuk. Mosfilm. 98 min.

Vzlet (The Take Off). d. Savva Kulish; sw. Oleg Osetinsky; c. Vladimir Klimov; m. Oleg Karavaichuk; with Larisa Kadochnikova, Albert Filozov, Evgeni Evtushenko, Elena Finogenova, Kirill Arbuzov, Vadim Aleksandrov, & Georgy Burkov. 136 min.

1982

Neskol'ko dnei iz zhizni I. I. Oblomova (Some Days in the Life of I. I. Oblomov). d. Mikhalkov;* sw. Alexandr Adabashian & Mikhalkov; au. Ivan Goncharov; c. Pavel Lebeshev; with Oleg Tabakov, Elena Solovei, Andrei Popov, & Yuri Bogatyrev. Mosfilm. 146 min.

Ostanovilsia poezd (The Train Stopped). d. Vadim Abdrashitov; sw. Alexander Mindadze; with Anatoli Solonitsyn. Mosfilm. 90 min.

Proshchanie (Farewell). d. Klimov;* sw. German,* Klimov, Shepitko,* & Rudolf Turin; au. Valentin Rasputin; c. Alexei Rodionov, Yuri Skhirtladze, & Sergei Taraskin; m. V. Artemev & A. Shnitke; with Stefania Staniuta, Lev Durov, Alexei Petrenko, Vadim Yokovenko, Yu. Katrin-Yortsev, Denis Luppov, & Maya Bulgakova. Mosfilm. 128 min.

Rodnia (Kinfolk). d. Mikhalkov;* sw. Victor Merezhko; c. Pavel Lebeshev; m. Eduard Artemiev; with Nonna Mordiukova, Svetlana Kruchkova, Andrei Petrov, & Yuri Bogatyrev. 97 min.

1983

Bez svidetelei (Without Witnesses). d. Mikhalkov;* sw. Mikhalkov, Sofia Prokofeva, & Ramiz Fataliev; au. Prokofeva; c. Pavel Lebeshev; m. Eduard Artemiev; with Irina Kupchenko & Mikhael Ulianov. Mosfilm.

Chastnaia zhizn (Private Life). d. Raizman;* sw. Anatoly Grebnev & Raizman; c. Nikolai Olonovsky; with Mikhail Ulianov, Iya Savina, Irina Gubanova, Tatiana Dogileva, Alexei Blokhin, Yelena Sanaeva, & Lilia Grintsenko. Mosfilm.

Liubimaia zhenshchina mekhanika Gavrilova (The Beloved Woman of Mechanic Gavri-

lov). d. Pyotr Todorovsky; sw. Sergei Bodrov. c. Evgeny Guslinsky; with Ludmila Gurchenko, Sergei Shakurov, Evgeny Evstigneev, A. Vasilev, Mikhail Svetin, Sbilowski, S. Ponomareva, Natalia Nazarova, & S. Sokolov. Mosfilm.

My iz dzhaza (Jazzman). d. Karen Shakhnazarov; sw. Alexander Borodyansky & Shakhnazarov; c. Vladimir Shevtsov; m. Anatoli Kroll; with Igor Skliar, Alexander Chorny, Nikolai Averiuskin, Pyotr Shcherbakov, Elena Tsyplakova, & Larisa Dolina. Mosfilm.

Patsany (Tough Kids). d. Dinara Asanova; sw. Yuri Kleptikov; with V. Priemykhov & M. Levtova. Lenfilm.

Slezy kapali (The Tears Were Flowing). d. Danelia;* sw. Danelia & Kir Bulychev; c. Yuri Klimenko; m. Gia Kancheli; with Evgeni Leonov, Iya Savina, Nina Grebeshkova, Olga Mashnaya, & Boris Andreev. Mosfilm.

Vassa. d. & sw. Panfilov;* au. Maxim Gorki; c. Leonid Kalashnikov; m. Vadim Bibergan; with Inna Churikova, Nikolai Skorobogatov, Valentina Telichkina, Valentina Yakunina, & Yana Poplavskaya. Mosfilm. 89 min.

Vokzal dlia dvoikh (A Train Station for Two). d. Riazanov;* sw. Riazanov & Emil Braginsky; c. Vadim Alisov; m. Andrei Petrov; with Gurchenko,* Oleg Basilashvili, Mikhalkov,* & Nonna Mordiukova.

1984

Agoniia (Agony/Rasputin), produced, 1975. d. Klimov;* sw. S. Lungin & I. Nusinov; c. L. Kalashnikov; with N. Petrenko, Alisa Freindlikh, & Leonid Bronevoi. Mosfilm.

Chuchelo (Scarecrow). d. Bykov;* sw. Bykov & Vladimir Zheleznikov; c. Anatoli Moukassey; with Christina Orbakaite & Yuri Nikulin. Mosfilm.

Den' dlinnee nochi (The Day Is Longer Than the Night). d. Gogoberidze;* sw. Gogoberidze & Zaira Arsenisvili; c. Nugzar Erkomaisvili; m. Gia Kancheli; with Darejan Kharchladze, Tamara Skhirtladze, Guram Pirtzkhalaya, & Irakli Khizanishvili. Gruziafilm, Tblisi.

Milyi, dorogoi, liubimyi, edistvennyi . . . (Dear, Dearest, Beloved, Only . . .). d. Dinara Asanova; sw. Valeri Priemykhov; c. Vladimir Il'in; m. Victor Kisine; with Valeri Priemyknov & Olga Mashnaia. Lenfilm.

Parad planet (Parade of Planets). d. Vadim Abdrashitov; sw. Alexander Mindadze; c. Vladimir Shevtsik; with Oleg Borisov, Peter Zaychenko, Alexei Zharkov, Sergei Nikonenko, Sergei Shakurov, & Alexander Pashutin. Mosfilm. 97 min.

Zhestoki romans (A Ruthless Romance). d. & sw. Riazanov;* c. Vadim Alisov; m. Andrei Petrov; with Mikhalkov,* Larisa Guseeva, Alisa Friendlikh, Andrei Miagkov, Alexei Petrenko, & Victor Proskurin. Mosfilm.

1985

Detskii sad (Kindergarten). d., sw., & au. Evgenii Evtushenko; c. Vladimir Palian; with Evtushenko, Nikolai Karachentsov, & Galina Stakhanova. Mosfilm.

Golubye gory, ili Nepravdopodobnaia istoriia (Blue Mountains, or An Improbable Story). d. Eldar Shengelaia; sw. Revaz Chishvili & Shengelaya; c. Levan Paatashvili, m. Gia Kancheli; with Ramaz Girogobiani, Vasili Kakhnishvili, Teimuraz Chirgadze, Ivan Savarelidze, & Darejan Sumbatashvili. Gruziafilm Studio. 97 min.

Idi i smotri (Come and See). d. Klimov;* sw. Klimov & Alexander Adamovich; au.

Adamovich; c. Alexei Rodionov; m. Oleg Yanchenko; with Alexei Kravchenko, Olga Mironova, Lubomiras Laucavicus, Vladas Bagdonas, & Victor Lorentz. Belarusfilm & Mosfilm. 142 min.

Moi drug Ivan Lapshin (*My Friend Ivan Lapshin*), produced 1983. d. German;* sw. Eduard Volodarski; c. Valeri Fedosov; with Andrei Boltnev, Nina Ruslsnova, Andrei Mironov, & Alexei Zharkov. Lenfilm.

1986

Legenda o Suramskoi kreposti (*The Legend of the Surami Fortress*), produced 1984. d. Parajanov* & Dodo Abashidze; sw. Vaya Gigashvili; c. Yuri Klimenko; with Levan Uchaneshvili, Zourab Kipchidze, Lela Alibegachvili, Abashidze, Veriko Andjaparidze, & Sofiko Chaurieli. Gruzia Films (Georgia Films). 89 min.

Pis'ma mertvogo cheloveka (*Letters from a Dead Man*). d. & sw. Konstantin Lopushansky; c. Nikolai Poloptsev; with Bykov.* Lenfilm.

Pliumbum, ili Opasnaia igra (*Pliumbum,* or *A Dangerous Game*). d. Vadim Abdrashitov; sw. Alexander Mindadze; c. Georgi Rerberg; with Anton Androsov, Elena Dmitrieva, Elena Yakovleva, Alexander Foklistov, Alexander Pashutin, Vladimir Steklov, Zoia Lirova, & Alexei Zaitsev. Mosfilm. 96 min.

Proverka na dorogakh (*The Trial on the Road* or *Check Point*), produced 1971. d. German;* sw. Eduard Volodarsky; m. Isaak Shvartz; with Bykov,* Vladimir Zamansky, Anatoli Solonitzyn, Oleg Borisov, and Anda Zaitzs. Lenfilm. 98 min.

1987

Komissar (*Commissar*), produced, 1967: d. & sw. Alexander Askoldov; au. Vasili Grossman; c. Valeri Ginzberg; with Nonna Mordiukova, Rolan Bykov, Raisa Niedashkovskaya, & Vasili Shukshin. Gorky. 110 min.

Krugovorot (*Turnover*) d. Gogoberidze;* sw. Gogberidze & Zaira Arsenishvili; c. Nugzar Erkomaishvili; with Leila Abashidze, Liya Eliana, Guram Pirtskhalava, Otar Megvinetukhutsesi, Ninel Chankvetadze, & Salome Alexi-Meskhishvili. Gruziafilm. 99 min.

Kurier (*Courier*). d. & au. Karen Shakhnazarov; sw. Alexander Borodyansky; c. Nikolai Nemoliaev; with Fedor Dunaevsky, Anastasia Nemoliaeva, Inna Churikova, Oleg Basilashvili, Svetlana Kryuchkova, & Vladimir Menshov. Mosfilm. 89 min.

Odinokii golos cheloveka (*A Man's Lonely Voice*), produced, 1978: d. Sokurov;* sw. Yuri Arabov; au. Andrei Platonov; with Andrei Gradov & Tatiana Goriacheva. Lenfilm. 90 min.

Skorbnoe beschuvstvie (*Solemn Heartlessness*). d. Sokurov;* sw. Jurij Arabov; au. George Bernard Shaw; c. Sergei Yurisditskii; with Ramaz Cchikvadze, Alla Osipenko, Tatiana Egoreva, Dimitri Briantsev, Vladimior Zamanski, Viktoria Amitova, Ilia Rivin, Irina Sokolova, Vadim Zuk, Andrej Resetin, P. Pribytko, L. An, & Y. Simonov. Lenfilm. 95 min.

1988

Assa. d. Sergei Soloviov; sw. Sergei Livnev; c. Pavel Lebeshev; with Tatiana Drubich, Stanislav Govorukhin, & Sergei Bugaev. Mosfilm. 150 min.

Korabl (*The Ship*). d. Alexander Ivanov-Sukharevsky; sw. Elena Lobachevskaya; c.

Sergei Taraskyn; with Vyacheslav Nevinny, Jr., Ekaterina Belikova, Denis Bannikov, Gleb Morozov, Oksana Fandera, & Maris Liepa. Mosfilm. 150 min.

Malenkaia Vera (Little Vera). d. Vasili Pichul; sw. Maria Khmelik; with Natalia Niegoda, Andrei Sokolov, Yuri Nazarov, Ludmila Zaitseva, & Alexander Niegreva. Mosfilm. 130 min.

Pokaianie *(Repentance)*, produced 1984: d. Abuladze;* sw. Abuladze, Nana Janelidze, & Rezo Kveselava; c. Mikhail Agranovich; with Avtandil Makharadze, Iya Ninidze, Merab Ninidze, Zeynab Botsvadze, Ketevan Abuladze, Edisher Giorgobiani, Kakhi Kavsadze, Nino Zakariadze, Nato Otahigava, Dato Kemkhadze, Veriko Anjaparidze, Boris Tsipuria. Gruzia-Film/Georgian State Television. 150 min.

1989

Ashik Kerib (The Demon). d. Parajanov;* sw. Georgi Badridze; au. Mikhail Lermentov; c. Albert Javurian; with Yuri Mgoian, Veronique Matomidze, Levan Natroshvili, & Sofiko Chaurieli. Gruzia. 90 min.

At the Close of the Night. d. Rodion Nakhapetov; sw. Oleg Rudnev & Igor Talankin; c. Vladimir Shevtsik; with Remigius Sabulis, Nele Klimene, Alexei Zharkov, Tynu Kark, & Smoktunovski.* Mosfilm.

Bumazhniya glaza Prishvina (Prishvin's Paper Eyes). d. & sw. Valery Ogorodnikov; c. Valery Mionov; with Alexander Romantsov, Oleg Kovalov, Irina Tsyvina, & Yuri Tsapnik. Lenfilm. 148 min.

Chomaya rosa—emblema bechali, b elaya rosa—emblema lyubvi (Black Rose Stands for Sadness, Red Rose Stands for Love). d. & sw. Sergei Solovyov; c. Yuri Klimenko; with Tatiana Drubich, Alexander Abdulov, Mikhail Rozanov, & Ludmila Savelieva. Mosfilm. 140 min.

Cold Summer of 1953. d. Alexander Proskin; sw. Edgar Dubrovsky; c. Boris Brozhovsky; with Valeri Priyenykhov, Anatoli Papnov, Victor Stepanov, Nina Usatova, & Zoya Buryak. Mosfilm.

Dvoye i Odna (Two Grownups and a Child). d. Eduard Gavrilov; sw. Galina Shcherbakova; c. Inna Zarafian; with Elena Mayorova, Georgi Burkov, Yuri Astfiev, & Nadezhda Fedosova. Central Gorky's Studio of Children's and Youth Films. 76 min.

A Forgotten Tune for the Flute. d. Riazanov;* s. Emil Braginsky & Riazanov; c. Vadim Alisov; with Leonid Filatov, Tatiana Dogileva, & Irina Kupchenko. Mosfilm.

Gorod zero (Zero City). d. Karen Shakhnazarov; sw. Alexander Borodynasky & Shakhnazarov; c. Nikolai Nemolyaev; with Leonid Filatov, Oleg Basilashvili, Vladimir Menshov, Armen Jigarkhanian, Evgeny Evstigneyev, Alexei Zharkov, Pyotr Shcherbakov, Elena Arzhanik, Tatiana Khvostikova, & Yuri Sherstnev. Mosfilm. 93 min.

Hey, Maestro!. d. Nodar Managadze; sw. Erlom Akhviediani, Managadze, & David Djavakhishvili; c. Levan Paatashvili; with Tengiz Amiridze, Dali Chitaladze, & Makvala Gonashvili. Gruziafilm (Georgia Film).

Karaul (The Guard). d. Alexander Rogozhkin; sw. Ivan Loshchilin; c. Valery Martynov; with Sergei Kuprianov, Alexei Buldakov, Taras Denisenko, Dmitry Iositov, Renat Ibraghimov, Alexei Poluian, Vasily Domrachev, & Nikita Mikhailovsky. Lenfilm.

Puteshestaviye v Visbaden (A Trip to Wisbaden). d. Evgeny Gerasimov; sw. A. Batalov;* c. Sergei Onutriyev; with Sergei Zhigunov, Elena Seropova, Natalia Lapina,

Zinovy Gerdt, Zeinab Botsvadze, & Gerasimov. Gorky Studios, ETO Ladya. 87 min.

Sto soldat i dve devushki (*A Hundred Soldiers and Two Girls*). d. & sw. Sergei Mikaelyan; with Maya Meldere, Alexander Timoshkin, & Alexander Saiko. Lenfilm. 100 min.

Straw Bells. d., sw., & c. Ilenko;* with Sergei Podgorny, Mikhail Goubovich, Les Serdiuk, Ludmilla Efimenko, & Natalia Sumskaia. Alexander Dovzhenko Studios, Kiev.

Utoli moi pechali (*Assuage My Sorrows*). d. Viktor Prokhorov & Alexander Alexandrov; sw. Alexandrov; with Sergei Koltakov, Varvara Soshalskaya, Elena Safonova, & Svetlana Voronina. Mosfilm. 94 min.

Vy chyo, starichyo (*Old Men Alone*). d. & sw. Heifitz;* au. Boris Vasilyev; c. Yuri Shaigardanov; with Mikhail Pakhomenko, Lev Borisov, Elena Melnikova, Tatyana Sharkova, Evgeny Krizhanovsky, Evgenia Kovalyova, Irina Rakshina, & Anatoly Kotenev. Lenfilm Studios. 100 min.

Zashchitnik Sedov (*Defense Counsel Sedov*). d. Evgeny Tsimbal; sw. Maria Zvereva; with Vladimir Ilyin & Vsevolod Larionov. Mosfilm. 46 min.

1990

Syn (*The Son*). d. Khalmamed Kakabayev; sw. Sergei Bodrov & Kakabayev; c. Sergei Shugarev; with Salikh Bayramov, Tamara Shaklrova, & Bekmurad Kutlymuradov. Turkmenfilm. 90 min.

2
Bruce R. S. Litte

POLAND

In the years since World War II, Poland has developed one of Europe's richest film cultures, despite its having experienced more than its share of political and social unrest, of economic hardships, of political repression, and above all of physical destruction and social dislocation of the war—greater than that of any other European country. Several decades ago, film historian Roger Manvell remarked that Polish filmmakers had the greatest amount of creative independence of any Communist country, the most room for "individual, personal expression." From the 1950s onwards "[u]nlike the Russians, they have used the film to precipitate, and perhaps alleviate, their unease, as well as their more active emotions. As a result, they have made some of the best films that have appeared in Europe since the war" (Manvell, 144). Despite periodic political crackdowns, a survey of Polish cinema from the perspective of the late 1980s will bear out Manvell's claim: at a time when Poland is opening up politically and artistically, with greater room for political and artistic expression, his observation is all the more applicable.

Film production in Poland goes back to the earliest years of this century. Permanent cinemas and foreign film import offices were established by 1910. During the interwar years about one hundred and fifty film production companies existed, and prior to World War II quite a large body of film had been made (Fuksiewicz, *Polish Cinema*, 9). However, it was not generally of high artistic merit, being a product of small, underfunded commercial facilities working in formulas derivative of Hollywood aesthetics and made for a restricted, undemanding domestic market. A typical production facility might quickly close after making less than a handful of films (Liehm and Liehm, 27–28). While some major directors, screenwriters, and cinematographers such as Aleksander Ford, Wanda Jakubowska, Antoni Bohdziewicz, and Leonard Buczkowski began their careers in the pre-war period, the really significant work in Polish film has been done in the post-war years through (and sometimes, despite) the state production

*Dedicated to Wojciech Kotaś

system. This chapter will glance at pre-war Polish cinema, but it will concentrate on the varied accomplishments in the Polish feature film industry since 1947, when the first post-war film appeared. In concentrating on feature films, it necessarily excludes other areas: shorts, documentaries (a particularly strong portion of the total picture), and most TV films.

Poland's highly developed literary traditions have contributed much to the development of Polish cinema from the earliest days to the present. In Poland, as in Russia, Hungary, and Czechoslovakia, flourishing native traditions, combined with strong French and Austrian influences, nurtured early film tradition, providing nourishment less available to Yugoslavia, Bulgaria, and Romania. Artists and writers like Karol Irzykowski (1873–1944) took the nascent genre of film seriously as an art form. (In fact, as Fuksiewicz notes, Polish film theory and criticism were more advanced than the films themselves (*Polish Cinema*, 10)). As an anti-realist and anti-positivist, as a member of "Young Poland," that first generation of creative voices that marked the beginning of modern Polish literature, Irzykowski, in a significant book entitled *The Tenth Muse* (*Dziesiąta Muza*), 1924, saw film as an independent art form, emphasizing the visual rather than the narrative and theatrical, seeing it as the art of motion, "lyricism of motion" (Fuksiewicz, *Polish Cinema*, 11–12).

Although Polish cinema arose in a culture possessing a strong national literary heritage—drawing inspiration from the most significant serious writers of the late nineteenth and early twentieth centuries: Sienkiewicz, Reymont, Prus, Zeromski, Wyspianski, and more recently from Andrzejewski, Iwaszkiewicz, Dabrowska, Dygat, Schulz, Brandys, Konwicki—nevertheless, the Polish cinema itself developed independently of the literary community. According to two leading film historians, literature occupied such a privileged position as a substitute for a national political movement that the new medium of film was confined to the cultural space in popular culture. The creative avant-garde community was too dispersed to make a significant contribution, too restricted by shaky production facilities (Liehm and Liehm, 27–28).

Of directors who later developed international careers, Alexander Ford was the most significant during the interwar period. Like a number of other directors, he came not from a literary background but an artistic one, from which he brought a strong visual sense to his films, and which he applied to social issues. About 1930 he joined a number of serious filmmakers in a non-commercial organization called START (Society of the Devotees of Artistic Film), which was designed to produce documentary films. Two products of his work with this organization were documentaries that are now considered classics: *Tetno Polskiego Manchesteru* (*Polish Manchester's Pulse*), 1928, an examination of working-class life of his birthplace, Lodz, and *Droga Mlodych* (*The Way of Youth*), 1936, a study of a sanitorium for Jewish children. This latter film was so controversial that it was banned in Poland as Communist propaganda and only shown in France. Film censorship, clearly, was not an entirely post-war phenomenon.

Despite unpropitious circumstances, some fiction films stand out. Ford, for one, wrote and directed *Legion Ulicy* (*The Street Legion*), 1932, which won the Polish Best Film of 1932 award, made a film in Palestine, *Sabra*, 1934, and co-directed with Jerzy Zarzycki a socially pointed adaptation of a contemporary novel, *Ludzie Wisly* (*People of the Vistula*), 1936, a film about laborers working along the main Polish river. A few films in the thirties even picked up international awards at festivals in Moscow and Venice.

And quite apart from the contributions of Ford and other members of START were a significant group of Yiddish films, reflecting the rich Jewish-Polish culture in the last years before the Holocaust, including Joseph Green's *Yidl Mitn Fidl* (*Yiddle With His Fiddle*), 1936; *Mamel*, 1938; and especially Waszynski's *Dybukk*, 1938, based on Jewish folklore. Green, a Jewish-American immigrant, produced high-quality films that are among the finest documents of an utterly vanished world. He employed the talents of the experienced Yiddish actress Molly Picon, who had been making Yiddish films since the early twenties and who, years later, would be seen in *Fiddler on the Roof*, 1971. Michael Waszynski's film is based on a turn-of-the-century play, originally written in Russian and performed at Stanislavsky's Moscow Art Theater, an expanded Yiddish version opening in Warsaw in 1920 (Goldberg, 887; Erens, 3459–3461).

World War II shattered the small film industry, destroying nearly all production facilities, and either killing or dispersing most filmmakers. Although documentary material was shot during the war (much of which footage was employed in war films by post-war directors), both commercial and artistic production stopped. But the war was hardly over when Poles began constructing a new film industry, the Provisional Government deciding to establish a nationalized film industry in 1945 and setting up Film Polski, managed by Aleksander Ford, which would coordinate film production, distribution, import, export, and education. As all old studios had been destroyed, Film Polski borrowed a covered sports stadium from the city of Lodz. This temporary loan turned into a permanent arrangement, and this recycled stadium continues to be the center of Polish film production (Michałek and Turaj, 3–4). More films and cinemas quickly became available. The government opened many new theaters, so that about six hundred were available by 1947. The distribution system possessed 158 films by 1946: 53 pre-war Polish, 84 Soviet, 16 English, and 5 French films (Michałek and Turaj, 3). A Young Filmmakers Workshop was established in Cracow, where Jerzy Passendorfer, Jerzy Kawalerowicz, Wojciech Has, and many others studied. This grew into a major educational institution, becoming the Higher School of Film, and was transferred to Lodz in 1948. There the school has since remained, the preeminent center of Polish film training, graduating hundreds of accomplished film professionals in the next twenty years.

Leonard Buczkowski, who had made nine comedies before the war, directed the first film for Film Polski, *Zakazane Piosenki* (*Forbidden Songs*), 1947, an immensely popular hit that used confrontations of Warsaw resistance fighters and Nazis as a vehicle for a collection of patriotic songs defiantly sung during the Occupation. Unfortunately, it was considered too soft on the Germans, and despite its popularity it had to be withdrawn. Buczkowski remade it, emphasizing the German brutality, and it was re-released in 1949. But it has remained one of the most popular Polish films, the second-most widely seen film, with 14 million viewers up to 1970 (Fuksiewicz, *Polish Cinema*, 14). Almost as popular was Buczkowski's *Skarb* (*Treasure*), 1949, the story of young Poles hunting for apartments in Warsaw during the reconstruction. Despite their popularity, neither of these films was artistically or technically adventurous.

But Ford's first post-war film, *Ulica Graniczna* (*Border Street*), 1949, was artistically and technically accomplished—a powerful statement against anti-Semitism, showing the solidarity of young Poles and Jews in occupied Warsaw: "Ford told the story according to the structure of Polish society at the time, telling the story through typical representatives of Polish social groups, whose unity under fire was to have been the source of a unified Poland" (Liehm and Liehm, 114–115). And so was Wanda Jakubowska's *Ostatni Etap* (*The Last Stage*), 1948. Jakubowska, who had been associated with the pre-war START group, remained in Poland during the Occupation, spending part of that time in Auschwitz, a horror that provided the germ for this film. Not simply content to present the brutality and degradation of the camp, with the directorial assistance of the young Jerzy Kawalerowicz and Jan Rybkowski, she also showed the power of friendship, the will to survive, and the love among the fellow-sufferers.

By the late 1940s the political climate was growing increasingly repressive, and filmmakers lost many opportunities for creative expression. This growth of Polish political centralization and repression, Polish Stalinism, affected every facet of Polish life. Its deadening approach could already be seen in Buczkowski's difficulties with *Forbidden Songs;* it seriously compromised many more films during the next five or six years. The watershed year was 1949, and when political diversity was squelched, so was cultural expression. The whip was cracked at the Congress of Wisła, a meeting of film and political leaders, which established the doctrine of socialist realism. According to this doctrine, films had to contribute to the advance of class struggle, eliminate bourgeois and petit bourgeois thought, overcome cosmopolitanism, and take a line on national unity that gave proper precedence to the Communist Party. This line applied not just to the development of a revolutionary society but also to the interpretation of the past, especially to the role of the Communists in fighting the Germans. The new dogma insisted that filmmakers highlight the role of the Communist underground and dismiss the contribution of the non-Communist resistance, that is, the Home Army, which was in fact the largest and most potent form of the resistance. Antoni Bohdziewicz, a leading filmmaker and teacher, who strenuously protested these decrees at the meeting, who "challenged the model of the positive hero and the whole idea of ideologically overloaded films," and who defended artistic freedom, was censured and not allowed to make any more films until 1957 (Michałek and Turaj, 10).

Two potentially good films got caught in the political changes. *Robinson Warszawaski,* by Jerzy Zarzycki, with a script by the notable writer Jerzy Andrzejewski, was condemned as "the first product of an erroneous conception of national solidarity" and for its "false ideological-esthetic overtones." Its plot had focused on a Warsaw citizen, a modern urban Robinson Crusoe, who had hidden in the ruins during the end of the Occupation; it had to be remade to emphasize how a Soviet radio operator heroically helped the Polish survivors. In a greatly bowdlerized version, it appeared in 1950 as *Miasto Nieujarzmione (Unvanquished City)* (Michałek and Turaj, 10). The change of title does tell a lot. A similar fate overtook Rybkowski's *Dom na Pustkowiu (A Home in the Wilderness)*, 1950, a subtle, intimate drama about two solitary women living near Warsaw who get filtered news about the Uprising reshaped as a heavy-handed political lesson. New films made to fit these imposed restrictions were aesthetic disasters. The classic instance of a doctrinaire social realist film was *Dwie Brygady (Two Brigades)*, 1950, supervised by Eugeniusz Cekalski (who had made the politically oppressive *Jasne Łany [Bright Fields]* three years earlier) and directed by a group of his students at Lodz. It involves two competitions— of factory workers trying to boost production and of young theatrical people deciding how best to transform this first competition to a stage presentation. Michałek and Turaj comment that "The premise was flimsy and the story anemic. There was not a single character developed in a believable way. Everything about it was artificial and false. Since its production it has stood as the perfect example of socialist realism" (11). Other films fared little better: *Pierwszy Start (The First Take-off)*, written by Ludwik Starski and directed by Buczkowski, is about a glider training camp; *Trzy Powiesci (Three Stories)*, which includes the uninspiring themes of eager youths being converted to socialism and fighting counterrevolutionary sabotage and bourgeois revisionism, was directed by Antoni Bohdziewicz, Czesław Petelski, and Ewa Poleska-Petelska. With *Zolnierz zwyciestwa (Soldier of Victory)*, Wanda Jakubowska dipped into the political hottub, producing a film that by all accounts was "an incredible cinematic fiasco," as she crammed together all the proper political themes of the 1940s into a chaotic muddle (Michałek and Turaj, 13). Rybkowski did not produce a socialist realist muddle, but his *Sprawa do zalatwienia (A Matter to Settle)* was a trivial comedy.

As reduced artistic freedom narrowed the range of approaches to contemporary issues, some directors successfully turned to a remoter and safer past, a phenomenom that has occurred more than once during the post-war period. Ford turned to Chopin, in *Młodość Chopina (The Young Chopin)*, the first post-war blockbuster. Although Ford pushed too hard the link between the music and progressive politics, "it is totally free of those stereotypes abounding in Western commercial films about artists." It boosted his career, solidifying "Ford's position as the foremost man of film in the Polish People's Republic" (Michałek and Turaj, 12). In *Warszawska Premiera (Warsaw Premiere)* Rybkowski turned to Moniuszko, the Polish national opera composer, the Polish Smetana, and recreated the era, tying the composer to folk roots and political context, while sympathetically portraying his creative personality (Michałek and Turaj, 13).

With the death of Stalin in 1953, Poland enjoyed a modest cultural relaxation that allowed films of greater substance. In 1954, assisted by the promising young Andrzej Wajda, Ford produced one of the Polish classics, *Piątka z Ulicy Barskiej* (*Five Boys from Barska Street*), a film about the popular subject of juvenile deliquency. He presented rounded characters, plausibly motivated—they belong to street gangs, they steal and kill because they were taught to by the war, because they had never known anything else, were completely alone, and received no help from the new society (Liehm and Liehm, 119). One critic, indeed, sees it as a beginning of the Polish New Wave cinema, "the earliest critical film movement to arise in Eastern Europe" (Hibbin, 1111).

Among the first major directors to benefit from the liberalization was Jerzy Kawalerowicz. His career warrants special consideration. He has been considered an atypical Polish filmmaker for having eschewed the problems of national existence, character, identity, and history, for having avoided historical bitterness, for having turned to more universal themes, and for employing a diversity of stylistic approaches. Trained in the fine arts, he began his professional film career as Buczkowski's assistant in *Forbidden Songs*. After directing a typically socialist realist film in the early fifties, *Gromada* (*The Village Mill*), he made a two-part neo-realistic film that exploded the restrictions of this genre: *Celuloza* (*A Night of Remembrance*) and *Pod Gwiazda Frygijska* (*Under the Phrygian Star*). The former is a coming-of-age story set in the 1930s, when a village boy is forced by poverty to leave his village, experience the difficulties of a new life among the town proletariat, and become a Communist Party activist. The latter focuses on his dramatic political activism. The film's power comes from its "full and complex presentation of the hero," from its "wide panorama of prewar Poland," and from its unusual concern for detail, all of which give the film "an almost epic character" (Fuksiewicz, *Polish Cinema*, 16). The diptych has an unusual richness of characterization and texture, in part from its sensitive response to its literary source, the novel by Igor Newerly, *Souvenir of Cellulose* (1952). His "surrender to literature, breaking through conventional filmic restrictions by giving priority to the literary material, later helped bring about profound reforms in the cinematic language employed by Polish directors" (Michałek and Turaj, 96–97).

Kawalerowicz based his next film, *Cien* (*Shadow*), on a script by Aleksander Ścibor-Rylski, a suspenseful story about post-war anti-government activities that plays with prevailing paranoid fantasies of subversive counterrevolutionary activities. Three years after the death of Stalin, we see a Polish director mocking central concerns of socialist realist dogma. Technically it is highly innovative, with superb camerawork by Jerzy Lipman, and an ambiguous narrative line that Western critics compared to Hitchcock's.

Kawalerowicz turned next, in *Prawdziwy Koniec Wielkiej Wojny* (*The True End of the Great War*), 1957, his only war film, to a psychological study of a woman (played by the director's wife, Lucyna Winnicka), her husband, an emotionally ravaged concentration camp survivor, and the man she turned to when she thought her husband dead. Though it painfully depicts the camp bar-

barities and the resulting human wreckage, it focuses on psychological analysis, on probing human portraits in vivid contexts. The solid psychological analysis, the creation of well-rounded characters, is another departure from the shallow characterizations of socialist realist cinema. Although not a great popular success, this film, in its treatment of unhealed and unhealable wounds, foreshadows works by Tadeusz Konwicki, Wojciech Has, and Andrzej Wajda (Michałek and Turaj, 100).

Kawalerowicz and Ford were supported by the political establishment, as Antonin Liehm and Mira Liehm point out, but new directors were influenced by belief in the authority of the people and the authority of truth, as well as the power of the creative individual. Poland, in its cinema, began to take a candid look at itself. And nothing better measures this scrutiny than Wajda's *Generation (Pokolenie)*, a cinematographic breakthrough:

Against the background of schematic determinism that revolutionary epics or social dramas were only rarely capable of avoiding, Wajda created the first tragedy in Eastern European cinematography. His romantic hero dies at the moment he has overcome his own fear, another tragic figure in Polish art, for whom nothing is left but a heroic suicide, and the first figure of pathos in Polish film. (Liehm and Liehm, 121)

Andrzej Wajda, far more than any other Polish director, has come to represent Polish cinema at home and abroad—Americans will be able to find some of his films available on video. Yet the foreign recognition might appear surprising, for Wajda is not a director whose films offer self-explanatory, universal themes in an easily recognizable frame of reference. His films require "effort, knowledge and imagination" because they are so firmly embedded in Polish history and culture. He has been less a cosmopolitan filmmaker than one whose interests, themes, and sensibilities are particularly Polish. Stylistically, he has been given to overstatement, spectacular effects and symbols, which have been frequently called "baroque." He has said, "I would gladly trade in this clutch of national symbols—sabres, white horses, red poppies, rowanberries—for a handful of sexual symbols from the Freudian textbook. The trouble is that I just wasn't brought up on Freud. My situation is hopeless—I caught on too late." Abstract terms—despair, baroque, bitterness, love of life—often used in discussing his films are less applicable than an understanding of national elements; his films are more typically reflections of national moods and anxieties than personal crises of despair or doubt (Michałek, *The Cinema of Andrzej Wajda* 7).

Generation, and Wajda's two following films, *Kanał (Canal)* and *Popiół i Diament (Ashes and Diamonds)*, often referred to as his "Trilogy," mark the early flowering of post-war Polish cinema. Wajda, like his master, Ford, studied Polish youth, but his characters are more convincing, less the stylized, positive socialist realist characters of all Eastern European cinema of the time (Whyte, 12). Wajda sees the Occupation, the backdrop of all three films, as less an opportunity for glib heroism than did many other war films, although he depicts both conscious and unconscious heroism, as well as "deep attachment to traditions or ideals to the extent of self-sacrifice" (Whyte, 12).

Generation tries to show that ordinary people are capable of extraordinary courage, for reasons other than purely ideological. Wajda focuses on the tragic young generation that came of age during the Occupation, those who sought their comfortable places in life and found themselves fighting. Wajda's first film is a coming-of-age story about moral choice, heroism and its evaluation, death, and love, "which in this tragic time is the only value on which one can count, and which is one of the few aids to finding oneself anew in a world of shattered illusions" (Fuksiewicz, *Polish Cinema,* 19). There were official objections to the rough street-wise hero, to the violent scenes, but nevertheless it opened in early 1955. However, it was coolly received—too half-heartedly radical for some, too unorthodox for others: critics and viewers, Michałek suggests, failed to recognize the abiding values, the depth of human concern, the freshness and power of its communication (*Wajda,* 22). Today, thirty-five years later, with Poland changing in extraordinary ways, it still makes for a powerful viewing experience.

Wajda's next film, *Canal,* achieved great popularity in Poland and earned praise abroad. His chronicle of the 1944 Warsaw Uprising focuses on the horrors experienced by a battalion of Resistance fighters fleeing the advancing Germans and escaping from their devastated neighborhood through the sewers of Warsaw, a fight that is powerfully wrenching. It is an adventure story laden with complex historical and political implications. Wajda offers an ambivalent attitude towards heroism—he admires the resistance fighters while he demythologizes their heroics; he presents an image of history wherein heroes are trapped and destroyed, history possessed of its "own logic which makes heroism and sacrifice pointless." These heroes may be aware of this futility but know they must make this sacrifice nevertheless (Fuksiewicz, *Polish Cinema,* 20).

The reassessment of history has played a crucial role in recent Polish cinema, and numerous post-war films have turned to historical events as a means of questioning contemporary political, social, and economic values. The Uprising was and still is particularly controversial: it was ordered by the Home Army (the non-Communist resistance) without coordination with the Soviet forces that were advancing towards the capital; the Soviet forces held back, permitting the Germans to concentrate on the destruction of the Uprising, killing several hundred thousand people, and burning the homes of over a million people after the city had been evacuated. Significantly, the smaller Communist resistance movement was not involved. Consequently, this bloodbath has been a continuing embarrassment for the Polish government and its relationship with the Soviet Union. *Canal* is a major film both artistically and politically, but it is no less important as an adumbration of films to come, those films that are manifestations of what has come to be called "the Polish School," lasting roughly from 1956 to 1962.

The third film of the "Trilogy," *Ashes and Diamonds,* a further demystification of heroics, has been called, justly I believe, the greatest achievement of post-war Polish cinema; it is further memorable for bringing Zbigniew Cybulski to stardom. Cybulski plays a counterrevolutionary guerrilla, Maciek, whose mission, on the last day of the war, is to shoot down the new Communist Party secretary. It is a suspenseful thriller, a straightforward story of violence and love, with the dimensions of high tragedy. Maciek can be seen as "a prisoner of a fate he is powerless to escape. At the very moment that he discovers . . . a love which regenerates and reprieves and has a foretaste of the flavour of happiness, he is summoned to kill and be killed" (Michałek, *Wajda,* 39). But *Ashes and Diamonds* works on other levels: on a social level it addresses the formation of a new national consciousness—the formation of a new social, cultural, and political identity. It illustrates Wajda's thorough immersion in Polish literary culture, for it was inspired by nineteenth-century Romanticism, by Cyprian Norwid—in a sense the Polish Melville (Miłosz, 266–280), whose poetry is quoted by the fighters and alluded to by the title, by the romantic verse drama of Juliusz Slowacki, by Stanisław Wyspianski, author of Wajda's favorite play, *Wesele (The Wedding)*—which he later made into a film. In fact, the closing dance sequence at dawn of *Ashes and Diamonds* duplicates the closing scene of the play. As Michałek observes, *Ashes and Diamonds* reflects messianic themes of the lofty nineteenth-century Romantic tradition in which Poland "was seen as hero, sage, saint, and above all, martyr . . . the Christ of nations, crucified to redeem them." This collective martyrdom necessitated individual martyrdom, as "Men were merely pawns on the chess-board of History, moved by invisible forces. Poland and the Poles were treated by this literature in a key of emotional extremes: from wild enthusiasm to furious condemnation, from gushing love to demented rage" (Michałek, *Wajda,* 46). Wajda himself has viewed the artist as playing a prominent role in this messianistic mission:

The artist of Polish Romanticism was not someone who fulfilled himself entirely in the fabric of his art—in poetry, painting or sculpture. He tried to outdo himself, and the historical situation came to his aid. He was something more than an author; he was the conscience of the nation, a prophet, and social institution. Poland in the nineteenth century was a country shorn of normal institutions: power, government, parliament, political life, public opinion. It was the poets who did duty for all these institutions. . . . In a sense it was, of course, an act of usurpation. (quoted in Michałek, *Wajda,* 47)

In post-war Poland, we might argue, filmmakers have usurped the poets, developing their cinematic creations as artistic expressions of the national conscience. Though most filmmakers would not actively espouse such a lofty role for the artist, yet it well defines the contribution of cinema to Polish life, exemplified particularly in Wajda's work.

The growing freedom of film expression was solidified by political events of 1956. An important result of the Poznan riots of June 1956 was a major political reorganization, from which Wladysław Gomułka was the immediate direct beneficiary, but which also benefited filmmakers. Gomułka had been imprisoned during the Stalinist purges in the very late 1940s through obvious Russian meddling, but was then released, rehabilitated, and brought to power with broad national support (for having defied the Russians). He permitted a moderate degree of liberalism. Closed issues were opened, such as the role of the Home Army, whose role in the liberation was now officially recognized. "Blood spilled for Poland, no matter by whom, is precious," he is supposed to have said (Michałek, *Wajda,* 19–20).

These political changes had an immediate impact on the film industry, which was decentralized in 1955, semi-autonomous "units" being established to boost production and increase creative freedom. Each unit was headed by a production chief, a screenwriter, and an artistic director—film experts rather than bureaucrats. Though these units were linked to a national Film Fund (and state financing) through the Ministry of Culture and Art on the one hand, and box office success on the other, yet they have been surprisingly, though unfortunately not consistently, free from government interference. Films have experienced politically motivated delays or been blocked entirely, and some directors have followed official doctrines with greater complicity than others. Any well-informed Pole would eagerly tell of the filmmakers who have readily bent with the political winds. But the striking feature of Polish cinema is the hard-won independence of many filmmakers. What Manvell wrote in the late sixties has continued to apply through the following years and despite the manifold difficulties: "Polish films . . . are films of intuition and ideas, not propaganda" (146).

Between 1955 and 1968, when further reorganization occurred, the film industry operated under the following structure. The Central Office of Cinematography, within the aforementioned ministry, contained four divisions: production, distribution, funding, and technical investment. The Production Division supervised the three feature film studios (at Lodz, Wrocław, and Warsaw) and nine film units. These units ("Iluzjion," "Kadr," "Rytm," "Start," "Studio," "Syrena," "Proprostu," "Kamera," and "Tor") were managed by some of the greatest figures in Polish cinema: the directors Starski and Petelski, Kawalerowicz, Rybkowski, Jakubowska, Ford, Zarzycki, Wohl, Bohdziewicz, and Różewicz; their literary managers were novelists and scriptwriters, including Dygat, Ścibor-Rylski, Bratny, Andrzejewski, Stawiński, and Zalewski. The Distribution Division controlled public cinemas, the Federation of Film Discussion Clubs, and amateur film clubs. The Economic Division controlled finances: box office returns went into the State Film Fund, which distributed money to the film units for the production of new films: the greater the receipts, the larger the funds for new productions. Distribution was controlled by the Film Repertory Councils, made up of cultural leaders and film critics who recommended films, both national and foreign, for distribution. Polish films, in the mid-sixties, comprised just over 10 percent of the films distributed (11.5 percent), with the bulk coming from the USSR (18 percent), France (15 percent), the United States (10.5 percent), Britain (10.5 percent), Czechoslovakia (9.5 percent), Italy (6 percent), East Germany (4 percent), West Germany (4 percent), and elsewhere (11 percent) (Cowie, 1965, 122).

The film production units increased the number of new films, the size of the audiences, and the artistic and professional skills of the filmmakers. Between 1946 and 1955 the number of full-length films had been averaging about five a year; between 1956 and 1968 it was averaging twenty a year; between 1969 and 1985 it would average twenty-eight annually. An enlarged audience also became a more discriminating audience; the better-trained filmmakers developed "a cinema... with its own style, its own themes, its own spiritual and esthetic identity—'The Polish School' " (Michałek and Turaj, 21). Michałek and Turaj see this "School" characterized by three trends: critical realism (honestly examining contemporary life), historical objectivity (involving controversial issues), and psychological depth (concentrating on inner rather than outer reality).

If Wajda was one beneficiary, Andrzej Munk was another. His vision differs markedly from Wajda's, being more rational, ironic, and skeptical, focusing, as Fuksiewicz notes, on the grotesque version of the tragedy of human fate and the absurd capriciousness of history (*Polish Cinema*, 23). His first major feature film, completed in 1957, was *Człowiek na Torze* (*The Man on the Track*), a fresh examination of labor problems centering on the mysterious death of an old engineer. Not at all the model socialist realist worker, he was proud, querulous, harsh towards his employees, and distrustful of change. Yet Munk grants him a certain nobility, while painting the young officials as petty representatives of a constricting new order. Munk's masterpiece, *Eroica,* appeared a year later. Inspired by Beethoven's symphony, it is a grim comedy in two episodes about heroism, offering a rational, skeptical approach that contrasts with Wajda's romanticism. The first episode focuses on a cowardly, drunken Warsaw antihero, who mocks heroic resistance fighters, who, "half-spiv, half-Schweik," displays a will to live, a "Sancho Panza [who] becomes a hero in a world where the Quixotes ride tanks and wield bombs" (Pearson, 198), but who, too, sacrifices himself to help the resistance, standing up for a lost cause, fully understanding the absurdity of his behavior. The second episode, ironic rather than comic, is set in a POW camp in 1944, Munk focusing not on German brutality but on the petty, conservative, authoritarian values of the prisoners. Yet these prisoners display solidarity, preserving the myth of an inmate whom the prisoners thought had escaped, but who had actually been hiding and had died in the camp. Three prisoners smuggle out the body, keeping quiet and maintaining the illusion of heroism (Whyte, 32–33).

Two more significant Munk films appeared prior to the director's untimely, accidental death in 1961, *Zezowate Szczescie* (*Cockeyed Luck*) and *Pasażerka* (*The Passenger*)—the latter unfinished at his death and assembled from fragments by Witold Lesiewicz. *Cockeyed Luck* is another ironic work about an anti-hero, modeled on Candide. With a script by Jerzy Stefan Stawiński, who had also scripted *Canal, The Man on the Track,* and *Eroica,* it consists of six flashbacks of a man "who always followed popular trends but always the wrong ones" (Whyte, 34). On the one hand, it presents, as Michałek and Turaj see it "a lampoon of a man who is an officious conformist, whose bad luck is caused by his fickle zealousness, his truckling to the times, his stupidity, his entanglement in national legends and myths, in short, his emotional instability." On the other hand, it also offers a highly critical view of Polish society, a society so absurdly changeable, that no ordinary Pole can adjust—a view resembling that of the great novelist Gombrowicz in *Ferydurke:* "Poles, their culture, their thinking, their politics are jejune and undeveloped, tangled up in myth and legend like the world as thought of by adolescents" (Michałek and Turaj, 125). *The Passenger* provides a persecutors' view of a concentration camp, the sadomasochistic relationship between a woman officer and a woman prisoner. Twenty years after the war, an elegant German woman aboard on ocean liner meets a young survivor of Auschwitz who had intrigued her when she was a Kapo. She claims that she had tried to help the youngster, but her memories show her having used severe mental torture upon the girl. The film is both technically and thematically innovative—Munk was the first director to explore the mixture of hatred and humanity of the camps (a prisoners' Bach recital counterpointed with the wails of extermination trains) (Cowie, 1965, 125–26). In this justly celebrated film, Munk "seemed desperately to want to discover the mystery of human suffering and human values under extreme tension" (Michałek and Turaj, 128).

Wajda and Munk were not the only members of the Polish School. Jerzy Passendorfer, Stanisław Lenartowicz, Stanisław Różewicz, and Kazimierz Kutz also explored questions of national identity, history, and heroism. Passendorfer's *Zamach* (*Answer to Violence*) examined the 1944 Warsaw assassination of a Gestapo general by the Home Army. Lenartowicz's *Pigulki dla Aurelii* (*Pills for Aurelia*) examined an ordinary day in the Occupation, though even this ordinary day involved issues of heroism inasmuch as an underground unit arms itself and rescues one of its members. In *Wolne Miasto* (*Free City*), Rozewicz examined the futile heroism of mailmen defending the Gdansk post office against the German onslaught in 1939.

Kutz made some particularly important contributions to this movement. He emphasized the isolation of his heroes, studying loneliness through portrait, landscape, and composition frames, transferring "the internal conflicts of his heroes to conflicts between man and objects," developing them in relation to simple objects like rooms and walls (Fuksiewicz, *Polish Cinema*, 28). In his 1959 debut film, *Krzyż Walecznych* (*Cross of Valor*), Kutz directed "a clear polemic" against Wajda, concentrating on ordinary soldiers who perform no great deeds: a peasant boy returns to his village full of military glory, only to find the village has vanished; a soldier who cannot carry out an order to shoot a German prison dog he has befriended; and soldiers in a post-war town trying to keep alive their cult of the glorious military commander by honoring his returning widow, who merely wants to live quietly in the present (Fuksiewicz, *Polish Cinema*, 24–25). Michałek stresses how Kutz introduces the common man as protagonist with a new warmth, in ways comparable to films by Czech directors Miloš Forman, Ivan Passer, and Vojtěch Jasný (Michałek and Turaj, 30). In *Nikt Nie Wola* (*No One Calling*), 1960, and *Ludzie z Pociagu* (*People on a Train*), 1961, he understatedly studies common people, refugees in a small town in western Poland in the first and, in the second, a crowd facing a threatening situation in a small provincial railway station. In both films, he displays "a quite extraordinary feeling for rhythm in film, which links many types of minute observations into a united whole, giving a dynamic flow to the most static scenes" (Fuksiewicz, *Polish Cinema*, 29).

One of the strongest cinema talents to appear in the late 1950s belonged to Tadeusz Konwicki. Having already made his mark as a witty, intelligent, paradoxical, and skeptical novelist and story writer, his literary interests flowed readily into film, a unified output that emphasizes three themes: "producing a nostalgic evocation of the past, despair for those who have been uprooted, and astonishment at the paradoxes of life in a totalitarian state" (Sobański, 79). He was the scriptwriter for Kawalerowicz's *Mother Joan of the Angels* and *The Pharoah*, making his directing debut in 1958 with *Ostatni Dzień Lata* (*The Last Day of Summer*), an intimate, lyrical film about a man and a woman on a beach, the themes of which are a failure of communication and post-war emotional dislocation (Michałek and Turaj, 31–32), concerns he expanded upon three years later in *Zaduszki* (*All Souls' Eve*).

In the closing years of this decade, Poland's master of comic film, Tadeusz Chmielewski, made his most accomplished film, *Ewa Chce Spać* (*Eve Wants to Sleep*), "a mad comedy out of a fantastic and grotesque world," a hilarious, sometimes slapstick view of contemporary Poland. "Comic inventiveness goes off pyrotechnically producing absurdity, paradox, and irony all in a basket of warm humor"; this frantic humor, a cross between Lubitsch and Monty Python, was new to Polish cinema, though not to the literature—it is the humor that one finds abundantly in Gombrowicz (Michałek and Turaj, 33). This film is a reminder that Polish cinema is not always intense and somber, not always absorbed in painful memories.

But somberness would not be surprising over the next several years. The optimism and liberalism of the early Gomułka years began to fade. Even by 1957 and 1958 censorship was reappearing: films were being closely examined, reworked, and postponed. A Wajda script about a young couple who close themselves off from the world, *We are Alone in the World*, was never filmed. Janusz Morgernstern made a politically sensitive film, *Życie Raz Jeszcze* (*Life Once Again*), that was withdrawn after several days, not to be shown again for twenty-one years. Though Stalinism did not return, "revisionism" was firmly resisted. In the early 1960s, though film production grew, the number of quality films declined; doors closed to young filmmakers, and established ones reworked safer themes—themes less political, less contemporary, and more private, more historical. Poles did not experience the rebirth of national cinema that occurred in the rest of Europe. According to the Liehms, Polish film had drifted to the periphery of Eastern European cinema, with no broad creative impulse replacing the discredited "Polish School" (369). But despite this chilly climate, some fine flowers flourished. The gifted Wojciech Has is a case in point.

While the films of most Polish directors have been closely related to shifting political and social realities, Has has pursued an independent career. His films have been psychological vehicles for his characters' self-discovery. Whether set in the past or the present, they employ rich visual effects and artistic direction in order to express, as Derek Elley writes, "A strong nostalgia—not for the social or material trapping of another age, but for the mysteries of the passage of time itself" (Cowie, 1975, 38). Fuksiewicz has elaborated this assessment, noting how Has has created an individualized, artistically polished cinema, one of rare moods and landscapes, of rich and complex feelings, of penetrating psychological experiences: "Has is a poet of the past fascinated by the fact of transcience, a keen observer of feelings which border between truth and deception. He is a chronicler of human hopes, longings and disasters" (*Polish Cinema*, 31). His characters are the obverse of all those obsessed by Polish history and national identity; they are defeated by life, inward-looking, often living deeply lonely in the past. In a 1963 interview, Has stated:

Each is bound to his past and often returns to it. It is a center to draw from, a source of lessons and experience. But the obsession with the past is not conscious in my films; it is more intuitive. Doubtless because I am like that myself. . . . It is my conception of the loneliness of modern man who can only overcome certain situations. My heroes are neither weak, cowardly or stupid. They would like to act but cannot; there are too many obstacles to overcome" (quoted by Elley in Cowie, 1975, 43–44; in this year IFG [International Film Guide] named him one of Five Directors of the Year).

This is not to say, however, that Has avoids social issues. Alcoholism, both a cause and a result of social isolation (as well as an index of larger-scale malaise), is the subject of *Pętla* (*The Noose*), his first feature film. It presents a single day in the life of an alcoholic vainly trying to go straight, emphasizing the loneliness of a man lost in a hostile, alien world, wandering the streets to escape from the confinement of his apartment.

Inadequate housing has long been another major Polish social problem, and this subject forms the social background of *Wspolny Pokój* (*The Common Room*), 1960, the story of a group of Warsaw bohemians. Fuksiewicz describes it as "a deeply moving picture of people hemmed by hopelessness and torpor, a vision of slow internal dying," in which people pretend to themselves and the world that they are actively alive (*Polish Cinema*, 31). Though this film is set in Warsaw of the 1930s, it could just as well be the 1960s—or the 1980s. Elley notes how it recalls Renoir and Clair in its ambience, with the characters fleeing their drab, tiny apartments for bars, drinking and "engaging in fruitless bombast." Indeed, "with its underlying sense of mystery," it is the most significant work of this time (40).

The artistic and literary intelligentsia are a special concern of Has' films, as in the lyrical and nostalgic *Farewells (Pozegmania)*, 1958, based on the novel by Stanisław Dygat about the pre-war intelligentsia. The troubled artist, emotionally crippled through his wartime entanglements with authorities, appears in *Jak Być Kochana (How to Be Loved)*, 1963, based on a Kazimierz Brandys story, with Zbigniew Cybulski playing a weak, narcissistic, mediocre actor living in the apartment of a young woman who loves him. Their relationship is revealed in flashback, as this woman, on a trip to Paris, remembers her disappointing romantic involvement with the man who had turned out to be a suicidally inclined buffoon and a compulsive liar. On a train she meets a seemingly dull traveler. But this meeting grows into a relationship, whereas the past one with the actor led to much melancholy. Fuksiewicz sees in this successful film the "motif of history making sport with people, mocking their dedication, and the motifs of the heroic myth and the impossibility of escaping the burden of the past" (*Polish Cinema*, 31-32). Of course, no Pole, not even Has, could avoid the war, which he uses in *Szyfry (The Code)*, 1966, to explore the paralysis resulting from conflicting war experiences: the relatively less brutal war in the West against the mass exterminations in the East.

One of the major trends of Polish cinema of the 1960s was the historical spectacular. Has contributed three immensely important films to this genre: *Rękopis Znaleziony w Saragossie (The Manuscript Found in Saragossa)*, 1965; *Lalka (The Doll)*, 1968; and slightly later, in 1973, *Sanatorium pod Klepsydrą (The Sanatorium Under the Sign of the Hourglass)*. All have literary roots, but each is "entirely cinematic in feel and structure," each demanding much of "the viewers' capacities for imagination and allegory," each involving "a labyrinthine journey" (Fuksiewicz, *Polish Cinema*, 41).

When Has turned from his earlier "chamber" movies, he did so in a big way. *The Manuscript Found in Saragossa*, adapted from an 1904 novel written in French by Count Jan Potocki, a Polish writer of the Enlightenment, is a complex, amusing tale of the fantastic tinged with wild black humor, a "philosophical story on the struggle of rationalism against superstition, prejudice and a belief in magic" (Fuksiewicz, *Polish Cinema*, 40). Structurally, it is a set of Chinese boxes (Elley counts as many as six narrative levels, 41-42). From Potocki's romanticism, Has turned to the naturalism of the late nineteenth-century novelist Bolesław Prus in *The Doll*, a story of the "tragic love of a parvenu for an impoverished aristocratic young lady." In it we see "the antinomy of Polish capitalism developing amidst traditions of romanticism, and paralysed to an equal degree by the policies of the countries which had partitioned Poland amongst themselves, and by the burden of a heritage of a feudal system of values" (Fuksiewicz, *Polish Cinema*, 40). And from Prus's naturalism, Has turned to the modernism of Bruno Schulz, a Polish Jew murdered in 1942, whose small corpus has been receiving considerable attention in the West in recent years—a writer having certain affinities with Kafka. His collection of phantasmagoric stories, *The Sanatorium Under the Sign of the Hourglass*, was a natural vehicle for Has' cinematographic imagination. Elley sees it as a loosely structured but "continuous fantasia on the theme of a young Jew's memories, childhood recollections and complexes.... a cinematic equivalent of Mahler's all-encompassing symphonies.... a baffling, exotic hymn to man's durability and capacity for adjustment." In all of these films the "central character undergoes various psychological trials before emerging a wiser, if somewhat baffled, person" (38).

For the genuinely large-scale historical epics, however, we must turn to directors who adapted the popular Polish classics, especially the historical and nationalistic novels of Henryk Sienkiewicz. In 1960 Ford made *Krzyżacy* (*Teutonic Knights*), the biggest Polish production to date and a tremendous popular success throughout all Eastern Europe. Celebrating the Polish defeat of the Germanic Teutonic Order at the fifteenth-century Battle of Grunwald, it remains the most frequently viewed Polish film. Two extremely successful films by Jerzy Hoffman, *Pan Wołodyjowski* (*Colonel Wolodyjowski*), 1969, and *Potop* (*The Deluge*), 1974, while not cinematic masterpieces, continued the celebration of an earlier history, when Poland was one of the largest and most progressive nations of Europe.

Two much greater historical films, undoubted masterpieces, came from Jerzy Kawalerowicz, *Matka Joanna od Aniołów* (*Mother Joan of the Angels*) and *Faraon* (*The Pharaoh*). The former was based on a story by Jaroslaw Iwaszkiewicz about the nuns of Loudon (subject of Aldous Huxley's book *The Devils of Loudon* and Ken Russell's film *The Devils*). Although the action is transposed to a seventeenth-century convent on the plains of eastern Poland, it is, on one level, an exorcism film about a supposedly possessed mother superior. But the real focus of this demystifying film is not demonic possession but external restrictions placed upon people by oppressive institutions, marking the director's rejection of religious fanaticism by pitting blind faith against "rebellion in the name of human freedom and dignity" (Fuksiewicz, *Polish Cinema*, 27), and making this historical subject a vehicle for thinly veiled political discourse. But it is more than an affirmation of secular humanism; it is a film of great formal beauty, "a classicist form... used to express gothic content, the combination yielding a film of complex esthetic maturity" (Michałek and Turaj, 104). Four years later Kawalerowicz began work on *The Pharaoh*, an extravagantly large historical film based on the turn-of-the-century novel by Bolesław Prus. Set in authentically recreated Egypt of the ninth century B.C., it is actually "about" national identity—"the function of the state, the sacrifices it requires, and the ideology it represents, developing all the doubts, questions, ironies, and grim humor that such reasoning can yield" (Michałek and Turaj, 105). He and Konwicki, scriptwriter for both this film and its predecessor, eschewed crowd-pleasing spectacles (e.g., great battles) and erotic conventions (no kissing—because of its assumed historical inauthenticity!).

In the mid-sixties Wajda also made a major Napoleonic film, *Popioły* (*Ashes*), faithfully adapted from the novel of Stefan Zeromski: "A giant historical and historical-philosophical fresco," which examines the tragedy of historical events, the role of the individual in history, "a salute to the brave, despairing resistance of a lost generation and—questionably—to progress" (Michałek, *Wajda*, 82). It is structured as a series of tableaux, beginning with Polish volunteers serving under Bonaparte in Italy in 1798 and ending with the disasterous retreat from Moscow. In "this intelligent and beautiful epic" Wajda, "the most reflective of directors, lingers despondently at the crumbling of an epoch" (Cowie, 1967, 137). It should be noted that the Poles had cast their lot with Napoleon because they saw him as the liberator from their traditional enemies, Prussia, Austria, and Russia, the three monarchies that had recently devoured the last pieces of independent Poland.

The 1960s also saw the appearance of a younger generation of directors, who, a decade younger than Wajda or Munk, had not experienced the war as adults and consequently whose attitude towards the war was different. Prominent among this generation were Roman Polański, Jerzy Skolimowski, Janusz Majewski, and Henryk Kluba.

Though Polański, by training, is a Polish director, much influenced by his student work with Wajda and Munk, most of his career has developed outside Poland, where he has achieved international fame. In fact, Polański made only one Polish feature film, *Knife in the Water* (*Nóż w Wodzie*), but this is probably the Polish film best known to a wide international audience. It is a tight, low-budget film with only three characters: a successful middle-aged sportswriter, his wife, and a young hitchhiker. It involves a power struggle between the two men, who may be seen as showing off for the wife as they cruise on the couple's sailboat, though Polański himself claims the young man is an accessory and the real conflict is between the couple (Weinberg, 33). Yet it is a struggle that does not emphasize the "violence, horror, and aberrant behavior that have become Polański landmarks" (Johnson, 1663). It is a subtle, restrained, psychologically and socially penetrating study, on one level, of class and generational conflict, the successful representative of a new Poland against a disaffected youth.

Skolimowski, a co-screenwriter for *Knife in the Water*, as well as for *Innocent Sorcerers*, like Polański left Poland, though the Polish segment of his filmmaking career was longer. His versatility is shown by the fact that in the mid-sixties he wrote, directed, and starred in his first feature film, *Rysopis* (*Identification Marks: None*), a legendary film about a hero who embodies a "lost and unfulfilled generation" (Fuksiewicz, Review, 1431), a film that has reminded critics of Godard (Paul, *Barrier*, 224). This was followed a year later by *Walkover*, a boxing film, a sport about which as an amateur boxing champion Skolimowski had intimate knowledge, and by his most significant Polish film, *Bariera* (*Barrier*). In its interweaving of reality and fantasy it reminds one critic of Fellini's *8½* (Paul, *Barrier*, 224); it employs an "unusual visual language, symbolic and brief like the lines of a modern poem, possessing all the intensity of modern graphics" (Michałek & Turaj, 43). In it Skolimowski shares with Wajda and Polański a thematic concern with the restlessness and alienation of youth, speaking for the younger generation that has "reacted against the heroism of [the war] and against the worship of the past. We have not tried to sacrifice our lives for a cause. That is where the barrier is in Poland today" (Skolimowski, quoted in Thomsen, 144). Skolimowski himself considers his next (and last) Polish film, *Ręce do Gory* (*Hands Up*), his best. It deals with the compromises of the successful, complacent middle-aged conformists who were once the idealistic leaders. But because it was "a provocation about political and social problems" or because of bureaucratic irrationality, it was withheld for sixteen years, until 1983. By this time Skolimowski had established his career in Western Europe, making *Deep End* (1970), *The Shout* (1975), and most notably *Moonlighting* (1982), in which, though it is about Polish workers in London, one easily spots allusions to the Solidarity movement.

Much less widely known abroad than Polański and Skolimowski, Janusz Majewski and Henryk Kluba have made some rewarding films. In the late sixties Majewski displayed a sense of the absurd and black humor in *Sublokator* (*The Lodger*) (which won prizes at international festivals in Mannheim, Cork, and Panama) and ingenuity in *Zbrodniarz Który Ukradł Zbrodnię* (*The Criminal Who Stole His Crime*). In his works of the late 1970s and early 1980s, including *Zazdrosc i Medycyna* (*Jealousy and Medicine*), *Lekcja Martwego Jezyka* (*A Lesson of Dead Language*), and *Epitafium dla Barbary Radziwiłłowny* (*The Epitaph for Barbara Radziwill*), he has created "complicated, sometimes stylized, psychological films, unfailingly brought off with good taste and exceptional craftsmanship" (Michałek and Turaj, 46). Kluba made a brilliant debut film in 1967, *Chudy i Inni* (*Skinny and Others*), set against the background of urbanization, a "ballad in which pathos goes hand in hand with humour, poetry with everyday human warmth, and epic style with documentary form and realism" (Fuksiewicz, *Polish Cinema*, 42). Kluba has continued working in this vein in *Słońce Wschodzi Raz na Dzień* (*The Sun Rises Once a Day*), 1967, a folk-ballad film, an allegorical presentation of the conflict between traditional present social structure and the new, revolutionary order brought in from the outside (Sobański, 70). Since this film had an "anarchistal tone," it got caught in crackdowns of the late 1960s and was not released until 1973.

These crackdowns, reflecting a serious national crisis, caused a major disruption of the film industry. The year 1968 brought the Czech Spring, the brief opening of the heavy doors of this neighbor's orthodoxy, slammed shut by the Soviet invasion in August. It was the year of political unrest in Western Europe and the United States. And it was a year of student demonstrations in Poland, occasioned in part, according to Michałek and Turaj, by the closing down of a classic piece of Polish theater, Michiewicz's *Dziady* (*Forefather's Eve*), for its supposedly anti-Soviet overtones. This student-sparked unrest led to major political and cultural purges, which hit the film industry with special severity, the Polish Film School coming under fierce political attack, Jerzy Toeplitz losing the Rectorship of the Lodz Film School, Jerzy Bossak being forced to resign from his artistic directorship of the Kamera Film Unit, and Ford losing his managership of the Studio Unit, getting stripped of his Party positions, and as a result of the widespread "anti-Zionist" campaign, leaving Poland (Turaj, "Poland," 129). About this time quite a few major figures in the film industry left Poland, including the great cinematographer Jerzy Lipman. All the film units that had survived from 1955 were collapsed into six short-lived units. These six were dissolved again in 1971, as a result of an even deeper political crisis that began in December 1970 with the worker riots in Gdańsk and Szczecin. The ensuing violence led to a political shakedown, Gomułka being outsted and replaced by Edward Gierek. Consumerism and massive borrowing, the beginnings of Poland's massive present indebtedness, characterized the newest political order.

Film production did not stabilize until the beginning of 1972, when "the imposed structures were dissolved and the former system of film units was reintroduced with broader freedom and more extensive production prerogatives." These new units had much greater autonomy, the government maintaining its right to veto scripts (Michałek and Turaj, 50). Sobański provides the following data (192–198). Seven film units were created or recreated, and some of these survived through the 1970s, though reorganized again during the Solidarity crisis of 1980–1981: "Iluzjion" (1972–1981; 1982–), managed by Czesław Petelski; "Kadr" (1972–) by Kawalerowicz; the short-lived "Panorama" (1972–1974) by Passendorfer; "Pryzmat" (1972–1978) by Ścibor-Rylski; "Silesia" (1972–1983) by Kutz (1972–1978) and Ernest Bryll (1978–1983); "Tor" (1972) by Różewicz (1972–1979), Zanussi (1979–1983), and Kieslowski (1984–); "X" (1972–1983) by Wajda. During the 1970s three more units were formed: "Profil" (1975–1981; 1981–), managed by Bohdan Poręba; "Nurt" (1976–1977) by Jerzy Antczak; "Perspektywa" by Morgenstern. More recently the surviving units were supplemented by "Krakow" (1980–1981), managed by Ryszard Filipski; "Zodiak" (1980–) by Jerzy Hoffman; "Aneks" (1981–1983) by Królikiewicz; "Rondo" (1981–) by Has; "Oko" (1984–) by Tadeusz Chmielewski; and "Dom" (1986–) by Zaorski. As of 1986, film production in Poland was being run by nine Film Units. The dissolutions, formations, and reformations are an index to the political flux in Poland. But it is worth noting that the artistic managers have included many of the great figures in Polish cinema and that the literary managers have included some leading writers: Jerzy Stefan Stawiński, Aleksander Ścibor-Rylski, Bolesław Michałek, and Tadeusz Konwicki.

Polish cinema not only survived these turmoils but came out strengthened. As Michałek and Turaj argue, "the seventies became . . . a thoroughly successful time for Polish film . . . [and] there began the extraordinary series of films, wave after wave of accomplished pieces in a succession not yet broken and only somewhat interrupted by the martial law events of 1981 and 1982" (50).

Although intelligent high-quality literary adaptations were characteristic of the early 1970s, several films of strong social orientation began a decade in which the films became increasingly attuned to contemporary issues. Kazimierz Kutz made two films set in the Silesian coal mines. *Sól Ziemi Czarnej* (*Salt of the Black Earth*), exploring industrial strikes of the 1930s, offered a fresh view "of a struggle for national liberation that is filmed in a surrealist style as a folk celebration, a bloody carnival, and a folk ballad set against the backdrop of real events" (Liehm and Liehm, 376); *Perła w Koronie* (*The Pearl in the Crown*) studies a regional uprising that caused the incorporation of this industrial region into the new Polish republic (Michałek and Turaj, 54).

The greatest director to emerge in these years was Krzysztof Zanussi, whose films have brought new philosophical depths to Polish cinema. His films involve moral choice, trying to discover meaningful values in the contemporary world, some order in present-day problems, moving from "rationalistic analysis and a logical structure to a penetrating moral unrest" (Liehm and Liehm, 379). *Struktura Kryształu* (*The Crystal Structure*), 1969, examines conflicts between public success and personal spiritual growth in two young scientists, one having achieved success in the technological elite, the other moral growth in an isolated rural career. The differences are explored rather than reconciled in a film that displays Zanussi's "ability to extract tension from the commonplace and lend it an intellectual and aesthetic dimension" (Fuksiewicz, *Polish Cinema*, 53). *Życie Rodzinne* (*Family Life*), 1971, focuses on a young engineer in the process of disassociating himself from a stifling family but finding such a break impossible: one remains tied to one's past. *Iluminacja* (*Illumination*), 1973, an elliptical meditation, an innovative translation of philosophy into cinema (Michałek and Turaj, 180), follows a young scientist's intellectual and moral quest for values to undergird his technological training as he questions "the ability of the natural sciences to explain . . . the phenomenon of human existence or define the human condition" (Michałek and Turaj, 176). *Illumination* brought Zanussi fame at home and recognition abroad. *Bilans Kwartalny* (*The Quarterly Balance-Taking*), a smaller-scale work, an extremely sensitive study of an ordinary working woman (brilliantly played by Maja Komorowska, who has starred in nearly all the Zanussi films), received wide viewing internationally. In the late 1970s Zanussi's work reached full maturity in four films of philosophical meditation: *Barwy Ochronne* (*Camouflage*), 1977; *Spirala* (*Spiral*), 1978; *Kontrakt* (*The Contract*), 1980; and *Constans* (*The Constant Factor*), 1980. *Camouflage* is a film of youth and age, of idealism and cynicism, the Mephistophelean idea of a moral young scientist tempted by a professor's worldly, successful survival; *Spiral* is a profound meditation on imminent death; *The Contract* is a study of a bride who chooses to say "No" at the altar, rejecting both the groom and a world of crass opportunism; and *The Constant Factor,* released just before the imposition of martial law, is a study of young veterans searching, in a world of chance and unpredictability, for "certain immutable values, constant factors, which remain the same irrespective of the changes of other elements" (Michałek and Turaj, 188).

The achievements of a Zanussi or a Wajda have not crowded out the competition, other younger, highly creative directors like Marek Piwowski, Andrzej Żuławski, and Grzegorz Królikiewicz. Piwowski contributed ingenious, flamboyant, wildly irreverent works in *Rejs* (*The Cruise*), 1970, and *Przepraszam, Czy Tu Bija?* (*Excuse Me, Do They Beat You Up Here?*), 1975. In 1970,

Żuławski's first film, *Diabeł* (*The Devil*), with similarities to Wajda's *Ashes*, was too violently radical for authorities and has never been released. His second film, *Trzecia Część Nocy* (*The Third Part of Night*), involving grotesque medical experimentation during the Occupation, was acclaimed two years later; his third, *Na Srebrnym Globie* (*On the Silver Globe*), was held up for more than a decade and was not completed and released until 1987. Królikiewicz, like Żuławski, combines expressionism and naturalistic detail, representing the avant-garde in the provocative, difficult 1973 film *Na Wylot* (*Through and Through*). This work, showing the "inner degeneration of people living lives of apathy and deterioration, appears to be set in the present," viewers not realizing until the end that the setting is 1933, forty years earlier (Liehm and Liehm, 377).

While Królikiewicz presented a subtly displaced present, directors in the midseventies increasingly were turning directly to the immediate present, to more direct social commentary in what has been called "the Cinema of Moral Concern" (Turaj; Michałek and Turaj, chapter 5). Filmmakers were drawing "inspiration directly from reality, without the mediation of literature" (Koniczek, 1978, 265) and looking for "a life in accordance with a higher moral imperative" (Koniczek, 1980, 257). At this time some of the most significant contemporary directors were beginning their careers: Feliks Falk, Janusz Zaorski, Agnieszka Holland, Janusz Kijowski, and Krzysztof Kieślowski. Showing the increased critically expressive possibilities, Falk's *Wodzirej* (*The Dance Leader*), 1978, depicts the corruption in show business, a miniaturization of his concern with the wider corruption of a society where "friendship, loyalty, and honesty" fall before "every form of hypocrisy and manipulation" (Turaj, 155). *Szansa* (*The Chance*), 1980, is a "philosophical duel" between two teachers, one "humane and liberal but naïve and ineffectual," the other an autocratic disciplinarian, "who struggle for their students' minds" (Turaj, 156). *Był Jazz* (*There Was Jazz*), 1981, examines how jazz was utilized in earlier post-war years (as is rock today) as a medium for dissent, an escape from Stalinist repression. Zaorski's *Pokój z Widokiem na Morze* (*The Room Overlooking the Sea*), 1978, deals with individual moral responsibility in the face of contemplated suicide—the potential victim is convinced to continue living not by those who attempt to dissuade him from jumping, but rather by the person who urges him to take moral responsibility for whichever choice he makes (Turaj, 155). Holland, one of the few women directors in Polish cinema, and one with strong political concerns, made powerful statements in 1978 about theatrical (and national) conformity, mediocrity, and potential liberation with *Aktorzy prowincjonalni* (*Provincial Actors*), about life among revoluntionaries (in 1905) with *Gorączka* (*A Fever*), 1981, and a working woman's misery in *Kobieta Samotna* (*The Lonely Woman*), 1985. Kieślowski made his mark in 1979 with *Amator* (*Camera Buff*), a cold, realistic look at "personal and social motives for behavior," a story of a young filmmaker who wants to portray his factory honestly. He gets official encouragement, but in attempting to understand and please his managers, he ties himself up in self-censorship, transforming his sponsors into his censors (Michałek and Turaj, 67), very much the appropriate metaphor for much artistic life in Eastern Europe of recent decades.

While these and other directors were establishing themselves, Wajda continued enlarging his enormously impressive mark. He had further explored war themes in the late fifties and early sixties in *Lotna,* 1959 (focusing on the controlling image of a white mare, symbol of Polish victory, and the theme of the tragic fatalism of history); *Samson,* 1961 (focusing on a young Jewish student embroiled and killed in the Warsaw ghetto); and, in 1970, the very significant *Krajobraz po Bitwie (Landscape After Battle).* This film has been viewed as Wajda's critical self-appraisal, containing his ambiguous feelings towards war, heroism, and tradition, uniting "a historical perspective of human fate with that of the personal one of the individual," a film in which "external determinants [are] complemented by internal ones, and the hero doomed by fate is replaced by an equally tragic hero who must define his own fate" (Fuksiewicz, *Polish Cinema,* 49). In 1969 he made a film about filmmaking (and a tribute to Cybulski), *Wszystko na Sprzedaż (Everything for Sale),* and a substantial comedy, *Polowanie na Muchy (Hunting Flies),* filled with "intelligent observation, acid humor, a sense of the absurd, knitted into a satirical picture of middle-class attitudes and bohemian snobberies" (Michałek, 116). He had also turned to literary sources, in *Brzezina (Birchwood),* 1970, probing more intensely than ever universal themes of love and death, his first film not confronting national and social myths, and *Wesele (The Wedding),* 1973, from Wyspianski's turn-of-the century play and one of Poland's major literary classics, Wajda producing a work with "realistic comedy and visionary symbolism interlocking into a single, magnificently functioning stage mechanism which glitters with scintillating effects" (Michałek, 157).

It is scarcely surprising that Wajda was a key contributor to the "Cinema of Moral Concern," especially with *Człowiek z Marmuru (Man of Marble),* 1977; *Bez Znieczulenia (Without Anesthesia),* 1978; and *Człowiek z Zelaza (Man of Iron),* 1981. In *Man of Marble* Wajda took quite a new path, producing a "paradocumentary fresco"—"primarily an image of the social and civilizational evolution of Polish Society" (Cowie, 1978, 267), with a dual focus on the Stalinism of the early fifties and the opportunities of the seventies. Thematically it is about both human repression and the repression of the truth. Despite official attempts to deprecate its significance, it immediately became the center of all Polish political discussions (Michałek and Turaj, 158). *Without Anesthesia* followed the journalistic approach of *Man of Iron,* with less of Wajda's previous baroque romanticism—a film about a crisis in the family and professional life of a successful journalist, "a drama of values expressed by a drama of existence" (Koniczek, 260). In *Man of Iron* Wajda created an account of the Solidarity crisis, a film that went "politically beyond anything that had ever been done" (Michałek and Turaj, 165). It was quickly made under tight deadlines, won the highest prize at the Cannes Film Festival, and was immensely popular in Poland during the eventful 1981, until the imposition of martial law on December 19, 1981, when it was immediately withdrawn.

Martial law briefly choked film production—and every other phase of Polish life. While the most severe constrictions were short-lived, post-Solidarity cinema did not soon breathe easily. Some directors, like Holland, emigrated and others, like Wajda (whose relations with authorities were poor and whose film unit "X" was dissolved in 1983) and Zanussi, worked abroad. Wajda made *Danton* in Paris and *Milosc w Niemczech* (*Love in Germany*) in Berlin—both of which splendid films are currently available to American viewers. While in Germany Zanussi made *Rok Spokojnego Słońca* (*The Year of the Quiet Sun*), a tragic love story of a post-war Polish-American romance, also currently available. Still, other major directors succeeded in producing significant films at home, especially Konwicki, with *Dolina Issy* (*The Issa Valley*) and Kawalerowicz, with *Austeria* (*The Inn*), which Konwicki helped script. The former is a beautiful, elegiac expansion of Milosz's novel, set in isolated pre-war Lithuania (homeland of both Milosz and Konwicki). The latter is based on a script Kawalerowicz and Konwicki had written back in the late sixties, one that could not be filmed then for political reasons. Set in Galicia (now in the Soviet Union) at the beginning of the century, it unfortunately may be more notable for its subject matter, the fall of East European Jewry, than its unqualified artistic merits (Abrahamson, 268).

Nonetheless, inventive, though now politically muted, films of younger directors soon appeared, although not without delays—Zaorski's *Matka Królów* (*Mother of the Krol Family*), completed in 1982, was not released until 1986. But two of Zaorski's politically less sensitive films did appear: *Baryton* (*The Baritone*), 1985, and *Jezioro Bodeńskie* (*Bodensee*), 1986,—perhaps because they were set in a safer past. In 1983 Barbara Sass made an intense film, *Krzyk* (*The Scream*), about a former woman prisoner whose fears and desperation lead her to murder an old man she is caring for, a man she has mistakenly assumed to belong to the corrupt old order. Andrzej Barański made an inventively crafted film about a simple, long-suffering woman, *Kobieta z Prowincji* (*A Provincial Woman*), 1985, that uses subtle narrative techniques to present the life of a typical Polish woman. Tomasz Zygadło, whose 1980 film *Cma* (*A Moth*) about the host of a nighttime talk show had been a significant contribution to the "Cinema of Moral Concern" (Michałek and Turaj, 72), made *Sceny Dzieciece z Życia Prowincji* (*Childhood Scenes from Provincial Life*), 1986, a well-received film about an old politician, supposedly modeled on Władysław Gomułka (Turaj, 168). In a very different vein Julian Machulski offered three inventive, ingenious films: *Vabank,* 1981; *Vabank II,* 1985; and *Seksmisja* (*Sex Mission*), 1984. Films like these three have brought a sparkling quality to the sometimes heavy-handed and problem-laden Polish cinema. Abrahamson has observed that *Vabank* moves "at an exhilarating vivace con brio pace and has a lightheadedness and a humour ... that is totally winning" (252). Finally, Feliks Falk in 1986 made a sequel to *Top Dog, Bohater roku* (*Hero of the Year*), that focuses on the theme of the manipulation of democracy, a film in which the master of ceremonies attempts to exploit a simple public hero, using him to "promote a carefully guided program of ersatz public criticism, a deceitful democratic openness, a controlled glasnost'' (Turaj, 170). The honest target, acute in his simplicity, sees the trap and refuses to compromise himself. This story of democratic blandishments and public awareness might be seen as a fitting narrative for Poland of the late eighties. The combination of wariness and integrity reflected in Falk's recent film, one more in a long series of affirmations by dozens of filmmakers of social, moral, or artistic integrity, is an indication that Polish filmmakers have remained, as Abrahamson remarked several years ago, "well anchored in a wide public and receive geniune support in their struggle for artistic integrity" (Cowie, 1984, 266).

The level of current film activity indicates the continued productivity of leading directors. Indicative of the public support and the continued vitality of Polish cinema is the very recent (June 1989) showing, at the Cracow International Short Film Festival, of the first truly independent film of post-war Poland, produced without any government support. It is a documentary by Leopold Nowak entitled *Genesis,* an account of the history of Polish Jewish culture. Indeed, films with Jewish themes are now prominent. Agnieszka Holland is directing a French-German co-production called *Hitler-Youth Shlomo* about a Jew who survived the war by adopting multiple identities. Andrzej Wajda is directing a film called *Korczak,* the story of the famous Polish-Jewish educational reformer who died in Treblinka, with Wojciech Pszoniak in the title role. And Krzysztof Zanussi has two upcoming films treating Jewish themes. *Dark Glasses* is to be based on his own mother's hiding of Jews during the Occupation; *Deep in the Heart* will be made for Israeli producer Menachem Golan, a film about a Gentile Texas couple who move to Israel, where the husband tries to get into the Israeli army. On a non-Jewish note, Zanussi is working on a French film about Napoleon, *Napoléon et l'Europe,* starring Jean-François Stevenin and Daniel Olbrychski, and has just completed a thoroughly Polish film, *Inventory,* starring Krystyna Janda and set in the Poland of 1989. It tells of a "former newspaper censor who is falling apart. A vestige of a repressive era, she embarks upon a tentative and difficult love affair with an idealistic youth" (Insdorf). Finally in 1989, Kieślowski had completed *Decalogue,* an ambiguous ten-film cycle that has been acclaimed at film festivals in Denver and Chicago. Basing it on the Ten Commandments, Kieślowski uses Mosiac Law to probe contemporary moral issues, offering a sweeping reassessment of all moral values on a scale commensurate with the profound changes moving through Poland.

With Poland now lurching toward democracy, the vestiges of repressive decades crumbling before an idealistic people, the struggle facing these experienced filmmakers and their successors will be much less with political repression and more with catastrophic economic decline. The task for Polish filmmakers, as for all Polish artists, will be the endeavor to help guide Poland into economic and environmental health, into a political and social rebirth, into a future that recaptures the progressive openness, generosity, and diversity that Poland once knew hundreds of years ago.

BIBLIOGRAPHY

Abrahamson, Kyell Albin. "Poland." Cowie. 1985: 258–260.
Chocitowski, Jerzy. *Contemporary Polish Cinema*. Warsaw: Polonia, 1962.
Cowie, Peter, ed. *International Film Guide* 1963–1988. London: Tantivy, pub. annually.
———. "Wajda Redux." *Sight and Sound* 49 (1980): 32–34.
Davies, Norman. *God's Playground: A History of Poland*. 2 vols. New York: Columbia University Press, 1982.
———. *Heart of Europe: A Short History of Poland*. Oxford: Oxford University Press, 1986.
Dyer, Peter John. Review of *Ashes and Diamond (Popiół i Diament)*, by Andrzej Wajda. *Sight and Sound* 28 (1959): 166–167.
Elley, Derek. "Wojciech Has." Cowie. 1975: 38–45.
Erens, Patricia. Review of *Yiddle With His Fiddle (Yidle Mit Fidl)*, by Joseph Green. *Magill's Survey of Cinema:* 3453–3461.
Fuksiewicz, Jacek. Review of *Identification Marks: None (Rysopis)*, by Jerzy Skolimowski. *Magill's Survey of Cinema:* 1426–1431.
———. *Polish Cinema*. Warsaw: Interpress, 1973.
Goldberg, Judith N. Review of *The Dybbuk*. *Magill's Survey of Cinema:* 887–891.
Hibben, Sally. Review of *Five Boys of Barska Street (Piątka z Ulicy Barskiej)*, by Andrzej Wajda. *Magill's Survey of Cinema:* 1109–1113.
Insdorf, Annette. "For Polish Film, a Mood of Cautious Optimism." *New York Times*, 23 July 1989: H20.
Janda, Krystyna and Edward Klosinski. "Biting cinema, biting people." Interview. *Sight and Sound*, Spring 1981: 88–90.
Johnson, Timothy W. Review of *Knife in the Water (Nóż w Wodzie)*. *Magill's Survey of Cinema:* 1663–1665.
Kieslowski, Krzystof. "No heroics, please." Interview. *Sight and Sound* 50 (1981): 88–90.
Koniczek, Ryszard. Review of *Without Anesthesia* by Andrzej Wajda. *(Bez Znieczulenia)*. Cowie. 1978: 264–269.
Liehm, Mira and Antonin J. Liehm. *The Most Important Art: Soviet and East European Film after 1945*. Berkeley: University of California Press, 1977.
Magill's Survey of Cinema: Foreign Language Films. 8 vols. Edited by Frank N. Magill. Englewood Cliffs, NJ: Salem, 1985.
Manville, Roger. *New Cinema in Europe*. New York: Dutton, 1966.
Mead, Gary. "Volksfilm for the 1980's: Prospects for Polish Cinema after Martial Law." *Sight and Sound* 52 (1983): 230–231.
Michałek, Bolesław. *The Cinema of Andrzej Wajda*. Edward Rothert, trans. London: Tantivy Press, 1973.
———. "Letter from Warsaw." *Sight and Sound* 30 (1961–1962): 16–17.
———. "The Polish Drama." *Sight and Sound* 29 (1960): 198–200.
———. "Warsaw Notes." *Sight and Sound* 33 (1964): 124.
Michałek, Bolesław and Frank Turaj. *The Modern Cinema of Poland*. Bloomington: Indiana University Press, 1988.
Miłosz, Czesław. *The History of Polish Literature*. Berkeley: University of California Press, 1983.
Moskowitz, Gene. "The Uneasy East: Aleksander Ford and the Polish Cinema." *Sight and Sound* 26 (1957–1958): 136–140.

Moszez, Gustaw. "Frozen Assets: Interviews on Polish Cinema." *Sight and Sound* 50 (1981): 86–87.
Paul, David M. Review of *Barrier (Bariera)*, by Jerzy Skolimowski. *Magill's Survey of Cinema:* 224–227.
———. Review of *Camouflage (Barwy Ochronne)*, by Krzysztof Zanussi. *Magill's Survey of Cinema:* 452–456.
———. Review of *Man of Iron (Człowiek z Zelaza)*, by Andrzej Wajda. *Magill's Survey of Cinema:* 1929–1934.
———. Review of *Man of Marble (Człowiek z Marmuru)*, by Andrzej Wajda. *Magill's Survey of Cinema:* 1935–1941.
Pearson, Gabriel. Review of *Eroica*, by Andrzej Munk. *Sight and Sound* 28 (1959): 197–198.
Robinson, David. "Gdansk 1980." *Sight and Sound* 50 (1980–1981): 38–39.
Rubenstein, Lenny. Review of *Ashes and Diamond (Popiół i Diament)*, by Andrzej Wajda. *Magill's Survey of Cinema:* 157–160.
———. Review of *The Passenger (Pasażerka)*, by Andrzej Munk. *Magill's Survey of Cinema:* 2367–2371.
———. Review of *Everything for Sale (Wszystko na Sprzedaz)*, by Andrzej Wajda. *Magill's Survey of Cinema:* 1116–1120.
———. Review of *Without Anesthesia (Bez Znieczulenia)*, by Andrzej Wajda. *Magill's Survey of Cinema:* 3409–3412.
Sinyard, Neil. Review of *Innocent Sorcerers (Niewinni Czarodzieje)*, by Andrzej Wajda. *Magill's Survey of Cinema:* 1500–1504.
Sobański, Oskar. *Polish Feature Films: A Reference Guide 1945–1985*. West Cornwall, Conn.: Locust Hill, 1987.
Thomsen, Christian Brad. "Skolimowski." *Sight and Sound* 37 (1968): 142–144.
Turaj, Frank. "Poland: The Cinema of Moral Concern." *Post New Wave Cinema in the Soviet Union and Eastern Europe*. Edited by Daniel J. Goulding. Bloomington: Indiana University Press, 1988: 149–171.
Toeplitz, Jerzy and Rafał Marszalek, eds. *Historia Filmu Polskiego*. 5 vols. Warsaw: Wydawnictwo Artystycene i Filmowe, 1974–1980.
Weinberg, Gretchen. "Roman Polański." *Sight and Sound* 33 (1963–1964): 32–33.
Whyte, Alistair. *New Cinema in Eastern Europe*. New York: Dutton, 1971.

BIOGRAPHICAL SKETCHES

ANDRZEJEWSKI, JERZY (1909–1983), novelist, screenwriter. Andrzejewski's most famous novel, *Popiół i Diament* (*Ashes and Diamonds*), 1948/1958,* was the basis of the classic Wajda film. He made his screenwriting debut with *Robinson Warszawski*, 1948, in conjunction with Czesław Miłosz and Jerzy Zarzycki—a film that ran afoul of the censors, was remade, and released in 1950 as *Miasto Nieujarzmione* (*Unvanquished City*),* though without Miłosz's further cooperation. He also wrote the scripts for Zarzycki's *Zagubione Uczucia* (*Lost Feelings*), 1957,* and Wajda's *Niewinni Czarodzieje* (*Innocent Sorcerers*), 1960,* with Jerzy Skolimowski.

ANTCZAK, JERZY (1929–), director, screenwriter, actor. Starting as a stage actor, Antczak went on to become a leading play director for Polish television, to head Polish TV Theater (1963–1975), to begin a film career in the early 1960s, to produce TV films in the 1970s, and to emigrate to the United States in 1980. He has directed *Labedzi Spiew* (*Swan Song*, 1962), part IV of *Spóźnieni Przechodnie* ("Stary Professor," "The Old Professor"), 1962;* *Hrabina Cosel* (*The Countess of Cosel*), 1968;* *Epilog Norymberski* (*The Nuremberg Epilogue*), 1971; *Noce i Dnie* (*Nights and Days*), 1975;* and *Mur* (*The Wall*), 1980, a Polish-American co-production, never released in Poland.

BAJON, FILIP (1947–), director, screenwriter. After making some innovative TV films in the late 1970s, Bajon made the successful *Aria dla Atlety* (*Aria for an Athlete*), 1979;* *Wizja Lokalna 1901* (*A Visit to the Scene of the Crime—1901*), 1980; and *Limuzyna Daimler-Benz* (*The Daimler-Benz Limousine*), 1983.* He is co-author of the screenplay (with Piotr Andrejew) for Andrejew's *Klincz* (*The Clinch*), 1979.*

BAJOR, MICHAŁ (1957–), actor. With a film career beginning in 1980, Bajor has already starred in films by some of the most significant directors: TV films by Holland and Morgenstern; studio films including Zebrowski's *W Biały*

Dzień (*In Broad Daylight*), 1981; Falk's *Był Jazz* (*There Was Jazz*), 1981/1984;* Bajon's *Limuzyna Daimler-Benz* (*Daimler-Benz Limousine*), 1983;* Kondratiuk's *Klakier* (*The Claqueur*), 1983;* and Kieślowski's *Bez Końca* (*Without End*),1984.*

BARAŃSKI, ANDRZEJ (1941–), director and screenwriter. With an original creative voice, Barański won the Polish Critics' Award for outstanding film in 1984 with *Niech Cie Odleci Mara* (*Let the Nightmare Fly*), 1982,* and equal recognition for *Kobieta z Prowincji* (*A Provincial Woman*), 1985.*

BINCZYCKI, JERZY (1937–), actor. A major stage and screen performer, he began appearing in major screen roles in the mid–1970s, most notably in Antczak's *Noce i Dnie* (*Nights and Days*), 1975;* Zebrowski's *W Biały Dzień* (*In Broad Daylight*), 1981;* and Hoffman's *Znachor* (*The Quack*), 1982.*

BOHDZIEWICZ, ANTONI (1906–1970), director, screenwriter, teacher. A wartime documentary filmmaker, founder of the first post-war film school, as manager of major units from 1957 to 1970 (''Po prostu'' and ''Tor''), and especially as a professor at the film school in Lodz, he taught the whole postwar generation of filmmakers.

BOROWCZYK, WALERIAN (1923–), director, screenwriter, painter. Although his career has mainly been in France, he made a major Polish film, *Dzieje Grzechu* (*The Story of Sin*), 1975.*

BRANDYS, KAZIMIERZ (1916–), novelist and screenwriter. Brandys has turned several of his novels into screenplays, beginning with *Samson*, the first volume of his tetralogy *Miedzy wojnami* (*Between the Wars*), 1948–1951, for Wajda's *Samson*, 1961.* He has also worked with Has on *Jak Być Kochana* (*How To Be Loved*), 1963,* and Rybkowski on *Sposob Bycia* (*A Manner of Behaving*), 1965. Several other of his works have been adapted for the screen by Majewski and Zaorski, notably the latter's *Matka Królów* (*Mother of the Krol Family*), 1982/1986*.

BRAUNEK, MALGORZATA (1947–), actress. An extremely popular star of the 1970s, Braunek is noted for her roles in Wajda's *Polowanie na Muchy* (*Hunting Flies*), 1969;* Majewski's *Lokis,* 1970;* Wajda's *Krajobraz po Bitwie* (*The Landscape after the Battle*), 1970;* Żuławski's *Trzecia Część Nocy* (*The Third Part of the Night*), 1972; and above all Hoffman's *Potop* (*The Deluge*), 1974.*

BUCZKOWSKI, LEONARD (1909–1967), director. He made a uniquely successful transition from a pre-war commercial career to the state system. His successes include *Zakazane Piosenki* (*Forbidden Songs*), 1947*/1948; *Pierwszy*

Start (The First Take Off), 1951;* and *Przygoda na Mariensztacie (Adventure in Mariensztat)*, 1954,* the first color Polish film.

BYRYLSKA, BARBARA (1941–   ), actress. Besides having leads in East German, Czech, Bulgarian, and Soviet films, Byrylska has notably starred in Kawalerowicz's *Faraon (The Pharaoh)*, 1966;* Hoffman's *Pan Wołodyjowski (Colonel Wolodyjowski)*, 1969;* Rybkowski's *Album Polski (The Polish Sketch-Book)*, 1970;* and Załuski's *Anatomia Miłości (The Anatomy of Love), 1972.*

CHMIELEWSKI, TADEUSZ (1927–   ), director, screenwriter, administrator. One of the most successful directors of comedy, Chmielewski has also served as vice-president of the Polish Filmmakers' Association since 1983 and manager of the "Oko" film unit since 1984. His films include *Ewa Chce Spać (Eve Wants to Sleep)*, 1958,* and *Gdzie Jest Generał? (Where Is the General?)*, 1964.*

CYBULSKI, ZBIGNIEW (1927–1967), actor. Still the legend of Polish cinema, Cybulski starred in numerous major films, starting with his debut in Wajda's *Pokolenie (Generation)*, 1955,* continuing with successes in important Wajda and Has films: Wajda's *Popiół i Diament (Ashes and Diamonds)*, 1958,* and *Niewinni Czarodzieje (Innocent Sorcerers)*, 1960;* Has' *Jak Być Kochana (How to Be Loved)*, 1963;* *Rękopis Znaleziony w Saragossie (The Manuscript Found in Saragossa)*, 1965;* and *Szyfry (The Code)*, 1966.* He also appeared in films by a cross-section of other leading directors, including Ford's *Ósmy Dzień Tygodnia (The Eighth Day of the Week)*, 1958/1983*; Kawalerowicz's *Pociąg (The Train)*, 1959;* Morgernstern's *Do Widzenia, Do Jutra (Farewell, Till Tomorrow)*, 1960,* and *Jowita,* 1967;* Ścibor-Rylski's *Ich Dzień Powszedni (Their Ordinary Days)*, 1963,* and *Morderca Zostawia Slad (The Murderer Leaves Traces)*, 1967, his last and uncompleted role; Nasfeter's *Zbrodniarz i Panna (A Criminal and a Maid)*, 1963; Kutz's *Milczenie (Silence)*, 1963;* Lenartowicz's *Giuseppe w Warszawie (Giuseppe in Warsaw)*, 1964;* and Konwicki's *Salto (The Somersault)*, 1965.*

CZYŻEWSKA, ELŻBIETA (1941–   ), actress. A leading star of the 1960s, Czyżewska has appeared in many major films before and since her emigration to the United States in 1967, including Has' *Złoto (Gold)*, 1962;* Munk's *Pasażerka (The Passenger)*, 1961–1963;* Kutz's *Milczenie (Silence)*, 1963;* Chmielewski's *Gdzie Jest Generał? (Where is the General?)*, 1964;* Lenartowicz's *Giuseppe w Warszawie (Giuseppe in Warsaw)*, 1964;* Ford's *Pierwszy Dzień Wolnosci (The First Day of Freedom)*, 1965;* Skolimowski's *Rysopis (Identification Marks: None)*, 1964;* Has' *Rękopis Znaleziony w Saragossie (The Manuscript Found in Saragossa)*, 1965;* Wajda's *Wszystko na Sprzedaz (Everything for Sale)*, 1969;* and Sass' *Debiutantka (The Debutante)*, 1982.*

DALKOWSKA, EWA (1947–), actress. A successful dramatic actress, Dalkowska has appeared in many successful films since 1975: Antczak's *Noce i Dnie (Nights and Days)*, 1975;* Jakubowska's *Biały Mazur (The Mazurka Danced at Dawn)*, 1979;* Wajda's *Bez Znieczulenia (Without Anesthesia)*, 1978;* Holland's *Aktorzy Prowincjonalni (Provincial Actors)*, 1979;* Zebrowski's *Szpital Przemienienia (The Hospital of the Transfiguration)*, 1979;* Zanussi's *Rok Spokojnego Słońca (The Year of the Quiet Sun)*, 1985;* and Barański's *Kobieta z Prowincji (A Provincial Woman)*, 1985.*

DMOCHOWSKI, MARIUSZ (1930–), actor. A highly successful character actor, Dmochowski's career began in the late 1950s with his debut in Munk's *Eroica*, 1958;* and continued in Antczak's *Hrabina Cosel (The Countess of Cosel)*, 1968;* Has' *Lalka (The Doll)*, 1968;* Hoffman's *Pan Wołodyjowski (Colonel Wolodyjowski)*, 1969;* Majewski's *Zazdrość i Medycyna (Jealousy and Medicine)*, 1973;* Zanussi's *Bilans Kwartalny (The Quarterly Balance-Taking)*, 1975,* and *Barwy Ochronne (Camouflage)*, 1977.*

DYGAT, STANISŁAW (1914–1978), novelist, screenwriter. A writer of gently satirical novels and stories, Dygat has written screenplays for Has' *Pozegnania (Farewells)*, 1958,* based on his own novel, and a five-part film based on his own stories, *Spoźnieni Przechodnie (Late Passers-By)*, 1962,* directed by Holoubek, Łapicki, Hanuszkiewicz, Antczak, and Rybkowski; he has also written dialogues for directors including Passendorfer and Has.

DYMNA, ANNA (1951–), actress. One of Poland's most popular contemporary stars, Dymna has starred in such films as Hoffman's *Tredowsata (She's a Leper)*, 1976; Różewicz's *Pasja (A Passion)*, 1978;* Hoffman's *Znachor (The Quack)*, 1982;* Konwicki's *Dolina Issy (Issa Valley)*, 1982;* and Has' *Osobisty Pamiętnik Grzesznika, Przez Niego Samego Spisany (The Personal Diary of a Sinner, Written in His Own Hand)*, 1986.*

FALK, FELIKS (1941–), director, screenwriter. Falk's career began in the early 1970s, his first full-length film appearing in 1975: *W Srodku Lata (In Midsummer)*,* followed by *Wodzirej (The Dance Leader)*, 1978;* *Szansa (The Chance)*, 1980;* *Był Jazz (There Was Jazz)*, 1981/1984;* and *Idol*, 1984. He has written screenplays for Holland, Kedzierski and Domaradzki's *Zdjęcia Próbne (Test Shots)*, 1977,* and Zaorski's *Baryton*, 1985.*

FORD, ALEKSANDER (1908–1980), director, screenwriter and administrator. With a career stretching back well before World War II and continuing through the post-war decades until he left Poland in 1968, Ford contributed immensely to Polish cinema. Besides very early success in *Legion Ulicy (The Street Legion)*, 1932, he directed *Ulica Graniczna (Border Street)*, 1949;* *Młodość Chopina (The Young Chopin)*, 1952;* *Piątka z Ulicy Barskiej (Five Boys from Barska*

Street), 1954;* *Ósmy Dzień Tygodnia—Der achte Wochentaq* (*The Eighth Day of the Week*), 1958/1983;* *Krzyżacy* (*Teutonic Knights*), 1960;* and *Pierwszy Dzień Wolnosci* (*The First Day of Freedom*), 1965.*

FRONCZEWSKI, PIOTR (1946–   ), actor. Beginning as a child actor, Fronczewski has gone on to become an extremely versatile, popular performer for TV and cinema. His appearances began in Różewicz's *Wolne Miasto* (*The Open City*), 1958,* and have also included Zebrowski's *Ocalenie* (*The Salvation*), 1972;* Zanussi's *Bilans Kwartalny* (*The Quarterly Balance-Taking*), 1975;* Zaorski's *Pokój z Widokiem na Morze* (*The Room Overlooking the Sea*), 1978;* and Zaorski's *Baryton* (*The Baritone*), 1985.*

HAS, WOJCIECH (1925–   ), director, screenwriter. An immensely original director, Has has been directing major films since the late 1950s, including *Pętla* (*The Noose*), 1958;* *Pozegnania* (*Farewells*), 1958;* *Wspólny Pokój* (*The Common Room*), 1960;* *Rozstanie* (*The Separation*), 1961;* *Złoto* (*Gold*), 1962;* *Jak Być Kochana* (*How to Be Loved*), 1963;* *Rękopis Znaleziony w Saragossie* (*The Manuscript Found in Saragossa*), 1965;* *Szyfry* (*The Code*), 1966;* *Lalka* (*The Doll*), 1968;* *Sanatorium pod Klepsydra* (*The Sanatorium Under the Sign of the Hourglass*), 1973;* *Nieciekawa Historia* (*An Uninteresting Story*), 1983;* *Pismak* (*The Hack*), 1985;* and *Osobisty Pamiętnik Grzesznika, Przez Niego Samego Spisany* (*The Personal Diary of a Sinner, Written in His Own Hand*), 1986.*

HOFFMAN, JERZY (1932–   ), director, scriptwriter, administrator. Especially successful in historical films, Hoffman's notable films include versions of two Sienkiewicz classics: *Pan Wołdyjowski* (*Colonel Wolodyjowski*), 1969,* and *Potop* (*The Deluge*), 1974*—two of the five top Polish box office successes—as well as *Znachor* (*The Quack*), 1982.*

HOLLAND, AGNIESZKA (1948–   ), director, screenwriter. As a leading but controversial director (who emigrated to France in 1982), Holland has made influential films: *Zdjęcia Próbne* (*Test Shots*), 1977,* with Falk, Pawel Kedzierski and Jerzy Domaradzki; *Aktorzy Prowincjonalni* (*Provincial Actors*), 1979; *Gorączka* (*A Fever*), 1981;* and *Kobieta Samotna* (*The Lonely Woman*), 1985.* As a screenwriter, she has worked on three Wajda films: *Bez Znieczulenia* (*Without Anesthesia*), 1978;* *Danton*, 1983;* and *Eine Liebe in Deutschland* (*A Love in Germany*), 1983.

HOLOUBEK, GUSTAW (1923–   ), actor. A prolific star, Holoubek has had leads in numerous major films, especially those of Has: *Pętla* (*The Noose*), 1958;* *Pozegnania* (*Farewells*), 1958;* *Wspólny Pokój* (*The Common Room*), 1960;* *Rozstanie* (*The Separation*), 1961;* *Rękopis Znaleziony w Saragossie* (*The Manuscript Found in Saragossa*), 1965;* *Sanatorium pod Klepsydra* (*The Sanatorium Under the Sign of the Hourglass*), 1973;* *Nieciekawa Historia* (*An

Uninteresting Story), 1983;* and *Pismak (The Hack)*, 1985.* Holoubek has also worked with Buczkowski, Zarzycki, Morgenstern, Hoffman, Konwicki, Rybkowski, Lenartowicz, Kawalerowicz, Zaorski, Żebrowski, and German director Vőlker Schlőndorff (*The Tin Drum*).

HÜBNER, ZYGMUNT (1930–), actor, director. As an actor specializing in restrained, intellectually cool roles, Hűbner has been appearing in important films since the late 1960s: Różewicz's *Westerplatte,* 1967;* Passendorfer's *Akcja "Brutus" (Operation "Brutus")*, 1971;* Wajda's *Smuga Cienia (The Shadow Line)*, 1976;* Żebrowski's *Szpital Przemienienia (The Hospital of the Transfiguration)*, 1979;* and Kieślowski's *Przypadek (By Accident)*, 1981.

IDZIAK, SLAWOMIR (1945–), cinematographer. Idziak is renowned for his work on films of leading directors, especially Zanussi's *Bilans Kwartalny (The Quarterly Balance-Taking)*, 1975;* *Kontrakt (The Contract)*, 1980;* *Rok Spokojnego Słońca (The Year of the Quiet Sun)*, 1985;* and Zaorski's *Partita na Instrument Drewniany (Partita for a Wooden Instrument)*, 1976.*

JAHODA, MIECYZSŁAW (1924–), cinematographer. Having photographed films for Has and Konwicki and known for his technical innovations—bringing Eastmancolor and Cinemascope to Polish films—Jahoda's work includes Has's *Pętla (The Noose)*, 1958;* *Pozegnania (Farewells)*, 1958;* *Rękopis Znaleziony w Saragossie (The Manuscript Found in Saragossa)*, 1965;* *Szyfry, (The Code)*, 1966;* and Konwicki's *Jak Daleko Stad, Jak Blisko (How Far from Here, How Near)*, 1972;* as well as Ford's *Krzyżacy (Teutonic Knights)*, 1960.*

JAKUBOWSKA, WANDA (1907–), director, screenwriter, administrator. As a co-founder of the START organization, she made a mark on pre-war Polish cinema; as a shaper of the post-war cinema production, in an exceptionally long career Jakubowska has continued to play an important part in Polish artistic life: her films include *Ostatni Etap (The Last Stage)*, 1948;* *Opowieść Atlantycka (The Atlantic Story)*, 1955;* *Biały Mazur (The Mazurka Danced at Dawn)*, 1979;* and *Zaproszenie do Tanca (Invitation to Dance)*, 1986.*

JANDA, KRYSTYNA (1952–), actress, particularly noted for her work with Wajda: *Człowiek z Marmuru (Man of Marble)*, 1977;* *Bez Znieczulenia (Without Anesthesia)*, 1978;* *Dyrygent (The Conductor)*, 1980;* *Człowiek z Zelaza (Man of Iron)*, 1981.* Janda has developed an international career in a variety of European films, such as the Hungarian Istvan Szabó's *Mephisto,* 1981.*

KAWALEROWICZ, JERZY (1922–), director, screenwriter, administrator. Kawalerowicz has long been one of Poland's leading directors, whose seminal films include *Celuloza (A Night of Remembrance)*, 1954,* *Pod Gwiazdą Frygijska (Under the Phrygian Star)*, 1954;* *Prawdziwy Koniec Wielkiej Wojny (The True

End of the Great War), 1957;* *Matka Joanna od Aniołów (Mother Joan of the Angels),* 1961;* *Faraon (The Pharaoh),* 1966;* and *Austeria (The Inn),* 1983.*

KIEŚLOWSKI, KRZYSZTOF (1941–), director, screenwriter. A highly innovative and controversial politically conscious filmmaker, Kieślowski has been writing and directing films since the mid 1970s: two politically sensitive TV films, *Personel (The Staff),* 1975; *Spokoj (Peace of Mind)* 1976–1980; feature films include *Blizna (A Scar),* 1976;* *Amator (Camera-Buff),* 1979;* *Przypadek (By Accident),* 1981; and *Bez Końca (Without End),* 1984.* In late 1989 reviews appeared for his massive *Decalogue,* a ten-film cycle that won acclaim at the 1989 Chicago Film festival.

KIJOWSKI, JANUSZ (1948–), director, screenwriter. One of the significant younger directors, Kijowski has already made his mark with *Indeks, (The Index)* 1977/1981;* *Kung Fu,* 1980;* and *Głosy (Voices),* 1982.*

KŁOSIŃSKI, EDWARD (1943–), cinematographer. Having been closely associated with the films of Wajda and Zanussi, he has photographed many significant films: Wajda's *Człowiek z Marmuru (Man of Marble),* 1977;* *Bez Znieczulenia (Without Anesthesia),* 1978;* *Panny z Wilka (The Maids of Wilko),* 1979;* *Człowiek z Zelaza (Man of Iron),* 1981;* and *Kronika Wypadków Miłosnych (A Chronicle of Amorous Accidents),* 1986;* Zanussi's *Iluminacja (The Illumination),* 1973;* and *Barwy Ochronne (Camouflage),* 1977.*

KLUBA, HENRYK (1931–), director and actor. With film experience ranging from acting in Polański's short *Dwaj Ludzie z Szafą (Two Men and a Wardrobe),* 1962, to serving as rector of the Lodz Film School, Kluba has also made some significant films: *Chudy i Inni (Skinny and Others),* 1967;* *Słońce Wschodzi Raz na Dzień (The Sun Rises Once a Day),* 1967/1973;* and *Sowizdrzał Świętokrzyski (The Merrymaker from Holy-Cross Mountains),* 1978–1980.

KOBIELA, BOGUMIL (1931–1969), actor. Though killed tragically young in an auto accident, Kobiela nevertheless had an important career, especially in films of Has, Munk, and Wajda: Has' *Pozegnania (Farewells),* 1958;* *Rozstanie (The Separation),* 1961;* *Rękopis Znaleziony w Saragossie (The Manuscript Found in Saragossa),* 1965;* *Lalka (The Doll),* 1968;* Munk's *Eroica,* 1958;* *Zezowate Szczęście (Cockeyed Luck),* 1960;* Wajda's *Popioł i Diament (Ashes and Diamonds),* 1958;* *Wszystko na Sprzedaz (Everything for Sale),* 1969;* also title role in Hoffman's *Pan Wołodyjowski (Colonel Wolodyjowski),* 1969.*

KOMOROWSKA, MAJA (1937–), actress. An immensely important talent, she made her fame in Zanussi's films, including *Za Sciana (Behind the Wall),* 1971; *Bilans Kwartalny (The Quarterly Balance-Taking),* 1975;* *Spirala (A Spi-*

ral), 1978;* Kontrakt (The Contract), 1980;* and Rok Spokojnego Słońca (The Year of Quiet Sun), 1985.*

KONWICKI, TADEUSZ (1926–), novelist, screenwriter, director. Besides having written several of the most extraordinary novels of modern Poland, Sennik wspolczesny (A Dreambook For Our Time), 1963, and Kompleks Polski (The Polish Complex), 1977, Konwicki has written and directed with equal distinction major films, including (with Jan Laskowski) Ostatni Dzień Lata (The Last Day of Summer), 1958;* Zaduszki (All Souls' Eve), 1961;* Salto (The Somersault), 1965;* Jak Daleko Stad, Jak Blisko (How Far from Here, How Near), 1972;* and Dolina Issy (Issa Valley), 1982.* His screenwriting contributions include scripts for Lenartowicz's Zimowy Zmierzch (Winter Dusk), 1957;* Kawalerowicz's Matka Joanna od Aniołów (Mother Joan of the Angels), 1961,* and Faraon (The Pharaoh), 1966;* Morgenstern's Jowita (based on Dygat's novel Disneyland), 1967;* Kawalerowicz's Austeria (The Inn), 1983;* and Wajda's Kronika Wypadków Miłosnych (A Chronicle of Amorous Accidents), 1986.*

KOWALSKI, WŁADYSŁAW (1936–), actor. With a long and diverse career, Kowalski has worked with many leading directors, including Has in Rozstanie (The Separation), 1961,* and Zoto (Gold), 1962;* Wajda in Samson, 1961;* Żebrowski in Szpital Przemienienia (The Hospital of the Transfiguration), 1979;* and W Biały Dzień (In Broad Daylight), 1981;* Sass in Bez Miłóśći (Without Love) 1980;* and Waldemar Dziki in Kartka z Podrozy (A Postcard from a Trip), 1982.

KRÓLIKIEWICZ, GRZEGORZ (1939–), director, screenwriter. A major avant-garde director, Królikiewicz has written and directed Na Wylot (Through and Through), 1973;* Klejnot Wolnego Sumienia (A Gem of Free Conscience), 1983;* and Zabicie Ciotki (The Killing of the Aunt), 1986.*

KUTZ, KAZIMIERZ (1929–), director, screenwriter. Beginning as an assistant to Wajda, Kawalerowicz, and Passendorfer, Kutz has developed into an original and inventive director whose films include Krzyż Walecznych (Cross of Valor), 1959;* Ludzie z Pociąqu (People on a Train), 1961;* Sól Ziemi Czarnej (Salt of the Black Earth), 1970;* Perła w Koronie (The Pearl in the Crown), 1972;* and Paciorki Jednego Różańca (Beads of the Same Rosary), 1979.

ŁAPICKI, ANDRZEJ (1924–), actor. One of the greatest Polish film stars, Łapicki's career has spanned more than forty years, starting with small parts in Buczkowski's Zakazane Piosenki (Forbidden Songs), 1947/1948, and Zarzycki's Miasto Nieujarzmionel (Unvanquished City), 1950,* continuing in films of many leading directors: Passendorfer's Powrot (The Return), 1960; Rybkowski's Dziś w Nocy Umrze Miasto (A Town Will Die Tonight), 1961;* Konwicki's Salto (The Somersault), 1965;* Batory's Lekarstwo na Miłośc (A Medicine for Love), 1966;

Has' *Lalka* (*The Doll*), 1968;* Wajda's *Wszystko na Sprzedaz* (*Everything for Sale*), 1969;* Konwicki's *Jak Daleko Stad, Jak Blisko* (*How Far from Here, How Near*), 1972;* Wajda's *Panny z Wilka* (*The Maids of Wilko*), 1979;* and Sass's *Debiutantka* (*The Debutante*), 1981.*

LENARTOWICZ, STANISŁAW (1921–), director, screenwriter. Lenartowicz's long career began with his segment "Nowela Kolarska" ("The Cyclist's Story") in *Trzy Starty* (*Three Starts*), 1955;* (*Spotkania Encounters*), 1957;* *Zimowy Zmierzch* (*Winter Dusk*), 1957;* *Cała Naprzód* (*Full Ahead*), 1967;* *Pigulki dla Aurelii* (*Pills for Aurelia*), 1958;* and *Opetanię* (*Obsession*), 1973.*

LIPMAN, JERZY (1922–1983), cinematographer. Making significant contributions to the Polish Film School before emigrating to Germany in 1969, Lipman worked with many leading directors: Wajda on *Pokolenie* (*Generation*), 1955;* *Kanał*, 1956;* *Lotna*, 1959;* *Popioły* (*Ashes*), 1965;* Kawalerowicz on *Cén* (*A Shadow*), 1956;* and *Prawdziwy Koniec Wielkiej Wojny* (*The True End of the Great War*), 1957;* Passendorfer on *Zamach* (*The Answer to Violence*), 1959;* Ford on *Ósmy Dzień Tygodnia* (*The Eighth Day of the Week*), 1958/1983;* Polanski on *Nóż w Wodzie* (*Knife in the Water*), 1962;* and Hoffman on *Pan Wołodyjowski* (*Colonel Wolodyjowski*), 1969.*

ŁOMNICKI, TADEUSZ (1927–), actor. In a long and varied career, Łomnicki has played in films by many leading directors: Ford's *Piątka z Ulicy Barskiej* (*Five Boys from Barska Street*), 1954;* Wajda's *Pokolenie* (*Generation*), 1955;* *Niewinni Czarodzieje* (*Innocent Sorcerers*), 1960;* and *Kronika Wypadków Miłosnych* (*A Chronicle of Amorous Accidents*), 1986;* Munk's *Eroica*, 1958;* Ford's *Pierwszy Dzień Wolnosci* (*The First Day of Freedom*), 1965;* Skolimowski's *Bariera* (*The Barrier*), 1966;* and *Ręce do Gory* (*Hands Up!*), 1967/1985;* Hoffman's *Pan Wołodyjowski* (*Colonel Wolodyjowski*), 1969;* and Zanussi's *Kontrakt* (*The Contract*), 1980.*

LUKASZEWICZ, OLGIERD (1946–), actor. Rising to fame with a lead in Kutz's *Sól Ziemi Czarnej* (*Salt of the Black Earth*), 1970,* and Wajda's *Brzezina* (*Birchwood*), 1970,* Lukaszewicz has continued to expand his career, working further with Kutz in *Perła w koronie* (*The Pearl in the Crown*), 1972;* with Wajda in *Weselel* (*The Wedding*), 1973;* with Majewski in *Lekcja Martwego Jezyke* (*A Lesson of Dead Language*), 1979;* and with Konwicki in *Dolina Issa* (*Issa Valley*), 1983.*

MACHULSKI, JULIUSZ (1955–), director. One of the rising young filmmakers, Machulski has achieved critical and popular success with *Vabank* 1982;* *Vabank II*, 1982;* and *Seksmisja* (*Sex Mission*), 1984.*

MAJEWSKI, JANUSZ (1931–   ), director, screenwriter. President of Polish Filmmakers' Association from 1983, Majewski has made many excellent literary adaptations, including *Sublokator (The Lodger)*, 1966;* *Zbrodniarz, Który Ukradł Zbrodnię (The Criminal Who Stole His Crime)*, 1969;* *Lekcja Martwego Jezyka (A Lesson of Dead Language)*, 1979;* and *Epitafium dla Barbary Radziwiłłowny (The Epitaph for Barbara Radziwill)*, 1983.*

MATYJASZKIEWICZ, STEFAN (1927–   ), cinematographer. Matyjaszkiewicz established his career working with Has on *Wspólny Pokój (The Common Room)*, 1960;* *Rozstanie (The Separation)*, 1960;* *Złoto (Gold)*, 1962;* *Jak Być Kochana (How to Be Loved)*, 1963;* *Lalka (The Doll)*, 1968*—as well as with Zanussi on *Struktura Kryształu (The Crystal Structure)*, 1969;* and Jakubowska on *Biały Mazur (The Mazurka Danced at Dawn)*, 1979.*

MICHAŁEK, BOLESŁAW (1925–   ), screenwriter, film critic. As a film critic since 1953, as editor of the weekly *Film* from 1961 to 1973, as president of the Polish Film Critics Union, as president of the International Film Critics Union from 1966 to 1970, and as literary manager of "X" film unit from 1973 to 1983 Michałek has played an important role in Polish filmmaking and done much to increase Western knowledge of it through his books and reviews; he contributed to scripts for Kawalerowicz's *Smierc Prezydenta (Death of the President)*, 1979,* and *Spotkanie na Atlantyku (A Meeting on the Atlantic)*, 1980, and for Wajda's *Danton*, 1983.*

MORGENSTERN, JANUSZ (1922–   ), director, screenwriter. Beginning as an assistant to Wajda, he has created a series of films of intelligent war reminiscences, highlighted by *Do Widzenia, Do Jutra (Farewell, Till Tomorrow)*, 1960;* *Jowita*, 1967;* *Trzeba Zabić Te Miłość (This Love Must Die)*, 1972; and *Życie Raz Jeszcze (Life Once Again)*, 1965/1986.*

MUNK, ANDRZEJ (1921–1961), director. His tragically early death cut short a great career, but he was a vital figure in the Polish Film School and left five major films: *Błekitny Krzyż (The Blue Cross)*, 1955;* *Człowiek na Torze (The Man on the Track)*, 1957;* *Eroica*, 1958;* *Zezowate Szczęście (Cockeyed Luck)*, 1960;* and *Pasażerka (The Passenger)*, 1961–1963.*

NOWICKI, JAN (1930–   ), actor. A major star of the 1970s and 1980s, he has developed an international career, especially in Hungarian films: leads in Wajda's *Popioły (Ashes)*, 1965,* Skolimowski's *Bariera (The Barrier)*, 1966;* Hoffman's *Pan Wołodyjowski (Colonel Wolodyjowski)*, 1969;* Zanussi's *Życie Rodzinne (Family Life)*, 1971;* Załuski's *Anatomia Miłości (The Anatomy of Love)*, 1972;* Has's *Sanatorium pod Klepsydra (The Sanatorium Under the Sign of the Hourglass)*, 1973;* and Zanussi's *Spirala (A Spiral)*, 1978.*

OLBRYCHSKI, DANIEL (1945–), actor. A Polish and international star, Olbrychski took on the mantle of Cybulski, making his mark in Wajda's films: *Popioły* (*Ashes*), 1965;* *Wszystko na Sprzedaz* (*Everything for Sale*), 1969;* *Polowanie na Muchy* (*Hunting Flies*), 1969;* *Brzezina* (*Birchwood*), 1970;* *Krajobraz po Bitwie* (*The Landscape after Battle*), 1970;* and *Panny z Wilka* (*The Maids of Wilko*), 1979.* But he has worked with many other major directors: Morgenstern in *Potem Nastapi Cisza* (*And The Silence Will Follow*), 1966;* and *Jowita*, 1967;* Zanussi in *Struktura Kryształu* (*The Crystal Structure*), 1969,* and *Życie Rodzinne* (*Family Life*), 1971;* and Hoffman in *Potop* (*The Deluge*), 1974.* Internationally, he has had important roles in such films as Volker Schlöndorff's *Die Blechtrommel* (*The Tin Drum*), 1980, and Joseph Losey's *La Truite* (*The Trout*), 1982.

PASSENDORFER, JERZY (1923–), director. Showing an interest in war and action stories, Passendorfer has made films that include *Zamach* (*The Answer to Violence*), 1959;* *Powrot* (*The Return*), 1960; *Barwy Walki* (*Colors of Struggle*), 1965; *Kierunek Berlin* (*Direction: Berlin*), 1968; *Ostatnie Dni* (*Last Days*), 1968; and *Akcja "Brutus"* (*Operation "Brutus"*), 1971.*

PETELSKA, EWA (1920–) AND CZESLAW PETELSKI (1922–), directors, administrators. They have had long directing careers as a husband-and-wife team, writing and directing such popular, basically establishment films as *Baza Ludzi Umarlych* (*The Deport of the Dead*), 1958, and *Ogniomistrz Kalen* (*Sergeant Kelen*), 1961.

PETRYCKI, JACEK (1948–), cinematographer. A politically conscious filmmaker, Petrycki was an integral part of the Cinema of Moral Anxiety of the 1970s, making many films with Holland, including *Aktorzy Prowincjonalni* (*The Provincial Actors*), 1979,* and with Kieślowski, including *Amator* (*Camera-Buff*), 1979,* and *Bez Końca* (*Without End*), 1984.*

PIECZKA, FRANCISZEK (1928–), actor. After having secondary roles in major films in the 1960s, in Kawalerowicz's *Matka Joanna od Aniołów* (*Mother Joan of the Angels*), 1961,* and Has' *Rękopis Znaleziony w Saragossie* (*The Manuscript Found in Saragossa*), 1965,* Pieczka broke into leads with Kluba's *Chudy i Inni* (*Skinny and Others*), 1967,* and Leszczyński's *Żywot Mateusza* (*The Life of Matthew*), 1968.* A few of his many successful roles have been in Kluba's *Słońce Wschodzi Raz na Dzień* (*The Sun Rises Once a Day*), 1967/1973;* Kutz's *Perła w Koronie* (*The Pearl in the Crown*), 1972;* Kieślowski's *Blizna* (*A Scar*), 1976;* Kawalerowicz's *Austeria* (*The Inn*), 1983;* and Zaorski's *Matka Królów* (*The Mother of the Krol Family*), 1982/1986.*

POLAŃSKI, ROMAN (1935–), director, screenwriter, actor. A major force in international cinema, most of his work has been abroad, apart from the short

Dwaj Ludzie z Szafą (Two Men and a Wardrobe), 1957, and *Nóż w Wodzie (Knife in the Water)*, 1962.* As an actor he appeared in Ewa Petelska's contribution to *Trzy Opowiesci (Three Stories)*, 1953; in Wajda's *Pokolenie (Generation)*, 1955;* and *Niewinni Czarodzieje (Innocent Sorcerers)*, 1960;* Morgenstern's *Do Widzenia, Do Jutra (Farewell, Till Tomorrow)*, 1960;* and Munks's *Zezowate Szczęście (Cockeyed Luck)*, 1960.*

PSZONIAK, WOJCIECH (1942–), actor. Major Wajda roles brought Pszoniak an international reputation; he emigrated to France in 1981. He played a lead in Wajda's German TV film *Pilatus und Andere—Ein Film for Karfreitag (Pilate and Others—A Film for Good Friday)*, 1972; in his *Wesele (The Wedding)*, 1973;* in *Ziemia Obiecana (The Promised Land)*, 1976;* in his Anglo-Polish production *Smuga Cienia (The Shadow Line)*, 1976;* and especially *Danton*, 1983.* He also appeared in films by Rybkowski, Sass, Jerzy Gruza, Zebrowski, and Kawalerowicz.

RADZIWILOWICZ, JERZY (1950–), actor. Catapulted to fame by important Wajda roles, he has starred in Wajda's *Człowiek z Marmuru (Man of Marble)*, 1977;* *Bez Znieczulenia (Without Anesthesia)*, 1978;* and *Człowiek z Zelaza (Man of Iron)*, 1981.*

RÓŻEWICZ, STANISŁAW (1924–), director and screenwriter. Noted for films that subtly examine moral and social problems, often written in conjunction with his brother, Tadeusz (1921–), a major poet, playwright, and screenwriter himself, Różewicz has been directing films since the early 1950s, including *Wolne Miasto (The Open Town)*, 1958;* *Głos z Tamtego Świata (A Voice from the Next World)*, 1962;* *Westerplatte* (his most famous film), 1967;* and *Kobieta w Kapeluscu (The Woman in a Hat)*, 1984.

RYBKOWSKI, JAN (1912–), director, screenwriter. With a long career behind him, Rybkowski has written and directed many comedies, melodramas, and literary classics, including *Warszawska Premiera (Warsaw Premiere)*, 1951;* *Pierwsze Dni (First Days)*, 1951; *Autobus Odjezdza 6.20 (The Bus Is Leaving at 6.20 A.M.)*, 1945; *Godziny Nadziei (Hours of Hope)*, 1955;* *Dziś w Nocy Umrze Miasto (A Town Will Die Tonight)*, 1961;* *Naprawde Wczoraj (Yesterday Indeed)*, 1964;* *Album Polski (The Polish Sketch-Book)*, 1970;* and *Granica (The Boundary)*, 1978.*

SASS, BARBARA (1936–), director, screenwriter. In the past decade, Sass has brought an articulate and powerful feminist voice to Polish cinema in *Bez Miłośći (Without Love)*, 1980;* *Debiutantka (The Debutante)*, 1982;* *Krzyk (The Scream)*, 1983;* and *Dziewczęta z Nowolipek, Rajska Jablon (The Girls from Nowolipki Street, The Apple Tree of Paradise)*, 1986.*

ŚCIBOR-RYLSKI, ALEKSANDER (1928–1983), writer, screenwriter. Ścibor-Rylski: transformed his own stories and novels into scripts for successful films, but he is best remembered for his work with Wajda on *Popioły* (*Ashes*), 1965;* *Lalka* (*The Doll*), 1968;* *Człowiek z Marmuru* (*Man of Marble*), 1977;* and *Człowiek z Zelaza* (*Man of Iron*), 1981.*

SEWERYN, ANDRZEJ (1946–), actor. Becoming one of the most successful Polish actors during the late 1970s before he emigrated to France in 1982, Seweryn appeared in films of various directors: Rybkowski's *Album Polski* (*The Polish Sketch-Book*), 1970;* Wajda's *Ziemia Obiecana* (*The Promised Land*), 1976;* Rybkowski's *Granica* (*The Boundary*), 1978;* Wajda's *Dyrygent* (*The Conductor*), 1980;* and *Człowiek z Zelaza* (*Man of Iron*), 1981.*

SIENKIEWICZ, HENRYK (1846–1916), novelist. Although not directly connected with Polish cinema, this most popular of all Polish novelists wrote works that have provided the basis for some of the most popular Polish films: for Bohdziewicz's *Szkice Weglem* (*Sketches in Charcoal*), 1957; for Hoffman's two extraordinarily popular films *Pan Wołodyjowski* (*Colonel Wolodyjowski*), 1969,* and *Potop* (*The Deluge*), 1974;* for Ford's *Krzyżacy* (*The Teutonic Knights*), 1960;* and for Rybkowski's *Rodzina Polanieckich* (*The Polaniecki Family*), 1978.

SKOLIMOWSKI, JERZY (1938–), director, screenwriter, actor. Making his mark with *Rysopis* (*Identification Marks: None*), 1964,* Skolimowski, before moving to England in 1970, made an impressive contribution to Polish cinema with *Walkower* (*Walkover*), 1965;* *Bariera* (*The Barrier*), 1966;* and *Reçe do Gory* (*Hands Up!*), 1967/1985.* His English film *Moonlighting*, 1982, indirectly casts light on the Solidarity movement. As an actor he has appeared in Wajda's *Niewinni Czarodzieje* (*Innocent Sorcerers*), 1960;* in Rybkowski's *Sposob Bycia* (*A Manner of Behaving*), 1966;* in his own *Rysopis*, *Walkover*, and *Ręce do Gory*, as well as in the American *White Nights* (1985). As a screenwriter he worked on Wajda's *Innocent Sorcerers* and Polański's *Knife in the Water*, 1962.*

SŁASKA, ALEKSANDRA (1925–), actress. As one of the greatest actresses of the 1950s and 1960s, Słaska won success in Jakubowska's *Ostatni Etap* (*The Last Stage*), 1948;* Rybkowski's *Dom na Pustkowiu* (*A Home in the Wilderness*), 1950;* Ford's *Młodość Chopina* (*The Young Chopin*), 1952,* and *Piątka z Ulicy Barskiej* (*Five Boys from Barska Street*), 1954;* Has' *Pętla* (*The Noose*), 1958;* and Munk's *Pasażerka* (*The Passenger*), 1961/1963.*

ŚLESICKI, WLADYSŁAW (1927–), director, screenwriter. Ślesicki is well known for a few very successful films, including *Ruchome Piaski* (*Moving Sands*), 1969, and especially *W Pustyni i w Puszczy* (*In the Desert and in a Wilderness*), 1973,* an immsensely popular version of a Sienkiewicz classic.

STARSKI, LUDWIK (1903-1984), screenwriter, writer. Having begun his career in the small pre-war commercial film industry, Starski successfully made the transition to the state industry with Buczkowski's *Zakazane Piosenki (Forbidden Songs)*, 1974;* *Skarb (A Treasure)*, 1948; and Ford's *Ulica Graniczna (Border Street)*, 1949,* going on to work on Buczkowski's *Pierwszy Start (The First Take Off)*, 1951,* and *Przygoda na Mariensztacie (Adventure in Mariensztat)*, 1954;* Rybkowski's *Nikodem Dyzma*, 1956; and concluding his career with Rzeszewski and Jahoda's *Hallo, Szpicbrodka, Czyli Ostatni Wystep Krola Kasiarzy (Hello, Pointed-Beard, or the Last Performance of Yeggs King)*, 1978.*

STAWIŃSKI, JERZY STEFAN (1921–), director, screenwriter, novelist. Recognized mainly as a screenwriter, Stawiński has written scripts for some of the most significant directors, many based on his own novels and stories: Wajda's *Kanal*, 1957;* Munk's *Człowiek na Torze (The Man on the Track)*, 1957,* *Eroica*, 1958,* and *Zezowate Szczęście (Cockeyed Luck)*, 1960;* Passendorfer's *Zamach (The Answer to Violence)*, 1959;* and Ford's Krzyżacy *(Teutonic Knights,)* 1960,* based on a Sienkiewicz novel.

STUHR, JERZY (1947–), actor. Among the very finest Polish actors, Stuhr has appeared in many of the greatest films since the mid–1970s: Kieślowski's *Blizna (A Scar)*, 1976;* Falk's *Wodzirej (The Dance Leader)*, 1978,* and his *Szansa (A Chance)*, 1980;* Holland's *Aktorzy Prowincjonalni (Provincial Actors)*, 1979;* Wajda's *Bez Znieczulenia (Without Anesthesia)*, 1978;* and Machulski's popular comedy *Seksmisja (Sex Mission)*, 1984.*

SZULKIN, PIOTR (1950–), director, screenwriter. An inventive, pessimistic visionary, Szulkin has made *Golem*, 1980;* *Wojna Światów—Nastepne Stulecie (The War of the Worlds—The Next Century)*, 1979; *O-bi, O-ba, Koniec Cywilizacji (. . . The End of Civilization)*, 1985;* and *Ga, Ga, Chwala Bohaterom (Ga, Ga, Glory to Heroes!)*, 1986.*

TYSZKIEWICZ, BEATA (1938–), actress. As Poland's most popular film star of the 1960s and as Wajda's wife, Tyszkiewicz developed a great national and international career, starring in Wajda's *Popioły (Ashes)*, 1965,* and *Wszystko na Sprzedaz (Everything for Sale)*, 1969,* as well as in Rybkowski's *Dziś w Nocy Umrze Miasto (A Town Will Die Tonight)*, 1961,* and *Naprawdę Wczoraj (Yesterday Indeed)*, 1964;* Konwicki's *Zaduszki (All Souls' Eve)* 1961;* and Ford's *Pierwszy Dzień Wolnosci (The First Day of Freedom)*, 1964.*

VOIT, MIECZYSLAW (1928–), actor. Voit has appeared in a large number of films, making his mark with the double lead in Kawalerowicz's *Matka Joanna od Aniołów (Mother Joan of the Angels)*, 1961,* then appearing in such films as Konwicki's *Zaduszki (All Souls' Eve)*, 1961;* Kawalerowicz's *Faraon (The*

Pharaoh), 1966;* Wajda's *Wesele (The Wedding)*, 1973;* Has' *Sanatorium pod Klepsydra (The Sanatorium Under the Sign of the Hourglass)*, 1973;* Hoffman's *Potop (The Deluge)*, 1974;* and Bajon's *Wizja Lokalna—1901 (The Visit to the Scene of the Crime—1901)*, 1980.*

WAJDA, ANDRZEJ (1926–), director, screenwriter. The most renowned of all Polish directors, with many major films to his credit, Wajda debuted in 1955 with *Pokolenie (Generation)*,* and nearly thirty films have followed, many recognized masterpieces: *Kanał*, 1957;* *Popioł i Diament (Ashes and Diamonds)*, 1958;* *Lotna*, 1959;* *Niewinni Czarodzieje (Innocent Sorcerers)*, 1960;* *Popioły (Ashes)*, 1965;* *Wszystko na Sprzedaz (Everything for Sale)*, 1969;* *Polowanie na Muchy (Hunting Flies)*, 1969;* *Krajobraz po Bitwie (Landscape after Battle)*, 1970;* *Brzezina (Birchwood)*, 1970;* *Wesele (The Wedding)*, 1973;* *Ziemia Obiecana (The Promised Land)*, 1976;* *Smuga Cienia (The Shadow Line)*, 1976;* *Człowiek z Marmuru (Man of Marble)*, 1977;* *Bez Znieczulenia (Without Anesthesia)*, 1978;* *Panny z Wilka (The Maids of Wilko)*, 1979;* *Dyrygent (The Conductor)*, 1980;* *Człowiek z Zelaza (Man of Iron)*, 1981;* *Danton*, 1983;* and *Kronika Wypadków Miłosnych (A Chronicle of Amorous Accidents)*, 1986.*

WILHELMI, ROMAN (1936–), actor. Becoming a star in the mid–1970s with leads in Borowczyk's *Dzieje Grzechu (The Story of Sin)*, 1975,* and Majewski's *Zaklete Rewiry—Dvoi Svĕt Hotelu Pacifik (The Enchanted Stations)*, 1975,* he has played many major roles during the past decade in Wajda's *Bez Znieczulenia (Without Anesthesia)*, 1978;* Bajon's *Aria Dla Atlety (Aria for an Athlete)*, 1979;* Szulkin's *Wojna Swiatow—Nastepne Stulecie (The War of the Worlds)*, 1981; and Batory's *Zapach Psiej Siersci (The Smell of a Dog's Coat)*, 1981.

WINNICKA, LUCYNA (1933–), actress. Winnicka first achieved acclaim in Kawalerowicz's (her husband's) films: *Pod Gwiazdą Frygijska (Under the Phrygian Star)*, 1954;* *Prawdziwy Koniec Wielkiej Wojny (The True End of the Great War)*, 1957;* and most memorably, *Matka Joanna od Aniołów (Mother Joan of the Angels)*, 1961;* her film career continued into the mid–1970s, when a career change brought her retirement from the screen.

WOHL, STANISŁAW (1912–1985), director, screenwriter, cinematographer. The premier post-war cinematographer, Wohl had a strong influence on many young directors; his contributions include Cekalski's *Jasne Łany (Bright Fields)*, 1947;* Rybkowski's *Dom na Pustkowiu (A Home in the Wilderness)*, 1950;* and three Jakubowska films: *Zołnierz Zwycięstwa (Soldier of Victory)*, 1953;* *Opowieść Atlantycka (The Atlantic Story)*, 1955;* and *Krol Macius I (King Matt the First)*, 1958.*

WÓJCIK, JERZY (1930–), cinematographer. As a prominent member of the Polish Film School he has worked on Munk's *Eroica*, 1958;* Wajda's *Popioł i*

Diament (Ashes and Diamonds), 1958,* and *Samson*, 1961;* Kawalerowicz's *Matka Joanna od Aniołów (Mother Joan of the Angels)*, 1961,* and *Faraon (The Pharaoh)*, 1966;* Morgenstern's *Życie Raz Jeszcze (Life Once Again)*, 1965,* and *Potem Nastapi Cisza (And The Silence Will Follow)*, 1966;* Różewicz's *Westerplatte*, 1967;* and Hoffman's *Potop (The Deluge)*, 1974.*

ZANUSSI, KRZYSZTOF (1939-   ), director, screenwriter, writer. Active on the international scene and one of the most profoundly creative of contemporary directors, Zanussi has brought moral, psychological, and philosophical depth to his films: *Struktura Kryształu (The Crystal Structure)*, 1969;* *Życie Rodzinne (Family Life)*, 1971;* *Iluminacja (The Illumination)*, 1973;* *Barwy Ochronne (Camouflage)*, 1977;* *Spirala (A Spiral)*, 1978;* *Constans (The Constant Factor)*, 1980;* *Kontrakt (The Contract)*, 1980;* and *Rok Spokojnego Słońca (The Year of the Quiet Sun)*, 1985.*

ZAORSKI, JANUSZ (1947-   ), director, screenwriter. A major and controversial younger director, Zaorski's films include *Partita na Instrument Drewniany (Partita for a Wooden Instrument)*, 1976;* *Pokój z Widokiem na Morze (The Room Overlooking the Sea)*, 1978;* *Baryton (The Baritone)*, 1985;* and *Matka Królów (The Mother of the Krol Family)*, 1982/1986.*

ZAPASIEWICZ, ZBIGNIEW (1934-   ), actor. Zapasiewicz has had a major film career for decades, beginning in the mid-1960s, working with Lomnicki, Batory, Skolimowski, Rybkowski, appearing in key Zanussi films, especially *Barwy Ochronne (Camouflage)*, 1977,* in Różewicz's *Pasja (A Passion)*, 1978;* in Wajda's *Bez Znieczulenia (Without Anesthesia)*, 1978,* in Zaorski's *Makta Królów (The Mother of the Krol Family)*, 1982/1986,* and *Baryton (The Baritone)*, 1985.*

ZAWADZKA, MAGDALENA (1944-   ), actress. Becoming a popular success in the late 1960s, Zawadzka has created some major parts in Passendorfer's *Mocne Uderzenie (The Big Beat)*, 1967; Majewski's *Sublokator (The Lodger)*, 1966;* Holoubek's *Mazepa*, 1975; and above all in Hoffman's *Pan Wołodyjowski (Colonel Wolodyjowski)*, 1969.*

ZEBROWSKI, EDWARD (1935-   ), director, screenwriter. Associated with scripts for Zanussi's TV films, Zebrowski has also directed several major films: *Ocalenie (The Salvation)*, 1972;* *Szpital Przemienienia (The Hospital of the Transfiguration)*, 1979;* and *W Biały Dzień (In Broad Daylight)*, 1981.*

ŻUŁAWSKI, ANDRZEJ (1940-   ), director, screenwriter. Beginning his career as Wajda's assistant on *Samson*, 1961,* Żuławski has spent much of his career in France, being too controversial an artist to survive in the Poland of recent history. His debut film, *Trzecia Część Nocy (The Third Part of Night)*,

1972,* was released, but *Diabeł* (*The Devil*), 1972, has not yet been released, and *Na Srebrynym Globie* (*On The Silver Globe*), begun in 1972, was released only in 1987.

ZYGADŁO, TOMASZ (1947-), director, screenwriter. Recognized as a major maker of documentary films, Zygadło has made some of the important recent feature films: *Rebus* (*Puzzle*), 1977;* *Cma* (*A Moth*), 1980;* and *Sceny Dzieciece z Życia Prowincji* (*Childhood Scenes from Provincial Life*), 1986.*

SELECTED FILMOGRAPHY

1947

Jasne Łany (Bright Fields). d. Eugeniusz Cękalski; sw. Krystyna Swinarska & Cękalski; c. Wohl* & Seweryn Kruszyński; with Hanna Bielicka, Jan Kurnakowicz, Kazimierz Dejmek, Łapicki,* Feliks Żukowski. "Film Polski." 112 m.

Zakazane Piosenki (Forbidden Songs). d. Buczkowski;* sw. Starski;* c. Adolf Forbert & Karol Chodura; with Danuta Szaflarska, Jerzy Duszyński, Janina Ordężanka, Jan Świderski, Jan Kurnakowicz, & Stanisław Łapiński. "Film Polski" 110 m.

1948

Ostatni Etap (The Last Stage). d. Jakubowska;* sw. Jakubowska & Gerda Schneider; c. Borys Monastyrski; with Barbara Drapińska, Alina Janowska, Zofia Mrozowska, & Śląska,* "Film Polski," 127 m.

1949

Ulica Graniczna. (Border Street), d. Ford;* sw. Jan Fethke, Ford, Starski;* c. Jaroslav Tuzar; with Maria Broniewska, Mieczysława Ćwiklińska, Władysław Godik, Jerzy Leszczyński, Władysław Walter, & Tadeusz Fijewski. "Film Polski." 125 m.

1950

Dom na Pustkowiu (A Home in the Wilderness). d. Rybkowski;* sw. Jarosław Iwaszkiewicz; c. Wohl;* with Śląska.* & Jerzy Śliwiński. WFF, Lodz. 91 m.

Miasto Nieujarzmione (Unvanquished City). d. Jerzy Zarzycki; sw. Andrezejewski* & Zarzycki; c. Jean Isnard; with Jan Kurnakowicz & Zofia Mrozowska. WFF, Lodz. 95 m.

1951

Pierwszy Start (The First Take Off). d. Buczkowski;* sw. Starski;* c. Seweryn Kruszyński; with Leopold Nowak, Jadwiga Chojnacka, Adam Mikołajewski, Jerzy Pietraszkiewicz, Władysław Woźniak, Bohdan Niewinowski, & Stanislaw Mikulski. WFF, Lodz. 112 m.

Warszawska Premiera (*Warsaw Premiż*). d. Rybkowski;* sw. Różewicz*, Rybkowski,* Jerzy Waldorff; c. Andrzej Ancuta; with Jan Koecher, Barbara Kostrzewska, Jerzy Duszyński, Danuta Szaflarska, Jan Kurnakowicz, & Stanislaw Żeleński. WFF, Lodz. 111 m.

1952

Gromada (*A Community*). d. Kawalerowicz;* sw. Kawalerowicz & Kazimierz Sumerski; c. Andrzej Ancuta; with Barbara Jakubowska, Ludwig Benoit, & Barbara Rachwalska; WFF, Lodz. 105 m.

Młodość Chopina (*The Young Chopin*). d. & sw. Ford;* c. Jaroslaw Tuzar; with Czeslaw Wołejko, Śląska,* & Jan Kurnakowicz. WFF, Lodz. 138 m.

1953

Sprawa Do Załatwienia (*A Matter To Settle*). d. Rybkowski;* sw. Stefania Grodzieńska, Zdzisław Gozdawa, & Waclaw Stępień; c. Adolf Forbert & Bogusław Lambach; with Adolf Dymsza (in 8 roles), Gizela Piotrowska, & Bohdan Niewinowski. WFF, Lodz. 97 m.

Zołnierz Zwycięstwa (*Soldier of Victory*). Pt. I "Lata walki" ("Years of Struggle"); Pt. II "Zwycięstwo" ("Victory"). d. & sw. Jakubowska;* c. Wohl;* with Jozef Wyszomirski, Barbara Drapińska, Tadeusz Schmidt, Krystyna Kamieńska, Tadeusz Janczar, Jacek Woszczerowicz (as Lenin), Kazimierz Wilamowski (as Stalin), Holoubek* (as Dzierżyński), Jerzy Kozłowski (as Bierut), Rafał Kajetanowicz (as Rokossowski), & Wladysław Hancza. WFF, Lodz. 100 & 116 m.

1954

Autobus Odjeżdża 6.20 (*The Bus Leaves at 6.20*). d. & sw. Rybkowski;* m. Stanislaw Skrowaczewski; c. Wohl;* with Śląska,* Jerzy Duszyński, Hanna Bielicka, Jan Ciecierski, Barbara Drapińska, Edward Dziewoński, Irena Netto. WFF, Lodz. 106 m.

Celuloza (*A Night of Rememberance*). d. Kawalerowicz;* sw. Kawalerowicz & Igor Newerly (from his novel *Pamiatka z Celulozy);* c. Seweryn Kruszyński; with Józef Nowak, Stanisław Milski, Zbigniew Skowroński, Jerzy Szpunar, Janusz Ściwiarski, Teresa Szmigielówna, Wojciech Pilarski, Tadeusz Kondrat, Halina Przybylska, Bronisław Pawlik, Hanna Bielicka, & Leon Niemczyk. WFF, Lodz. 124 m.

Piątka z Ulicy Barskiej (*Five Boys from Barska Street*). d. & sw. Ford* (Wajda* one of the assistant directors); c. Jaroslaw Tuzar & Karol Chodura; with Śląska*, Tadeusz Janczar, Łomnicki*, Marian Rulka, Miecysław Stoor, Andrzej Kozak, Jerzy Szpunar, Ewa Krasnodębska, Zofia Malynicz, Hanna Skarżanka, Ludwik Benoit, & Stanislaw Łapiński. WFF, Lodz. 124 m.

Pod Gwiazdą Frygijska (*Under the Phrygian Star*). Pt. II of *A Night of Remembrance*. d. Kawalerowicz;* sw. Newerly & Kawalerowicz; c. Seweryn Knuszyński; m. Stanisław Skrowaczewski; with Winnicka,* Józef Nowak, Stanisław Milski, Halina Przybylska, Jerzy Szpunar, Zofia Perczynska, Józef Gliński, Bronisław Pawlik, Janusz Jaron, Tadeusz Kondrat, & Aleksander Sewruk. WFF Lodz. 122m.

Przygoda na Mariensztacie (Adventure in Mariensztat). d. Buczkowski;* sw. Starski;* c. Seweryn Kruszyński & Franciszek Fuchs; with Lidia Korsakówna, Tadeusz Schmidt, Adam Mikolajewski, Tadeusz Kondrat, Stanisław Winczewski, Barbara Rachwalska, Wanda Bojarska, & Edward Dziewoński. WFF, Lodz. 109 m.

1955

Błękitny Krzyż (The Blue Cross). d. & sw. Munk;* au. Adam Liberak; c. Sergiusz Sprudin; with Stanisław Byrcyn Gąsienica, Stanisław Wawrytko, & Stanisław Marusarz. WFD, Warsaw. 61 m.

Godziny Nadziei (Hours of Hope). d. Rybkowski;* sw. Jerzy Pomianowski (after his novel); c. Wladyslaw Forbert; with Zbigniew Józefowicz, Krystyna Kamieńska, Stanisław Mikulski, Jadwiga Chojnacka, Bronisław Pawlik, Zofia Marozowska, Bohdan Ejmont, Stanisław Milski, & Jerzy Kaliszewski. WFF, Lodz. 102 m.

Kariera (The Career). d. Jan Koecher; sw. Konwicki* & Kazimierz Sumerski; c. Kazimierz Wawrzyniak; m. Stanisław Skrowaczewski; with Jan Świderski, Lidia Korsakóvna, Tadeusz Janczar, Andrzej Hrydzewicz, Teresa Szmigielówna, Adam Mularczyk, Wanda Łuczycka, Bronislaw Dardziński, Tadeusz Woźniak, Stanisław Kwaskowski, Jerzy Pietraszkiewicz, & Bohdan Ejmont. WFF, Lodz. 77 m.

Opowieść Atlantycka (The Atlantic Story). d. Jakubowska;* sw. Mirosław Żuławski; c. Wohl;* m. Stanisław Skrowaczewski; with Damian Damięcki, Michel Bustamente, Mieczysław Stoor, Henryk Szletyński, Stanisław Kwaskowski, & Irena Netto. WFF, Lodz. 84 m.

Pokolenie (Generation). d. Wajda* (with Ford*); sw. Bohdan Czeszko; c. Lipman;* with Łomnicki,* Tadeusz Janczar, Urszula Modrzyńska, Janusz Paluszkiewicz, Ryszard Kotas, Polański,* & Cybulski.* WFF, Wrocław. 90 m.

Trzy Starty (Three Starts). sw. Leopold Tyrmand, Marian Promiński, Bohdziewicz,* Stanisław Lenartowicz, E. & C. Petelski;* Pt. I d. E. Petelska;* c. Zbigniew Czajkowski; with Elżbieta Polkowska, Zdzisław Karczewski, Ryszard Ostałowski, Kobiela,* Barbara Rachwalska, & Adam Danielewicz; pt. II d. C. Petelski;* c. Czeslaw Świrta; with Antczak,* Janusz Kłowinski, & Katarzyna Łaniewska; pt. III d. Stanislaw Lenartowicz; c. Antoni Wójtowicz; with Cybulski*, Jerzy Smyk, Adam Brodzisz, Krystyna Denisiuk, & Henryk Łoza. WFF, Lodz. 102 m.

1956

Cién (A Shadow). d. Kawalerowicz;* sw. Ścibor-Rylski;* c. Lipman;* with Zygmunt Kęstowicz, Adolf Chronicki, Emil Karewicz, Ignacy Machowski, & Tadeusz Jerasz. WFF, Lodz. 97 m.

1957

Człowiek na Torze (The Man on the Track). d. Munk;* sw. Stawiński* & Munk; with Kazimierz Opalinski, Zygmunt Maciejewski, Zygmunt Zintel, Zygmunt Listkiewicz, & Roman Kłosowski. "Kadr." 87 m.

Kanal (Canal). d. Wajda;* sw. Stawiński;* c. Lipman;* with Teresa Iżewska, Tadeusz

Janczar, Emil Karewicz, Wieńczysław Gliński, Władysław Sheybal, Tadeusz Gwiazdowski, Stanisław Mikulski, & Teresa Berezowska. "Kadr." 95 m.

Prawdziwy Koniec Wielkiej Wojny (The True End of the Great War). d. Kawalerowicz;* au. Jerzy Zawieyski; sw. Kawalerowicz & Zawieyski; c. Lipman;* with Winnicka,* Roland Głowacki, Janina Sokołowska, Andrzej Szalawski, & Olga Bielska. "Kadr." 89 m.

Spotkania (Encounters). d. & sw. Lenartowicz;* au. Makuszyński, Iwaszkiewicz, & Dygat;* c. Jahoda;* with Alicja Jankowska, Mieczyslaw Gajda, Barbara Modelska, Wienczyslaw Gliński, Kazimierz Orzechowski, Emil Karewicz, Urzula Modrzyńska, Bogusz Bilewski, Maria Kaniewska, & Tadeusz Woźniak. "Rytm." 84m.

Szkice Weglem (Chalk Sketches). d. Bohdziewicz;* au. Sienkiewicz;* sw. Buczkowski* & Ariadna Demkowska; with Barbara Walkowna, Wiesław Golas, Józef Zbigród, Stanisław Woliński, Joanna Poraska, Tadeusz Chmielewski, & Aleksander Michałowski. "Rytm." 97 m.

Zagubione Uczucia (Lost Feelings). d. Jerzy Zarzycki; au. Mortkowicz-Olczak; sw. Andrzejewski*, Julian Dziedzina; with Maria Klejdysz & Andrzej Jurczak. "Syrena." 75 m.

Zemia (The Land). d. Jerzy Zarzycki; sw. Danuta Ścibor-Rylska; c. Antoni Wójtowicz; with Janusz Strachocki, Zofia Malynicz, Jadwiga Andrzejewska, Stanisław Milski, Wacław Kowalski, Andrzej Kozak, Ryszard Wojciechowski, Zygmunt Zintel, Kazimierz Fabisiak, Mieczysław Stoor. "Syrena." 99 m.

Zimowy Zmierzch (Winter Dusk). d. Lenartowicz;* sw. Konwicki;* c. Jahoda;* with Włodzimierz Ziembiński, Maria Kierzkowa, Zugmunt Zintel, Lidia Borowczyk, Bogusz Bilewski, Maria Ciesielska, Zbigniew Stokowski, Marian Nowak, Janina Niczewska, & Tamara Paslawska. "Rytm." 94 m.

1958

Eroica. d. Munk;* sw. Stawiński*; c. Wójcik*; with (Pt. I "Scherzo alla polacca") Edward Dziewoński, Barbara Połomska, Ignacy Machowski, Leon Niemczyk, & Kazimierz Opaliński; (Pt. II "Ostinato lugubre") Kazimierz Rudzki, Mariusz Dmochowski, Roman Kłtosowski, Kobiela,* Łomnicki,* & Wojciech Siemion. "Kadr." 86 m.

Ewa Chce Spać (Eve Wants to Sleep). d. Chmielewski,* sw. Chmielewski & Andrzej Czekalski, c. Matyjaszkiewicz;* with Barbara Kwiatkowska, Stanisław Mikulski, Ludwik Benoit, Zygmunt Zintel, & Maria Kaniewska. "Syrena." 103 m.

Krol Macius I (King Mat I). d. Jakobowska;* au. Janusz Korczak; c. Wohl;* m. Stanisław Skrowaczewski; with Juliusz Wyrzykowski, Ludwik Halicz, Elżbieta Buczek, Jan Koecher, Tadeusz Białoszczyński, Janusz Jaron, Józef Kondrat, Henryk Borowski, Stanisław Kwaskowski, Szczepan Baczyński, Jan Kurnakowicz, Mieczystaw Stoor, Adam Mularczyk, & Ignacy Gogolewski. "Start." 93m.

Ostatni Dzień Lata (The Last Day of Summer). d. Konwicki* & Jan Laskowski; sw. Konwicki; c. Laskowski; with Irena Laskowska & Jan Machulski. "Kadr." 66 m.

Pętla (The Noose). d. Has; au. Marek Hłasko; sw. Hłasko & Has; c. Jahoda; with Holoubek,* Śląska,* Teresa Szmigielówna, & Tadeusz Fijewski. "Iluzjion." 104 m.

Pigulki Dla Aurelii (Pills for Aurelia). d. Lenartowicz;* sw. Ścibor-Rylski* with Jerzy

Adamczak, Andrzej Hrydzewicz, Jarosław Kuszewski, Ryszard Pietruski, Zdzisław Kuzniar, & Barbara Modelska. "Rytm." 92 m.

Popioł i Diament (Ashes and Diamonds): d. Wajda;* sw. Andrzejewski;* c. Wójcik* with Cybulski,* Ewa Krzyżewska, Wacław Zastrzeżyński, Adam Pawlikowski, Kobiela,* Jan Ciecierski, Stanislaw Milski, Zbigniew Skowroński, & Barbara Krafftówna. "Kadr." 106 m.

Pozegnania (Farewells). d. Has;* sw. Dygat;* c. Jahoda;* with Maria Wachowiak, Tadeusz Janczar, Holoubek;* Stanisław Jaworski, Stanisław Milski, Irena Netto, Jozef Pieracki, Irena Starkówna, Helena Sokołowska, & Hanna Skarżanka. "Syrena." 102 m.

Wolne Miasto (The Open City). d. Różewicz;* sw. Jan Jozef Szczepański, c. Wladyslaw Forbert, with Wlodzimierz Ziembinski, Bronisław Dardziński, Hanna Zembrzuska, Jan Machulski, Irena Netto, Adam Kwiatkowski, & Fronczewski.* "Rytm." 103 m.

1959

Krzyż Walecznych (Cross of Valor). d. Kutz;* sw. Józef Hen; c. Wójcik;* with Jerzy Turek, Aleksander Fogiel, Bronisław Pawlik, Andrzej May, Grażyna Staniszewska, Adolf Chronicki, & Cybulski.* "Kadr." 84 m.

Lotna. d. Wajda;* sw. Wojciech Zukrowski; c. Lipman;* with Jerzy Pichelski, Adam Pawlikowski, Jerzy Moes, Mieczysław Loza, & Bożena Kurowska. "Kadr." 89 m.

Ostatni Strzal (The Last Shot). d. Rybkowski;* sw. Ścibor-Rylski;* c. Bogusaw Lambach; with Stanisław Jasiukiewicz, Emil Karewicz, & Urszula Modrzynska. "Rytm." 86 m.

Pociąg (Night Train). d. Kawalerowicz;* sw. Jerzy Lutowski & Kawalerowicz; c. Jan Laskowski; with Winnicka,* Leon Niemczyk, Teresa Szmigielówna, & Cybulski.* "Kadr." 101 m.

Sygnały (Signals). d. Passendorfer;* sw. Zdzisław Skowroński; c. Kaszimierz Konrad; with Danuta Starczewska, Stanisław Mikulski, Teresa Szmigielówna, & Leon Niemczyk. "Iluzion." 88 m.

Zamach (The Answer to Violence). d. Passendorfer;* sw. Stawiński;* c. Lipman;* with Andrzej May, Bozena Kurowska, Grazyna Staniszewska, Wojciech Siemion, Łomnicki,* Roman Kłosowski, Tomasz Zaliwski, Jerzy Nasierowski, & Andrzej Kostenko. "Iluzjon." 81 m.

1960

Do Widzenia, Do Jutra (Farewell, Till Tomorrow). d. Morgenstern;* sw. Cybulski,* Kobiela,* & Wilhelm Mach; c. Jan Laskowski; with Teresa Tuszyńska, Cybulski, Grażyna Muszyńska, Barbara Baranowska, & Polański.* "Kadr." 91 m.

Krzyżacy (Teutonic Knights): d. Ford;* au. Sienkiewicz;* sw. Stawiński* & Ford; c. Jahoda;* with Andrzej Szalawski, Grażyna Staniszewska, Aleksander Fogiel, Urszula Modrzyńska, Emil Karewicz, Tadeusz Białoszczyński, Winnicka,* Stanisław Jasiukiewicz, Voit,* Henryk Borowski, Leon Niemczyk, & Mieczysław Stoor. Eastmancolor & dyaliscope. "Studio." 173 m.

Niewinni Czarodzieje (Innocent Sorcerers). d. Wajda;* sw. Andrzejewski* & Skoli-

mowski;* c. Krzysztof Winiewicz; with Krystyna Stypułkowska, Łomnicki,* Cybulski,* & Polański.* "Kadr." 86 m.
Nikt Nie Woła (No One Calling). d. Kutz;* sw. Józef Hen; c. Wójcik;* with Zofia Marcinkowska, Henryk Boukołowski, Barbara Krafftówna, Halina Mikołajska, & Aleksander Fogiel. "Kadr." 85 m.
Wspólny Pokój (The Common Room). d. & sw. Has;* c. Matyjaszkiewicz;* with Mieccczysław Gajda, Holoubek,* Adam Pawlikowski, Anna Łubienska, Tyszkiewicz,* Irena Netto, & Zdzisław Maklakiewicz. "Kamera." 92 m.
Zezowate Szczęście (Cockeyed Luck). d. Munk;* sw. Stawiński;* c. Lipman* & Krzysztof Winiewicz; with Kobiela,* Maria Ciesielska, Helena Dąbrowska, Barbara Kwiatkowska, Krystyna Karkowska, Barbara Połomska, & Irena Stalończyk. "Kamera." 115 m.

1961

Dziś w Nocy Umrze Miasto (A Town Will Die Tonight). d. Rybkowski;* sw. Leon Kruczkowski & Rybkowski; c. Bogusław Lambach; with Łapicki* & Tyszkiewicz.* "Rytm." 95 m.
Ludzie z Pociągu (People on a Train). d. Kutz;* sw. Marian Brandys & Ludwika Woznicka; au. Brandys; c. Kurt Weber; with Jerzy Block, Maciej Damięcki, Małgosia Dziedzic, Danuta Szalfarska, Andrzej May, & Aleksander Fogiel. "Kadr." 98 m.
Matka Joanna od Aniołów (Mother Joan of the Angels). d. Kawalerowicz;* sw. Konwicki* & Kawalerowicz; c. Wójcik;* with Winnicka,* Voit,* Anna Ciepielewska, Zygmunt Zintel, Kazimierz Fabisiak, & Pieczka.* "Kadr." 109 m.
Rozstanie (The Separation). d. Has;* sw. Jadwiga Żylińska; c. Matyjaskiewicz;* with Lidia Wysocka, Kowalski,* Holoubek,* Irena Netto, Adam Pawlikowski, Danuta Krawczyńska, Cybulski,* & Kobiela.* "Kamera." 78 m.
Samson. d. Wajda;* sw. Brandys* (from his novel) & Wajda; c. Wojcik;* with Serge Merlin, Alina Janowska, Jan Ciecierski, Tadeusz Bartosik, Elżbieta Kępińska, & Kowalski.* "Droga" & "Kadr." 117 m.
Zaduszki (All Souls' Eve). d. & sw. Konwicki;* c. Kurt Weber; with Ewa Krzyzewska, Edmund Fetting, Jadwiga Chojnacka, Tyszkiewicz,* Czyżewska,* Andrzej May, Voit,* Pieczka,* Ryszard Ronczewski, & Kazimierz Opaliński. "Kadr." 97 m.

1962

Dziewczyna Z Dobrego Domu (A Girl of Good Family). d. Bohdziewicz;* sw. Mieczyslaw Piotrowski; c. Stanisław Loth; with Krystyna Stypulkowska, Tadeusz Janczar, Ignacy Gogolewski, Czyżewska,* Władysław Krasnowiecki, Wanda Jaroszewska, & Jerzy Przybylski. "Droga." 96 m.
Głos z Tamtego Świata (A Voice from the Next World). d. Różewicz;* sw. Różewicz & Kornel Filipowicz; c. Władysław Forbert; with Kazimierz Rudzki, Wanda Łuczycka, Tatiana Czechowska, Danuta Szaflarska, Barbara Modelska, Krystyna Feldman, Maria Homerska, & Marta Lipinska. "Rytm." 116 m.
Jutro Premiera (Opening Tomorrow). d. Morgernstern;* sw. Jerzy Jurandot & Morgenstern; c. Kurt Weber; with Irena Malkiewicz, Wienczysław Gliński, Aleksander Bardini, Kalina Jędrusik, Holoubek,* Edward Dziewoński, Aleksander Dzwon-

kowski, Barbara Krafftówna, Wanda Luczycka, Wojciech Siemion, & Tadeusz Janczar. "Kadr." 90 m.

Mój Stary (My Old Man). d. Janusz Nasfeter; sw. Teresa and Janusz Nasfeter; c. Wójcik;* with Adolf Dymsza, Krystyna Lubienska, Tadeusz Wiśniewski, Wiesław Michnikowski, Tadeusz Bartosik, & Barbara Drapińska. "Studio." 73 m.

Nóż w Wodzie (Knife in the Water). d. Polański;* sw. Polański, Skolimowski,* & Jakub Goldberg; c. Lipman;* with Jolanta Umecka, Leon Niemczyk, & Zygmunt Malanowicz. "Kamera." 101 m.

Spotkanie w "Bajce" (The Meeting in the Cafe "Tale"). d. Rybkowski;* sw. Michał Tonecki & Rybkowski; c. Jahoda;* with Śląska,* Holoubek,* Łapicki,* Teresa Iżewska, Maria Wachowiak, Barbara Kościeszanka, Aleksander Fogiel, Beata Barszczewska, & Mieczysław Pawlikowski. "Rytm." 78 m.

Spóźnieni Przechodnie (Late Passers-By). d. Rybkowski;* sw. Dygat* (from his own stories); c. Jahoda:* I. "Czas przybliża, czas oddala" ("The Time Unites or Divides"): d. Holoubek;* with Kalina Jędrusik, Maria Wachowiak, Holoubek, & Wienczysław Gliński; II. "Krąg istnienia" ("The Existence Circle"): d. Łapicki;* with Tyszkiewicz,* Jerzy Jogałła, Maria Homerska, Kobiela,* Irena Netto, Wanda Łuczycka, & Aleksander Dzwonkowski; III. "Paryz" ("Paris"): d. Adam Hanuszkiewicz; with Lidia Korsakówna & Adam Hanuszkiewicz; IV. "Stary professor" ("The Old Professor"): d. Antczak;* with Kazimierz Opaliński, Zofia Kucówna, Michał Pawlicki, & Ignacy Machowski; V. "Nauczycielka" ("The Teacher"): d. Rybkowski;* with Alina Janowska, Krzysztof Chamiec, Mieczysław Pawlikowski, Łapicki,* Holoubek,* Dygat,* Tyszkiewicz,* Rybkowski, & Cybulski.* "Rytm." 94 m.

Złoto (Gold). d. Has;* sw. Bohdan Czeszko; c. Matyjaszkiewicz;* with Kowalski,* Krzysztof Chamiec, Barbara Krafftówna, Adam Pawlikowski, Tadeusz Fijewski, Aleksander Fogiel, Czyżewska,* Danuta Korolewicz, & Halina Dobrucka. "Kamera." 98 m.

1963

Ich Dzień Powszedni (Their Ordinary Days). d. & sw. Ścibor-Rylski;* c. Jan Janiszewski; with Cybulski,* Śląska,* Pola Raksa, Barbara Krafftówna, Pieczka,* Leon Niemczyk, Zbigniew Józefowicz, Zofia Kucówna, Zbigniew Koczanowicz, Brylska.* "Rytm." 97 m.

Jak Być Kochana (How to Be Loved). d. Has;* sw. Brandys;* c. Matyjaszkiewicz;* with Barbara Krafftówna, Cybulski,* Artur Młodnicki, Wienczysław Gliński, Zdzisław Maklakiewicz, & Wiesława Kwasniewska. "Kamera." 101 m.

Milczenie (Silence). d. Kutz;* sw. Jerzy Szczygieł & Kutz; c. Wiesław Zdort; with Kazimierz Fabisiak, Mirosław Kobierzycki, Czyżewska,* Maria Zbyszewska, Cybulski,* Tadeusz Kalinowski, Edward Rączkowski, & Halina Ludczewska. "Kadr." 99 m.

Pasażerka (The Passenger). d. & sw. Munk;* c. Krzysztof Winiewicz; with Śląska,* Anna Ciepielewska, Jan Kreczmar, Marek Walczewski, Irena Malkiewicz, Maria Kościałkowska, Leon Pietraszkiewicz, & Janusz Bylczyński. "Kamera." 43 m.

1964

Dwa Żebra Adama (*The Second Rib*). d. Morgenstern;* sw. Józef Hen; c. Bogusław Lambach; with Zygmunt Kęstowicz, Ewa Wawrzón, Joanna Kostusiewicz, Renata Kossobudzka, & Bohdan Ejmont. "Syrena." 86 m.

Echo (*The Echo*). d. Różewicz;* sw. Tadeusz and Stanislaw Różewicz; c. Wójcik;* with Wienczysław Gliński, Barbara Horawianka, Jacek Blawut, Stanisław Milski, Piotr Pawlowski, Ewa Wawrzoń, & Bronisław Dardziński. "Rytm." 96 m.

Gdzie Jest Generał? (*Where Is the General*)?. d. & sw. Chmielewski;* c. Jerzy Stawicki; with Czyzewska,* Jerzy Turek, Bolesław Płotnicki, Stanisław Miłski, & Wacław Kowalski. "Start." 96 m.

Giuseppe w Warszawie (*Giuseppe in Warsaw*). d. Lenartowicz;* sw. Jacek Wejroch; c. Antoni Nurzynski; with Czyżewska,* Antonio Cifariello, Cybulski,* Jarema Stępowski, Krystyna Borowicz, & Aleksander Fogiel. "Kadr." 83 m.

Koniec Naszego Świata (*The End of Our World*). d. & sw. Jakubowska;* c. Kazimierz Wawrzyniak; with Lech Skolimowski, Teresa Wicinska, & Krystyn Wójcik. "Start." 155 m.

Naganiacz (*The Beater*). d. C. & E. Petelski;* sw. Roman Bratny; c. Matyjaszkiewicz;* with Bronisław Pawlik, Maria Wachowiak, Wacław Kowalski, Ryszard Pietruski, Krystyna Borowicz, Aleksander Fogiel, & Bohdan Ejmont. "Kamera." 86 m.

Naprawdę Wczoraj (*Yesterday Indeed*). d. Rybkowski;* sw. Leopold Tyrmand; c. Jahoda;* with Łapicki,* Tyszkiewicz,* Ewa Krzyzowska, Holoubek,* & Aleksander Fogiel. "Rytm." 90 m.

Rozwodów Nie Bedzie (*There Won't Be Any More Divorces*). d. & sw. Stawiński;* c. Lipman;* with (Pt. I) Marta Lipinska, Kowalski,* Brylska,* Wienczyslaw Gliński; (pt. II) Teresa Tuszyńska, Zbigniew Dobrzyński, Elżbieta Kepińska, Pola Raksa, Andrzej Szajewski, Tadeusz Kalinowski, Adam Pawlikowski, Elżbieta Świecicka; (pt. III) Magda Zawadzka, Paweł Galia, Cybulski,* Zdzisław Maklakiewicz, & Teresa Iżewska. "Kamera." 99 m.

Rysopis (*Identification Marks: None*). d. & sw. Skolimowski;* c. Witold Mickiewicz; with Skolimowski & Czyżewska.* "PWSF." 73 m.

1965

Pierwszy Dzień Wolnosci (*The First Day of Freedom*). d. Ford;* sw. Bohdan Czeszko; c. Tadeusz Wiezan; with Tadeusz Łomnicki, Tyszkiewicz,* Tadeusz Fijewski, Krzysztof Chamiec, Roman Kłosowski, Mieczysław Stoor, & Czyżewska;* "Studio." 93 m.

Pingwin (*Penguin*). d. & sw. Stawiński;* c. Matyjaszkiewicz;* with Andrzej Kozak, Krystyna Konarska, Cybulski,* Janina Kałuska-Szudłowska, Mieczysław Milecki, Wojciech Duryasz, Andrzej Szczepkowski, & Stanisław Tym. "Kamera." 97 m.

Popioły (*Ashes*). d. Wajda;* sw. Ścibor-Rylski;* c. Lipman;* with Olbrychski,* Bogusław Kierc, Piotr Wysocki, Tyszkiewicz,* Pola Raksa, Jan Koecher, & Władysław Hancza. "Rytm." 233 m.

Rękopis Znaleziony w Saragossie (*The Manuscript Found in Saragossa*): d. Has;* sw. Tadeusz Kwiatkowski; c. Jahoda;* with Cybulski,* Iga Cembrzyńska, Joanna Jędryka, Kazimierz Opaliński, Aleksander Fogiel, Pieczka,* Ludwik Benoit, Barbara

Krafftówna, Pola Raksa, August Kowalczyk, Adam Pawlikowski, Tyszkiewicz*, Holoubek,* & Leon Niemczyk. "Kamera." 181 m.

Salto (The Somersault). d. & sw. Konwicki;* c. Kurt Weber; with Cybulski,* Holoubek,* Marta Lipińska, Irena Laskowska, Włodzimierz Borunski, Łapicki,* Zdzisław Maklakiewicz, & Iga Cembrzyńska. "Kadr." 103 m.

Walkower (Walkover). d. & sw. Skolimowski;* c. Antoni Nurzyński; with Skolimowski, Aleksandra Zawieruszanka, Krzysztof Chamiec, Pieczka,* Kluba,* & Tadeusz Kondrat. "Syrena." 76 m.

1966

Bariera (The Barrier). d. & sw. Skolimowski;* c. Jan Laskowski; with Nowicki,* Joanna Szczerbic, Łomnicki,* Zdzisław Maklakiewicz, Ryszard Pietruski, Maria Malicka, Małgorzata Lorentowicz, & Andrzej Herder. "Kamera." 83 m.

Faraon (The Pharaoh). d. Kawalerowicz;* sw. Konwicki* & Kawalerowicz; c. Wójcik;* with Jerzy Zelnik, Andrzej Girtler, Wiesława Mazurkiewicz, Piotr Pawłowski, Stanisław Milski, Józef Czerniawski, Voit,* Brylska,* Krystyna Mikolajewska, Ewa Krzyzewska, & Ryszard Ronczewski. "Kadr." 183 m.

Niedziela Sprawiedliwości (Sunday of Justice). d. Passendorfer;* sw. Roman Bratny; c. Lambach; with Krzysztof Chamiec, Magdalena Zawadzka, Jerzy Przybylski, Wojciech Pilarski, Mieczysław Waskowski, & Michał Szewczyk. "Iluzjion." 85 m.

Pieklo i Niebo (Heaven and Hell). d. Różewicz;* sw. Filipowicz & Różewicz;* c. Kurt Weber; with Kazimierz Opaliński, Józef Fratczak, Andrzej Szczepkowski, Wiesław Michnikowski, Irena Szczurowska, Marta Lipinska, Tadeusz Płucinski, & Zygmunt Zintel. "Rytm." 96 m.

Potem Nastapi Cisza (And The Silence Will Follow). d. Morgenstern;* sw. Zbigniew Safian & Morgenstern;* c. Wójcik;* with Łomnicki,* Marek Perepeczko, Olbrychski,* Brylski,* Barbara Sołtysik & Kazimierz Fabisiak. "Syrena." 92 m.

Sposob Bycia (A Manner of Behaving). d. Rybkowski;* sw. Brandys* & Jerzy Markuszewski; c. Lipman;* with Łapicki,* Winnicka,* Irena Szczurowska, Ewa Krzyzewska, Zbigniew Zapasiewicz, Leon Niemczyk, Skolimowski,* & Bronisław Pawlik. "Rytm." 80 m.

Sublokator (The Lodger). d. & sw. Janusz Majewski;* c. Kurt Weber; with Jan Machulski, Barbara Ludwiżanka, Katarzyna Łaniewska, Magdalena Zawadzka, Teresa Lipowska, & Krystyna Feldman. "Kamera." 99 m.

Szyfry (The Code). d. Has;* sw. Andrzej Kojowski; c. Jahoda;* m. Krzysztof Penderecki; with Jan Kreczmar, Cybulski,* Irena Eichlerówna, Irena Horecka, Ignacy Gogolewski, Janusz Kłosiński, Barbara Krafftówna, & Wacław Kowalski. "Kamera." 84 m.

1967

Cała Naprzód (Full Ahead). d. Lenartowicz;* sw. Ewa Szumańska, Lenartowicz; c. Tadeusz Wieżan & Jerzy Stawicki; with Cybulski,* Zdzisław Maklakiewicz, Teresa Tyszyńska, Krzysztof Litwin, Leon Niemczyk, & Jerzy Nowak. "Kadr." 89 m.

Chudy i Inni (Skinny and Others). d. Kluba;* sw. Wiesław Dymny; c. Wiesław Zdort;

with Wiesław Golas, Pieczka,* Mieczysław Stoor, Ryszard Pietruski, Ryszard Filipski, Edward Rączkowski, Leon Niemczyk, Krystyna Chmielewska, Janusz Sykutera, Andrzej Firtler, & Zdzislaw Leśniak. "Syrena." 95 m.

Jowita. d. Morgenstern;* sw. Konwicki;* au. Dygat;* c. Jan Laskowski; with Olbrychski,* Barbara Kwiatkowska, Kalina Jędrusik, Cybulski,* Ignacy Gogolewski, Anna Pieskaczwska, Ewa Ciepiela, Iga Cembrzynska, Aleksander Fogiel, & Ryszard Filipski. "Syrena." 95 m.

Kontrybucja (The Contribution). d. Łomnicki;* sw. Roman Bratny; c. Bogusław Lambach; with Wojciech Zasadzinski, Krystyna Mikołajewska, Jan Englert, Henryk Bak, Władysław Rozanski, Maciej Rayzacher, Anna Polony, Leonard Andrzejewski, Leon Pietraszkiewicz, & Tadeusz Łomnicki. "Iluzion." 94 m.

Westerplatte. d. Różewicz;* sw. Szczepański; c. Wójcik;* with Hübner,* Arkadiusz Bazak, Tadeusz Schmidt, Józef Nowak, Tadeusz Pluciński, Andrzej Zaorski, Bohdan Niewinowski, Józef Nalberczak, Bohdan Ejmont, & Janusz Paluszkiewicz. "Rytm." 99 m.

1968

Hrabina Cosel (The Countess of Cosel). d. Antczak;* c. Bogusław Lambach & Jan Janiszewski; with Jadwiga Barańska, Dmochowski,* & Stanisław Jasiukiewicz.

Lalka (The Doll). d. & sw. Has* (from novel of Boleslaw Prus); c. Matyjaszkiewicz;* with Tyszkiewicz,* Dmochowski,* Jan Kreczmar, Tadeusz Fijewski, Janina Romanowna, Łapicki,* & Jan Machulski. "Kamera." 159 m.

Żywot Mateusza (The Life of Matthew). d. Witold Leszczyński; with Pieczka.*

1969

Wszystko na Sprzedaz (Everything for Sale). d. & sw. Wajda;* c. Witold Sobocinski; with Łapicki, Tyszkiewicz,* Czyżewska,* & Olbrychski.* "Kamera." 105 m.

Czerwone i Zlote (Red And Gold). d. Lenartowicz;* with Jadwiga Chojnacka & Zdzisław Karczewski.

Gra (A Game). d. Kawalerowicz;* with Holoubek* & Winnicka.*

Pan Wołodyjowski (Colonel Wolodyjowski). d. & sw. Hoffman* (from the novel of Sienkiewicz*); with Łomnicki,* Magdalena Zawadzka,* Mieczysław Pawlikowski, & Olbrychski.*

Polowanie na Muchy (Hunting Flies). d. Wajda;* sw. Janusz Głowacki; c. Zygmunt Samosiuk; with Braunek,* Zygmunt Malanowicz, Ewa and Hanna Skarżanka, Józef Pieracki, & Olbrychski.* "Zespoly Filmowe." 108 m.

Struktura Kryształu (The Crystal Structure). d. Zanussi;* with Jan Mysłowicz & Andrzej Żarnecki.

Zbrodniarz, Który Ukradł Zbrodnię (The Criminal Who Stole His Crime). d. Majewski;* with Hübner* & Brylska.*

1970

Album Polski (The Polish Sketch-Book). d. Rybkowski;* with Brylska* & Seweryn.*

Brzezina (The Birchwood). d. Wajda;* sw. Jarosław Iwaszkiewicz (from his own story); c. Zygmunt Samosiuk; with Emilia Krakowsaka, Łukaszewicz,* Olbrychski,* & Mieczysław Stoor. "Tor." 99 m.

Krajobraz po Bitwie (Landscape After Battle). d. & sw. Wajda* (from stories of Tadeusz Borowski); c. Zygmunt Samosiuk; with Olbrychski*, Stanisława Celinska, Tadeusz Janczar, Mieczysław Stoor, Zygmunt Malanowicz, Leszek Drogosz, Braunek,* & Józef Pieracki. "Wektor." 109 m.
Lokis. d. Majewski;* with Braunek* & Józef Duriasz.
Rejs (The Cruise). d. Marek Piwowski; with Zdzisław Makakiewicz & Stanisław Tym.
Sól Ziemi Czarnej (Salt of the Black Earth). d. Kutz;* with Lukaszewicz* & Jan Englert.

1971

Akcja "Brutus" (Operation "Brutus"). d. Passendorfer;* with Hübner* & Ewa Krzyżewska.
Kardiogram (A Cardiogram). d. Roman Załuski; with Tadeusz Borowski & Anna Seniuk.
Życie Rodzinne (Family Life). d. Zanussi;* with Olbrychski,* Komorowska,* Jan Kreczmar, & Nowicki.*

1972

Anatomia Miłowści (The Anatomy of Love). d. Roman Załuski; with Brylska* & Nowicki*.
Jak Daleko Stad, Jak Blisko (How Far from Here, How Near). d. Konwicki;* with Łapicki* & Holoubek.*
Ocalenie (The Salvation). d. Żebrowski;* with Zapasiewicz.* "Tor."
Perła w Koronie (The Pearl in the Crown). d. Kutz;* with Łukaszewicz* & Pieczka.*
Trzecia Część Nocy (The Third Part of the Night). d. Andrzej Żuławski; with Braunek* & Leszek Teleszynski.
Zaraza (The Plaque). d. Roman Załuski; with Tadeusz Borowski & Janusz Bukowski.

1973

Chłopi (Peasants). d. Rybkowski;* sw. Rybkowski & Kosiński;* with Władysław Hancza, Ignacy Gogolewski, Emilia Krakowska, Krystyna Królówna, Jadwiga Chojnacka, & Tadeusz Fijewski. "Kadr."
Iluminacja (The Illumination). d. Zanussi;* with Stanislaw Latałło, Małgorzata Pritulak, Monika Dzienisiewicz-Olbrychska, & Edward Żebrowski. "Tor."
Na Wylot (Through and Through). d. & sw. Królikiewicz;* with Franciszek Trzeciak & Anna Nieborowska.
Opętanie (Obsession). d. Lenartowicz;* sw. Andrzej Szczypiorski; with Alicja Jachiewicz & Stanislaw Mikulski. "Pryzmat."
Palec Boży (God's Finger). d. Antoni Krauze; with Marian Opania & Zaorski.*
Sanatorium pod Klepsydra (The Sanatorium Under the Sign of the HourGlass). d. & sw. Has* (from the Bruno Schulz novel); c. Witold Sobocinski; with Nowicki,* Tadeusz Kondrat, Holoubek,* Halina Kowalska, Voit,* & Ludwik Benoit. "Silesia." 124 m.
Sekret (A Secret). d. Roman Załuski; with Antonina Gordon-Górecka, Lidia Wysocka, & Fronczewski.*
Słońce Wschodzi Raz na Dzień (The Sun Rises Once a Day). d. Kluba;* with Pieczka;* produced 1967.
W Pustyni i w Puszczy (In the Desert and in a Wilderness). d. & sw. Ślesicki* (from the Sienkiewicz* novel); with Thomas Medrzak & Monika Rosca.

Wesele (*The Wedding*). d. Wajda;* sw. Andrzej Kijowski (from the classic play by Stanisław Wyspianski); c. Witold Sobocinski; with Olbrychski,* Ewa Ziętek, Małgorzata Lorentowicz, Łapicki,* Pszoniak,* Pieczka, Emilia Krakowska, Voit,* Hanna Skarżanka, & Mieczysław Stoor. "X." 106 m.
Zazdrość i Medycyna (*Jealousy and Medicine*). d. & sw. Janusz Majewski;* with Dmochowski* & Ewa Krzyżewska.

1974

Drzwi w Murze (*A Door in the Wall*). d. Różewicz;* sw. Tadeusz Różewicz; with Zbigniew Zapasiewicz & Wanda Neuman. "Tor."
Gniazdo (*The Nest*). d. Rybkowski;* with Pszoniak* & Wanda Neumann.
Nagrody i Odznaczenia (*Prizes and Distinctions*). d. Łomnicki;* with Witold Dębicki & Jadwiga Jankowska-Cieślak.
Opowieść w Czerwieni (*A Story in Red*). d. Kluba;* with Nowicki* & Alicja Jachiewicz.
Potop (*The Deluge*). d. & sw. Hoffman* (from the novel of Sienkiewicz*); with Olbrychski* & Braunek.*

1975

Awans (*The Promotion*). d. Zaorski;* with Marian Opania & Bożena Dykiel.
Bilans Kwartalny (*The Quarterly Balance-Taking*). d. Zanussi;* with Komorowska,* Fronczewski,* & Marek Piwowski.
Dzieje Grzechu (*The Story of Sin*). d. & sw. Borowczyk;* with Grażyna Długołęcka, Łukaszewicz,* Jerzy Zelnik, & Wilhelmi.* 128 m.
Linia (*The Line*). d. Kutz;* with Czesław Jaroszyński & Teresa Lipowska.
Noce i Dnie (*Nights and Days*). d. & sw. Antczak* (based on a novel by Maria Dabrowska); with Jadwiga Barańska & Jerzy Bińczycki.
W Srodku Lata (*In Midsummer*). d. Falk;* with Teresa Budzisz-Krzyżanowska & Andrzej Chrzanowski.
Zaklęte Rewiry—Dvoi Svět Hotelu Pacifik (*The Enchanted Stations*). d. Majewski;* with Marek Kondrat & Wilhelmi.*

1976

Blizna (*A Scar*). d. Kieślowski;* with Pieczka,* Dmochowski,* & Stuhr.* "Tor."
Partita na Instrument Drewniany (*Partita for a Wooden Instrument*). d. Zaorski;* with Jerzy Turek, & Fronczewski.*
Przepraszam, Czy Tu Bija? (*Excuse Me, Do They Beat You Up Here?*). d. Marek Piwowski; with Zdzistaw Rychter, Jerzy Kulej, & Jan Szczepański.
Smuga Cienia (*The Shadow Line*). d. Wajda* (from Conrad's novel); with Graham Lines & Marek Kondrat. Poland-Great Britain.
Ziemia Obiecana (*The Promised Land*). d. Wajda;* au. Wladysław Reymont; with Olbrychski,* Pszoniak,* Seweryn,* Łapicki,* Tadeusz Białoszczynski, & Anna Nehrebecka. "X."

1977

Barwy Ochronne (*Camouflage*). d. & sw. Zanussi;* c. Kłosiński;* with Piotr Garlicki, Zbigniew Zapasiewicz, Dmochowski,* & Christine Paul. "Tor." 106 m.

Człowiek z Marmuru (Man of Marble). d. Wajda;* sw. Ścibor-Rylski;* c. Kłosiński;* with Janda,* Radziwilowicz,* Tadeusz and Jacek Łomnicki, Michal Tarkowski, Piotr Cieslak, & Krystyna Zachwatowicz. "X." 165 m.
Rebus (Puzzle). d. Zygadło;* sw. Maria Horodecka; c. Witold Stok; with Zbigniew Buchkowski, Marek Frackowiak, Zbigniew Pietrykowski. "Tor."
Zdjęcia Próbne (Test Shots). d. Holland,* Kędzierski, & Domaradzki; with Daria Trafankowska & Andrzej Pieczynski. "X."

1978

Antyki (Antiquities). d. Wojciechowski; with Leonard Mokicz & Januariusz Gosciminski.
Azyl (The Asylum). d. & sw. Roman Załuski; c. Janusz Pawlowski; with Marek Frąckowiak, Ewa Lemańska, & Zofia Rysiowna.
Bez Znieczulenia (Without Anesthesia). d. Wajda;* sw. Holland;* c. Kłosiński;* with Zapasiewicz*, Ewa Dałkowska, Seweryn,* Janda,* Emilia Krakowska, Wilhelmi,* & Stuhr.* "X." 115 m.
Granica (The Boundary). d. Rybkowski;* with Janda* & Seweryn.*
Pasja (A Passion). d. Różewicz;* sw. Andrzej Kojowski; c. Wójcik;* with Piotr Garlicki, Zbigniew Zapasiewicz, Bogusław Smela, Wojciech Alaborski, Henryk Machalica, Voit,* & Dymna.* "Tor."
Pokój z Widokiem na Morze (The Room Overlooking the Sea). d. Zaorski;* with Fronczewski* & Holoubek.*
Rekolekcje (Spiritual Retreats). d. Witold Leszczyński; with Ryszard Cieślak & Pszoniak.*
Rdza (Rust). d. Roman Załuski; with Hübner.*
Spirala (A Spiral). d. & sw. Zanussi;* c. Kłosiński;* with Nowicki,* Komorowska,* & Zofia Kucowna. "Tor." 90 m.
Wodzirej (The Dance Leader). d. & sw. Falk;* c. Kłosiński;* with Stuhr,* Michał Tarkowski, Slawa Kwasniewska, Bogusław Sobczuk, & Wiktor Sadecki. "X." 115 m.
Wśród Nocnej Ciszy (Silent Night). d. Chmielewski;* with Tomasz Zaliwski & Piotr Łysak.

1979

Aktorzy Prowincjonalni (Provincial Actors). d. & sw. Holland;* c. Jacek Petrycki; with Tadeusz Huk, Halina Łabonarska, & Jan Ciecierski. "X." 108 m.
Amator (Camera-Buff). d. & sw. Kieślowski;* c. Jacek Petrycki; with Stuhr,* Małgorzata Zabkowska, Ewa Pokas, Zanussi,* & Krzysztos Jurga. "Tor."
Aria dla Atlety (Aria for an Athlete). d. & sw. Bajon;* Jerzy Zieliński; with Krzysztof Majchrzak, Pola Raksa, Wilhelmi,* Bogusz Bilewski, & Pszoniak.* "Tor." 103 m.
Biały Mazur (The Mazurka Danced at Dawn). d. Jakubowska;* with Dałkowska* Tomasz Grochoczynski, & Anna Chodakowska.
Klincz (The Clinch). d. & sw. Bajon;* c. Mieroslawski; with Tomasz Lengren, Bolesław Smela, Zdzisław Lesniewicz, & Janusz Sykutera. "Kadr." 97 m.
Lekcja Martwego Jezyka (A Lesson of Dead Language). d. Majewski;* with Lukaszewicz.*
Panny z Wilka—Les Demoiselles de Wilko (The Maids of Wilko). d. Wajda;* with Olbrychski,* Anna Seniuk, Komorowska,* Stanisława Celinska, & Christine Pascal.

Smierc Prezydenta (Death of the President). d. Kawalerowicz;* sw. Michałek;* c. Witold Sobociński; with Zdzisław Mrozewski, Marek Walczewski, Henryk Bista, Czesław Bydzewski, Jerzy Duszński, & Edmund Fetting. "Kadr." 142 m.
Szpital Przemienienia (The Hospital of the Transfiguration). d. Żebrowski;* with Dałkowska,* Piotr Dejmek, Henryk Bista, & Hübner.*
Zmory (Nightmares). d. Stanisław Marczewski; with Piotr Lysak.

1980

Bez Miłośći (Without Love). d. Sass;* with Dorota Stalińska, Zdzisław Wardejn, & Kowalski.*
Constans (The Constant Factor). d. & sw. Zanussi;* c. Idziak;* with Tadeusz Bradecki, Zofia Mrozowska, Małgorzata Zajaczkowska, & Cezary Morawski. "Tor." 105 m.
Cma (A Moth). d. Zygadło;* with Wilhelmi.*
Dyrygent (The Conductor). d. Wajda;* with John Gielgud, Janda,* & Seweryn.* "X."
Golem. d. Szulkin; with Marek Walczewski & Janda.*
Kontrakt (The Contract). d. & sw. Zanussi;* c. Idziak;* with Łomnicki,* Komorowska,* Leslie Caron, Tyszkiewicz*, & Nina Andrycz. "Tor."
Kung Fu. d. & sw. Kijowski;* c. Krzysztof Wyszynski; w. Teresa Sawicka, Fronczewski,* Olbrychski,* & Seweryn.* "X."
Rog Brzeskiej i Capri (On the Corner of Brzeska and Capri Streets). d. Krzysztof Wojciechowski; with Janina Kondracka, Zbigniew Bartosiewicz, & Edward Narkiewicz.
Rycerz (A Knight). d. Majewski;* with Piotr Skarga & Olbrychski.* *Sowizdrzał Świętokrzyski (The Merrymaker from Holy-Cross Mountains)*. d. Kluba;* with Łukaszewicz* & Tyszkiewicz.*
Szansa (The Chance). d. & sw. Falk;* c. Kłosiński;* with Stuhr,* Tomasz Zieciowski, Andrzej Buszewicz, & Krzysztof Zaleski: "X."
Wściekły (Rabid). d. Roman Załuski; with Bronisław Cieślak & Brylska.*

1981

Człowiek z Zelaza (Man of Iron). d. Wajda;* sw. Ścibor-Rylski;* c. Kłosiński;* with Marian Opania, Radziwiłowicz,* Janda,* & Irena Byrska: "X." 140 m.
Gorączka (A Fever). d. Holland;* with Adam Ferency & Barbara Grabowska.
Indeks (The Index). d. Kijowski;* with Krzysztof Zalewski, & Ewa Żukowska.
Miś (The Bear). d. Stanisław Bareja; with Stanisław Tym, & Barbara Burska.
Mniejsze Niebo (Limited Sky). d. Morgenstern;* with Wilhelmi* & Tyszkiewicz.*
W Biały Dzień (In Broad Daylight). d. & sw. Żebrowski;* c. Witold Stok; with Bajor,* Janda,* Holoubek,* Krzysztof Kolberger, Władysław Kowalski, Nowicki,* Radziwiłowicz,* & Zapasiewicz.*
Wizja Lokalna–1901 (The Visit to the Scene of the Crime–1901). d. Bajon;* w. Łomnicki,* Olbrychski,* & Andrzej Zarnecki; "Tor."

1982

Debiutantka (The Debutante). d. Sass;* with Dorota Stalińska, Łapicki,* & Czyżewska.*
Dolina Issy (Issa Valley). d. & sw. Konwicki* (from the Miłosz novel); c. Jerzy Łuka-

szewicz; with Maria Pakulnis, Danuta Szaflarska, Ewa Wisniewska, Maciej Mazurkiewicz, Dymna,* & Edward Dziewoński. "Perspektywa." 110 m.
Głosy (Voices). d. Kijowski;* with Ewa Dałkowska & Krzysztof Zaleski.
Konopielka (Konopielka). d. & sw. Witold Leszczynski; p. Zbigniew Napiorkowski; with Krzysztof Majchrzak, Anna Seniuk, Jerzy Block, Marek Siudym, Tomek Jarosiński, Joanna Sienkiewicz, Pieczka,* & Anna Milewska. "Perspektwa." 92 m.
Niech Cie Odleci Mara (Let the Nightmare Fly). d. Andrzej Barański; with Marek Probosz, Anna Ciepielewska, & Bronislaw Pawlik.
Rys (The Lynx). d. & sw. Rozewicz* (from an Iwaszkiewicz story); c. Wojcik;* with Radziwilowicz,* Franciszek Pieczka,* & Piotr Bajor. "Tor." 84 m.
Vabank. d. Machulski;* with Jan Machulski, Leonard Pietraszak, & Witold Pyrkosz.
Vabank II, Czyli Riposta (The Riposte). d. Machulski;* with Jan Machulski, Leonard Pietraszak, & Witold Pyrkosz.
Znachor (The Quack). d. Hoffman;* with Jerzy Binczycki & Dymna.*

1983

Austeria (The Inn). d. Kawalerowicz;* sw. Konwicki* & Kawalerowicz (from novel of Julian Stryjkowski); with Pieczka,* Pszoniak,* Jan Szurmiej, & Ewa Domańska: "Kadr." 104 m.
Danton. d. Wajda; with Gerard Depardieu & Pszoniak.*
Dreszcze (Thrills). d. Wojciech Marczewski; with Tomasz Hudziec, Teresa Marczewska, & Marek Kondrat.
Epitafium dla Barbary Radziwiłłowny (The Epitaph for Barbara Radziwill). d. Majewski;* with Dymna,* Jerzy Zelnik, Śląska.*
Jesli Sie Odnajdziemy (If We Meet Again). d. Roman Załuski; with Krzysztof Kolberger & Barbara Klimkiewicz.
Klakier (The Claqueur). d. Kondratiuk;* with Zuzanna Łozińska & Michal Bajor.
Klejnot Wolnego Sumienia (A Gem of Free Conscience). d. Królikiewicz;* with Voit* & Jerzy Prażmowski.
Krzyk (The Scream). d. & sw. Sass;* c. Wieslaw Zdort; with Dorota Stalińska, Krzysztof Pieczyński, Iga Cembrayńska, & Anna Romantowska. "Kadr."
Limuzyna Daimler-Benz (The Daimler-Benz Limousine). d. Bajon;* with Michał Bajor & Piotr Bajor.
Nieciekawa Historia (An Uninteresting Story). d. Has;* with Holoubek* & Hanna Mikuć.
Ósmy Dzień Tygodnia—Der achte Wochentaq (The Eighth Day of the Week). d. Ford;* sw. Ford & Marek Hłasko; c. Lipman; with Sonja Ziemann, Cybulski,* Łomnicki,* & Zbigniew Wójcik. "Studio" and CCC-Film, Berlin. 84 m.
Zasieki (Abatises). d. Andrzej J. Piotrowski; with Damian Damiecki, Andrzej Wojaczek, & Łukaszewicz.*

1984

Bez Końca (Without End). d. Kieślowski;* with Grażyna Szapołowska, Aleksander Bardini, Michał Bajor, & Jerzy Radziwiłowicz.
Był Jazz (There Was Jazz): d. & sw. Falk;* c. Witold Sobociński; with Bożena Adamkowna, Michał Bajor, & Andrzej Grabarczyk. "X." 107 m.
Seksmisja (Sex Mission). d. Machulski;* sw. Machulski, Jolanta Hartwig, & Pawel Hajny;

c. Jerzy Lukaszewicz; with Stuhr,* Lukaszewicz,* Bożena Stryjkowna, Bogusława Pawelec, Hanna Stankowna, & Tyszkiewicz,* "Kadr."
To Tylko Rock (It's Only Rock 'n Roll). d. Pavel Karpinski; with Janda,* Grazyna Trela-Stawska, & Zdzisław Wardejn.

1985

Baryton (The Baritone). d. Zaorski;* with Zbigniew Zapasiewicz, Fronczewski,* & Małgorzata Pieczynska.
Fetysz (The Fetish). d. Krzysztof Wojciechowski; with Jan Prochyra & Ewa Zietek.
Idol (The Idol). d. Falk;* with Krzysztof Pieczynski & Ewa Żukowska.
Kobieta Samotna (The Lonely Woman). d. Holland;* with Maria Chwalibog & Bogusław Linda. "X."
Kobieta z Prowincji (A Provincial Woman). d. Andrzej Barański; with Ewa Dałkowska.
O-bi, O-ba, Koniec Cywilizacji (...The End of Civilization). d. Szulkin;* with Stuhr* & Janda.*
Pismak (The Hack). d. Has;* with Wojciech Wysocki, Janusz Michałowski, & Jan Peszek.
Ręce do Gory (Hands Up!). Skolimowski;* with Skolimowski, Bogumił Kobiela, Joanna Szczerbic, Łomnicki,* & Adam Hanuszkiewicz; produced 1967.
Rok Spokojnego Słońca (The Year of Quiet Sun). d. Zanussi;* with Komorowska* & Scott Wilson. Poland-U.S.

1986

Bohater roku (Hero of the Year). d. Falk;* with Stuhr.*
Dziewczęta z Nowolipek, Rajska Jabłon (The Girls from Nowolipki Street, The Apple Tree of Paradise). d. Sass;* with Ewa Kasprzyk, Isabela Drobotowicz-Orkisz, Maria Ciunelis, Marta Klubowicz, & Piotr Bajor.
Ga, Ga, Chwała Bohaterom (Ga, Ga, Glory to Heroes). d. Szulkin;* with Olbrychski,* Agnieszka Fatyga, Stuhr,* & Nowicki.*
Jezioro Bodeńskie (Bodensee). d. Zaorski;* with Holoubek* & Krzysztof Pieczynski.
Kronika Wypadków Miłosnych (A Chronicle of Amorous Accidents). d. Wajda;* sw. & au. Konwicki;* with Paulina Mlynarska, Piotr Wawrzynczak, & Konwicki.* "Perspektywa."
Matka Królów (The Mother of the Krol Family). d. Zaorski;* with Zbigniew Zapasiewicz, Bogusław Linda, & Magda Teresa Wójcik; produced 1982.
Osobisty Pamiętnik Grzesznika, Przez Niego Samego Spisany (The Personal Diary of a Sinner, Written in His Own Hand). d. Has;* with Piotr Bajor
Sceny Dzieciece z Życia Prowincji (Childhood Scenes from Provincial Life). d. Zygadło;* with Dariusz Siatkowski & Beata Paluch; produced 1984.
Wielki Bieg (The Big Run). d. Jerzy Domaradzki; with Jarosław Kopaczewski & Tadeusz Bradecki; produced 1981.
Zabicie Ciotki (The Killing of the Aunt). d. Królikiewicz;* with Robert Herubin & Maria Kleydysz.
Zaproszenie do Tanca (Invitation to Dance). d. Jakubowska;* with Antonina Gordon-Górecka & Maria Probosz.

Życie Raz Jeszcze (*Life Once Again*). d. Morgenstern;* sw. Roman Bratny; c. Wójcik;* with Łomnicki,* Ewa Wisniewska, Łapicki,* Edmund Fetting, & Tadeusz Kalinowski; "Syrena"; produced 1965: 96 m.

Zygfryd (*Siegfried*). d. Andrzej Domalik; with Holoubek* & Tomasz Hudziec.

3

Thomas J. Slater

CZECHOSLOVAKIA

Czechoslovakia is a small, land-locked Central European nation made up of two dominant nationalities, the Czechs and Slovaks (who speak two different, though related, languages), that has been constantly overpowered by its neighbors, the Germans and Russians. Yet, even after Soviet tanks rolled into Prague in August of 1968, crushing Alexander Dubček's attempts to lead his country down its own distinct road towards socialism and reimposing a Stalinist government, Czech dissidents grimly fought on until the country finally achieved its return to democracy, along with most of Eastern and Central Europe, in 1989. Yet, despite this remarkable change, which has included the rise of playwright Václav Havel to the presidency, most Westerners are unfamiliar with the central role that Czech artists and writers have played in their country's struggle for freedom. As the novelist Josef Škvorecký has stated, "When Jaroslav Seifert in 1956 proclaimed that Czechoslovak writers were the 'conscience of the nation,' he was only reiterating a very old notion" ("Czech Writers," 44).

Throughout this century, it has continually been artists such as Škvorecký and Havel who have led the fight against political oppression. Turning to Czech literature and film in particular (though the other arts may be very similar), the elements of satire and irony that have helped the nation survive become most visible, all of it derived from the two early giants of the nation's literature, Franz Kafka and Jaroslav Hašek, author of *The Good Soldier Švejk*. From Kafka, the Czechs received a picture of an incomprehensible world that they have continually been able to apply to their situation by combining it with the biting satire of *Švejk*. This combination has produced a "style of storytelling" which involves "people who are weak, who are almost imperceptible, who seemingly are dumb—but only seemingly; who are average from all points of view except in their spirit; and who can effectively ridicule those who pretend to be powerful, those who pretend to be wise and have all the answers" (Daniel, 55).

These central characters tend to be the figures like Peter of Miloš Forman's *Cerný Petr* (*Black Peter*, 1963) who stare at the world in their own quiet, uncomprehending ways, attempting to fit in yet ultimately unwilling to give up their dignity in order to do so. Even in Czechoslovak films in the eighties, such characters keep appearing as in Jiří Menzel's *Věsničko má, středisková* (*My Sweet Little Village*, 1986). Through such characters, Czech directors have developed a solid tradition of examining their culture and society with lyricism, seriousness, and a sense of humor sometimes developing into Kafkaesque black comedy. Always, there seems in the best works to have been the desire to reveal, understand, and develop common-sense responses from the viewers. The films state, "This is how life is. Let's go about it with some compassion." These desires go beyond the goal of mere entertainment and relate directly to the Czech history of political oppression, a condition that would not tend to produce aggressive personalities, but has given birth to a great pride in national identity and cultural achievements. In other words, the Czechoslovakian situation is one that would naturally tend to uphold the value of understanding, and Czech and Slovak artists have done so throughout their long history of great accomplishments.

In the history of Czechoslovak film, in particular, a number of these characteristics are evident. Working in reverse chronological order, we can find the impulses for examining society in the influences on the Czechoslovak New Wave of the sixties from Italian neo-realism and English "realists." In just about the only pre–1950s Czech film available for viewing in the West, Gustav Machatý's *Extase* (*Ecstasy*, 1933), we find an examination of the conflict between social roles and personal desires and an understanding for the characters who are dominated by either. Out of this conflict, Machatý develops a solution that goes beyond the individual characters to the entire society. (I wish to discuss this film in greater depth later. But, for now, I would just like to mention that film scholars can be grateful to Machatý for including the famous nude scene of Hedy Kiesler [later known as Hedy Lamarr], providing a reason for its availability in America, even though a wrong one.) Finally, the desire of Czech filmmakers to examine and reveal their society is what has given Czech film a history older than this century. For, in 1896, architect and amateur photographer Jan Křízenecký brought the nation's first Lumière movie camera from Paris to Prague. In June 1898 he presented a show of three filmstrips, *Dostaveníčko ve mlynici* (*Rendezvous at the Mill*), *Pláčo a smích* (*Laughing and Crying*), and *Výstavní parkar a lepič plakátů* (*The Exhibition Sausage Vender*).

Like the earliest films in France and America, these were very simple documentary shorts whose titles explained the contents exactly. Nevertheless, Křízenecký was already making use of close-ups and beginning the process of developing a needed national cinema. Langdon Dewey reports that Czech audiences "found imported films difficult because the Czech language is a polybrid, inflectatory communicatory system having little to link it with, say, French subtitles" (*Outline*, 7). Thus, Czech film was tied directly to the national culture and identity right from the beginning. Czech interest in film has always been inordinately large for the size of the country. From some reason, perhaps a natural desire to develop an art form that could help bind the people's cultural identity more tightly, the Czechs took to the new medium almost as soon as it was invented and thereafter steadily contributed to its development.

Certainly, the driving force behind the growth of the Czech film industry was the profit motive, which only makes its story similar to those of many other national film industries. This force produced the establishment of several film studios during the first three decades of the century, which had an artistic benefit as Czech technicians, directors, and performers sought ways to produce superior films. For example, several excellent cameramen emerged from this period. Otto Heller begin shooting films in 1919 and eventually produced a celebrated anti-Nazi film, *Bílá nemoc* (*The White Plague*), with Czech director Hugo Haas in 1937 as well as working with Olivier and Ophuls later in his career (Dewey, *Outline*, 12). Karel Degl shot an ambitious Faustian period film called *Stavitel chrámu* (*The Builder of the Cathedral*) with co-director Antonín Novotný in 1919, continued by working on documentaries well into the forties, and later became an instructor at the national film academy, FAMU (Dewey, *Outline*, 13). Václav Vích shot many important Czech silent films, most significantly Machatý's *Erotikon* (1929), which, through its exceptional lighting, softness, and atmosphere, established the notion of a "Czech photography" (Dewey, *Outline*, 27). Finally, Jan Stalich became world famous for his work on *Ecstasy* and Josef Rovenský's *Řeka* (*The River*), both of which were sensations at the 1934 Vienna Film Festival. Stalich went on to have a long career and also eventually teach at FAMU (Dewey, *Outline*, 41). In the area of sound, Josef Šlechta developed a device in 1929 for directly recording sound onto motion picture film. This innovation significantly lowered the cost of producing sound films, which led to a boom in Eastern European production over the next decade (Stoil, 49).

While these important technicians worked at improving how film recorded, Czech artists and writers often turned to national culture and traditions to improve what it recorded. The popularity of specifically Czech themes was evident in the early post-World War I years following the nation's establishment in 1918. Superpatriotism was a major genre at this time (Škvorecký, *All the Bright*, 3). But the story of the first all-Czech language sound film, *Fidlovačka* (Svatopluk Innemann, 1931), reveals the close ties between pride in national identity and the development of Czech film art. Studios were hesitant about producing such a film, since the population for it was so small that its profit potentiality was considered dim. Nevertheless, *Fidlovačka* made use of a number of Czech folk songs and was a big success (Dewey, *Outline*, 32). František Daniel explains that Czech cinema flourished during the early days of sound film, because for Czechs, "language is closely tied up with the national tradition; the defense of the language is something that runs through a thousand years of history, and every Czech has been taught that the language must be preserved if the national culture is to survive" (52). Thus, for Czechs, Daniel states, film has long been, "in the fullest sense, part of the national culture" (52).

From at least the late teens, Czech film has always had close ties with other arts as well. Even before then, the Czech art world was taking the medium seriously. In 1908, Václav Tille wrote *Kinema*, an early work of film theory that discussed such advanced notions as linking shots together and film as art. In the early twenties, the Czech avant-garde published a flurry of enthusiastic articles about film. Karel Tiege produced another work of theory, *Film*, in 1925, arguing that film should be like a mobile optical poem, a view that valued the individual vision and looks forward to the lyrical style (Liehm and Liehm, 10, 23).

A key influence on the development of Czech film was the "Devětsil" avant-garde movement of the late twenties. As Peter Hames states, "Devoted to revolution in art, life, and politics, the Devětsil linked itself to the Communist Party, advocated work of a consciously avant-garde nature, and attempted to promote the cinema as an art form" (*The Czechoslovak*, 11). Its members included Tiege, the poet Vitezslav Nezval (who collaborated with Machatý on *Erotikon* and *From Saturday to Sunday*), the novelist Vladislav Vančura, and film director Martin Frič (Hames, *The Czechoslovak*, 11-12). Vančura moved into directing himself, producing five films, including *Před maturitou* (*Before Graduation*, 1932), which became an international success. A study of youth, noted for some excellent performances, it is still considered a fine film from the decade (Dewey, *Outline*, 42). Nezval and Vančura (who was killed by the Nazis in 1942) still had influence in the sixties when the films *Markéta Lazarová* (František Vláčil, 1967), *Rozmarné léto* (*Capricious Summer*, Jiří Menzel, 1968), and *Valérie a týden divů* (*Valerie and Her Week of Wonders*, Jaromil Jireš, 1969) were all produced from their works (Hames, *The Czechoslovak*, 12).

Martin Frič began working in films in 1919, moving into directing in 1928. He was the first director to win the title of National Artist and became known as the head of the "improvisatory trend" in Czech film (as opposed to the lyrical trend) (Dewey, *Outline*, 34, 29). Among his most notable works out of a long filmography were *Jánošík*, (1935); two films with the great Czech comedy team of Jiri Voskovec and Jan Werich, *Hej rup!* (*Heave Ho!*, 1934) and the antifascist *Svět patří-nám* (*The World Belongs to Us*, 1937); the first Czech color film, *Reiterate the Warning* (1947), which also marked the beginning of Slovakian feature production; and perhaps the only notable films of the early fifties, *Císařův pekář* (*The Emporer's Baker*) and *Pekařův císař* (*The Baker's Emporer*, 1951), starring Jan Werich and based on an old Czech legend. He also helped start the career of and inspire the young Miloš Forman, who worked with him on the script of a 1955 film, *Nechte to na mne* (*Leave It to Me*) (Liehm, *Miloš Forman*, 14–15).

Voskovec and Werich, as well known in Czechoslovakia, even in the sixties, as Laurel and Hardy were in America, deserve some special attention. Describing their achievements, Škvorecký writes,

Together with Jaroslav Ježek, the father of Czech jazz, they moulded dadaism, circus, jazz, Chaplin, Buster Keaton, and American vaudeville into a new art form. They created a new kind of intellectual-political musical. Never before had anything like that existed in Bohemia, and it was a quarter of a century after the Nazis had closed the Voskovec and Werich theatre, before it appeared again in the Semafor Theatre of Jiří Suchý and Jiří Šlitr. (*All the Bright*, 23-4)

Besides *Heave Ho!* and *The World Belongs to Us*, their other films in the thirties were *Pudr a benzín* (*Powder and Gasoline*, 1931), and *Peníze nebo život* (*Your Money or Your Life*, 1932), both directed by Jindřich Honzl.

The most important connection between Devětsil and Czech filmmakers was the collaboration of Nezval and Machatý. But Machatý was an absolutely serious artist long before his contacts with the Devětsil group. In the early twenties he worked in Hollywood, reportedly with both D. W. Griffith and Erich von Stroheim. Returning to Czechoslovakia in 1925, he helped organize the new Kavalírka Company and produced his first feature as director, an adaptation of Tolstoi's *Kreutzerova sonáta* (*The Kreutzer Sonata*, 1926). Then, following a failed version of *Švejk*, Machatý began his important work with Nezval.

Their two films together along with *Ecstasy* can be considered as a trilogy, providing "a clever and often subtle analysis of male-female relations" (Hames, *The Czechoslovak*, 13). Though *Erotikon* featured the first Czech nude (Yugoslav actress Ita Rina) and a powerfully sensuous opening sequence, its morality was entirely conventional in upholding the values of family life. Nevertheless, it boldly presented a sympathetic heroine governed by passion and drew attention to the cinematography of Václav Vích (Hames, *The Czechoslovak*, 13-14). Of Machatý's next film, Hames writes, "In comparison with both *Erotikon* and *Ecstasy, From Saturday to Sunday* is a much more mature work. The credit must go to Nezval's script, which attempts both greater depth of characterization and makes a more convincing effort to deal with the problems of everyday reality" (*The Czechoslovak*, 15).

Ecstasy, however, is also a film that artistically goes far beyond the reputation it has earned on the basis of Hedy Kiesler-Lamarr's nude scene. In it, the viewer can see Machatý struggling to blend the lyricism he apparently achieved in his silent films with the demands of using sound. Throughout the film, his contrast of lifeless social and artistic forms with an active engagement with life establishes a thematic basis for the final scene, which shows a road crew rhythmically clearing the land for a new road. Thus, Machatý makes his beliefs about the path to ecstasy clear. It is to be hoped that more students in the future can become similarly engaged with his work and discover that he had more to offer than just a scene of a naked woman running through the woods.

Two other important directors from the thirties were Otakar Vávra and Hugo Haas. Vávra, the founder of the Prague Film Academy, where he taught several members of the Czechoslovak New Wave of the sixties, and also the guiding force behind the nationalization of Czechoslovak film in the late forties, has been a leading adaptor of literary works and continually innovative throughout his career, being the most daring director of the sixties in his use of nudity (Škvorecký, *All the Bright*, 17). After providing scripts throughout the thirties for Rovenský, Frič, and Haas, Vávra achieved notoriety as a director with *Cech panen kutno-horských* (*Guild of the Kutná Hora Maidens*), which won an award at the Venice Festival (Hames, *The Czechoslovak*, 31). His other achievements as a director included *Krakatit* (1948, based on the utopian novel by Karel Čapek), *Romance pro křídlovku* (*Romance for Flugelhorn*, 1967, winner of the Gold Prize at the San Sebastian film festival), and *Kladivo na čarodějnice* (*Hammer Against Witches*, 1970, "a savage study of the last witch-burnings in Bohemia") (Dewey, *Outline*, 49).

Hugo Haas first gained attention as a comic actor in Innemann's *Muži v offsidu* (*Men Offside*, 1932), a soccer comedy. He achieved success in a number of other comedies as well, but gained his greatest acclaim for directing the antifascist *The White Plague*, 1937, based on a play by Karel Čapek with a script by Vávra. In 1939, Haas barely left in time to escape the Nazis. Though certainly grief-stricken, he eventually made it to Hollywood, where he had a successful acting career and directed a total of fourteen films (Škvorecký, *All the Bright*, 1922).

This brief survey of Czech film until 1940, although only touching the surface of what was accomplished, attempts to reveal some of the richness of the nation's cinematic history, one that has been too much neglected in the West. It deserves a greater awareness from both scholars and the public. Though I have not discussed the rise and fall of various studios or the pioneering work of certain producers, there are two more performers who deserve mention. One was a comedian named Vlasta Burian, who appeared in some of Martin Frič's comedies, *Revizor* (*The Inspector General*) and *U snědeného krámu* (*The Ruined Shopkeeper*), both 1933. Mainly a stage performer, Škvorecký says of him, "If the Czech cabaret ever had a genius, it was Burian" (*All the Bright*, 22). Certainly these films deserve some exposure. Another was the versatile actress Anny Ondráková, the most popular pre-war screen star, who also made two films in 1929 with Alfred Hitchcock, *Manxman* and *Blackmail* (which is now available in video). She later achieved additional fame by marrying heavyweight boxing champion Max Schmeling. One last film that deserves recognition is Karel Anton's *Tonka šibenice* (*Tonka, Tart of the Gallows*, 1930). Starring Ita Rina and Josef Rovenský, the film focused on a popular prostitute who is brought to death row to fulfill the final wishes of a condemned man, and is rewarded for her compassion with rejection by her lover and mockery from the other whores (Hames, *The Czechoslovak*, 16–17). Dewey writes that "the psychological approaches to this melodramatic story were surprisingly subtle" (*Outline*, 31).

Despite these accomplishments, Czech film, like most other national cinemas, was far from existing on a consistently high level of quality during its first forty years. Generally, the number of commercially oriented lightweight works far outnumbered those of serious artistic intent (whether comedies or dramas). Up until 1920, Czech filmmakers produced few notable works. Križenecký's documentary *Svatojanské proudy* (*The St. Johan's Rapids*) won a Gold Medal at the 1912 Vienna Film Exposition. Antonin Fencl's comedies *Zlaté srdéčko* (*The Golden Heart*, 1916) and *Pražští Adamité* (*The Prague Adamites*, 1917) won popularity by striking nationalistic chords, as did Karel Degl's *O děvčicu* (*The Little Girl*, 1918) (Brož, *The Path* 7, 9). The next year saw the production of the internationally successful *The Builder of the Cathedral*, but it was the exception to the rule. Financial insecurity during the early years of Czech nationhood hurt both the quality and quantity of film production (Brož, *The Path*, 10). Heavy competition from foreign imports dropped domestic production to just eight features in 1924 (Dewey, *Outline*, 14), and the films of these years were so commercially oriented that film became an insignificant part of cultural life (Brož, *The Path*, 13).

Following some signs of revival in the late twenties, a difficult period of adjustment again set in with the coming of sound, and production once more dipped to just eight features in 1930. Sound also contributed to the box office failures of Junghans' *Such is Life* and Jan Kolár's monumental epic *Svatý Václav* (*St. Wenceslas*, 1929) (Broz, *The Path*, 15). Still, the ability to export films by Machatý and Innemann gave Czech film the most vitality of any national cinema in East-Central Europe at this time (Stoil, 49). Continued success at international festivals during the 1930s and the influx of both native avant-gardists and others entering the country from Russia and Germany brought new levels of intensity to Czech life and film (Liehm and Leihm, 24). The Czech film industry responded to the challenges of the times and, by 1938, stood on the brink of international recognition (Liehm and Liehm, 25).

But then came the infamous Munich Conference and its aftermath in 1938–1939 in which Czechoslovakia's supposed European allies agreed to the establishment of a German "protectorate" over the nation. Slovakia formed a separate state under the German nation. The following occupation by the Nazis led to the slaughter of thousands of Czechs and Slovaks, persecution for thousands more, and terrible hardships for the rest as the country was looted of most of its goods. But, amazingly enough, the film industry was able to come through all the devastation in good shape. The Nazis wanted to maintain the Czech studios for producing their own films during and after the war. Therefore, the Barrandov Studios in Prague were not only preserved but also expanded under the Germans. In addition, an experimental studio for animated films was established in Prague, producing its first feature-length work, *Wedding in the Coral Sea*, late in the war. The existing studio for short works in Zlin also continued functioning (Liehm and Liehm, 26–27).

Throughout the occupation, Czech filmmakers were able to lay the groundwork for the post-war industry as well. As early as 1935, Vávra, Vančura, and a group of other artists had established the Czechoslovak Film Society, dedicated to increasing the aesthetic level of production through publishing articles and holding screenings of acclaimed international productions. During the war, this group continued to work on plans for nationalization of the industry, and a decree to that effect was signed in August of 1945 by president in exile Eduard Beneš.

This development was tied more to Czech and Slovak culture than to the Communist Party (Hames, *The Czechoslovak,* 31–32). But these traditions were ones that the Party and Stalin were eventually able to exploit, with a terrible detriment to the Czechs and Slovaks. In fact, the potential for an independent Czech communism only increased the amount of Stalinist repression (Hames, *The Czechoslovak,* 25). Thus another period of potential greatness was aborted during the fifties.

Not only had the film industry emerged from the war with established facilities and a production plan, but it also had new talent. Vávra and Frič had continued to work during the occupation, producing some fine films. They had been joined by new directors Frantisek Čáp and Václav Krška, who became one of the most notable figures of the fifties. In addition, the Nazis' closings of the universities had driven many young intellectuals into the film industry (Liehm and Liehm, 26–27). These events culminated in the establishment of the Prague Film School (FAMU) in 1945 and the release of several films immediately after the war.

Of these, most were undistinguished productions rushed to completion under difficult conditions, but Čáp's *Muži bez křídel (Men Without Wings,* 1946) received a prize at Cannes and Karel Steklý's *Siréna (The Strike,* 1947) won a Grand Prize at Venice. Čáp soon emigrated to Yugoslavia and Steklý never made another notable film. But other new directors were emerging at the time who would have a good deal of influence over the next two decades. Jiří Weiss demonstrated an original style in his first feature *Uloupená hranice (The Stolen Frontier,* 1947) (Liehm and Liehm, 97, 99). Jiří Krejčík's third film, *Svědomí (Conscience,* 1948) was a penetrating study of a man's failed attempt to redeem some tragic errors he has made. Despite acting in an entirely appropriate manner, he can never undo the suffering he has caused. The film was eventually condemned by the authorities (Hames, *The Czechoslovak,* 42–43). Jan Kadár's Slovak production *Katka (Cathy,* 1949) was a debut film that, according to the Liehms, "remains surprisingly fresh" (101–102). However, after its poor reception, Kadár moved to Prague and began his long, successful partnership with Elmar Klos. In addition, the veterans Frič and Vávra also remained very active. Frič's immediate post-war productions included "a successful parody of a commercial tear jerker," *Pytlákova schovanka (The Poacher's Ward,* 1948). Vávra's best from this period, *Němá barikáda (Silent Barricade,* 1948) adopted a neorealist style to tell about the brief Prague uprising against the Nazis in May of 1945.

But the one Czech film from this time to truly reach a level of greatness was Alfred Radok's *Daleká cesta (The Long Journey,* 1949). Radok's film was a darkly brilliant tale of which Škvorecký states, "I am not aware of any comparable work created at that time in world cinematography" (*All the Bright,* 41). Unfortunately, the film was not given much exposure and Radok was only allowed to complete two more films after that, one of them being *Dědeček automobil (Grandfather Automobile,* 1957), on which Miloš Forman gained his first experience as an assistant director. Thus, although thrown back to its infancy by the war, the Czech film industry showed all indications in the late 1940s of having firm legs and being ready to run.

What happened next was the result of several factors. During the war, Beneš's government in exile in London and the Czechoslovak Communists in Moscow reached a level of agreement. However, following popular elections in which they did well, the Communists forced Beneš's abdication and assumed power in February 1948 (Hames, *The Czechoslovak*, 36). But visions of a distinctly Czechoslovak road to socialism soon evaporated, and a Zhdanovist cultural policy was imposed, a development that naturally resulted in the banning of most of the best recent films (Liehm and Liehm, 101). It also produced some of the most horribly comic productions of the Soviet socialist realist style in the early years of the decade (Škvorecký, *All the Bright*, 35). Some avant-gardists reacted to these developments with suicide and emigration (Liehm and Liehm, 101), and Stoil suggests that the Party also used the threat of charging directors with collaboration during the war to keep them in line (107).

But part of the decline in both quantity and quality during the early fifties was also a result of Czechoslovak directors' honestly attempting to find ways to work within the new guidelines. Many, such as Weiss, who artfully expressed his ideas in *Vstanou noví bojovníci* (*New Fighters Will Arise*, 1950), strongly believed in the Soviet socialist ideology (Hames, *The Czechoslovak*, 39). Miloš Forman later said that during the fifties he also believed in the possibility of working within socialist realist guidelines (Slater, 11). One immediate impact of the new policies was to drop production to an all-time low of eight films in 1951. Yet, the production of Frič's *The Emperor's Baker* and *The Baker's Emperor* during this year and the debuts of Weiss, Miroslav Hubáček (*V trestnem území*, *In the Penalty Zone*), and Karel Kachyňa and Vojtěch Jasný (*Není stále zamračeno*, *The Clouds Will Roll Away*) show that Zhdanovism was not always thoroughly applied (Liehm and Leihm, 103–104). Another impact was to push directors even further towards working with national history and traditions. The best directors moved in this direction, with Vávra going as far back as the sixteenth century to find source material (Škvorecký, *All the Bright*, 36).

But much of the impulse to work with national history and culture as a source was also natural, partly because of feelings about restoring national pride following the war and partly owing to Czechoslovakia's deep humanistic traditions. Nationalization helped feed this impulse, as Czech and Slovak directors were now free to explore political themes without fear of having to be successful at the box office (Hames, *The Czechoslovak*, 37). This factor was a boon to quality as well, since directors could now spend more time on a production (Škvorecký, *All the Bright*, 28). One crucial area in which nationalization had an important impact was in animation and puppet films. These could have never been produced if their makers, mainly the internationally famous Jiří Trnka and Karel Zeman, had been forced to rely on private funding. But, most importantly, they helped carry on the Czech humanist ideals throughout the difficult decade of the fifties and established a production system that formed the basis for the outstanding feature films of the sixties. Creating an animated film is a craft that requires a small group of workers over whom the director must have complete quality control. This fact, and the international fame of these two artists, left little room for official interference in their work. In the 1960s the transformation of the entire film industry into similar small production groups made the Czechoslovak New Wave possible.

The other significant filmmaker of the period in which socialist realism held sway, which was only six or seven years, was Václav Krška, who also drew on national history and culture. From 1947 through 1952, Krška made several biographical films about Czech artists, writers, and inventors and a large historical epic, *Revoluční rok 1848* (*The Revolutionary Year, 1848*, 1949) (Dewey, *Outline*, 53–54). Then in 1953 and 1954, Krška produced adaptations of two works by Fráňa Šrámek, *Měsíc nad řekou* (*Moon over the River*) and *Stříbrný vítr* (*Silvery Wind*). Dealing with the frustrations and sexual awakenings of youth, these films received strong disapproval from the authorities. Šrámek's favorable status in the early fifties apparently helped *Moon over the River* survive, but *Silvery Wind* was delayed in its release for two years (Liehm and Liehm, 111). In 1958, Krška further challenged official conventions in *Zde jsou lvi* (*Hic Sunt Leones* [*Scars of the Past*]), in which a team of doctors' efforts to save a severely injured man are contrasted with the inconsideration that led to his accident, raising the question of why there is not equal concern for the active and healthy as there is for the sick and dying. As Peter Hames states, Krška "was a director who might well have acquired an international reputation had the times been different, and he is regarded by his pupil, Jan Němec, as one of the first to develop a style revealing his own personality, a predecessor of Antonioni" (*The Czechoslovak*, 43).

By now readers must have a number of questions about this period in Czechoslovak film history because, even though the fifties were a dreary decade for the nation during which the rest of the world hardly even knew that Czech film existed, there is still a good amount of quality to be found from the beginning of this period right up to the start of the New Wave in 1963. New directors were continually emerging and Czechoslovak films were taking occasional prizes at international festivals. With the speech of Soviet Premier Nikita Khrushchev revealing the crimes of Stalin at the 20th Congress of the Soviet Communist Party in 1956, socialist realism was further weakened and even more exceptional films were produced. Czechoslovak directors were ordered to stop imitating empty Soviet models, and new encouragement was given to youth. The years 1957–1961 saw some of the best work of Vojtěch Jasný, *Zářijové noci* (*September Nights*, 1957), *Touha* (*Desire*, 1958), *Přežil jsem svou smrt* (*I Survived My Death*, 1960), and *Procesí k panence* (*Pilgrimage to the Virgin*, 1961); Jiří Weiss, *Vlčí jáma* (*Wolf Trap*, 1958) and *Romeo, Julie, a tma* (*Romeo, Juliet and the Darkness*, 1960); Zbyněk Brynych, *Žižkovská romance* (*A Local Romance*, 1958), and *Smyk* (*Skid*, 1960); Jiří Krejčík, *Probuzení* (*Awakening*, 1959) and *Vyšší princíp* (*The Higher Principle*, 1960); Ladislav Helge, *Škola otců*

(*School for Fathers*, 1957) and *Velká samota* (*The Great Seclusion*, 1959); and Ján Kadár and Elmar Klos, *Tam na konečné* (*House at the Terminus*, 1957) and *Třetí přání* (*The Third Wish*, 1958).

Though not as innovative on the whole as the films of the New Wave, these productions still often give deeply probing and dramatic pictures of Czech society. *House at the Terminus*, for example, presented "the loneliness, cynicism, and compromise that . . . are supposed to be either eliminated or exceptional cases within a socialist society" (Hames, *The Czechoslovak*, 48). Moreover, this list, and the contributions by several of these directors to the New Wave, indicate only the surface of what was and could have been produced during these years. As Peter Hames explains, "the fact that a film like *House at the Terminus* could be made without condemnation suggests two things. The first is the extent to which the banned films must have been overt in their criticism. The second is a generally felt need to confront the realities of everyday life that probably went beyond the immediate individual interests and objectives of Kadár and Klos" (*The Czechoslovak*, 48).

But how could such a film even be allowed into production? What qualities did these films possess that made their social criticisms palatable over an untold number of other projects that did not survive? Certainly, the situation reveals that there were no exact guidelines, as there never can be in art. Some films, like Krška's *Moon Over the River* and *Silvery Wind*, could get by on their connection with an acceptable writer. The puppet films benefited from their unique production requirements. All of which means that the random censorship cannot be explained as a specifically devised tactic to keep the filmmakers on edge. If the authorities could have taken the alternative of banning any and all objectionable works, they probably would have. So there was no consciously chosen strategy of randomness.

One possible explanation for what was allowed involves the idea of using national history, traditions, and art as source material, which has always been a source of vitality for Czech and Slovak films. Stalinist-Zhdanovist philosophy seems mainly to have encouraged and/or allowed the expression of nationalist ideas based on well-established cultural and artistic traditions, while vigorously suppressing any expressions that attempted to develop new artistic movements. This approach would help a country like Czechoslovakia maintain an illusion of independence from Moscow while effectively preventing it from strengthening a truly autonomous identity. Thus, from 1948 to 1957, only Trnka, Zeman, and Krška were able to develop distinct personal styles. Within these restrictions, the Czechs would have some room for artistic expression based on their achievements in animation and the development of the lyrical style. But this trend is evident in all Czech post-war film right up to the present, with Jiří Menzel's *My Sweet Little Village* being a recent example. It influenced Miloš Forman's first film, *Konkurs* (*Competition*), for example. This film involved the conflict between traditional brass band music and the young culture of motorcycles and rock and roll, which, Forman states, "the authorities hated with a passion" (personal letter). Anything outside these safe, backwards-looking traditions was suppressed whenever the political climate allowed it.

The crackdown on filmmakers and other artists at the 1959 Banska Bystrica Conference reveals more of the thinking behind official censorship. The Stalinists in power had been looking to reassert a firm control ever since Khrushchev's speech, and early in the year they began selectively attacking a broad range of artists. In film, Kadár and Klos's *The Third Wish* was singled out for particular condemnation, but not because it was necessarily critical of the regime or socialism in general. Instead, the attack was made as part of a "battle against the remnants of bourgeois thought" (Škvorecký, *All the Bright,* 59) and the two directors were the right age to have been influenced by pre-war culture. A number of the other films just mentioned as some of the brightest examples of this period were also criticized, and, although the charges made were not the severe antisocialist accusations that would have come under Stalin, the directors involved still had to pay strong penalties. Kadár and Klos were prevented from working for two years, and Ladislav Helge was dealt an effective psychological blow that crippled his work for a number of years (Škvorecký, *All the Bright,* 58–64).

Still, this setback was only able to delay, but not prevent, the New Wave, and perhaps only made its emergence more remarkable since it appeared to rise so suddenly out of nothing. This fact caused it to become known as "the Czechoslovak film miracle" and led to countless questions of how it happened. The reasons are many and include the long, deep history of filmmaking in Czechoslovakia, the country's rich cultural and humanistic traditions, and the preservation of its studios through the war. But a final, crucial element was the film school, FAMU. Though the influence of the school on the New Wave directors cannot be defined specifically, FAMU was important for providing a large group of young film artists with a place where they could see a lot of movies from all over the world, discuss their ideas with each other, and work on short films without the pressure of having to achieve critical or box office success. Thus, the young students were able to relate to both national and international traditions and trends in cinema and did not have to feel like they were working in isolation. This was crucial at a time when they were very likely, as Forman described, to have strong doubts about their own ideas that deviated from socialist realism. They were able to find justification for what they wanted to do in what had been done elsewhere and receive encouragement to pursue their innovations.

Certainly, their stylistic experiments are what distinguish the New Wave from the previous era, and these can be related to their different attitudes towards socialism. While there were several directors of the older generation who contributed notable works to the Czechoslovak "film miracle," production in the sixties was dominated by a group of young directors who astounded the world through their honest looks at contemporary Czechoslovak society. For them, politics was of only a secondary concern at best, and thus, influenced by all the contemporary trends in international filmmaking, they set out to express their personal visions. A brief discussion of a notable Slovak film from 1963 that is not considered part of the New Wave should help reveal the differences. Peter Solan's *Boxer and the Death* is an interesting study of a concentration camp commander who chooses a prisoner as a sparring partner, allowing him good food and special privileges so that he will prove a worthy opponent. The prisoner, however, eventually wins and is rewarded with his freedom, but gives it up in order to return and save the others. It seems the commandant has pulled the escape alarm to cover his absence, and punishments will be sure to follow.

Though Solan's film won a prize at the San Francisco Film Festival, it is an entirely conventional socialist film in many ways. The main characters have personal struggles, but the evil fascist naturally makes the wrong selfish choice, while the good socialist chooses the group over personal freedom. Good and evil are never hard to distinguish. More disturbing is that none of the prisoners are Jewish and Jews are never referred to, though perhaps there were some camps in which all the prisoners were Czech or Slovak.

Another film dealing with the Nazi occupation made the previous year shows a closer relationship to the New Wave because of its stylistic differences. Zbyněk Brynych's *Transport z ráje* (*Transport From Paradise,* 1962) was based on a number of stories by Arnost Lustig, an important literary source for the New Wave. The film deals with an approximate twenty-four-hour period in the Nazi-created Jewish settlement of Terezin. While the Nazis are again almost entirely evil, the difference here is that they do not weaken. Several Jews do what they can to resist, for example by refusing to collaborate and running a clandestine printing press. But the Nazis snuff out all these efforts and punish those involved. The Germans are cocky and confident and never lose their grip. At the end, the transport train leaves for the concentration camp, and the German commanders plan a party to celebrate a job well done.

Throughout the film, there is no discernible story line, no central character, and no hero. The camera simply observes, creating a portrait of evil at its height. Occasionally, one of the Jews will be caught in a freeze frame forming a memorable picture of injustice. The pace is slow and steady, like the entire process of oppression, and the mood is always gray and gloomy. There was nothing to celebrate about this period.

These qualities of honest, patient observation and an apparent refusal to bend reality to the demands of a narrative mark the differences of the New Wave. Two other early breaks from socialist realism were Frantisek Vláčil's *Holubice* (*The White Dove,* 1960) and the Slovak Štefan Uher's *Slnko v sieti* (*Sunshine in a Net,* 1962). Both diverged from official standards mainly in terms of their striving for poetic presentations. But it was in 1963 that the New Wave truly first began to make its mark.

That year saw the release of Miloš Forman's *Black Peter* and *Competition,* Věra Chytilová's *O něčem jiném* (*About Something Else*), and Jaromil Jireš's *Křik* (*The Cry*). Forman and Chytilová, along with Jiří Menzel, Evald Schorm, and Jan Němec, were to become the major directors in the Czech film phenomenon. In their work, they were able to play off the Czech lyrical traditions and draw on Czech literature and culture, just as their country's filmmakers have always been able to do. But the mark of their distinction came from going beyond all that; they had learned to look directly at their society and report accurately and honestly on what they saw. In doing so, they were able to draw on contemporary trends such as Italian neorealism and cinéma-vérité, but these were only slight influences, strongly modified by their love of Hollywood movies as well.

Miloš Forman was the first and foremost at putting these influences into his own distinctive approach. His ideas about working with actors says a lot about his methods in general. Forman has said that in working with an actor, he will first rehearse the situation and see how the actor performs. Then he will decide on how to shoot the scene based on what the actor has done. But just as he would not move a building, he will also not artificially move an actor (Gelmis, 131). The method suggests Forman's constant concern with making his works of fiction as believable as possible and explains his frequent use of non-actors. Forman has said that in his work he likes to get as close to actual life as possible (Forman, "Closer").

In fact, his first film, *Competition,* originated from simply going down to Prague's popular Semafor Theatre and filming the people on the streets. This material became a forty-five-minute story about young girls auditioning. It produced a portrait of Czech youth, part cruelly honest and part sympathetic, that had never been seen on the nation's screens before. Later Forman received permission to film a second forty-five-minute production, this one about brass bands, and the two films were released as a single feature. In the second film, Forman again used footage from actual events, brass band rehearsals and a motorcycle race, to construct a story about the conflicts between youth culture and traditional culture.

Forman's two most famous Czech films, the Academy Award nominated *Lásky jedné plavovlásky* (*Loves of a Blonde,* 1965) and *Hoří, má panenko!* (*The Firemen's Ball,* 1967), both had similar origins. The first began when Forman picked up a teen-age girl hitchhiking in Prague at 3 a.m. She was trying to find the apartment of a boy she had met only once before, who had given her a false address. This became the story of the film. *The Firemen's Ball* was inspired by a visit to an actual firemen's ball, after which Forman and his co-writers, Ivan Passer and Jaroslav Papoušek (who also became skilled directors in their own right), simply brainstormed about all the things that could have happened. In these films as well, Forman's camera takes on the role of a simple observer, revealing with cruelty and sympathy, the hypocrisy of the society in its attempts to order people around, succeeding at nothing but making their lives more miserable.

Forman's first feature, *Černý Peter,* ironically originated from a novel by Papoušek. But the setting was moved from 1945 to 1963 when Forman discovered that his young actors performed much better when they could just be themselves. Oddly enough, that does not involve much. Peter (Ladislav Jakim), especially, spends the film awkwardly trying to please his girlfriend Paula (Pavla Martinková), his demanding father, and his boss. Through all this, the camera again simply watches as Peter struggles to maintain his dignity while the adults go about making fools of themselves. In each of his Czech films, Forman uses large crowd scenes, usually in a ballroom, to allow his camera to simply observe a large cross-section of society. These scenes manage to reveal a great deal about human behavior without the use of any dialogue.

Věra Chytilová began similar to Forman with *About Something Else,* an unusual documentary that parallels the lives of two totally unrelated women, one an ordinary housewife and the other a world champion gymnast. Much of it consisted of cinéma-vérité material and attempted to get the audience to sympathize with the sufferings from hard work and boredom that each experienced. In her other two films from the sixties, Chytilová dropped the documentary aspect of her work but kept the unusual qualities. *Sedmikrásky (Daisies,* 1966) must be, in fact, one of the most unusual films ever produced. It focuses on two girls, Marie I and Marie II, who decide that nothing matters and become involved in a series of nihilistic episodes, many of them involving food. But, in actuality, the film has no conventional chronology, logical narrative, or psychological development. As Peter Hames writes, "The point of the film is to make a single interpretation impossible, to force a conclusion that what has been seen constitutes only part of 'the truth.' The film's conception is a provocation in the context of conventional audience expectations, and the film usually has precisely that effect both in Czechoslovakia and elsewhere" *(The Czechoslovak,* 222–223). Similarly, her next film, *Ovoce stromů rajských jíme (We Eat the Fruit of the Trees of Paradise,* 1969)

is genuinely experimental in that it explores unconventional and "impossible" associations, and Chytilová's strength lies in the confidence with which she approaches just such impossibilities. Even more than in *Daisies,* it is a film in which the visual qualities are dominant. Whereas the "aesthetics" of *Daisies* may have arisen partly by accident and as a result of its critical approach, *The Fruit of Paradise* is clearly a deliberate exploration and celebration of formal effects. (Hames, 227)

Perhaps the most internationally famous film of the period was Jiří Menzel's *Ostře sledované vlaky (Closely Watched Trains,* 1966). Like Forman, Menzel takes a comic approach to his material, but there are serious issues involved. In his Oscar-winning work, set at a rural Czech train station during the Nazi occupation, Menzel's point seems to be that we need to be mainly concerned with creating and enjoying life. When we insist too much on order, like the Nazis, we miss what is really important and only cause destruction.

Menzel's other films completed or started before the Soviet invasion, in which his "all-pervading theme is the vicissitudes of sex" were *Rozmarné léto (Capricious Summer,* 1967), *Zločin v šantánu (Crime in the Nightclub,* 1968), and *Skřivánci na niti (Larks on a String,* 1969). The final film was banned before release and prevented Menzel from returning to the studios until the mid-seventies. (It was finally viewed at the 1990 Berlin Film Festival.)

Like Brynych in *Transport From Paradise,* Jan Němec also raises serious questions about relationships between oppressors and the oppressed in *O slávnosti a hostech* (*Report on the Party and the Guests,* 1966). The most haunting aspect of Němec's film is not how the party leader (intended to refer directly to the Party leader in this allegory) is really an evil man who skillfully strips his guests of their freedom, but how the guests cooperate so willingly. Němec, who also directed a film of Lustig's works, *Démanty noci* (*Diamonds of the Night,* 1964), shows how all the guests quickly begin placing themselves in debt to the host who has trapped them and whom they do not even know. The guests just want to enjoy themselves, possess nice things, and avoid conflict, and the host promises all this as long as they do not upset him. It seems like a fair trade. But in the end, they are all trapped in what appears to be a comfortable prison, and the one man who wants to be different is being hunted down by dogs. The guests blow out the candles themselves, and the host promises to relight them later. This dim hope seems to be enough for everyone involved, but no one has stood up to the host. Even the man who slipped away can only be admired for valuing his independence. Certainly, as with *Transport From Paradise,* the question arises whether more could be done. In his other feature, *Mučedníci lásky* (*Martyrs of Love,* 1966) Němec, like Chytilová, asserted his creative freedom by producing a poetically ambiguous work that Peter Hames refers to as "a dream world equivalent to the fantasies of popular song" (*The Czechoslovak,* 205). In 1968, Němec began work on a documentary of Czech life that became completely changed by the invasion of the tanks. It was completed as *Oratorio for Prague* and concluded Němec's Czech film career.

One final director who deserves specific attention as a major figure of the New Wave is Evald Schorm, who portrayed the nonconformist in *Party and the Guests* though his style is entirely different from Němec's. Schorm is mainly concerned with ideas rather than style. His first feature, *Každý den odvahu* (*Courage for Every Day,* 1964) dealt with the human consequences of Stalinism. Though criticized as a slander against the revolution, Schorm's film is actually sympathetic towards its Stalinist hero. *Návrat ztraceného syna* (*The Return of the Prodigal Son,* 1966) related the problems of an eventual suicide victim to those faced by most people. Schorm criticized the malaise of an advanced socialist society through visual devices emphasizing fear and isolation. In *Pět holek na krku* (*Five Girls to Deal With,* 1967), Schorm comments on the cruelty and emptiness of bureaucratic parents, jealous teen-agers, and street alcoholics but manages to do so with humor and understanding. *Farářův konec* (*End of a Priest,* 1969), made in collaboration with Josef Škvorecký, is a comedy upholding Christian morality over socialist half-truths (Hames, 49–111). Schorms' final film of the sixties, *Den sedmý, osmá noc* (*Seventh Day, Eighth Night,* 1969) was banned.

Other significant young directors to emerge during the sixties included Forman's colleagues Ivan Passer and Jaroslav Papoušek, fellow Czechs Jaromil Jireš, Hynek Bočan, Antonín Máša, Oldřich Lipský, and Jan Schmidt, and the Slovaks Juraj Jakubisko and Juraj Herz. Their styles ranged widely from the careful observation of Forman to the more experimental style of Chytilová. In 1965, several of these directors contributed short films based on the stories of Bohumil Hrabal (author of *Closely Watched Trains*) to a compilation film entitled *Perličky na dně* (*Pearls at the Bottom*). Throughout the decade, the short film continued to be an important form in Czechoslovakia, as it does today. In fact, one of the nation's most talented current directors, Jan Švankmajer, began his career as a director of shorts in 1964 and continues to work in that form. It is probably his use of this largely unnoticed form that has allowed him to complete many of his films, though he has not been free from censorship. Peter Hames reports that "Švankmajer has characterized his work as surrealist investigation—an attempt to liberate feelings of fear and anguish using weapons of sarcasm, objective humor, and black comedy" ("After the Spring," 132).

Several older directors such as Otakar Vávra, Vojtěch Jasný, Jiří Weiss, and Karel Kachyňa also created excellent works throughout the sixties. František Vláčil endured powerful physical and psychological hardships to create a monumental work on a fourteenth-century struggle between Christian and pagan forces in *Markéta Lazarová* (1967). He followed that with two other impressive films *Údolí včel* (*Valley of the Bees*, 1968) and *Adelheid* (1969). The first was also set in medieval times, the last at the end of World War II. Reading accounts of these films in Hames's book, one gets the impression that had Vláčil worked in the West, he would be internationally recognized today as a master of the cinema.

Certainly, no discussion of the New Wave can be complete without some focus on the beautiful Oscar-winning Slovak-language film of Ján Kadár and Elmar Klos, *Obchod na korse* (*The Shop on Main Street*, 1965). Again set during the Nazi occupation, the film once more deals with the failure of individuals to resist because of their selfish concerns. The main character, Tono Britka, never makes a decision except when it is too late, and then he does so violently. This quality produces the film's tragic climax in which Tono kills an old Jewish woman and then hangs himself. The conclusion then shows these two victims waltzing down the street together in beatific peace. But by indicating that such harmony can only exist after death, Kadár and Klos significantly undercut the Czechoslovak lyrical tradition.

Throughout the sixties, the Stalinist regime of Antonín Novotný became increasingly discredited and unable to handle the mounting liberalism in Czechoslovak society. At the June 1967 Writers' Congress, several leading authors and philosophers including Milan Kundera, Karel Kusík, and Ludvik Vaculík called for an alternative brand of socialism, giving support to the intellectuals and artists of the time (Hames, *The Czechoslovak*, 279–280). In December the Novotný regime finally capitulated to the reform movement led by the new general secretary, the Slovak Alexander Dubček. What followed for the next eight months became known as the Prague Spring, a time in which the government and intellectuals were finally working together to address the nation's problems, and the dreams of a responsive and compassionate socialism that could allow freedom of expression once more seemed possible. However, on August 20, 1968, Soviet tanks rolled into Prague, putting a quick end to Dubček's experiment and establishing a new regime under Gustav Husák that would bring the nation back under firm Soviet control. It had to be a terrible irony to the Czechoslovakians, twenty years later, when Mikhail Gorbachev began following many of the policies that the Soviets had crushed in Prague while still defending that action.

Initially, "normalization," as the Soviets termed it, had absolutely no impact on the film industry. In fact, "the aesthetic level of filmmaking in 1968–69 probably surpassed that of the earlier achievements of the New Wave" (Hames, *The Czechoslovak*, 257). This year saw new releases by many of the decade's greatest figures, including *Všichni dobří rodáci (All Those Good Countrymen)*, by Vojtěch Jasný. Subsequently banned, the film was a fitting conclusion to the decade and this era of Czechoslovak history.

Jasný sketches out the decline of a small village from 1945 to about 1960, in which Stalinism appears to be the great evil. But the narrator wonders at the end about where they all went wrong. How did they dig their own graves? They began with a good community. But, while some of them saw communism as a path towards an ideal, others saw it as a system that could be exploited for personal gain. They tried to force the community to go where they wanted it to and only destroyed it and anyone who stood up to them. At the end, one of the original Party leaders leaves town on his bicycle. The beautiful countryside is still there. But the faith embodied in the opening scene, set in a church where hymns to Stalin and God get equal time, is gone.

The appropriateness of this conclusion to the destruction of the Prague Spring may not be entirely coincidental. Karel Pryl has pointed out that many of the remarkable films of 1968–1969 were not ones that had simply started production before the invasion and concluded afterwards but "conscious demonstrations of a refusal to give in" (126). Eventually, however, several productions were stopped, several completed works banned, and four films (*The Firemen's Ball, End of a Priest, A Report on the Party and the Guests,* and *All Those Good Countrymen*) were banned "forever" (Hames, *The Czechoslovak*, 257–258). The new regime then made some important changes to assure that Czech and Slovak film would again return to a level of dismal mediocrity.

In 1970 the managing directors of both the Barrandov studios and the Koliba studios in Bratislava were deprived of their posts, and the five autonomous production groups and their script advisory boards were abolished. The production plan for 1970 was canceled and the Union of Czechoslovak Film and Television Artists dissolved. Alois Poledňák, the director of Barrandov, who was appointed after the reorganizations that followed Banská Bystrica in 1959, was arrested in September 1970 for "anti-socialist activities." He was held without trial until the summer of 1971 when he was sentenced to two years in jail for "endangering state secrets" (Hames, *The Czechoslovak,* 258)

The result was a decade of movies like Dušan Klein's *Summons for the Queen* (1975), a detective film in which the point seems to be that the police have assistants everywhere and trying to beat the system is no use. Though Klein does show a seedy side to Czechoslovak life, the good people are completely disgusted by that. Progressively speaking, the film does present some lawbreakers sympathetically. But the crime operation's kingpin, played by Vladimír Menšík, who also appeared in *Loves of a Blonde* and *All Those Good Countrymen,* is a sly manipulator who gets what he deserves. In the end, everything comes out right for the police and society.

Nevertheless, despite the renewed standards of mediocrity, Czechoslovak film did have some bright spots in the 1970s. A few directors, including Otakar Vávra, who became the first to declare his allegiance to the post-'68 regime, were able to continue having distinctive careers. As in the fifties, films that looked back to cultural traditions and achievements in the past were acceptable to the regime. Vávra, who has made a great number of such films, returned to the genre to create a World War II trilogy *Dny zrady* (*Days of Betrayal,* 1972), *Sokolovo* (1975), and *Osvobození Prahy* (*The Liberation of Prague,* 1977) that matched his Hussite trilogy of the fifties for blandness. But, looked at carefully, it can be seen as containing more honesty than the regime would probably like to see (Hames, *The Czechoslovak,* 263). Other directors working in this area included František Vláčil with *Koncert na konci léta* (*Concert at the End of the Summer,* 1979), a tribute to Dvořák, and Jiří Krejčík with *Božská Ema* (*The Divine Emma,* 1979), based on the life of Emmy Destin, a pre-World War I opera star who was successful in the United States. Czech and Slovak films generally benefited from fine technical work since the government's restrictions affected directors, but not cinematographers or sound engineers.

In addition, as throughout its history, Czechoslovak film has begun its climb back towards legitimacy with the assistance of some fine writers. Bohumil Hrabal, who contributed so much to the sixties, collaborated on two films with Jiří Menzel, *Postřižiny* (*Cutting it Short,* 1981) and *Slávnosti sněženek* (*The Snowdrop Festival,* 1983). Hames writes of *Postřižiny,* "there is no doubt that it is Menzel's best film since the sixties and, on every level, the most successful Czech film of the post-invasion period" ("After the Spring," 119). Another important new screenwriter, Zdeněk Svěrák, collaborated with Menzel on two other films *Na samotě u lesa* (*Seclusion Near a Forest,* 1976) and *Vesničko má, středisková* (*My Sweet Little Village,* 1986). As successfully entertaining comedies, these films are not merely exceptions to a rule of mediocrity, but also evocative of the spirit of the sixties in ways that are relevant to the present. Like Czech films of the fifties, those of the post-invasion decades also deserve to be evaluated on their own terms and not merely in comparison with the New Wave or flawed by political restrictions.

Svěrák has also continued working with Ladislav Smoljak, his collaborator on plays for the Jára Cimrman Theatre, a leading theatre of the sixties. Together, they have written a number of films, including two for the veteran comedy director, Oldřich Lipský. In the eighties, Smoljak himself turned to directing and began bringing several of their works to the screen. Another writer who has been a significant source of inspiration is the novelist Vladimír Páral. Two films by the Slovak Jaromil Jireš based on his works, *Mladý muž a bíla velryba* (*Young Man and the White Whale*, 1978) and *Katapult* (*Catapult*, 1983), have helped move Czech film closer to dealing with social realities.

Jireš was another of the few directors to maintain a distinct identity throughout the seventies and created what is probably the most powerful Czech film of the decade, *A pozdravuji vlaštovky* (*And Give My Love to the Swallows*, 1971). Based on the diaries of a young resistance fighter, Maruška Kudeříková, a national heroine who was imprisoned, tortured, and executed by the Nazis, the film reveals her deep humanity, optimism, and love even for her captors. Hames writes, "*And Give My Love to the Swallows* is surely a message of hope and sustenance produced for a period of spiritual and intellectual despair and disillusion. In place of empty slogans and bureaucratic conformism, it offered something rather subversive—a genuine belief and commitment" (*The Czechoslovak*, 266).

Another veteran Czech director making some notable films since the Prague Spring has been František Vláčil with *Dym bramborové ňate* (*Smoke on the Potato Fields*, 1976), *Stíny horkého léta* (*Shadows of a Hot Summer*, 1978), and *Stín kapradiny* (*The Shades of Ferns*, 1985). Significant Slovak contributions have come from Dušan Hanák with *Ružové sny* (*Rose-Tinted Dreams*, 1976) and *Tichá radosť* (*Silent Joy*, 1985); Juraj Jakubisko with *Postav dom, zasaď strom* (*Build a House, Plant a Tree*, 1980) and *Tisícročná v čela* (*The Millennial Bee*, 1983); and Štefan Uher with *Keby som mal pušku* (*If I Had a Gun*, 1971) and *Pásla kone na betóne* (*Concrete Pastures*, 1982).

Each of these directors has also made other films, which, while not up to their highest standards, must also possess interest by reflecting some of their talent. In addition, sixties veterans such as the Czech Karel Kachyňa and the Slovak Juraj Herz also contributed new works during the seventies. Though probably not thrilling works, Hames's comments on Vávra and the screening of Oldřich Lipský's *Adela ještě nevečeřela* (*Adela Hasn't Had Supper Yet/Dinner for Adele*, 1978) at the 1982 University of Oklahoma Czech Film Festival indicate that once again there is probably a lot more quality in Czech and Slovak film during the last two decades than the world has noticed. Lipský's film, which has not been mentioned in any writing about recent Czechoslovak film that I have seen, is a hilarious comedy about the American detective Nick Carter in Prague and involves a people-eating plant much like the one seen a decade later in Frank Oz's hit *The Little Shop of Horrors*. Taking the response of an audience of Oklahoma college students as an indication, Lipský's film could have been another foreign success. But, once again, the xenophobic policies of America's commercial theaters have limited its audience's cultural horizons.

The Czechoslovak film situation in the late eighties showed the continued relevance of Ivan Passer's comment that while transgressing ideological restraints may be more dangerous than breaking economic restrictions, it is also more possible since political guidelines cannot be as specific as monetary ones (Liehm, *Closely Watched*, 378). A representative example of the expressiveness possible in Czech film throughout that period is represented in Jiří Menzel's Oscar-nominated *My Sweet Little Village*. The film beautifully evokes the Czech lyrical tradition and all the charm of a closely knit village. Furthermore, it ends with a vision of harmony and apparent optimism that these traditions will survive. But, throughout the film, the villagers are constantly threatened by modern technology, the socialist system, and Prague executives, who wish to transform their houses into weekend retreats. Characters are run over by farm machinery and cars, cooperative farmworkers habitually drink on the job, and those closest to power are the most corrupt and least sensitive to human suffering. Despite these problems, the people miraculously survive. The film provides a tribute to their spirit, still alive from the sixties, which Menzel evokes with cinematic references to *Closely Watched Trains* and *Loves of a Blonde*. On the whole, Menzel's point is that maintaining an independent identity is greatly preferable to being part of the system.

For Czech and Slovak filmmakers, this task has been difficult, and a purist could maintain that there is something hypocritical in espousing independence while relying on the system for the means of production. Yet all filmmakers must get money from somewhere, and Western directors commonly make films attacking the economic system that has provided their life support. Therefore, when Otakar Vávra immediately proclaimed his allegiance to the new regime following the Soviet invasion and other directors later followed suit with statements of confession about past errors and dedication to the new system, they were simply making the kinds of proclamations that they had to in order to keep working. The directors must have felt that they could accomplish more by producing films than by remaining idle, and therefore they should be judged by their films and not by their pledges of allegiance.

Evidence for the validity of this approach lies in the continuing presence of Věra Chytilová at the forefront of Czechoslovak film. After a layoff of several years because of political animosities, Chytilová has since returned to make several films, which, while far more conventional than her work in the sixties, still challenge the society "to look at itself and the nature of its morality and material preoccupations" (Hames, "After the Spring," 127). Moreover, her films also contribute strong feminist attitudes to the culture and continue to reveal her commitment to experimentation. Chytilová's post-invasion films include *Hra o jablko* (*The Apple Game*, 1976), *Panelstory* (*Prefab Story*, 1979), *Kalamita* (*Calamity*, 1979), *Faunovo příliš pozdní odpoledne* (*The Very Late Afternoon of a Faun*, 1983), *Vlčí bouda* (*Wolf's Cabin*, 1986), and *Šašek a královna* (*The Jester and the Queen*, 1987). Chytilová has defended the integrity of her work by claiming that she has control of her editing, and she has also stated that this was a freedom shared by her colleagues. She adds, "But most of them have a conventional approach and edit the way they have been taught.... I want to give new meaning to a film with my editing—I want to put things together in a new way" (Hames, "After the Spring," 129).

Along with Ladislav Smoljak, another new director who has established a distinct body of work is Jiří Svoboda. His films are marked by a strong visual style, impressive casts in challenging roles, and simple themes that are capable of wider resonance, a la František Vláčil (Hames, "After the Spring," 135). Other notable young film directors include Vladimír Drha, Karel Smyczek, Jaroslav Soukup, Zdenek Flidr, Zdeněk Troška, and Vladimír Balco (Hames, "After the Spring," 136–137). The 1988 Karlovy Vary Film Festival featured impressive new works by several of these people which once again combined honest examinations of Czechoslovak society with artistic innovations. These films included Smeyczek's *Why?*, Drha's *Sensitive Spot,* and Soukup's *Disco Story*. The sensation of the festival seems to have been Vít Olmer's *Bony a klid* (*Big Money*), a story of the black market currency trade. But there were also impressive new films by Miloš Zábranský (*A House for Two*), Zdeněk Zaoral (*Cobwebs* and *Pilgrims*), Stanislav Látal (*Švejk,* a documentary), and several by women directors: *Out of Love* by Helena Třeštíková, *Deadly Sunday* by Drahomíra Vihanová, and *Life is at the End,* a nine-part series on pregnancy made for television by the sisters Yvonne Vávrova and Lenka Střelecká. In addition, the festival's program notes indicated a new positive attitude towards the accomplishments of the New Wave, and Evald Schorm has now completed his first feature since 1969 (Hames, "Czech List"). Finally, working from the beginning of the New Wave right through the present, Jan Švankmajer has continued to show how Czech animators have always possessed the freedom to create works that challenge official conventions at every level. Even with the downfall of the Communists, Švankmajer's films, which he refers to as "surrealistic investigations of reality," will probably continue to be in conflict with conventional standards. But at least now, Czechs and Slovaks should have more opportunities to see them. Under the old regime, they were mainly produced for export only (Hames, "After the Spring," 130–134).

Even before the Communist downfall in 1989, reality was finally making its invasion of the country, inspired by Gorbachev and a new unity among dissidents within the population at large: "Thanks to the authorities, they [were] getting to know each other in prison cells, in collective trials, in joint efforts to defend their imprisoned members" (Laber, 40). But the government still had imprisonment as a tool, and, even in 1989, both Josef Škvorecký and Antonín J. Liehm saw a long time until the conditions of the sixties could return (personal letters). With the new freedoms being implemented, conditions certainly are not the same, since no one knows what kinds of effects market forces might now have on the shape of the Czechoslovak film industry and the content of its products. Yet, the release of *Skylarks on a String* and Jiří Strecha's *The Velvet Revolution,* a documentary about the change of power in 1989 (Dash), indicate that the emphasis in Czechoslovak film on carefully examining reality might still be alive. With their rich heritage to draw on, and the ability to now fully re-examine the triumphs of the sixties, the possibility definitely exists that Czech filmmakers could astound the world once again.

BIBLIOGRAPHY

Adamic, Oldřích. *The Czechoslovak Film, 1963-64*. Prague: Československý Filmexport, 1964.
———. *The Czechoslovak Film, 1965-66*. Prague: Československý Filmexport, 1966.
Boček, Jaroslav. *Looking Back on the New Wave*. Prague: Československý Filmexport, 1967.
———. *Modern Czechoslovak Film, 1945-1965*. Prague: Artia, 1965.
Bond, Kirk. "The New Czech Film." *Film Comment* 5 (Fall 1968):70-79.
Brož, Jaroslav. "Grass Roots." *Films and Filming* 11 (June 1965):39-42.
———. *The Path of Fame of the Czechoslovak Film*. Prague: Československý Filmexport, 1967.
Cargin, Peter. "Some Hope Still for Czechoslovakian Cinema." *Film* 67 (Autumn 1972):6.
Chytilová, Věra. "I Want to Work." *Index on Censorship* 5.2 (Summer 1976):17-20.
Clouzot, Claire. "Sons of Kafka." *Sight and Sound* 36 (Winter 1966-67):35-37.
Daniel, Frantisek. "The Czech Difference." *Politics, Art, and Commitment in the East European Cinema*. Edited by David W. Paul. New York: St. Martin's Press, 1983:49-56.
Dash, Sean. "Breakouts." *Film Comment* (May-June 1990):4-5.
Dewey, Langdon. "The Czechoslovak Cinema: Go! Stop! Go! Go?" *Film* 52 (Autumn 1968):20-32
———. "Czechoslovakia: Silence into Sound." *Film* 60 (Autumn 1970):4-7.
———. *An Index to Czechoslovak Directors*. London: British Federation of Film Societies, 1968.
———. *Outline of Czechoslovakian Cinema*. London: Informatics, 1971.
Elley, Derek. "Ripples From a Dying Wave." *Films & Filming* 20.10 (July 1974):32-36.
Forman, Miloš. "Closer to Things." *Cahier du Cinema in English* (January 1967):57-8.
Gelmis, Joseph. *The Film Director as Superstar*. Garden City, N.Y.: Doubleday & Co., 1970.
Gillett, John. "A Visit to Prague." *Sight and Sound* 29 (Winter 1959-60):22.
———. "The Czechs at Karlovy Vary." *Film* ser.2. 108 (September 1982):6-7.
Grenier, Cynthia. "East-West Meeting Ground." *Sight and Sound* 29 (Autumn 1960):182-183.
Haller, R. A. "Interview with Ján Kadár." *Film Heritage* 8.3 (Spring 1973):27-31.
Hames, Peter. "Czech Cinema: Encouraging Signs." *Film* ser.2. 66 (October 1978):7.
———. "Czech List." *Sight and Sound* (Autumn 1988):225-226.
———. "Czech Mates." *Films and Filming* 20 (April 1974):54-57.
———. *The Czechoslovak New Wave*. Berkeley: University of California Press, 1985.
———. "Czechoslovakia: After the Spring." *Post New Wave Cinema in the Soviet*

Union and Eastern Europe. Edited by Daniel J. Goulding. Bloomington: Indiana University Press, 1989: 102–42.

Janousek, Jiri, ed. *3½: Chytilová, Forman, Jireš, Juráček*. Prague: Orbis, 1965.

Laber, Jeri. "Fighting Back in Prague." *The New York Review of Books*. 27 April 1989:39–41.

Liehm, Antonín J. *Closely Watched Films: The Czechoslovak Experience*. New York: International Arts and Sciences Press, 1974.

———. *The Miloš Forman Stories*. New York: International Arts and Sciences Press, 1975.

———. *The Politics of Culture*. New York: Grove Press, 1973.

———. "The Reckoning of a Miracle." *Film Comment* 5 (Fall 1968): 64–69.

———. "Success on the Screen." *Survey* 59 (April 1966):12–30.

———. "Triumph of the Untalented." *Index on Censorship* 5.3 (August 1976): 57–60.

Liehm, Antonín J., and Mira Liehm. *The Most Important Art: Eastern European Film After 1945*. Berkeley: University of California Press, 1977.

Madsen, Axel. "This Year in Marienbad." *Sight and Sound* 36 (Autumn 1967): 176–77.

Orna, Bernard. "These Puppets Were So Real." *Films and Filming* 4 (April 1958): 30–31.

———. "A Czech Touch of Neo-Realism." *Films and Filming* 6 (May 1960): 34.

Paul, David W. ed. *Politics, Art, and Commitment in the East European Cinema*. New York: St. Martin's Press, 1983.

Pryl, Karel (pseud.). "Swan Song." *Sight and Sound* 40 (Summer 1971): 125–26.

Purs, Jiří. "Czechoslovak Cinema in 1985, A Year of Jubilee." *Czech Film* 1 (Winter 1985): 1–3.

Robinson, David. "Magic Lantern." *Sight and Sound* 30 (Spring 1961):91.

Škvorecký, Josef. *All the Bright Young Men and Women: A Personal History of the Czech Cinema*. Toronto: Peter Martin Associates, 1971.

———. "The Birth and Death of the Czech New Wave." *Take One* 2.8 (1970):10.

———. "Czech Writers: Politicians in Spite of Themselves." *New York Times Book Review* (10 December 1989): 1, 43–45.

———. "Czechoslovakia." *World Cinema Since 1945*. Edited by William Luhr. New York: Ungar Publishing Co., 1987: 154–69.

———. *Jiří Menzel and the History of the Closely Watched Trains*. Boulder, Colo.: East European Monographs, 1982.

Slater, Thomas J. "Miloš Forman, An Interview, Part II." *Post Script* 5.1 (Fall 1985): 2–16.

Štábla, Zdeněk. "The First Cinema Shows in the Czech Lands." *Film History* 3.3 (1989): 203–21.

Steigerwald, Karel. "Schools, Films, and Festivals" (interview with Professor A. M. Brousil). *Screen Education* 46 (September–October 1968): 88–92.

Stoil, Michael Jon. *Cinema Beyond the Danube: The Camera and Politics*. Metuchen, N.J.: The Scarecrow Press, 1974.

Toman, Ludvík. "Czech Feature Films: Variety of Genres and Subjects." *Czechoslovak Film* 1.2 (1972):6–13.

Váňová, Libuse, ed. *The Czechoslovak Film, 1968*. Prague: Československý Filmexport, 1968.

Weiss, Jiří. "Czech Cinema Has Arrived." *Films and Filming* 5 (March 1959): 8, 34.

———. "Mixing It." *Films and Filming* 11 (June 1965):46–48.
———. "My Friend the Gypsy." *Films and Filming* 1 (June 1955):14–15.
Whyte, Alistar. *New Cinema in Eastern Europe*. London: Studio Vista/Dutton, 1971.
Žalman, Ján. *Films and Filmmakers in Czechoslovakia*. Prague: Orbis, 1968.
———. "Question Marks on the New Czechoslovak Cinema." *Film Quarterly* (Winter 1967–68):18–27.
Zvonicek, Stanislav, ed. *Modern Czechoslovak Film, 1945–1965*. Prague: Artia, 1965.

BIOGRAPHICAL SKETCHES

BOČAN, HYNEK (1935–), director. More traditional in his approach than most of the New Wave, Bočan turned to fine literature to produce some highly professional work, including *Nikdo se nebude smát* (*Nobody Shall Be Laughing*), 1965;* *Soukromá víchřice* (*Private Hurricane*), 1967;* and *Čest a sláva* (*Honor and Glory*), 1969.

BREJCHOVÁ, JANA (1940–), actress. Beginning her career at the age of 13, Brejchová first gained international attention four years later in Weiss's *Vlčí jáma* (*Wolf Trap*), 1958.* Forman's first wife, she has won numerous awards, including most popular actress, 1968. Her films include Brynych's *Žižkovská romance* (*A Local Romance*), 1958;* Krejčík's *Probuzení* (*Awakening*), 1959;* Kachyňa's *Noc nevěsty* (*The Night of the Bride*), 1967; Schorm's *Každý den odvahu* (*Courage for Every Day*), 1964;* *Návrat ztraceného syna* (*The Return of the Prodigal Son*), 1966;* and *Farářův konec,* (*End of a Priest*) 1969;* Lipský's *Gentlemen, I Have Killed Einstein*, 1969; Schmidt's *Luk královny Dorotky* (*The Bow of Queen Dorothy*), 1969; and Svoboda's *Schůzka se stíny* (*A Meeting With Shadows*), 1982.

BRYNYCH, ZBYNĚK (1927–), director. Though he has produced some disasters, Brynych has also created some powerful examinations of fascism, human relationships, and people's relationships to their environment. These include *Žižkovská romance* (*A Local Romance*), 1958;* *Transport z ráje* (*Transport from Paradise*), 1962;* and *. . . A pátý jezdec je strach* (*. . . the Fifth Horseman Is Fear*), 1964.*

BURIAN, E. F., theater director. Member of the avant-garde Devětsil group and influential artist during the thirties, he later loaned his theater for rehearsals to a company led by the young Miloš Forman.

BURIAN, VLASTA, actor. A comic genius but political simpleton, Burian made several films in the twenties and thirties with artists such as Anny Ondráková, Voskovec and Werich, Martin Frič, and Hugo Haas, but allowed himself to be used by the Nazis and later struggled on with his career under the Communists until his death in the fifties.

ČAPEK, KAREL (1890–1938), author. "The Father of Czech Drama," originator of the word "robot," and novelist, Čapek fired the imaginations of his fellow countrymen both artistically and politically. As his work progressed, he became increasingly anti-militarist and anti-fascist, creating the play that became the basis for Hugo Haas' *Bílá nemoc* (*The White Plague*), 1937.*

CHYTILOVÁ, VĚRA, (1929–), director. A major force of the New Wave, on the cutting edge of experimentation in *Sedmikrásky* (*Daisies*), 1966,* and *Ovoce stromů rajských jíme* (*We Eat the Fruit of the Trees of Paradise*), 1969.* Before and since, she has been less eccentric, but is producing some of the most fascinating Czech films. Other films include *Strop* (*The Ceiling*), 1961;* *Pytel blech* (*A Bagful of Fleas*), 1962,* combined with *The Ceiling* and released as *U stropu je pytel blech* (*There's a Bagful of Fleas at the Ceiling*), 1962;* *O něčem jiném* (*About Something Else*), 1963;* *Hra o jablko* (*The Apple Game*), 1976;* *Panelstory* (*Prefab Story*), 1979;* *Kalamita* (*Calamity*), 1979;* *Faunovo příliš pozdní odpoledne* (*The Very Late Afternoon of a Faun*), 1983;* *Vlčí bouda* (*Wolf's Cabin*), 1986;* and *Šašek a královna* (*The Jester and the Queen*), 1987.*

ČUŘÍK, JAN (1924–), cinematographer. An important contributor from the pre-New Wave up through the present. Dewey states, "His technical expertise encompasses quasi-documentary realism, lyricism, and even exaggerated simplicity to underline a director's larger implications" (*Outline,* 80). Films include Brynych's *Žižkovská romance* (*A Local Romance*), 1958,* and *Transport z ráje* (*Transport from Paradise*), 1962;* Vláčil's *Holubice* (*The White Dove*), 1960;* Chytilová's *O něčem jiném* (*About Something Else*), 1963;* Juráček's *Josef Kilian* 1964;* Schorm's *Každý den odvahu* (*Courage for Every Day*), 1964,* and *Pět holek na krku* (*Five Girls to Deal With*), 1967;* and Jireš's *Žert* (*The Joke*), 1969;* *Valérie a týden divů* (*Valerie and Her Week of Wonders*), 1969;* *A pozdravuji vlaštovky* (*And Give My Love to the Swallows*), 1971;* and *Lidé z metra* (*People of the Metro*), 1974.

DEGL, KAREL (1896–1951), producer, cinematographer. Beginning his career with Fencl's *Zlaté srdéčko* (*The Golden Heart*), 1916, Degl began a production company with his brother Emanuel in 1918, helping many important figures, including Frič, get their start. As a cinematographer he worked with many important directors, including Rovenský throughout the thirties. He also co-directed the ambitious *Stavitel chrámu* (*The Builder of the Cathedral*), 1919,* with Antonín Novotný.

FORMAN, MILOŠ (1932–), director. The most well-known figure in Czech cinema, not only because of his Academy Awards for *One Flew Over the Cuckoo's Nest* (1975) and *Amadeus* (1984) but because his Czech films took an honest look at society, particularly the young, with humor, compassion, and criticism. He earned Academy Award nominations for his last two Czech films, *Lásky jedné plavovlásky* (*Loves of a Blonde*), 1965,* and *Hoří, má panenko* (*The Firemen's Ball*), 1967.* However, his first two films, *Konkurs* (*Competition*), Pt. I: *Kdyby ty muziky nebyly* (*If There Were No Music*), Pt. II: *Konkurs* (*Competition*), 1963,* and *Černý Petr* (*Peter and Paula/Black Peter*), 1963,* also showed Czech audiences something entirely new.

FRIČ, MARTIN (1902–1968), director. The most prolific figure in Czech film history, starting his career in 1919 and moving into directing in 1928. His best productions were *Varhaník u Sv. Víta* (*The Organist of Saint Vitas*), 1929;* *Hej rup!* (*Heave Ho!*), 1934;* *Jánošík*, 1935;* *Svět patří nám* (*The World Belongs to Us*), 1937; *Císařův pekář* (*The Emperor's Baker*) and *Pekařův císař* (*The Baker's Emperor*), 1951;* and *Hvězda zvaná pelynek* (*A Star Called Wormwood*), 1964. Frič also gave Forman his first screenwriting opportunity with *Nechte to na mně* (*Leave It to Me*), 1955.

HAAS, HUGO (1902–1969), actor-director. Known for his comic talents in such films as Innemann's *Muži v offsidu* (*Men Off-Side*), 1931,* Haas also became a powerful dramatic actor and director, producing the anti-fascist *Bílá nemoc* (*The White Plague*), 1937,* which later forced him to flee for his life. He successfully continued his career in America (with mostly "B" movies) until the mid-sixties, when he attempted once more to work in Czechoslovakia, but met only with frustration.

HACKENSCHMIED (later HAMMID), ALEXANDER, set designer, editor, director. Hackenschmied's work primarily in documentaries and the avant-garde, along with his reluctance to take major credits, kept him fairly unknown but does not diminish his large contributions. His own directorial efforts included *Bezúčelná procházka* (*Aimless Walk*), 1930, and *Na Pražském hrade* (*Prague Castle*), 1932. He worked with Machatý as scene designer on *Erotikon*, 1929,* and as "artistic collaborator" on *Ze soboty na neděli* (*From Saturday to Sunday*), 1931,* and as editor with Plicka on *Through Mountains—Through Valleys*, 1932, and *Zem spieva* (*The Earth Is Singing*), 1933.* In America, he co-directed the classic avant-garde film *Meshes of the Afternoon* with his then-wife Maya Deren.

HANÁK, DUŠAN, director. Slovak creator of international award-winning documentaries and the 1969 Mannheim prize-winning feature *322*. Hanák also made one of the best films of the seventies, *Ružové sny* (*Rose-Tinted Dreams*), 1976,* the 1989 Silver Bear winner at the Berlin Film Festival; *Ja milujem, ty* miluješ (*I Love, You Love*), produced in 1980;* and the notable feminist feature *Tichá radosť* (*Silent Joy*), 1985.*

HAŠEK, JAROSLAV, (1883–1923), author. Creator of the classic work of Czech comedy, *The Good Soldier Švejk*. Repeatedly filmed and an inspiration for countless other works, *Švejk*'s cultural status placed it beyond the reach of censors though it defied all the socialist ideals.

HELGE, LADISLAV (1927–), director. A powerful influence on young directors while at FAMU in the late fifties, Helge also directed the award-winning *Škola otců* (*School for Fathers*), 1957,* and the politically controversial *Velká samota* (*Great Seclusion*), 1960,* for which he was severly censored, returning to form only in 1968 with the effective and very similar *Stud* (*Shame*). The Soviet invasion of 1968, however, silenced him even more effectively.

HELLER, OTTO (1896–1970), cinematographer. After experience in the teens and twenties with companies such as Lucernafilm, Weteb, and Pragafilm, working often with Karel Lamač and Anny Ondráková, Heller contributed to the anti-Nazi films *Hej rup!* (*Heave Ho!*), 1934,* by Frič, and Haas' *Bílá nemoc* (*The White Plague*), 1937,* forcing him to flee when the Germans came. But he continued to be extremely successful in the West, with his most notable work coming on Sir Laurence Olivier's *Richard III*.

HERZ, JURAJ (1934–), actor, director. A Slovak director who works in Prague, Herz began at the culturally significant Semafor Theatre and showed a great deal of variety in his three notable films from the sixties, *Znamení Raka* (*The Sign of the Crab*), 1967; *Kulhavý ďábel* (*The Lame Devil*), 1968; and *Spalovač mrtvol* (*The Cremator of Corpses*), 1969.* The first was a psychological detective film, the second a period-piece comedy, and the third a dark character study. Recently, he has also directed the concentration camp film *Zastihla mě noc* (*I Was Caught by the Night*), 1986.*

HRABAL, BOHUMIL (1914–), author. Major literary source for the New Wave directors, who paid him a great tribute with the omnibus *Perličky na dně* (*Pearls at Bottom*), 1965,* for which seven filmmakers each adapted one of his short stories. Hrabal has worked most often with Menzel, the two collaborating on *Ostře sledované vlaky* (*Closely Watched Trains*), 1966;* *Skřivánci na niti* (*Skylarks on a String*), 1969;* *Postřižiny* (*Cutting It Short*), 1981;* and *Slávnosti sněženek* (*The Snowdrop Festival*), 1983.*

HRUŠÍNSKÝ, RUDOLF (1920–), actor. Beginning on the stage in 1935 and continuing through the eighties, Hrušínský's presence in a film is always a guarantee of some quality. His roles include ones in Čáp's *Noční motýl* (*The Night Moth*), 1941;* Herz's *Spalovač mrtvol* (*The Cremator of Corpses*), 1969;*

and Menzel's *Rozmarné léto* (*Capricious Summer*), 1967,* and *Vesničko má, středisková* (*My Sweet Little Village*), 1986.*

ILLÍK, JOSEF (1919–), cinematographer. An important contributor particularly to the work of Kachyňa, for whom he shot *Kočár do Vídně* (*The Coach to Vienna*), 1966;* *Noc nevěsty* (*The Night of the Bride*), 1967; and *Vlak do stanice nebe* (*The Train to Heaven Station*), 1973, among others. Illík has garnered many awards, including ones for Krška's *The Day the Tree Will Bloom*, 1961, and Kachyňa's *Trápení* (*Worries*), 1961. His other notable works include Vávra's *Kladivo na čarodějnice* (*Hammer Against Witches*), 1970.* He is particularly adept at capturing atmosphere.

INNEMANN, SVATOPLUK, director. Important early figure because of the quantity of his work and his consistent collaboration with top-quality artists. His cameramen included Václav Vich, Jan Stalich, and Karel Degl. Elmar Klos wrote his scripts in the early thirties, and he later collaborated with Vladislav Vančura.

JAKUBISKO, JURAJ (1938–), director. A proficient technician who achieved some remarkable cinematographic effects both with cameraman Igor Luther and on his own, Jakubisco inaugurated a distinctly Slovak style. His first feature, *Kristove roky* (*Crucial Years*), 1966,* won several awards. It was followed by *Zbehovia a pútnici* (*The Deserter and the Nomads*), 1968;* *Vtáčkovia, siroty a blázni* (*Birds, Orphans, and Fools*), 1969;* and *See You in Hell, Fellows!*, 1970, which he was not allowed to finish. Allowed to make only documentaries until the late 1970s, he has since returned with a flourish, completing six films since then. These have included *Tisícročna včela* (*The Millennial Bee*), 1983,* Golden Phoenix award winner at the Venice Film Festival; *Perinbaba*, 1985, a fairy-tale awarded a Gondola at Venice; and *Ledim na konari a je mi dobre* (*Flying High*), 1989,* a great success at the Venice Film Festival and the national entry for the Best Foreign Film Oscar.

JASNÝ, VOJTĚCH (1925–), director. A graduate of FAMU, Jasný reached a distinctively expressive style six years before the New Wave and later directed the perfect summary film for the sixties, *Všichni dobří rodáci* (*All Those Good Countrymen*), 1969.* His other films were *Zářijové noci* (*September Nights*), 1957;* *Touha* (*Desire*), 1958;* *Prezil jsem svou smrt* (*I Survived My Death*), 1960; *Procesi k panence* (*Pilgrimage to the Virgin*), 1961; and *Až přijde kocour* (*Cassandra Cat*), 1963.*

JIREŠ, JAROMIL (1935–), director. A talented filmmaker whose work has been equally balanced between the social and the personal, reality and fantasy, and the sublime and the grotesque. His works include *Křik* (*The Cry*), 1963;* *Žert* (*The Joke*), 1969;* *Valérie a týden divů* (*Valerie and Her Week of Wonders*),

1969;* A pozdravuji vlaštovky (And Give My Love to the Swallows), 1971;* Mladý muž a bíla velryba (Young Man and the White Whale), 1978; Causa králik (The Rabbit Case), 1979;* Neuplne zatmeni (Incomplete Eclipse), 1980; Katapult (Catapult), 1983; and Prodloužený čas (Prolonged Time), 1985. For some of his works, Kireš has drawn on top Czech authors like Kundera, Nezval, and Vladimir Páral.

JOHN, RADEK, writer. A prolific figure who scripted both of the big successes at the 1989 Karlovy Vary Film Festival, Karel Smyczek's Proč? (Why?),1987,* and Olmer's Bony a Klid (Big Money), 1988.* He also wrote Smyczek's Jen si tak trochu písknout (Just a Little Whistle), 1980, and Viktor Polsný's Poločas rozpadu (Half Time), 1985.

JUNGHANS, KARL (1897–?), director. German filmmaker, known primarily for creating the Czech silent masterpiece Takový je život (That's Life), 1929.*

KÁČER, JAN, actor, director. Leading actor in some of the top New Wave films, Káčer made his directorial debut in the early seventies. His performances included roles in Schorm's Každý den odvahu (Courage for Every Day), 1964,* and Návrat ztraceného syna (The Return of the Prodigal Son), 1966;* Vláčil's Údolí včel (Valley of the Bees), 1968,* and Adelheid, 1969;* and Bočan's Nikdo se nebude smát (Nobody Shall Be Laughing), 1965.*

KACHYŇA, KAREL (1924–   ), director. Along with Jasný, one of the first FAMU graduates in 1951. The two collaborated for four years until looser political conditions allowed them to develop their own styles. In the sixties, Kachyňa began a long association with screenwriter Jan Procházka, among the highpoints of which were Trápení (Worries), 1961; Ať žije republika! (Long Live the Republic!), 1965;* Kočár do Vídne (The Coach to Vienna), 1966;* Noc nevěsty (The Night of the Bride), 1967; Směšný pán (The Funny Man), 1969;* and Ucho (The Ear), 1971. He also made the internationally recognized children's film Už zase skáču přes kaluže (I'm Jumping Over Puddles Again), 1971.*

KADÁR, JAN (1918–1979), and **ELMAR KLOS** 1910–), directors. This team began making distinctive films in the early fifties, reaching a pinnacle with their Academy Award-winning Obchod na korze (The Shop on Main Street), 1965,* and culminating with Hrst vody (Adrift), 1969.* Their earlier works included Hudba z marsu (Music from Mars), 1954;* Tam na konečné (At the Terminal Station), 1957;* Smrť sa volá Engelchen (Death is Called "Engelchen"), 1963;* and Obžalovaný (The Accused), 1964.

KOLÁR, JAN STANISLAV (1896–   ), director, actor, scenario-writer, author, and film historian. Beginning a long and distinguished career in the teens, Kolár wrote, directed, and acted in a series that became known as the Polykarp comedies (1917). Developing an early association with Karel Lamač, the two appeared in *Učitel orientálnich jazyků* (*The Teacher of Oriental Languages*), 1918,* and *Akord smrti* (*Chord of Death*), 1919,* both of which Kolár also co-scripted and co-directed. In 1929, he directed the monumental *Svatý Václav* (*Saint Wenceslas*),* and then worked mainly as an actor for the remainder of his career, appearing in Radok's *Dědeček automobil* (*Grandfather Automobile*), 1956.*

KREJČÍK, JIŘÍ (1918–), director. An accomplished director of the immediate post-war era with a wide range of styles, Krejčík was also an early practitioner of the objective realism developed by Forman, Passer, and Papoušek in the New Wave. He received official reprimands for *Svědomí* (*Conscience*), 1949.* But it was later acclaimed, as were his features *Týden v tichém domě* (*Week in the Quiet House*), 1947;* *Ves v pohraničí* (*The Village on the Frontier*), 1948;* *Probuzení* (*Awakening*), 1959;* *Vyšší princíp* (*Higher Principle*), 1960;* and *Penzion pro svobodné pány* (*Boarding House for Bachelors*), 1968. In the seventies, he made *Lásky hry šálivé* (*Tricks of Deceptive Love*) and *Božská Ema* (*The Divine Ema*), 1979.

KŘESADLOVÁ, VERA, actress. Strikingly beautiful, Křesadlová began as a singer at the Semafor Theatre, appeared in Forman's *Konkurs* (*Competition*), 1963,* married him, and then appeared in the films of his collaborators, Passer— *Intimní osvětlení* (*Intimate Lighting*), 1965*—and Papoušek—*Nejkrásnější věk* (*The Most Beautiful Age*), 1969,* and *Ecce Homo Homolka,* 1969.* She also made two films with Menzel, *Zločin v dívčí škole* (*Crime in the Girl's School*), 1965, and *Skřivánci na niti* (*Skylarks on a String*), 1969,* and appeared in Jireš's *Žert* (*The Joke*), 1969.* She is also the mother of Forman's twin sons.

KŘIŽENECKÝ, JAN (1868–1921), director. Really a pioneer. Křiženecký was an architect and amateur photographer who first brought Lumière cameras to Prague in 1896 and thus fathered the nation's film industry. In June of 1898, he presented the first three films for Czech audiences, *Dostaveníčko ve mlynici* (*Rendezvous at the Mill*)*, *Pláčo a smích* (*Laughing and Crying*),* and *Výstavní parkar a lepič plakátů* (*The Exhibition Sausage Vendor*).*

KRŠKA, VÁCLAV (1900–), director. A literary and theatrical figure, Krška achieved the nearly impossible by defining a personal style during the fifties. He was strongly assisted by drawing on the works of the author Fráňa Šrámek. His films include *Řeka čaruje* (*The Spell of the River*), 1945; *Revoluční rok 1848* (*The Revolutionary Year, 1848*), 1949; *Měsíc nad řekou* (*Moon Over the River*), 1953;* *Stříbrný vítr* (*The Silvery Wind*), 1954* (banned until 1956); *Hic Sunt Leones* (*Scars of the Past*), 1958;* and *The Day the Trees Will Bloom,* 1961.

KRUMBACHOVÁ, ESTER (1923–), set designer, designer, screen writer, director. This important and versatile member of the New Wave made her directorial debut in 1970 with *The Murder of Mr. Devil,* but has only had one screenplay produced since then, Chytilová's *Faunovo příliš pozdní odpoledne (The Very Late Afternoon of a Faun),* 1983.* During the sixties, she also produced scripts for Chytilová's *Sedmikrásky (Daisies),* 1966,* and *Ovoce stromů rajských jíme (We Eat the Fruit of the Trees of Paradise),* 1969;* Němec's *O slávnosti a hostech (Report on the Party and the Guests),* 1966,* and *Mučedníci lásky (Martyrs of Love),* 1966;* Brynych's *. . . A pátý jezdec je strach (. . . the Fifth Horseman Is Fear),* 1964;* Vávra's *Kladivo na čarodejnice (Hammer Against Witches),* 1970;* and Jireš' *Valérie a týden divů (Valerie and Her Week of Wonders),* 1969.* She was a set or costume designer on Jasny's *Až přijdě kocour (Cassandra Cat),* 1963,* and *Všichni dobří rodáci (All Those Good Countrymen),* 1969;* Němec's *Démanty noci (Diamonds of the Night),* 1964;* and Kachyňa's *Kočár do Vídne (The Coach to Vienna),* 1966.*

KUČERA, JAROSLAV (1929–   ), cinematographer. A major figure of the New Wave, known for his adventurous technical experiments, Kučera shot all of Jasný's films excepting the international production *Dýmky (Pipes),* 1966, and all of Chytilová's, whom he also married, excepting *O něčem jiném (About Something Else),* 1963. Other work for this prolific artist included Jireš's *Křik (The Cry),* 1963;* Němec's *Démanty noci (Diamonds of the Night),* 1964;* the omnibus *Perličky na dně (Pearls at Bottom),* 1965;* the haunting adaptation of Arnost Lustig's *Dita Saxová,* 1967, by Antonín Moskalyk; and Herz's *Morgiana,* 1972.*

KUNDERA, MILAN (1929–   ), author. An important spiritual force for the New Wave as well as all of Czech culture, his works provided the basis for Bočan's *Nikdo se nebude smát (Nobody Shall Be Laughing),* 1965,* and Jireš' *Žert (The Joke),* 1969.*

LIPSKÝ, OLDŘICH (1924–1986), director. Primarily the creator of comedies, he reached success in his take-offs on Westerns, *Limonádový Joe (Lemonade Joe),* 1964;* science fiction, *Gentlemen, I Have Killed Einstein,* 1969; and detective films, *Adela ještě nevečeřela (Adela Hasn't Had Supper Yet),* 1978.* In the seventies, he also collaborated with the important new writing team of Ladislav Smoljak and Zdeněk Svěrák on *Jáchyme, hod ho do stroje (Joachim, Put It in the Machine),* 1974, and *Mařečku, podejtě mi péro (Mařeček, Pass Me a Pen),* 1976.

LUSTIG, ARNOST (1926–   ), author. Survivor of the Holocaust and another major literary source for the New Wave, Lustig now lives and works in Washington, D.C. His stories of the Nazi persecution formed the basis for Brynych's *Transport z ráje (Transport From Paradise),* 1962;* Němec's *Sousto (A Loaf of Bread),* 1960, and *Démanty noci (Diamonds of the Night),* 1964;* and Antonín Moskalyk's *Dita Saxová,* 1967.

MACHATÝ, GUSTAV (1901–1962), director. A major figure in Czech film, whose artistry is sometimes neglected because of the nude scene with Hedy Lamarr in the 1932 *Extase (Ecstasy),** which made both of them famous. Having spent four years in Hollywood, and reportedly having worked with Griffith and von Stroheim, he returned to make some of the greatest Czech films of the era, including *Kreutzerova sonáta (Kreutzer Sonata)*, 1926;* *Erotikon*, 1929;* and *Ze soboty na neděli (From Saturday to Sunday)*, 1931.* In 1945, he did a mild, low-budget remake of *Ecstasy* titled *Jealousy*.

MENZEL, JIŘÍ (1938–), director, actor. Still a major figure in Czech film, Menzel gained international fame by winning an Academy Award with his first film *Ostře sledované vlaky (Closely Watched Trains)*, 1966.* Known for his wry sense of humor, Menzel also makes touching and significant commentary on Czech history and society and the human condition. He was nominated for a second Academy Award in 1986 for *Věsničko má, středisková (My Sweet Little Village),** The rest of his filmography as a director includes *Rozmarné léto (Capricious Summer)*, 1967;* *Zločin v šantánu (Crime in the Night Club)*, 1968; *Skřivánci na niti (Skylarks on a String)*, 1969;* *Kdo hledá zlaté dno? (Who Looks for Gold?)*, 1975; *Na samotě u lesa (Seclusion Near a Forest)*, 1976;* *Báječní muži s klikou (Those Wonderful Movie Cranks)*, 1978; *Postřižiny (Cutting It Short)*, 1981;* and *Slávnosti sněženek (The Snowdrop Festival)*, 1983.* He has also made many appearances as an actor, several times in his own films and at least twice in works by Chytilová.

NĚMEC, JAN (1936–), director. Another major figure of the New Wave, whose allegorical *O slávnosti a hostech (Report on the Party and the Guests)*, 1966,* was his most famous film. Němec also made bold stylistic and structural experiments in *Démanty noci (Diamonds of the Night)*, 1964,* and *Mučedníci lásky (Martyrs of Love)*, 1966.* His other works included a prize-winning debut with *Sousto (A Loaf of Bread)*, 1960, and the documentary *Oratorio for Prague*, 1969, which included footage of the Soviet invasion.

NEZVAL, VÍTĚZSLAV (1900–?), poet, novelist. Exponent of surrealism, poetism, member of the Devětsil group, and supporter of cinema art, Nezval contributed to the scripts for Machatý's *Erotikon*, 1929, and *Ze soboty na neděli (From Saturday to Sunday)*, 1931,* and for Frič's *Varhaník u Sv. Víta (The Organist of Saint. Vitus)*, 1929.* His novel was the basis for Jireš' *Valérie a týden divů (Valerie and Her Week of Wonders)*, 1969.*

OLMER, VÍT (1947–), actor, director. A performer throughout the sixties, Olmer turned to directing in the eighties, producing the biggest success of the 1988 Karlovy Vary Film Festival, *Bony a klid (Big Money)*, 1988.* Taking a very Western-style commercial approach, his other films have included *Jako jed (Like Poison)*, 1985,* and *Antonyho šance (Anthony's Chance)*, 1986.*

ONDRÁKOVÁ, ANNY (1903–1987), actress. Possessing the talent and beauty to perform in a wide variety of roles and gain international fame, Ondráková eventually worked throughout Europe, including with Alfred Hitchcock in England. Married first to Karel Lamač, she later had a long marriage with boxing champion Max Schmeling. Her Czech films included a debut at the age of sixteen in Kolár and Lamač's *Dáma s malou nožkou* (*The Lady With the Small Foot*), 1919;* Kolár's *Zpěv zlata* (*The Song of Gold*), 1920;* and Anton's *Únos bankéře Fuxe* (*The Kidnapping of Banker Fux*), 1923.*

ONDŘÍČEK, MIROSLAV (1933–), cinematographer. Principally known as Miloš Forman's cinematographer, Ondříček shot all of Forman's Czech films except *Černý Petr* (*Black Peter/Peter and Paula*), 1963,* and has shot most of his American ones. But he has also contributed to many other Czech films and continues to work for many directors both in his home country and throughout the world. His other works have included Jireš' *Křik* (*The Cry*), 1963;* Passer's *Intimní osvětlení* (*Intimate Lighting*), 1965;* Němec's *Mučedníci lásky* (*Martyrs of Love*), 1966;* and Krejčík's *Božská Ema* (*The Divine Ema*), 1979.

PAPOUŠEK, JAROSLAV, director, screenwriter. One-third of the creative trio that also included Forman and Passer, Papoušek was originally a sculptor and writer, whose novel formed the basis for Forman's *Černý Petr* (*Black Peter/Peter and Paula*), 1963.* He later became an accomplished creator of comic realism in his own right, using several of Forman's ex-cast members and even his sons and ex-wife. These films included *Nejkrásnější věk* (*The Most Beautiful Age*), 1969,* and *Ecce homo Homolka*, 1969.*

PASSER, IVAN (1933–), director. After getting started with the Forman team, Passer began creating his own intimate and personal films in 1965 with *Fádní odpoledne* (*A Boring Afternoon*).* His only other Czech directorial effort was the highly acclaimed *Intimní osvětlení* (*Intimate Lighting*), 1965.* He has since created several American films, the most successful being *Born to Win* (1971) and *Cutter's Way* (1978).

PECH, ANTONÍN (1874–1928). One of the pioneers of Czech cinema, Pech served in many roles: accountant, director, producer, and photographer. He is most important for founding the earliest production company, Kinofa, in 1908, which lasted until 1912.

PLICKA, KAREL, cinematographer, teacher. Creator of two highly acclaimed Slovakian documentaries, *Through Mountains—Through Valleys,* 1932, and *Zem spieva* (*The Earth Is Singing*), 1933,* Plicka went on to become an instructor in Bratislava and later at FAMU.

PROCHÁZKA, JAN (1929–1971), screenwriter. Capitalizing on a favorable relationship with the Novotný regime of the sixties, Procházka assisted the New Wave directors with the authorities and created several notable screenplays for Karel Kachyňa, including *Trápení (Worries)*, 1961; *Ať žije republika! (Long Live the Republic!)*, 1965;* *Kočár do Vídně (The Coach to Vienna)*, 1966;* *Noc nevěsty (The Night of the Bride)*, 1967; *Směšný pán (The Funny Man)*, 1969;* and *Ucho (The Ear)*, 1971. By the end of his life, although persecuted by the new Soviet-installed authorities, he was highly revered by the artistic elite. Though the police tried to block admission to his funeral, it was attended by many artistic leaders anyhow, including Václav Havel.

RADOK, ALFRED (1914–?), director. Besides being the creator of the multi-media *Laterna Magica (Magic Lantern)*, which captured international attention at the Brussels Exposition of 1958 and became a well-known tourist attraction thereafter, Radok was responsible for only three films, but one of them, *Daleká cesta (*The Long Journey), 1949,* has been praised by Škvorecký as the most remarkable film of the forties to be made anywhere. He was also able to create *Divotvorný klobouk (The Magical Hat)*, 1952, and *Dědeček automobil (Grandfather Automobile)*, 1956,* and to help get Miloš Forman started before running into endless frustration. After 1968, he finally left for Sweden and died of a heart attack in the early seventies.

ROVENSKÝ, JOSEF (1894–1937), actor, director. A major figure of the twenties and thirties. As an actor, he was known as the Czech Emil Jannings and carried the lead role in *Tonka šibenice (Tonka, Tart of the Gallows)*, 1930,* one of the best silent Czech films. As a director, he was a leading figure in establishing the Czech "lyrical tradition" with *Řeka (The River)*, 1933.* He also completed *Maryša*, 1935,* and, before his early death, began *Panenství (Virginity)*, 1937, which was completed by Vávra.

SCHMIDT, JAN (1934), director. Schmidt began his career in collaboration with Pavel Juráček. Together, they created the Kafkaesque *Josef Kilian*, 1964.* Schmidt then directed *Konec srpna v hotelu Ozón (The End of August at the Hotel Ozone)*, 1966,* from a Juráček script and *Kolonie Lanfieri (The Lanfieri Colony)*, 1969. After a period of inactivity shared with many of his colleagues, he returned to work in the mid-seventies.

SCHORM, EVALD (1931–   ), director, actor. Still practicing both of his talents, Schorm was a major figure of the New Wave who has only recently returned to the director's chair after a long layoff. His great films of the sixties included *Každý den odvahu (Courage for Every Day)*, 1964;* *Návrat ztraceného syna (The Return of the Prodigal Son)*, 1966;* *Pět holek na krku (Five Girls to Deal With)*, 1967;* *Farářův konec (End of a Priest)*, 1969;* and *Den sedmý, osmá noc (Seventh Day, Eighth Night)*, 1969. Schorm will also be long remembered as the quietly rebelious guest in Němec's *O slávnosti a hostech* (*Report on the Party and the Guests*), 1966.*

ŠKVORECKÝ, JOSEF (1924–), author. Perhaps the best-known current Czech writer, Škvorecký worked closely with the New Wave from its pre-history through the end. Appearing in a few films, he also wrote the screenplays for Menzel's *Zločin v šantánu* (*Crime in the Night Club*), 1968, and Schorm's *Farářův konec* (*End of a Priest*), 1969.* Škvorecký has also written several personal accounts of the New Wave, including the major work *All the Bright Young Men and Women*. He now writes, teaches, and co-directs a publishing company for other expatriate writers in Toronto.

ŠLITR, JIŘÍ and JIŘÍ SUCHÝ. An important musical-comedy team, their Semafor Theatre was a great source of inspiration for the New Wave and provided the setting for Forman's debut, *Konkurs* (*Competition*), 1963,* in which they also appeared. Another appearance came at the end of the New Wave in Menzel's *Zločin v šantánu* (*Crime in the Night Club*), 1968. In 1970, Suchý turned to directing, but Šlitr did not survive long into the decade.

SMOLJAK, LADISLAV. See SVĚRÁK, ZDENĚK.

SOFR, JAROMÍR, cinematographer. Sofr has added the appropriate mood to a great number of important works from the beginning of the New Wave and beyond. His works include Chytilová's *Strop* (*The Ceiling*), 1961;* Kachyňa's *Ať žije republika!* (*Long Live the Republic!*), 1965;* Němec's *O slávnosti a hostech* (*Report on the Party and the Guests*), 1966;* Schorm's *Farářův konec* (*End of a Priest*), 1969;* and Menzel's *Rozmarné léto* (*Capricious Summer*), 1967,* and *Na samotě u lesa* (*Seclusion Near a Forest*), 1976.*

STALICH, JAN (1907–), cinematographer. Beginning his career at the age of fourteen, Stalich hit an unbelievable peak in 1932–1933 when he shot Machatý's *Extase* (*Ecstasy*)* and Rovenský's *Řeka* (*The River*)* and contributed to Cikan's *Dům na předměstí* (*A House in the Suburbs*).* Following the war, Stalich helped Czech cinema achieve what few successes it could with some of the first color cinematography in Czechoslovakia, and on specific works like Čáp's *Muži bez křídel* (*Men Without Wings*), 1946;* Krška's *Revoluční rok, 1848* (*The Revolutionary Year, 1848*), 1949; and Frič's *Císařův pekař* (*The Emporer's Baker*) and *Pekařův císař* (*The Baker's Emperor*), 1951.*

ŠVANKMAJER, JAN (1934–), director. The foremost contemporary Czech animator, and the most politically unrestricted filmmaker of the seventies and eighties, Švankmajer refers to his work as "surrealist investigation—an attempt to liberate feelings of fear and anguish using the weapons of sarcasm, objective humor, and black comedy" (Hames, "After the Spring," 132). A filmmaker mainly for export during the years of repression, his work has received little distribution in his own country. His most famous film is *Možnosti dialogu (Dimensions of Dialogue)*, 1982.* His other works include *Poslední trik pána Edgara a pána Schwarzwalda (Mr. Edgar's Last Trick)*, 1964; *Rakvičkárna (Punch and Judy)*, 1966;* *Byt (The Flat)*, 1968; *Záhrada (The Garden)*, 1968;* *Tichý týden v dome (A Quiet Week at Home)*, 1969;* *Jabberwocky*, 1971; *Leonarduv deník (Leonardo's Diary)*, 1972;* *Zánik domu Usheru (The Fall of the House of Usher)*, 1981;* *Kyvadlo, jáma a naděje (The Pit, the Pendulum, and Hope)*, 1983;* and *Do sklepa (Down to the Cellar)*, 1983.*

SVĚRÁK, ZDENĚK, writer, actor, and **SMOLJAK, LADISLAV** director, writer, actor. Principal playwrights of the absurdist Jára Cimrman Theatre of the sixties, Svěrák and Smoljak have injected their particular brand of black humor into a series of works, collaborating as authors on the scripts for Menzel's *Na samotě u lesa (Seclusion Near a Forest)*, 1976,* and Lipský's *Jáchyme, hod ho do stroje (Joachim, Put It in the Machine)*, 1974, and *Mařečku, podejtě mi péro (Mařeček, Pass Me a Pen)*, 1976. Svěrák also authored the script for Menzel's *Vesničko má, středisková (My Sweet Little Village)*, 1986.* As a writer/director team, they have created successful comedies such as *Vrchní, prchni (Run, Waiter, Run)*, 1980;* *Jára Cimrman, Lying Asleep*, 1983; and *Rozpustený a vypustený (Dissolved and Let Out)*, 1984. Each has also appeared as actors in recent films.

SVOBODA, JIŘÍ, director. One of the few new directors to create a recognizable body of work in the eighties, Svoboda's films are characterized by a strong visual style and significant roles for some of the best Czech performers. His works include *Schůzka se stíny (A Meeting with Shadows)*, 1982; *Zánik samoty Berhof (The End of the Lonely Farm Berhof)*, 1983;* and *Skalpel, prosím (Scalpel, Please)*, 1985.*

TRNKA, JIŘÍ (1912–1970), animation director. One of the foremost creators of puppet films ever, along with fellow East Europeans George Pal and Vladislav Starevich, Trnka was able to respond to the political and social problems that other artists could not by virtue of working with this *children's* artform. Following influences from master puppeteer Josef Skupa and training in the animation studio established during World War II, Trnka gained international acclaim with films such as *Špalíček (The Czech Year)*, 1947; *Císařův slavík (The Emporer's Nightingale)*, 1948; *Arie prérie (Song of the Prairie)*, 1949; *Bayaya*, 1950; *Staré pověsti české (Old Czech Legends)*, 1953; *Švejk*, 1955; *Sen noci svatojanské (A Midsummer Night's Dream)*, 1959; *Vášeň (Obsession)*, 1960; *Kybernetická babička (Cybernetic Grandma)*, 1962; *Archandél Gabriel a pani Husa (The Archangel Gabriel and Mother Goose)*, 1964; and *Ruka (The Hand)*, 1966.

UHER, ŠTEFAN (1930–), director. A Slovak artist, Uher's *Slnko v sieti (Sunshine in a Net)*, 1962,* was one of the first outstanding films of the New

Wave. After directing *Organ (The Organ)*, 1965, he struggled through the rest of the sixties, but still maintained a considerable reputation, which he has since been able to add to with films such as *Keby som mal pušku (If I Had a Gun)*, 1971,* and the internationally recognized *Pásla kone na betóne (Concrete Pastures)*, 1982.*

URBAN, MAX (1882–?), producer, director, cinematographer. Architect and amateur photographer, Urban founded the Fotokinema Company in 1911, which became ASUM the following year and lasted until 1917. His productions included *Šaty dělají člověka (Clothes Make the Man)*, 1912, loosely based on Shakespeare's *Much Ado About Nothing,* and a silent version of the Smetana opera *Prodaná nevěsta (The Bartered Bride)*, 1913,* probably the first film ever seen by the young Miloš Forman.

VANČURA, VLADISLAV (1891–1942), novelist, director. Producing a vital influence on Czech culture, Vančura turned to directing in the thirties, creating the notable study of youth *Před maturitou (Before Graduation)*, 1932,* and the less successful *Na sluneční straně (On the Sunny Side)*, 1933, and *Marijka nevěrnice (The Unfaithful Marijka)*, 1934. His novels provided the sources for Vláčil's *Markéta Lazarová*, 1967,* and Menzel's *Rozmarné léto (Capricious Summer)*, 1968.* He was executed by the Nazis.

VÁVRA, OTAKAR (1911–), director. One of Czechoslovakia's most prolific directors, matched perhaps only by Frič, with whom he shared the ability to adjust to various political authorities, continuing to work even under the Nazis. Vávra began in the thirties, produced some fine work early in his career, and has naturally shown great versatility, resorting to the safe historical epic genre in the most repressive times. But he proved his talent most convincingly during the sixties, when some of his films, such as *Romance pro křidlovku (Romance for Flugelhorn)*, 1966, and *Kladivo na čarodějnice (Hammer Against Witches)*, 1970,* were far more bold than many of those produced by the young members of the New Wave.

VLÁČIL, FRANTIŠEK (1924–), director. Still working, Vláčil has a deep artistic background, made one of the first breakthrough films of the sixties, *Holubice (The White Dove)*, 1960,* and put himself through extreme life-threatening adversities in order to make the Dark Ages epic *Markéta Lazarová*, 1967,* as authentic as possible. He followed that with the also remarkable *Údolí včel (Valley of the Bees)*, 1968,* and *Adelheid*, 1969.* During the repressive years of the seventies and eighties, he still managed to direct the noteworthy *Dym bramborové ňate (Smoke on the Potato Fields)*, 1976;* *Stíny horkého léta (Shadows of a Hot Summer)*, 1978; and *Stín kapradiny (The Shades of Ferns)*, 1985.

VOSKOVEC, JIŘÍ (GEORGE) (1905–1981) and **JAN WERICH** (1905–), actors. A comedy team, affectionately known throughout the nation as V and

W, they are the Czech equivalents of Laurel and Hardy, though perhaps broader in their range of talents. During the thirties they made a string of successful comedies, the most highly regarded being *Hej rup!* (*Heave Ho!*), 1934.* The others were *Pudr a benzín* (*Powder and Gasoline*), 1931;* *Peníze nebo život* (*Your Money or Your Life*), 1932;* and *Svět patří nám* (*The World Belongs to Us*), 1937. During the forties, Voskovec continued his career in America as George Voskovec, appearing in several films well into the sixties. Werich appeared in Frič's *Císařův pekař* (*The Emperor's Baker*)* and *Pekařův císař* (*The Baker's Emperor*),* both 1951.

WEISS, JIŘÍ (1913–), director. Weiss possessed an unusual career in that he was one of only a very few directors to build a distinctive body of work in the fifties, but he then declined in the sixties. His most notable works were *Uloupená hranice* (*The Stolen Frontier*), 1947; *Vstanou noví bojovníci* (*New Fighters Shall Arise*), 1950;* *Hra o život* (*Life Was the Stake*), 1956; *Vlčí jáma* (*Wolf Trap*), 1958;* and *Romeo, Júlie a tma* (*Romeo, Juliet, and the Darkness*), 1960.*

SELECTED FILMOGRAPHY

1898

Dostaveníčko ve mlynici (Rendezvous at the Mill). d. Křiženecký.*
Pláčo a smích (Laughing and Crying). d. Křiženecký.*
Výstavní parkar a lepič plakátů (The Exhibition Sausage Vendor). d. Křiženecký.*

1913

Prodaná nevěsta (The Bartered Bride). d. Urban,* a silent version of the Bedřich Smetana opera. ASU.

1916

Zlaté srdéčko (The Golden Heart). d. Antonín Fencl; sw. Josef Šváb-Malostránský; with Fencl, Šváb-Malostránský, & Ema Švandová-Kadlecová. Lucernafilm.

1918

Alois vyhral na los (Alois Won the Sweepstakes). d. Richard F. Branald; sw. Kolár;* with Kolár, Karel Lamač, & Machatý* (his screen debut).
Učitel orientálních jazyků (The Teacher of Oriental Languages). d. Kolár* and Olga Rautenkrancová; with Kolár and Karel Lamač.

1919

Akord smrti (Chord of Death). d. Kolár* and Karel Lamač; sw. Kolár; c. Svatopluk Innemann; sets: Ferdinand Fiala; with Kolár, Lamač, Přemysl Pražský, Rovenský,* & Machatý.*
Dáma s malou nožkou (The Lady with the Small Foot). d. Kolár;* sw. Machatý* (his first);* with Ondráková (Annie Ondra).*
Stavitel chrámu (The Builder of the Cathedral). d. Degl* & Antonín Novotný. Degl Brothers Co.
Teddy by kouřil (Teddy'd Like a Smoke). d. Machatý* (his directorial debut).

1920

Setřele písmo (*The Faded Writing*). d. Rovenský* (his directorial debut).
Zpěv zlata (*The Song of Gold*). d. Kolár;* c. Heller;* with Ondráková.* AB Uniohrady Co.

1921

Jánošík. d. Jaroslav Siakel and František Horlivý; sw. Ziak-Marusiak. First Slovak feature.

1923

Únos bankéře Fuxe (*The Kidnapping of Banker Fux*). d. Karel Anton; with Ondráková.*

1926

Kreutzerova sonáta (*Kreutzer Sonata*). d. Machatý;* au. Leo Tolstoi; c. Heller;* sets: Vilem Rittershain; with Eva Byron & Jan Petrovich. M. S. Films (Germany). 45 min.
Pohádka máje (*The May Story*). d. Karel Anton; with Voskovec* in his screen debut.

1927

Batalion. d. Přemysl Pražský; au. Josef Hais-Týnecký; c. Jaroslav Blažek; set: Alois Mecera; with Karel Hašler, Bronislava Lívia, Karel Noll, Eman Fiala, Evžen Wiesner, Roman Roda-Ruzicha, & Vladimír Pospišil-Born. AB and Kavalírka Studios.

1928

Páter Vojtěch (*Father Vojtech*). d. Frič* (his directorial debut); c. Heller.*

1929

Erotikon. d. Machatý;* c. Václar Vích; sets: Alexander Hackenschmied and Julius Borsódy; with Ita Rina, Olaf Fjord, Luigi Servanti, Theodoro Pištek, Charlotte Suza, & S. Sleichert. Kavalírka Studios. 78 min.
Svatý Václav (*Saint Wenceslas*). d. Kolár;* c. Stalich,* Heller,* and Vladimír Vich; costumes: J. M. Gottlieb; with Zdeněk Štepánek.
Takový je život (*That's Life*). d. Junghans;* c. Lazslo Schaffer; sets Ernest Meiwers; with Věra Baranovská, Theodor Pištek, Wolfgang Zilzer, & Valeská Gert. Kavalírka Studios. 6 reels.
Varhaník u Sv. Víta (*The Organist of Saint Vitus*). d. Frič;* sw. Nezval;* au. Frič and Václav Wasserman; c. Jaroslav Blažek; with Karel Hašler. Kavalírka Studios.

1930

C. a k. polní maršálek (*The Field Marshal*). d Karel Lamač (first Czech sound comedy); with Viasta Burian.*

Když struny lkají (*When the Strings Weep*). d. Friedrich Fehér (first Czech language film).
Tonka šibenice (*Tonka, Tart of the Gallows*). d. Karel Anton; au. Egon Ervin Kisch; with Ita Rina, Rovenský,* and Věra Baranovskaia. First Czech sound film. Kavalírka Studios.

1931

Fidlovačka (first entirely Czech language sound film). d. Innemann;* c. Václav Vích; with Antonie Nedošinská, Rovenský,* Eman Fiala, Slávka Tauberová, Jiří Sedláček, Čeněk Siegl, & Jindřich Plachta. 80 min.
Muži v offsidu (*Men Off-Side*). d. Innemann;* au. Karel Poláček; with Haas.*
Pudr a benzín (*Powder and Gasoline*). d. Jindřich Honzl; first Voskovec and Werich* film.
Ze soboty na neděli (*From Saturday to Sunday*). d Machatý;* au. Nezval;* c. Vladimir Vích; sets: Alexander Hackenschmied; with Magda Máderová, Ladislav H. Struna, & Jiřina Šejbalová.

1932

Extase (*Ecstasy*). d. Machatý;* au. Nezval;* c. Stalich;* sets: Bohumil Hes; with Hedy Keissler (Hedy Lamarr), Andre Nox, Pierre Nay, & Jaromír Roguz. Elektra Film. 82 min.
Peníze nebo život (*Your Money or Your Life*). d. Jindřich Honzl; with Voskovec and Werich.*
Před maturitou (*Before Graduation*). d. Vančura* and Innemann;* with Jindřich Plachta.

1933

Dům na předměstí (*A House in the Suburbs*). d. Miroslav Cikán; au. Karel Poláček and Haas;* c. Stalich,* Vladimír Vích, & Ferdinand Pečenka; with Eman Fiala and Antonie Nedošinská.
Řeka (*The River*). d. Rovenský;* c. Stalich;* sets Ferdinand Fiala.
Zem spieva (*The Earth Is Singing*). d. Plicka;* ed. Alexander Hackenschmied. A Slovak film.

1934

Hej rup! (*Heave Ho!*). d. Frič;* with Voskovec and Werich.*

1935

Jánošík. d. Frič;* sw. Frič, Karel Hašler, and Karel Plicka; with Palo Bielik, Theodor Pištek, J. W. Speerger, & Ladislav H. Struna. Slovak language film.
Maryša. d. Rovenský;* au. Alois and Vilém Mrštík, with script contributions from Vávra;* c. Degl;* with Jiřina Štěpničková and Vladimír Borský.

1937

Bílá nemoc (*The White Plague*). d. Haas;* au. Čapek;* c. Heller;* with Vladimír Šmeral and Ladislav Boháč.

1938

Cech panen kutnohorských (*Guild of the Kutná Hora Maidens*). d. Vávra;* sw. Vávra and Zdeněk Štěpánek; art d. Štepán Kopecký; with Štěpánek, Jiřina Šejbalová, & Adina Mandlová.

1939

Ohnive leto (*Fiery Summer*). d. František Čáp and Krška.*

1941

Noční motýl (*The Night Moth*). d. František Čáp; c. Ferdinand Pečenka; with Gustav Nezval, Marie Glazrová, Hrušinský,* and Adina Mandlová.

1946

Muži bez křídel (*Men Without Wings*). d. František Čáp; c. Stalich.*
Rozina sebranec (*Rosina the Foundling*). d. & au. Vávra;* sw. Václav Řezáč; with Marie Glazrová, Zdeněk Štěpánek, Francis Kreuzman, Ladislav Boháč, Jan Pivec, Gustav Hilmar, Saša Rašilov, Antonin Solo, & Zdenka Baldová. Barrandov. 100 min.

1947

Siréna (*The Strike*). d. & sw. Karel Steklý; au. Marie Majerová; c. Jaroslav Tuzar; with Ladislav Boháč, Marie Vášová, Pavla Suchá, Nada Mauerová, Oleg Reif, Bedřich Karen, Josef Bek, Miloš Nedbal, & Bohumil Machník. Miloš Masník/Zdeněk Reimann Group/Barrandov.
Týden v tichém domě (*Week in the Quiet House*). d. Krejčík;* au. Jan Neruda; sw. Krejčík and J. A. Novotný. Barrandov Studios.

1948

Ves v pohraničí (*The Village on the Frontier*). d. Krejčík;* au. Frantisek Dvořák and Zdenka Infeldová; sw. Dvořák and Vladimír Tůma. Barrandov Studios.

1949

Daleká cesta (*The Long Journey*). d. Radok;* sw. Radok, Erik Kolář & Mojmír Drvota; c. Josef Střecha; with Blanka Waleská, Otomar Krejča, Viktor Ocásek, Zdenka Baldová, Jiří Spirit, & Eduard Kohout. Barrandov. 95 min.
Svědomí (*Conscience*). d. Krejčík;* au. Vladimír Valenta; sw. Jiří Fried and J. A. Novotný; with Miloš Nedbal and Marie Vášová. Barrandov Studios.

1950

Vstanou noví bojovníci (*New Fighters Shall Arise*). d. Weiss;* au. Antonín Zápotocký (Czechoslovak president); sw. Jaroslav Tuzar.

CZECHOSLOVAKIA

1951

Císařův pekář (*The Emperor's Baker*). *Pekařův císař* (*The Baker's Emperor*, combined and rereleased in 1955 as *The Emporer and the Golem*). d. Frič;* sw. Frič, Werich,* & Jiří Brdečka; c. Stalich* & Bohumil Hába; with Werich, Marie Vášová, Nataša Gollová, Jiří Plachý, František Černý, Bohuš Záhorský, Zdeněk Štěpánek, František Filipovský, & Chytilová.* Barrandov. 110 min. (1955 version).

1952

Únos (*Kidnapped*). d. Kadár and Klos;* au. Kadár, Klos, & F. B. Kunc; c. Rudolf Milič; m. Jiří Šust; with J. Dohnal, L. Pešek, Jaroslav Mareš, & B. Obrová.

1953

Měsíc nad řekou (*Moon over the River*). d. Krška; au. Fráňa Šrámek; with Zdeněk Štepánek, Dana Medřická, & Eduard Cupák.

1954

Hudba z marsu (*Music from Mars*). d. Kadár and Klos;* sw. Vratislav Blažek & Kadár; m. Jan Rychlík, Jiří Sternwald, D. C. Vackář, Tibor Andrašovan, Jaroslav Moravec, & Julius Fučík; with J. Marvan, Oldřich Nový, Alena Vránová, & Josef Bek.

1955

Cesta do pravěku (*A Journey to the Primeval Time*). d. Karel Zeman; sw. Zeman, Antonín Novotný, William Cayton, & Fred Ladd; c. Vaclav Pazderník, Antonín Horák, & Anthony Huston; with Vladimir Bejval, Peter Hermann, Zdeněk Husták, Josef Lukáš, James Lucas, Victor Betral, & Charles Goldsmith. Gottwaldov Film Studio/New Trend Associates-Childhood Productions. 87 min.

1956

Dědeček automobil (*Grandfather Automobile*). d. Radok;* sw. Adolf Branold; asst. d. Forman;* with Kolár,* Radovan Lukavský, Luděk Munzar, Ginette Pigeon, Raymond Bussieres, & Josef Hlinomaz. Barrandov. 98 min.
Střibrný vítr (*The Silvery Wind*), produced in 1954. d. Krška;* au. Fráňa Šrámek; with Eduard Cupák.

1957

Škola otců (*School for Fathers*). d. Helge;* with Karel Höger.
Tam na konečné (*At the Terminal Station*). d. Kadár and Klos;* au. Ludvik Askenázy; c. Rudolf Stahl; with Eva Očenásová, Vladimír Ráž, Martin Růžek, Jana Dítěťová, & Anna Melíšková. Barrandov. 98 min.
Zářijové noci (*September Nights*). d. Jasný;* au. Pavel Kohout; c. Kučera;* with Jiří Vala, Marie Tomášová, Václav Lohniský, L. Pešek, & S. Remunda.

1958

Touha (Desire). d. Jasný;* sw. Jasný & Vladimir Valenta; c. Kučera;* with Jan Jakeš, Brejchová,* Jiří Vala, Věra Tichánková, Anna Melišková, Václav Babka, & Václav Lohniský. Barrandov. 95 min.
Třetí přání (The Third Wish). d. Kadár and Klos;* au. Vratislav Blažek; sw. Kadár, Klos, & Blažek; c. Rudolf Stahl; m. Jiří Sternwald; with R. Markovič, T. Beljaková, & B. Záhorský.
Vlčí jáma (Wolf Trap). d. Weiss;* sw. Weiss, J. Brdečka, & Jarmila Glazarová; au. Glazarová; with Jiřina Šejbalová, Brejchová*, & Miroslav Doležal. Barrandov. 95 min.
Vynález zkázy (Invention for Destruction). d. Karel Zeman; sw. Zeman & František Hrubín; au. Jules Verne; c. Jiří Tarantík; with Arnošt Navrátil, Lůbor Tokoš, Miloslav Holub, & Jana Zatloukalová. Czech State Film. 85 min.
Zde jsou lvi (Hic Sunt Leones [Scars of the Past]). d. Krška;* sw. Oldřich Daněk; with Karel Höger & Dana Medřická.
Žižkovská romance (A Local Romance). d. Brynych;* au. Vladimír Kalina; c. Čuřík;* m. Jiří Sternwald; with Renata Olárová, Jiří Vala, Brejchová,* & Eduard Cupák. Barrandov. 100 min.

1959

Probuzení (Awakening). d. Krejčík;* with Brejchová* & Peter Kostka.
Velká samota (The Great Seclusion). d. Helge;* au. and sw. Ivan Kříž; asst. d. Passer;* with Július Pántik.

1960

Holubice (The White Dove). d. Vláčil;* au. Otakar Kirchner; c. Čuřík;* with Kateřina Irmanovová, Hans-Peter Reinicke, Karel Symczak, Vjačeslav Irmanov, & Gustav Puttjer. Československý Film. 76 min.
Romeo, Julie a tma (Romeo, Júliet and the Darkness). d. Weiss;* sw. Weiss & Jan Otčenášek; au. Otčenášek; c. Václav Hanuš; with Ivan Mistrík, Dana Smutná, Jiřina Šejbalová, František Smolík, & Jiří Kodet. Czech State Film. 95 min.
Smyk (Skid). d. Brynych;* au. Brynych and Jiří Vala; sw. Brynych, Vala, & Pavel Kohout; c. Jan Kališ; asst. d. Passer;* m. Jiří Sternwald; with Vala, Jiřina Švorcová, J. Jirásková, & W. Taub.
Vyšší princip (The Higher Principle). d. Krejčík;* au. Jan Drda; with Brejchová,* Ivan Mistrík, & Marie Vášová.

1961

Ďáblová past (The Devil's Trap). d. Vlačil;* sw. F. A. Dvořák & Miloš Kratochvíl; c. Rudolf Milič; with Vítezslav Vejrážka, Miroslav Macháček, Olmer,* Karla Chadimová, Vlastimil Hašek, & Čestmír Řanda. Czech State Film. 85 min.
Strop (The Ceiling). d. Chytilová;* c. Sofr;* m. Jan Klusák & Šlitr;* with Menzel* and Jakubisko.*

CZECHOSLOVAKIA

1962

Pytel blech (*A Bagful of Fleas*). d. Chytilová* (released with *Ceiling* as *U stropu je pytel blech—There's a Bagful of Fleas at the Ceiling*).
Slnko v sieti (*Sunshine in a Net*) d. Uher;* sw. Alfonz Bednár; c. Stanislav Szomolányi. Slovak film.
Transport z ráje (*Transport from Paradise*). d. Brynych;* au. Lustig;* a.d. Herz;* c. Čuřík;* m. Jiří Sternwald; w. Zdeněk Štepánek, Ilja Prachař, L. Pešek, and H. Čočková. Barrandov. 94 min.

1963

Až přijdé kocour (*Cassandra Cat*). d. Jasný;* sw. Jasný and Jiří Brdečka; c. Kučera;* asst. d. Passer;* with. Werich, Vlastimil Brodský, Jiří Sovák, and Emília Vášáryová.
Černý Petr (*Black Peter/Peter and Paula*). d. Forman;* au. Papoušek;* sw. Papoušek and Forman; asst. d. Passer;* c. Jan Němeček; m. Šlitr;* w. Ladislav Jakim, Pavla Martinková, Vladimír Pucholt, & Jan Vostrčil. Barrandov.
Konkurs (*Competition*), Pt. I: *Kdyby ty muziky nebyly* (*If There Were No Music*), Pt. II: *Konkurs* (*Competition*). d. Forman;* s. Forman and Passer;* c. Ondříček;* m. Suchý and Šlitr;* w (Pt. 1). Václav Blumenthal, Vladimír Pucholt, Jan Vostrčil, and František Zeman, and (Pt. 2) Ladislav Jakim, Markéta Krátká, Křesadlová,* Šlitr and Suchý. Barrandov.
Křik (*The Cry*). d. Jireš;* au. Ludvik Aškenázy; sw. Askenázy and Jireš; c. Kučera* and Ondříček;* w. Josef Abrhám, Eva Límanová, & Eva Kpecká. Czech State Film. 80 min.
O něčem jiném (*About Something Else*). d. Chytilová;* c. Čuřík;* with Eva Bosáková, Věra Uzelacová, & Josef Langmiler. Czech State Film. 90 min.
Smrť sa volá Engelchen (*Death is Called "Engelchen"*). d. Kadár and Klos;* au. Ladislav Mnačko; c. Rudolf Milič; m. Zdenek Liška; with Káčer,* Eva Poláková, Blažena Holišová, Martin Rusch, & Vlado Müller. 160 min. Slovak language film.

1964

...A pátý jezdec je strach (*...the Fifth Horseman Is Fear*). d. Brynych;* au. Hana Bělohradská; sw. Bělohradská, Brynych, & Krumbachová;* c. Jan Kališ; m. Jiří Sternwald; with Miroslav Macháček, Ilja Prachař, Jiří Adamíra, O. Scheinflugová, Josef Vinklář, Jiří Vršťala, & Zdenka Prochákozva. Barrandov. 95 min.
Démanty noci (*Diamonds of the Night*). d. Němec;* au. Lustig;* c. Kučera;* asst. d. Bočan;* costumes: Krumbachová;* with Ladislav Jánský & Antonín Kumbera. Barrandov. 64 min.
Josef Kilian. d. Pavel Juráček and Jan Schmidt; sw. Juráček; c. Čuřík;* m. Viliam Bukový; with K. Vašíček & P. Bártl.
Každý den odvahu (*Courage for Every Day*). d. Schorm;* sw. Antonin Máša; with Káčer,* Brejchová,* Menzel,* J. Jirásková, Vlastimil Brodský, & Josef Abrhám. Barrandov. 90 min.
Limonádový Joe (*Lemonade Joe*). d. Lipský;* sw. Jiří Brdečka; c. Vladimír Novotný; with Karel Fiala, Waldemar Matuška, Květa Fialová, & Olga Schoberová. Barrandov. 95 min.
Starci na chmelu (*The Hop-Pickers*). d. Ladislav Rychman; sw. Vratislav Blažek; with

Vladimír Pucholt, Miloš Zavadil, Ivana Pavlová, Irena Kačírková, & Josef Kemr. Czech State Film. 90 min.

1965

Ať žije republika! (*Long Live the Republic!*). d. Kachyňa;* s. Procházka;* c. Sofr;* m. Zdeněk Liška; with Zdeněk Lstibúrek, Vlado Müller, N. Gajerová, Gustav Valack, Iva Janžurová, & Josef Karlík. Barrandov. 123 min.
Bloudění (*Wandering*). d. Máša and Čuřík;* sw. Antonin Máša; c. Čuřík and Ivan Slapeta; w. Jiří Pleskot, Jiřina Jirásková, Jaromír Hanzlík, Brejchová,* Vladimír Šmeral, Miroslav Macháček, and Káčer.* Czech State Film. 80 min.
Fádní odpoledne (*A Boring Afternoon*). d. Passer;* au. Hrabal;* sw. Hrabal and Passer; c. Kučera;* with Kamila Turková, Josef Vanista, Miloš Končický, & Leopold Smolík.
Intimní osvětlení (*Intimate Lighting*). d. Passer;* au. and sw. Passer, Papoušek,* & Václav Šašek; c. Josef Strecha & Ondříček;* with Karel Blažek, Zdeněk Bezůšek, Jaroslava Štedrá, Vlastimila Vlková, Křesadlová,* and Jan Vostrčil. Barrandov. 70 min.
Lásky jedné plavovlásky (*Loves of a Blonde*). d. Forman;* sw. Papoušek,* Passer,* and Forman; asst. d. Passer; m. Evžen Illin; with Hana Brejchová, Vladimír Menšík, Vladimír Pucholt, Milada Ježková, Josef Šebánek, and Jan Vostrčil. Barrandov.
Nikdo se nebude smát (*Nobody Shall Be Laughing*). d. Bočan;* au. Kundera;* sw. Bočan* & Pavel Juráček; c. Jan Němec;* with Káčer,* Štěpánka Řeháková, Josef Chvalina, Radoslav Brzobohatý, & Menzel.* Czech State Film. 80 min.
Obchod na korze (*Shop on Main Street*). d. Kadár and Klos;* au. Ladislav Grosman; c. Vladimír Novotný; m. Zdeněk Liška; with Jozef Króner, Ida Kaminská, Martin Hollý, & František Zvarík. Barrandov. 125 min. Slovak language film.
Perličky na dně (*Pearls at the Bottom*). au. Hrabal;* Pt. I: *Smrt pána Baltazára* (*The Death of Mr. Balthazar*): d. Menzel;* c. Kučera;* m. Jan Klusák; with E. Izerle, Ferdinand Kruta, Pavla Maršálková, M. Nohýnek, & M. Španková; Pt. II: *Podvodníci* (*Imposters*): d. Němec;* c. Kučera;* m. Jiří Šust; with M. Čtrnácty, F. Havel, J. Hejl, & J. Vasák; Pt. III: *Dům radosti* (*The House of Joy*): d. Schorm;* c. Kučera;* m. Klusák; with J. Pechlatová, Václav Žák, Ivan Vyskočil, & C. Pokorný; Pt. IV: *Automat svět* (*The World Snack Bar*): d. Chytilová;* c. Kučera;* m. Klusák; with V. Mrázková, V. Boudnik, & A. Laštovková; Pt. V: *Romance*: d. Jireš;* c. Kučera;* m. Šust; with D. Valtová, Vyskočil, & K. Jeřábek. Barrandov. 105 min.
Zlatá reneta (*The Golden Rennet*). d. Vávra;* au. František Hrubín; sw. Vávra, Hrubín; c. Andrej Barla; m. Jiří Srnka; with Karel Höger, S. Budínová, Eva Límanová, Ilja Prachař, V. Tichánková, B. Holišová, & V. Obručová. Barrandov. 90 min.

1966

Hotel pro cizince (*Hotel for Strangers*). d., au., & sw. Antonin Máša; c. Ivan Slapeta; m. Svatopluk Havelka; with Petr Čepek, Vladimír Šmeral, Taťána Fischerova, Marta Krásová, Josef Somr, Schorm,* and Menzel.* Barrandov. 103 min.
Konéc srpna v hotelu Ozón (*End of August in Hotel Ozone*). d. Jan Schmidt; sw. & au. Pavel Juráček; c. Jiří Macák; with Ondrej Jariabek, Betta Poničanová, Magda Seidlerová, Hana Vítkova, Jana Nováková, Vanda Kalinová, Natalie Malsovová,

Irina Licarová, Jitka Hořejší, & Alena Leppertová. Czech Army Film Studios. 87 min.
Kočár do Vídně (*The Coach to Vienna*). d. Kachyňa;* sw. Procházka;* c. Illík;* m. Jan Novák; with Iva Janžurová, Jaromír Hanzlík, & Luděk Munzar. Barrandov. 75 min.
Kristové roky (*Crucial Years*). d. Jakubisko;* sw. Jakubisko* & Lúbor Dohnal; c. Igor Luther; w. Jiří Sýkora, Vlado Müller, & Miriam Kantorková. Koliba Studios (Bratislava). 100 min.
Mučedníci lásky (*Martyrs of Love*). d. Němec;* sw. Němec & Krumbachová*; c. Ondříček;* with Eva Olmerová, Karel Gott, Marta Kubišová, Jan Hammer, Miroslav Vitouš, Jan Klusák, Josef Koníček, & Lindsay Anderson. Barrandov. 70 min.
Návrat ztraceného syna (*The Return of the Prodigal Son*). d. Schorm;* m. Jan Klusák; with Jan Káčer, Brejchová,* Dana Medřická, Menzel,* Milan Morávek, & Jiřina Trebiček. Barrandov. 90 min.
O slávnosti a hostech (*Report on the Party and the Guests*). d. Němec;* sw. Němec & Krumbachová;* c. Sofr;* with Schorm;* Jan Klusák, Ivan Vyskočil, Karel Mareš, Jiří Němec, Pavel Bošek, Helena Pejsková, Škvorecký,* & Zdena Škvorecká. Barrandov. 70 min.
Ostře sledované vlaky (*Closely Watched Trains*). d. Menzel;* au. Hrabal;* c. Sofr;* with Václav Neckář, Jitka Bendová, Vladimír Valenta, Josef Somr, Vlastimil Brodský, Milada Ježková, & Menzel. Barrandov. 75 min.
Rakvičkárna (*Punch and Judy*), animated. d. & sw. Švankmajer;* c. J. Šafář; voices: Procházka,* N. Munzarová, & B. Šrámek. Krátky Films. 10 min.
Sedmikrásky (*Daisies*). d. Chytilová;* sw. Chytilová & Krumbachová;* c. Kučera;* with Jan Klusák, Ivana Karbanová, Jitka Cerhová, & Julius Albert. Barrandov. 74 min.

1967

Hoří, má panenko (*Firemen's Ball*). d. Forman;* sw. Forman, Papoušek,* & Passer;* asst. d. Papoušek; c. Ondříček;* m. Karel Mareš; with Milada Ježková, Josef Sebánek, & Jan Vostrčil.
Markéta Lazarová. d. Vláčil;* au. Vančura;* sw. Vláčil & František Pavlíček; c. Bedřich Batka; with Magda Vášáryová, František Velecký, Vlastimil Harapes, Pavla Polásková, & Vladimír Menšík. Barrandov. 180 min.
Pět holek na krku (*Five Girls to Deal With*). d. Schorm;* s. Schorm & Iva Hercíkova; c. Čuřík;* with Andrea Čunderlíková, Jana Krupičková, Lucie Žulová, Dana Matejková, Markéta Křenková, & Martin Vedra. Czech State Film/Svabik-Prochazka. 90 min.
Rozmarné léto (*Capricious Summer*). d. Menzel;* sw. Menzel & Václav Nyvt; au. Vančura;* c. Sofr;* with Hrušinský,* Vlastimil Brodský, František Rehák, Míla Mysliková, Jana Drchalová, & Menzel. Czech State Film/Smída-Fikár. 75 min.
Soukromá víchřice (*Private Hurricane*). d. Bočan;* au. Vladimír Páral; c. Jan Nemeček; with Josef Somr, Pavel Landovský, Daniela Kolárová, Menzel;* Míla Mysliková, & Josef Chvalina. Barrandov. 90 min.

1968

Údolí včel (*Valley of the Bees*). d. Vláčil;* sw. Vláčil and Vladimír Korner; c. František Uldrych; with Petr Cěpek, Jan Káčer, Antonín Pražák, and Věra Galatíková.

Záhrada (The Garden). d. & sw. Švankmajer;* c. Sv. Malý; with J. Hálek, L. Kopřiva, M. Myslíková, V. Borovicka, & F. Husák. Krátky Films. 17 min.

Zbehovia a pútnici (Deserters and the Nomads). d. & c. Jakubisko;* sw. Ladislav Ťažký & Jakubisko; with Imrich Weczulic, Maria Grandtnerová, & Helena Anysova (banned; released 1989). Slovak Film/Studio Cinema Bratislava. 55 min.

1969

Adelheid. d. Vláčil;* au. Vladimír Korner; sw. Vláčil and Korner; c. František Oldrich; with Petr Čepek, Emma Černá, Pavel Landovský, Jan Vostrčil, & Jan Káčer.*

Don Sancho, animated. d. & sw. Švankmajer;* au. Franz Liszt; c. S. Malý; voices: V. Kuschmit, M. Krajník, J. Podsekník, & M. Volková. Krátky Films. 33 min.

Ecce homo Homolka. d. Papoušek;* with Josef Sebánek, Petr Forman, Matej Forman, Helena Ružičková, Maric Motlová, & František Husák. Barrandov. 82 min.

Farářův konec (End of a Priest). d. Schorm;* sw. Škvorecký;* c. Sofr;* with Vlastimil Brodský, Jan Libiček, Jaroslav Satoranský, Zdena Škvorecká, Josefa Pechlatová, Václav Kotva, Gueye Cheick, Vladimír Valenta, & Brejchová.* Barrandov. 97 min.

Hrst vody (Adrift). d. Kadár and Klos;* au. Lajos Zilaly; sw. Imre Gyongyossy; c. Vladimír Novotný; with Rade Markevic & Milena Dravic.

Nejkrásnější věk (The Most Beautiful Age). d. & sw. Papoušek;* c. Josef Ort-Snep; with Hana Brejchová, Křesadlová,* Ladislav Jakim, Jan Stockl, Anna Pisáriková, Jiří Hálek, Vladimír Šmeral, Milada Ježková, Josef Sebánek, & Josef Kolb. Barrandov. 80 min.

Ovoce stromů rajských jíme (We Eat the Fruit of the Trees of Paradise). d. Chytilová;* sw. Chytilová & Krumbachová;* c. Kučera;* m. Zdenek Liška; with Jitka Nováková & Karel Novák.

Skřivánci na niti (Skylarks on a String). d. Menzel; au. Hrabal*; w. Křesadlova* (banned, released in 1990).

Směšný pán (The Funny Man). d. Kachyňa;* sw. Procházka;* c. Josef Pávek; with Vladimír Šmeral, Jiří Adamíra, Danuše Klichová, Zdeněk Kryžánek, & Evelyn Steimarová. A Švábik-Procházka Production. 78 min.

Spalovač mrtvol (The Cremator of Corpses). d. Herz;* au. Ladislav Fuks; m. Zdeněk Liška; with Hrušinský,* Menzel,* Vlasta Chramostová, Jana Stehnová, Miloš Vognič, Ilja Prachř, Jiří Lír, Eduard Kohout, & Jan Vlček. Czech State Film/Sebor-Bor. 100 min.

Tichý týden v dome (A Quiet Week at Home), animated. d. & sw. Švankmajer;* c. S. Malý & K. Suzan; animation, Z. Sob; with V. Borovička. Krátky Films. 20 min.

Valérie a týden divů (Valerie and Her Week of Wonders). d. Jireš;* sw. Jireš and Krumbachová;* au. Nezval;* c. Čuřík;* m. Luboš Fišer; with Jaroslava Schallerová, Helena Anýzová, Petr Kopřiva, Jiří Prymek, & Jan Klusák. Barrandov. 85 min.

Všichni dobří rodáci (All Those Good Countrymen). d. & sw. Jasný;* c. Kučera;* costumes: Krumbachová;* with Radoslav Brzobohatý, Vlastimil Brodský, Vladimír Menšík, Drahoslavo Hofman, & Pavel Pavlovský. Barrandov. 126 min.

Vtáčkovia, siroty a blázni (Birds, Orphans, and Fools). d. Jakubisko;* c. Igor Luther; with Jiří Sýkora, Phillipe Avron, & Magda Vášáryová (banned).

Žert (The Joke). d. Jireš;* au. Kundera;* sw. Jireš; c. Čuřík;* with Josef Somr, Jana Dítětova, Luděk Munzar, & Schorm.* Barrandov. 80 min.

1970

Kladivo na čarodějnice (*Hammer Against Witches*). d. Vávra;* sw. Vávra and Krumbachova;* c. Illík;* with Vladimír Šmeral, Elo Romančík, Soňa Valentová, L. Skrbková, Jiřina Štepnicka, Lůbor Tokoš, Blažena Holišová, Eduard Cupák, & Blanka Waleská. Barrandov. 110 min.

Kostnice (*The Ossuary*). d. & sw. Švankmajer;* c. Sv. Malý. Krátky Films. 11 min.

Případ pro začínajícího kata (*The Case for the New Hangman*). d. Pavel Juráček; au. Jonathan Swift (adapted from *Gulliver's Travels*); c. Jan Kališ; with Lubomír Kostelka, Klára Jerneková, Milena Zahrynowská, Radovan Lukavský, Jindřich Janda, Miloš Vávra, & Miroslav Macháček (banned). Barrandov. 100 min.

1971

A pozdravuji vlaštovky (*And Give My Love to the Swallows*). d. & sw. Jireš;* au. Maruška Kudeřiková; c. Čuřík;* with Magda Vášáryová, Viera Strnisková, Július Vašek, Hanna Pastejříková, & Dagmar Bláhová. Czech State Film/Barrandov. 90 min.

Keby som mal pušku (*If I Had a Gun*). d. Uher;* sw. Milan Ferko; c. Stanislav Szomolányi; with Marián Dernát, Jozef Gróf, Ľudovít Króner, Emília Došeková, & Hana Grissová. Slovak State Film. 90 min.

Petrolejove lampy (*Kerosene Lamps*). d. Herz;* sw. Václav Šašek, Lubor Dohnal, & Herz; au. Jaroslav Havlíček; c. Dodo Simončič; with Iva Janžurová, Petr Čepek, Marie Rosůlková, Ota Sklenčka, Vladimír Jedenáctik, Karel Černoch, & Jana Plichthová. Czech State Film/Barrandov. 97 min.

Už zase skáču přes kaluže (*I'm Jumping Over Puddles Again*). d. Kachyňa;* sw. Kachyňa, Ota Hofman, Vladimir Dlouhý, Zdenka Hadrbolcova, & Lubor Vraspír. Barrandov. 90 min.

1972

Leonarduv deník (*Leonardo's Diary*), animated. d. & sw. Švankmajer;* c. J. Šafár; animation: V. Kladiva & K. Chocholin. Studio Jiřiho Trnky (Prague)/Corona Cinematografica (Rome). 12 min.

Morgiana d. & sw. Herz;* au. Alexander Grin; c. Kučera;* with Iva Janžurová, Josef Abrham, Petr Čepek, Nina Divíškova, & Ivan Palúch. Barrandov. 95 min.

1976

Dym bramborové ňate (*Smoke on the Potato Fields*). d. Vláčil;* sw. Vláčil & Václav Nyvlt; c. František Oldřich; w. Hrušínský,* Věra Galatíková, Alois Švehlík, Jana Dítěťová, Vítezslav Jandák, Marie Logoidová, Josef Somr, & Václav Lohnický. Czech Film/Barrandov. 95 min.

Hra o jablko (*The Apple Game*). d. Chytilová;* with Dagmar Bláhová, Menzel,* & Jitka Cerhová.

Na samotě u lesa (*Seclusion Near a Forest*). d. Menzel;* sw. Svěrák* and Smoljak;* c. Sofr*; m. Jiří Šust; with Josef Kemr, Svěrák, Smoljak, Jan Tříska, & Naďa Urbánková. Czech State Film/Barrandov. 92 min.

Ružové sny (*Rose-Tinted Dreams*). d. & sw. Dušan Hanák; c. Dodo Šimončič; with Iva Bittová, Juraj Nvota, Josef Hlinomaz, Marie Molová, Arpád Rigo, Hana Slivková,

Sally Salingová, Ľudovít Króner, & Václav Babka. Slovak Film/Koliba Studios (Bratislava). 85 min.

1978

Adela ještě nevečeřela (*Adele Hasn't Had Supper Yet/Nick Carter in Prague*). d. Lipský;* sw. Jiří Brdečka; c. Kučera;* with Michal Dočolomanský, Hrušínský,* Miloš Kopecký, Ladislav Pešek, Naďa Konvalinková, Martin Růžek, Václav Lonhnisky, Olga Schoberová, & Květa Fialová. Barrandov. 100 min.

1979

Causa králik (*The Rabbit Case*). d. Jireš;* Jaroslav Dietl; c. Sofr;* with Miloš Kopecký, Alena Vránová, Zlata Adamovská, Marie Brožová, Jaroslav Satoranský, & Martin Růžek. Czech State Film/Barrandov. 85 min.
Kalamita (*Calamity*). d. Chytilová;* c. Ivan Slapeta; with Boleslav Polívak, Dagmar Bláhová, & Zdeněk Dítě.
Panelstory (*Prefab Story*). d. Chytilová;* sw. Chytilová & Eva Kačírková; c. Sofr;* with Lukáš Bech, Antonín Vanha, Michal Nesvadba, Kačírková, J. Kodet, & Alena Rycová. Barrandov. 90 min.

1980

Ja miujem, ty miluješ (*I Love, You Love*). d. Dušan Hanák; sw. Jozef Ort-Šnep; with R. Klasowsik, Junžurova, & V. Babka. (recently released; winner of the Silver Bear at the 1989 Berlin Film Festival). Slovak Film (Bratislava).
Postav dom, zasaď strom (*Build a House, Plant a Tree*). d. Jakubisko;* sw. Mikuláš Kováč & Lýdia Ragtová; c. Stanislav Doršic; with Jozef Matúš, Jana Siniaková, Ondřej Pavelka, & Virsitzender Simiak. Slovenský Film (Bratislava). 90 min.
Vrchní, prchni (*Run, Waiter, Run*). d. Smoljak;* sw. Svěrák;* c. Ivan Slapeta; with Josef Abrham, Libuše Šafránková, Svěrák, Eliška Balzerová, Dagmar Patrasová, Jiří Kodet, Karel Augusta, & Zuzana Fišerová. Barrandov.

1981

Postřižiny (*Cutting It Short*). d. Menzel;* au. and sw. Hrabal;* with Jaromír Hanzlík, Jiří Schmitzer, Hrušínský,* Oldřich Vlach, Petr Čepek, Magda Vášáryová, František Řehák, Miloslav Stibich, Alois Liskutin, Pavel Vondruška, Jaroslava Kretschmerová, & Oldřich Vezner. Barrandov. 96 min.
Zánik domu Usheru (*The Fall of the House of Usher*), (animated). d. Švankmajer.*

1982

Možnosti dialogu (*Dimensions of Dialogue*), (animated). d. Švankmajer.*
Pásla kone na betóne (*Concrete Pastures*), d. Uher;* sw. Milka Zimková & Uher; au. Zimková; c. Stanislav Szomolányi; with Zimková, Veronika Jeníková, Peter Vons, Peter Staník, Mikuláš Las, & Ferdinand Macurák. Koliba Studios (Bratislava). Slovak Film. 82 min.
Vítr v kapse (*Wind in My Pocket*). d. Jaroslav Soukup; sw. Soukup & Miroslav Valc; c.

Sofr;* with Lukáš Vaculík, Sagvan Tofi, Ivana Andrlová, Karel Augusta, Karel Bochoc, Bronislav Poloczek, Zora Kesslerová, Karolína Slunečková, Ilonka Svobodová, Jiří Kalužný, & Ferdinand Kruta. 81 min.

1983

Do sklepa (*Down to the Cellar*) (animated). d. Švankmajer.*
Faunovo příliš pozdní odpoledne (*The Very Late Afternoon of a Faun*). d. Chytilová;* au. Jiří Brdečka; sw. Krumbachová;* c. Jan Malíř; m. Miroslav Kořínek & Jiří Stivín; with Leoš Suchařípa, Libuše Pospíšilová, Vlasta Špicnerová, & Jiří Hálek. Krátký Film.
Kyvadlo, jáma a naděje (*The Pit, the Pendulum and Hope*), animated. d. & sw. Švankmajer;* au. Edgar Allan Poe; c. Miloslav Spálai, animation: Bedřich Glaser. Krátky Films/Studio Jiřiho Trnky. 15 min.
Slávnosti sněženek (*The Snowdrop Festival*). d. Menzel;* sw. Hrabal;* with Hrušínský,* Jaromír Hanzlík, Jiří Schmitzer, Libuše Šafránková, & Josef Somr.
Tisícročna včela (*The Millennial Bee*). d. Jakubisko;* sw. Jakubisko & Petr Jaroš; au. Jaroš; c. Stanislav Doršic; with Jozef Króner, Štefan Kvietik, Ivana Valešová, Michal Dočolomanský, Eva Jakoubková, & Jana Janovská. Slovenský Film (Bratislava). 175 min. Pt. 1: 98 min. Pt. 2: 77 min. Awarded Golden Phoenix at Venice Film Festival.
Zánik samoty Berhof (*The End of the Lonely Farm Berhof*). d. Svoboda;* sw. Vladimír Korner & Svoboda; au. Korner; c. Vladimír Smutný; with Brejchová,* Ladislav Kriváček, Evelyna Steimarova, Milan Kňažko, Marek Probosz, Zbigniew Suszynski, Leon Niemczyk, Petronela Vancíková, Lubomír Kostelka, Vít Pohanka, & Štefan Mišovič. Barrandov, 2nd Production Group. 91 min.

1985

Jako jed (*Like Poison*). d. Olmer;* s. Olmer, Jiří Just, & Karel Žídek; au. Žídek; with Svěrák,* Ivona Krajčovičová, Libuše Švormova, Laďka Kozderková, Václav Švorc, František Řehák, Vlado Durdík, & Jaromíra Milová. Barrandov. 76 min.
Skalpel, prosím (*Scalpel, Please*). d. & sw. Svoboda;* au. Valia Stýblová; c. Vladimír Smutný; with Miroslav Macháček, Brejchová,* Radoslav Brzobohatý, & Frantisek Řehak. Barrandov. 110 min.
Tichá radosť (*Silent Joy*). d. Dušan Hanák; sw. Hanák & Ondrej Šulaj; c. Viktor Svoboda; with Magda Vášáryová, Jiři Bartoška, Brejchová,* Juraj Nvota, Robert Koltai, Erzsi Pasztor, Ferencz Bencao, & Maroš Brachna. Slovak Film-Making, Studio for Fiction Films, 2nd Group. 88 min.

1986

Antonyho šance (*Anthony's Chance*). d. Olmer;* sw. Olmer & Rudolf Ráž; c. Ota Kopřiva; m. Jiří Stivín; with Luboš Veselý, Veronika Jeníkova, & Barbara Straková. Barrandov.
Vesničko má, středisková (*My Sweet Little Village*). d. Menzel;* sw. Svěrák;* c. Sofr;* m. Jiří Šust; with János Bán, Marián Labuda, Svěrák, Hrušínský,* Milena Dvorská, Ladislav Županič, Petr Čepek, & Libuše Šafránkova. Barrandov. 101 min.
Vlčí bouda (*Wolf's Cabin*). d. Chytilová;* sw. Chytilová & Daniela Fischerova; c. Sofr;*

with Miroslav Macháček, Štepánka Červenková, Rita Dudusová, Káčer,* & Tomáš Platy. Barrandov. 92 min.
Zastihla mě noc (*I Was Caught by the Night*). d. Herz;* sw. Herz & Jaromíra Kolárova; c. Viktor Ružička; Michael Kocáb; with Jana Řiháková, Brejchová,* Andrea Bogušovská, Jana Paulová, Sylva Turbová, Jana Svobodová, Hrušínský,* & Radoslav Brzobohatý. Barrandov. 129 min.

1987

Proč? (*Why?*). d. Karel Smyczek; sw. Smyczek & John;* c. Jaroslav Brabec; m. Michal Pavlíček; with Martin Dejdar, Jan Potměšil, Pavlína Mourková, Martin Sobotka, & Markéta Zmožková. Barrandov. 68 min.
Šašek a královna (*The Jester and the Queen*). d. Chytilová;* au. Boleslav Polívka; c. Jan Malíř; with Polívka, Chantal Poulain, & Jiří Kodet. Barrandov.
Svět nic nevi (*The World Knows Nothing*). d. Jiří Svoboda; sw. Vaclav Šašek; au. Miroslav Nohejl; c. Josef Vaniš; with Radoslav Brzobohatý, Emil Horváth, Petra Vančíoková, Milan Kňažko, & Magda Vašáryová. Barrandov. 3,068 m.

1988

Bony a klid (*Big Money*). d. Olmer;* sw. Olmer and John;* c. Ota Kopřiva; with Jan Potměšil, Veronika Jeníková, Josef Nedorost, Tomáš Hanák, & Roman Skamene. Barrandov.
Citlivá místa (*Sensitive Spot*). d. Vladimír Drha; sw. Katarína Slobodová; c. Josef Pávek; with Brejchová,* Terezá Brodska, & Ivan Urbánek. Barrandov.
Geometrickou radou. d. Chytilová;* sw. Chytilová & Pavel Škapík; c. Jaroslav Brabec; with Tomáš Hanák, Milan Steindler, David Vávra, Tereza Kučerová, Bára Dlouhá, Renata Becerová, & Chantal Poullain-Polívková. Barrandov.
Kamarád do deště (*A Good Pal*). d. Jaroslav Soukup; sw. Miroslav Vaic & Soukup; c. Vladimír Smutný; with Sagvan Tofi, Lukáš Vaculik, Beata Andraszewicz, Karel Augusta, Karol Strasburger, Ivan Vyskočil, & Alena Vránová. Barrandov. 2,600 m.
Kopytem sem, kopytem tam (*Snowball Reaction*). d. Chytilová;* sw. Pavel Škapík & Chytilová; au. Skapik; c. Jaroslav Brabec; with Milan Šteindler, Tomáš Hanák, David Vávra, Tereza Kučerová, Barbora Dlouhá, Ivana Kuntová, Renata Becerrová, & Chantal Poullain. Barrandov. 3,675 m.
Nejistá sezóna (*Uncertain Season*). d. Smoljak;* sw. Smoljak & Svěrák;* c. Richard Valenta; with Smoljak, Svěrák, Jaroslav Weigel, Jan Hraveta, Jaroslav Vozab, Miloš Čepelka, Petr Brukner, Josef Vondráček, Genadij Rumlena, Michal Weigel, Jr., & Jan Kašpar. Barrandov. 88 min.
Oznamuje so láskám vašim (*Let It Be Known to All Your Loves*). d. & sw. Kachyňa;* au. Karel Zitek; c. Richard Valenta; with Lukáš Vaculik, Markéta Hrubešová, Antonín Procházka, Pavel Nový, Ladislav Lakomý, Bohumila Dolejšová, & Miroslav Moravec. Barrandov. 2,579 m.
Pehavý max a strašidlá (*Freckles and Ghosts*). d. Jakubisko;* sw. Jaroslav Dietl, Joachim Hammann, Jakubisko, & Jozef Paštéka; au. A. R. Petterson; c. Ján Ďuriš; with Martin Hrebeň, Ferdy Maine, Barbara de Ross, Gerhardt Karzel, Andrej Hryc, Boleslav Polivka, Viveca Lindfors, Jacques Herlin, Eddie Constantine, Flavio

Bucci, Tilo Prückner, Roman Skamene, Mercedes Samietro, & Sancho Gracia. Koliba, Bratislava.

Spravca Skanzenu (Down to Earth). d. Uher;* sw. & au. Uher & Ondrej Šulaj; c. Zoltán Weigl; with Pavol Mikulik, Valerie Zawadská, Stanislav Štepka, Peter Bzdúch, Lucia Križnaová, Alexandra Zaborská, & Marek Szabó. Slovak Film, Bratislava. 2,470 m.

1989

Blázni a děvčátka (Young Girls, Crazy Guys). d. & sw. Kachyňa;* c. Ján Čuřík;* with Radim Špaček, Pavel Nový, Milan Šimáček, Zdeněk Žák, Josef Somr, Stanislav Tříska, & Jan Hrabéta. Barrandov. 2,362 m.

Divoká srdce (Famous Duels). d. Jaroslav Soukup; sw. Kamil Pixa & Jaroslav Vokřál; c. Vladimir Smutný; with Boris Rosner, Zdeněk Ornest, Jan Vávra, Antonín Procházka, Marek Vašut, Zlata Adamovská, Karel Greif, Jiří Bartoška, & Lukáš Vaculík. Barrandov. 2,943 m.

Evropa tančila valčík (Europe Danced the Waltz). d. Vávra;* s. Milos Kratochvíl & Vavra; au. Kratochvíl; c. Andrej Barla; with Hrušínský,* Jiří Bartoška, Martin Růžek, Josef Vinklář, Josef Somr, & Svatopluk Beneš. Barrandov. 2,814 m.

Konec starých časů (The End of Old Times). d. Menzel;* sw. Jiří Bažek; au. Vančura;* c. Jaromír Šofr; with Josef Abrhám, Jaromir Hanzlik, Jan Hartl, Marián Labuda, Hrušínský,* Barbara Leichnerová, Tereza Chudobová, Chantal Poullain, Alice Dvořáková, Ljuba Krbová, & Pavel Zvarič. Barrandov. 2,652 m.

Masseba (A Message of Times Past and Future). d. Miloš Zábranský; sw. Miroslav Vaic & Zábranský; c. Roman Pavliček; with Karel Roden, Victoria Kidane, Václav Postránecký, Vladimír Marek, Radan Rusev, Jana Dolanská, Miloslav Štibich, Martin Dejdar, Vlastimil Venclik, & Lenka Machoninová. Barrandov. 2,589 m.

Muka obraznosti (Tortured Imagination). d. Vladimir Drha; sw. Václav Šašek; au. Vladimir Páral; c. Emil Sirotek; with Jiří Pomeja, Dasha Blahová, Jiří Bartoška, Pavel Pipal, Taťána Medvecká, Luděk Randal, Nella Boudová, & Josef Bláha. Barrandov. 2,368 m.

Nemocný bílý sion (The Sick White Elephant). d. Karel Smyczek; sw. Ivan Bednář & Mirko Halm; c. Ivan Šlapeta; with Oldřich Navrátil, Marie Durnová, Miloslav Štibich, František Rehák, & Sinoman Stašová. Barrandov. 2,790 m.

Sedím na konóri... (Flying High). d. Jakubisko;* sw. Jakubisko & Josef Paštéka; c. Ladislav Kraus; with Boleslav Polivka, Ondřej Pavelka, Markéta Hrubešová, Deana Horváthová, Miroslav Macháček, & Štefan Kvietik. Slovak Film, Bratislava. 3,447 m.

4

Daniel J. Goulding

YUGOSLAVIA

Yugoslavia, a multi-national federation of socialist republics approximately the size of Wyoming with a population of nearly 24 million, is a complex and fragile mosaic of diverse nationalities and ethnic peoples whose histories and cultures have been differently shaped and influenced by ancient Greece and Rome, Byzantium, the Turkish Empire, and Western and Central Europe. Yugoslavia is divided into six republics, corresponding to the main Slav-speaking national groups, and two autonomous regions. The republics are Serbia, Croatia, Bosnia-Hercegovina, Slovenia, Macedonia, and Montenegro. The autonomous region of Kosovo contains mainly Albanian-speakers and Serbs, and the autonomous region of Vojvodina has a mixed population of Serbs, Hungarians, and other minorities. The two autonomous regions are under the general suzerainty of Serbia. The country, whose capital is Belgrade, borders seven nations. At its northern limits is a short frontier with Italy giving way (in clockwise succession) to borders with Austria, Hungary, Romania, Bulgaria, Greece, and Albania.

The major groups of Yugoslav peoples—Serbs, Croats, Slovenes, Bosnian Muslims, Macedonians and Montenegrins—constitute more than four-fifths of the population. Of the non-Slav population, the Albanians are the predominant group, while the Hungarians comprise a much smaller but, nonetheless, significant minority. Other small but important minorities (together comprising less than 5 percent of the population) are Turks, Romanians, Gypsies, Slovaks, Bulgarians, Germans, Ruthenians (Ukrainians), Czechs, and Italians, as well as even smaller Polish, Austrian, Greek, and Jewish groups. Some nine-tenths of the people speak Slavic languages, and three-quarters of these speak Serbo-Croatian. The Serbs use the Cyrillic alphabet and the Croats use the Latin (with diacritical markings), but conversion is relatively simple.

In religion, the country is about one-third Roman Catholic, one-tenth Muslim, and the rest Eastern Orthodox. Roman Catholic traditions are strong among the Slovenes and Croats, Eastern Orthodox among the Serbs, Montenegrins, and Macedonians, while Muslim influences are felt most strongly in Bosnia and among Albanians.

Acute economic disparities exist on a roughly north/south axis. The more prosperous regions of Yugoslavia are found in Slovenia, Croatia (including the Dalmatian coast along the Adriatic), the autonomous region of Vojvodina, and parts of Serbia and Bosnia-Hercegovina. The poorer regions are found in Montenegro, Macedonia, the autonomous region of Kosovo, and parts of Serbia and Bosnia-Hercegovina. Economic disparities, coupled with religious differences, and differing linguistic and ethnic identities and affiliations have strongly molded the country's social and political development and have often led to fierce conflicts and profound internecine strife.

The first Yugoslav state was born out of the ashes of World War I and the ruins of the Austro-Hungarian Empire. Officially founded in 1918 as the Kingdom of Serbs, Croats, and Slovenes, the name was changed in 1929 to Yugoslavia ("Land of the South Slavs") by the initiative of King Alexander. During World War II the boundaries of Yugoslavia were obliterated by multiple enemy occupiers and contending domestic foes, and its former existence erased. At the end of the war, Yugoslavia was reborn as a Federation of Socialist Republics under the leadership of Josip Broz Tito, victorious marshall of the Yugoslav National War of Liberation.

It was not until the end of World War II that Yugoslavia began to build the infrastructure (in production, distribution, and theatrical exhibition) and to evolve a film culture (artists, critics, technicians, producers) capable of sustaining a continuous multinational domestic film industry. And it was not until the late 1950s and early 1960s that the best Yugoslav films began to attract significant international critical attention and awards, and to take their place among the most interesting ones being made in Eastern Europe at that time. From the late 1950s to the present, Yugoslavia has managed, often against considerable odds, to produce at least some films which transcend national boundaries to speak with artistic integrity, humor, and social relevance to filmgoers everywhere. The story of the evolution and development of film in Yugoslavia is often as complex and multidimensional as the peoples and cultures it mirrors on the screen. The narrative of this chapter focuses upon the development of Yugoslav film following World War II. The brief synopsis at the end of this book includes highlights of the most significant earlier developments.

ESTABLISHMENT AND EVOLUTION OF A NATIONAL CINEMA, 1945–1990

It is difficult to envision a more unpromising set of conditions for establishing a national film industry than those which existed in Yugoslavia immediately following World War II. Shorn of a sophisticated film history and film tradition such as that of other newly formed socialist governments in Hungary, Poland, and Czechoslovakia, Yugoslavia found itself after the war with an almost complete lack of trained film professionals, with film equipment which was scarce and antiquated, and with practically nonexistent systems of film production and distribution. There were fewer than four hundred and fifty film theaters in Yugoslavia, many of which were damaged by the war and ill equipped.

Not only were the conditions and resources for the development of film in Yugoslavia scarce or nonexistent, they were also framed by a country savaged by a war of resistance against multiple occupying forces and a fierce civil war waged by the Partisans against Chetniks and Ustashis. With the exception of Poland, no country had experienced such wide loss of life and destruction of its basic economic infrastructure. It is a significant testimonial to the high importance which the new socialist regime placed on film that the first systematic efforts to establish and to build a national cinema occurred in these early years of struggle against severe odds and deprivations.

Birth and Early Struggles, 1945–1950

In less than a year after the war, the central government formed a separate committee for cinematography as the highest state organ for the development of film and placed at its head the well-known Yugoslav writer Aleksandar Vučo, who was appointed by Tito himself and given broad discretionary powers. When the committee was disbanded in April 1951 in favor of a more decentralized film structure, the committee could lay claim to a number of impressive achievements—achievements all the more impressive when seen in the context of the shattered condition of the country immediately after the war and of the severe economic and political crisis which occurred following Yugoslavia's dramatic break with the Soviet Union in 1948. During the nearly five-year period in which film activities were centered in the hands of the federal committee for cinematography and its surrogate republican organizations, a sufficiently modern organization and material base had been established to support the annual and continuous production of domestic films. Separate film studios had been established in all six republics, an enterprise (which later evolved into Jugoslavija film) had been formed to regulate the import and export of films, and a new Film City (*Filmski grad*) was built and equipped at Košutnjak, on the wooded outskirts of Belgrade. In addition, the committee established the first film school in Belgrade and two technical schools in Belgrade and Zagreb for the training of film technicians, as well as establishing a serious monthly journal, *Film,* as an outlet for film discussion, criticism, and polemics.

Film production had risen to levels which exceeded by several times the annual production of pre-war Yugoslavia and included the production of 13 feature films, 270 documentary and short films, and more than 300 numbers of film news and journals. Moreover, production had expanded during this period to include all of Yugoslavia's six republics, including a modest output by the smallest of its republics, Montenegro. The network of film theaters had increased substantially, from 576 in 1946 to more than 920 by April 1951, and viewers had increased from 31,520,000 in 1946 to more than double that number by the end of 1950, 67,926,000. During the same period, state investments in the development of all areas of film activity had grown by more than ten times (Goulding, *Liberated,* 6–7).

The first period of establishing a national cinema in Yugoslavia was dominated by the Soviet model of hierarchical and centralized organization under strict party control. Films were conceived of as a powerful mass medium for serving heuristic and propagandistic purposes, as well as for reflecting the development of a distinctive socialist art based upon the principles of nationalist realism—Yugoslavia's variant of the Stalinist-Zhdanov narrowly conceived socialist realism dogma. None of the films made during this period escaped entirely from this ideologically rigid and deforming aesthetic. In their most sterile realization, the films are replete with course propagandizing, ideological posturing, and sloganeering set in the context of socially important but banal content; involve a mechanical analysis of reality through sharply defined antinomies such as reactionary-revolutionary, individual-social, subjective-collective; provide assessments of situations, past or present, which are ultimately optimistic; and deny any connection with worldwide artistic traditions.

The short films, documentaries, and newsreel segments made toward the end of the war and its immediate aftermath often provided searing, first-hand visual accounts of the war-torn villages, cities, and countryside of Yugoslavia and documented the early efforts to rebuild the shattered country. It was not until 1947, however, that the first feature film, *Slavica,* produced by Avala film of Belgrade and directed by Vjekoslav Afrić, was completed. Cast in an optimistic heroic mold which was emulated by other Partisan films of the period, *Slavica* is set on the Adriatic coast and covers the whole span of the war. The film abounds in simplistic melodramatic sequences, acted out with theatrical flourish and excess and accompanied by very simple stereotyping of collaborators and satraps; of evil, indolent, pleasure-loving Italian occupiers; of harsh, unfeeling Germans; of exceptionally brave, fair, enthusiastic, ever-victorious Partisans joining hands and hearts in song and heroic deeds; and of simple, strong fisherfolk, learning for the first time the magic legendary name of "Tito" and discovering the real meaning of the National War of Liberation, in which their own destinies are merged with a new Yugoslavia reborn from the ashes of the old and characterized by "brotherhood and unity" (*bratsvo i jedinstvo*), and victory for all of the peoples of the country.

Despite its naïveté and crude propagandizing, the film, nonetheless, does capture well the Dalmatian coastal setting and the dialects and the authentic culture of the region. It is made with obvious enthusiasm, and was received enthusiastically by audiences throughout the country. In its first year, *Slavica* attracted nearly 2 million viewers throughout all regions of Yugoslavia. This strong showing was not matched by other early Partisan films made in the same naive, epic mold. These were nonetheless widely viewed, with the second feature film, *Živjeće ovaj narod* (*This People Must Live*), by the Croatian director Nikola Popovic, attracting in its first year over 1.2 million viewers, and *Besmrtna mladost* (*Immortal Youth*), directed by Vojislav Nanović and produced by Avala film in 1948, attracting nearly 750,000 viewers in less than six months (Goulding, *Liberated*, 20).

At the same time, the more discerning critics and members of the Yugoslav film community (Eli Finci, Teodor Balk, and Jovan Popović, among others) expressed increasing impatience with the level of technical and artistic achievements revealed in these early efforts. In the second issue of *Film*, Teodor Balk asserted that cliché-ridden texts, character representation, dialogue, and thematic oversimplification might be the death of film in Yugoslavia—not only of "artistic values but also the death of their social utility and effectiveness" (Balk, "Problemi" 5–7). Writing toward the end of this period, Jovan Popović asserted that the complex and rich materials suggested by Yugoslavia's immediate revolutionary past and socialist reconstruction had too often received only surface film treatment abounding in repetitive stereotypes and formulaic rigidity (Popović, 3–18).

Of the small number of feature films produced in Yugoslavia during the initial five-year period following World War II, only three stand out as suggesting deeper and more mature possibilities for future filmic development: France Štiglic's *On Their Own Ground*, dealing with Partisan war themes; Vladimir Pogačić's *Story of a Factory*, centered on post-war socialist reconstruction; and Radoš Novaković's *Sofka*—adapted from the classic Serbian novel *Nečista krv* (*Impure Blood*) by Bora Stanković—the only film produced during the period which effectively suggests the possibility of filmically portraying pre-war historical subjects and adapting traditional Yugoslav literary sources to the screen.

It is not surprising that, in the initial five-year period of the establishment and evolution of a national cinema in Yugoslavia, the predominant energies of its leadership were directed toward creating the necessary organizational, material, and technical means for continuous independent film production. While the films produced were virtually ignored by the international film community, they nonetheless revealed a vibrant nationalism and a striving to express, to reinforce, and to legitimize a unique and complex national experience which had been forged on the anvil of a brutal war and the hardships of nationalist reconstruction. In the process a small but growing vanguard of skilled film artists had gained their experience, and the rudiments of a distinctive film culture had begun to take shape. There were already signs of increasing impatience to break the confining mold of socialist realist dogma, to expand, diversify, and deepen the possibilities of filmic expression, and to move toward greater flexibility and decentralization of film organization and production.

Decentralization and Liberation, 1951–1960

The second period of Yugoslavia's evolution of a national cinema is infinitely more complex and richly textured than the first struggling period after the war. It was a period characterized by a general evolution toward decentralizing the organization and control of the Yugoslav film industry through the introduction, quite slow in the beginning, of the principles and practices of workers' self-management into all phases of film production and film distribution. Partly as a consequence of these changes and partly as a consequence of the generally improved economic conditions and economic growth which occurred in Yugoslavia at the end of the decade, this period witnessed a considerable maturation in the infrastructure and material base for film production; the elaboration of more sophisticated networks of film distribution and exhibition; a steady rise in the professionalization of film technicians and artists; the development of a livelier, "freer," and more informed group of film critics, who were able to express their views in a proliferating number of serious journals, newspapers, and weeklies; a progressive opening of Yugoslavia to cultural influences from the West; and a significant increase in the number, range, and genres of films produced.

The initial phase of this period was characterized by polemic and ideological efforts to stretch or to break the narrow propagandistic mold of the first period and was followed by increasing experimentation with new styles of realism and greater thematic complexity, variety of genres, and emphasis upon character development and psychological individualization. It was during this period as well that Yugoslav film began to gain an increasing international audience and recognition, with recognition primarily occurring in the realm of short, documentary, and animated films and secondarily, and to a lesser extent, accruing to a relatively small number of "quality"-produced feature films.

In the early 1950s, Yugoslavia developed its unique brand of self-management socialism based on the concept of a socialist market economy, in which ownership is neither private (except in the case of small service establishments) nor solely in the hands of a centralized state. Under such a system, workers in each enterprise theoretically become trustees of that portion of socially owned property committed to their hands, and this trusteeship is exercised through elected workers' councils. For Yugoslavia's fledgling film industry, this system led to the dissolution of the centralized committee of cinematography at the end of 1950 in favor of developing increasingly decentralized and autonomous film production, distribution, and exhibition enterprises.

Partly as a result of these changes, and partly as a result of the strong economic growth which Yugoslavia experienced at the end of the 1950s, the annual production of domestically produced feature films more than doubled in the latter half of the decade—from an annual rate of six films through 1954 to an average of fourteen films in the years from 1957 through 1960. Then 1954 marked the first year that Yugoslavia entered into favorable co-equal financial and artistic film production with foreign studios, and by the end of the decade, nineteen co-productions had been completed—many of them with Western countries involving internationally well-known film directors (Liehm and Liehm, 247–248).

During the same decade, admissions for domestically produced films more than tripled—from 5,656,000 in 1951 to 17,133,000 in 1960. Admissions to imported foreign films also experienced a strong surge, almost doubling from 57,875,000 in 1951 to 112,991,000 in 1960 (Goulding, *Liberated*, 37). The rise in domestic viewing of foreign films was tied to the dramatic opening and growth of film imports from the United States and Western Europe. In the years immediately following the war, the USSR clearly dominated the market, with only a small trickle of films from the United States, Great Britain, and Italy and a somewhat larger share from France. Beginning in 1950, however, this picture was reversed, with the United States emerging as the dominant exporter of films to Yugoslavia, followed by France and Italy (Kosanović, *Dvadeset,* 84).

The most immediate change from the first period's heuristic and propagandistic films about the War of Liberation and socialist reconstruction was the expansion of the range of subject matter and genres. The 1950s ushered in films of light comedy and satire, children's films, action-adventure films, and historical-literary films, as well as transformed in various ways the subject matter and filmic approach to the Partisan war experience.

Two of the most popular and successful film comedies of the period were *Vesna* (1953), directed by the emigré Czech filmmaker František Čap (top prize winner at the first annual festival of feature films at Pula, 1954), and *Pop Čira i pop Spira* (*Father Čira and Father Spira*), 1957, the debut film of Yugoslavia's first woman feature film director, Soja Jovanović. Based on the classical light comedy of Steven Sremac, it was the first Yugoslav feature film shot in color, won first prize at the 1957 Pula festival, and was one of the largest box office attractions of its time. The most sophisticated literary-historical films of the period were directed by Fedor Hanžeković; *Bakonja Fra Brne* (*Monk Brne's Pupil*), 1951, based on the 1892 story by the Croatian Simo Matavulj; and *Svoga tela gospodar* (*Master of One's Own Body*), 1956, Hanžeković's subtle film adaptation of Slavko Kolar's play—a poignant satirical comedy set in a small rural village north of Zagreb (circa 1928). The most prolific and successful director of action-adventure films during this period was the Serbian Živorad (Žika) Mitrović. Two of his immensely popular films, *Ešalon Doktora M* (*Echelon of Dr. M*), 1955, and *Kapetan Leši* (*Captain Leši*), 1960, were action-adventure transformations of Partisan war themes. His most interesting film of the period, however, was *Mis Ston* (*Miss Stone,* 1958), which depicted the adventures of an American missionary who is caught up in the maelstrom of Macedonian resistance to Turkish domination in the nineteenth century. Several imaginative feature films for children were made during this period, including *Kekec,* 1951, directed by the Slovenian Jože Gale (winner of first prize in the category of children's films at the 1952 Venice Film Festival), and two highly popular films directed by the versatile and talented Croatian Branko Bauer, *Sinji galeb* (*Grey Seagull*), 1953, and *Milijuni na otoku* (*Millions on an Island*), 1955.

Accompanying the growth and widening of popular themes and genres of film expression which occurred during this period was a searching re-examination of the war experience and its aftermath. The revolutionary past began to take on an increasingly tragic and human dimension in the films of such directors as France Štiglic, Branko Bauer, Stole Janković, Vladimir Pogačić, Radoš Novaković, and Veljko Bulajić. The abstract and idealized epics of the first period were replaced by intimate psychological portraiture and realistic, sometimes brutally naturalistic, depictions of war and its aftermath. Interesting problems of human survival and the cruel moral dilemmas of war are posed in concrete and eventful stories in which film narrative is advanced by freely linked visual sequences and is shorn of postured set speeches and abstract heroics.

One of the first Partisan films of this type was directed by Radoš Novaković, who had already established his credentials as one of Yugoslavia's leading directors with his first film, *Sofka*. His film *Daleko je sunce* (*The Sun Is Far Away*), 1953, is based on Dobrica Ćosić's influential post-war novel of the same name. Ćosić was one of the most important of the post-war Yugoslav writers and among the first to penetrate the official idealization and purity of the War of Liberation—to expose its sometimes disillusioning, cruel, and bitter side. Other films which transformed the Partisan myth from the idealized to the real were Pogačić's films *Veliki i mali* (*Big and Small*), 1956, and *Sam* (*Alone*), 1959; France Štiglic's *Deveti krug* (*The Ninth Circle*), 1960; Branko Bauer's *Ne okreći se, sine* (*Don't Turn Round, My Son*), 1956; and Stole Janković's *Partizanske priče* (*Partisan Stories*), 1960.

Pogačić was the only director of the period to extend the new spirit of critical realism to contemporary life and problems with his sensitive and well-made film *Subotom uveče* (*On Saturday Evening*), 1957. The Croatian Veljko Bulajić, who received his training at the Centro Sperimentale in Rome under the tutelage of Cesare Zavattini, also expanded the possibilities of film realism with his two Italian neo-realist inspired films about the immediate post-war years, *Vlak bez voznog reda* (*Train Without a Time Schedule*), 1959, and *Uzavreli grad* (*City in Ferment*), 1961.

The most significant film experimentation in Yugoslavia in the 1950s and early 1960s, however, occurred not in the realm of feature film production but in the areas of film animation and documentary and short films and in the growing sophistication of the amateur film movement.

During the late 1950s, animated film production in Yugoslavia was concentrated in the specialized studio of Zagreb film, founded in 1953 as a successor to Duga film, which had pioneered post-war Yugoslav experimentation in animation under the inspiration of the versatile talents of Croatian Fadil Hadžić. Reaching its most fecund and imaginative period in the late 1950s and early 1960s, Zagreb animated films transcended national boundaries and achieved wide international recognition and renown. Less a "school" than a loose collective or "family" or imaginative artists, Zagreb film animators produced a remarkable series of witty, abstract, ingeniously designed meditations on the tragi-comic paradoxes and ironies of modern life; satires of popular art forms; and poignant evocations of contemporary humanity's frustrations, helplessness, and limitations. The most visible of the early leaders of Zagreb film were the Montenegrin Dušan Vukotić and the Croatian writer-director Vatroslav Mimica. Vukotić's films have now entered the classical repertoire of animated films, and his work was recognized by many international prizes, including the first Academy Award for animation granted outside the United States, for his film *Surogat* (*Ersatz*), 1961. Mimica likewise directed a series of highly recognized animated films, including *Samac* (*Alone*), 1958, which won the studio's first international prize at the Venice Film Festival; *Kod fotografa* (*At the Photographer's*), 1958; *Jaje* (*The Egg*), 1960; and *Mala kronika* (*A Little Story*), 1962. Other highly gifted animators associated with Zagreb film who also won numerous international prizes and recognition in the early 1960s included Nikola Kostelac, Vladimir Kristl, Aleksandar Marks, Vladimir Jutriša, Zlatko Burek, Boris Kolar, Borivoj Dovniković, Zlatko Grgić, and Pavao Štalter. Mimica alone among the Zagreb film animators successfully experimented with both animated film and feature films and became a leading figure in the *new film* movement of the 1960s.

Another source of experimentation and the development of original new talent in the late fifties and early sixties was found in the realm of documentary and short film production. The most important "schools" or centers of film production during this period were the Belgrade school associated with Dunav film, the Sarajevo group associated with Bosna studio, and the Zagreb documentarists, associated mainly with Jadran film and later with the influential FAS—Film Authors' Studio—which was disbanded in 1973 for financial reasons. Garnering numerous international prizes and recognition, several of the prominent Yugoslav and short film directors later emerged in the vanguard of feature film directors of the sixties, including, among others, Matjaž Klopčič, Puriša Đorđević, Ante Babaja, Aleksandar Petrović, Bato Čengić, and Krsto Papić.

Another source of stylistic filmic experimentation and the development of film artists was the Yugoslav amateur film movement, which began quite modestly in the late forties and early fifties but by the end of the fifties had attracted to its activities some of those who would become the most prominent feature film directors (as well as writers, directors of photography, and film editors) associated with *new film* tendencies of the sixties, including Dušan Makavejev, Živojin Pavlović, Kokan Rakonjac, Boštjan Hladnik, and Želimir Žilnik.

With all of its polemic ups and downs, the decade of the fifties had witnessed a quickening and ripening of the Yugoslav cultural scene, which, in the realm of film, had led to imaginative breakthroughs in animated film and in documentary, short, and experimental films. Feature films had likewise broadened the "acceptable" boundaries of film expression. Moreover, the economic and material conditions for an accelerated rate of film production and film organization had been achieved, and by the end of the fifties, Yugoslav film was poised and ready to enter upon its most fecund and creative period.

New Film and Republican Ascendancy, 1961–1972

For Yugoslavia's young domestic film industry, the 1960s began with high ambition and enthusiasm, evolved over a turbulent decade full of contradictions and struggles, and reached its lowest ebb in the beginning of the seventies—

with its vanguard creators silenced or dispersed and the industry itself dispirited and beset with severe economic difficulties and challenges.

The sixties witnessed a further decentralization and democratization of Yugoslav self-management enterprises and a shift toward greater republican autonomy in the organization and dispersal of financial resources for film production, distribution, and exhibition. By the end of the decade, two additional centers of film production were established in the autonomous regions of Vojvodina and Kosovo.

In 1961, feature film production leaped to more than twice the annual level it had achieved in the previous decade, with thirty-two domestically produced feature films and one co-production. This number, however, was not matched nor exceeded until the peak years of the decade, 1967, 1968, and 1969 when 35 to 39 feature films and co-productions were completed each year. The dramatic rise in feature film production and the relatively free and decentralized structure of Yugoslav film enterprises opened the way for a new generation of filmmakers, who were quick to seize upon the opportunities presented to them (Goulding, *Liberated*, 63–64).

The vanguard of Yugoslav film critics, theorists, and film artists in the sixties rallied loosely and with varying degrees of commitment under the banner of *novi film* (*new film* or *open cinema*). While eschewing a specific program or forced aesthetic conformity, the advocates of *new film* sought: (1) to increase the latitude for individual and collective artistic expression and to free film from dogmatism and bureaucratic control; (2) to promote stylistic experimentation in film form and film language—influenced initially by early 1960s films associated with French *nouvelle vague* and vanguard Italian cinema, and later in the sixties by *new wave* tendencies in Eastern European countries, most notably Hungary, Czechoslovakia, and Poland; (3) to involve film in the expression of *savremene teme* (contemporary themes), including the right to critique the darker, ironic, alienated, and gloomier side of human, societal, and political existence; and (4) to do all of these things within the context and premises of a Marxist-socialist state—at a time in Yugoslavia's evolution when these very premises were a focal point for heated philosophical and ideological debate. *New film* was associated with the larger trends of the period toward greater democratization of Yugoslav society, sometimes referred to as Yugoslavia's "second revolution." Dušan Stojanović, one of Yugoslavia's leading film theoreticians and critics, perhaps best expressed the "spirit" and thrust of the *new film* movement when he stated that the most valued distinction of the new Yugoslav film is that it extends the possibility "of transforming a single collective mythology into a multitude of private mythologies" (Stojanović, 170).

Of the thirty-two feature films produced in 1961, two were singled out as representing the birth of *new film* tendencies in Yugoslav feature film production and as making a sharp break with the past: *Dvoje* (*Two*), directed by Aleksandar Petrović, and *Ples v dežju* (*Dance in the Rain*), directed by Boštjan Hladnik. Both films were anti-optimistic manifestos which explored failed love relationships, played out in an alienated urban environment. Both were personal, intimate films which experimented in very different ways with new possibilities for film language, in which intricate visual metaphors replaced traditional narrative structure. Both were the subject of heated debate and controversy. Advocates of *new film* praised them as "the most filmic films yet produced in Yugoslavian cinema" and as representing significant breakthroughs in contemporary thematics and film form. Skeptics regarded them as imitative, pale reflections of French and Italian *nouvelle vague* tendencies which were alien to the distinctive cultural roots and contemporary conditions of socialist Yugoslavia. Hladnik's film was condemned by some critics for "aestheticism" or preoccupation with form over content, for the negative and sterile view of modern life and relationships which it presented, and for offering visual complexity without philosophical depth. Others praised the film for its poetic and visually arresting style, for its complex filmic exploration of the ambiguous borders between dream and waking, reality and illusion, and, as in the case of Petrović's film, for opening up new paths of development in Yugoslav feature films.

Undaunted by the controversy that surrounded their first works, Petrović and Hladnik followed them with second films which elicited even more vociferous attacks. Petrović's second film, *Dani (Days)*, 1963, departed even further from conventional narrative structure in favor of creating a melancholy visual meditation on the empty life of an ordinary young woman, whose inner boredom finds visual equivalents in the cold sterility of her Novi Beograd suburban apartment and soul-less urban surroundings. Hladnik's second film, *Peščeni grad (Sand Castle)*, 1962, is an intensely personal and stylized psychological study of three young people, one of whom had been born in a concentration camp during the war, who find the realities of their life so harsh and alienating that they escape into a world of illusion and games. Neither of these films was accepted for official showing at the annual festival at Pula for Yugoslav feature films, and the *new film* tendencies they represented were sharply attacked by top Party officials.

Other films to fall into official disfavor in the early sixties were the multi-episode feature films directed by three amateur film directors associated with the Belgrade kino klub group, Živojin Pavlović, Kokan Rakonjac, and Marko Babac. Their first film, *Kapi, vode, ratnici (Raindrops, Waters, Warriors)*, 1962, consists of three different episodes, which portray in a veristic, grainy, naturalistic way somber stories from the war years and contemporary life. Their second film, *Grad (The City)*, 1963, was officially banned by the district court in Sarajevo, and the film negative and all copies impounded. Aleksandar Petrović sharply criticized the judgment of the court and stated that because of "a lack of comprehension and understanding, one of Yugoslavia's best films was tossed into the wastebasket" (Petrović, 175).

The well-known Belgrade painter Miča Popović also came under scathing attack with his first feature film, *Čovek iz hrastove šume (Man from the Oak Forest)*, 1963, which was subjected to several re-edits before eventually being released. Živojin Pavlović's film *Povratak* (*The Return*), made in 1963, was also held up for three years before finally being released in 1966.

Despite these early struggles and setbacks, the triumph of *new film* tendencies was clearly evident at the 1965 annual festival of Yugoslav feature films at Pula. The festival was highlighted by Aleksandar Petrović's third feature film, *Tri* (*Three*), one of his most mature and effective films, which captured first prize and earned international critical acclaim and widespread popular acceptance. Dušan Makavejev, the most original film director of the period, and the best known internationally, made his feature debut with the film *Čovek nije tica* (*Man Is Not a Bird*). One of the leading creative spirits of the Belgrade kino klub group, Kokan Rakonjac, screened his second independently directed feature film, *Klakson* (*Horn*). Živojin Pavlović, whose first feature film, *The Return*, was delayed in its release until the following year, stirred renewed controversy with the screening of his second film, *Neprijatelj* (*The Enemy*). The gifted Belgrade director Puriša Đorđević offered the first of his surrealist-inspired tetralogy about the war years and their aftermath with his film *Devojka* (*Girl*). The ripening of *new film* tendencies which these works represented inspired one of the most eloquent advocates of such tendencies, Dušan Stojanović, to declare that "at last we have thematic freedom and lively film" (Goulding, *Liberated*, 73).

On the larger political stage, the fall from power in 1966 of Aleksandar Ranković, chief of the State Security Service, secretary of the LCY (League of Communists of Yugoslavia), and a member of Tito's inner circle, was widely interpreted as a further triumph of the "progressive" or "liberal" wing of the Communist Party. The forced retirement of Ranković was only one more sign of the progressive liberalization of Yugoslav economic, political, and cultural life which took place in the late sixties. In this increasingly liberalized atmosphere, *new film* directors and film artists continued to widen thematic horizons and to become more provocative in their critique of contemporary conditions.

The Belgrade Nexus

At the cutting edge of *new film* expression and experimentation were the three Belgrade-based film directors Dušan Makavejev, Aleksandar Petrović, and Živojin Pavlović. Pavlović, a short-story writer, novelist, film critic, and essayist, was from his earliest days as an amateur filmmaker a focus of heated debate and polemics. He provoked and sometimes enraged his critics with an unrelenting assault on received myths and popular shibboleths. His was a scorched-earth policy, a demonic urge to find in film the means to shake complacency, to purge away the dross of collective memory, to confront unpleasant truths, and to explore relentlessly the dark corners of the soul and the broken promises of the new socialist order. He was a pessimistic harbinger of unwanted news and unwelcome visions. His style was naturalistic, often brutally so, but at moments was illuminated by a dark lyricism and poetry. His most important films on contemporary themes were *Budjenje pacova* (*Awakening of the Rats*), 1967, a somber and evocative record of human spirits broken on the yoke of the past and living out shattered lives in the contemporary slums of Belgrade, and *Kad budem mrtav i beo* (*When I Am Pale and Dead*), 1967, about the human cost of industrialization. His most controversial film, *Zaseda* (*The Ambush*), 1969, was a mordantly witty and bitter recounting of the years immediately after the war, when Stalinism reigned supreme; in it a young, idealistic revolutionary is casually shot on a lonely road by the Yugoslav secret police. In the context of the film, it was not only the young boy who was "ambushed" but the revolution itself. Pavlović's film *Rdeče klasje* (*The Red Wheat*), 1970, is also set in the immediate postwar period and debunks the failures of collectivization.

If Pavlović was the stern teacher who drove his lessons forward to their relentless conclusion, Makavejev was the ironic, irreverent, sophisticated, and playful gadfly who stung with wit and cunning, lifted the veil of public pomp to expose its empty interior, debunked the rituals of reification and cant, exposed the obscenity of repressive power even when it was dressed in the illusory garb of sanctioned bureaucratic niceties, and celebrated the uniqueness and liberating spirit of the individual. During this period, Makavejev experimented with increasingly complex and multi-layered film collages which challenged the viewer to move freely within the films' open spaces and multiple imagistic associations; *Čovek nije tica* (*Man Is Not a Bird*), 1965; *Ljubavni slučaj ili tragedija službenice PTT* (*Love Affair or the Tragedy of a Switchboard Operator*), 1967; *Nevinost bez zaštite* (*Innocence Unprotected*), 1968; and *WR: Mysterije organizma* (*WR: Mysteries of the Organism*), 1971. In the two films which won the greatest international attention and awards, *Love Affair* and *WR: Mysteries of the Organism*, Makavejev imaginatively explores the actual and metaphorical regions of eroticism as a foil to the obscenities of repressive power. In *WR*, he delivers an ironic and satiric double critique of the degeneration of Communist ideals and practice in the East, and the trivialization of human values, excessive self-interest, and consumer-oriented narcissism and commodity fetishism in the West.

Aleksandar Petrović probed with increasing complexity and sophistication the regions between human freedom and fulfillment and the sometimes confining and harsh demands of social and historical realities which penetrate the soul and pinion the spirit. He was, among his peers, perhaps the consummate film craftsman. His most important films of the period, all of which won widespread international critical attention and awards, were *Tri* (*Three*), 1965, a powerful anti-heroic film treatment of the Partisan war experience; *Skupljači perja* (*I Even Met Happy Gypsies*), 1967, which unfolds a tragic story of Gypsies portrayed in the contemporary setting of Vojvodina and Belgrade; and *Biće skoro propast sveta* (*It Rains on My Village*), 1969, which eschews picturesqueness and naïve romantic visions of village life to portray a ruined world of evil, backwardness, and isolation. His last and most controversial film of the period, *Majstor i Margarita* (*The Master and Margaret*), 1972, based on the well-known and long suppressed Russian novel by Mikhail Bulgakov, is set in Moscow during the beginning of Stalin's reign and explores the complex relationships of creative freedom and expression in an increasingly Kafkaesque and repressive atmosphere. An analogy is implicitly drawn between this period and the events which were then unfolding in Yugoslavia under the banner of *black film,* and Petrović uses the occasion to savage his contemporary critics.

Other important Belgrade-based contributors to *new film* tendencies were the directors Puriša Đorđević, Kokan Rakonjac, and Miča Popović. Popović, a well-known Belgrade painter, followed a unique path of filmic development and contributed visually distinctive, psychologically complex, and highly controversial perspectives on the war years in his films *Čovek iz hrastove šume (Man from the Oak Forest),* 1964, and *Delije (The Toughs),* 1968. Puriša Đorđević's most important contribution to the period, as previously mentioned, was his surrealistic tetralogy on the War of Liberation and its aftermath: *Devojka (Girl),* 1965; *San (Dream),* 1966; *Jutro (Morning),* 1967; and *Podne (Noon),* 1968. Kokan Rakonjac made his first feature film with a negative hero *Izdajnik (Traitor)* in 1964, followed by *Klakson (Horn),* 1965, an offbeat portrayal of a small group of guests at a holiday lodge in the mountains who vainly attempt to overcome isolation and alienation. Rakonjac's promising career was cut short by his sudden death in 1969 at age thirty-three. Just before his death, he completed the film *Zazidani (Pent-up),* a searing examination of prison life with strong political overtones.

Toward the end of the decade, Belgrade's influence reached out to embrace the Novi Sad group of film creators associated with the newly established Neoplanta film. The most important director of this group was Želimir Žilnik, whose film *Rani radovi (Early Works),* 1969, named after Marx's own *Early Works,* was singled out for strong attack and held up as a perfect example of *black film*—a film so radically disaffiliated from mainstream assumptions about socialist reality that it was effectively banned from domestic distribution after winning first prize at the Berlin international film festival. A sharply satirical Godardian reflection on the failures of the Yugoslav socialist revolution, Žilnik's film was closer than any film of the period to the Yugoslav radical student movement of the late sixties—especially in its attack on official complacency and corruption, and societal surrender to bourgeois materialism.

The Zagreb Group

The second most important center of *new film* experimentation and creation was Zagreb. Directors who worked out of the studios in Zagreb tended to be less radical politically than their colleagues in Belgrade but were no less inventive in pushing forward the boundaries of film stylistics and expression.

The most restlessly creative and versatile of the Zagreb filmmakers was Vatroslav Mimica, who produced an interesting and varied series of films during this period. His *Prometej sa otoka Viševice (Prometheus from Vishevica Island),* 1964, provides a sympathetic but melancholy portrayal of a middle-aged *stari borac* (old fighter), who had spent his youth in the mountains with rifle in hand

and whose contemporary efforts to bring the blessings of electrification and modernization to the island of his birth are met with incomprehension and conservative resistance. The present is infused with memories of the past and brings with it disillusionment and pain. A stylistically more inventive film is *Ponedeljak ili utorak* (*Monday or Tuesday*), 1966, an abstract meditation on urban ennui, in which a journalist's daydreams punctuate the deadly and monotonous rhythm of his days. Even more abstract and visually compelling is Mimica's film *Kaja, ubit ću te* (*Kaja, I'll Kill You*), 1967, which universalizes the terror and degradation of war and occupation by framing the sudden and brutal death of an ordinary shopkeeper with visually stylized renderings of parched walls, windswept, narrow, empty streets, and the sound of jackboots on cobbled stone in a nameless Dalmatian town. In his film *Događaj* (*The Event*), 1969, Mimica makes greater concessions to narrative structure and creates a minutely ritualistic and dark tale of greed and violence. In his last film of the period, *Hranjenik* (*Nourishee*), 1971, Mimica experiments with changing shades and gradations of color to transform a concentration camp into a philosophical metaphor where helpless victims try over and over again to achieve a bit of freedom.

Other major contributions to *new film* tendencies by the Zagreb group were made by Ante Babaja, Zvonimir Berković, and Krsto Papić. Babaja's most important film of the period is *Breza* (*The Birch Tree*), 1967, a visually rich film inspired by Croatian folk painting, which recounts the tragic death of a beautiful but frail peasant girl, who is metaphorically linked to the slender and vulnerable birch tree of the film's title. The talented scriptwriter and musician Zvonimir Berković made his debut as a director with *Rondo* (1966), which remains his most important film. A literary and cinematic variation on a rondo by Mozart, the film creates a sophisticated ambience in which a chess game becomes a metaphor for an urbane love triangle. One of Yugoslavia's foremost documentary filmmakers, Krsto Papić, achieved international acclaim with his third feature film, *Lisice* (*Handcuffs*), 1969, which skillfully recreates the uncertainty, tension, and pervasive ambiguity of the period immediately following Tito's dramatic break with Stalin in 1948. It is the first and only film of the period to suggest that the spirit of Stalinism existed not only in those being purged, but also in those who were doing the purging.

Other Visions, Other Voices

Ljubljana continued, as in earlier periods, to be a vital source for film experimentation. The two most important Slovenian film directors associated with *new film* tendencies were Boštjan Hladnik and Matjaž Klopčič. Hladnik's major contributions to modernist film expression, as already indicated, occurred in the early sixties with his two films *Dance in the Rain* and *Sand Castle*. After making these, Hladnik went to West Germany, where he completed two features, and upon his return to Yugoslavia he never recaptured a leading role in *new film* development. In the middle sixties, Hladnik was eclipsed by the versatile and stylistic inventive contributions of Klopčič, who had studied film and literature in Paris, and had apprenticed with Godard and other leading French directors. His most important films of the period were *Na papirnatih avionih* (*On Wings of Paper*), 1967, and *Oksigen* (*Oxygen*), 1970.

Among the smaller republican centers for film production (Montenegro, Macedonia, and Bosnia-Hercegovina), only Bosna film in Sarajevo contributed substantially to *new film* tendencies. In the late fifties, the documentary group in Sarajevo had established a well-deserved international reputation for stylistic inventiveness and political boldness. Two of its leading documentarists, Bato Čengić and Boro Drašković, emerged at the end of the sixties as leading feature film directors. Čengić provoked widespread critical attention and controversy with his films *Mali vojnici* (*Little Soldiers*), 1967; *Uloga moje porodice u svetskoj revoluciji* (*The Role of My Family in the World Revolution*), 1970; and *Slike iz života udarnika* (*Scenes from the Life of Shock Workers*), 1972. Drašković made an auspicious debut with his first feature film, *Horoskop* (*Horoscope*), 1969, which depicts the emptiness of life in a small town, where pent-up youthful vitality erupts into violence.

No brief survey of *new film* tendencies would be complete without acknowledging the gifted directors of photography who contributed substantially to the creative realization of modernist film expression. Among the most important of these were Tomislav Pinter, Aleksandar Petković, Milorad Jakšić-Fanđo, Rudi Vavpotić, Karpo Aćimović-Godina, Frano Vodopiveć, and Mihajlo Popović.

While films associated with *new film* tendencies provoked the greatest controversy within Yugoslavia and garnered the greatest attention outside her borders, they coexisted with a much larger number of films produced during the same period which were made strictly for entertainment, or which affirmed more orthodox aesthetic values and thematic perspectives. Among the traditional directors who continued to make well-crafted and often quite popular films during this period were France Štiglic, Veljko Bulajić, Branko Bauer, and Žika Mitrović.

Counteroffensive

From about 1969 to 1972, the counteroffensive against *new film* tendencies was renewed and intensified under the banner of *black film*. The most radical films of the period were attacked for their nihilistic and pessimistic view of Yugoslav socialist development and for anarcho-individualistic non-conformism. The campaign was stimulated, in part, by events occurring on the larger political stage: the 1968 student demonstrations in Belgrade, the Warsaw Pact invasion of Czechoslovakia, and especially the Croatian nationalist-separatist crisis of 1971. These events ushered in a period of increasing ideological stringency, aimed at nonestablishment Marxists (especially philosophers associated with the internationally acclaimed journal *Praxis*), members of the non-Marxist "humanistic intelligentsia," radical student leaders, and artists. In the area of film, this campaign led to banning some films and subjecting others to more subtle styles of bureaucratic intervention. Makavejev was expelled from the Party and left Yugoslavia to continue film work in the West following the controversy surrounding *WR: Mysteries of the Organism*. After a three-month hearing in 1973, Petrović, who was not a party member, was dismissed from his position at the film academy for contributing to a negative atmosphere at the school and for "extreme political negligence." The hearing was precipitated by a diploma film, *Plastični Isus (Plastic Jesus)*, which was officially banned following the trial and conviction of its young director, Lazar Stojanović. Stojanović was not jailed for making the film, but for expressing anti-Titoist statements while serving his obligatory term in the Yugoslav army after graduating from the film academy. Pavlović was also expelled from the film academy the next year but was later reinstated without faculty rank or teaching duties.

The mounting political pressures against *new film* creators coincided with a severe and deepening economic crisis in the Yugoslav film industry. The rapid growth of television in Yugoslavia during the sixties took a heavy toll on film attendance, which experienced its strongest decline in the late sixties and early seventies. The highest point of total film viewing occurred in 1960, with 130,124,000 admissions, but by 1971 this number had fallen 38 percent to 80,874,000. Toward the end of the sixties there was also a deterioration in the ratio of admissions to domestic films to admissions to imported foreign films. From 1961, the peak year for admissions to domestic films (21,075,000), the numbers fell by 1971 to only 6,100,000, a drop of 71 percent (Goulding, *Liberated*, 64). These trends reached crisis proportions in the early seventies and were further exacerbated by a drop in foreign earnings on the export of Yugoslav films, which had experienced a significant growth throughout most of the sixties.

These generally negative trends led to a reduction in overall feature film production in the early seventies and created a significant crisis in the areas of film distribution and exhibition as well. The dynamic implications of these adverse economic trends were combined with the tightening ideological climate of the late sixties and early seventies, and together they formed the twin millstones upon which *new film* tendencies were ground to a halt.

The period from 1973 to 1977 marked Yugoslavia's lowest ebb of domestic feature film production since the beginning of the sixties—with an average of 18 feature films produced annually during those years. It was not until the end of the seventies and the beginning of the eighties that annual production levels recovered to a 25 to 30 films-per-year level.

The low and flat profile of film production in the mid-seventies was matched by a general lack of thematic boldness and cinematic experimentation. Heroic Partisan films (which had already begun to weary domestic viewers with their worn clichés, xenophobic excesses, and repetitive formulas), light comedies, action-adventure films, and historical dramas once again rose to the forefront, and *new film* radicalism receded to the vanishing point. Some spark of it remained in Krsto Papić's *Predstava Hamleta u selu Mrduša Donja (A Village Performance of Hamlet)*, 1973, based on the witty and controversial play of the same name by Ivo Brešan. The Pula festival of 1973, however, was dominated by an empty, expensively produced, three-hour melodramatic color spectacle of the famous Partisan battle at Sutjeska, which starred Richard Burton as Marshall Tito. In 1974, Živojin Pavlović, unable to secure film projects in Serbia and in political trouble at the film academy in Belgrade, went to northeast Slovenia in the Prekomurje to make *Let mrtve ptice* (*The Flight of a Dead Bird*), a passionate and melancholy tale of the collapse of a family of seasonal farm workers under the pressures of modernization and contemporary ethics. A year later, in 1975, Puriša Đorđević stirred up a storm of controversy with his film *Pavle Pavlović*, a biting and irreverent depiction of corruption and illegal acquisition of wealth within the socialist system. Even though Đorđević's film was made on the heels of an official campaign against these same practices led by Tito himself, it was accused of "ridiculing the system of self-government" and was prohibited from competing in the Yugoslav film festival at Pula (Liehm and Liehm, 420).

Revival and Resurgence (1976–1990)

It was not until the late seventies and early eighties that a significant rebirth and revitalization of Yugoslav cinema took place. Feature film production rose to levels (25 to 30 annually) which rivaled the high watermark of the late sixties, and a new generation of film artists stimulated the revival of artistically and socially more interesting films.

Paradoxically, the comeback of Yugoslav film has occurred in a decade of multiple and deepening political and economic crises. At the center of Yugoslavia's current "time of troubles" are deteriorating economic conditions characterized by a high and persistent inflation rate, a huge balance of payments deficit, a precipitous drop in the living standards of many Yugoslavs, and the declining productivity of workers. Economic difficulties have been exacerbated by political paralysis at the federal level and the steady devolution of power to regional and republican centers whose interests do not always coincide with all-Yugoslav plans of social and economic stabilization and growth.

Added to these woes have been the re-emergence of nationality problems and inter-ethnic strife and the multiple stresses carried in the wake of Yugoslavia's rapid transition from a predominantly agrarian economy at the end of the war to a predominantly urbanized and industrialized one today. Longstanding dilemmas in Yugoslavia's rapid urbanization and industrialization have been heightened by recent worsening economic and social conditions. The winds of change which are sweeping across former East Bloc countries have buffeted Yugoslavia in unique ways. The relatively more prosperous republics of Slovenia and Croatia lying to the northwest have been the quickest to move toward pluralism and democratization. The largest republic, Serbia, however, is, at the time of this writing (mid–1990), still under the sway of a charismatic Communist leader, Slobodan Milošević, who favors centralization and greater Serbian control over the autonomous regions of Kosovo (with its 90 percent Albanian population) and Vojvodina (with its quite mixed and varied population). The strong line which Milošević has taken against Albanian nationalists-separatists in Kosovo has raised fears in Slovenia and Croatia of old-style Serbian chauvinism. In early 1991, both Slovenia and Croatia voted autonomous status for their republics and affirmed their right to secede altogether from Yugoslavia if circumstances warrant. While it is certainly possible that Yugoslavia may break up into separate small countries, it appears more likely, at the time of this writing, that it will move toward a reconstituted looser confederation of autonomous republics.

This pessimistic litany of unresolved woes and dilemmas must be balanced against the resilience and independence of the peoples of Yugoslavia and the pride and resourcefulness they have shown in finding innovative solutions to seemingly intractable problems in the past. Yugoslav films have recently played a significant role in the present critical revisioning of Yugoslavia's revolutionary past and in imaginatively reflecting the subtle, complex, and rapidly changing contours of her evolving present.

The comeback of Yugoslav film in the late seventies and early eighties was initially spearheaded by a new generation of filmmakers who had studied together at FAMU, the professional film school in Prague, and became known collectively as the "Czech group," or the "Prague group," of Yugoslav directors. Members of the original group are the directors Goran Paskaljević (b. 1947), Srđan Karanović (b. 1945), Goran Marković (b. 1946), Rajko Grlić (b. 1947), and Lordan Zafranović (b. 1944), as well as the cinematographers Živko Zalar and Vilko Filač. They shared and continue to share a common interest in making well-crafted films which communicate effectively with the audience as well as make sharp and meaningful comments on the complexities and contradictions of contemporary life in Yugoslavia. The best of their films combine absurdist social satire (imbibed in part from their Czech mentors) and sharply observed social realism. Free of political dogmatism, the *new Yugoslav cinema* is informed by a broad humanism which depicts the foibles and contradictions of human nature and explores the regions of human imagination and freedom playing against the labyrinthine, sometimes coercive, and infinitely complex surfaces of Yugoslav reality.

Goran Paskaljević was the first film director of the "Czech group" to make a significant breakthrough in Yugoslav feature film production with his popular and critically acclaimed debut *Čuvar plaže u zimskom periodu (Beach Guard in Winter)*, 1976. The film depicts an appealing and offbeat romance between two young people whose youthful aspirations for marriage and career are crushed on the wheels of social and familial constraints. In his next film *Pas koji je voleo vozove (The Dog Who Loved Trains)*, 1978, Paskaljević explores the distaff side of the social order (its misfits and fringe dwellers) with irony and wit, exposes the sometimes rough and brutal edges of contemporary reality, and does so within the context of imaginative cinematography and a dramatically interesting narrative structure. His last two films of the late seventies, *Zemaljski dani teku (Days on Earth Are Flowing By)*, 1979, and *Poseban tretman (Special Treat-*

ment), 1980, deal respectively with institutional approaches to caring for the aged and the treatment of alcoholics. Paskaljević's most significant film of the eighties, *Anđeo čuvar (Guardian Angel)*, 1987, is a sensitive, cinematically rich, and compassionate dramatization of the real-life plight of young Yugoslav Gypsy children sold into bondage in Italy as beggars, prostitutes, and petty thieves. Shot on location in Italy and in the Gypsy settlement of Ciganmala near Niš, Yugoslavia, the film paints an unromanticized and ethnographically authentic portrait of Gypsy life in a region where Gypsies lead a sedentary, segregated, and economically depressed existence. The film depicts the unsuccessful efforts of a well-intentioned journalist to expose the inner workings of this modern trade in white slavery, and to gain the love and acceptance of a young Gypsy boy, Šaina. In the brutal conclusion of the film the journalist is savagely and fatally beaten by members of the Gypsy community and his dead body is tossed on the rubbish heap outside the settlement. The rich imagery of the film is significantly enhanced by the skillfully edited musical sound track created by the versatile and talented Zoran Simjanović.

One of the most consistently original and cinematically inventive of the "Czech group" of Yugoslav directors, Srđan Karanović—*Društvena igra (Social Games)*, 1972; *Miris poljskog cveća (The Scent of Wild Flowers)*, 1977; winner of the coveted critics prize, FIPRESCI, at Cannes; *Petrijin venac (Petrija's Wreath)*, 1980—has made two recent films which critically evoke the tensions, contradictions, and sense of crisis and inertia which characterized Yugoslavia in the eighties. *Nešto između (Something In-Between)*, 1982, for which he also wrote the scenario in collaboration with Milosav Marinović and the American Andrew Horton, is an engaging portrayal of a young American woman journalist who, in a brief six-week stay in Belgrade, finds herself caught "in-between" her sexual and sentimental attachments to two Yugoslav men. At a deeper level, the film explores the ambivalent posture of Yugoslavia, herself trapped "in-between" the political tensions of East and West and the cultural and economic collisions of North and South. Karanović was awarded first prize for best direction at the Pula festival in 1983, and won the top prize at the fourth international film festival in Valencia, Spain. His next film, *Jagode u grlu (A Throatful of Strawberries)*, 1985, for which he wrote the script in collaboration with Rajko Grlić, conveys a somewhat more somber image of contemporary malaise. With dark humor and pungent social commentary, the film is built around the reunion of four old friends in their late thirties who have followed very different paths since their student days in the sixties. Despite the forced *joie de vivre*, the pervasive mood of the film is one of malaise, fragmentation, and drift. The four companions of the film were all born in 1945, the "beginning of a new era," and have grown into disillusioned and troubled middle age, along with the social system of which they are a part. Karanović's most recent film, *Za sada bez dobrog naslova (Still Lacking a Good Title)*, 1988, is the first film to tackle the sensitive issue of the Albanian nationalist-separatist movement in Kosovo. It is a complex depiction of the strong and primitive passions which flow between the Albanian majority and the Serb minority in the region. As with other Karanović works, there are also added layers of self-reflexivity in the film's structure as he portrays the ethics and self-management obstructionism which the filmmaker-protagonist must endure as he attempts to make the very film which the audience is now watching.

One of the most highly regarded of the "Czech group" directors, Goran Marković, has made a series of films characterized by sharp social commentary and satire—*Specijalno vaspitanje (Special Education)*, 1977; *Nacionalna klasa do 785 cm (National Category up to 785 cm)*, 1979; *Majstori, majstori*, 1980; *Variola Vera*, 1982; and *Tajvanska kanasta (Taiwan Canasta)*, 1985. Two of the most impressive of these films are *Special Education* (First Prize, Mannheim Festival) which depicts the efforts of an unorthodox and maverick counselor in a home for juvenile delinquents to break through the wall of silence erected by a sensitive and troubled youth; and *Variola Vera,* a dark social satire which depicts personal venality and corruption in the medical and public health professions when a virulent outbreak occurs of a rare and fatal strain of smallpox with the medical name "Variola Vera." Marković, who both wrote and directed the film, was awarded first prize for best director and best screenplay at the 1982 Valencia film festival. In his most recent film *Već viđeno (Déjà Vu)*, 1987, Marković departs from social commentary and satire to create a tautly conceived and stylistically compelling psychological portrait of a once-brilliant pianist who is haunted by childhood psychosexual traumas. A love affair with a beautiful young woman, Olga, prompts him to relive these tortured memories, shatters his fragile façade of "normalcy," and leads him to brutally murder Olga and her father. Olga's younger brother witnesses these murders from his hiding place, and the cycle of neurotic disturbance is repeated in him. Marković's film exemplifies the high level of technical and artistic mastery which characterize the best of the *new Yugoslav cinema* and the steadily ripening relationships which have developed between the writer-director Marković, the cinematographer Živko Zalar, the music director Zoran Simjanović, and a seasoned cast of excellent actors and actresses.

Rajko Grlić has contributed several of the most interesting and important films of the "Czech group's" offerings: *Kud puklo da puklo (Whichever Way the Ball Bounces)*, 1974; *Bravo Maestro*, 1978; *Samo jednom se ljubi (You Only Love Once)*, 1981, released under the English title *The Melody Haunts My Memory; U raljama života (The Jaws of Life)*, 1984; and *Za sreću je potrebno troje (Three's Happiness)*, 1986. *Bravo Maestro* is a masterful portrayal of a brilliant young composer who sacrifices his personal integrity to achieve fame and empty applause. *You Only Love Once* is the most caustic and searchingly critical film dealing with Yugoslavia's immediate post-war Stalinist period since Pavlović's *Ambush*. The film depicts the physical and psychological disintegration of the protagonist, a bright young Partisan hero, as he becomes progressively alienated from the new Stalinist order established immediately after the war, and as he becomes passionately involved with Beba, the beautiful daughter of a suspected wartime collaborator. The film imaginatively captures the spartan existence of the times and the political and social contradictions which eventually tear the protagonist Tomislav apart. On one level, there is the political contradiction of revolutionary elan rubbing up against the emergence of special privileges and an increasingly intolerant new social and political structure. At another level there is the class conflict between Tomislav's peasant upbringing and the professional middle-class refinements of Beba's family. It is the complex cinematic representation of these class and sociopolitical vortices which lifts the love story above the level of melodrama, and makes the suicide of Tomislav at the end of the film both poignant and dramatically effective. Grlić's *The Jaws of Life,* directed from a script written in collaboration with the talented female novelist Dubravka Ugrešić, is a biting social comedy which interweaves the fate of a middle-aged female television director and the tv character she has created. The film deals more explicitly than any other Yugoslav film of the eighties with new feminist sensibilities and with newly evolved ambiguities in contemporary relations between the sexes. Grlić's most recent film is a British-Yugoslav co-production, *The Summer of White Roses,* 1989, set in an idyllic lakeside resort at the beginning of World War II.

The most elegant visual stylist of the "Czech group" is Lordan Zafranović—*Nedelja II (Sunday II)*, 1969; *Dalmatinska kronika (Dalmatian Chronicle)*, 1972; *Muke po mati (The Matthew Passions)*, 1975; *Okupacija u 26 slika (Occupation in 26 Pictures)*, 1978; *Pad Italije (The Fall of Italy)*, 1981; *Ujed Andela (The Angel's Bite)*, 1984; *Večernja zvona (Evening Bells)*, 1986; and *Praznik kurvi (Whore's Holiday)*, 1988. One of the most dramatically compelling and evocative recollections of the war years is Zafranović's powerful *Occupation in 26 Pictures,* set in the beautiful city of Dubrovnik on the southern part of the eastern Adriatic coast during the successive occupations of Germans, Italians, and Ustashis. In a manner structurally related to Vatroslav Mimica's earlier experimental *Kaja, I'll Kill You,* Zafranović's film creates an ever-enlarging metaphor of evil. The rigid mechanism of fascism, with its goose-stepping soldiers, inflated oratory, Mussolini posturing, false pomp, anticultural vulgarity, and unspeakable Ustashi atrocities, is played antipodally against the graceful ease and lyrical beauty of Dubrovnik's Mediterranean culture. Zafranović's film received widespread critical praise at international film festivals and captured first prize at the Pula festival. In his thematically and stylistically most mature film of the eighties, *Večernja zvona (Evening Bells)*, 1986, based on the award-winning novel by Mirko Kovač, Zafranović provides a complex rendering of the period from 1926 to 1948 in which the protagonist Tomislav K., in the final sequences of the film, senselessly loses his life in prison after being falsely arrested as a Stalinist sympathizer.

While the "Czech group" of Yugoslav film directors provided the yeast for leavening and quickening the resurgence of Yugoslav film expression in the late seventies and early eighties, numerous other creative sources have nurtured its continued maturation and growth during the last few years. The two most important and visible new directors to emerge in the eighties are the Serbian Slobodan Šijan (b. 1946) and the Bosnian Emir Kusturica (b. 1954).

One of the brightest and most inventive films of the eighties is Slobodan Šijan's debut film *Ko to tamo peva (Who's That Singing Over There?)*, 1980, directed in collaboration with the scenarist Dušan Kovačević and the cinematographer Božidar Nikolić. The film wittily portrays a group of provincials making their way to Belgrade in a rickety bus, unaware of the tragedy that awaits them on that fatal day, Sunday, April 6, 1941, when Nazi Germany launched its savage bombing attack on Belgrade under the code name "Operation Punishment." Šijan's cinematic portrait-in-miniature of pre-war Yugoslavia is informed by tolerance and a humanistic embrace of all the colorful characters who share this last fateful ride together. Sharp satire blends with nostalgic remembrance of a time past, a more innocent time, a decaying epoch which ends in flames and rubble. A strong critical and popular success, Šijan's film won for him the coveted George Sadoul award for best debut film by a foreign director in 1981. Another impressive critical and popular success was his film *Davitelj protiv davitelja (Strangler Versus Strangler)*, 1984, directed from an original script which he wrote with Nebojša Pajkić. The film is both an elaborate parody of a Hitchcockian psychological thriller and a witty, bizarre, surrealistic, and mordant satire on urban decadence, moral relativism, youthful iconoclasm, and the breakdown of public civility. Especially well captured is the anarchic and iconoclastic spirit of a segment of Yugoslavia's youth which is radically disaffiliated from mainstream values and sacred myths. Unlike the politically explicit radical youth movements in Yugoslavia during the late sixties, youthful disaffection in the eighties has often been deflected into various rock, *new wave,* and punk styles. The most radical of these new styles celebrate the values of anarchy, surrender, decline, and societal exile, voluntarily assumed (Goulding, *Post,* 270–271). Šijan's film wittily and satirically captures these cutting edge attitudes more fully than any other film of the decade, and remains a strong favorite of youthful urban filmgoers to the present—having acquired something of a cult status.

Emir Kusturica, who also received his film training at FAMU in Prague, has directed three feature films, all of which have won major international awards and strong critical acclaim—*Sjećas li se Dolly Bell (Do You Remember Dolly Bell?)*, 1981; *Otac na službenom putu (When Father Was Away on Business)*, 1985; and *Dom za vešanje (Time of the Gypsies)*, 1989. Kusturica's debut film *Do You Remember Dolly Bell?,* made in collaboration with the Bosnian poet Abdulah Sidran as screenwriter and FAMU-trained Vilko Filač as cinematographer, is a richly detailed portrayal of a young boy coming of age in a Moslem family on the outskirts of Sarajevo. Kusturica's film vividly depicts the forces of modernity and Western cultural influences colliding with traditional cultural norms and values of the region, and of older forms of Marxist political orthodoxy clashing with steadily strengthening forces of socialist pragmatism and political and economic experimentation. The play of these larger socio-cultural and political forces is framed against a skillfully drawn portrait of a sixteen-year-old boy, Dino Zolje, who lives with his poor family on the outskirts of Sarajevo, and whose painful process of growing into young manhood is poignantly assisted by a tender sexual liaison with a young prostitute, Dolly Bell. Kusturica's debut film was an enormous popular and critical success and captured the Golden Lion for best first film at the 1981 Venice film festival.

Kusturica's second film, *When Father Was Away on Business,* also made in collaboration with Sidran and Filač, achieved even greater international critical acclaim, winning the *Palme d'Or* for best feature film at the 1985 Cannes film festival. The film imaginatively depicts the tensions and the moral and political ambiguities which prevailed in Yugoslavia after the break with Stalin, as these impacted on a Moslem family living in Sarajevo. The time of the film is condensed from the summer of 1950 to the summer of 1952, a period in which Yugoslavia weathered the harshest diplomatic, economic and military threats against her independence, and steadily gained in strength. The dramatic structure of the film mirrors and reflects this steady progress toward reconciliation and transcendence as seen from the innocent, precocious, and mischievous perspective of the film's six-year-old child narrator, Malik. The film is filled with humor, ranging from the situational to the satiric and mordant, which serves to undercut and punch holes in official as well as personal solemnities. Kusturica avoids political and socio-cultural didacticism about the period in favor of a subtle blending of social realism and Chagallian surrealism in which the cruel ambiguities of the time and the face of repression are countered with humor, magic, lyricism, and the elasticity of the human spirit. In the final scene, when young Malik is miraculously levitated above the rooftops and trees, he has symbolically transcended the particularities of his family and of the times, and has entered what Eliade calls the ''sacred'' time of myth—a time which is recurrently present and which exists both in and out of history.

Kusturica's latest film, *Time of the Gypsies,* based on an original script by Yugoslavia's leading scenarist Gordan Mihić, won for Kusturica the best director's award at the 1989 Cannes film festival. In this film, Kusturica moves even further in the direction of blending veristic filmic evocations of gypsy life with magical realism and illusion. His narrative structure is more experimental and poetic in form—influenced, in part, by such South American writers as Marquez, Llosa, Cortazar, and Borges.

Other feature film directors who emerged in the eighties and contributed substantially to the development of the *new Yugoslav cinema* are the Macedonian Stole Popov (b. 1950), whose uneven first film, *Crveni konj (The Red Horse),* 1981, was followed by his internationally successful *Srećna nova '49 (Happy New Year 1949),* 1986, a darker evocation of the period immediately following Tito's split with Stalin than presented in Kusturica's more celebrated film; the Montenegrin Branko Baletić (b. 1946), whose relatively slight first film, *Sok od šljiva (Plum Juice),* 1980, was followed by his witty and accomplished *Balkan ekspres (Balkan Express),* 1983; the talented Slovenian cinematographer-turned-director Karpo Godina (b. 1943), whose visually stylish, dadaist-inspired period film *Splav meduze* (*The Raft of Medusa*), 1980, was followed by the interesting but comparatively less successful *Rdeči boogie* (*Red Boogie*), 1983; Božidar Nikolić (b. 1942), the talented cinematographer, and Dušan Kovačević (b. 1948), the gifted comedy playwright and scenarist, co-directed *Balkanski špijun* (*The Balkan Spy*), 1984, one of the most biting satires and darkest social comedies of the eighties; and the Slovenian scenarist and director Filip Robar-Dorin (b. 1940), whose debut film, *Ovni in mamuti* (*Sheep and Mammoths*), 1985, earned widespread critical praise.

Several directors who contributed substantially to *new film* tendencies in the sixties (the Serbians Živojin [Žika] Pavlović, Puriša Đorđević, Miloš Radivojević, and Želimir Žilnik; the Croatians Vatroslav Mimica, Krsto Papić, Branko Ivanda, Ante Babaja, and Zvonimir Berković; the Slovenians Boštjan Hladnik and Matjaž Klopčič; and the Bosnians Boro Drašković and Bato Čengić) have all directed films in the eighties, in some cases after a long absence from feature film production. Among the most significant of these recent films are *Zadah tela* (*Body Scent*), 1983, directed by Žika Pavlović, winner of the Golden Arena award for best film at the 1983 Pula feature film festival, which explores the dark underside of socialism in the characteristic style of Pavlović's most important films of the sixties; *Dediščina, (The Heritage)*, 1984, directed by Matjaž Klopčič, featured in the Certain Regard section of the 1985 Cannes festival, a cinematically complex rendering of the period from 1914 to 1944 and the tragedy which overtakes three generations of the Vrhunc family; *Život je lep* (*Life Is Beautiful*), 1985, a dark metaphor of social breakdown and spiritual paralysis in contemporary Yugoslavia, directed by Boro Drašković; *Živeti kao sav normalan svet* (*Living Like the Rest of Us*), 1982, directed by Miloš Radivojević, a compelling cinematic study of a talented and idealistic music student from the provinces who is progressively disillusioned by the subtle politics and corrupt lifestyles which he finds in the professional conservatory of music in Belgrade; and *Život sa stricem* (*My Uncle's Legacy*), 1988, Krsto Papić's most important film of the eighties.

One of the foremost directors of the sixties, Aleksandar Petrović, has not directed a film in Yugoslavia since his controversial *The Master and Margaret* (1972). He has, however, received French funding for a major a tv and film project, *Migrations,* which he partially shot in Yugoslavia. Dušan Makavejev, the best-known Yugoslav director internationally (*Sweet Movie, Montenegro, The Coca Cola Kid,* and *Manifesto*), has not made a film in Yugoslavia since *WR: Mysteries of the Organism*. He has, however, recently returned to Yugoslavia several times for guest appearances, and *WR: Mysteries of the Organism* has enjoyed special screenings in Yugoslavia with enthusiastic audience response. His most recent film, *Manifesto* (1988), is a U.S.-Yugoslav co-production, and was shot in Slovenia.

Also contributing to the enlivening of Yugoslav film in the eighties have been the avant-garde experiments in visual form and what Yugoslav critics call the "new narrativity" which have taken place in the usually more conservative realm of television drama, especially in Belgrade (Goulding, *Post,* 252–253). Animated film, no longer exclusively centered in Zagreb, has also remained a lively source of artistic experimentation. Among the most significant of these recent animated films are *Satiemania,* 1978, directed by Zdenko Gašparović, and inspired by the mocking, lyrical music of Erik Satie. Sketches, reminiscent of the best impressionistic drawings of the twenties, integrate graphic movement with humor and detached spleen. *Riblje oko (Fisheye),* 1982, directed by Joško Marušić, depicts a cruel reversal of nature in which monster fish invade and demolish a village. This macabre vision is executed with woodcuts creating a vivid black-and-white pictorial effect. *Opsesija (Obsession),* 1983, directed by Aleksandar Marks, uses exaggerated expressionistic drawings to create a nightmarish world based on Edgar Allan Poe's short story "The Black Cat." *Kuća br. 42 (House No. 42),* 1984, directed by Pavao Štalter, employs a cinematic reconstruction of a daguerreotype showing an old building in downtown Zagreb. Using soft focus and subtle time-lapse, the stationary picture turns into a peopled city scene which nostalgically captures petit-bourgeois behavior and turn-of-the-century romantic atmosphere.

It should also be emphasized that liberated cinematic tendencies in Yugoslavia, as in past periods, exist at the thin edge of a much larger politically conformist and commercially oriented cinema. The most popular films with the domestic audience in the eighties have been light social comedies with contemporary settings. The most successful director of the genre, Zoran Čalić, has made seven films based on a continuing cast of characters, beginning with *Lude godine (Crazy Years),* 1977, which have all been enormous box office successes. Another film in this genre which broke all previous domestic box office records is *Tesna koža (The Tight Spot),* 1983, directed by Mića Milošević. Several commercially oriented imitators of this trend, however, have failed to reach even the relatively low level of audience taste at which these films are aimed. It is important to note, however, that, unlike in other East European countries, there is a very strong audience in Yugoslavia for domestically produced films. Indeed, domestic films often outstrip the box office receipts for even the most popular foreign imports (Goulding, *Post,* 282).

Conclusion

It is difficult to assess whether the cinematic accomplishments of Yugoslavia's recently touted *new Yugoslav cinema* can be sustained into the nineties. There has perhaps never been a period in Yugoslavia's post-war film development in which there have been so many seasoned, artistically gifted, and professionally well-trained film directors, cinematographers, scenarists, actresses, actors, and other film artists and technicians eager to further strengthen the artistic integrity of Yugoslav films and to expand the international audience for them. Levels of feature film production have remained high despite very serious economic problems, creating healthy opportunities for new and relatively untried directors and other film artists to express themselves.

Film projects, however, must be guided through an increasingly fissiparous system, with film production enterprises (many of them small and underfinanced) spread throughout Yugoslavia's six republics and two autonomous regions. More significantly, the fortunes of Yugoslav film are inevitably held hostage to the complex drama currently being acted out in the larger socio-cultural and political arena. It is difficult, if not impossible, to predict whether Yugoslavia will find a way out of her present quandaries. There are strong and opposing forces at work for fragmentation and unity; devolution and centralization; liberality and repression; openness and closure; and rival views of the meanings and lessons to be learned from Yugoslavia's often turbulent and dramatic past. It is a remarkable tribute to a relatively small film industry that each year some films are produced which not only reflect Yugoslavia's unique cultural and political experience, but which also transcend republican and national boundaries to imaginatively address filmgoers everywhere.

BIBLIOGRAPHY

Books

Čolić, Milutin. *Jugoslovenski ratni film*. 2 vols. Belgrade: Institut za film, 1984.
Goulding, Daniel J. *Liberated Cinema: The Yugoslav Experience*. Bloomington: Indiana University Press, 1985.
———, ed. *Post New Wave Cinema in the Soviet Union and Eastern Europe*. Bloomington: Indiana University Press, 1989.
Holloway, Ronald. *Z is for Zagreb*. Cranbury, N.J.: A. S. Barnes, 1972.
Ilić, Momčilo, ed. *Filmografija jugoslovenskog filma, 1945–1965*. Belgrade: Institut za film, 1970.
———. *Filmografija jugoslovenskog filma, 1966–1970*. Belgrade: Institut za film, 1974.
Kosanović, Dejan. *Dvadeset godina jugoslovenskog filma, 1945–1965*. Belgrade: Savez filmskih radnika jugoslavije i festival jugoslovenskog filma, 1966.
———. *Počeci kinematografija na tlu Jugoslavije 1896–1918*. Belgrade: Institut za film, 1986.
Liehm, Mira, and Antonín J. Liehm. *The Most Important Art: East European Film After 1945*. Berkeley: University of California Press, 1977.
Makavejev, Dušan. *WR: Mysteries of the Organism*. New York: Avon Books, 1972.
Obradović, Branislav, ed. *Filmografija jugoslovenskog igranog filma, 1945–1980*. Belgrade: Institut za film, 1981.
———. *Filmografija jugoslovenskog igranog filma, 1981–1985*. Belgrade: Institut za film, 1987.
Pavlović, Zivojin. *Davolji film*. Belgrade: Institut za film, 1969.
Petrović, Aleksandar. *Novi film*. Belgrade: Institut za film, 1971.
Ramet, Pedro, ed. *Yugoslavia in the 1980s*. Boulder and London: Westview Press, 1985.
Sher, Gerson S. *Praxis: Marxist Criticism and Dissent in Socialist Yugoslavia*. Bloomington: Indiana University Press, 1977.

Stojanović, Dušan. *Velika avantura film*. Belgrade: n.p., 1970.
Tasić, Zoran and Jean-Loup Passek, eds. *Le Cinéma Yougoslave*. Paris: Centre Georges Pompidou, 1986.
Volk, Petar. *Istorija jugoslovenskog filma 1896–1982*. Belgrade: Institut za film, 1986.

Articles

Balk, Teodor. "Problemi našeg filma i film naših problema." *Film* 2 (March 1947): 5–7.
———. "Festival of Yugoslav Feature Films in Pula." *Bulletin* (1965–1989).
Holloway, Ronald. "Slovenian Film." *Kino* (Special Issue, 1985).
———. "Yugoslavia." In *International Film Guide, 1987*. Edited by Peter Cowie. New York: A. S. Barnes, 1987.
Horton, Andrew. "The New Serbo-Creationism." *American Film*, 11. 4 (January-February 1986): 24–30.
———. "Yugoslavia: Multi-Faceted Cinema." In *World Cinema Since 1945*. Edited by William Luhr. New York: Ungar, 1987.
Jovičić, Vladimir. "Crni talas u našem filmu." *Borba Reflektor*, August 3, 1969, pp. 22–29.
"Le Film Yougoslave en 1985" (Special French Edition), *Filmograf* 11.34 (spring 1986).
Popović, Jovan. "Iskustva iz šest naših prvih umetničkih filmova i pouke za dalji rad." *Film* 1–2 (July 1949): 3–49.
Schöpflin, George. "Yugoslavia's Uncertain Future," "The Yugoslav Crisis," and "Yugoslavia's Growing Crisis." In, respectively, *Soviet Analyst* 11.13 (30 June 1982), 12.2 (26 January 1983), and 14.25 (19 December 1984).
Shaplen, Robert. "A Reporter at Large: Tito's Legacy—I." *The New Yorker* (5 March 1984), pp. 110–25.
———. "A Reporter at Large: Tito's Legacy—II." *The New Yorker* (12 March 1984), pp. 79–119.
Tirnanić, Bogdan. "Paralelna istorija jugoslovenskog filma" (a ten part series on Yugoslav film in the sixties). *NIN* (May 18, 25; June 1, 8, 15, 22, 29; and July 6, 13, 20, 1986).

BIOGRAPHICAL SKETCHES

AFRIĆ, VJEKOSLAV (1906–1980), scenarist and theater and film director. Apprenticed with the Soviet director Abram Room on his film *U planinama Jugoslavije* (*In The Mountains of Yugoslavia*), 1946, and directed the first postwar feature film, a naíve, heroic Partisan film, *Slavica* (1947).*

BABAJA, ANTE (1927–   ), scenarist and director. Studied economics before working with Jacques Becker in Paris as an assistant director. His documentary films have won several important prizes. His best feature film is *Breza* (*The Birch Tree*), 1967.* Since 1968 he has taught at the Zagreb Academy of Theater and Film Arts.

BALETIĆ, BRANKO (1946–   ), television and film director. Graduated in film from the Belgrade Academy of Dramatic Arts. His most popular and critically praised film is *Balkan ekspres* (*Balkan Express*), 1983.*

BAUER, BRANKO (1921–   ), scenarist and director. Began as a documentary filmmaker in the late forties. He made two critically successful and popular feature films for children and an important film on World War II, *Ne okreći se, sine* (*Don't Turn Round, My Son*) in the fifties, and two of his best films *Prekobrojna* (*Superfluous*) and *Licem u lice* (*Face to Face*)* in the sixties.

BULAJIĆ, VELJKO (1928–   ), scenarist and director. One of Yugoslavia's most popular and successful filmmakers. Studied at the Centro Sperimentale in Rome with Cesare Zavattini. After several successful years as a documentarist, Bulajić made his influential debut film *Vlak bez voznog reda* (*Train Without a Time Schedule*), 1959.* His most popular and internationally awarded films are the two war epics *Kozara*, 1962,* and *Bitka na Neretvi* (*Battle on the River Neretva*), 1969.

ČENGIĆ, BATO (1931–), director. Studied at the School of Art Design in Sarajevo, and film in London with Schlesinger and Reisz. An important and internationally awarded documentarist in the fifties and sixties, Čengić also directed three controversial and significant feature films; *Mali vojnici (Little Soldiers)*, 1967;* *Uloga moje porodice u svetskoj revoluciji (The Role of My Family in the World Revolution)*, 1970; and *Slike iz života udarnika (Scenes from the Life of Shock Workers)*, 1972.*

ĐORĐEVIĆ, PURIŠA (1925–), scenarist and director. Studied art history and worked as a journalist. In 1947 he began his long and successful career in film as a documentarist. An influential figure in the *new film* movement of the sixties, Đorđević is best known for his surrealist-inspired tetralogy on the war years and its aftermath: *Devojka (Girl)*, 1965;* *San (Dream)*, 1966;* *Jutro (Morning)*, 1967;* and *Podne (Noon)*, 1968.*

DRAŠKOVIĆ, BORO (1935–), theater and film director. Studied philosophy in Sarajevo, film and theater direction in Belgrade, and apprenticed with Wajda and Kawalerowicz in Poland. Drašković has won critical acclaim for his work in theater, television, and film. His most important and internationally awarded recent feature film is *Život je lep (Life is Beautiful)*, 1985.*

GILIĆ, VLATKO (1935–), scenarist, director, and designer. Graduated from the School of Architecture in Belgrade. Yugoslavia's leading director of short films, Gilić has won numerous awards for his inspired works: *Homo sapiens, Homo homini, In continuo, Moc (Power), Ljubav (Love), Dan vise (One More Day)*.

GODINA, KARPO (1943–), cinematographer and director. Graduate of film and theater direction from the Ljubljana Academy of Dramatic Arts, Godina has won many awards as a cinematographer and short film scenarist and director. His most important feature film is *Splav Meduze (The Raft of Medusa)*, 1980,* for which he served as both director and cinematographer.

GRLIĆ, RAJKO (1947–), scenarist and director. Graduated from FAMU in Prague with Marković, Karanović, Paskaljević and Zafranović. A member of the "Prague group" of Yugoslav film directors, Grlić has made a number of critically acclaimed documentaries, short films, and television dramas. Among his most significant and highly acclaimed feature films are *Bravo Maestro*, 1978;* *Samo jednom se ljubi (You Only Love Once)*, 1981;* and *U raljama života (The Jaws of Life)*, 1984.*

HADŽIĆ, FADIL (1922–), scenarist, director and playwright. Graduated from the Academy of Art in Zagreb. In the late forties he was editor of the satirical journal *Kerumpuh*, which attracted several of Yugoslavia's leading animators. In the early fifties he served as director of Duga film, precursor to the internationally famous Zagreb film. Hadžić has written over thirty plays and directed fourteen feature films.

HLADNIK, BOŠTJAN (1929–), director. Graduated from the Academy of Dramatic Art in Ljubljana and apprenticed as an assistant director with Claude Chabrol, Philippe de Broca, and Robert Siodmak in Paris. His short films won many international prizes. He helped to initiate *new film* tendencies in Yugoslavia with his feature films *Ples v dežju* (*Dance in the Rain*), 1961,* and *Peščeni grad* (*Sand Castle*), 1962.*

JANKOVIĆ, STOLE (1925–), scenarist and director. His most popular and critically acclaimed feature films deal with the war years, *Partizanske priče* (*Partisan Stories*), 1960, and *Radopolje,* 1963.

KARANOVIĆ, SRĐAN (1945–), scenarist and film and television director. A graduate of FAMU, Karanović is a leading figure in the "Prague group" of Yugoslav directors. In addition to making many critically acclaimed short films and television dramas, he has won several international prizes for his feature films. Among the most important of his feature films are *Miris poljskog cveća* (*The Scent of Wild Flowers*), 1977;* *Petrijin venac* (*Petrija's Wreath*), 1980;* *Nešto između* (*Something In-Between*), 1982;* and *Jagode u grlu* (*A Throatful of Strawberries*), 1985.*

KLOPČIČ, MATJAŽ (1934–), scenarist and director. Graduated in architecture and apprenticed in film with Godard and Dassin in Paris. He contributed significantly to *new film* tendencies with his films *Na papirnatih avionih* (*On Wings of Paper*), 1967,* and *Oksigen* (*Oxygen*), 1970. His most acclaimed recent film is *Dediščina* (*The Inheritance*), 1984.*

KOVAČEVIĆ, DUŠAN (1948–), playwright, scenarist, and director. Graduated from the Academy of Dramatic Art in Belgrade. An award-winning comedy playwright, Kovačević also wrote the scenario for the highly successful feature film *Ko to tamo peva* (*Who's That Singing Over There?*), 1980,* and wrote the scenario and co-directed the black film comedy *Balkanski špijun* (*The Balkan Spy*), 1984.*

KUSTURICA, EMIR (1954–), director. A graduate of FAMU, Kusturica has been the most successful of the younger generation of directors. All of his feature films have won major international prizes; *Sjećas li se Dolly Bell* (*Do You Remember Dolly Bell?*), 1981;* *Otac na službenom putu* (*When Father Was Away on Business*), 1985;* and *Dom za vešanje* (*Time of the Gypsies*), 1989.*

MAKAVEJEV, DUŠAN (1932–), director. Studied psychology and graduated from the Academy of Dramatic Art in Belgrade. His amateur films and documentaries won many prizes, and his social and sexual film satires were among the most controversial and internationally well known of the *new film* period; *Čovek nije tica* (*Man Is Not a Bird*), 1965;* *Ljubavni slučaj* (*Love Affair*), 1967;* *Nevinost bez zaštite* (*Innocence Unprotected*), 1968;* and *WR: Misterije organizma* (*WR: Mysteries of the Organism*), 1971.* In the West, he made *Sweet Movie*, 1974; *Montenegro*, 1981; *The Coca-Cola Kid*, 1985; and *Manifesto*, 1988.

MARKOVIĆ, GORAN (1946–): Director. A FAMU graduate, Marković contributed substantially to the rebirth of Yugoslav cinema in the late seventies and eighties. His most celebrated and awarded films are *Specijalno vaspitanje* (*Special Education*), 1977;* *Variola Vera*, 1982;* and *Već viđeno* (*Déjà Vu*), 1987.*

MIHIĆ, GORDAN (1938–): Scenarist and director. Yugoslavia's most prolific and important scenarist, Mihić has written 29 feature film scenarios, 16 television series, 8 television dramas, 40 radio dramas, and 5 plays. His most recent critical success is the film scenario for *Dom za vešanje* (*Time of the Gypsies*), 1989.*

MIMICA, VATROSLAV (1923–), scenarist and director. Studied medicine before becoming involved in film. One of the founders of Zagreb film, and one of its foremost directors of animated films, Mimica also made a series of important experimental feature films in the *new film* period. The most impressive and artistically intricate of these is *Kaja, ubit ću te* (*Kaja, I'll Kill You*), 1967.*

NIKOLIĆ, BOŽIDAR (1941–), cinematographer and director. Graduated from the Academy of Dramatic Art in Belgrade. His major accomplishments have been as the cinematographer for several important feature films. He also co-directed and served as cinematographer for the popular and critically successful black comedy *Balkanski špijun* (*The Balkan Spy*), 1984.*

NIKOLIĆ, ŽIVKO (1942–), director. A graduate of the Academy of Dramatic Art in Belgrade, Nikolić has won many prizes for his short films. His feature films are experimental and strikingly original. His most accessible and important recent film is *U ime naroda* (*In the Name of the People*), 1987.*

NOVAKOVIĆ, RADOŠ (1915–1979), director. One of the most important of the first generation of post-war film directors, Novaković made several of the best films of the late forties and early fifties. He taught at the Academy of Dramatic Art in Belgrade until his death.

PAPIĆ, KRSTO (1933–), director. Literature graduate from Zagreb. Papić was an internationally acclaimed documentarist before he began making feature films in 1965. His most impressive and internationally acclaimed feature film is *Lisice* (*Handcuffs*), 1969.* His most important recent film is *Život sa stricem* (*My Uncle's Legacy*), 1988.*

PASKALJEVIĆ, GORAN (1947–), scenarist and film and television director. A graduate of FAMU, Pakaljević led the revival of Yugoslav cinema in the late seventies with his film *Čuvar plaže u zimskom periodu* (*Beach Guard in Winter*), 1976.* His most impressive film of the eighties is *Anđeo čuvar* (*Guardian Angel*), 1987.*

PAVLOVIĆ, ŽIVOJIN (1933–), writer, essayist, scenarist, and director. A graduate in fine arts, Pavlović is both a major writer and film director. A leader of *new film* tendencies, his most impressive and controversial films of the sixties are *Budjenje pacova* (*Awakening of the Rats*), 1967;* *Kad budem mrtav i beo* (*When I am Pale and Dead*), 1967;* and *Zaseda* (*Ambush*), 1969.* His most important film of the eighties is *Zadah tela* (*Body Scent*), 1983.*

PETROVIĆ, ALEKSANDAR (1929–), director. Graduated in the history of art in Belgrade, and studied film in Prague. One of the most powerful and influential leaders of *new film* tendencies, Petrović made several of the key films of the period; *Dvoje* (*Two*), 1961;* *Dani* (*Days*), 1962;* *Tri* (*Three*), 1965;* *Skupljači perja* (*I Even Met Happy Gypsies*), 1967;* *Biće skoro propast sveta* (*It Rains on My Village*), 1968;* and *Majstor i Margarita* (*The Master and Margaret*), 1972.*

POGAČIĆ, VLADIMIR (1919–), director. Studied history of art in Zagreb. One of Yugoslavia's most influential directors of the fifties, whose most influential films are *Veliki i mali* (*Big and Small*), 1956;* *Subotom uveče* (*On Saturday Evening*), 1957;* and *Sam* (*Alone*), 1959.*

POPOV, STOLE (1950–), scenarist and director. A graduate of the Academy of Dramatic Art in Belgrade, Popov won several important international prizes for his documentary films before making his first feature film *Crveni konj* (*The Red Horse*) in 1981. His most celebrated feature film is *Srećna nova—'49* (*Happy New Year, 1949*), 1986.*

RADIVOJEVIĆ, MILOŠ (1939–), scenarist and director. Graduated from the Academy of Dramatic Art in Belgrade. Strikingly original and inventive, one of Radivojević's early films *Bez* (*Without*), 1972, is a full-length feature film without a word of dialogue or narration. Among his most significant recent films are *Kvar* (*Breakdown*), 1978,* and *Živeti kao sav normalan svet* (*Living Like the Rest of Us*), 1982.

ŠIJAN, SLOBODAN (1946–), director. A graduate in both painting and film direction in Belgrade, Šijan has directed some of the wittiest and most biting social satires of the eighties; *Ko to tamo peva (Who's That Singing Over There?)*, 1980;* *Maratonci trče posčasni krug (The Marathon Runner)*, 1981; *Kako sam sistematski uništen od idiota (How I Was Systematically Destroyed by an Idiot)*, 1983; and *Davitelj protiv davitelja (Strangler Versus Strangler)*, 1984.*

ŠTIGLIC, FRANCE (1919–), scenarist and Director. One of Yugoslavia's most venerable directors, Štiglic has been an active filmmaker for four decades. His most enduring films are from the fifties and early sixties, especially *Deveti krug (The Ninth Circle)*, 1960,* and *Balada o trobenti in oblaku (Ballad of a Trumpet and a Cloud)*, 1961.

VUKOTIĆ, DUŠAN (1927–), scenarist, designer, animator and director of animated and fiction films. Studied architecture before beginning his career as an animator in 1951. One of the founders of Zagreb film, Vukotić is the most honored and internationally famous of the several outstanding animation artists associated with Zagreb film. He has won over forty major domestic and international awards including the Academy Award in 1962 for *Surogat (Ersatz)*, 1961.

ZAFRANOVIĆ, LORDAN (1944–), scenarist and director. Studied literature and the history of art in Split, and film at FAMU in Prague. One of the members of the "Prague group" of Yugoslav directors, Zafranović's most impressive and visually stylish and complex films are *Okupacija u 26 slika (Occupation in 26 Pictures)*, 1978,* and *Večernja zvona (Evening Bells)*, 1986.*

ŽILNIK, ŽELIMIR (1942–), scenarist and director. Beginning in the early sixties Žilnik has made a number of award-winning documentaries, short films, and television programs. His most radical and important feature film remains *Rani radovi (Early Works)*, 1969,* which won first prize at the Berlin international film festival.

ŽIŽIĆ, BOGDAN (1934–), director. Graduated in law in Zagreb before beginning his professional film career in 1964. Žižić has won many domestic and international prizes for his documentary films. He achieved his greatest critical success as a director of feature films with *Ne naginji se van (Don't Lean Out the Window)*, 1977, a dramatization of the plight of the Yugoslav *Gastarbeiter* (guest worker) in West Germany.

SELECTED FILMOGRAPHY

1947

Slavica. d. Vjekoslav Afrić;* sw. Vjekoslav Afrić; c. Žorž Skrigin; with Irena Kolesar, Dubravko Dujšin, Marijan Lovrić, Carka Jovanović, Ljibiša Jovanović, Jozo Laurenčić, Boža Nikolić, Ivka Rutić, & Dejan Dubajić. Avala film (Belgrade).

1948

Sofka. d. Radoš Novaković;* sw. Aleksandar Vučo, from the novel *Nečista krv* by Bora Stanković; c. Stevan Misković; with Vera Gregović, Milivoje Živanović, Marija Crnobori, Tomislav Tanhofer, Rade Marković, Marko Marinković, Marija Taborska, & Mila Dimitrijević. Avala film (Belgrade).

1956

Veliki i mali (*Big and Small*). d. Vladimir Pogačić;* sw. Miodrag Đurđević; c. Aleksandar Sekulović; with Jozo Laurenčić, Ljuba Tadić, Severin Bijelić, Nikola Ivković, & Milan Srdoč. Avala film (Belgrade).

1957

Subotom uveče (*On Saturday Evening*). d. Vladimir Pogačić;* sw. Dragoslav Ilić; c. Aleksandar Sekulović; with (I) Zoran Stojiljković & Radmila Radovanović; (II) Milan Srdoč & Pavle Vuisić; (III) Dejan Durović, Snežana Mihajlović, & Smiljka Ilić. Avala film (Belgrade).

1959

Sam (*Alone*). d. Vladimir Pogačić;* sw. Vladimir Pogačić;* c. Aleksandar Sekulović; with Milan Puzić, Nikola Simić, Radmila Radovanović-Andrić, Pavle Vuisić, Severin Bijelić, Milan Srdoč. Avala film (Belgrade).

Vlak bez voznog reda (*Train Without a Time Schedule*). d. Veljko Bulajić;* sw. Veljko Bulajić, Stjepan Perović, Ivo Braut, & Elio Petri; c. Krešo Grčević; with Olivera Marković, Ivica Pajer, Inge Ilin, Ljiljana Vajler, Milan Milošević, Stojan Aranđelović, Velimir (Bata) Zivojinović, & Lia Rho-Barbieri. Jadran film (Zagreb).

1960

Deveti krug (*The Ninth Circle*). d. France Štiglic;* sw. Zora Dirnbach; c. Ivan Marinček; with Dušica Žegarac, Boris Dvornik, Desanka (Beba) Lončar, Dragan Milivojević, Ervina Dragman, Branko Tatić, & Mihajlo Kostić. Jadran film (Zagreb).

1961

Dvoje (*Two*). d. Aleksandar Petrović;* sw. Aleksandar Petrović; c. Ivan Marinček; with Beba Lončar, Miha Baloh. Avala film (Belgrade).

Ples v dežju (*Dance in the Rain*). d. Boštjan Hladnik;* sw. Boštjan Hladnik, from the novel *Črni Dveni in bel dan* by Dominik Smole; c. Janez Kališnik; with Duša Počkaj, Miha Baloh, Rado Nakrst, Ali Raner, & Jože Zupan. Triglav film (Ljubljana).

1962

Dani (*Days*). d. Aleksandar Petrović;* sw. Aleksandar Petrović; c. Aleksandar Petković; with Olga Vujadinović, Ljubisša Samardžić, Mila Dimitrijević, & Tatjana Lukijanova. Avala film (Belgrade).

Kozara, d. Veljko Bulajić;* sw. Ratko Đurović, Stevan Bulajić and Veljko Bulajić; c. Aleksandar Sekulović; with Olivera Marković, Milena Dravić, Velimir (Bata) Zivojinović, Bert Sotlar, Dragomir Felba, Ljubiša Samardžić, Mihajlo Kostić, Milan Milošević, & Tamara Miletić. Bosna film (Sarajevo).

Peščeni grad (*Sand Castle*). d. Boštjan Hladnik;* sw. Boštjan Hladnik; c. Janez Kališnik; with Milena Dravić, Ali Raner, Ljubiša Samardžić, Spela Rozin, & Janez Albreht. Reflex-Viba film (Ljubljana).

1963

Licem u lice (*Face to Face*). d. Branko Bauer;* sw. Bogdan Jovanović; c. Branko Blažina; with Ilija Džuvalekovski, Vladimir Popović, Husein Čokić, Milan Srdoč, & Boris Dvornik. Jadran film (Zagreb).

1964

Prometej s otoka Viševice (*Prometheus from the Island of Vishevica*). d. Vatroslav Mimica;* sw. Vatroslav Mimica, Slavko Goldstein, & Krunoslav Quien; c. Tomislav Pinter; with Slobodan Dimitrijević, Mira Sardoč, Janez Vrhovec, Dina Rutić, Pavle Vuisić, Husein Čokić, & Dragomir Felba. Jadran film (Zagreb).

1965

Čovek nije tica (*Man Is Not a Bird*). d. Dušan Makavejev;* sw. Dušan Makavejev; c. Aleksandar Petković; with Janez Vrhovec, Milena Dravić, Boris Svornik, Stojan Aranđelović, & Eva Ras. Avala film (Belgrade).

Devojka (*Girl*). d. Mladomir (Puriša) Đorđević;* sw. Mladomir (Puriša) Đorđević; c. Branko Perak; with Milena Dravić, Ljubiša Samardžić, Rade Marković, Siniša Ivetić, Bekim Fehmiu, & Mija Aleksić. Avala film (Belgrade).

Tri (*Three*). d. Aleksandar Petrović;* sw. Antonije Isaković & Aleksandar Petrović from the novel *Paprat i vatra* by Antonije Isaković; c. Tomislav Pinter; with Velimir (Bata) Živojinović, Senka Veletanlić-Petrović, Woja Mirić, Ali Raner, Slobodan Perović, & Mića Tomić. Avala film (Belgrade).

1966

Rondo. d. Zvonimir Berković; sw. Zvonimir Berković; c. Tomislav Pinter; with Stevo Žigon, Milena Dravić, Relja Bašić, Zvonimir Rogoz, Rudolf Kukić, Boris Festini. Jadran film (Zagreb).

San (Dream). d. Mladomir (Puriša) Đorđević;* sw. Mladomir (Puriša) Đorđević; c. Mihailo Popović; with Ljubiša Samardžić, Mihailo Janketić, Olivera Vučo, Mija Aleksić, Ljuba Tadić, Siniša Ivetić, Aleksandar Stojković, Velimir (Bata) Živojinović, & Stojan Aranđelović. Avala film (Belgrade).

1967

Breza (Birch Tree). d. Ante Babaja;* sw. Slavko Kolar, Ante Babaja, & Božidar Violić; c. Tomislav Pinter; with Manca Košir, Fabijan Šovagović, Velimir (Bata) Živojinović, Nela Eržišnik, & Stane Sever. Jadran film (Zagreb).

Budjenje pacova (Awakening of the Rats). d. Živojin Pavlović;* sw. Gordan Mihić* & Ljubiša Kozomara, from the novel *Neznanka* by Momčilo Milankov; c. Milorad Jakšić-Fanđo; with Slobodan Perović, Duriša Žegarac, Severin Bijelić, Mirjana Blašković, Mića Tomić, Nikola Milić, & Pavle Vuisić. FRZ (Belgrade).

Jutro (Morning). d. Mladomir (Puriša) Đorđević;* sw. Mladomir (Puriša) Đorđević; c. Mihailo Popović; with Milena Dravić, Ljubiša Samardžić, Mija Aleksić, Neda Arnerić, Ljuba Tadić, Olga Jančevecka, Jelena Jovanović-Žigon, Neda Spasojević, Faruk Begolli. Dunav film (Belgrade).

Kad budem mrtav i beo (When I am Pale and Dead). d. Živojin Pavlović;* sw. Gordan Mihić* & Ljubiša Kozomara; c. Milorad Jakšić-Fanđo; with Dragan Nikolić, Ružica Sokić, Dara Čalenić, Neda Spasojević, Severin Bijelić, Nikola Milić, Zorica Šumadinac, & Slobodan Aligrudić. FRZ (Belgrade).

Kaja, ubit ću te (Kaja, I'll Kill You). d. Vatroslav Mimica;* sw. Vatroslav Mimica & Krunoslav Quien, from the novel (same title) by Krunoslav Quien; c. Frano Vodopivec; with Zaim Muzaferija, Ugljesa Kojadinović, Antun Nalis, Jolanda Djačić, Izet Hajdarhadžić, & Husein Čokić. FRZ, Jadran film (Zagreb).

Ljubavni slučaj ili tragedija službenice PTT (Love Affair or the Tragedy of a Switchboard Operator). d. Dušan Makavejev;* sw. Dušan Makavejev; c. Aleksandar Petković; with Eva Ras, Slobodan Aligrudić, Ružica Sokić, & Miodrag Andrić. Avala film (Belgrade).

Mali vojnici (Little Soldiers). d. Bahrudin (Bato) Čengić;* sw. Mirko Kovač; c. Aleksandar Vesligaj; with Stojan Aranđelović, Marija Tocinoski, Zaim Muzaferija, Zlatko Madunić, Mija Aleksić, Darko Cesar, Gordan Kulić, Sead Čakal, & Mirsad Ibrišević. Bosna film (Sarajevo).

Na papirnatih avionih (On Wings of Paper). d. Matjaž Klopčič;* sw. Matjaž Klopčič; c. Rudi Vavpotić; with Leopold (Polde) Bibič, Snežana Nikšić, Dare Ulaga, Mirko Bogataj, Stanislava Pešić, Nuša Svetina, Katja Levstik, & Štefka Drolc. Viba film (Ljubljana).

Skupljači perja (I Even Met Happy Gypsies). d. Aleksandar Petrović;* sw. Aleksandar

Petrović; c. Tomislav Pinter; with Bekim Fehmiu, Velimir (Bata) Živojinović, Olivera Vučo, Gordana Jovanović, Mija Aleksić, & Rahela Ferari. Avala film (Belgrade).

1968

Biće skoro propast sveta (*It Rains on My Village*). d. Aleksandar Petrović;* sw. Aleksandar Petrović; c. Đorđe Nikolić; with Annie Girardot, Ivan Paluch, Mija Aleksić, Dragomir Bojanić, & Eva Ras. Avala film (Belgrade) and Artistes associés (Paris).
Nevinost bez zaštite (*Innocence Unprotected*). d. Dušan Makavejev;* sw. Dušan Makavejev; c. Branko Perak; with Dragoljub Aleksić, Ana Milosavljević, Vera Jovanović, Bratoljub Gligorijević, Ivan Živković, Pera Milosavljević, & Stevan Mišković. Avala film (Belgrade).
Podne (*Noon*). d. Mladomir (Puriša) Đorđević;* sw. Mladomir (Puriša) Đorđević; c. Mihailo Popović & Jovan Jovanović; with Ljubiša Samardžić, Neda Arnerić, Faruk Begolli, Ljuba Tadić, Mija Aleksić, Dušica Žegarac, Olga Jančevecka, Elena Barbieri, & Husein Čokić. Dunav film and Avala film (Belgrade).

1969

Horoskop (*Horoscope*). d. Boro Drašković;* sw. Boro Drašković and Zulfikar (Zuko) Džumhur; c. Ognjen Milićević; with Milena Dravić, Pavle Vuisić, Dragan Nikolić, Miloš Kandić, Dragan Zarić, Mihailo Janketić, & Josif Tatić. Bosna film and Kinema (Sarajevo).
Lisice (*Handcuffs*). d. Krsto Papić;* sw. Mirko Kovač & Krsto Papić; c. Vjenceslav Orešković; with Fabijan Šovagorić, Adem Čejvan, Jagoda Kaloper, Ilija Ivezić, Fahro Konjhodžić, Edo Peročević, Zlatko Madunić, Ivica Vidović, Branko Špoljar, & Zaim Muzaferija. Jadran film (Zagreb).
Rani radovi (*Early Works*). d. Želimir Žilnik;* sw. Želimir Žilnik & Branko Vučičević; c. Karpo Aćimović-Godina;* with Milja Vujanović, Bogdan Tirnanić, Marko Nikolić, Čedomir Radović, & Slobodan Aligrudić. Neoplanta film (Novi Sad) and Avala film (Belgrade).
Vrane (*Crows*). d. Ljubiša Kozomara & Gordan Mihić;* sw. Ljubiša Kozomara & Gordan Mihić; c. Jerzy Wójcik; with Slobodan Perović, Milan Jelić, Ana Matić, Jelisaveta Sablić, Ivan Đurđević, Ines Fančović, Verga Ignjatović, Jovanka Kotlajić, Marica Popović, & Severin Bijelić. Avala film (Belgrade).
Zaseda (*Ambush*). d. Živojin Pavlović;* sw. Živojin Pavlović from the novels, *Po treći put* by Antonije Isaković and *Legende* by Živojin Pavlović; c. Milorad Jakšić-Fanđo; with Milena Dravić, Ivica Vidović, Slobodan Aligrudić, Severin Bijelić, Pavle Vuisić, Dragomir Felba, Marija Milutinović, & Mirjana Blašković. FRZ (Belgrade).

1970

Rdeče klasje / *Crveno klasje* (*The Red Wheat*). d. Živojin Pavlović;* sw. Živojin Pavlović, from *Na kmeith* by Ivan Potrč; c. Miodrag Jakšić-Fanđo; with Majda Potokar, Rade Šerbedžija, Irena Glonar, Majda Grbac, Arnold Tovornik, Angelica Hlebce, & Jože Zupan. Viba film (Ljubljana) and Centar FRZ SR Srbije (Belgrade).

1971

WR: Misterije organizma (*WR: Mysteries of the Organism*). d. Dušan Makavejev;* sw. Dušan Makavejev; c. Predrag Popović & Aleksandar Petković; with Milena Dravić, Jagoda Kaloper, Ivica Vidović, Zoran Radmilović, & Miodrag Andrić. Neoplanta film (Novi Sad).

1972

Majstor i Margarita (*The Master and Margaret*). d. Aleksandar Petrović;* sw. Aleksandar Petrović, Amadea Pagani, & Barbare Pagani, from the novel by Mikhail Bulgakov; c. Roberto Gerardi; with Ugo Tognazzi, Mimsy Farmer, Alain Cuny, Velimir (Bata) Živojinović, Pavle Vuisić, Ljuba Tadić, Eva Ras, Fabijan Šovagović, Taško Načić, Danilo Stojković, Zlatko Madunić, Fahro Konjhodžić, & Janez Vrhovec. Dunav film (Belgrade) and Euro Iternational film S.P.A. (Rome).

Slike iz života udarnika (*Scenes from the Life of Shock Workers*). d. Bahrudin (Bato) Čengić;* sw. Branko Vučičević & Bahrudin (Bato) Čengić; c. Karpo Aćimović-Godina;* with Adem Čejvan, Stojan Aranđelović, Zaim Muzaferija, Ilija Bašić, Mida Stevanović, Dragomir Bojanić, Helena Buljan, Štefka Drolc, & Alija Sirotanović. Studio film (Sarajevo).

1973

Predstava Hamleta u selu Mrduša Donja (*A Village Performance of Hamlet*). d. Krsto Papić;* sw. Krsto Papić & Ivo Brešan, from the play by Ivo Brešan; c. Vjenceslav Orešković; with Rade Šerbedžija, Milena Dravić, Fabijan Šovagović, & Ljubiša Samardžić. Jadran film (Zagreb).

1974

Let mrtve ptice (*The Flight of a Dead Bird*). d. Živojin Pavlović;* sw. Branko Šömen; c. Milorad Jakšić-Fanđo; with Leopold (Polde) Bibič, Rudi Kosmač, Janez Vrhovec, Marko Simčić, Peter Ternovšek, Jožica Avbelj, Ivanka Mežan, Majda Grbac, Arnold Tovornik, Jože Zupan, & Tone Gogala. Viba film (Ljubljana).

1976

Čuvar plaže u zimskom periodu (*Beach Guard in Winter*). d. Goran Paskaljević;* sw. Gordan Mihić;* c. Aleksandar Petković; with Irfan Mensur, Gordana Kosanović, Danilo Stojković, Mira Banjac, Dara Čalenić, Velimir (Bata) Živojinović, Ružica Sokić, Pavle Vuisić, Faruk Begolli, & Janez Vrhovec. Centar FRZ SR Srbije (Belgrade).

Vdovstvo Karoline Žašler (*The Widowhood of Karolina Žašler*). d. Matjaž Klopčič;* sw. Tone Partljić; c. Tomislav Pinter; with Milena Zupančič, Radko Polič, Leopold (Polde) Bibič, Boris Cavazza, Zlatko Šogman, Miranda Zaharija, Dare Ulaga, & Marijeta Gregorač. Viba film and Vesna film (Ljubljana).

1977

Miris poljskog cveća (*The Scent of Wild Flowers*). d. Srđan Karanović;* sw. Srđan Karanović & Rajko Grlić;* c. Živko Zalar; with Ljuba Tadić, Sonja Divac, Aleksandar Berček, Olga Spiridonović, Bogdan Diklić, Branko Cvejić, Slobodan Aligrudić, Miodrag Radovanović, Čedomir Petrović, Gorica Popović, & Ljubomir Čipranić. Centar FRZ SR Srbije (Belgrade).

Specijalno vaspitanje (*Special Education*). d. Goran Marković;* sw. Goran Marković & Miroslav Simić; c. Živko Zalar; with Slavko Štimac, Bekim Fehmiu, Ljubiša Samardžić, Aleksandar Berček, & Cvijeta Mesić. Centar FRZ SR Srbije (Belgrade).

1978

Bravo Maestro. d. Rajko Grlić;* sw. Rajko Grlić & Srđan Karanović;* c. Živko Zalar; with Rade Šerbedžija, Aleksandar Berček, Koraljka Hrs, Božidar Boban, Radojka Šverko, Mladen Budiščak, Ante Vican, Zvonimir Lepetić, Izet Hajdarhadžić, Angel Palašev, & Zlata Petković. Jadran film and Croatia film (Zagreb).

Kvar (*Breakdown*). d. Miloš Radivojević;* sw. Svetozar Vlajković & Miloč Radivojević; c. Aleksandar Petković; with Aleksandar Berček, Neda Arnerić, Milena Dravić, Dušan Janićijević, Ljuba Tadić, Olga Spiridonović, Đorđe Jelisić, & Irfan Mensur. Film Danas (Belgrade).

Okupacija u 26 slika (*Occupation in 26 Pictures*). d. Lordan Zafranović;* sw. Mirko Kovač & Lordan Zafranović; c. Karpo Aćimović-Godina; with Boris Kralj, Milan Štrljić, Stevo Žigon, Zvonimir Lepetić, Tanja Poberžnik, Frano Lasić, Ivan Klemenc, Gordana Pavlov, Milan Erak, Boris Dvornik, & Dušica Žegarac. Jadran film (Zagreb).

1979

Nacionalna klasa do 785 cm (*National Category up to 785 cm*). d. Goran Marković;* sw. Goran Marković; c. Živko Zalar; with Dragan Nikolić, Bogdan Diklić, Gorica Popović, Aleksandar Berček, Rade Marković, Mića Tomić, Olivera Marković, Bora Todorović, Vojislav Brajović, Irfan Mensur, Danilo Stojković, Ana Krasojević, Maja Lalević, & Jelica Sretenović. Centar film (Belgrade).

Zemaljski dani teku (*Days on Earth Are Flowing By*). d. Goran Paskaljević;* sw. Goran Paskaljević; c. Milan Spasić; with Dimitrije Vujović, Obren Helcer, Šarlota Pešić, & Mila Keča. Centar film and RTV (Belgrade).

1980

Ko to tamo peva (*Who's That Singing Over There?*). d. Slobodan Šijan;* sw. Dušan Kovačević.* c. Božidar Nikolić;* with Pavle Vuisić, Dragan Nikolić, Danilo Stojković, Aleksandar Berček, Neda Arnerić, Taško Načić, Slavko Štimac, & Bora Stjepanović. Centar film (Belgrade).

Majstori, majstori (*Teacher, Teacher*). d. Goran Marković;* sw. Goran Marković & Miroslav Simić; c. Milan Spasić; with Semka Sokolović-Bertok, Bogdan Diklić, Pavle Vuisić, Snežana Nikšić, Predrag Laković, Olivera Marković, Zoran Radmilović, Tatjana Bošković, Mića Tomić, Mirjana Karanović, Aleksandar Berček, Stojan Dečermić, Rade Marković, Miodrag Andrić, Mira Banjac, Dobrila Cirković, & Branko Cvejić. Art film, Union film, Inex film, Zvezda film (Belgrade) and Kinema (Sarajevo).

Petrijin venac (*Petrija's Wreath*). d. Srđan Karanović;* sw. Srđan Karanović, from the novel (same title) by Dragoslav Mihajlović; c. Tomislav Pinter; with Mirjana Karanović, Dragan Maksimović, Marko Nikolić, Ljiljana Krstić, Pavle Vuisić, Veljko Mandić, Olivera Marković, & Mića Tomić. Centar film (Belgrade).

Poseban tretman (Special Treatment). d. Goran Paskaljević;* sw. Dušan Kovačević;* c. Aleksandar Petković; with Ljuba Tadić, Danilo Stojković, Dušica Žegarac, Petar Kralj, Milena Dravić, Milan Srdoč, Radmila Zivković, Bora Todorović, Predrag Bijelić, & Pavle Vuisić. Centar film (Belgrade) and Dan Tana Productions (Los Angeles).

Splav Meduze (The Raft of Medusa). d. Karpo Aćimović-Godina;* sw. Branko Vučičević; c. Karpo Aćimović-Godina; with Olga Kacjan-Srdić, Vladislava Milosavljević, Boris Komnenić, Frano Lasić, Erol Kadić, Miloš Battelino, & Radmila Živković. Viba film (Ljubljana) and RTV (Belgrade).

1981

Pad Italije (The Fall of Italy). d. Lordan Zafranović;* sw. Mirko Kovač & Lordan Zafranović; c. Božidar Nikolić;* with Daniel Olbrychski, Ena Begović, Gorica Popović, Dragan Maksimović, Mirjana Karanović, Miodrag Krivokapić, Dušan Jančijević;, Ljiljana Krstić, Velimir (Bata) Živojinović, Frano Lasić, Snežana Savić, & Izet Hajdarhodžić. Jadran film (Zagreb) and Centar film (Belgrade).

Samo jednom se ljubi (You Only Love Once). d. Rajko Grlić;* sw. Rajko Grlić, Branko Šömen, & Srđan Karanović;* c. Tomislav Pinter; with Predrag Manojlović, Vladica Milosavijević, Mladen Budiščak, Zijah Sokolović, & Erland Josephson. Jadran film (Zagreb).

Sjećas li se Dolly Bell (Do You Remember Dolly Bell?). d. Emir Kusturica;* sw. Abdulah Sidran; c. Vilko Filač; with Slavko Štimac, Ljiljana Blagojević, Mira Banjac, & Slobodan Aligrudić. Sutjeska film and Televizija Sarajevo (Sarajevo).

1982

Nešto između (Something In-Between). d. Srđan Karanović;* sw. Srđan Karanović, Milosav Marinović, & Andrew Horton; c. Živko Zalar; with Caris Corfman, Predrag Manojlović, Dragan Nikolić, Zorka Dorknic-Manojlović, & Renata Ulmanski. Centar film (Belgrade).

Variola Vera. d. Goran Marković;* sw. Goran Marković; c. Radoslav Vladić; with Rade Šerbedžija, Rade Marković, Semka Sokolović-Bertok, Erland Josephson, Bogdan Diklić, & Vladica Milosavljević. Art film (Belgrade).

1983

Balkan ekspres (Balkan Express). d. Branko Baletić;* sw. Gordan Mihić;* c. Živko Zalar; with Dragan Nikolić, Bora Todorović, Tanja Bošković, Olivera Marković, Velimir (Bata) Živojinović, & Ratko Polič. Art film 80 and Inex film (Belgrade).

Zadah tela (Body Scent). d. Živojin Pavlović;* sw. Slobodan Leman & Živojin Pavlović, from the novel (same title) by Živojin Pavlović; c. Aleksandar Petković; with Dušan Janjicijević, Metka Franko, Rade Šerbedžija, Ljiljana Medjasi, Ziah Sokolović, Ivo Ban, & Stole Aranđelović. Film Danas (Belgrade) and Viba film (Ljubljana).

1984

Balkanski špijun (The Balkan Spy). d. Božidar Nikolić* & Dušan Kovačević;* sw. Dušan Kovačević; c. Božidar Nikolić; with Danilo (Bata) Stojković, Mira Banjac, Bora Todorović, & Zvonko Lepetić. Ro Slavija film and OOUR Union film (Belgrade).

Davitelj protiv davitelja (Strangler Versus Strangler). d. Slobodan Šijan;* sw. Slobodan Šijan & Nebojša Pajkić; c. Milorad Glušica; with Taško Načić, Nikola Simić, Srđan Šaper, Sonja Savić, Rahela Ferari, Pavle Minčić, Marija Baksa, & Branislav Zeremski. Centar film (Belgrade).

Dediščina (Heritage). d. Matjaž Klopčič;* sw. Matjaž Klopčič; c. Tomislav Pinter; with Milena Zupančič, Leopold (Polde) Bibič, Bernarda Oman, Radko Polič, Bine Matoh, Majda Potokar, & Boris Ostan. Viba film (Ljubljana).

Mala pljačka vlaka (The Small Train Robbery). d. Dejan Šorak; sw. Dejan Šorak; c. Karpo Aćimović-Godina;* with Velimir (Bata) Živojinovič, Miodrag Krivokapić, Mustafa Nadarević, Kruno Šarić, Danko Ljuština, Fabijan Šovagović, & Tatjana Bošković. Jadran film (Zagreb) and Kinema (Sarajevo).

U raljama života (The Jaws of Life). d. Rajko Grlić;* sw. Rajko Grlić & Dubravka Ugrešić, from the novel (same title) by Dubravka Ugrešić; c. Tomislav Pinter; with Gorica Popović, Vitomira Lončar, Bogdan Diklić, Miodrag Krivokapić, & Koraljka Hrs. Art film, Croatia film, Jadran film, Union film and Kinematografi (Belgrade).

1985

Jagode u grlu (A Throatful of Strawberries). d. Srđan Karanović;* sw. Srđan Karanović & Rajko Grlić;* c. Živko Zalar; with Branko Cvejić, Predrag (Miki) Manojlović, Aleksandar Berček, Bogdan Diklić, Mira Banjac, Gordana Marić, & Dobrila Stojnić. Avala pro film (Belgrade).

Otac na službenom putu (When Father Was Away on Business). d. Emir Kusturica;* sw. Abdulah Sidran; c. Vilko Filač; with Predrag (Miki) Manojlović, Mirjana Karanović, Moreno d'e Bartolli, Mustafa Nadarević, Pavle Vuisić, Mira Furlan, & Predrag Laković. Forum (Sarajevo).

Ovni in mamuti (Sheep and Mammoths). d. Filip Robar-Dorin; sw. Filip Robar-Dorin; c. Karpo Aćimović-Godina;* with Slavko Štimac, Božidar Bunjevac, & Marko Derganc. Viba film (Ljubljana) and RZ filmske alternative (Novo Mesto).

Tajvanska kanasta (Taiwan Canasta). d. Goran Marković;* sw. Milan Nikolić & Goran Marković; c. Miloš Spasojević; with Boris Komnenić, Neda Amerić, Gordana Gadžić, Radko Polić, & Predrag (Miki) Manojlović. Centar film (Belgrade).

Život je lep (Life is Beautiful). d. Boro Drašković;* sw. Boro Drašković; c. Božidar Nikolić;* with Rade Šerbedžija, Sonja Savić, Dragan Nikolić, Ljubiša Samardžić, Pavle Vuisić, Predrag Laković, Milan Erak, & Snežana Savić. Neoplanta film (Novi Sad), Slavija film and OOUR Union film (Belgrade).

1986

Bal na vodi (Dancing on Water, released in U.S. as *Hey Babu Riba).* d. Jovan Aćin; sw. Jovan Aćin; c. Tomislav Pinter; with Gala Videnović, Dragan Bjelogrlić, Goran Radaković, Nebojša Bakočević, Srđan Todorović, Milan Štrljić, Relja Bašić, & Marko Todorović. Avala film and Inex film (Belgrade).

YUGOSLAVIA

Srećna nova Godina—'49 (Happy New Year—1949). d. Stole Popov;* sw. Gordan Mihić;* c. Mišo Samoilovski; with Svetozar Cvetković, Meto Jovanovski, Vladica Milosavljević, & Aco Đorčev. Vardar film, Makedonija film, and Gradski kina (Skopje), Union film (Belgrade).

Večernja zvona (Evening Bells). d. Lordan Zafranović;* sw. Mirko Kovač; c. Andrija Pivčević; with Rade Šerbedžija, Petar Božović, Miodrag Krivokapić, Neda Arnerić, Ljiljana Blagojević, & Mustafa Nadarević. Jadran film and Jugoart (Zagreb), Montenegroexport (Nikšić).

Za sreću je potrebno troje (Three's Happiness). d. Rajko Grlić;* sw. Rajko Grlić & Dubravka Ugrešić; c. Živko Zalar; with Predrag (Miki) Manojlović, Mira Furlan, Dubravka Ostojić, Bogdan Diklić, Vanja Drach, & Ksenija Pajić. Jadran film (Zagreb) and Centar film (Belgrade).

1987

Anđeo čuvar (Guardian Angel). d. Goran Paskaljević;* sw. Goran Paskaljević; c. Milan Spasić; with Ljubiša Samardžić, Neda Arnerić, Šaban Bajramović, & Jakup Amzić. Trz otvoreni atelje Beograda singidunum and Morava (Belgrade), Jugoart (Zagreb).

U ime naroda (In the Name of the People). d. Živko Nikolić;* sw. Živko Nikolić & Dragan Nikolić; c. Savo Jovanović; with Miodrag Krivokapić, Savina Geršak, Petar Božović, & Vesna Pećanac. Zeta film (Budva), Avala pro-film and Centar film (Belgrade), Montex (Nikšić).

Već viđeno (Déjà Vu). d. Goran Marković;* sw. Goran Marković; c. Živko Zalar; with Mustafa Nadarević, Anica Dobra, & Miroslav Mandić. Art film 80 and CFS Avala film (Belgrade), Croatia film (Zagreb), Smart Egg Pictures (London).

1988

Praznik kurvi (Whore's Holiday). d. Lordan Zafranović;* sw. Veljko Barbieri & Lordan Zafranović; c. Andrija Pivčević; with Ranko Zidarić, Neda Arnerić, Stevo Žigon, & Dušica Žegarac. Jadran film and Televizija Zagreb (Zagreb).

Za sada bez dobrog naslova (Still Lacking a Good Title). d. Srđan Karanović;* sw. Srđan Karanović; c. Božidar Nikolić;* with Mira Furlan, Meto Jovanovski, Sonja Jačevska, Čedo Orobabić, & Boro Begović. Beograd film and Centar film (Belgrade).

Život sa stricem (My Uncle's Legacy). d. Krsto Papić;* sw. Ivan Aralica, Krsto Papić; c. Boris Turković; with Davor Janjić, Alma Prica, Miodrag Krivokapić, Anica Dobra, Branislav Lečić, & Ivo Gregurević. Urania film and Kinematografi (Zagreb), Avala film (Belgrade), Strassen Productions (Los Angeles).

1989

Dom za vešanje (Time of the Gypsies). d. Emir Kusturica;* sw. Gordan Mihić;* c. Vilko Filač; with Davor Dujimović, Bora Todorović, Ljubica Adžović, Husnija Hašimović, Sinolička Trpkova, Zabit Memedov, Elvira Sali, Suada Karišik, Predrag Laković, Mirsad Zulić, Ajnur Redžepi, Bedrije Halim, Edin Rizvanović, Ibro

Zulić, Murat Jagli, Nazifa Ahmetović, Šaban Rojan, Marijeta Gregorač, Advija Redžepi, Irfan Jagli, Albert Mamutović, Branko Đurić, Boris Juh, Emir Ćerin, Julijana Demirović, & Jadranka Adžović. Forum and Televizija Sarajevo (Sarajevo).

5   *Tomasz Warchoł*

HUNGARY

For a country the size of the state of Maine and a population of roughly ten million, Hungary can boast a uniquely rich film tradition and a lively film industry.[1] Since the mid–1960s, Hungarian cinematography has regularly produced about twenty feature films annually, half of which typically represented thoughtful, honest, artistically challenging innovative filmmaking. It is, therefore, the most consistently reliable and satisfying national cinema of Europe. It has gained that reputation thanks to a relative political stability and the comparatively enlightened Communist patronage of the film industry during the last twenty-odd years under János Kádár, a period marked by mild censorship and the filmmakers' tacit recognition of the boundaries of the permissible.

To understand Hungary's special devotion to cinema, one needs to look at the country's painful and complex history. For four hundred years, ever since Hungary lost its independence and status of the most powerful nation in Central Europe, its people, overcome first by ruthless Turks, then dominated by Austrians, had to struggle for the preservation of their national heritage and identity. When, with the break-up of the Hapsburg Empire, it regained its independence, the 1920 Treaty of Trianon reduced its territory by two-thirds and left more than three million Magyars in what was now Czechoslovakia, Romania, and Yugoslavia. For its appointed new leader, the unimaginative and autocratic Admiral Horthy, development of national cinema, or for that matter promotion of any serious culture, was the last thing on his mind. Horthy served the interests of the aristocracy and the military and did his best to keep the old feudal social structure intact. His regime's stifling censorship together with foreign monopoly of the film market effectively buried any hopes for an original native cinema. Ironically, Hungary had to go through another world war to revive that hope and turned it into reality when the country became "liberated" by the Soviet Red Army and joined the newly formed Communist Bloc. Hungarian filmmakers quickly recognized that just as the Soviets used film for heavy-handed ideological propaganda, they finally had the medium to express their national character by propagating their intricate history and culture. It is also through that medium of cinema and its universal visual imagery that they could effectively transcend their linguistic isolation (Hungarian language does not even share Indo-European roots) and enter the common European consciousness. In the last twenty-five years, Hungarian films have penetrated and enriched that consciousness.

The beginnings of cinema in Hungary were very auspicious; first films were shown at the Velence Cafe in Budapest already in 1896. Two years later, the cafe owner founded the first Hungarian film company, the Projectograph. The release of one of its productions *Ma és holnap* (*Today and Tomorrow*), directed probably by Mihály Kertész and shown on October 14, 1912, marks the official birth of the truly Hungarian dramatic art/fiction cinema. By 1912, Hungary had its first film studio, Hunnia, which, despite early failure, was followed by the emergence of other more successful ones. Before the outbreak of World War I, Hungary had more than 120 permanent cinemas and between 1907 and 1920 published at least seventeen periodicals devoted exclusively to film. In most of them, film was treated as a unique, autonomous art form of revolutionary potential. In addition, many daily newspapers and literary journals carried regular sections on the art of film. Much of this early criticism predates later fully developed theories of Béla Balázs and Rudolf Arnheim (Liehm and Liehm, 9).

Over thirty directors were making films in Hungary before the end of World War I. Most of them moved to cinema from journalism, photography, or theater. Two most prominent were Mihály Kertész and Sándor Korda, who between 1912 and 1919 made thirty-nine and twenty-four films respectively (little of their work has survived, though). The latter edited a number of film journals and ran Budapest's largest studio, Corvin, before he left Hungary in 1919 to become, as Alexander Korda, England's leading director and film producer of the thirties and forties. For his contributions, he became the first filmmaker to receive British knighthood. His two talented brothers, Vincent and Zoltán, followed him abroad and into successful careers in film. Kertész left Hungary in the spring of 1918 to work on a project in Vienna and never returned, frustrated by the unstable and unfavorable political situation in his homeland. After some years of exile, he settled in the United States, where under the name of Michael Curtiz he launched an impressive Hollywood career, directing such memorable films as *Casablanca* and *Yankee Doodle Dandy*.

Most of the films from that early period were adaptations of Hungarian literary classics, part of an ambitious program to familiarize Hungarians with their cultural heritage. For that purpose the studios created the unique position of a literary editor who overlooked the transformation of literary texts into film scripts. If Korda's Hungarian films reflected that trend, Kertész's represented a welcome departure, as most of his were based on original scripts and involved dynamic action giving him greater freedom to explore the kinetic potential of cinema.

In October 1918, Hungary emerged as an independent nation—ironically from the ruins of the defeated Austro-Hungarian Empire. In the fragile, chaotic political situation that followed, Hungary experienced a period of violent social strife and radical changes. After a few months, by early spring of 1919, the liberal government of Count Károlyi was ousted by the leftist radicals whose leader, Béla Kun, a participant in the Russian October Revolution, proclaimed the creation of the Hungarian Republic of Councils under the consolidated power of the Hungarian Communist Party. In the process of a sweeping and comprehensive restructuring of the entire socio-political system, Kun's regime also nationalized the film industry, pre-dating a similar move in the Soviet Union by five months. But Kun's control did not last long either, even though the four months of his rule saw the release of thirty-one quite original films (Nemeskürty, 44–51). By August 1919 his often bloody revolution was put down with the help of the Romanian army (just as Kossuth's 1848 heroic peasant rebellion was crushed with the help of the Russian army). In another grim irony of those times, Kun, reluctant to enlist Soviet involvement, retreated first to Slovakia, then fled to the Soviet Union, where he later became one of the victims of the Stalinist purges.

The new government quickly undid the changes by restoring monarchy, paradoxically without a monarch, as it was led by the appointed regent, Admiral Miklós Horthy. Horthy's ruthless "white terror" gradually forced many artists and intellectuals, especially those involved in the Republic of Councils, to flee repression abroad and make new homes either in one of the major capitals of Europe or in the United States, as was, for example, the case with Béla Lugosi. Many others were imprisoned. As for filmmakers, "not a single one of the pioneers was still active in 1925" (Liehm and Liehm, 31). When other countries produced masterpieces of silent cinema, Hungary had no industry at all.

The industry was revived in the early thirties with the introduction of sound, largely to satisfy the demand for Hungarian-spoken films. The subsidies came from taxes imposed on the many distributors of foreign films. The monopolistic, centralized character of that system exluded, however, any hopes for original, critical cinema. The government was the only state film company, owning all studios and equipment. Before funding production, the regime's own Film Industry Fund, made up of people with no artistic concerns, had to approve the script. As a result, it naturally functioned as a heavily restrictive censorship office. At the same time, no ambitious Hungarian had the financial resources to work outside that system. The Liehms illustrate the extent and absurdity of that control. No film could show horse's hooves raising dust on the road, because Hungarian roads were not supposed to be dusty, "nor could high-level Hungarian officials be shown running up or down stairs in a hurry [because] 'a representative of our country never behaves in an undignified manner' " (31). No wonder, therefore, that almost none of 132 films made between 1931 and 1938 distinguished itself in any way. Seventy percent of those films were shallow comedies set mostly in contemporary Hungary; others were melodramatic operettas (with an obligatory dose of the czardas, the native folk dance) adapted from trashy romances nostalgically glorifying the aristocratic past. In short, all were reactionary, trivial entertainment produced ad nauseam by a handful of loyal craftsmen. For example, a quarter of them were directed by István Székely (later known as Steve Sekely, a minor Hollywood director), half were scripted by Károlyi Nóti, and all used a very limited pool of players.

A notable exception to that uniform mediocrity was Pál Fejős' *Tavaszi zápor* (*Spring Shower*, shown as *Marie* in Western Europe), made in 1932. For a change, the protagonist was a peasant girl employed as a maid by a local landowner. The plot, though melodramatic, conveyed strong social criticism. The heroine is seduced, made pregnant, and abandoned by the suitor of the rich family's daughter. She is also rejected by her village and has to give birth in a brothel, the only place where she finds compassion and safety. When she returns to the village, she is again cruelly mistreated and abused until she dies. The film ends with a hopeful image that her daughter will be able to avoid her mother's tragic fate. Through the victimization and exploitation of its heroine, the film exposes the hypocrisy and selfishness of the bourgeoisie, the intolerance and narrow-mindedness of the peasants, and the total indifference of the system. Fejős' film was naturally attacked by the regime's press as giving a negative and false picture of Hungarian society, forcing the director to make most of his later films abroad. His other Hungarian feature, *Ítél a Balaton* (*The Verdict of Lake Balaton*), about the harsh lives of fishermen, has been lost.

As the country was drifting towards fascism, the outbreak of World War II found Hungary allied with Hitler's Germany and Mussolini's Italy. As a result, French, British, and American films were no longer shown, which put their distributors out of business. This situation expanded the market for Hungarian features, most of which were blatantly propagandistic. One film, though, deserves special attention—István Szőts' *Emberek a havason* (*People from the Alps*), made in 1942 and awarded for best debut at the prestigious (even under Mussolini) Venice Film Festival, the first such international recognition for a Hungarian film. Without excessive sentimentality, in beautifully captured Alpine landscapes, it tells a simple, intelligently edited story of mountain people mercilessly exploited by local landowners. Concentrating on the tragedy of one family, Szőts shows how the death of the wife and the destruction of their dwelling turn a passive community of foresters into an active rebellious force. When the husband out of despair kills the landowner, the message is unmistakably clear—the poor masses will not stand for the injustice much longer.

The international respect for his film brought Szőts only trouble at home. He was virtually banned from filmmaking after his request to make an adaptation of the pacifist novel *Ének a búzamezőkről* (*Song of the Cornfields*) was denied. Ironically, when he was allowed to adapt that script (co-written by Béla Balázs) in 1947, the finished film was banned from distribution by the Communists as "non-Marxist" and "ideologically erroneous" (Liehm and Liehm, 149). His next worthy project, a film entitled *Talpalatnyi föld* (*The Soil under Your Feet*), was taken away from him and assigned to Frigyes Bán. Szőts, whose great talent was suppressed by his own Hungarian orthodox rightists and doctrinaire leftists, made two more films during a brief post-Stalinist thaw of 1954–1956, and left the country for good when the Soviet army cruelly crushed the Hungarian revolution of November 1956. He has lived in Austria ever since. Now that Communism has finally collapsed, he intends to return to his homeland.

In the years immediately following World War II, from 1945 to the beginning of 1948, Hungary, even though Communist, was still run, as was Poland, by a coalition government made up of four parties: Peasant, Social Democratic, Communist, and Smallholders, but like other Soviet-liberated countries could not resist enforced nationalization and centralization for very long. Before the film industry fell under exclusive Communist control and its party, on Stalin's orders, established monopolistic power, Hungary released just seven feature films, one of which, *Valahol Európában* (*Somewhere in Europe*), 1947, remains a remarkable masterpiece of neorealist cinema, its impact equal to De Sica's famous *Bicycle Thieves*, Rosselini's *Open City*, or Buñuel's *Los Olvidados*. *Somewhere in Europe*, directed by the well-traveled and experienced Géza Radványi and co-written by Béla Balázs, put Hungary firmly on the map of international cinema.

The film, set in post-war Hungary, tells of a group of children, orphans of various ages, roaming the countryside, fighting for survival by looting the neighboring farms whose owners treat them like pests that need to be eradicated. Radványi's narration, though restrained and objective, clearly identifies with the children—their depravity a result of conditions created by adults. The children are the innocent, desperate victims rejected by the inhuman, indifferent world. That condemnation is reinforced when, in the second half, the children take over the partly ruined castle inhabited by an old musician. The old man, though initially their prisoner, gradually wins them over by providing them with food and shelter, organizing their lives, dividing responsibilities, and teaching them moral values. He gives them a sense of purpose, community, and dignity and brings them back to civilization. But the hostile villagers want to put the children in prison, and the film ends with the old man pleading for their care and guidance. As Graham Petrie observes, "Not a word or an image in the film rings false, the acting is superlative throughout, and the humanity and compassion that permeate it speak just as clearly today as they did thirty years ago" (*History*, 8–9). Radványi, who was active in cinema before and during the war, was the first in Hungary to introduce modern editing and a mobile camera. He also pioneered Stanislavsky's "method acting." *Somewhere in Europe* was Radványi's only Hungarian film until 1979, when he briefly returned to his homeland to make *Circus Maximus*.

For the next five years, Hungarian cinema choked under the crude propaganda of Soviet cultural administrator A. A. Zhdanov's "socialist realism" and no worthy films were produced. Instead, the country suffered its worst terror: forced collectivization of farms and nationalization of industry, confiscation of churches, mass deportations and purges culminating in the show trial and execution of László Rajk, the Minister of the Interior and one of Stalin's staunchest supporters. The country was like one big prison with anybody guilty upon arrest.

Right after Stalin's death, Hungary was first to come up for air. The liberally minded Imre Nagy succeeded as Prime Minister the country's most hated man, Mátyás Rákosi (who still headed the Party). Most political prisoners were released, Rajk and other victims were rehabilitated, liberal Communists and opposition leaders regained their voices, borders were opened, collectivization stopped, and plans for economic recovery were instituted. But this bloodless gradual transformation of the totalitarian system was stalled in 1955 when in the Soviet Union the liberal Malenkov was replaced by Khrushchev and the Hungarian old guard led by Rákosi forced Nagy, accused of "rightist deviations," out of office.

But Rákosi's days were numbered. After Khrushchev's public revelations of Stalin's "errors and distortions," Hungarians were determined to reclaim their freedoms and win independence. At the end of October 1956, Hungarian revolt broke out. Nagy was reinstated, György Lukács, a famous Marxist critic, replaced József Révai, another Soviet puppet, as the Minister of Culture, and János Kádár, one of many Communists jailed under Rákosi, became the Party's First Secretary. The popular government called for a multiparty democracy and the departure of Soviet troops stationed in the country. What happened a few days later added yet another bitter chapter to Hungary's tragic history. Instead of withdrawing, more Soviet troops crossed the Hungarian border and mercilessly crushed Hungary's peaceful revolution. The government was arrested, the Communist Party dismantled, Nagy and 500 others executed, more than 13,000 killed, over 10,000 deported, and almost a quarter of a million forced to flee the country.

A small number of films made between 1954 and 1957 reflected these social and political tensions by challenging the crude social realist conventions. They paved the way for a wave of outstanding works that were to attract international following in the mid-sixties and throughout the seventies. Two of them were made by Zoltán Fábri, who is still active in Hungarian cinema. The first, *Körhinta* (*Merry-Go-Round*), 1955, is a sort of *Romeo and Juliet* without its tragic dimension. Its plot still follows predictable recipes. A daughter of a stubborn private farmer falls in love, against her parents' will, with a young man working in a collective farm. After their relationship ends in marriage, the father (portrayed rather unsympathetically) reluctantly joins the cooperative to be close to his daughter. Even though Fábri makes it clear that in following her lover, the girl opts for a bright Communist future and against the backward past, his attention is primarily devoted to the evolution of the couple's relationship, their feelings for each other rather than the underlying ideological conflict. But Fábri's unconventionality in this film is first and foremost formal, seen in his unorthodox editing (including flashbacks), camera movement, and convincing acting.

Fábri's next film, *Hannibál tanár úr* (*Professor Hannibal*), made a year later, was much bolder. Through a tragicomic story, set in the period of Horthy's "white terror," about a timid history teacher unwittingly caught up in the regime's paranoid propaganda campaign, Fábri unmistakably alludes to the fresh reality of the Stalinist "red terror" of widespread fear and oppression: of the denunciations, forced confessions, show trials, arbitrary imprisonments, deportations, and executions. With his film, Fábri, unknowingly, introduced what was to become the most pervasive theme of the best Hungarian (and one might add Polish) films in the following decades: an individual's struggle for identity and autonomy in the world of uncompromising historical and political pressures.

Other films from that dramatic period that are worth addressing include Félix Máriássy's *Külvárosi legenda* (*Suburban Legend*), 1957; Tamás Banovich's *Az eltüsszentett birodalom* (*The Empire Gone with a Sneeze*), 1956; and Imre Fehér's *Bakaruhaban* (*A Sunday Romance*), 1957. *Suburban Legend*, scripted by Máriássy's wife, Judit, was to be set in contemporary Hungary, but because of its depressing portrayal of the existence of the working class, the censors approved it only after its action was moved into the thirties. Even then, the completed film was soon banned while the Máriássys had to offer public self-criticism and face carefully orchestrated primitive ideological attacks (Liehm and Liehm, 168).

Banovich's film, a biting satire on Stalin's personality cult presented in the veiled form of "a fairy-tale allegory about a tyrant whose entire kingdom had to bend to his will," did not fare much better (Liehm and Liehm, 168). Its brief appearance shortly before the Soviet aggression thwarted its potential popular success. With the revolution crushed, the film was naturally banned and Banovich barred from filmmaking until the sixties.

The third of the films, *A Sunday Romance,* was, just like the earlier two, its director's best film. This one was politically safe since its action took place during World War I, but it is memorable for its sensitive handling of a love affair between an upper-class journalist in the army and a maid, both trapped in their rigid hierarchical society which dooms their relationship. Remarkable is the woman's reaction to the public exposure of their affair. Although she loses her job and suffers humiliation, she proudly asserts her independence and rejects the man's belated pleas for forgiveness and reconciliation. The acting of Margit Bara and Iván Darvas as protagonists is superlative and the recreation of the last years of Austro-Hunagarian monarchy very vivid and objective.

Of the reformist 1956 government, the occupying Soviet forces spared János Kádár, entrusting him with "the restoration of order" and rebuilding the demoralized and depleted new Party, now called the Hungarian Socialist Workers' Party. Therefore, as a result of the widespread repression that followed the tragic revolution, Hungarians did not experience their post-Stalinist thaw until the early sixties. However, once the regime felt securely entrenched and gave in to liberalization, the thaw continued with only minor tensions well into the eighties. By the early seventies, Kádár's policies of the gradual appeasement of intellectuals, decentralization of the economy, limited privatization of businesses, incentives for private farming, and other state-controlled market mechanisms turned Hungary into the most stable, liberal, and westernized country of the Soviet Bloc.

A small but outspoken film community was at the head of the reform process, quickly instituting critical changes in their own industry. The most remarkable of them was the establishment of the Béla Balázs Studio (named after the famous film aesthetician who died in 1949 hounded by Stalinists), which after a false start in 1958 was revived in 1961. There, graduates of the Budapest Academy of Theater and Film Art could make their first, usually short, independent films free from government interference, even though supported by state funds. Such contemporary prominent directors as István Szabó, Pál Gábor, and Sándor Sára, all students of older filmmakers like Félix Máriássy, co-founded the Studio and began their outstanding careers there.

Also in the early sixties, the state film production company, Mafilm, created four autonomous film units (studios)—Dialóg, Objektiv, Hunnia, and Budapest—each with an administrative director, a vice-director (usually a major filmmaker), and an advisory council of other filmmakers who selected scripts for production. A director was free to work with any of the studios. By the mid-sixties each studio could produce about five low-budget feature films a year. Naturally, all films had to be ultimately approved by the Ministry of Culture, which allocated all studios' budgets and employed the entire film community, but only a few were shelved or heavily censored. This rather unique and efficient system has continued through 1989, and one can only hope it will survive in some form in the new political reality of the nineties.

The best way to illustrate the rich and diverse achievement of Hungarian cinema after the mid-sixties is to discuss the best work of its major directors as well as outstanding individual films by others.

Certainly, no director attracted greater critical attention and contributed more to the European interest in Hungarian film than Miklós Jancsó, whose singular brand of cinema made him if not the most original, then surely the most bewildering contemporary filmmaker. When Jancsó made his first internationally acclaimed ground-breaking *Szegénylegények* (*The Round-Up*) in 1965, he was already forty-four, with three feature films and numerous documentaries to his credit. Having graduated from the Academy of Theater and Film Art in 1950, he was a typical product of the times—a fanatical Communist impressed by the revolutionary social makeover and assured the future of mankind was spelled out by Marxist-Leninist ideology. His films until the 1962 *Oldás és kötés* (*Cantata*) reflect those naïve convictions. Even though *Cantata,* being an existentialist psychological drama, does not anticipate Jancsó's characteristic style and themes, it shows the strong influence of Antonioni and Bergman and as such has been, in the Liehms' words, "considered an overture to the Hungarian film renaissance of the sixties" (173).

His next film, the semi-autobiographical *Igy jöttem* (*My Way Home*), 1964, however, at least thematically opens the way for the Jancsó genre. The action takes place at the end of World War II and follows a sixteen-year-old deserter from the Hungarian army (which fought on the Nazi side) as he tries to return home. On his way he is confronted by various military groups—Cossacks, the Red Army, Hungarian guerrillas, and desperate fascists—all representing the forces vying for political control, each abusing the boy in one manner or another. After he is arrested by the advancing Soviets, he becomes friends with a young

Russian soldier to whom he is assigned. When, towards the end, the Russian dies of an earlier wound, the boy puts on his uniform, only to be later beaten by his countrymen as a traitor. Even though the boy's story may be viewed as a metaphor for Hungary hopelessly struggling for its autonomy (its home), victimized by internal and external forces, and eventually accepting Russians as its liberators (the boy's mute friendship with the Russian and the symbolic gesture of putting on his uniform), Jancsó's film develops themes and employs some images treated later in an increasingly abstract, symbolic fashion: man's inherent, self-perpetuating violence; the arbitrariness and insignificance of human life; the futility of rebellion; the corruption by power; the barren flat landscapes of the Puszta (the Hungarian Plain); the circular, ritualistic movements of the distant human figures conditioned by history and politics to play their assigned roles. *My Way Home,* called by one critic "the gentlest . . . and the most engaging" of his films, may serve as an appropriate introduction to Jancsó's artistic evolution and also as a reminder to those frustrated by that evolution that he is clearly capable of creating emotionally engaging cinema (Price, 193).

The Round-Up, perhaps Jancsó's most celebrated film, convincingly justifies his radical departure from mainstream narrative by adopting an original, meaningful structure and style to expose his themes and illustrate his message. The film is set about twenty years after the crushed 1848 peasant rebellion, a period of intensive repression of the still-active followers of Kossuth and Śandor Rózsa. The entire action of the film, however, happens in and around the prison built somewhere in the vast Puszta, where rounded-up peasants are selectively interrogated by Austrian military officials. The distinction between the oppressors and the oppressed is immediately evident. The former wear uniforms, carry weapons, and have complete power over the destinies of their passive, hopeless, and haggard victims (the original title means "the desperate [hopeless] ones").

Jancsó does not allow the audience any identification with the peasants, treating them only as a repressed mass. Even when he isolates and follows any of the victims, his camera does not individualize them, refusing to register their reactions or suggest their emotional condition. It remains detached, coldly objective, keeping a safe distance with its predominantly traveling, circular, long pan shots. The oppressors are even more abstract—their features indistinguishable from each other, their movements conditioned by years of military discipline, their interactions reflecting strict military hierarchy, their articulation limited to mechanically delivered commands and directions. The dialogue is in fact so rudimentary that Gyula Hernádi's script did not even include it (Armes, 145). Instead, the plot, represented as a pattern of successive confrontations between the interrogators and the prisoners, naturally presupposes those basic verbal exchanges.

But Jancsó's conscious disengagement from his work goes even farther—he witholds any moral judgment of his characters and any comment about their background or the reasons for their actions. His films end without conclusions or clear resolutions, and he consistently refuses to justify his work both formally and thematically. As a result of such strategy, he paradoxically demands a peculiar intellectual involvement of the viewer, who must integrate the series of episodes into a coherent pattern and recognize it as variations exploring Jancsó's principal subject—a study of power and oppression and the idea of revolution. In the words of Graham Petrie, the most patient and penetrating of Jancsó's Western critics, Jancsó's style "enhances the audience's awareness of the film as a product and of its own responsibility for interpretation and assessment." Jancsó subverts traditional narrative so thoroughly—"denying us the normal satisfaction of emotional identification and sympathy; of scene-setting and background explanation; of psychological motivation and analysis; and of narrative logic, climax and resolution—that the process of watching a film becomes radically defamiliarized" (Petrie, "Jancsó," 193).

The Round-Up, unlike some of his later films, clearly separates the victims from the oppressors, a distinction determined by the clear-cut conflict of the film (manifested in contrasting black and white). Moreover, because the audience quickly realizes that the purpose of the successive interrogations is the identification of Rózsa's rebels, the film still develops a partially traditional plot that with each episode moves steadily towards its outcome. In that process, Jancsó shows us a horrifying array of insidious methods—delayed executions, false promises of freedom, public torture, forced confessions, and fraudulent proclamations—that the interrogators use to identify their victims. Jancsó's oppressors take sadistic pleasure in manipulating and deceiving their captives, in enjoying complete control over their lives, in making them cooperate in their own destruction. Their satisfaction seems proportionate to the degree of the victim's humiliation. In *The Round-Up* suicidal defiance is inconsequential, rebellion impossible, oppression inescapable.

Jancsó's next film *Csillagosok, katonák* (*The Red and the White*), 1967, through another historical context, further examines the questions of power, oppression, and violence as a deterministic experience of humanity. The year is 1918 and the "plot" follows a series of bloody encounters between the Whites and a detachment of Hungarian Reds fighting in the Russian Civil War.

The film was a Soviet-Hungarian coproduction "commissioned" from Jancsó for a celebration of the fiftieth anniversary of the October Revolution, but since Jancsó refuses to take sides in the conflict or distinguish between the violence of the Reds and the Whites, all that the film "celebrated" was humanity's degradation, a senseless, self-perpetuating cruelty of one human being to another. Add to that the fact that the Reds speak Hungarian (naturally) and the Whites Russian, and we can understand why despite heavy editing of the Russian version, Jancsó's anti-propagandistic film was never distributed in the Soviet Union (Liehm and Liehm, 395). After all, Jancsó's purpose is not to legitimize any ideology or political system but to expose their destructive consequences.

In *The Red and the White* "the exigencies of warfare rule out the possibility of delaying the gratification of power . . . : prisoners have to be eliminated before they have a chance to participate in the always imminent reversal of the situation"

(Petrie, *History*, 44). Reality of the war obliterates morality as Jancsó demonstrates how easily the helpless victims can become oppressors, how the capacity for evil exists in all. In the brutal world of the film, one cannot be neutral to survive, and there is no resolution of the perpetual violence.

Formally, *The Red and the White* refines the style of *The Round-Up*. The action is less contextualized, the narrative more fragmented, the dialogue even more reductive, the movement of characters more ritualistic, exceedingly choreographed. The long circular shots again dominate the film, but they have become more complex and extended, reflecting the film's atmosphere of entrapment and encirclement. The addition of music and dance further upset narrative continuity. In short, *The Red and the White* moves towards increasing abstraction and symbolization (e.g., female nudity representing vulnerability and humiliation, and in his later films also liberation) that eventually turned his art into a sort of revolutionary ballet or pantomime.

With *Csend és kiáltás* (*Silence and Cry*), 1968, Jancsó takes us to another violent period of Hungarian history—the "white terror" following the short-lived Republic of Councils. The action is almost entirely confined to one family's farmhouse chosen as refuge by an escaped revolutionary and traces the enigmatic relationship between a White officer and the fugitive and its impact on the life of the family.

For the first time, but certainly not the last, Jancsó takes his experimentation with narrative so far that he systematically frustrates the viewer's speculations and leaves the viewer no clues to the behavior of his characters (Petrie, *History*, 66). The audience does not know why the White commandant, having discovered the fugitive, refuses to arrest him (does he want to savor his role of an oppressor, or have they met before?), why the woman and her sister poisoned the mother-in-law and now do the same to a husband of one of them, why a realization of this upsets the fugitive so much that he reports it to the authorities and thus reveals his presence, why the officer ulimately decides not to kill his victim (tired of his role as oppressor?), why he hands him the pistol (a gesture of reconciliation?), and why the Red prisoner simply shoots him with it (inevitably taking on the role of the oppressor?). Other "background" scenes raise similar basic questions: we do not know who the victims are, what their crimes might have been, or why they are being punished. If all this is meant to illustrate Jancsó's "world of random and casual violence" (Petrie, *History*, 66), then it also alienates the viewer who, denied most fundamental principles of narrative structure, feels abandoned by the artist.

Fényes szelek (*The Confrontation*), completed later the same year, marks the beginning of the second stage in the development of Jancsó's oeuvre in which he attempts, according to Petrie, to overcome the impasse reached in *Silence and Cry* ("Jancsó," 194) by moving from the portrayal of the senseless and irredeemable violence and his nihilistic message to the "systematic exploration of the morality of violence" (Petrie, *History*, 46).

The subject of the film is more contemporary, recalling Jancsó's youth and not so distant Hungarian past. The story, set in 1947, relates the ideological conflict between the passive, conservative students from the seminary and the often fanatical revolutionaries filled with idealistic ideas about establishing a socialist educational system with which they want to convert the seminarians to their faith. For much of the film we watch the various tactics the young radicals employ to achieve their end and the corresponding power struggle within their ranks. However, their illusory independence ends abruptly when both police and Party forces, until then only observing the developments from a distance, step in and authoritatively impose a compromise. Despite such an ending, in contrast to his earlier films, Jancsó not only examines the ideological dimensions of his conflict but also shows some emotional involvement—the film's ending clearly reflects his sympathy for the young, passionate radicals in spite of their often brutal intolerance.

The Confrontation moves in the direction of further ritualization of narrative as most of the action develops through carefully choreographed dances, gestures, songs, and poetic recitals, all integrated and increasingly charged with symbolic meaning. The individual sequences become longer (often of ten minutes or more) and more elaborate, reflecting their function as self-contained illustrations of the film's ideological arguments.

Beginning with *Sirokkó* (*Sirocco,* also known in English as *Winter Wind,* an absurd title that means the opposite of the original), a French-Hungarian co-production completed in 1969, Jancsó has made most of his films abroad with foreign casts and, except for *Sirocco* itself, in foreign settings and on foreign subjects. *Sirocco* also begins a period of Jancsó's artistic decline, of his steadily deteriorating international reputation when his films, increasingly impenetrable and incoherent, gradually alienated most of his (until then) patient critics and faithful admirers. *Sirocco,* and especially Hungarian-made *Égi bárány* (*Agnus Dei*), 1970, followed by Italian productions *La Pacifista,* 1970; *La tecnica ed il rito* (*Technique and Rite*), 1971; *Roma rivuole Cesare* (*Rome Wants Another Caesar*), 1973; and again Hungarian *Szerelmem, Elektra* (*Elektreia*), 1974, all break any remaining communication lines with the audience with their unrelated, fragmented images, cryptic symbols, metaphors without contexts, and dry, formalistic, rootless designs.

The theme of "the morality of violence and the possibility of genuine, uncontaminated revolution" that the aforementioned films apparently examined is much more convincingly represented in *Még kér a nép* (*Red Psalm*), 1971, Jancsó's last outstanding and critically acclaimed film (Petrie, "Jancsó," 196). According to Petrie, "it brings language and theme together in almost perfect synthesis" (ibid., 197). Made in Hungary and awarded for best direction at Cannes in 1972, *Red Psalm* argues, through a series of stunningly powerful, dialectical sequences, that violent revolution born of despair from years of relentless oppression and intolerable suffering must be the only moral action left to take. To illustrate his point, Jancsó, instead of setting a concrete historical context, creates a historical paradigm in which a group of hypothetical peasants is variously victimized and exploited by the forces of oppressive authority representing the church, the military, and the landowners.

Jancsó's most popular film thus far and one that certainly deserves critical attention is his 1976 Italian production *Vizi privati, pubbliche virtù* (*Private Vices, Public Virtues*), 1976. Its popularity was undoubtedly caused by its subject matter—a story of a rebellious prince who, trapped in his luxurious environment, attempts to upset the authoritarian socio-political system by indulging in sexual promiscuity and breaking sexual taboos. His perverse practices are tolerated by his father, the emperor, for as long as they can be contained as harmless provocations. But when the prince's subversion, by way of corrupting young aristocracy, turns against and humiliates the emperor and his officials, he sends the military that kills the prince and his closest associates. *Private Vices, Public Virtues* is then another exploration of the theme of revolution, this time in openly sexual terms. Its conclusion leaves no doubt that sexual freedom cannot challenge an authoritative political system. Revolution through sexual liberation, as Jancsó clearly demonstrates, is anarchic, limited, personal at best, and ultimately self-exhausting. It cannot substitute for "disciplined revolutionary thought and action" (Petrie, "Jancsó," 204).

In 1978 Jancsó completed two parts of a planned trilogy covering almost fifty years of Hungarian history, from the beginnings of the century through the late 1940s, viewed through "the career of Endre Bajcsy-Zsilinszky, a politician of aristocratic background who moved from an extreme conservative position to a sympathy with socialist ideas in the 1930s and was finally executed in 1944 for plotting to kill Hitler" (Petrie, "Jancsó," 205). Entitled *Magyar rapszódia* (*Hungarian Rhapsody*) and *Allegro Barbaro,* the two films were the most costly productions in the history of Hungarian cinema. The money was never retrieved, as the film had almost no audience and met with little, mostly hostile, critical reaction including this comment from Penelope Houston, the editor of *Sight and Sound* and one of Jancsó's most tolerant critics: "the total effect, for me, is one of almost stupefying monotony . . . can the pageant, with its simplifications, its ritual, its reliance on purely formal and repetitive elements, any longer speak in a significant way to . . . [an] audience? One doubts it" (Petrie, "Jancsó," 210). No wonder that Jancsó never went back to complete the trilogy. Symptomatically, as if to intimate that Jancsó's career was a closed chapter, the jury at the 1979 Cannes Festival where *Hungarian Rhapsody* was screened recognized him for his entire work.

In the eighties, Jancsó's work fell into even greater obscurity. *A zsarnok szíve* (*The Tyrant's Heart*), 1981; the French-made *L'Aube* (*The Dawn*), 1985; and a 1986 *Szörnyek évadja* (*Season of Monsters*) were all irritatingly manneristic and predictably incongruous. Even if they contained some isolated unforgettable images (i.e., beautifully photographed female nudity in *Season of Monsters*), the individual segments were like signifiers without the signified, known perhaps only to Jancsó himself.

Jancsó's most recent film, *Jézus Krisztus horoszkópja* (*Jesus Christ's Horo-*

scope), 1989, however, if sufficiently publicized and properly distributed, may win him back his audiences. It's a horrifying vision of a totalitarian Orwellian reality in which a modern-day Joseph K. chooses to take desperate action to assert himself as an individual. With its conflict and its focus on a single protagonist, this new film implies Jancsó's considerable emotional involvement, very atypical of his work so far.

The main difficulty in properly assessing Jancsó's entire career is that only a handful of critics have been able to follow its evolution. Jancsó's foreign films have disappeared from international screens just days after their releases and are virtually unavailable. His Hungarian films are shown sporadically (mostly in Europe) and selectively (without the context of others) and are thus by and large misinterpreted. In North America Jancsó is still an obscure figure, a handful of his films known only to the most devoted filmgoers. Graham Petrie may be the only film scholar and critic this side of the Atlantic who has seen almost all of Jancsó's work and can, therefore, competently share his interpretations of it with us. Until Jancsó's films are made available on video cassettes to engage a critical discussion of his work, Petrie's will remain the only authoritative voice on the subject.

Of the Jancsó generation, now considered veterans of Hungarian cinema, no one deserves greater attention than Károly Makk, who, before debuting as a director in 1954 (*Liliomfi*), worked as an assistant on such films as *Somewhere in Europe, The Soil under Your Feet,* and Zoltán Várkonyi's *Simon Menyhért születése* (*The Birth of Menyhert Simon*), 1954. His 1955 *A 9-es kórterem* (*Ward No. 9*), a neorealistic-existentialist drama, established him on the domestic market, but it was not until 1970 when he completed *Szerelem* (*Love*) that his work attracted international attention. Makk was ready to make that film already in 1965 but had to fight a protracted battle with the censors (quite typical of his earlier films, which suffered from obvious concessions to the regime's ideological pressures) while waiting for a more favorable political climate.

Based on two short stories by Tibor Déry, a famous contemporary writer whose works have been frequently adapted for the screen, *Love* takes place in Rákosi's 1950s and centers on the difficult relationship between an old bedridden woman and her daughter-in-law, hoping for the return of their son and husband. The old woman does not know, however, that her son has been arrested and "disappeared" as one of many innocent victims of Stalinist paranoia, and the young woman makes sure her mother-in-law does not learn the truth, which would kill her. To keep alive in the face of the constant humiliations (such as losing her job, being followed, and having her apartment searched) she is put through, the young woman creates a fictitious life for her husband (complete with imaginary correspondence which she regularly reads to the old woman) in which he is a successful film director in America.

Love masterfully combines scenes of hostile reality outside which the young woman has to constantly confront, with the emotionally charged private world of the women's complex relationship. These are also subtly interspersed with the old woman's lyrical reminiscences and visions of her son. The film's ending only enriches its dramatic complexity. The husband returns, released as arbitrarily as he was arrested, but his mother did not live to see him—all he is left with is a bundle of her most prized possessions, reflections of her and their past. At least she died knowing he was happy and successful, believing in his myth. The critics at the 1971 Cannes Film Festival where the film was shown recognized its emotional power and subtlety, awarding both actresses, Mari Törőcsik and Lili Darvas, for their outstanding performances.

Makk's next film, *Macskajáték* (*Catsplay*), 1974, even though nominated for an Academy Award, was beautifully shot but left the audiences indifferent. As Petrie put it, "it is almost as though he were trying too hard to repeat the success of *Love*" (*History*, 184). It was not until over a decade later that Makk again created a masterpiece, the 1982 *Egymásra nézve* (*Another Way*), a socially bold psychological drama set in 1958, just two years after the trauma of the Revolution.

As in *Love*, Makk focuses on two women, both young journalist-reporters, and traces their relationship powerfully shaped by outside political circumstances. One of the women, formerly blacklisted, who has just joined the staff of a weekly magazine ironically named *Truth*, discovers on her assignment that a subject of her story, a chairman of an exemplary cooperative farm, has achieved his success by coercing peasants to join it through blackmail and threats. When she wants to publish her revelations, she confronts the cowardice of her editor and the cynical conformism of the publisher. After her text is extensively rewritten, she resigns, rightly anticipating her formal expulsion. But Makk uses this dramatic story mainly as background for his primary plot, which follows the evolution of the lesbian relationship between the heroine and her fellow reporter, played by the beautiful Polish actress, Grażyna Szapołowska. As the protagonist's rebelliousness exposes the hypocrisy and authoritarian nature of the system, Makk convincingly involves us in the heroine's obsessive attraction to the other woman and the impact it has on their lives. Makk's story ends tragically—the woman, wounded by her impulsive husband outraged at her infidelity, recovers in the hospital, while the heroine is shot dead trying to cross the border to the West.

Another Way speaks powerfully against the intolerance, corruption, and injustice that destroy love, truth, and dignity. With his film, which so brilliantly combines hard realism and lyricism, Makk proves again that, given the right material, he is certainly one of the most sensitive European filmmakers. His extraordinary ability to create complex female characters by drawing such painfully real performances from his actresses was recognized by the jury of the 1982 Cannes Festival: Jadwiga Jankowska-Cieślak, another Polish actress, who played the defiant reporter, received the Best Actress Award while the critics gathered there gave Makk's film their prestigious FIPRESCI Prize.

Makk's most recent film was a 1984 American coproduction, *Lily in Love*, a subtly drawn commercial venture, more typical of his less memorable films.

Another veteran director of Hungarian cinema, actually the same age as Makk, who made a few outstanding films in his more consistent output is András Kovács. Unlike Makk, he did not debut as a director until 1960. His films are also stylistically and thematically very different—almost all share a documentary character and an objective, detached tone.

Kovács' first international success came with the release of *Hideg napok* (*Cold Days*), 1966, a stark black-and-white fictional recreation of one of the most shameless chapters in Hungarian modern history—the massacre of over 3,000 Serbian and Hungarian nationals, mostly Jewish, of Novi Sad, now part of Yugoslavia, in 1942. Kovács builds his narrative from memories of the four men who actively participated in the mass murder and now, that is, in 1946, the present time of action, await trial. The horror of the massacre itself is compounded by Kovács' narrative strategy. As each prisoner recounts the circumstances of his involvement and the killings themselves, each denies his complicity in what happened, claiming he only obeyed the orders. But Kovács patterns the story to let the audience see the inconsistencies and contradictions among their recollections, their pitiful attempts to justify their situation and shift the blame to others (in one episode Kovács makes it clear that the refusal to carry out orders wasn't punished by death).

It is the individual images, though, that accuse with greatest force: the rounded-up, passive villagers shivering in the cold as their executioners prepare holes in the ice-covered river where they will dispose of the bodies; the continuous off-screen shots ringing in our ears; and the figures of soldiers, half-shrouded in the river mist, dragging the dead across the ice. Even then Kovács' style is unobtrusive and distant. His method of confronting the audience with the characters, their stories, and his images demands our moral response. In a sense, he implicates us by universalizing the moral dimensions of the tragedy. Predictably, some critics saw Kovács' film as an oblique condemnation of Stalinist atrocities.

Kovács' other important film, *Bekötött szemmel* (*Blindfold*), 1974, which earned him a Jury's Prize at San Sebastian, is a story of a young priest caught up in the political struggle during World War II and driven to madness when his faith and moral values are being challenged by a military court demanding only unequivocally simple answers during his interrogation. More recently, two other of his films, *A ménesgazda* (*The Stud Farm*), 1978, and *A vörös grófnő* (*The Red Countess*), 1984, attracted considerable international attention. With the first one, Kovács included his voice in the investigation of the political tensions of the Stalinist 1950s, variously addressed by other older and younger Hungarian filmmakers. *The Stud Farm,* his first color film, focuses on the conflict between a new, ignorant Party manager of a horse-breeding farm and its experienced pre-war employees set against the backdrop of ruthless collectivization. *The Red Countess* is an expensive two-part drama spanning the first two decades of this century's Hungarian history by following the relationship between Count Mihály Károlyi, a liberal aristocrat, who became for a brief period the first and only president of post-World War I Hungary, and Countess Katinka Andrássy, later his wife, from whose autobiography Kovacs developed his script.

One of the most popular and prolific directors of the Hungarian older generation is Péter Bacsó, who like Kovács did not go behind the camera until the early 1960s. Since then, however, Bacsó has regularly done one film a year, and almost all have been, if not critically, then certainly commercially, successful. They consistently expose the absurdities of Hungarian everyday life in a documentary style with satirical, often farcical, plots, a welcome antidote to the otherwise overwhelmingly serious intellectual tone of Hungarian productions. His protagonists are often simple workers pitted against the inefficient, corrupt, and ultimately repressive bureaucracy. Bacsó prefers to work with non-actors in actual locations of factories, offices, streets, and apartments. The character of his films explains their popularity with the domestic audience, which readily sympathizes with his heroes, relates to the familiar situations, and spontaneously responds to his broad, absurdist humor. For those same reasons, however, his films do not communicate well abroad. Deprived of their audience and social context, their absurdist humor becomes absurd, their realism turns merely representational, while their plots lose their potential universality in the heavy concreteness of the everyday.

At least four of his films, however, are especially memorable. The 1970 *Kitörés* (*Outbreak*) tells the story of a disgruntled worker whose frustrations over housing shortages (he has no private place to spend the night with his girlfriend) and a dead-end job drive him to increasingly outspoken protests against the authorities. Tolerated for a while, he eventually loses his job, his girlfriend, and most of his supporters when the authorities decide his visibility may create unnecessary trouble. At the end of the film, a fellow worker advises him "to learn to navigate" if he wants to survive.

Harmadik nekifutás (*The Last Chance*), 1973, which received a Grand Prix in San Remo in 1974, exploits the comedy of a situation where a factory manager, insisting on taking responsibility for his inefficiency, joins the ranks of common workers to convince himself and others that a position of authority must be earned, not simply given. Everybody, however, treats him as a loony. Bacsó's most famous film is *A tanu* (*The Witness*) completed in 1969 but shelved until 1978. It follows the rise and fall of another tragicomic antihero who thanks to a friend in high places moves, during Rákosi's 1950s, from one important position to another, being equally unprepared for each. His demise comes when, hired to give false testimony at one of the show trials, he forgets his lines.

Bacsó's most popular recent film is also a tragicomedy entitled *Banánhéjeringő* (*Banana Skin Waltz*), 1986. Through its absurdist, often hilarious plot, the film convincingly shows how an organized life of a successful young surgeon loses ground when on the way to his wedding, on a national holiday, he puts his coat over a naked woman, who stressed by her job ran out into the street. *Banana Skin Waltz* and his newest work, a 1988 scathing, perfectly timed satire on Ceausescu's mad dictatorship, *Titania, Titania,* seem to develop situations and address topics familiar enough to Western audiences to promise wider international distribution.

Such international visibility was quickly and easily established by Márta Mészáros, whose work has been frequently awarded at prestigious festivals abroad but, until recently, unfairly criticized at home. That largely negative reaction of her native audience has a lot to do with the subjects and themes of her films. Most of her earlier work consistently deals with the independently minded unsettled woman whose struggles for self-realization, fulfillment, or mere preservation of identity, aggressively challenge traditional morality and confront Hungarians with the conservative and chauvinistic nature of their society, a truth apparently uncomfortable to admit.[2] Regardless of her frustrating domestic misunderstanding, today Mészáros is, together with István Szabó, Hungary's most respected and famous filmmaker and, perhaps, the most admired and accomplished woman director in the world.

Mészáros belongs to the oldest generation active in Hungarian cinema only by virtue of her age (she will turn sixty in 1991) because, unlike her peers, she could not make her first feature film until 1968. Her unusual background also places her in a category of her own. Born in Budapest, she was only four when her parents (her father was a well-known sculptor) fleeing Horthy's persecutions emigrated to the Soviet Union, only to meet a more cruel fate when her father died from torture as one of countless victims of Stalinist genocide. She could not return to her homeland until the end of the war, but soon, having been offered a scholarship to study film in Moscow, she seized an opportunity to fulfill her life's passion. Graduating in the ill-fated 1956, she spent three years in Romania, working for its film industry, so she did not settle back in her homeland until 1959. In the sixties she was married to Miklós Jancsó, who certainly helped launch her career, which, in turn, paved the way for other Hungarian women directors, whose representation in the Hungarian film industry is still very marginal, a situation typical in most other countries as well.

Mészáros' first feature film, *Eltávozott nap* (*The Girl*), introduced her plain, unassuming, realistic style and the subject matter of her films in the seventies—the predicament of women in the Hungarian contemporary society. Documenting the daily life of an alienated and tenacious factory worker, raised in an orphanage and looking for her father and her identity, Mészáros involves us imperceptibly in the heroine's instinctual search for a meaningful existence in a world she learned not to trust.

Three films later Mészáros made *Örökbefogadás* (*Adoption*), 1975, which, awarded in Berlin and Chicago, won her instant international prestige and a reputation of a feminist filmmaker (which she is, but only within an inevitably political context of Central-Eastern Europe). *Adoption* is about a strange friendship between a middle-aged woman in a relationship with a married man by whom she would like to have a child and a young rebellious girl from a nearby state-run housing project, herself dating a boy she wishes to marry. The wedding eventually takes place despite the opposition of the girl's parents, and the last scene shows the older woman returning home with an adopted baby. Seemingly, both women have found what they desired, but now separated they will have to deal with the consequences of their choices alone. Mészáros subtly suggests that the young girl's independence is incompatible with the sadly traditional reality of her marriage, while the older woman looks pathetic and forlorn holding on to her infant on a cold and bleak day.

Kilenc hónap (*Nine Months*), 1976, and *Ők ketten* (*The Two of Them/Women*), 1977, Mészáros' first color films, followed the success of *Adoption*. Both also introduce a pair of Mészáros' favorite performers: Lili Monori (replaced in her recent *Diary* trilogy by Zsuzsa Czinkóczi, who incidentally played Monori's daughter in *The Two of Them*) and Jan Nowicki, a Polish actor. *Nine Months*, awarded by Cannes critics, is perhaps her most feminist film. It focuses again on a young and proud working-class girl who agrees to a love affair with her foreman but refuses to marry him. He soon discovers she has a child who lives with her parents in the country. Possessive and jealous, he demands explanations and verbally abuses her, still insisting, however, on their marriage. But she does not change her mind even when he makes her pregnant. His discovery that she is on good terms with the father of her child leads to more arguments. After he humiliates her in front of his rich family and then beats her, she simply leaves him despite his threats that he will not support their unborn child. The final sequence showing her delivering a baby in another town is intercut with the man despairing over losing her and frustrated that he cannot find her.

The Two of Them, like *Adoption*, deals with a relationship of two women, one younger, one older. The older one supervises a home for girls, and the younger, separated from her alcoholic husband, insists against the rules on keeping her child with her. Their friendship confronts the older woman with the emptiness and aimlessness of her own marriage and the younger one with the necessity of bringing up her child alone as her husband fails to control his addiction. Both realize, however, that they need each other to deal with their circumstances.

The fact that the two films present men as ineffectual, insensitive, abusive, or weak-willed and show them as destructive burdens in the women's lives conveys a fatalistic view of a woman's condition. That message may perhaps best explain the negative reaction those and other of Mészáros' films received in Hungary.

Discouraged by such reception, Mészáros made her next three films in collaboration with foreign producers. Most successful of these was the French-Hungarian production, *Örökség* (*The Heiresses*), 1980, with Isabelle Huppert, Lili Monori, and naturally Jan Nowicki. It is about a wealthy but sterile woman who during World War II "persuades a Jew to have a child by her husband in order to inherit her father's estate. The husband eventually falls in love with the surrogate wife, and his real wife responds by having the husband arrested for violating the Nuremberg Laws and the Jewish woman deported to Auschwitz"

(Cook, 711). Mészáros returned to a more liberal Hungary, undergoing rapid democratization influenced by Poland's Solidarity movement, and there embarked on a project she had been contemplating for nearly twenty years—an autobiographical trilogy, a tripartite film-diary, the work that secured her the status of one of the outstanding filmmakers of the eighties.

The first in the sequence was *Napló gyermekeimnek* (*Diary for My Children*) completed in 1982 but released two years later and then celebrated with prizes in Cannes, Chicago, Munich, and finally in Budapest where it won awards for best film and best direction. Skillfully combining semi-fictionalized autobiography with documentary footage and meaningfully contrasting black-and-white and color photography, the film follows an adolescent protagonist Juli, Mészáros' alter ego (Zsuzsa Czinkóczi) from her return to Hungary in 1946 through 1953, the peak of Stalinist oppression. Orphaned (her father died during the Soviet purges, her mother, shortly before she left for Hungary—all these and other past experiences are conveyed in dream-like soft-focus color flashbacks), Juli moves in with a family friend, Magda, employed by the security police as a prison commander. In Magda's friend, János, a handsome, middle-aged, open-minded engineer, Juli sees her lost idolized father and a welcome antidote to the hypocritical and doctrinaire Magda. When János is arrested for his open non-conformity and thrown into Magda's prison, and Magda refuses to help, Juli, powerless, can only protest by packing her belongings and leaving the opportunistic Magda.

Napló szerelmeimnek (*Diary for My Loves*), 1987, continues the story of Juli's intellectual and emotional maturation through the political events from 1953 until 1956. Following her passion for cinema already suggested in the first *Diary*, Juli tries to gain admittance to the Budapest Film School, but, rejected as a woman, has to accept help from Magda, who arranges for her to study in Moscow. Russia is in the apex of the personality cult, and the intense indoctrination corrupts even Juli: together with others she cries at Stalin's death. Later she searches for news of her father, only to learn he died in his prison cell. She never finds his grave. At least now, after he has been rehabilitated, she can openly cherish his memory. In her dreams, he has the face and gestures of János, but he always fades away from her. Her life as an odd one in Moscow is intercut with scenes of János' suffering in prison. In a heart-rending, emotionally almost unbearable sequence, Juli with her grandfather visit him in prison. Later, after being freed, János realizes he can no longer be free, unable to forget the tormenting experiences of human brutality and degradation. The film ends with Juli returning to Moscow to receive her diploma and the news of the breakout of the Hungarian Revolution. The Hungarian borders are closed and Juli, confused, realizes she cannot return home.

The last part of the trilogy, *Napló apámnak, anyámnak* (*Diary for My Father and Mother*), just recently released in Hungary (1990), will soon reach international audiences. The film opens with the toppling of Stalin's statue in Budapest and shots of revolutionary crowds celebrating in the streets and ends with the trial and death of Juli's beloved János, one of the leaders of the Revolution. He is buried in an unmarked grave. When Kádár celebrates the restored communist power, Magda, recovered from her temporary crisis, is in the crowd, chanting new slogans. Juli remains the center of the film, documenting the plight of her people with her camera. In the film's coda, an emotionally charged epilogue, we see János' wife and her son a few years later going to the grave of their husband and father, but the police drive them brutally away.

The *Diaries* are an extraordinary achievement. Brilliantly photographed by her son, Miklós (Nyika) Jancsó, Jr., perfectly combining dramatic autobiographical story, historical document, and political commentary, the trilogy is a unique personal journey through Hungary's recent tortured past matched in its impact and scope only by Wajda's *Człowiek z marmuru* and *Człowiek z żelaza* (*Man of Marble, Man of Iron*). Just like Wajda's two films, Mészáros' *Diaries* are a powerful condemnation of the ideological imprisonment of humanity and its devastating consequences and, at the same time, a tribute to those who resisted those forces and helped others recover from the captivity.

Diaries, though so highly praised, were not the only films Mészáros made in the last decade. She took a break between the first two parts to make a successful adaptation of Gogol's play *The Inspector General* entitled *Délibábok országa* (*Land of Miracles*), 1983. In 1989, before shooting the third part, Mészáros completed *Piroska és a farkas* (*Bye-Bye Red Riding Hood*), a lyrical recollection of childhood creatively adapted from the famous fairy tale. Mészáros seems to be at the peak of her powers, and her new films are awaited with great anticipation.

It is time now to review the achievement of the prominent graduates of the Béla Balázs Studio to whom Hungary's cinema owed its recognition abroad in the sixties.

Most famous of them is undoubtedly István Szabó, who already at twenty-five distinguished himself with two short films produced through the Béla Balázs Studio. One of them, *Te* (*You,* 1963), still remains the most awarded short film in Hungarian film history. His feature-length debut came a year later with *Álmodozások kora* (*The Age of Daydreaming*), a film clearly influenced by early Truffaut and Godard. It portrays his own generation as it follows the lives of five young college graduates and shows how their aspirations and idealistic enthusiasm are slowly dissipated when they confront the real world of frustrating social, political, economic, and personal limitations, what Goethe called "the muddled business of living."

His next film *Apa* (*Father*), 1966, is also his most personal and, by his own admission, his favorite (Paul, "Szabó," 6). It was highly acclaimed in Hungary and abroad, collecting awards at festivals in Moscow, Locarno, Acapulco, and Valladolid. Constructed as a series of intricately patterned flashbacks that weave in and out of the narrative present, the film follows a young boy's evolving fantasies of his idolized dead father as they reflect his difficult passage from childhood through adolescence and into manhood. Knowing very little of his father's past, the boy creates him into a mythic, heroic figure whose imagined exploits and superhuman abilities become the core of the boy's identity. At that stage his stories and fantasies help him define himself and win authority among his schoolmates. As the boy matures into a young man, the idolatry slowly gives in to reality as the protagonist confronts his heroic vision of the father with the memories of those who remembered him. The demythologizing process corresponds here with the young man's liberation from what has, by then, become a disabling memory, an obstacle to his self-assertion as an individual. The dramatic events of 1956 only accelerate that realization. In the last, clearly symbolic, sequence of the film we see him swimming across the Danube, a feat his father never accomplished. As the camera shows him reaching his goal, it gradually retreats into a long shot that shows many other swimmers beside and behind him, thus suggesting the universality of the protagonist's experience (*The Age of Daydreaming* also ended with shots universalizing the individual destinies).

Made in 1970, Szabó's *Szerelmesfilm* (*Love Film*) received much less publicity. It was considered disappointing by most critics, who blamed it for heavy-handed didacticism, pretentious narrative structure, artificial dialogue, and unconvincing acting. On the other hand, David Paul claims it is Szabó's most underrated film ("Hungary," 186), while Graham Petrie's extensive analysis of the film clearly reflects his admiration for its form and the lyricism of its content.

The film's present action follows Jancsi, a young man on his train journey to France to see his lover and childhood sweetheart, Kata, from whom he was separated by the tragedy of 1956, when she chose to emigrate while he stayed behind. Before they are reunited, however, Szabó takes us on a different journey—Jancsi's fragmented recollections about their relationship, the particular times retrieved from his memory. As Jancsi reintegrates his life by recreating his past experiences with Kata, the audience similarly organizes those memories into a coherent narrative pattern. But the film is also about the inevitable imperfection, selectivity, and deception of our memory. Jancsi finds that much of what he thinks he remembers is vague and disconnected, often distorted into what he wished had happened. When the two lovers finally meet, they realize that the relationship to their country that divides them is stronger than their relationship to each other. Jancsi cannot see himself uprooted from his society and culture; Kata has transplanted herself into a new, less burdensome ground. Jancsi is willing to live with his memories as the foundation of his identity, in a reality that has formed him, while Kata will nurture those memories to build her new self.

Love Film was Szabó's first color film and as usual starred his favorite actor, András Bálint. Like his two earlier films, it also ended with a sequence that made the protagonist's individual experience a collective one. After his return to Budapest, Jancsi sends a telegram to Kata, and the camera shows long lines of other people at the post office sending messages to loved ones separated from them by the cruel verdicts of politics and history.

Szabó's most enigmatic and difficult film is probably *Tűzoltó utca 25* (*25*

Fireman Street), completed in 1973 and awarded the Grand Prix at Locarno the following year. The setting this time is an old house slated for demolition, and as Szabó patterns its history from the memories of those who have lived in it, we realize that the house is, strangely enough, a sort of composite protagonist animated with its own identity through the lives of its residents. Recent Hungarian history forms again an important background as Szabó shows how his different characters behaved under trying circumstances. He distinguishes between those who conformed and compromised themselves and those who stood by their moral principles, preserving their dignity. *25 Fireman Street,* like all Szabó's films, requires a very attentive viewing, as it often blurs the boundaries between memory and fantasy, past and present.

The 1979 *Bizalom (Confidence)*, awarded at the Berlin festival and nominated for an Oscar, marks a definite movement away from earlier modernist experimentation with narrative time and space towards a linear, conventional storyline. It tells a dramatic story of a war-time relationship between a man and a woman, both members of the resistance, forced to stay in hiding from the authorities. Initially strangers to each other, they have to assume false identities and pretend they are husband and wife. Living in constant fear of being discovered and uncertain about the future, they first realize they have to depend on each other and soon become lovers. Their greatest test, ironically, comes with the liberation, the day they have been both waiting for. They are now free, but they are apprehensive about the new, unfamiliar reality. Szabó suspends the resolution. We can only wonder what will happen to them and their relationship.

Watching Szabó's earlier films including *Confidence* and admiring their subtle psychology, their existential reflectiveness, and demanding narrative composition, no one would have anticipated the international success Szabó achieved with his three most recent films, all German-Hungarian coproductions: *Mephisto*, 1981; *Redl Ezredes/Oberst Redl (Colonel Redl)*, 1984; and *Hanussen*, 1988.

Examined together, all three films share such remarkable thematic and stylistic unity separating them from his earlier films that they can be easily considered a kind of a trilogy. In each Szabó studies a fictionalized historical figure (played by Klaus-Maria Brandauer) whose social rise is promoted and then manipulated by the increasingly oppressive political circumstances which confront him with fundamental moral and ethical choices and question his identity and integrity. Each of the protagonists is also a parvenu, an outsider blinded by his apparent power, wealth, or influence until he can no longer control the consequences of his actions or his destiny.

Szabó's rich and complex development of his characters through their complicated circumstances involves the audience in powerful existentialist dramas that easily relate to our own lives. His characters cannot be simply dismissed as opportunists or conformists. They have some of our sympathy as we discover they possess some of our characteristics.

Mephisto is the most celebrated of the three. It received two awards at Cannes, an Academy Award as Best Foreign Film of 1982, and similar distinctions in

Italy and England. It is also Szabó's only literary adaptation, as it is loosely based on Klaus Mann's novel by the same title. *Mephisto* follows a career of Hendrik Hőfgen (Mann's fictionalized Gustav Grűndgens), who became the director of German National Theater under the Nazis.

The setting of *Colonel Redl* is the last years of the Hapsburg Empire, and it is based on the life of Alfred Redl, who rose to a position as the head of the Austro-Hungarian police but like Hőfgen became the victim of his own game. *Hanussen* fictionalizes the life of a well-known psychic during the time of the Nazi takeover of the German Reich, but unlike the two earlier films, it still has not received the extensive critical attention it greatly deserves.

Szabó is not a prolific director, but he remains continually active, carefully planning each new project. Like no other director, he puts most of his time into meticulous scripting of his stories, close cooperation with his major actors and actresses, and with Lajos Koltai, his cinematographer. The result of such a detailed preparation is reflected on the screen: his last three films combine excellent acting, rich meaningful imagery, and intense dialogue with superbly recreated atmosphere of the periods to produce some of the intellectually most intriguing works in cinema history. His newest project, tentatively entitled *Opera Europa,* a Hungarian-British co-production shot in Paris and Budapest, is a modern transformation of the Tower of Babel story.

Unlike Szabó's, István Gaál's career seemed to have reached its peak in the early seventies. Five years older than Szabó, Gaál was also one of the founders and first graduates of the Béla Balázs Studio. His debut, *Sodrásban (Current)*, 1963, was very well received at home and abroad. Like Szabó's *The Age of Daydreaming,* it was a "generational" film examining, in a more dramatic context, the reactions of a group of teen-agers on a country trip to the apparent drowning of one of them. The film is most convincing when it studies the psychological impact of the tragedy on each of the youngsters and the group as a whole.

Gaál's two most famous films are *Magasiskola (The Falcons)*, 1970, and *Holt vidék (Dead Landscape)*, 1971. The former, his first film in color, awarded the prestigious Jury's Prize at Cannes, is a subtle metaphor on the nature of totalitarianism. The setting is a falconry station where the falcons are trained to control the local bird population. We enter that isolated world as outsiders together with a young student, a newcomer to the camp, whose point of view is maintained throughout the film. The manager of the station is fanatically devoted to his job and exerts authoritarian control not only over the conditioning of the wild birds but also over the people who work under him. Together with the boy, we are at first strangely fascinated by the skills of the trainers, the beauty and the obedience of the falcons, and the efficiency of the program, but as the aesthetic awe gives way to the inevitably moral questions, we become aware of the inhuman, oppressive character of the entire system. Feeling the increasing entrapment within that horrifying reality, the student, unable to challenge it, escapes, refusing to be implicated in its destructive influence.

Gaál's *Dead Landscape* also conveys metaphorical implications through an unusual setting. It follows the gradual disintegration of a relationship between a husband and wife who become the only inhabitants of a deserted village. The film's main character is the wife who, after the death of the old woman, her only remaining human contact in the village, spends most of her days alone while her husband works in the neighboring town. The isolation and emptiness of the place become gradually so oppressive that they upset her both mentally and emotionally. Gaál dramatically demonstrates how the abandoned, decaying landscape pulls the husband and wife apart until one of their violent arguments ends in her accidental death. The film powerfully speaks of the need for human communication and social interaction as fundamental to our existence.

Pál Gábor's first major film, *Horizont* (*Horizon*), 1971, is also a generational statement. Its protagonist is a rebellious, angry young man, frustrated with the economic and social limitations of his existence. Instinctively searching for freedom and opportunity which he cannot find, he is doomed to fail. Returned to his factory after undergoing psychiatric evaluation, he is "no more reconciled to his fate than he was before" (Petrie, *History,* 211). Gábor followed this film with the thematically similar *Utazás Jakabbal* (*Journeys with Jacob*), 1972, awarded at Locarno, a free-wheeling "road movie" about two young fire equipment inspectors traveling across the Hungarian provinces trying to add excitement to their routine jobs.

Gábor's spectacular success came with the release of *Angi Vera,* 1978, which to date remains the most highly praised and the most internationally rewarded Hungarian film, having received major prizes at festivals in Cannes (FIPRESCI), San Sebastian, Chicago, São Paulo, Oslo, Rome, London, and Figuera da Foz. Set in 1948, at the time of the Stalinist consolidation of power, it follows the process of the ideological indoctrination of an attractive teen-age girl who is still unable to comprehend its corrosive impact on her fragile identity. The film's lyrical yet objective tone moves us with its story and subtly presented images. It accuses without didacticism, intellectual arguments, or propaganda. Like no other political film, *Angi Vera* condemns the shameful past without ever showing police interrogations, mass arrests, torture, or deaths.

Gábor's death of a heart attack in 1987 put an end to a career that would have certainly given us more films of *Angi Vera* caliber. In the Hungarian film community, he will also be remembered as one of the most popular and respected professors at Budapest's Academy of Theater and Film.

Another director whose very promising career was stopped by an untimely death (1981) is Zoltán Huszárik, a graduate of the Béla Balázs Studio, who brought to Hungarian cinema his unique talent as an artist and painter. He secured his special place in Hungarian film history with his very original film *Szindbád* (*Sindbad*), made in 1971. In a series of visually sumptuous flashbacks, sensual recollections of the aging hedonist of the title, the film gives us a nostalgic, refined vision of the turn-of-the-century Budapest. Gradually, the separate images combine to reflect the personality of their author—a sensual, yet superficial man, a lover of women and good food who can now sustain his appetite only by relishing the past. *Sindbad* is pure style; its director, like his protagonist, communicates almost exclusively on the aesthetic level, sharing images for our sensual consumption. Petrie himself found the film almost like a meal, "too rich to absorb at one sitting" (*History*, 207).

Other directors representing the first wave of the Balázs Studio generation include Imre Gyöngyössy, Zsolt Kézdi-Kovács, Ferenc Kósa, Pál Sándor, and Sándor Sára, all familiar names in Hungary but relatively unknown abroad.

Most of Gyöngyössy's work is documentaries, one of which, a 1985 Hungarian-German TV production, *Add tudtul fiadnak* (*That Ye Inherit/The Land of the Miraculous Rabbis*), has been called "the best documentary ever made about the survivors of the Nazi camps" (Cook, 717). His feature films exhibit intricate narrative structure and challenging "Eisensteinian" editing which make them quite inaccessible. His best and commercially most successful film is *Jób lázadása* (*Job's Revolt*), 1983, co-directed with Barna Kabay, a moving story of an elderly Jewish-Hungarian couple who in the face of the rising anti-Semitism in 1943 adopt a seven-year-old Christian boy to pass on to him their wisdom, traditions, and property before they become victims of the imminent genocide. The film touchingly recreates the life of a Jewish rural community in the shadow of political developments that will inevitably destroy it. The film's sense of the impending doom becomes more poignant because we view the events from the young boy's perspective. *Job's Revolt* ends with the coming of the Nazis, the unimaginable nightmare come true.

Zsolt Kézdi-Kovács, who began his film career as Jancsó's assistant, has made about ten films thus far, but his second one, *Romantika* (*Romanticism*), 1972, may still be his best. It distinguishes itself with its cerebral tone, affected style, and its subject matter: in the early 1800s, an idealistic young aristocrat filled with noble and lofty Enlightenment ideas and Romantic sensibilities returns to his father's country estate where he is frustrated by their incongruity with real life. Like *Sindbad*, *Romanticism* is masterfully photographed and stylized, its aestheticism often outweighing the content, a reflection of Jancsó's influence.

Kézdi-Kovács' *Ha megjön József* (*When Joseph Returns*), 1975, is a striking departure from the style and theme of *Romanticism*. It is a realistic contemporary story of a marriage that cannot survive because the husband, a seaman, is away from his wife for ten months of every year. The film focuses on the lonely, restricted, and unfulfilling life of the wife, who must live in her mother-in-law's apartment, trapped in a social limbo from which there seems no escape.

Ferenc Kósa's best film was his stunning debut, *Tizezer nap* (*Ten Thousand Suns*), awarded the Grand Prix at Cannes. Even though finished in 1965, the film was shelved for two years of frustrating negotiations with the censors. Regardless of how much of the original had to be cut, the film is still one of the boldest commentaries on modern Hungarian history. By following the thirty harsh years of a peasant's life—from pre-war poverty and army war service through forced collectivization, imprisonment during Stalinism, and subsequent release until the crushed revolution of 1956—the film shows the disintegration of a family whose future has been blighted by the scars that can never heal. No other film of that time offered such a bleak and impassioned vision of Communist blessings.

Pál Sándor's most notable film is *Szerencsés Dániel* (*Daniel Takes a Train*), 1982, which received a FIPRESCI award at Cannes a year later. It is one of a host of films made since the late seventies that objectively and openly deal with the previously unmentionable tragic events of the 1956 revolution and follows two friends trying to leave Budapest in the days of the Soviet invasion.

One of the most active, respected, and versatile filmmakers in Hungary has undoubtedly been Sándor Sára, another pioneer Béla Balázs Studio graduate. He has earned this reputation first as an outstanding cinematographer for such films as Gaál's *Current*, Kósa's *Ten Thousand Suns*, Szabó's *Father* and *25 Fireman Street*, and Huszárik's *Sindbad*, all recognized internationally for their outstanding photography. As a director he distinguished himself with at least two significant films, *Feldobott kő* (*The Upthrown Stone*), 1968, and *Holnap lesz fácán* (*Pheasant Tomorrow*), 1974. Finally, since the early eighties he has become a major figure of the "Budapest Documentary School," directing a number of hard-hitting "film-essays" that exposed some shameful chapters of the nation's Communist past.

The Upthrown Stone, like all of his films, deals with sensitive, provocative socio-political issues suppressed by the official propaganda. Set in Rákosi's 1950s, it vividly depicts the oppressive and paranoid atmosphere of terror and fear, of denunciations, arbitrary imprisonments, and show trials, of brutal collectivization and repression of minorities (Gypsies). Its young hero eventually turns against the system by exposing its inhuman character. The title metaphorically warns that the suffering inflicted on the oppressed will come down like "upthrown stones" to punish the oppressors. Sára's film had a powerful impact on the radicalization of Hungarian society. Together with Kósa's *Ten Thousand Suns* it was the most openly critical film of the sixties.

Six years later, Sára again took the director's chair to make *Pheasant Tomorrow*, another honest and bold political film, this time a subtly veiled, lightly served allegory on the nature of ideological manipulation and authoritarian mentality. Its radical message denounces human willingness to "escape from freedom" as well as political machinery that suppresses our free will.

Of the later graduates of the Balázs Studio, two directors deserve special recognition: István Dárday and Péter Gothár. Dárday's best-known film is his 1974 debut, *Jutalomutazás* (*Holiday in Britain*), a satirical comedy about a peasant boy selected for a government-sponsored trip to England whose future is manipulated by his traditional parents, his community, and the authorities, each representing a closed-mindedness of its own. But Dárday's influence went beyond his films. As one of the most talented documentarists, he established the

Társulás Studio (1981), which produced dozens of unique sociographic "film-essays" establishing the now famous Budapest Documentary School. Reviewing their achievement goes beyond the scope of this chapter.

Péter Gothár's first two films, *Ajándék ez a nap* (*A Priceless Day*), 1979, and *Megáll az idő* (*Time Stands Still*), 1981, were both very successful, the former more so at home, the latter largely in the West, where it received a handful of festival awards. *A Priceless Day* is a contemporary black comedy exposing the country's eternal housing shortage and its demoralizing impact on the young generation. *Time Stands Still* looks at the Hungarian lost generation of 1956, shattered by the failed revolution, longing for freedom and an escape from the drab, depressing reality of their lives.

Despite the deepening recession further aggravated by the difficult transition from communism to democracy and a market economy, the Hungarian cinema in the later eighties was kept alive and well, maintaining its high standards with quality films by both the established and youngest directors. Among the new talents is Péter Gárdos, director of *Szamárköhögés* (*Whooping Cough*), a 1986 hit which brought him instant international recognition. It views the atmosphere and events of the Soviet invasion of Budapest in 1956 through the eyes of a ten-year-old boy, baffled by the frantic behavior of his parents and excited by the unexpected vacation from school. The film dramatically exploits the grim humor and the tragic potential of the situation.

Other distinguished new talents include Pál Erdőss, whose *Adj király katonát!* (*The Princess*), 1982, received a "Golden Camera" at Cannes; András Jeles, author of the thoughtful allegorical *Angyali üdvözlet* (*The Annunciation*), 1984; Péter Timár, *Egészséges erótika* (*Sound Eroticism*), 1985; János Xantus, *Hülyeség nem akadály* (*Idiots May Apply*), 1985; and Géza Bereményi, a long-time scriptwriter turned director whose technically stunning *Eldorádó* (*The Midas Touch/El Dorado*), 1988, fully deserved its five nominations for the 1989 European "Oscar."

Perhaps the most promising of the recent debuts, however, is Ildikó Enyedi's *Az én XX századom* (*My 20th Century*), 1989, a captivating, masterfully narrated story about very different separated twins and the man who loves them both thinking they are one. With awards from Cannes ("Golden Camera" for Best First Feature), Edinburgh, and Las Vegas, Enyedi's film is likely to receive wide international distribution.

This necessarily general overview of the evolution and accomplishments of Hungarian cinema clearly attests to its vitality, diversity, and originality, all reflected in the continuously maintained high international reputation. It is primarily an "auteur" cinema, shaped and dominated by the particular sensibilities and styles of its talented directors. The contributions of performers are considered secondary, so much so that Hungarofilm, the country's export/advertising agency, has no single publication on its film actors and actresses. The entire metropolis' film industry is located in Budapest, Hungary's monopolistic metropole. As a result, the Hungarian film community is very close-knit and tightly integrated through years of common education, extensive professional cooperation, and frequent intermarriages. Standards for admission to the Budapest Academy of Theater and Film are most rigorous, with a ratio of more than thirty outstanding applicants for one position. Once accepted, students are taken through a challenging course of study that involves all aspects of film art from theory, through screenwriting, to actual directing, which explains why 80 percent of Hungarian films since the mid-sixties are based on original scripts, written mostly by their directors. As graduates and established filmmakers, directors are paid regular salaries as state employees and earn more only during the actual film productions, most of which are commissioned for television. Many of the directors are also encouraged to teach in the Academy and share administrative responsibilites in the individual studios.

Those structures have loosened up considerably in the months following the effective dismantling of Communist-run socialism. William Fisher reports in *Sight and Sound* that "four fledgling independent distributors sprang up last year [1989]. Since they entered the market, the number of American pictures has leapt from 30 a year (shown two years after their U.S. release) to nearly 80 (shown at the same time as in Western Europe)" (160). As a result, the state film companies Mafilm and Mokep, now faced with powerful, open-market competition, have to make do on reduced government subsidies, forcing them to invest in more popular films, such as contemporary light comedies with a lot of sex, and share the profits from their successful distribution. By the same rule, more than half of the recent annual productions were documentaries simply because they could be made on small budgets and for large TV audiences hungry for such investigative material.

In spite of the current, continuous economic difficulties, the future of Hungarian cinema looks more optimistic than, say, that of Poland, or Yugoslavia, not to mention Bulgaria or Romania. For one thing, the film community in Budapest is determined to fight for its artistic integrity and a reasonable system of partial subsidies. Throughout the late seventies and the eighties, Hungary, unlike other Eastern Bloc countries, has established not only a sound technological and institutional base but also many important cooperations with producers and distributors in Germany, Italy, and France, which will prove critical to the survival of Hungarian cinema in these transitional years. More and more of Hungarian films will be released as international co-productions, and more and more foreign films will be shot in Hungary. These tendencies, enforced by the rules of capitalist economy, will no doubt continue to promote the ambitious intellectual cinema of István Szabó and the sensitive psychological dramas of Márta Mészáros, but they will surely discourage any commercial producers from investing money in a new film by Miklós Jancsó.

NOTES

1. I would like to thank Professor Graham Petrie of the McMaster University Drama Department, Dr. Lia Somogyi of the Hungarofilm, Budapest, Mr. Béla Szombati, First

Secretary of the Hungarian Embassy in Washington, D.C., and my friend, Dr. Gautam Kundu, formerly of Louisiana State University and now joining my English Department at Georgia Southern University, for supplying me with many essential materials without which I would not have been able to undertake this assignment.

2. In an interview for a Hungarian journal *Hitel,* quoted by Catherine Portuges in her essay "Between Worlds: Re-Placing Hungarian Cinema," Mészáros said, "All my earlier films were political, though not overtly so, addressing political themes from a psychological perspective. The general public despised *The Two of Them, Nine Months,* and *The Heiresses* because these films described people who were different from them. They called attention to democratic problems such as women's right to independence, to live their own lives. These are especially important themes today in Hungary, for I know no other country that is so conservative about these issues" (66).

BIBLIOGRAPHY

The following bibliography does not include reviews of current Hungarian films published quite regularly in the Budapest-based *The New Hungarian Quarterly* since the journal's inception in 1960. It also does not include about twenty reviews of major Hungarian films that have appeared in the Foreign Films Series of *The Magill's Survey of Cinema.*

Armes, Roy. *The Ambiguous Image: Narrative Style in Modern European Cinema.* Bloomington: Indiana University Press, 1976. 141–153.
Bachmann, Gideon. "Jancsó Plain." *Sight and Sound* 43 (Fall 1974): 217–221.
———. "Letter from Hungary." *Take One* 4:10(1975): 24–26.
Bickley, Daniel. "Socialism and Humanism: The Contemporary Hungarian Cinema." *Cineaste* 9:2(1979): 30–35.
Biró, Yvette. "The Hungarian Film Style and Its Variations." *New Hungarian Quarterly* 9:32(1968): 3–8.
Christensen, Peter G. "Collaboration in Isvtán Szabó's *Mephisto.*" *Film Criticism* 12:3(1988): 20–32.
Cook, David. *A History of Narrative Film.* New York: Norton, 1990. 699–724.
Crick, Philip. "Three East European Directors: Makaveyev, Menzel, Jancsó." *Screen* 11:2(1970): 64–71.
Czigány, Lorant. "Jancsó Country." *Film Quarterly* 26 (Fall 1972): 44–50.
Fisher, William. "Prague/Budapest." *Sight and Sound* 59 (Summer 1990): 158–161.
Hoberman, J. "Budapest's Business." *Film Comment* 22:3(1986): 68–71.
———. "Interview with Márta Mészáros." *The Village Voice,* 6 November 1984.
Houston, Penelope. "The Horizontal Man." *Sight and Sound* 38 (Summer 1969): 116–120.
Ignotus, Paul. *Hungary.* New York: Praeger, 1972.
Jaehne, Karen, and William Kelly. "*Hungarian Rhapsody* and *Allegro Barbaro.*" *Film Quarterly* 34 (Fall 1980): 47–56.
Jaehne, Karen. "István Szabó: Dreams of Memories." *Film Quarterly* 32 (Fall 1978): 30–41.
Kolker, Robert Phillip. *The Altering Eye: Contemporary International Cinema.* New York: Oxford University Press, 1983.
Liehm, Antonin, and Mira Liehm. *The Most Important Art: Eastern European Film After 1945.* Berkeley: University of California Press, 1977.

Nemeskürty, István. *Word and Image: History of Hungarian Cinema*. Budapest: Corvina Press, 1974.
Paul, David. "The Esthetics of Courage." *Cinéaste* 14:4(1986): 16–22.
———. "Hungary." In *Post New Wave Cinema in the Soviet Union and Eastern Europe*. Edited by Daniel J. Goulding. Bloomington: Indiana University Press, 1989. 172–214.
———. "Interview with István Szabó." *Columbia Film View* 1 (Winter 1985): 4–6.
Petrie, Graham. *History Must Answer to Man: The Contemporary Hungarian Cinema*. Budapest: Corvina Press, 1978.
———. "István Gaál and *The Falcons*." *Film Quarterly* 27 (Spring 1974): 20–26.
———. "Miklós Jancsó: Decline and Fall?" in *Politics, Art and Commitment in the East European Cinema*. Edited by David Paul. London: The Macmillan Press, 1983. 189–210.
———. "New Cinema from Eastern Europe." *Film Comment* 11:6(1975): 48–51.
———. "Two Years of Hungarian Cinema, 1975–1977." *New Hungarian Quarterly* 19:72(1978): 210–221.
———. "Why the Hungarian Cinema Matters." *New Hungarian Quarterly* 18:68(1977): 215–218.
Portuges, Catherine. "Between Worlds: Re-Placing Hungarian Cinema." In *Before the Wall Came Down: Soviet and East European Filmmakers Working in the West*. Edited by Graham Petrie and Ruth Dwyer. Lanham, Md.: University Press of America, 1990. 63–70.
Price, James. "Polarities: The Films of Miklós Jancsó." *London Magazine* 9(1969): 189–194.
Quart, Barbara Koenig. "*Diary for My Children*." *Film Quarterly* 38 (Spring 1985): 46–49.
Riegel, O. W. "What Is 'Hungarian' in the Hungarian Cinema?" *New Hungarian Quarterly* 17:63(1976): 185–193, 17:64(1976): 206–215, 18:65(1976): 201–210. A three-part article.
Robinson, David. "Quite Apart from Miklós Jancsó." *Sight and Sound* 39 (Spring 1970): 84–89.
Sitton, Bob. "Hungarian Director Discusses His Film *Father*." *Film Comment* 5 (Fall 1968): 58–63.
Stoil, Michael Jon. *Cinema Beyond the Danube*. Metuchen, N.J.: The Scarecrow Press, 1974.
Vas, Robert. "Out of the Plain." *Sight and Sound* 35 (Summer 1966): 151–153.
———. "Yesterday and Tomorrow: New Hungarian Film." *Sight and Sound* 29 (Winter 1959/60): 31–34.
Whyte, Alistair. *New Cinema in Eastern Europe*. London: Studio Vista, 1971.
Young, Vernon. "Film Chronicle: Natural and Unnatural History." *Hudson Review* 25(1972–73): 93–100.

BIOGRAPHICAL SKETCHES

Since Hungarofilm in Budapest has never published information on Hungarian actors and actresses, the following notes include entries devoted mostly to film directors and cinematographers. Eventually, Hungarofilm promises to have a comprehensive biographical lexicon of its performers, many of whom need to be added to this section. Among those missing are such great artists as Andrea Drahota, Kati Kovács, Zsuzsa Czinkóczi, Veronika Papp, Károly Eperjes, Dorottya Udvaros, and Juli Básti, not to mention a host of Polish actors and actresses such as Jan Nowicki, Anna Polony, Grażyna Szapołowska, and Jadwiga Jankowska-Cieślak whose unforgettable roles in many Hungarian films represent some of the best work in their careers. Films with an asterisk are treated in the filmography section and are identified by their English titles only. The Academy stands for the Budapest Theater and Film Academy.

ANDOR, TAMÁS (1937–   ), cinematographer. Started in the documentary; later worked with such directors as Mészáros (*On the Move,** 1979; *Mother and Daughter/Anna,** 1981), Makk (*Another Way,** 1982; *Lily in Love,** 1984), and Bacsó (*Banana Skin Waltz,** 1986; *Titania, Titania,** 1988).

BACSÓ, PÉTER (1928–   ), director. Started as scriptwriter and literary editor in the 1950s; has taught in the Academy; has served as the Managing Director of the Dialóg Studio; since 1963 Bacsó has made more than twenty feature films including *Fejlövés* (*Fatal Shot*), 1968; *A tanu* (*The Witness*), 1969, released 1978; *Outbreak,** 1970; *Jelenidő* (*Present Indicative*), 1971; *The Last Chance,** 1973; *Te rongyos élet!* (*Oh, Bloody Life*), 1983; *Banana Skin Waltz,** 1986; and *Titania, Titania,** 1988.

BALÁZS, BÉLA (1884–1949), film theoretician, writer, and poet. Active in the Bela Kun's Republic of Councils, Balázs left for Austria and Germany when Horthy's regime took over; published *Der Geist des Films* in 1930; worked with Pabst, Brecht, and Leni Riefenstahl; left Germany in 1932; lived in the Soviet

Union until 1945 teaching film theory; returned to Hungary working on scripts for *Somewhere in Europe*,* 1947, and *Ének a búzamezökröl* (*The Song of the Cornfields*), 1947; continuous harassment under Stalinism hastened his death. His *Film—Werden und Wesen einer neue Kunst* (1948) was published in English in 1952 as *Theory of the Film: Character and Growth of a New Art*. The famous Béla Balázs Studio was named after him.

BÁLINT, ANDRÁS (1943–   ), actor. Graduated from the Academy in 1965; played leading roles in Szabó's films (*The Age of Daydreaming*,* 1964; *Father*,* 1966; *Love Film*,* 1970; *25 Fireman Street*,* 1973) as well as Jancsó's *Confrontation*,* 1968; *Red Psalm*,* 1971; and *Season of Monsters*,* 1986.

BÁNSÁGI, ILDIKÓ (1947–   ), actress. Graduated from the Academy in 1972; played major roles in *Sindbad*,* 1971; *Journeys with Jacob*,* 1972; Szabó's *Confidence*,* 1979, *Mephisto*,* 1981, and *Hanussen*,* 1988, as well as Jancsó's *Jesus Christ's Horoscope*,* 1989, and Mészáros' *Diary for My Father and Mother*,* 1990. She also starred in a number of Romanian films.

BARA, MARGIT (1928–   ), actress. Graduated in 1955; famous for her astonishing performance in *A Sunday Romance*,* 1957; later appeared in films by Makk and Kovács; abandoned film career in the seventies.

BEREMÉNYI, GÉZA (1946–   ), scriptwriter and director. Published several volumes of short stories and plays and wrote scripts for Kézdi-Kovács and Gothár among others. His first two films—*The Disciples*,* 1985, and *The Midas Touch/El Dorado*,* 1988—were enthusiastically received by both critics and audiences.

BÓDY, GÁBOR (1946–1985), director. Graduated from Budapest University with a degree in film semantics; involved in the establishment of the Béla Balázs Studio; attended the Academy from 1971 to 1975; gained instant recognition with two modernist feature films: *American Torso*,* 1975, and *The Dog's Night Song*,* 1983; committed suicide.

CSERHALMI, GYÖRGY (1948–   ), actor. Graduated from the Academy in 1972; starred in films of many outstanding directors, both young and old, including Jancsó, Makk, Fábri, Sára, Bódy, Gothár, Bereményi, and Szabó; major films include *Red Psalm*,* 1971; *American Torso*,* 1975; Makk's *Egy erkölcsös éjszaka* (*A Very Moral Night*, 1977); *Mephisto*,* 1981; *Flowers of Reverie*,* 1984; *The Disciples*,* 1985; *Season of Monsters*,* 1986; *Just Like Amerika*,* 1987.

DÁRDAY, ISTVÁN (1940–   ), director. Leading figure of the "Budapest Documentary School"; established Társulás Studio in 1981; his major fiction film is *Holiday in Britain*,* 1974.

DARVAS, IVÁN (1925–), actor. Imprisoned in 1957; major roles in Makk's *Liliomfi*, 1955; *A Sunday Romance*,* 1957; *Cold Days*,* 1966; *Love*,* 1970. Darvas is perhaps Hungary's most popular and respected actor, thanks mainly to television and radio performances.

FÁBRI, ZOLTÁN (1917–), director. Started his studies in 1935; graduated as actor in 1941; became a member of National Theater; worked as stage manager for Zoltán Várkonyi; since mid-seventies Fábri has taught at the Academy; for many years he was the president of the Federation of Hungarian Film and Television Artists. He made over twenty-five feature films, mostly literary adaptations, including *Merry-Go-Round*,* 1955; *Professor Hannibal*,* 1956; *Két félidő a pokolban* (*Two Half-Times in Hell*), 1961; *Húsz óra* (*Twenty Hours*), 1965; *A Pál utcai fiúk* (*The Boys of Paul Street*), 1968; *Isten hozta, őrnagy úr* (*The Toth Family*), 1969; *141 perc A befejezetlen mondatból* (*The Unfinished Sentence*), 1974; *Az ötödik pecsét* (*The Fifth Seal*), 1976; *Magyarok* (*The Hungarians*), 1977; *Fabian Balint talalkozasa istennel* (*Balint Fabian Meets God*), 1980; and *Requiem*, 1981.

FEJŐS, PÁL (1897–1963), director. Worked in Hungary between 1920–23 and then in 1932, when he made *Spring Shower*, first Hungarian film to attract critical attention abroad; later worked in the United States, Europe, and the Far East.

GAÁL, ISTVÁN (1933–), director. Graduated from the Academy in 1958; spent two years in Rome's Centro Sperimentale on scholarship; worked as cameraman for Sándor Sára. Major films include *Current*,* 1963; *Green Years*,* 1965; *The Falcons*,* 1970; and *Dead Landscape*,* 1971.

GÁBOR, PÁL (1932–1987), director. One of the co-founders of the Béla Balázs Studio; since the late 1960s, Gábor has taught in the Academy. Major films include *Horizon*,* 1971; *Journeys with Jacob*,* 1972; and *Angi Vera*,* 1978. Died of heart attack.

GOTHÁR, PÉTER (1947–), director. Began as TV assistant; graduated from the Academy in the late 1970s; active in both theater and film directing. Major films include *A Priceless Day*,* 1979; *Time Stands Still*,* 1981; *Idő van* (*Time*), 1985; and *Just Like Amerika*,* 1987.

GYÖNGYÖSSY, IMRE (1930–), director. A victim of Stalinist show trials, Gyöngyössy was imprisoned until 1955. Officially rehabilitated, he continued his studies in the Academy; wrote film scripts and plays; started as director in 1966; from the mid–1970s, he has worked with Barna Kabay on documentaries for TV and theaters. His highly metaphysical, structurally intricate fiction films include *Virágvasárnap* (*Palm Sunday*), 1969; *Meztelen vagy* (*Legend about the Death and Resurrection of Two Young Men*), 1971; and *Job's Revolt*,* 1983.

HERNÁDI, GYULA (1926–), scriptwriter and playwright. Author of scripts for all of Jancsó's Hungarian films and for Mészáros' *Adoption*,* 1975; *Nine Months*,* 1976; and *Mother and Daughter/Anna*,* 1981. See Jancsó, below.

HUSZÁRIK, ZOLTÁN (1931–1981), director. One of the co-founders of the Béla Balázs Studio, Huszárik received training in graphic arts and designing which he used magnificently in his memorable *Sindbad*,* 1971, and then in *Csontváry*, 1979, a poetic, visionary tribute to a classic Hungarian painter.

JANCSÓ, MIKLÓS (1921–), director. Studied law and folk art before World War II; POW during the war; graduated from the Academy in 1950; shot propaganda newsreels and documentaries in the 1950s; spent most of the seventies in Italy; devotes half of his time to professional theater working with his permanent partner, scriptwriter and playwright Gyula Hernádi. His films include *Cantata*,* 1962; *My Way Home*,* 1964; *The Round-Up*,* 1965; *The Red and the White*,* 1967; *Silence and Cry*,* 1968; *The Confrontation*,* 1968; *Red Psalm*,* 1971; *Elektreia*,* 1974; *Private Vices, Public Virtues*,* 1976; *Magyar rapszódia-Allegro Barbaro* (*Hungarian Rhapsody-Allegro Barbaro*), 1978; *Season of Monsters*,* 1986; and *Jesus Christ's Horoscope*,* 1989.

JANCSÓ, MIKLÓS "NYIKA," JR. (1952–), cinematographer. Son of Márta Mészáros and Miklós Jancsó; graduated from the Academy in 1979; famous for his photography in Mészáros' recent films: *Diary for My Children*,* 1984 (1982); *Diary for My Loves*,* 1987; *Bye-Bye Red Riding Hood*,* 1989; and *Diary for My Father and Mother*,* 1990.

KENDE, JÁNOS (1941–), cinematographer. Graduated from the Academy in 1965; has shot most of Jancsó's films and selected films of Mészáros, Gábor, Gyöngyössy, and Kézdi-Kovács. Major achievements include *Silence and Cry*,* 1968; *Red Psalm*,* 1971; *Journeys with Jacob*,* 1972; *Romanticism*,* 1972; *When Joseph Returns*,* 1975; *Nine Months*,* 1976; *Season of Monsters*,* 1986; and *Jesus Christ's Horoscope*,* 1989.

KÉZDI-KOVÁCS, ZSOLT (1936–), director. Studied under Félix Máriássy in the Academy; one of the first graduates of the Béla Balázs Studio; worked as Jancsó's assistant in the 1960s. Major films include *Romanticism*,* 1972; *When Joseph Returns*,* 1975; *A kedves szomszéd* (*The Nice Neighbor*), 1979; *A rejtőzködő* (*The Absentee*), 1985; and *Kiáltás és kiáltás* (*Cry and Cry Again*), 1987.

KOLTAI, LAJOS (1946–), cinematographer. Next to Kende, Koltai is Hungary's most famous cameraman. Studied at the Academy between 1965 and 1970 where he now teaches; can adapt to styles of radically different directors; most well-known work includes *Holiday in Britain*,* 1974; *Adoption*,* 1975; *Just Like at Home*,* 1978; *The Stud Farm*,* 1978; *Angi Vera*,* 1978; *Confidence*,* 1979;

*A Priceless Day,** 1979; *Mephisto,** 1981; *Time Stands Still,** 1981; *The Princess,** 1982; *Colonel Redl,** 1984; and *Hanussen,** 1988.

KÓSA, FERENC (1937–), director. Graduated from the Béla Balázs Studio with the memorable *Ten Thousand Suns,** 1965. Other films include *Í télet* (*Judgment*), 1970, and *A másik ember* (*The Other Person*), 1987.

KOVÁCS, ANDRÁS (1925–), director. Graduated from the Academy in 1950; worked as scriptwriter until late 1950s; since 1981 he has been the president of the Association of Hungarian Film and TV Artists. His best films include *Cold Days,** 1966; *Fallow Land,** 1972; *Blindfold,** 1974; *The Stud Farm,** 1978; *Szeretők* (*An Afternoon Affair*), 1983; and *The Red Countess,** 1984.

KOZÁK, ANDRÁS (1943–), actor. Graduated from the Academy in 1965; played major roles in the films of Jancsó, Kovács, Szabó, Mészáros, Gaál, and Kósa. They include *Current,** 1963; *My Way Home,** 1964; *Ten Thousand Suns,** 1965; *The Round-Up,** 1965; *Father,** 1966; *The Red and the White,** 1967; *The Girl,** 1968; *The Confrontation,** 1968; *Silence and Cry,** 1968; *Blindfold,** 1974; and *Season of Monsters,** 1986.

LATINOVITS, ZOLTÁN (1931–1976), actor. Played complex, ambiguous characters in such memorable films as *Cantata,** 1962; *The Round-Up,** 1965; *Cold Days,** 1966; *Silence and Cry,** 1968; *Sindbad,** 1971; *Fallow Land,** 1972; and Fábri's *Az ötödik pecsét* (*The Fifth Seal*), 1976.

MADARAS, JÓZSEF (1937–), actor. Started his acting career in 1957; appeared in over fifty films including almost all of Jancsó's Hungarian films; major roles in *Silence and Cry,** 1968; *The Confrontation,** 1968; *Horizon,** 1971; *Red Psalm,** 1971; *Romanticism,** 1972; *The Last Chance,** 1973; *Blindfold,** 1974; *Elektreia,** 1974; *The Stud Farm,** 1978; and *Season of Monsters,** 1986.

MAKK, KÁROLY (1925–), director. One of the very first students of the Academy, Makk worked as assistant director on Radványi's *Somewhere in Europe** and with Szőts and Ban on *Talpalatnyi föld* (*The Soil under Your Feet*), 1948; co-directed *Simon Menyhért születése* (*The Birth of Menyhert Simon*), 1954, with Várkonyi; has taught at the Academy for over thirty years; has been the art director of Dialog Studio since its beginnings; together with Fabri, Makk is Hungary's most distinguished director. His best films include *Liliomfi,* 1954; *A 9-es kórterem* (*Ward No.9*), 1955; *Megszállottak* (*The Fanatics*), 1961; *Love,** 1970; *Macskajáték* (*Catsplay*), 1974; *Egy erkölcsös éjszaka* (*A Very Moral Night*), 1977; *Another Way,** 1982; and *Lily in Love,** 1984.

MÁRIÁSSY, FÉLIX (1919–1975), director. Professor of Theater and Film Academy since 1948, Máriássy educated the entire generation of Hungarian filmmakers; suffered from serious heart trouble since 1968; long-time president of the International Federation of Film Art Academies. Major films include *Egy pikoló világos* (*A Glass of Beer*), 1955; *Budapesti tavasz* (*Springtime in Budapest*), 1955; and *Suburban Legend*,* 1957.

MÉSZÁROS, MÁRTA (1931–), director. Lived in the Soviet Union since 1935; returned to Hungary after the war; studied film in Moscow Film Academy (VGIK) until 1956; her first marriage took her to Romania, where between 1956 and 1959 she made documentary films; after returning to Hungary, she spent ten more years making documentary, educational, and art films; since her 1968 feature-length debut, Mészáros has gradually established herself as the most outstanding woman director in Europe. Her films include *The Girl*,* 1968; *Holdudvar* (*Binding Sentiments*), 1969; *Szabad lélegzet* (*Riddance*), 1973; *Adoption*,* 1975; *Nine Months*,* 1976; *The Two of Them/Women*,* 1977; *Just Like at Home*,* 1978; *On the Move*,* 1979; *The Heiresses*,* 1980; *Mother and Daughter/Anna*,* 1981; *Diary for My Children*,* 1984 (1982); *Diary for My Loves*,* 1987; *Bye-Bye Red Riding Hood*,* 1989; and *Diary for My Father and Mother*,* 1990.

MONORI, LILI (1945–), actress. Graduated from the Academy in 1969; Monori attained instant international recognition through her leading roles in Meszaros' films. Her most famous performances include *When Joseph Returns*,* 1975; *Nine Months*,* 1976; *The Two of Them/Women*,* 1977; *A tanu* (*The Witness*), 1978 (1969); and *The Heiresses*,* 1980.

RADVÁNYI, GÉZA (1907–1987), director. Started his film career in the thirties; before the war worked also as journalist and foreign correspondent in Paris, Geneva, Madrid, and London; returned to Hungary in 1939 where he debuted as director; worked in Rome between 1941 and 1943; was instrumental in establishing Hungarian film industry after 1945, introducing Hungarian filmmakers to modern editing, mobile camera, Stanislavsky's "method acting," and Italian neo-realism; became first professor of the Academy; made one of the first color films; left Hungary at the onset of Stalinism, working in France, Germany, and Italy; returned to Hungary in 1979; his most famous film remains the influential, ground-breaking *Somewhere in Europe*,* 1947.

RUTTKAI, ÉVA (1927–1985), actress. Started acting before the war; joined the National Theater in 1948; taught in the Academy between 1951 and 1953; appeared in more than thirty films including *Liliomfi*, 1954; *Egy pikoló világos* (*A Glass of Beer*), 1955; *Budapesti tavasz* (*Springtime in Budapest*), 1955; *Sindbad*,* 1971; and *When Joseph Returns*,* 1975.

SÁNDOR, PÁL (1939–), director. Graduated from the Academy in 1964; began with short films in the Béla Balázs Studio; first feature film in 1967. Among his dozen films, the two best-known are *Daniel Takes a Train*,* 1982, and *Miss Arizona*, 1988, a Hungarian-Italian production with Marcello Mastroianni.

SÁRA, SÁNDOR (1933–), cinematographer and director. One of the founders and first graduates of the Béla Balázs Studio; as cinematographer, Sará worked on many different films of his friends including Gaál's *Current*,* 1963; Kósa's *Ten Thousand Suns*,* 1965, and *I télet* (*Judgement*), 1970; Szabó's *Father*,* 1966, and *25 Firemen Street*,* 1973; and Huszárik's *Sindbad*,* 1971. Since mid-seventies, Sára has made a number of ground-breaking documentaries which established him as the pioneer and leader of the famous Budapest Documentary School as well as one of the most respected Hungarian film artists in his country. His feature films include *The Upthrown Stone*,* 1968, and *Pheasant Tomorrow*,* 1974.

SOMLÓ, TAMÁS (1929–), cinematographer and director. Graduated as cameraman already in 1949; directed and shot over a hundred educational and popular science films; received international recognition for his work on Jancsó's early films: *Cantata*,* 1962; *My Way Home*,* 1964; *The Round-Up*,* 1965; and *The Confrontation*,* 1968. Somló also shot Mészáros' debut, *The Girl*,* 1968; since mid-seventies concentrated exclusively on directing and producing shorts.

SZABÓ, ISTVÁN (1938–), director. Thanks to a remarkable debut, *Te* (*You*, 1963), which he shot during his apprenticeship at the Béla Balázs Studio, Szabó made his first feature *The Age of Daydreaming*,* 1964, when he was only twenty-six. In the eighties he has become the best-known Hungarian filmmaker. His films include *Father*,* 1966; *Love Film*,* 1970; *25 Fireman Street*,* 1973; *Confidence*,* 1979; *Mephisto*,* 1981; *Colonel Redl*,* 1984; and *Hanussen*,* 1988.

SZIRTES, ÁDÁM (1925–1989), actor. Studied at the Academy between 1945 and 1950; appeared in major roles in over eighty Hungarian films including memorable performances in *Talpalatnyi föld* (*The Soil under Your Feet*), 1948; *Simon Menyhért születése* (*The Birth of Menyhert Simon*), 1954; *Merry-Go-Round*,* 1955; *A Sunday Romance*,* 1957; *Húsz óra* (*Twenty Hours*), 1964; *Cold Days*,* 1966; *The Girl*,* 1968; *Romanticism*,* 1972; and *Pheasant Tomorrow*,* 1974.

SZŐTS, ISTVÁN (1912–), director. His *People from the Alps*,* 1942, was the first Hungarian film to be recognized abroad. He ran afoul of the Communist authorities and his *Ének a búzamezökröl* (*Song of the Cornfields*), 1947, was never released, while his *Talpalatnyi föld* (*The Soil under Your Feet*), 1948, was taken away from him. Szőts made two films during the thaw of 1954–1956 and then, like many others, left Hungary when it was invaded by the Soviet army. He has lived in Austria in relative obscurity ever since.

TÖRŐCSIK, MARI (1935–), actress. Undoubtedly the most famous and distinguished Hungarian performer, Törőcsik played in about a hundred films. Graduated from the Academy in 1957; has been a member of the National Theater since 1958; major roles in such films as *Merry-Go-Round,** 1955; *Suburban Legend,** 1957; *Silence and Cry,** 1968; *Love,** 1970; *Dead Landscape,** 1971; *Elektreia,** 1974; *Macskajáték (Catsplay)*, 1974; *Déryné, hol van? (Mrs. Dery, Where Are You?)*, 1975; *Whooping Cough,** 1986; and *Diary for My Father and Mother,** 1990.

VARKONYI, ZOLTÁN (1912–1979), director. Began as a successful actor in the late 1930s; worked as translator of German and French literature; repressed by fascists before and during the war; since 1949 taught in the Academy and became its managing director in 1974; worked regularly for stage, radio, and TV; made first feature film in 1951; among his eighteen films, many are adaptations of literature. His best-known work remains *Simon Menyhért születése (The Birth of Menyhert Simon)*, 1954.

ZOLNAY, PÁL (1928–), director and actor. Gave up a career in diplomacy to study film; made his first feature in 1961; his best films are *Photography,** 1972, and *Embryos,** 1985; his most recent role was in Mészáros' first two *Diaries* (1984, 1987); contributes documentaries and literary programs for TV.

ZSOMBOLYAI, JÁNOS (1939–), cinematographer and director. Shot all films directed by Bacsó before 1986 as well as Gaál's *Dead Landscape,** 1971, and Gábor's *Horizon,** 1971.

SELECTED FILMOGRAPHY

The filmography that follows includes basic information on major Hungarian feature films (excluding documentary) made between 1932 and 1990. It is adapted from a number of issues of the *Hungarofilm Bulletin* published quarterly in Budapest. The year refers to the time of the film's release; year of production is given in parentheses if the release was delayed.

1932

Tavaszi zápor (Spring Shower/Marie). d. Fejős;* sw. Ilona Fülöp; c. István Eiben & Marley Pawerel; with Annabella, István Gyergyai, & Ilona Dajbukát.

1942

Emberek a havason (People from the Alps). d. Szőts;* sw. Szőts; c. Ferenc Fekete; with János Görbe & Alice Szellay. 90 min.

1947

Valahol Európában (Somewhere in Europe). d. Radványi;* sw. Balázs,* Radványi, Judit Máriássy, & Félix Máriássy;* c. Barnabás Hegyi; with Artur Somlay, Miklós Gábor, & Zsuzsa Bánki. 102 min.

1955

Körhinta (Merry-Go-Round). d. Fábri;* sw. Fábri & László Nádasy; c. Barnabás Hegyi; with Törőcsik,* Béla Barsi, Manyi Kiss, Imre Sóos, & Szirtes.* 101 min.

1956

Hannibál tanár úr (Professor Hannibal). d. Fábri;* sw. Fábri, István Gyenes, & Péter Szás; c. Ferenc Szécsényi; au. Ferenc Móra; with Ernő Szabó, Manyi Kiss, & Noemi Apor. 92 min.

HUNGARY

1957

Bakaruhaban (A Sunday Romance). d. Imre Fehér; sw. Miklós Hubay; c. János Badal; au. Sándor Hunyady; with Bara* & Darvas.* 98 min.

Külvárosi legenda (Suburban Legend). d. Máriássy;* sw. Judit Máriássy; c. István Eiben; with Géza Tordy, Imre Sinkovits, & Törőcsik.*

1962

Oldás és kötés (Cantata). d. Jancsó;* sw. Jancsó; c. Somló;* with Latinovits,* Andor Altay, & Béla Barsi. 98 min.

1963

Sodrásban (Current). d. Gaál;* sw. Gaál; c. Sára;* with Marianne Móor, Andrea Drahota, & Kozák.* 89 min.

1964

Álmodozások kora (The Age of Daydreaming). d. Szabó;* sw. Szabó; c. Tamás Vámos; with Bálint,* Ilona Béres, Judit Halász, & Cecilia Esztergályos. 102 min.

Igy jöttem (My Way Home). d. Jancsó;* sw. Hernádi;* c. Somló;* with Kozák,* Sergei Nikonenko, János Görbe, & Madaras.* 106 min.

1965

Szegénylegények (The Round-Up). d. Jancsó;* sw. Hernádi;* c. Somló;* with János Görbe, Tibor Molnár, Kozák,* & Latinovits.*

Zöldár (The Green Years). d. Gaál;* sw. Gaál & Gyöngyössy;* c. Miklós Herczenik; with Benedek Tóth, Virág Darab, & Gábor Koncz. 108 min.

1966

Apa (Father). d. Szabó;* sw. Szabó; c. Sára;* with Miklós Gábor & Bálint.* 96 min.

Hideg napok (Cold Days). d. Kovács;* sw. Kovács; c. Ferenc Szécsényi; au. Tibor Cseres; with Latinovits,* Darvas,* Bara,* Szirtes.* 101 min.

1967

Tizezer nap (Ten Thousand Suns, 1965). d. Kósa;* sw. Kósa & Gyöngyössy,* & Sándor Csóori; c. Sára;* with Tibor Molnár, Kozák,* Gyöngyi Buros. 109 min.

Csillagosok, katonák (The Red and the White). d. Jancsó;* sw. Jancsó, Hernádi,* & Georgi Mdivani; c. Somló;* with Krystyna Mikołajewska, Tibor Molnár, Kozák,* & Madaras.* 92 min.

1968

Csend és kiáltás (Silence and Cry). d. Jancsó;* sw. Hernádi;* c. Kende;* with Kozák,* Madaras,* Törőcsik,* Latinovits,* & Andrea Drahota. 80 min.

Eltávozott nap (*The Girl*). d. Mészáros;* sw. Mészáros; c. Somló;* with Kati Kovács, Kozák,* & Szirtes.* 82 min.
Feldobott kő (*The Upthrown Stone*). d. Sára;* sw. Sára, Kósa,* & Sándor Csóori; c. Sára;* with Lajos Balazsovits, Katalin Berek, & János Pásztor. 90 min.
Fényes szelek (*The Confrontation*). d. Jancsó;* sw. Hernádi;* c. Somló;* with Andrea Drahota, Kati Kovács, Kozák,* Madaras,* Bálint,* & Lajos Balazsovits. 80 min.

1970

Kitörés (*Outbreak*). d. Bacsó;* sw. György Konrád & Bacsó; c. Zsombolyai;* with Sándor Oszter & Edit Lendvai. 113 min.
Magasiskola (*The Falcons*). d. Gaál;* sw. Gaál; c. Elemér Ragályi; au. Miklós Mészöly; with Ivan Andonov, György Bánffy, & Judit Meszléry. 88 min.
Szerelem (*Love*). d. Makk;* sw. Tibor Déry; c. János Tóth; w. Lili Darvas, Törőcsik,* Iván Darvas.* 92 min.
Szerelmesfilm (*Love Film*). d. Szabó;* sw. Szabó; c. Bálint* & Judit Halász. 143 min.

1971

Holt vidék (*Dead Landscape*). d. Gaál;* sw. Gaál; c. Zsombolyai;* with István Ferenczy & Törőcsik.* 94 min.
Horizont (*Horizon*). d. Gábor;* sw. Gábor & Gyula Marosi; c. Zsombolyai;* with Péter Fried, Szilvia Marossy, & Madaras.* 84 min.
Még kér a nép (*Red Psalm*). d. Jancsó;* sw. Hernádi;* c. Kende;* with Andrea Drahota, Madaras,* Bálint,* & Tibor Molnár. 88 min.
Szindbád (*Sindbad*). d. Huszárik;* sw. Huszárik; c. Sára;* au. Gyula Krudy; with Latinovits,* Ruttkai,* Margit Dayka, & Bánsági.* 98 min.

1972

Fotográfia (*Photography*). d. Zolnay;* sw. Orsolya Székely & Zolnay; c. Elemér Ragályi; with István Iglódi & Márk Zala. 82 min.
A magyar ugaron (*Fallow Land*). d. Kovács;* s. Kovács; c. György Illés; with Andrea Drahota, Latinovits,* & Sándor Horváth.
Romantika (*Romanticism*). d. Kézdi-Kovács;* sw. Bereményi;* c. Kende;* with Szirtes,* Madaras,* & István Szegő. 87 min.
Utazás Jakabbal (*Journeys with Jacob*). d. Gábor;* sw. István Császár & Gábor; c. Kende;* with Péter Huszti, Erika Bodnár, & Bánsági.* 88 min.

1973

Harmadik nekifutás (*The Last Chance*). d. Bacsó;* sw. Bacsó & Péter Zimre; c. Zsombolyai;* with István Avar, Ilona Kassai, & Madaras.* 106 min.
Tűzoltó utca 25 (*25 Fireman Street*). d. Szabó;* sw. Szabó; c. Sára;* with Lucyna Winnicka, Bálint,* & Rita Békés. 97 min.

1974

Bekötött szemmel (*Blindfold*). d. Kovács;* sw. Kovács; c. Ferenc Szécsényi; with Kozák,* Madaras,* & Sándor Horváth. 85 min.

Holnap lesz fácán (Pheasant Tomorrow). d. Sára;* sw. Sára & Géza Paskandy; c. Sára & Péter Jankura; with Lóránd Lohinszky, Erika Szegedi, & Szirtes.* 83 min.
Jutalomutazás (Holiday in Britain). d. Dárday;* sw. Dárday & György Szalai; c. Koltai;* with Kálmán Tamás & Mrs. Tamás. 87 min.
Szerelmem, Elektra (Elektreia). d. Jancsó;* sw. Hernádi* & László Gyurko; c. Kende;* with Törőcsik,* Madaras,* & Cserhalmi.* 76 min.

1975

Amerikai anzix (American Torso/American Fragment). d. Bódy;* sw. Bódy; c. Bódy, István Lugossy, & Péter Timár; au. Ambrose Bierce; with Cserhalmi* & András Fekete.
Ha megjön József (When Joseph Returns). d. Kézdi-Kovács;* sw. Kézdi-Kovács; c. Kende;* with Monori* & Ruttkai.*
Örökbefogadás (Adoption). d. Mészáros;* sw. Mészáros* & Hernádi;* c. Koltai;* with Kati Berek & László Szabó. 89 min.

1976

Kilenc hónap (Nine Months). d. Mészáros;* sw. Mészáros, Hernádi,* & Ildikó Koródy; c. Kende;* with Monori* & Jan Nowicki. 93 min.
Vizi privati, pubbliche virtù (Private Vices, Public Virtues). d. Jancsó;* sw. Ginovanna Gagliardo; c. Tomislav Pinter; with Lajos Balazsovits, Pamela Villoresi, & Teresa Ann Savoy. 104 min. Italian-Yugoslav production.

1977

Ők ketten (The Two of Them/Women). d. Mészáros;* sw. Ildikó Koródy, József Balázs, & Bereményi;* c. Kende;* with Marina Vlady, Monori,* Jan Nowicki, & Zsuzsa Czinkóczi.

1978

Angi Vera. d. Gábor;* sw. Gábor; c. Koltai;* au. Endre Vészi; with Veronika Papp, Éva Szabó, Erzsi Pásztor, & Tamás Dunai. 96 min.
A ménesgazda (The Stud Farm). d. Kovács;* sw. Kovács; c. Koltai;* au. István Gall; with Madaras,* Sándor Horváth, & Ferenc Fábián. 100 min.
Olyan, mint otthon (Just Like at Home). d. Mészáros;* sw. Ildikó Koródy; c. Koltai; with Zsuzsa Czinkóczi, Jan Nowicki, & Anna Karina. 108 min.

1979

Ajándék ez a nap (A Priceless Day). d. Gothár;* sw. Gothár & Péter Zimre; c. Koltai;* with Cecilia Esztergályos, Pál Hetényi, & Judit Pogány. 89 min.
Bizalom (Confidence). d. Szabó;* sw. Szabó & Erika Szántó; c. Koltai;* with Bánsági* & Péter Andorai. 117 min.
Utközben (On the Move). d. Mészáros;* sw. Mészáros,* Jan Nowicki, & Marek Piwowski; c. Andor;* with Delphine Seyrig, Jan Nowicki, & Beata Tyszkiewicz. 104 min. Polish-Hungarian production.

1980

Örökség (The Heiresses). d. Mészáros;* sw. Ildikó Koródy & Mészáros; c. Elemér Rágalyi; with Isabelle Huppert, Monori,* & Jan Nowicki. 104 min. French-Hungarian production.

1981

Anna (Mother and Daughter/Anna). d. Mészáros;* sw. Hernádi* & Mészáros; c. Andor;* with Marie-José Nat & Jan Nowicki. 92 min. French-Hungarian production.

Megáll az idő (Time Stands Still). d. Gothár;* sw. Bereményi* & Gothár; c. Koltai;* with István Znamenak & Henrik Pauer. 99 min.

Mephisto. d. Szabó;* sw. Szabó & Péter Dobai; c. Koltai;* au. Klaus Mann; with Klaus Maria Brandauer, Bánsági,* Cserhalmi,* & Krystyna Janda. 144 min. German-Hungarian production.

1982

Adj király katonát! (The Princess). d. Pál Erdőss; sw. István Kardos; c. Koltai,* Ferenc Pap, & Gábor Szabó; with Erika Ozsda & Andrea Szandrei. 113 min.

Egymásra nézve (Another Way). d. Makk;* sw. Makk & Erzsébet Galgóczi; c. Andor;* with Jadwiga Jankowska-Cieślak, Grażyna Szapołowska, Péter Andorai. 107 min.

Szerencsés Dániel (Daniel Takes a Train). d. Sándor;* sw. Zsuzsa Tóth; c. Elemér Rágalyi; with Péter Rudolf, Sándor Zsőter, Kati Szerb, & Törőcsik.* 93 min.

1983

Jób lázadása (Job's Revolt). d. Gyöngyössy* & Barna Kabay; sw. Gyöngyössy, Barna Kabay, & Katalin Petényi; c. Gábor Szabó; with Ferenc Zenthe, Hédi Temesy, & Gábor Fehér. 105 min.

Kutya éji dala (The Dog's Night Song). d. Bódy;* sw. Bódy & Sándor Erdélyi; c. Johanna Heer; with Bódy, András Fekete, & Gabriella Seres. 147 min.

1984

Angyali üdvözlet (The Annunciation). d. András Jeles; sw. András Jeles; c. Sándor Kardos; with Péter Bocsor, Julia Mérő, & Eszter Gyalog. 100 min.

Jatszani kell (Lily in Love). d. Makk;* sw. Frank Cucci; c. Andor;* with Maggie Smith, Christopher Plummer, & Elke Sommer. 107 min. Hungarian-American production.

Napló gyermekeimnek (Diary for My Children, 1982). d. Mészáros;* sw. Mészáros; c. Miklós (Nyika) Jancsó, Jr.;* with Zsuzsa Czinkóczi, Anna Polony, Jan Nowicki, & Zolnay.* 108 min.

Redl ezredes (Colonel Redl). d. Szabó;* sw. Szabó & Péter Dobai; c. Koltai;* with Klaus Maria Brandauer, Armin Muller-Stahl, Dorottya Udvaros, Gudrun Landgrebe, Károly Eperjes, & Bálint.* 149 min. Hungarian-German production.

Szirmok, viragok, koszoruk (Flowers of Reverie). d. László Lugossy; sw. István Kardos, & László Lugossy; c. Elemér Rágalyi; with Cserhalmi,* Grażyna Szapołowska, & Bogusław Linda. 106 min.

A vörös grófnő (The Red Countess). d. Kovács;* sw. Kovács; c. Miklós Biró; au. Countess Katinka Károlyi; with Juli Bśti & Ferenc Bács. 152 min.

1985

Egészséges erótika (Sound Eroticism). d. Péter Timár; sw. Péter Timár; c. Sándor Kardos; with Adam Rajhona, Róbert Koltai, Judit Németh, & Kati Kristóf. 94 min.
Embriók (Embryos). d. Zolnay;* sw. Zolnay & Orsolya Székely; c. Elemér Rágalyi, Tamás Sas, & Gábor Halász; with Erzsébet Gaál & Kati Lázár. 86 min.
A tanítványok (The Disciples). d. Bereményi;* sw. Bereményi; c. Sándor Kardos; with Károlyi Eperjes, Cserhalmi,* & Juli Básti. 103 min.

1986

Banánhéjkeringő (Banana Skin Waltz). d. Bacsó;* sw. Bacsó; c. Andor;* with Mihaaly Dés, Juli Básti, & Dorottya Udvaros. 102 min.
Szamárköhögés (Whooping Cough). d. Péter Gárdos; sw. Péter Gárdos & András Osvát; c. Tibor Máthe; with Marcell Tóth, Eszter Karász, Judit Hernádi, Károlyi Eperjes, & Törőcsik.* 90 min.
Szörnyek évadja (Season of Monsters). d. Jancsó;* sw. Hernádi* & Jancsó; c. Kende;* with Cserhalmi,* Madaras,* Katarzyna Figura, Kozák,* & Bálint.* 90 min.

1987

Napló szerelmeimnek (Diary for My Loves). d. Mészáros;* sw. Mészáros & Éva Pataki; c. "Nyika" Jancsó;* with Zsuzsa Czinkóczi, Anna Polony, Jan Nowicki, & Zolnay.* 130 min.
Tiszta Amerika (Just Like Amerika). d. Gothár;* sw. Péter Esterházy & Gothár; c. Zoltán Dávid; with Andor Lukáts, Erika Bodnár, Szirtes,* & Cserhalmi.* 119 min. Hungarian-Japanese production.

1988

Eldorádo (The Midas Touch/El Dorado). d. Bereményi;* sw. Bereményi; c. Sándor Kardos; with Károly Eperjes & Judit Pogány. 110 min.
Hanussen. d. Szabó;* sw. Szabó & Péter Dobai; c. Koltai;* with Klaus Maria Brandauer, Erland Josephson, Bánsági,* Károly Eperjes, Grażyna Szapołowska, Cserhalmi,* & Adriana Biedrzyńska. 140 min. Hungarian-German production.
Titania, Titania. d. Bacsó;* sw. Bacsó; c. Andor;* with Gyula Bodrogi, Dorottya Udvaros, & Andrea Kiss. 138 min.

1989

Az en XX. szazadom (My 20th Century). d. Ildikó Enyedi; sw. Enyedi; c. Tibor Máthe; with Dorotha Segda, Oleg Jankovsky, & Gábor Máté. 104 min.
Jézus Krisztus horoszkópja (Jesus Christ's Horoscope). d. Jancsó;* sw. Hernádi;* c. Kende;* with Cserhalmi,* Juli Básti, Bánsági,* Dorottya Udvaros, Bálint,* & Kozák.* 94 min.
Piroska és a farkas (Bye-Bye Red Riding Hood). d. Mészáros;* sw. Mészáros, Éva Pataki,

& Jan Nowicki; c. "Nyika" Jancsó* & Thomas Vámos; with Fanny Lauzier, Pamela Collier, & Jan Nowicki. 96 min. Hungarian-Canadian production.

1990

Napló apámnak, anyámnak (*Diary for My Father and Mother*). d. Mészáros;* sw. Mészáros & Éva Pataki; c. "Nyika" Jancsó;* with Zsuzsa Czinkóczi, Jan Nowicki, Törőcsik,* Bánsági,* & Anna Polony. 93 min.

6

Judith Roof

EAST GERMANY

Though, as a political unit, the German Democratic Republic did not come into existence until 1949, the heritage of East German cinema began long before. When directors and writers such as Wolfgang Staudte, Slatan Dudow, Erich Engel, Gerhard Lamprecht, and Friedrich Wolf began working in the Soviet sector of Germany after World War II, they brought with them the heritage of the pre-war German cinema, including an expressionist aesthetic, a Brechtian eye to social and political activism, and the best of a German theater influenced by Max Reinhardt. Staudte, who had begun making films shortly before the war, had worked with both Reinhardt and Piscator in German theater. Engel, a theatrical director who had directed Brecht's *Threepenny Opera,* began to make films for the budding socialist republic. The Bulgarian Dudow had directed the well-regarded film *Kühle Wampe* before the war and had worked with Sergei Eisenstein in the Soviet Union. Lamprecht, an old hand at the cinematic adaptation of novels, provided an expertise in the stolid narrative film techniques of pre-war Germany.

Despite its strong surviving ties both to a robust cinema tradition and the practice of a socialist aesthetic, East Germany's film industry had to grow from nearly nothing. Like all of Germany, East Germany was ravaged and destitute at the end of the war and the conquering Soviet army continued to take machinery, including film equipment, as war restitution. The Soviet sector that became East Germany was, however, fortunate to still have the film studios at Babelsburg, the Agfa film stock factory, and studios in Berlin that could function as the physical and technological base for a new industry. And the new industry began almost without delay, spurred by the enthusiasm and political commitment of photographers like Kurt Maetzig, who moved immediately to document the ruins of war. Using the Althoff studios in Berlin, Maetzig began to make newsreels with a socialist realist slant. Capturing the piles of rubble and the last-ditch destruction wrought by the Nazis, Maetzig and the Filmactiv Group made *Augenzeuge* or "eyewitness" newsreels, promoted with the slogan: "See for Yourself, Hear for Yourself, and Judge for Yourself." The pretense of strict objectivity that characterized these films set a receptive mood for the dictates of an ideologically pure socialist realism soon to be imposed by Party committees in charge of film production and cultural affairs.

While Maetzig's newsreels catalogued destruction, Maetzig and five others began to reconstruct a film industry with an eye toward more than documentary. Rebuilding began in November 1945 as Maetzig, Wolfgang Staudte, Georg Klaren, Boleslaw Barlog, and Friedrich Wolf formed the core of DEFA (Deutsche Film Aktiengesellschaft) (Liehm and Liehm, 76). Licensed by the Soviets, DEFA became the only film production unit in East Germany, taking over surviving production facilities and moving into the old UFA office building in Berlin. The film group's function in what would soon become the German Democratic Republic was, according to Colonel Tulpanov, Soviet cultural adviser, to aid in "the struggle for the democratic construction of Germany, the effort to educate the German people, . . . in the meaning of true democracy and humanism" (Liehm and Liehm, 76). Thus, commencing with a broad charge, DEFA and her artists began the almost fifty-year struggle with artistic restrictions, government censorship, ideological conformity, and the repression of individual vision that would plague the East German film industry, keeping it from reaching its potential and often preventing excellence. The history of East German film traces the ebb and flow of ideological freezes and thaws that determine the variety, originality, and vision of an industry posed as a tool for the propagation and maintenance of a healthy and correct socialist *weltanschauung*.

The primary reason, in fact, for the East German film industry's inconsistency was that it was completely subject to the vagaries of party policy. Through its years as a film monopoly, DEFA was controlled and managed variously by Soviet attachés, the government, the official party SED (Sozialistische Einheitspartei Deutschlands), or combinations of these in a complex and changing committee structure. DEFA policy followed the ideological imperatives of the moment, using film to correct and enforce a "proper" socialist perspective. Conflicts between artists and DEFA most often resulted in the emigration of the artist or censorship, and the result was a tradition of competent but often "flat" films that served their Party and state by rarely ever doing more than instructively illustrating the evils of war and fascism, the problems of a socialist existence in an imperialist world, the victories of the socialist worker, the history of the German people as they struggled against fascism, or the dilemmas of young people and people in love in a socialist state.

Even though party doctrine held that cinema was an important arm of the socialist movement, DEFA's consistently meager production figures have never been able to program fully German cinemas. Instead East Germans have seen a mixture of Nazi-era films deemed ideologically harmless, Soviet films, films from other Eastern European countries, and finally films from Western Europe along with a large measure of documentary and newsreels. The growth of DEFA, also subject to political fortune, was slow despite its ready-made studios at Babelsburg; beginning with only two films in 1946, production rose to twelve in 1949 during the period of its stewardship by proponents of the more liberal "Leningrad group." By 1949, when the German Democratic Republic officially became a sovereign nation, the Soviets held 80 percent of the shares in DEFA. Production slowed to a low of six films per year in 1952, reflecting changes in DEFA philosophy, but rose to highs of 15 in 1954, 21 in 1957, and 25 in 1958, the result of a brief period of ideological thaw. In the sixties, production figures were more consistent settling to about 20 features per year by the seventies, and reduced to about 16 per year in the 1980s.

DEFA also became a multi-purpose film organization. By the mid-sixties it had developed seven specialized institutions in addition to its main production facilities; these sub-units covered all aspects of film making from the technical to the educational, including DEFA-Kopierwerke (Printing Works), the Apparatus Works, the Studio for Synchronization, the State Film Archives, the Film School at Potsdam, the DEFA Studio for Popular Science Films, and the Animation Film Studio. Babelsburg itself contains nine studios located on 120 acres with a production capacity of 50 feature films per year. DEFA even handles foreign distribution through DEFA-Aussenhandel and the distribution company "Progress." By the 1970s all of this was managed by the Main Board of Film within the Ministry of Culture.

IDEOLOGICAL IDEALISM: 1946–1952

At least DEFA as an organization thrived as the East German film monopoly. Building from the 56 cinemas standing in Berlin at the end of the war, DEFA slowly began to produce feature films that illustrated the problems of contemporary life in the rubble of war. These Trümmerfilme or "rubble films" used the contemporary, almost expressionistic setting of post-war Berlin as the backdrop for the exploration of dilemmas facing those who live through a war and who wish to build a new and ideologically different nation on the ruins of the old. The first of these films was the 1946 film *Die Mörder sind unter uns* (*The Murderers Are Among Us*), directed by Wolfgang Staudte. Expressionist in style, Staudte's film uses the haunting ruins of Berlin as the graphic setting for the story of a returning Berliner's attempt to have a war criminal punished. *Die Mörder* combines the desire for retributive justice with the pathos of destroyed lives in a way that might have provided an inventive model for DEFA's mission of educating and exhorting the populace about socialist ideas while retaining an artistic integrity and vision.

DEFA, however, because of its rapid changes in leadership and its tendency to reflect the doctrinaire uncertainties of the unseasoned government, did not follow through with more films of the quality of *Die Mörder*. Its other first offering was *Irgendwo in Berlin* (*Somewhere in Berlin*), directed by veteran Gerhard Lamprecht. A typical "rubble film," *Irgendwo* chronicles the struggles of children left in Berlin's ruins; it would be more characteristic of DEFA's "rubble films" and other realist extensions of the *Augenzeuge* newsreels that included "reconstruction" films illustrating the direction of socialist change, anti-fascist films demonstrating the new Germany's break with the past, and some lighter entertainment that would soon bear the brunt of complaints of ideological impurity.

The three broad genres—rubble films, reconstruction films, and anti-fascist films—contributed the majority of DEFA's production between 1946 and 1952, the period during which DEFA experienced its first shifts in leadership and philosophy. Films such as *Unser täglich Brot* (*Our Daily Bread*), 1949, and *Buntkarierten* (*The Checkered Bedspread*), 1949, explored themes of destruction and reconstruction. *Unser täglich Brot,* directed by the veteran of socialist aesthetics, Slatan Dudow, is reminiscent of the artist's earlier film, *Kühle Wampe,* but follows the more obvious ideological line of Zhdanovian realism, tracing a post-war family's mixed efforts to pick up the pieces of their lives (Liehm and Liehm, 80). The epic *Buntkarierten,* Kurt Maetzig's second feature film, traces a family of workers from the nineteenth century to the post-war present, as they embody the virtues of tireless labor and selfless devotion to the state. Continuing to develop a socialist realist expressionism, DEFA's films took both contemporary and pre-war Germany as their setting, using both present and increasingly the past to illustrate the virtues of a socialist existence.

But DEFA's changing leadership reigned in any creative fervor that might have ranged beyond Zhdanovian dictates. Colonel Tulpanov, a Leningrad liberal who guided cultural affairs in 1946 and 1947, oversaw the production of such promising films as Maetzig's *Ehe im Schatten* (*Marriage in the Shadow*), 1947, which commenced the subgenre of anti-fascist films. Dipping into pre-war history, *Ehe im Schatten* tells the story of Joachim Gottschalk who chose to die with his Jewish wife, thus indicting the anti-Semitism of Nazi Germany. When Tulpanov was removed from his post in 1947, DEFA experienced month-to-month changes in personnel that prevented the development of any consistent aesthetic line deviating from strict socialist realism and from the limited topics found useful for promoting political lessons. While 1948 and 1949 witnessed a broadening of DEFA's offerings, as documentaries and even comedies joined the rubble films, neither newer form represented any substantial evolution in aesthetic philosophy or any greater certainty in direction. Andrew Thorndike's documentaries were certainly the most conservative possibilities, risking nothing in their "objective" exposition of social and historical ills. Thorndike began production of his rigidly orthodox films, *Der 13. Oktober* (*The 13th October*) and *Von Hamburg bis Stralsund* (*From Hamburg to Stralsund*) in 1949. Characterized by an archival method, Thorndike's documentaries used old footage and narration to reshape Germany in an ideologically acceptable way, beginning a staunch tradition of polemical documentaries that would become a continuously influential form throughout the history of East German film.

The most zealous expressions of socialist purity represented by documentaries were produced along with films such as *Wozzeck* that attempted to enlarge the stylistic confines of socialist realism. Based on Büchner's novel and directed by

Georg Klaren, one of the original founders of DEFA, *Wozzeck* is a markedly expressionistic film. Staudte also contributed a realist/expressionist film in the same vein, the satire *Die seltsamen Abenteuer des (Herrn) Fridolin B. (The Strange Adventure of Herr Fridolin B.)*, 1948, which made fun of "bureaucratism and the petty bourgeoisie" (Liehm and Liehm, 82). Erich Engel, another member of the pre-war German avant-garde, made *Affäre Blum (The Blum Affair)*, 1948, which used its Weimar Republic setting to explore a case of miscarried justice, helping to establish the tradition of an anti-fascist genre. But Engel's second film, *Der Biberpelz (Beaver Coat)*, 1949, like *Figaros Hochzeit (The Marriage of Figaro)*, 1949, was criticized by DEFA's new head Sepp Schwab as having "crossed over to a platform of neutrality between East and West" (quoted in Liehm and Liehm, 85).

Finding where the lines between orthodoxy and decadence would be drawn, early East German directors did not need to venture far into stylistic extremes or fits of personal vision. Schwab's repressive mandates made it clear that DEFA's role was limited to the very narrow function of ideological illustration made within the accepted stylistic confines of socialist realism. As he took over DEFA's leadership in 1949, Schwab indicated that DEFA's ideological purity was more important than its artists, claiming that to overcome the "disruptive efforts" of films such as Engel's *Der Biberpelz*, "DEFA had to relinquish some of its collaborators" (quoted in Liehm and Liehm, 85). The "collaborators" he is referring to are Engel and veteran Arthur Rabenalt, who was guilty of directing entertaining films without sufficient social value such as *Das Mädchen Christine (The Girl Christine)*, 1949, which had been, according to Schwab, influenced by "the old forces" into a "false line." Not only did Engel and Rabenalt leave, so did Lamprecht, after an East German career of one film, and Boleslaw Barlog, another of DEFA's original founders (Liehm and Liehm, 85). So began the exodus that would periodically plague East German cinema as many of its most promising directors would leave for the West when DEFA's dictates became too oppressive.

Those directors who remained after Schwab took control toed the party line with more reconstruction and anti-fascist films illustrating a socialist consciousness that attempted to address the problems of contemporary Germany in an ideologically correct way. While the last "lightweight" entertainment film, *Das kalte herz (The Cold Heart)*, was made by Paul Verhoeven in 1950, Klaren, who had deviated a bit in his adaptation of *Wozzeck*, returned to the party line with the rigidly doctrinaire *Semmelweis—Retter der Mütter (Semmelweis—Savior of Mothers)*, 1949. Staudte, whose creativity often found more compelling and original ways of fulfilling party expectations, directed *Rotation*, 1949, which mixed subjective and objective perspectives in the anti-fascist story of a son who informs on his father (Liehm and Liehm, 84). Staudte also directed a film based on a Heinrich Mann novel, *Der Untertan (The Kaiser's Lackey)*, 1951, which continued his earlier satire of the bourgeoisie.

Kurt Maetzig, Slatan Dudow, and Martin Hellberg used their creative talents to exemplify DEFA's filmic ideals. Maetzig directed *Rat der Götter* (*Divine Councils*), 1950, scripted by Friedrich Wolf, and illustrating in grand terms the Nuremberg Trials and the German-American collaboration in war crimes. He also directed *Roman einer Ehe* (*Story of a Young Couple*), 1951, that traced the marital and ideological conflict of a married couple split between East and West who ultimately decide for the superiority of the East (Liehm and Liehm, 89). Propaganda films like these were also artfully produced by Dudow, who directed *Familie Benthin* (*The Benthin Family*), 1950, considered a "great" expression of the socialist ideal. Dudow also directed *Frauenschicksale* (*Women's Destiny*), 1952, the dark story of the decadent effects of the West on two young girls from the East. Hellberg, a newcomer, seemed to fit easily into the governing propagandistic aesthetic, making two films in this period, *Das verurteilte Dorf* (*The Condemned Village*), 1951, about life in an East German village, and *Geheimakten Solvay* (*The Solvay Dossier,*) 1952, about the trial of management of a German factory (Liehm and Liehm, 91).

These films were the best of a field of DEFA productions that illustrated in crude terms the superiority of the East and of socialism. Other films of the period such as *Der Auftrag Höglers* (*By Mandate of Högler*), 1949, by Gustav von Wagenheim; Klaren's *Sonnenbrucks*, 1950; *Kein Platz Für Liebe* (*No Place for Love*), 1950, by Hans Deppe; *Die Meere rufen* (*The Oceans Are Calling*), 1951, by Eduard Kubat; and *Schatten über Inseln* (*Shadows Over Islands*), 1952, by Otto Meyer extended the list of mediocre films made by unremarkable and soon-to-be-forgotten directors who could neither thrive in nor challenge the ruling system. This stream of commonplace films accompanied Thorndike's prolific documentary production, as he turned out film after film, including *Freundschaft Siegt* (*Friendship Wins*), 1951, *Wilhelm Pieck—das Leben unseres Präsidenten* (*Wilhelm Pieck—The Life of Our President*), 1951; and *Die Prüfung* (*The Examination*), 1952, all exemplary versions of documentary polemic.

THAW AND FREEZE IN THE FIFTIES

In the fifties, filmmakers continued sorting the relation between film, creativity, and party policy as political events catalyzed ideological thaws and freezes. The death of Stalin in 1953 occasioned a general thaw that would last until 1956, but even as policy appeared to become less restrictive, other events such as the East German workers' strikes of 1953 and the Hungarian revolution of 1956 would freeze the creative environment before it really had a chance to nurture a cinema that could combine the best of German tradition with the creative possibilities of a socialist art. The resulting tension between hints of liberalization and threats of greater restriction forced filmmakers into a middle ground of safe socialist realist formulas that tended merely to elaborate East German cinema's first five years.

By 1953, with so many experienced filmmakers gone, it was both timely and necessary for new East German filmmakers to take up the struggle to define the

East German cinema. While veterans such as Maetzig, Dudow, and Thorndike continued to direct heroic fare such as Maetzig's two-part biographical epic *Ernst Thälmann—Sohn seiner Klasse* (*Ernst Thälmann, Son of his Class*), 1954, and *Ernst Thälmann—Führer seiner Klasse* (*Ernst Thälmann, Leader of His Class*), 1955; Dudow's classic anti-Nazi film, *Stärker als die Nacht* (*Stronger Than the Night*), 1954; and Thorndike's *Sieben vom Rhein* (*Seven from the Rhine*), 1954, Hellberg took advantage of the brief post-Stalin thaw to try his hand at socialist romance in *Das kleine und das grosse Glück* (*Little and Big Happiness*), 1953. But even that genre required compliance with committee-formulated directives, and quickly the advent of the workers' strike forced the re-imposition of the old restrictions under the rubric of the "new course" that made room only for a kind of socialist entertainment film that could compete effectively against the inroads of West German television (Liehm and Liehm, 95). The films that resulted from the odd compromise of ideology—that which illustrated the highest ideals of socialist practice in the struggles of the people to form a new and better existence—and commercial competition that featured fantasy and escapism managed to do no more than to envelope a tepid romance within a large dose of party philosophy. Such films as E. W. Fiedler's *Rauschende Melodien* (*Swelling Melodies*), 1954; Kurt Jung-Alsen's *Wer seine Frau lieb hat* (*Whoever Loves His Wife*), 1955; and Hans Müller's *Zar und Zimmermann*, (*Tsar and Carpenter*), 1956, typified this genre, adding only box office receipts to DEFA's developing style (Liehm and Liehm, 95). And the old propaganda films continued to be made, with von Wagenheim's *Die gefährliche Fracht* (*Dangerous Load*), 1953, and Arthur Pohl's *Die Unbesiegbaren* (*The Undefeatable*), 1953.

Filmmakers beginning their careers in the 1950s were left with a very narrow line of creative ideological compliance within which to make their mark. And some did. Konrad Wolf, son of playwright and founding member of DEFA Friedrich Wolf, returned to East Germany from the Soviet Union to begin making a series of films that would distinguish themselves as products of perhaps the most unique vision in East German cinema. His first film, *Einmal ist keinmal* (*Once is Nonce*), 1953, was a comedy that proved to be an inauspicious beginning for one of the more innovative and visionary filmmakers of East Germany who would go on later in the decade to make the first critically acclaimed East German film, *Sterne* (*Stars*), 1959. Gerhard Klein and Joachim Kunert who both came to feature filmmaking from documentaries, made their feature debuts in 1955 with *Alarm im Zirkus* (*Alarm in the Circus*) and *Special Peculiarities: None*, respectively.

While younger filmmakers struggled to begin, what was left of a slight thaw manifested itself briefly in the development of an international cooperation in filmmaking. Stimulated by post-Stalin openness, but not completed until 1958, films such as *Die Elenden* (*Les Misérables*), directed by Frenchman Jean-Paul Le Chanois, and *Die Hexen von Salem* (*The Crucible*), directed by Raymond Rouleau, represented attempts to create evidence of a multi-national belief in socialist ideals.

The year 1956, however, saw the beginning of even more restrictive ideological control that affected even those who thought themselves hard-line dévotés of the new government. The harassment of intellectuals and fear of reprising the events of Hungary convinced German leader Ulbricht to tighten the reigns, making his "new course" an even more rigid version of the old. By 1956, even Staudte, who had worked successfully within the limits of the original East German system, gave up and returned to the West after directing *Die Geschichte vom kleinen Muck* (*Little Mook*), 1953, a children's film, and *Leuchtfeuer* (*Beacon*), 1954, two less-than-stunning attempts to comply with DEFA's committee directives.

Despite tighter control, which meant that ideas, outlines, scripts, and films had to undergo and survive layers of committee scrutiny, the new generation of East German filmmakers thrived slightly during the period from 1956 to 1959. Wolf's talents became more evident in *Genesung* (*Recovery*), 1956, and *Lissy*, 1957, culminating in the brilliant Bulgarian co-production *Sterne* (*Stars*), 1959, another anti-fascist film about the marriage between a German and a Jewish woman during World War II so well filmed that it won the Special Jury prize at Cannes. Wolf's sensitive realism manages to convey the mood, the time, and the anguish of the soldier who begins to recognize the wrongs of his country as he falls in love with a Greek Jewess and decides to join the Partisans and fight against the Nazis. Gerhard Klein made two more films, *Eine Berliner Romanze* (*Berlin Romance*), 1956, and *Berlin, Ecke Schönhauser* (*Berlin, Schoenhauser Corner*), 1957, that fulfilled the objectives of the socialist romance—asserting the superiority of socialist existence and the inevitable fulfillment awaiting couples who work together for the larger social weal—while their unrelenting realism imaged "shadier" aspects of East German existence (Liehm and Liehm, 261). Another neophyte, Frank Beyer, also made his debut during this period, beginning a prolific and successful career with *Zwei Mütter* (*Two Mothers*), 1957.

By 1958 it was clear that there would be little space for artistic invention, vision, or originality. Experienced filmmakers such as Maetzig sought variety to make up for lack of experimentation. Working in different genres, Maetzig made *Schlösser und Katen* (*Palaces and Huts*), 1957, a propaganda postcard of an East German town; *Das Lied der Matrosen* (*Sailors' Song*), 1958, a historical film for the anniversary of the Russian revolution; the science fiction film *First Spaceship on Venus*, 1958, co-produced with Poland; and the comedy *Vergesst mir meine Traudel nicht* (*Don't Forget My Traudel*), 1957. Dudow, an old hand at socialist realism, switched to comedy, making the satire *Der Hauptmann von Köln* (*The Captain of Cologne*), 1956, filled with comic gags, and finished his career with the comedy, *Verwirrung der Liebe* (*Craziness of Love*), 1959.

Workmanly filmmakers such as Hellberg and Thorndike continued the production of ideological illustrations, Hellberg with a collection of historical films and romances including *Richter von Zalamea* (*The Judge of Salamea*), 1955; *Emilia Galotti*, 1957; *Kapitäne bleiben an Bord* (*Captains Do Not Leave the Ship*), 1958; *Kabale und Liebe* (*Intrigue and Love*), 1959; and *Senta auf Abwegen*

(*Senta Goes Astray*), 1959. Thorndike, now teamed with his wife, Annelie, continued with large documentary projects such as *Du und mancher Kamerad . . . (The German Story/You and Other Comrades)*, 1956; *Urlaub auf Sylt (Holiday on Sylt)*, 1957; and *Unternehmen Teutonenschwert (Operation Teutonic Sword)*, 1958, from *The Archives Testify* series.

Against this late-fifties panorama of limited variety and stalled creativity, less experienced filmmakers such as Kunert, Beyer, Janos Veiczi, Günter Reisch, and Heiner Carow joined returning veteran Erich Engel in producing a series of propaganda films, each bringing to them some elements of their developing personal style. Kunert directed *It Happened in Berlin,* 1957, and *The Lottery Swede,* 1958, while Beyer made *Eine alte Liebe (An Old Love)*, 1959. Veiczi directed *The Benderath Incident,* 1956, and *Reportage 1957,* 1959, and Reisch began his career co-directing *Das Lied der Matrosen (Sailors' Song)*, 1958, with Maetzig and making the feature film *Maibowle,* 1959. Carow made his debut with the impressive *Sie nannten ihn amigo (They Called Him Amigo)*, 1959, an innovative film that mixed expressionism with a subjective perspective (Liehm and Liehm, 265). Engel's last film, *Geschwader Fledermaus (Fledermaus Squadron)*, 1958, was a propaganda work about Vietnam.

1960S, CENSORSHIP, AND SOCIALIST CONTEMPORARY FILMS

The uncertainties of the 1950s most often resulted in the filmmaker's retreat to pre-war Germany as a safe setting for ideological dramas. While socialist romances threatened dangerous contemporaneity, filmmakers hardly dared to treat present-day Germany, since such a setting would produce a difficult, if not impossible, committee gamut. But the ideological dictates of a socialist praxis also demanded relevance, so in the relatively stable period of the early 1960s, filmmakers began to make "*sozialistische Gegenwartsfilme*" or "socialist contemporary" films. The emphasis on the present did not come without its price. The 1960s began with the banning of Wolf's film about uranium miners, *Die Sonnensucher (The Sun Seekers)*, made in 1957, released in 1959 and not screened until 1972. The reason for the film's repression was not any offensive content, but rather Ulbricht's desire to fall in line with the new Soviet policy against nuclear weapons (Liehm and Liehm, 259).

While East Germany began a period of relative isolation signaled by the 1961 building of the Berlin wall, the feeling of greater security provided by such extreme measures battled against the dissatisfaction that had necessitated a wall to keep East Germans in Germany in the first place. A slight economic revival in the early 1960s pushed the number of DEFA feature productions to its highest level, and many of these were unremarkable, ideologically conformist films about the virtues of contemporary life in East Germany. The most successful of these were the contemporary romances that continued to illustrate the felicitous union of love and duty, a combination that spoke to both emotions and patriotism. Films such as Maetzig's *Septemberliebe (September Love)*, 1960; *Königskinder*

(*Invincible Love*), 1962, directed by Beyer; *Une deine Liebe auch* (*And Your Love Too*), 1962, and *Julia lebt* (*Julia Lives*), 1963, directed by beginner Frank Vogel; Konrad Wolf's adaptation of Christa Wolf's novel *Der Geteilte Himmel* (*The Divided Sky*), 1964; and Egon Günther's *Lot's Weib* (*Lot's Wife*), 1964, brought together questions of responsibility and love that sometimes veered toward the line of political impropriety since they flirted with the touchy present.

The socialist romances were joined by films from another "safer" realm, the military, whose interpersonal issues of duty, patriotism, and right and wrong were intriguing, but inevitably clearer. These army films were often a form of the "buddy" film, tracing the plight of comrades in arms as they face conflicting struggles on the battlefield. Army films also avoided the present, usually taking place in the past of World War II, where dilemmas had already been determined by the course of history. Though Frank Beyer returned to the Spanish Civil War for material for his film *Fünf Patronenhülsen* (*Five Cartridges*), 1960, other army films were more contemporary, treating the plights of friends in such works as *Die heute über vierzig sind* (*Those Over Forty Today*), 1960, directed by Kurt Jung-Alsen, who had made the first army buddy film, *Betrogen bis zum Jüngsten Tag* (*Duped till Doomsday*), in 1957. Perhaps the best army film was *Die Abenteuer des Werner Holt* (*The Adventures of Werner Holt*), 1964, directed by Joachim Kunert, tracing the different choices of two Nazi soldiers at the end of the war. Beyer, however, who had also directed another army film, *Karbid und Sauerampfer* (*Guns and Sorrell*), 1963, went a slightly different direction, combining the anti-fascism of the concentration camp with the conflicts of war in *Nackt unter Wölfen* (*Naked Among Wolves*), 1962, the story of a Buchenwald revolt.

The slight inroads into contemporary issues made in the early 1960s were halted by the deliberations of the Eleventh Plenary Session of the SED which resoundingly reaffirmed the filmmakers' necessary adherence to strict ideological conformity. While ascribing to an ideal of artistic freedom, such freedom was defined only as that work completely in line with state ideology. Attacks against intellectuals recommenced in the name of purity, and films that had begun to explore critically contemporary issues, such as Kurt Maetzig's *Das Kaninchen bin ich* (*The Rabbit Is Me*), 1965, were seen as leading toward a dangerous zone of unproductive and misleading criticism. Referred to as the "rabbit films," this group of mid–1960s productions, derived from the socialist romances, was banned as deviating from the positive role of cinema in the socialist state. Films such as Günther Stahnke's *Der Frühling braucht Zeit* (*Spring Needs Time*), 1965; romance director Frank Vogel's *Denk bloss nicht, ich heule* (*Just Don't Think I'm Crying*), 1965; Kurt Barthel's *Fräulein Schmetterling* (*Miss Butterfly*), 1965; and Frank Beyer's *Spur der Steine* (*Track of Stones*), 1965, were all banned before or shortly after screening.

What filled up screen space in the mid–1960s was more neutral and even regressive fare, including a large dose of westerns such as *Die Söhne der grossen Bärin* (*Sons of the Great Bear*), 1965, and its sequels, directed by Josef Mach.

Also possible were such historical epics as Maetzig's *Die Fahne von Krivoy Rog* (*The Flag at Krivoy Rog*), 1967, and other dramas taking place in history instead of on the dangerous ground of the present. Egon Günther chose pre-World War I Germany as the setting for *Abschied* (*Farewell*), 1968, and Konrad Wolf made his autobiographical film *Ich war neunzehn* (*I Was Nineteen*), 1967, about his experiences after World War II. Comedies also re-emerged, including *Mir nach Canaillen!* (*Follow Me, Mob!*), 1966, directed by Ralf Kirsten and Wolfgang Luderer's *My Friend Sybille*, 1967.

The curtailment of filmic explorations into social problems also made more prominent the thriving documentary industry, as the Thorndikes and many other documentary directors, including Walter Heynowski, continued to produce topical films that reproduced the proper socialist perspective. The prominence of the documentary style even spurred the development of another film sub-genre, a documentary realism that appeared in the late 1960s to take the place of the quashed contemporary films. Replacing restrictive narrative formulas and the confines of socialist realism with the slightly expanded vision accorded the documentary, documentary realist films could focus on individuals in relatively unmediated glimpses of the work place and thus present both contemporary problems and questions of personal conflict within the larger scheme of German labor without being accused of individualism, incorrect subject matter, or a skewed emphasis. Films such as Frank Vogel's *Das siebente Jahr* (*Seventh Year*), 1968; Siegfried Kühn's *Im Spannungsfeld* (*In the Field of Tension*), 1969; Ralf Kirsten's *Netzwerk* (*Network*), 1969; and *Dr. Med Sommer II*, 1970, represented this newest sub-genre as East German cinema began to be less restrictive in the early 1970s (Liehm and Liehm, 364).

REALITY, FANTASY, THE 1970S, AND THE 1980S

Several conditions shifted in the late 1960s that enabled a slight relaxation of cinematic restrictions in the 1970s. East Germany adopted a new constitution in 1968, marking its final adjustment to independent existence. Television gained in importance, displacing cinema as the primary instrument of social education, and leaving cinema more to its own devices. Those devices again included filmic forays into the world of contemporary social problems in films retaining the documentary realist slant. East German film of the 1970s and 1980s did diversify from its anti-fascist and documentary mainstream, but mainly in continuations of previous traditions such as literary adaptations, fantasy films, and films treating the problems of women. Though in the early 1980s an attempt was made to make at least 50 percent of the films DEFA produced treatments of contemporary situations, these films either reiterated anti-fascist themes, remade the same socialist formulas, or went toward the realm of biography. The documentary influence remained clear; its antithesis was the trend toward fantasy that entered the cinema via children's films.

By the mid-sixties, DEFA was governed by the Main Board of Film within the Ministry for Education, and headed by the Deputy Minister of Culture. It had developed an efficient studio system with experienced screenwriters, actors, and cinematographers who worked permanently at the DEFA studios. Writers such as Wolfgang Kohlhaase, Günther Rücker, Jochen Nestler, Manfred Freitag, and Helmut Baierl worked in teams with such seasoned cinematographers as Claus Neumann, Werner Bergmann (who often teamed with Wolf), and Jürgen Brauer, and with performers such as Erwin Geschonneck, Jutta Hoffman, Jutta Wachowiak, Günther Simon, Cox Habbema, and Rolf Hoppe. The result was efficiency, but at the price of too much consistency as the same people tended to make films with similar texture, theme, and style.

DEFA mainly continued to produce anti-fascist fare, while increasing contemporary offerings in the seventies and eighties. Thus the norm for DEFA was films such as Maetzig's *Januskopf*, 1971; Günther's *Anlauf (Start)*, 1971, and *Die Leiden des jungen Werthers (The Sorrows of Young Werther)*, 1975; Seeman's *Reife Kirschen (Ripe Cherries)*, 1972; Warneke's *Die Unverbesserliche Barbara (Incorrigible Barbara)*, 1977; Oehme's *Asta mein Engelchen (Asta my Angel)*, 1980; Rücker's *Die Verlobte (The Fiancée)*, 1982; Heymann's *Schwierig sich zu verloben (Difficult to Get Engaged)*, 1984; and Craef's *Haus am Fluss (House on the River)*, 1987, which continued the formulas of romance and social commitment typical of the East German mainstream. Gathering a new set of DEFA-trained directors such as Seemann, Warneke, Heymann, Ulrich Weiss, and Hermann Zschoche, the East German film industry did begin to vary its formula by adding more comic elements in films such as Kühn's *Das zweite Leben des Friedrich Wilhelm Georg Platow (The Second Life of Friedrich Wilhelm Georg Platow)*, 1973, and Rainer Simon's *Das Luftschiff (Airship)*, 1984. It also attempted more serious verbal fare such as Kühn's adaptation of Goethe in the 1975 film *Wahlverwandtschaften (Elective Affinities)* or Lothar Warneke's study of a cancer victim's search for the meaning of life in *Apprehension*, 1983.

With this steady stream of contemporary, romantic, sometimes comic, sometimes tragic, always ideologically pure dramas also developed three sets of overlapping sub-genres that would dominate both seventies and eighties East German cinema. The "woman's film" had existed since Slatan Dudow's early *Frauenschicksale (Women's Destiny)*, 1952. Emerging in the seventies and eighties as a major form, the woman's film was the perfect format for exploring both social and romantic issues as they affect the lives of individual characters. Picking up from Egon Günther's mid-sixties film, *Lots Weib (Lot's Wife)*, 1964, the seventies commenced with Günther's *Junge Frau von 1914 (A Young Woman of 1914)*, 1970, followed by two better-than-average films, Günther's *Der Dritte (The Third One)*, 1972, and Heiner Carow's *Die Legende von Paul und Paula (The Legend of Paul and Paula)*, 1973, both about "young, independent women" who struggle to raise children (Liehm and Liehm, 366–367). Günther would continue to make films on the topic, including the famous first East/West German co-production *Lotte in Weimar*, 1975, starring Lili Palmer and Jutta Hoffman. The trend continued in the late seventies and early eighties with Warneke's *Die*

Unverbesserliche Barbara (*Incorrigible Barbara*), 1978; Zschoche's *Bürgschaft für ein Jahr* (*Warranty for One Year*), 1980, also about the struggles of a young, independent woman to raise children alone; Warneke's *Apprehension*, 1983, which focuses on a young woman's struggle with the threat of cancer; Horst Seemann's popular *Arztinnen* (*Lady Doctors*), 1984; Zschoche's *The Solo Sailor*, 1987, another film about the demands placed on a single woman raising a child; and Erwin Stranka's *Liane*, 1987, about the problems of a young woman working in technology.

In the same way that the topicality of the woman's film permitted the safe exploration of contemporary problems, so did the sub-genre of biographical films which could combine the documentary nature of biography with illustrative examples of people who either did or did not find satisfactory answers to the difficulties of oppression, imperialism, greed, or opportunism. Prefaced, as were women's films, by early successes in the genre such as Maetzig's grandiose *Ernst Thälmann* films, filmmakers in the seventies focused on the lives of scientists, artists, and socialist leaders. Though Günter Reisch's film on Lenin, *Unterwegs zu Lenin* (*On the Way to Lenin*), 1970, was not immensely popular at the box office, it recommenced an interest in biographical filmmaking linked both to tradition and to the more recent style of documentary realism (Liehm and Liehm, 366). Konrad Wolf made the first successful seventies biography in his adaptation of Lion Feuchtwanger's study of Goya in *Goya* (1971), a topic that enabled Wolf to consider questions about the role of the artist in society. Horst Seemann made another popular biography of an artist in *Beethoven—Tage aus einem Leben* (*Beethoven—Days from a Life*), 1975, and Peter Schamoni contributed *Frühlingssinfonie* (*Spring Symphony*), 1983, on the life of Schumann. Lothar Warneke explored the lives of scientists in two films, *Es ist eine alte Geschichte* (*It Is an Old Story*), 1972, and *Leben mit Uwe* (*Life with Uwe*), 1974, while Frank Vogel filmed a study of the life of Johannes Kepler in *Putzt das Licht der Vernunft* (*Clean Up the Light of Common Sense*), 1975. Political leaders gained interest in another film on the life of Ernst Thälmann, in Bernard Stephan's *Aus meiner Kindheit* (*My Childhood*), 1975, and in a film on Wolz, Reisch's *Wolz—Leben und Verklarung eines deutschen Anarchisten* (*Wolz—The Life and work of a German Anarchist*), 1975.

Literary adaptations also became more prominent as a desirable form, since filming appropriate literary works often promised, though didn't always deliver, a good film. Wolf's *Goya* was a success, as was Egon Günther's adaptation of Goethe's *Die Leiden des jungen Werthers* (*The Sorrows of Young Werther*), 1976, while Kühn's *Die Wahlverwandtschaften* (*Elective Affinities*), 1974, another adaptation of Goethe, was less effective. Other adaptation films include Günther's *Junge Frau von 1914* (*A Young Woman of 1914*), 1970, based on a work by Arnold Zweig; Kirsten's *Die Elixiere des Teufels*, 1974, adapted from a work by E. T. A. Hoffman; Günther's *Lotte in Weimar*, 1975, after a novel by Thomas Mann; and Horst Seemann's *Levin's Mühle* (*Levin's Mill*), 1982, based on a novel by Bobrowski.

Literature also led to the realm of fantasy, as it did in Jürgen Brauer's adaptation of Bettina von Arnim in *Gritta vom Rattenschloss* (*Gritta of the Castle of Rats*), 1986, derived from the tradition of children's films begun with films like Staudte's *Die Geschichte vom kleinen Muck* (*Little Mook*), 1953. The seventies and eighties urge toward the fantastical represents, however, a newer phase in East German film art, where the fantastic is finally seen as a metaphorical possibility in the illustration of ideological truths. Though these films like Günter Reisch's *Anton der Zauberer* (*Anton the Magician*), 1977, and Erwin Stranka's *Der kleine Zauberer und die grosse Fünf* (*The Little Magician and the Bad Mark*), 1977, most often appealed to children, they still drew large audiences. Closer to pure entertainment also were the several musicals, operettas, and ballets produced during the past two decades, including Horst Bonnet's *Orpheus in der Unterwelt* (*Orfeus in the Underworld*), 1974; Karl Heymann's *May I Call You Petrushka?*, 1980, a ballet film; and the musical *Zille und ich* (*Zillie and Me*), 1984.

Even within the norms of East Germany's anti-fascist, socialist contemporary, and other sub-genres, several excellent films stood out in the seventies and eighties. Frank Beyer's 1975 film, *Jakob der Lügner* (*Jacob the Liar*) was nominated for an Oscar for the Best Foreign Picture. A much better-than-average anti-fascist film, *Jakob der Lügner* focuses on a character in a Jewish ghetto in Poland who pretends he has a contraband radio. Both comic and poignant, Beyer's film manages, through honest writing and excellent acting, to merge the best possibilities of socialist realist filmmaking. Another popular film was Konrad Wolf and Wolfgang Kohlhaase's film, *Solo Sunny*, 1979. Starring Renate Krössner, the film traces the career of a factory worker who becomes a successful pop singer, studying the tensions among individual ambition, group success, artistic freedom, and the emergence of decadent Western culture in the center of East Germany.

In the almost fifty years of its existence DEFA created a new film tradition that reflected the tenets of socialism as it developed in East Germany. The links to political ideology both helped the film industry establish itself, and hindered it from ever creating a widely varied, artistically interesting body of films. Though East Germany might boast a number of competent filmmakers, only a very few—like Konrad Wolf—stand out as directors whose vision could transform even the strict dictates of committee-run production. As Liehm and Liehm point out at the end of their study of East German film, the seventies promised "no change at all" (368). Their prediction proved to be true as the films of the seventies and eighties merely retraced the line settled upon in the late sixties. The events of 1989–1990 ended the independent tradition of East German cinema as the two Germanies merged. What will remain of East Germany's socialist realist tradition is difficult to determine, but it is most likely that emergence into the greater Western European market will force more competitive and less doctrinarian cinematic practices. Perhaps the best aspects of a socially responsible film tradition will not be lost, but will in a more open environment finally come to fruition.

BIBLIOGRAPHY

Bawden, Liz-Anne, ed. *The Oxford Companion to Film*. New York: Oxford University Press, 1976.
Bergan, Ronald, and Robyn Karney, ed. *The Holt Foreign Film Guide*. New York: Henry Holt, 1988.
Boussinot, Roger, ed. *L'Encyclopédie du cinéma*. Paris: Bordas, 1989.
Cowie, Peter, ed. *International Film Guide*. London: Tantivy, 1970–1989.
DEFA. *Film und fernsehkunst der DDR*. Berlin: Henschelverlag, 1979.
Ellis, Jack. *A History of Film*. Englewood Cliffs, N.J.: Prentice-Hall, 1979.
Hibbin, Nina. *Eastern Europe: An Illustrated Guide*. New York: A. S. Barnes, 1969.
Katz, Ephraim, ed. *The Film Encyclopedia*. New York: Crowell, 1979.
Leonhard, Sigrun. "Testing the Borders: East German Film between Individualism and Social Commitment." Daniel Goulding, ed. *Post New Wave Cinema in the Soviet Union and Eastern Europe*. Bloomington: Indiana University Press, (1989): 51–101.
Liehm, Mira, and Antonin Liehm. *The Most Important Art: Eastern European Film After 1945*. Berkeley: University of California Press, 1977.
Lyon, Christopher, ed. *The International Directory of Films and Filmmakers. Vol. II, Directors/Filmmakers*. Chicago: MacMillan, 1984.
Magill, Frank, ed. *Magill's Survey of Cinema, Foreign Language Films*. Englewood Cliffs, N.J.: Salem Press, 1985.
Manvell, Roger, and Heinrich Fraenkel. *The German Cinema*. New York: Praeger, 1971.
Manvell, Roger, ed. *International Encyclopedia of Film*. New York: Crown, 1972.
Sadoul, Georges. *Dictionary of Film Makers*. Berkeley: University of California Press, 1972.
Slide, Anthony, ed. *The International Film Industry: A Historical Dictionary*. New York: Greenwood, 1989.
Stoil, Michael Jon. *Cinema Beyond the Danube: The Camera and Politics*. Metuchen, N.J.: Scarecrow, 1974.
Whyte, Alistair. *New Cinema in Eastern Europe*. London: Dutton, 1971.

BIOGRAPHICAL SKETCHES

BEYER, FRANK (1932–   ). Beyer studied drama in Berlin, then attended film school in Prague, graduating in 1957. He worked as assistant director under Kurt Maetzig, then began a dual career as film and theater director. Beyer began to direct his own films in 1957, became Director of Staatstheater in Dresden in 1966, and at the same time became involved in television production. His films include *Zwei Mütter (Two Mothers)*,* 1957; *Eine alte Liebe (An Old Love)*,* 1959; *Fünf Patronenhülsen (Five Cartridges)*,* 1960; *Königskinder* (Invincible Love),* 1962; *Nackt unter Wölfen (Naked Among Wolves)*,* 1962; *Karbid und Sauerampfer*,* 1963; *Spur der Steine (Track of Stones)*,* 1965; *Jakob der Lügner (Jacob the Liar)*,* 1974, nominated for an Oscar; *Der Auftenhalt (The Turning Point)*,* 1983; and *Bockshorn** (1984).

CAROW, HEINER (1929–   ). After working in youth theater, Carow studied directing at the DEFA Training studio. Working first at Popular Science Studios, Carow soon became a feature director, making *Sheriff Teddy*,* 1957; *Das Leben beginnt (Life Begins)*,* 1959; *Sie nannten ihn amigo (They Called Him Amigo)*,* 1959; *The Länneken Wedding*,* 1963; *Die Reise nach Sundevit (The Trip to Sundevit)*,* 1966; *The Russians Are Coming*,* 1967; *Die Legende von Paul und Paula (The Legend of Paul and Paula)*,* 1973; *Bis dass der Tod euch scheidet ('Til Death Do Us Part)*,* 1986.

DUDOW, SLATAN (1903–1963). Born in Zaribrod, Bulgaria, the son of a railway worker, Slatan Dudow went to Berlin in 1922 to study architecture. Becoming interested in theater and politics, Dudow switched from architecture to the dramatic school of Emanuel Reicher in 1923, and then in 1925 to the Institute of Theatrical Studies in Berlin. A part of the progressive worker's culture alive before the reign of Hitler, Dudow organized a workers' theater. In 1929 he visited the Soviet Union where he met director Sergei Eisenstein and became familiar with Eisenstein's theories of montage. Returning to Germany, he collaborated with Bertolt Brecht, directing the short *Seifenblasen (Soap Bubbles)*,

1929. While editor and assistant to documentary director Victor Blum, Dudow made his own documentary, *Wie der Berliner Arbeiter wohnt* (*How the Berlin Worker Lives*), 1930. He also continued working with Brecht, co-scripting Brecht's *Die Dreigroschenoper* (*Threepenny Opera*) and directing *Kühle Wampe*, 1932, his first and perhaps most famous film, co-written by Brecht. The controversial nature of *Kühle Wampe* caused his exile from Germany in 1934. Temporarily abandoning filmmaking, Dudow went first to Paris where he directed several Brecht plays, then to Switzerland in 1939 where he spent the years during World War II. Returning to Berlin in 1946, he again began directing and scripting films for DEFA, including *Unser Täglich Brot* (*Our Daily Bread*),* 1949, and *Stärker als die Nacht* (*Stronger than the Night*),* 1954, an anti-Nazi film. Dudow was killed in an automobile accident on August 12, 1963, while working on his last film, *Christine*. Other East German films include *Familie Benthin* (*The Benthin Family*),* 1950; *Das Beil von Wandsbek* (*The Axe of Wandsbek*),* 1951; *Frauenschicksale* (*Women's Destiny*),* 1952; *Der Hauptmann von Köln* (*The Captain of Cologne*),* 1956; and *Verwirrung der Liebe* (*Craziness of Love*),* 1959.

ENGEL, ERICH (1891–1966). Beginning his career in theater, Engel directed the first performance of the *Threepenny Opera* in 1928, worked with Max Reinhardt, and was director of the State Theater in Munich (1945). A member of the German avant-garde of the twenties and thirties, Engel moved to East Berlin as a stage director when Brecht was offered a theater there. While Engel still was not known primarily as a film director, his film *Affäre Blum* (*The Blum Affair*),* 1948, was an important work in the nascent East German cinema. He also directed *Der Biberpelz* (*Beaver Coat*),* 1949, for DEFA before returning to West Germany. His final film for DEFA was the 1958 movie *Geschwader Fledermaus* (*Fledermaus Squadron*).*

GÜNTHER, EGON (1927–). The versatile Günther, who has written four novels, has also been a teacher, scriptwriter, editor, and scholar, studying German philology and educational theory. The first to direct an East-West German co-production, Günther began his directing career with *Lot's Weib* (*Lot's Wife*),* 1962. He also directed *Wenn du gross bist, lieber Adam* (*When You Grow Up, Dear Adam*),* 1965; *Abschied* (*Farewell*),* 1968; *Junge Frau von 1914* (*A Young Woman of 1914*)* 1970; *Anlauf* (*Start*),* 1971; *Der Dritte* (*The Third One*)* 1972; *Die Schlüssel* (*The Keys*),* 1974; *Lotte in Weimar,* East-West co-production, 1975; and *Die Leiden des jungen Werthers* (*The Sorrows of Young Werther*),* 1976.

HELLBERG, MARTIN (1905–). Experienced as a stage and film actor and director, Hellberg served as professor at the DEFA film school at Potsdam and wrote a book on stage and film art. A talented director, Hellberg tried to make the most of the range of conditions imposed by state film committees. His films include *Das verurteilte Dorf (The Condemned Village)*,* 1951; *Geheimakten Solvay (The Solvay Dossier)*,* 1952; *Das kleine und das grosse Glück (Little and Big Happiness)*,* 1953; *Richter von Zalamea (The Judge of Salamea)*,* 1955; *Emilia Galotti*,* 1957; *Kapitäne bleiben an Bord (Captains Do Not Leave the Ship)*,* 1958; *Kabale und Liebe (Intrigue and Love)*,* 1959; and *Senta auf Abwegen (Senta Goes Astray)*,* 1959, before he returned to acting, performing in Egon Günther's film *Lotte in Weimar*,* 1975, among others.

KLEIN, GERHARD (1920–1970). A student of theater and cinema, Klein made short films and worked on documentaries before becoming a feature director whose films often approached excellence within the limited field of permissible East German film genres. His films include *Alarm im Zirkus (Alarm in the Circus)*,* 1955; *Eine Berliner Romanze (Berlin Romance)*,* 1956; *Berlin, Ecke Schönhauser (Berlin, Schoenhauser Corner)*,* 1957; *Der Fall Gleiwitz (The Gleiwitz Case)*,* 1961; and the screenplay for *Leichensache Zernik (The Zernik Affair)*,* 1970.

KÜHN, SIEGFRIED (1936–   ). A member of the second generation of East German film directors, Kühn made several influential films, including *Im Spannungsfeld (In the Field of Tension)*,* 1969; *Zeit der Störche (Time of the Storks)*,* 1970; *Das zweite Leben des Friedrich Wilhelm Georg Platow (The Second Life of Friedrich Wilhelm Georg Platow)*,* 1973; *Die Wahlverwandtschaften (Elective Affinities)*,* 1974; and *Childhood*,* 1987.

KUNERT, JOACHIM (1929–   ). Beginning as an assistant director, Kunert also made documentary and newreel films. He made his first feature film, *Special Peculiarities: None*,* in 1955. Other films include *It Happened in Berlin*,* 1957; *The Lottery Swede*,* 1958; *Lorenz v. Lorenz*,* 1959; *No. 8 Seiler Street*,* 1960; *The Second Track*,* 1962; *Die Abenteuer des Werner Holt (The Adventures of Werner Holt)*,* 1964; and *Die Toten bleiben jung (The Dead Stay Young)*,* 1967.

MAETZIG, KURT (1911–   ). One of the founders of DEFA, Maetzig became a photographer after studying philosophy and law. He began the Filmactiv Group that made early post-war *Augenzeuge* or "eyewitness" documentaries of the Berlin rubble. A prolific and versatile filmmaker, Maetzig has been director of the Potsdam Film School since 1955. His feature films include *Ehe im Schatten (Marriage in the Shadow)*,* 1947; *Buntkarierten (The Checkered Bedspread)*,* 1949; *Familie Benthin (The Benthin Family)*,* 1950; *Rat der Götter (Divine Councils)*,* 1950; *Roman einer Ehe (Story of a Young Couple)*,* 1951; *Ernst Thälmann—Sohn seiner Klasse (Ernst Thälmann, Son of His Class)*,* 1954; *Ernst Thälmann—Führer seiner Klasse (Ernst Thälmann, Leader of His Class)*,* 1955; *Schlösser und Katen (Palaces and Huts)*,* 1957; *Vergesst mir meine Traudel nicht (Don't Forget My Traudel)*,* 1957; *Das Lied der Matrosen (Sailors' Song)*,* 1958; *(First Spaceship on Venus)*,* 1958; *Septemberliebe (September Love)*,*

1960; *Das Kaninchen bin ich (The Rabbit Is Me)*,* 1965; *Die Fahne von Krivoy Rog (The Flag at Krivoy Rog)*,* 1967; *Girl on the Diving Board*), 1967; and *Januskopf,** 1971.

REISCH, GÜNTER (1927–   ). After being a prisoner of war in World War II, Reisch continued school, graduating from high school and helping to found the Potsdam Free German Youth. He studied at the East Berlin School of Drama and received training at the DEFA film school. He began his film career as assistant to Gerhard Lamprecht and Kurt Maetzig, and served as a member of the Party Executive office of DEFA. His films include *Das Lied der Matrosen (Sailors' Song)** with Kurt Maetzig, 1958; *Maibowle,** 1959; *Silvesterpunsch (New Year's Punch),** 1960; *Solange Leben in mir ist (So Long As I Live),** 1965; *Unterwegs zu Lenin (On the Way to Lenin),** 1970; *Trotz Alledam (In Spite of It All),** 1971; *Wolz,** 1975; *Anton der Zauberer (Anton the Magician),** 1977; and *Die Verlobte (The Fiancée),** 1982.

RÜCKER, GÜNTHER (1924–   ). Educated at the Music Academy in Leipzig, Rücker became a radio producer and playwright. He colloborated with the Thorndikes, scripting many of their documentaries, including *Du und mancher Kamerad (The German Story/You and Other Comrades),** 1956; *Urlaub auf Sylt (Holiday on Sylt),** 1957; *Unternehmen Teutonenschwert (Operation Teutonic Sword),** 1958; and *Das Russische Wunder (The Russian Miracle),** 1963. He also scripted feature films such as *Der Fall Gleiwitz (The Gleiwitz Case),** 1961; *Wolz,** 1975; and directed two excellent films, *Die besten Jahre (The Best Years),** 1965; and *Die Verlobte (The Fiancée),** 1982, with Günter Reisch.

SEEMANN, HORST (1937–   ). After studying film direction at the DEFA film school in Potsdam and serving in the army, Seemann began directing feature films. His works include *Zeit zum leben (The Time for Life),** 1969; *Reife Kirschen (Ripe Cherries),** 1972; *Beethoven—Tage aus einem Leben (Beethoven—Days from a Life),** 1976; *Levin's Mühle (Levin's Mill),** 1982; *Hotel Polan und seine Gäste (The Polan Hotel and its Guests),** 1982; and *Arztinnen (Lady Doctors),** 1984.

STAUDTE, WOLFGANG (1906–   ). Born in Saarbrücken, Germany, Staudte began his career by following in the footsteps of his father, a stage and screen director. Staudte studied theater at the Technical Institute, Oldenburg, worked as a member of the Berlin leftist workers' theater, Volksbühne, and was a stage actor for both Max Reinhardt and Erwin Piscator in the 1920s. His career in film began with film acting in 1931, after which he began to script and direct commercials and shorts. He directed his first feature film, *Akrobat schö-ö-ön (Beauti-i-ful Acrobat)*, released in 1943, after having been selected in a competition for promising young directors by the Tobis firm. He made two other light comedies before the end of the war and began his practice of writing his own film scripts. As one of the only directors left in Berlin after the war, Staudte made his most famous film, *Die Mörder sind unter uns* (*The Murderers Are Among Us*),* 1946. The first film produced by the newly formed DEFA, *Die Mörder* was praised as a penetrating "Trümmerfilme" or "rubble film" in which Staudte combined expressionist elements with documentary realism in a bitter denunciation of the Nazis and an insightful exploration of post-war conditions. Though he was given more license by DEFA than other directors, tensions with the production company forced him to move to West Berlin in 1955, where he continued to direct films. A political artist who combined social commitment and satire with documentary realism, Staudte was considered a successor to Lang and Pabst. Other films Staudte made in East Germany include *Die Seltsamen Abenteuer des (Herrn) Fridolin B.* (*The Strange Adventures of Herr Fridolin B*),* 1948; *Rotation,** 1949; *Der Untertan* (*The Kaiser's Lackey [The Underdog] [The Submissive]*),* 1951; *Die Geschichte des kleinen Muck* (*Little Mook*),* 1953; and *Leuchtfeuer* (*Beacon*),* 1954.

THORNDIKE, ANDREW (1909–   ). Beginning in the advertising department of UFA making industrial shorts, Andrew Thorndike became the leading East German documentarist. Accused of subverting troops and other anti-fascist activities during World War II, Thorndike was sent to the Russian front, where he became a prisoner of war for four years in the USSR. In 1948 he began making newsreels and documentaries for DEFA, composing his first compilation documentary *Wilhelm Pieck* (1951). Known for his polemical style, Thorndike, since 1951 with his wife, Annelie, made a number of documentaries, and documentary series, such as the *Aus unseren Tagen* (*From Our Times*) and *The Archives Testify* series. His films include *Der 13. Oktober* (*The 13th October*),* 1949; *Von Hamburg bis Stralsund* (*From Hamburg to Stralsund*)* in the *Aus unseren Tagen* series, 1949; *Der Weg nach oben* (*The Way Up*),* 1950; *Freundschaft Siegt* (*Friendship Wins*),* 1951; *Wilhelm Pieck—das Leben unseres Präsidenten* (*Wilhelm Pieck—The Life of Our President*),* 1951; *Die Prüfung* (*The Examination*),* 1952; *Sieben vom Rhein* (*Seven from the Rhine*),* 1954; *Du und mancher Kamerad . . .* (*The German Story/You and Other Comrades*),* 1956; *Urlaub auf Sylt* (*Holiday on Sylt*)* in *The Archives Testify* series, 1957; *Unternehmen Teutonenschwert* (*Operation Teutonic Sword*)* in *The Archives Testify* series, 1958; *Das Russische Wunder* (*The Russian Miracle*), two parts, 1963; *Tito in Deutschland* (*Life in Germany*),* 1965; and *Du bist mein, ein Deutsches Tagesbuch* (*You Are Mine, A German Diary*),* 1969.

WARNEKE, LOTHAR. After studying evangelical theology and working in the textile industry, Warneke studied at the Potsdam Film School in the early 1960s. He became an assistant feature director, then graduated to features with such films as *Dr. Med Sommer II,** 1970; *Es ist eine alte Geschichte* (*It Is an Old Story*),* 1972; *Leben mit Uwe* (*Life with Uwe*),* 1974; *Die Unverbesserliche Barbara* (*Incorrigible Barbara*),* 1977; *Unser Kurzes Leben* (*Our Short Life*)*

1980; *Apprehension,** 1983; *Eine sonderbare Liebe (A Strange Love Affair),** 1984; and *Bear Ye One Another's Burdens,** 1984.

WOLF, KONRAD (1925–1982). Son of dramatist Friedrich Wolf, Konrad Wolf was born in Hechingen, Germany. He moved to Moscow in 1933 after the Nazis took over Germany and in 1945, after service in the Red Army, he returned to Berlin, where he helped found *Berliner Zeitung* for which he was a reporter and worked at the House of Soviet Culture until 1949. From 1949 to 1954, he studied film at the VGIK Institute of Cinematography in Moscow, where he studied with Grogori Alexandrov, Sergei Gerasimov, and acted as an assistant director for Kurt Maetzig and Joris Ivans. Returning to Germany, he made his first feature film for DEFA, *Einmal ist keinmal (Once is Nonce),** 1955. Often collaborating with Wolfgang Kohlhaase, Wolf made a series of films before serving as the president of the Academy of the Arts of GDR from 1965. In 1959, Wolf's film *Sterne (Stars)** won Special Jury Prize at Cannes. In 1975 a special Wolf retrospective was held in Moscow. Considered a skilled filmmaker, Wolf was concerned with the political role of the artist in society as is reflected in such films as *Goya,* 1971, and the more introspective *Ich war neunzehn (I Was Nineteen),** 1968. Other films include *Genesung (Recovery),** 1955; *Die Sonnensucher (The Sun Seekers),** 1957; *Leute mit Flügeln (People With Wings),** 1960; *Professor Mamlock,** 1961; *Der Geteilte Himmel (The Divided Sky),** 1964; *Der nackte Mann auf dem Sportplatz (The Naked Man on the Athletic Field),** 1974; *Mama, ich lebe (Mum, I'm Alive),** 1977; and *Solo Sunny,** 1979.

SELECTED FILMOGRAPHY

1946

Berlin im Aufbau (Berlin Under Construction). d. Kurt Maetzig;* sw. Marion Keller; c. Harry Bremer, Otto Baeker, Erich Nitzschmann, Heinz Jaworsky, Walter Fehdmer, Kurt Krigar, Herbert Körner, C. Schlawe, and Alfred Westphal.

Die Mörder sind unter uns (The Murderers Are Among Us). d. Wolfgang Staudte;* sw. Staudte; c. Friedl Behn-Grund, and Eugen Klagemann; m. Ernst Roters; with Hildegard Neff, Ernst Wilhelm Borchert, and Arno Paulsen. First feature made in Germany after World War II.

Freies Land (Free Land). d. Milo Harbich; sw. Harbich and Kurt Hahne; c. Otto Baecker, with Ursula Voss, Fritz Wagner, and Herbert Wilk.

Irgendwo in Berlin (Somewhere in Berlin). d. Gerhard Lamprecht; sw. Lamprecht; c. Werner Krien; with Harry Hindemith, Hedda Sarnow, and Paul Bildt.

1947

Ehe im Schatten (Marriage in the Shadow). d. and sw. Maetzig;* c. Friedl Behn-Grund and Eugen Klagemann; with Paul Klinger and Ilse Steppat.

Razzia (Round-Up). d. Werner Klingler.

Wozzeck. d. Georg Klaren; au. Büchner; with Kurt Meisel.

1948

Affäre Blum (The Blum Affair). d. Erich Engel;* sw. Robert Stemmle; c. Friedl Behn-Grund, and Karl Plintzner; with Kurt Erhardt, and Karin Evans.

Die seltsamen Abenteuer des (Herrn) Fridolin B. *(The Strange Adventures of Herr Fridolin B);* d. and sw. Staudte.*

Träum nicht, Annette (Don't Dream Annette).

1949

Buntkarierten (The Checkered Bedspread [Life in the Ticking]). d. Maetzig;* sw. Berta Waterstradt; c. Friedl Behn-Grund and Karl Plintzner; with Camilla Spira and Werner Hinz.

EAST GERMANY

Das Mädchen Christine (*The Girl Christine*). d. Arthur Rabenalt.
Der Auftrag Höglers (*By Mandate of Högler*). d. Gustav von Wagenheim.
Der Biberpelz (*Beaver Coat*). d. Engel;* au. Gerhardt Hauptmann.
Der 13. Oktober (*The 13th October*). d. and sw. Andrew Thorndike;* c. Werner Bergmann and Kurt Stanke.
Figaros Hochzeit (*The Marriage of Figaro*).
Rotation. d. Staudte;* sw. Staudte and Erwin Klein; c. Bruno Mondi; with Paul Esser and Irene Korb.
Semmelweis—Retter der Mütter (*Semmelweis—Savior of Mothers*). d. Georg Klaren.
Unser täglich Brot (*Our Daily Bread*). d. Dudow;* sw. Dudow, Hans Joachim Beyer, and Ludwig Turek; c. Robert Baberske; with Paul Bildt and Viktoria von Ballasko; m. Kurt Eisler.
Von Hamburg bis Stralsund (*From Hamburg to Stralsund*). d. Andrew Thorndike* (in *Aus Unseren Tagen* series).

1950

Das kalte Herz (*The Cold Heart*). d. Paul Verhoeven.
Der Weg nach oben (*The Way Up*). d. Andrew Thorndike.*
Familie Benthin (*The Benthin Family*). co-d. Dudow* and Maetzig;* sw. Dudow; c. Karl Plintzner.
Kein Platz für Liebe (*No Place for Love*). d. Hans Deppe.
Rat der Götter (*Divine Councils*); [*Council of the Gods*] d. Maetzig;* sw. Friedrich Wolf, and Philipp Gecht; c. Friedl Behn-Grund; with Paul Bildt and Fritz Tillmann.
Sonnenbrucks. d. Georg Klaren.

1951

Das Beil von Wandsbek (*The Axe of Wandsbek*). d. Dudow* and Falk Harnack; co-sw. Staudte;* au. Arnold Zweig. Not shown until 1962.
Das verurteilte Dorf (*The Condemned Village*). d. Hellberg;* sw. Jeanne and Kurt Stern.
Die Meere rufen (*The Oceans Are Calling*). d. Eduard Kubat.
Der Untertan (*The Kaiser's Lackey* [*The Underdog*] [*The Submissive*]). d. Staudte;* sw. Staudte and Fritz Staudte; au. Heinrich Mann; c. Robert Baberske; with Werner Peters, and Paul Esser.
Freundschaft siegt (*Friendship Wins*). d. Andrew Thorndike.*
Roman einer Ehe (*Story of a Young Couple*). d. Maetzig.*
Wilhelm Pieck—das Leben unseres Präsidenten (*Wilhelm Pieck—The Life of Our President*). d. Andrew Thorndike.*

1952

Die Prüfung (*The Examination*). d. Andrew Thorndike.*
Frauenschicksale (*Women's Destiny* [*Fates of Women*]). d. Dudow;* sw. Dudow, Ursula Rumin, and Gerhard Bengsch; c. Robert Baberske and Hans Hauptmann; with Sonja Sutter, Lotte Loebinger, and Anneliese Book.
Geheimakten Solvay (*The Solvay Dossier*). d. Hellberg.*
Schatten über Inseln (*Shadows Over Islands*). d. Otto Meyer.

1953

Das kleine und das grosse Glück (Little and Big Happiness). d. Hellberg;* sw. Paul Wiens.
Die gefährliche Fracht (Dangerous Load). d. Gustav von Wagenheim.
Die Geschichte vom kleinen Muck (Little Mook). d. Staudte;* co-sw. Staudte.
Die Unbesiegbaren (The Undefeatable). d. Arthur Pohl.
Einmal ist keinmal (Once is Nonce). d. Wolf.* Debut film with DEFA.

1954

Ernst Thälmann—Sohn seiner Klasse (Ernst Thälmann, Son of his Class) (Part One). d. Maetzig;* sw. Willi Bredel, Michael Tschesno-Hell, and Maetzig; c. Karl Plintzner; with Günther Simon and Hans-Peter Minetti.
Leuchtfeuer (Beacon). d. Staudte;* co-sw. Staudte.
Rauschende Melodien (Swelling Melodies). d. E. W. Fiedler; m. Strauss.
Sieben vom Rhein (Seven from the Rhine). d. Andrew Thorndike.*
Stärker als die Nacht (Stronger Than the Night). d. Dudow;* sw. Jeanne Stern and Kurt Stern; c. Karl Plintzner, and Horst Brandt; with Wilhelm Koch-Hooge and Helga Göring.

1955

Alarm in Zirkus (Alarm in the Circus). d. Gerhard Klein;* sw. Wolfgang Kohlhaase and Hans Kubisch; c. Werner Bergmann; with Erwin Geschonneck and Uwe-Jens Pape.
Ernst Thälmann—Führer seiner Klasse (Ernst Thälmann, Leader of His Class) (Part Two). d. Maetzig;* sw. Willi Bredel, Michael Tschesno-Hell, and Maetzig; c. Karl Plintzner and Horst Brandt; with Günther Simon, and Hans-Peter Minetti.
Richter von Zalamea (The Judge of Salamea). d. Hellberg;* au. Calderon.
Special Peculiarities: None. d. Kunert.*
Wer seine Frau lieb hat (Whoever Loves His Wife). d. Kurt Jung-Alsen.

1956

Der Hauptmann von Köln (The Captain of Cologne). d. Dudow;* sw. Dudow, Henryk Keisch, and Michael Tschesno-Hell; c. Werner Bergmann; with Rolf Ludwig, Erwin Geschonneck, and Else Wolz.
Du und mancher Kamerad (The German Story/You and Other Comrades). d. Andrew Thorndike* and Annelie Thorndike; sw. Karl-Eduard von Schnitzler, Annelie Thorndike, Andrew Thorndike, and Günther Rücker; c. Kurt Stanke, Waldemar Ruge, Walter Fuchs, Joachim Lubnau, Ernst Kunstmann, Vera Kunstmann, Rudolf Ehrlich, and Harry Kadoch.
Eine Berliner Romanze (Berlin Romance). d. Gerhard Klein;* sw. Wolfgang Kohlhaase; c. Wolf Göthe; with Annekathrin Bürger, and Ulrich Thein.
Genesung (Recovery). d. Wolf;* sw. and au. Karl-Georg Egel and Paul Wiens.
The Benderath Incident. d. Janos Veiczi.
Zar und Zimmermann (Tsar and Carpenter). d. Hans Müller.

1957

Berlin, Ecke Schönhauser (Berlin, Schoenhauser Corner). d. Klein;* with Ekkehard Schall and Gerhard Rachold.
Betrogen bis zum Jüngsten Tag (Duped till Doomsday). d. Kurt Jung-Alsen; sw. Kurt Bortfeldt; au. Franz Fühmann; c. Walter Fehdmer; with Rudolf Ulrich and Wolfgang Kieling.
Die Abenteuer des Till Ulenspiegel (The Adventures of Till Ulenspiegel). d. Gérard Philippe. Product of international cooperation.
Emilia Galotti. d. Hellberg;* au. Lessing.
It Happened in Berlin. d. Kunert.*
Lissy. d. Wolf;* co-sw. Wolf.
Schlösser und Katen (Palaces and Huts [Castles and Cottages]). d. Maetzig;* sw. Kuba & Maetzig; c. Otto Merz; with Raimund Schlcher, Erika Dunkelmann, & Erwin Geschonneck.
Sheriff Teddy. d. Carow.*
Urlaub auf Sylt (Holiday on Sylt). d. Annelie Thorndike & Andrew Thorndike;* sw. Thorndike, Thorndike, & Günter Rücker;* c. Archivmaterial, Walter Fuchs.
Vergesst mir meine Traudel nicht (Don't Forget My Traudel). d. Maetzig.*
Zwei Mütter (Two Mothers). d. Beyer.*

1958

Das Lied der Matrosen (Sailors' Song). d. Maetzig* & Günter Reisch.*
Die Elenden (Les Misérables). d. Jean-Paul Le Chanois; au. V. Hugo. Product of international cooperation.
Die Hexen von Salem (The Crucible). d. Raymond Rouleau; au. Arthur Miller. Product of international cooperation.
First Spaceship on Venus. d. Maetzig.* Polish and East German collaboration. Science fiction.
Geschwader Fledermaus (Fledermaus Squadron). d. Engel.*
Kapitäne bleiben an Bord (Captains Do Not Leave the Ship). d. Hellberg.*
The Lottery Swede. d. Kunert.*
Unternehmen Teutonenschwert (Operation Teutonic Sword). d. Andrew Thorndike; sw. Rücker.* (In *The Archives Testify* series.)

1959

Das Leben beginnt (Life Begins). d. Carow.*
Die Sonnensucher (The Sun Seekers). d. Wolf;* sw. Karl Georg Egel & Paul Wiens; c. Werner Bergmann; with Ulrike Germer, Günther Simon, & Erwin Geschonneck. Made in 1957, release delayed two years, then banned and not screened until 1972.
Eine alte Liebe (An Old Love). d. Beyer;* sw. Werner Reinowski & Beyer; c. Günter Marczinkowski; with Gisela May & Erich Franz.
Kabale und Liebe (Intrigue and Love). d. Hellberg;* au. Schiller.
Lorenz v. Lorenz. d. Kunert.*
Maibowle. d. Reisch.*
Reportage 1957. d. Janos Veiczi.

Sie nannten ihn amigo (They Called Him Amigo). d. Carow;* sw. Wera and Claus Küchenmeister & Carow; c. Helmut Bergmann; with Ernst-Georg Schwill, Erich Franz, & Fred Düren.
Senta auf Abwegen (Senta Goes Astray). d. Hellberg.*
Sterne (Stars). d. Wolf* & Rangel Vulchanov; sw. Angel Wagenstein; c. Werner Bergmann; with Sasha Kruscharska & Jürgen Frohriep. Product of cooperation with Bulgaria. Wolf received first Jury Prize, Cannes, 1959.
Verwirrung der Liebe (Craziness of Love). d. Dudow;* sw. Dudow; c. Helmut Bergmann; with Annekathrin Bürger & Angelica Domröse.

1960

Die heute über vierzig sind (Those Over Forty Today). d. Kurt Jung-Alsen.
Fünf Patronenhülsen (Five Cartridges). d. Beyer;* sw. Walter Gorrish; c. Günter Marczinowski; with Erwin Geschonneck & Ulrich Thein.
Leute mit Flügeln (People With Wings). d. Wolf.*
No. 8 Seiler Street. d. Kunert.*
Septemberliebe (September Love). d. Maetzig.*
Silvesterpunsch (New Year's Punch). d. Reisch.*
Step by Step. d. Janos Veiczi.

1961

Auf der Sonnenseite. d. Ralf Kirsten; sw. Heinz Kahlau, Gisela Steineckert, & Kirsten; c. Hans Heinrich; with Manfred Krug & Marita Böhme.
Der Fall Gleiwitz (The Gleiwitz Case). d. Klein;* sw. Rücker;* c. Jan Curik.
Professor Mamlock. d. Wolf;* co-sw. Wolf.

1962

Nackt unter Wölfen (Naked Among Wolves). d. Beyer;* sw. Bruno Apitz & Beyer; c. Günther Marczinowski; with Erwin Geschonneck & Gerry Wolff.
Königskinder (Invincible Love). d. Beyer.*
The Second Track. d. Kunert.*
Une deine Liebe auch (And Your Love Too). d. Frank Vogel.

1963

Beschreibung eines Sommers (Description of a Summer). d. & au. Karl-Heinz Jakob.
Das Russische Wunder (The Russian Miracle); d. Thorndike,* Annelie Thorndike; sw. Thorndike, Thorndike, & Rücker;* c. Sergej Kisseljow, Wladimir Kopalin, Wolfgang Randel, Alexander Kotschetow, & Peter Süring. (In *The Archives Testify* series.)
Streng geheim (Top Secret). d. Janos Veiczi; sw. Harry Thürk & Veiczi; c. Karl Plintzner; with Alfred Müller & Helmut Schreiber.
Julia lebt (Julia Lives). d. Frank Vogel; sw. Manfred Freitag & Joachim Nestler.
Karbid und Sauerampfer (Guns and Sorrell). d. Beyer;* sw. Hans Oliva & Beyer. c. Günter Marczinkowski; with Erwin Geschonneck & Marita Böhme.
The Länneken Wedding. d. Carow.*

Der geteilte Himmel (The Divided Sky). d. Wolf;* sw. Christa & Gerhard Wolf, Konrad Wolf, Willi Brückner, & Kurt Bartel; au. Christa Wolf; c. Werner Bergmann; with Renate Blume & Eberhard Esche.
Die Abenteuer des Werner Holt (The Adventures of Werner Holt). d. Kunert;* sw. Joachim Kunert & Claus Kuechenmeister; au. Dieter Noll; c. Rolf Sohre; with Klause-Peter Thiele, Arno Wyzniewski, Manfred Karge, & Günter Junghans.
Lots Weib (Lot's Wife). d. Günther;* sw. Günther & Helga Schütz; c. Otto Merz; with Marita Böhme, Günther Simon, & Gerry Wolff.
O.K. d. Walter Heynowski.

1965

Das Kaninchen bin ich (The Rabbit Is Me). d. Maetzig;* au. Manfred Bieler.
Der Frühling braucht Zeit (Spring Needs Time). d. Günther Stahnke; sw. Stahnke & Konrad Schwalbe. Banned.
Denk bloss nicht, ich heule (Just Don't Think I'm Crying). d. Frank Vogel; sw. Manfred Freitag & Joachim Nestler. Banned.
Die besten Jahre (The Best Years). d. Rücker;* sw. Rücker & Peter Krause; c. Peter Krause; with Horst Drinda, Rolf Hoppe, & Harry Hindemith.
Die Söhne der grossen Bärin (Sons of the Great Bear). d. Josef Mach.
Fräulein Schmetterling (Miss Butterfly). d. Kurt Barthel; sw. & au. Christa Wolf. Banned.
Karla. d. Herman Zschoche; sw. Ulrich Plenzdorf.
Solange Leben in mir ist (So Long As I Live). d. Reisch.*
Spur der Steine (Track of Stones). d. Beyer;* au. Erich Neutsch. Banned after three days.
Tito in Deutschland (Life in Germany); in two parts. d. Andrew Thorndike.*
Wenn du gross bist, lieber Adam (When You Grow Up, Dear Adam). d. Günther.* Banned.

1966

Die Reise nach Sundevit (The Trip to Sundevit). d. Carow.*
Mir nach Canaillen! (Follow Me, Mob!). d. Ralf Kirsten.

1967

Der lachende Mann (The Laughing Man). d. Walter Heynowski & Gerhard Scheumann; c. Peter Hellmich; sw. (English) John Peet & Stanley Forman.
Die Fahne von Krivoy Rog (The Flag at Krivoy Rog). d. Maetzig.*
Die gofrorenen Blitze (Frozen Lightening). d. Janos Veiczi; sw. Harry Thürk & Veiczi; c. Günter Haubold; with Alfred Müller, Leon Niemczyk, & Dietrich Körner.
Die Toten bleiben jung (The Dead Stay Young). d. Kunert;* au. Anna Seghers.
Girl on the Diving Board; d. Maetzig.*
Ich war neunzehn (I Was Nineteen). d. Wolf;* sw. Wolf & Wolfgang Kohlhaase; c. Werner Bergmann; with Jaecki Schwarz, Wassili Liwanow, Rolf Hoppe, Alexei Ejboshenko, Galina Polskich, & Jenny Gröllmann.
My Friend Sybille. d. Wolfgang Luderer.
Stories of that Night.
The Valley of the Seven Moons. d. Gottfried Kolditz.
The Corporal's Gun. d. Rolf Losansky.

The Russians Are Coming. d. Carow;* sw. Carow & Claus Küchenmeister.
Hochzeits Nacht im Regen (Wedding-Night in the Rain). d. Horst Seemann.*

1968

Abschied (Farewell). d. Günther;* sw. Günther & Günter Kunert; au. Johannes Becher; c. Günter Marczinkowski; with Rolf Ludwig & Katharina Lind.
Das siebente Jahr (Seventh Year). d. Frank Vogel.
Piloten im Pyjama (Pilots in Pajamas). d. Walter Haynowski & Gerhard Scheumann.
Spur des Falken (Clue of the Falcon). d. Josef Mach.

1969

Du bist mein, ein Deutsches Tagesbuch (You Are Mine, A German Diary). d. Andrew Thorndike.*
Feine Spielwaren—Made in USA (Superior Toys—Made in the USA). d. Günter Raetz.
Im Spannungsfeld (In the Field of Tension). d. Kühn.*
Netzwerk. d. Ralf Kirsten; sw. Kirsten; c. Claus Neumann; with Alfred Müller, Jutta Wachowiak & Manfred Krug.
Tödlicher Irrtum (Fatal Error). d. Josef Mach.
Weisse Wölfe (White Wolves). d. Josef Mach.
Zeit zum Leben (The Time for Life). d. Seemann.*

1970

Dr. Med. Sommer II. d. Warneke;* sw. Hannes Hütter & Warneke; c. Roland Gräf, with Werner Tietze & Juliane Koren.
Junge Frau von 1914 (A Young Woman of 1914). d. Günther;* au. Arnold Zweig.
Leichensache Zernik (The Zernik Affair). d. Helmut Nitzschke; sw. Gerhard Klein,* W. Kohlhaase, J. Plötner & H. Nitzschke; c. Claus Neumann; with Alexander Lang & Gert Gütschow.
Unterwegs zu Lenin (On the Way to Lenin). d. Reisch;* sw. Helmuit Baierl & Jewgeni Gabrilowitsch; au. Kurella; c. Jïgen Brauer & Waleri Wladimirow; with Gottfried Richter & Michail Uljanow.
Zeit der Stuörche (Time of the Storks). d. Kühn.*

1971

Anlauf (Start). d. Günther.*
Eolomea. d. Hermann Zschoches; sw. Angel Wagenstein; c. Gñter Jaeuthe; with Wsewolod Sanajew & Cox Habbema.
Goya. d. Wolf;* co-p. GDR/USA or DEFA/Lenfilm; sw. Angel Wagenstein; au. Lion Feuchtwanger; c. Werner Bergmann & Konstantin Ryshow; with Donatas Banionis & Olivera Katerina.
Hut ab, wenn du Küsst (Take Care When You Kiss). d. Rolf Losansky; sw. Maurycy Janowski; c. Wolfgang Braumann; with Angelika Waller & Alexander Lang.
Januskopf (Janus's Head). d. Maetzig;* sw. Hans-Albert Pederzani & Helfried Schreiter; c. Werner Bergmann & Jürgen Brauer; with Horst Schulze & Ludmilla Kasjanowa.

Käsebier oder die gestohlene Schlacht (*Cheese Beer or the Stolen Battle*). d. Erwin Stranka; p. DEFA/Filmstudio Barrandov (Prague); sw. Stranka; c. Otto Hanisch; with Manfred Krug & Herwart Grosse.

Laut und leise ist die Liebe (*Loud and Soft Is Love*). d. Helmut Dzuiba; sw. Wolfgang Ebeling & Dzuiba; c. Hans-Jürgen Sasse; with Margot Busse & Werner Tietze.

Lützower. d. Werner Wallroth; sw. Wallroth; c. Hans-Jürgen Kruse; with Jürgen Reuter & Herta Knoll.

Männer ohne Bart (*Men Without Beards*). d. Rainer Simon; sw. Inge Wüste & Simon; au. Uwe Kant; c. Claus Neumann; with Hermann Beyer & Manfred Böhme.

Mein lieber Robinson (*My Dear Robinson*). d. Roland Gräf; sw. Gräf & Klaus Poche; c. Gräf; with Jan Bereska & Gabriele Simon.

Schwarzer Zwieback (*Black Zwieback*). d. Herbert Rappaports; sw. Michail Blejman, Edith Gorrish, & Rappaport; au. J. Drabkina; c. Eduard Rosowski & Rolf Schrade; with Natalja Warlej & Rüdiger Joswig.

Trotz alledem (*In Spite of It All*). d. Reisch;* sw. Michael Tschesno-Hell; c. Jürgen Brauer; with Horst Schulze & Ludmilla Kasjanowa.

1972

Der Dritte (*The Third One*). d. Günther;* sw. Egon Panitz; c. Erich Gusko; with Jutta Hoffmann, Barbara Dittus, & Rolf Ludwig.

Der Mann, der nach der oma kam (*The Man Who Came After the Grandmother*). d. Roland Oehme; sw. Oehme, Maurycy Janowski, & Lothar Kusche; au. Renate Holland-Moritz; c. Wolfgang Braumann; with Winfred Glatzeder, Rolf Herricht, & Marita Böhme.

Es ist eine alte Geschichte (*It Is an Old Story*). d. Lothar Warneke; sw. Warneke & Hannes Hüttner; c. Claus Neumann; with Katharina Thalbach, Cox Habbema, Benjamin Besson, & Christian Steyer.

Reife Kirschen (*Ripe Cherries*). d. Seemann;* sw. Seemann & Manfred Richter; c. Helmut Bergmann; with Günther Simon & Helga Raumer.

1973

Das zweite Leben des Friedrich Wilhelm Georg Platow (*The Second Life of Friedrich Wilhelm Georg Platow*). d. Kühn;* sw. Helmut Baierl & Kühn; c. Roland Dressel; with Fritz Marquardt, Juergen Holtz, Gisela Hess, & Hermann Beyer.

Die Legende von Paul und Paula (*The Legend of Paul and Paula*). d. Carow;* sw. Ulrich Plenzdorf & Carow; c. Jürgen Brauer; with Angelica Domröse & Winifried Glatzeder.

1974

Apachen. d. Goddfried Kolditz; sw. Gojko Mitic & Kolditz; c. Helmut Bergmann; with Gojko Mitic & Beli; Produced by DEFA/BUFTEA (Bucharest)/MOSFILM.

Aus dem Leben eines Taugenichts (*From the Life of a Good-for-nothing*). d. Celino Bleiweiss; sw. Wera & Claus Küchenmeister; au. Joseph Freiherr von Eichendorff; c. Günter Jaeuthe; with Dean Reed & Anna Dziadyk.

Der Wüstenkönig von Brandenburg (*The Desolate King of Brandenburg*). d. Hans Kratz-

ert; sw. Dieter Schubert & Inge Wüstle; c. Wolfgang Braumann; with Klaus Winter & Hilmar Baumann.
Der nackte Mann auf dem Sportplatz (*The Naked Man on the Athletic Field*). d. Wolf;* sw. Wolf & Wolfgang Kohlhaase; c. Werner Bergmann; with Kurt Böwe & Ursula Karusseit.
Die Schlüssel (*The Keys*). d. Günther;* sw. Günther & Helga Schütz; c. Erich Gusko; with Jutta Hoffmann & Jaecki Schwarz.
Die Hosen des Ritters von Bredow (*The Pants of the Knight from Bredow*). d. Konrad Patzold; sw. Günter Kaltofen; au. Willibald Alexis; c. Hans Heinrich; with Rolf Hoppe & Lissy Tempelhof.
Die Wahlverwandtschaften (*Elective Affinities*). d. Kühn;* sw. Kühn & Regine Kühn; au. Goethe; c. Claus Neumann; with Beata Tyszkiewiecz & Hilmar Thate.
Die vereiste Brücke (*The Frozen Bridge*). d. Christo Chrisov; produced by DEFA/Studio Sofia/MOSFILM; sw. Christov & Wolfgang Ebeling; c. Atanas Tessev; with Stefan Getzov & Martin Flörchinger.
Die Elixiere des Teufels (*The Elixir of the Devil*). d. Ralf Kirsten; sw. Brigitte Kirsten; au. E. T. A. Hoffman; c. Claus Neumann; with Benjamin Besson & Jaroslava Schallerova.
Für die Liebe noch zu mager? (*Too Skinny for Love?*). d. Bernhard Stephan; sw. J. Nestler & M. Freitag; c. Hans-Juergen Kruse; with Simone v. Zglinicki & Christian Steyer.
Jakob der Lügner (*Jacob the Liar*). d. Beyer;* sw. Gerd Gericke; c. Günther Marczinkowski; with Vlastimil Brodsky, Erwin Geschonneck, & Manuela Simon. Nominated for an Academy Award for the Best Foreign Language Film.
Leben mit Uwe (*Life with Uwe*). d. Warneke;* sw. Siegfried Pitschmann & Warneke; c. Claus Neumann; with Cox Habbema & Eberhard Esche.
Nicht Schummeln, Liebling! (*Don't Cheat, Darling!*). d. Jo Hasler; sw. Hasler & Heinz Kahlow; c. Jo Hasler; with Dorit Gäbler & Karel Fiala.
Orpheus in der Unterwelt (*Orfeus in the Underworld*). d. Horst Bonnet; sw. Bonnet; au. Hector Cremieux/Jacques Offenbach; c. Otto Hanisch; with Gerry Wolff, & Dorit Gäbler.
Ritter Blaubart (*Bluebeard the Knight*). d. Walter Felsenstein; sw. Felsenstein & Georg Mielke; au. Offenbach; c. Otto Merz & Hans-Jürgen Reinecke; with Hanns Nocker & Melitta Muszeli.
Susanne und der Zauberring (*Suzanne and the Magic Ring*). d. Erwin Stranka; sw. Rose Klein, Stranka, & L. Gerber; c. Lothar Gerber; with Monika Wolf & Stefan Lisewski.
. . . verdammt, ich bin erwachsen (*. . . Shucks, I'm Grown Up*). d. Rolf Losansky; sw. Losansky, & Günter Mehnert; au. Joachim Novotny; c. Peter Süring; with Ralf Sclösser & Angelika Herrmann.

1975

Auf meiner Kindheit (*My Childhood*). d. Bernard Stephan.
Bankett für Achilles (*A Banquet for Achilles*). d. Roland Gräf; sw. Martin Stephan; c. Jürgen Lenz; with Erwin Geschonneck & Elsa Grube-Deister.
Hans Röckle und der Teufel (*Hans Rockle and the Devil*). d. Hans Kratzert; sw. Gudrun Deubner; with Rolf Hoppe & Peter Aust.

Liebe mit 16 (*Love at 16*). d. Herrmann Zschoche; with Simone Zglinicki & Heinz-Peter Linse.
Lotte in Weimar. d. Günther; sw. Günther; au. Thomas Mann; c. Erich Gusko; with Lilli Palmer, Martin Hellberg, & Jutta Hoffman. First East and West German co-production.
Putzt das Licht der Vernunft (*Clean Up the Light of Common Sense*). d. Frank Vogel.
Till Eulenspiegel. d. Rainer Simon; sw. Christa & Gerhard Wolf; with Winfried Glatzeder & Cox Habbema.
Ulzana (*Apachen, Pt. 2*). d. Gottfried Kolditz; produced by DEFA/BUFTEA (Bucharest); sw. Gojko Mitic & Kolditz; c. Helmut Bergmann; with Gohko Mitic & Renate Blume.
Unterm Birnbaum (*Under the Pear Tree*). d. Ralf Kirsten; sw. Brigitte & Ralf Kirsten; au. Theodor Fontane; c. Wolfgang Braumann; with Angelica Domroese & Erik S. Klein.
Wie fuettert man einen Esel? (*How Does One Feed an Ass?*). d. Roland Oehme; produced by DEFA in cooperation with studios and actors in Czechoslovakia, Hungary, Romania, Bulgaria; sw. Maurycy Janowski & Oehme; c. Emil Sirotek; with Manfred Krug & Karla Chadimova.
Wolz—Leben und Verklarung eines deutschen Anarchisten (*Wolz—The Life and Work of a German Anarchist*). d. Reisch;* sw. Rücker;* c. Jürgen Brauer; with Regimantas Adomaitas & Heidemarie Wenzel.

1976

Beethoven—Tage aus einem Leben (*Beethoven—Days from a Life*). d. Seemann;* sw. Günter Kunert & Seemann; c. Otto Hanisch; with Donatas Banionis & Stefan Lisewski.
Die Leiden des jungen Werthers (*The Sorrows of Young Werther*). d. Günther;* sw. Helga Schütz; au. Goethe; c. Erich Gusko; with Hans-Jürgen Wolf & Katharina Thalbach.
Eine Pyramide für mich (*A Pyramid for Me*). d. Ralf Kirsten; sw. Karl-Heinz Jacobs & Kirsten; c. Hans-Jürgen Kruse; with Justus Fritzsche & Günter Junghans.

1977

Anton der Zauberer (*Anton the Magician*). d. Reisch;* with Ulrich Thein & Barbara Dittus.
Der kleine Zauberer und die grosse Fünf (*The Little Magician and the Bad Mark*). d. Erwin Stranka; sw. Stranka; c. Peter Brand; with Jürgen Heinrich & Karin Schröder.
Die Flucht (*The Flight*). d. Roland Gräf; sw. Hannes Hüttner; c. Claus Neumann; with Armin Mueller-Stahl & Jenny Gröllmann.
Die unverbesserliche Barbara (*Incorrigible Barbara*). d. Warneke;* sw. Warneke; c. Jürgen Lenz; with Cox Habbema & Peter Aust.
Mama, ich lebe (*Mum, I'm Alive*). d. Wolf;* sw. Wolfgang Kohlhaase; c. Werner Bergmann; with Peter Prager & Uwe Zerbst.

1979

Solo Sunny. d. Wolf* & Wolfgang Kohlhaase; sw. Kohlhaase; c. Eberhard Geick; with Renate Krössner & Alexander Lang.

1980

Asta mein Engelchen (Asta my Angel). d. Roland Oehme; sw. Manfred Wolter; with Erwin Geschonneck.
May I Call You Petrushka? d. Karl-Heinz Heymann; c. Werner Bergmann; with Hannelore Bey & Frank Bey.
Unser kurzes Leben (Our Short Life). d. Warneke;* sw. Regine Kühn; au. Brigitte Reimann; with Simone Frost.
Pugowitza. d. Jürgen Brauer; au. Alfred Wellm.
Bürgschaft für ein Jahr (Warranty for One Year). d. Hermann Zschoche.
Your Unknown Brother. sw. Wolfgang Trampe; au. Willi Bredel.

1982

Die Verlobte (The Fiancée). d. Rücker* & Reisch;* c. Jürgen Brauer; with Jutta Wachowiak.
Levin's Mühle (Levin's Mill). d. Seemann;* au. Bobrowski.
Hotel Polan und seine Gäste (The Polan Hotel and its Guests). d. Seemann.*

1983

Apprehension. d. Warneke;* sw. Helga Schubert; c. Thomas Plehnert; with Christine Schorn.
Exploring the Marches of Brandenburg. d. Roland Gräf; au. Günter de Bruyn; with Hermann Beyer.
Frühlingssinfonie (Spring Symphony). d. Peter Schamoni; produced by Allianz/ZDF/ DEFA/Greentree/Schamoni; sw. Schamoni; c. Gerard Vandenberg; with Nastassja Kinski, Herbert Grönemeyer, & Rolf Hoppe.
Sabine Kleist, 7 Jahre (Sabine Kleist, 7). d. Helmut Dzuiba; sw. Dzuiba; with Petra Lämmel.
Der Aufenthalt (The Turning Point). d. Beyer;* sw. Wolfgang Kohlhaase; au. Hermann Kant.

1984

Das Luftschiff (Airship). d. Rainer Simon; c. Roland Dresse; with Jörg Gudzuhn.
Ärztinnen (Lady Doctors). d. Seemann;* au. Rolf Hochhuth; with Judy Winter, Inge Keller, Rolf Hoppe, & Walther Reyer.
Bockshorn (Taken for a Ride). d. Beyer;* sw. Ulrich Plenzdorf; au. Christoph Meckel; with Jeff Dominiak & Bert Löper.
Eine sonderbare Liebe (A Strange Love Affair). d. Warneke.*
Schwierig sich zu verloben (Difficult to Get Engaged). d. Karl Heinz Heymann.
Erscheinen Pflicht (Attendance Compulsory). d. Helmet Dzuiba.
Fariaho. d. Roland Graf; with Franciszek Pieczka.
Insel der Schwäne (Island of Swans). d. Hermann Zschoche; sw. Ulrich Plenzdorf; au. Benno Pludra.
Isabel auf der Treppe (Isabel on the Stairs). d. Unterberg. Children's film.
Ole Henry. d. Ulrich Weiss; sw. Dieter Schubert.

EAST GERMANY

Verzeihung, sehen sie Fussball? (Excuse me—Are You Watching Football?). d. Gunther Scholz; with Jutta Wachowiak.
Zille und ich (Zillie and Me).

1985

Die Frau und der Fremde (The Woman and the Stranger). d. Rainer Simon.

1986

Der Prinz hinter den sieben Meeren (The Prince Behind the Seven Seas). d. Walter Beck. Children's film.
Ete and Ali. d. Peter Kahane; sw. Waltruad Maienreis & Henry Schneider.
Gritta vom Rattenschloss (Gritta of the Castle of Rats). d. Jürgen Brauer; au. Bettina von Arnim; with Hermann Beyer.
Ab heute erwachsen (Grown Up, as from Today). d. Gunter Scholz; sw. Helga Schubert.
Karl and Anna. d. Rainer Simon; au. Leonhard Frank.
Your Unknown Brother. d. Ulrich Weiss.

1987

Bis dass der Tod euch scheidet (Til Death Do Us Part). d. Carow.*
Haus am Fluss (House on the River). d. Roland Craef.
Die Gänze von Bützow (The Geese of Bützow). d. Frank Vogel.
So Many Dreams. d. Carow;* with Jutta Wachowiak.
The Solo Sailor. d. Hermann Zschoche; with Christina Powileit.
Liane. d. Erwin Stranka; sw. Stranka; au. Daniela Dahn; with Ariane Borbach.
Interrogation of the Witnesses. d. Gunther Scholtz; c. Claus Neumann.
Wengler and Sons. d. Rainer Simon.
Childhood. d. Kühn.*
Käthe Kollwitz—Pictures of a Life. d. Ralf Kirsten; with Jutta Wachowiak.

1988

Bear Ye One Another's Burdens. d. Warneke;* sw. Wolfgang Held; with Manfred Möck & Jörg Post.

7

Judith Roof

ROMANIA

Like Romania itself, Romanian cinema has remained obscure. The sparse international distribution of its films has made it remote and unfamiliar. Until recently, it has been aesthetically insignificant, adhering rigidly to the somewhat formulaic necessities imposed by film's illustrative and ideological functions in a totalitarian regime. For these reasons Romanian cinema has not gained the world stature of other Eastern European cinemas, notably Czechoslovakia. A promising art in a country that values its literature, the course of the development of Romanian cinema has been determined more by the country's economic and political conditions than by its enthusiasm, pool of talent, audience interest, or, after World War II, available technology. While relatively few films were produced in Romania before World War II, the post-war development of a distinctly Romanian cinema traces a subtle history of the warring impulses of artistic vision and doctrinal exigency.

It is fair to say that Romanians became practiced cinema viewers before they became proficient at film production, though they approached both sides of the screen with caution. Their unsettled political position throughout the first half of the twentieth century, their retention of a rural economy, and their cultural reliance upon Western Europe favored the importation of foreign films over the development of their own industry. Early twentieth-century Romania was stalled in the middle of a transformation from a feudal society begun in the late nineteenth century with the 1864 emancipation of the peasants; 80 percent of the population of Romania was still rural and mainly impoverished. Because of financial difficulties, international disputes, constant changes in territory, and bad treaties, Romania did not develop a substantial industrial base. A peasant uprising in 1907, a constantly shifting government, and a series of wars—including the first and second Balkan wars (1912 and 1913) and World War I—made it difficult for Romania, sensitively located at one of the cruxes of dispute, to concentrate on improving domestic conditions. In addition, only after World War I was Romania able to consolidate substantial territory occupied by Romanian-speaking peoples, including Bulkovia to the north, Transylvania to the west, and Bessarabia to the east.

Though an attempt was made in the late 1930s to organize film production through the creation of a National Cinematograph Office under the auspices of the National Touring Office, political unrest and economic backwardness made it nearly impossible to develop a film industry until a relatively more stable Communist government was formed in 1948. Following the Russian model, the series of governments in power from 1948 to 1990 regarded the cinema as a powerful tool for educating the people and extolling the virtues of a socialist existence. After World War II, not only did the new government step up industrialization, but they instituted a national film industry with the building of sumptuous Bucareşti studios at Buftea, and the establishment of a film school in the I. L. Caragiale Institute of Theatrical Art. Gradually implementing a socialist model for group film production at specialized studios, feature films were produced at Bucareşti, short subjects at the Alexandru Sahia, and animations at Animafilm Studios. A central committee who planned both topics and resources coordinated film production.

By the end of World War II only fifty full-length films had been made in Romania, an average of one per year from the date of the first film shown in Bucharest. The first films were screened in "a programme of Romanian landscapes" as early as 1893, and Romania certainly did not lag far behind the initial cinemaphilia of the rest of Europe, viewing newsreels in Bucharest in May 1896 (Hibbin, 117). The first permanent theater designed for film screenings, however, was not built until 1910 when the Carmen Sylvia Theater, named after the wife of King Carol I, opened in Bucharest. Though the first Romanian film production company, Romania Film, founded by Constantin Theodorescu began in the same year, throughout the history of Romanian cinema, distribution far exceeds production. By 1930, there were 279 cinemas in Romania, though film production rarely exceeded seven full-length features per annum with a full complement of shorts, documentaries, newsreels, and the animated films, a form in which Romanians were pioneers. From 1948 when there were a reported 383 cinemas, to 1969 when there were 573 permanent 35mm cinemas and 5,700 16mm facilities and mobile units, film production rose to about 15 full-length features per year. By 1987 there were 630 35mm cinemas, and film production rose to approximately 25 full-length features per year. Though the figures are often conflicting, cinema attendance has always been substantial, though increasing audience interest in the 1970s and 1980s doubled attendance from 40 million in 1973 to 95 million in 1989.

THE EARLY YEARS

In what turned out not to be a harbinger of a rapid development of cinema in Romania, Romanians in Bucharest saw the Lumière brothers' show on May 27, 1896, only five months after its December 1895 premiere in Paris. But Romanian filmmakers did not rapidly advance beyond primitive cinema's initial predilection for documentary and animation. Romanian Paul Menu began producing newsreels soon after the Lumière showing, and films of the Romanian countryside were featured in 1897. Entrepreneur and director Nicolae Barbelian began his film career in 1911, screening films in his own mobile cinema and working on documentaries both as a cameraman and director. A shortage of resources necessary for the development of a film production industry and strict censorship rather than any lack of audience forced some artists such as Lupu Pick and Jean Negulesco (director of such Hollywood films as *Johnny Belinda* and *How to Marry a Millionaire*) to ply their talents elsewhere and others such as Jean Georgescu to act and direct in the thriving French film industry, gaining experience that enabled him to return to Romania to make films when conditions for a filmmaking there had improved.

Those who remained in Romania set the standard that would shape the Romanian film industry until the end of World War II. While filmmakers such as Barbelian and Paul Călinescu made documentary films, and pioneer animators Aurel Petrescu and Marin Iorda began Romania's acclaimed animation industry, few filmmakers made notable fiction films. Only thirty silent fiction films were produced in Romania by 1930, and of those, few were memorable, generally following the patriotism of director Grigore Brezeanu's second film, *War for Independence*, 1912 (Liehm and Liehm, 22). Brezeanu also held the distinction of directing Romania's first fiction film, *Fatal Love*, made in 1911.

Romania's silent fiction films, like its pre-war talkies, tended to stick to a single pattern, revealing a propensity for adaptations of literature or "Romanian versions" of popular films made elsewhere. The two most noted fiction filmmakers of the pre-war era, Jean Mihail (1896–1963) and Jean Georgescu (1904-), tended to specialize in adaptations. Mihail directed three silent films, two adaptations of the work of I. L. Caragiale, *Pagat (Sin)*, 1924, and *Manasse*, 1925, and *Lia*, 1927, a film that focuses on the impoverished working class in contrast to the affluence of the privileged upper classes. Georgescu, who worked as actor, cameraman, and director in France, directed the comedy *O Noapte Furtunosa (Stormy Night)* in 1942 upon his return to Romania. Also adapted from the work of nineteenth-century writer I. L. Caragiale's play, *Stormy Night* is a farce still heavily indebted to Georgescu's French influences, manifesting a taste for overly theatrical effects (Liehm and Liehm, 22).

By the beginning of World War II, Romania had developed a film industry noted only for some achievement in documentary filmmaking; Paul Călinescu's film *Țara Molițor (The Country of Motzi)* was commended at the 1938 Venice film festival. Călinescu's documentaries, including *Bucharest*, 1936; *How to Do a Radio Report*, 1942; and *How to Do a Film Report* 1943, were the product of the National Cinematograph Office established in 1936 by the National Touring Office which attempted to provide state support for film production. Modeled after similar programs in other countries, the national office sought to bring together the best Romanian production professionals to stimulate the production of Romanian films. Most of what was created under its auspices, however, were documentaries and newsreels.

THE EMERGENCE OF A NATIONAL INDUSTRY

While film production was nationalized in 1948 on the heels of the establishment of a socialist republic, film production did not return to even its meager pre-war levels until 1955. While several privately produced comedies appeared in the interim—Cornel Dimitrescu's *Pădurea indragostitilor (The Forest of Lovers)*, 1946, and Viktor Gertler's Romanian-Hungarian co-production *Doua lumi si o dragoste (Two Worlds and One Love)*, 1947—the ten years between 1945 and 1955 were spent establishing an industry that had almost no pre-war antecedents in a cultural environment confused by the sudden government-inspired shift from a traditional Romanian partiality to the French to the socialist realism of Zhdanovian prescriptions. Led by Soviet-influenced party leaders, the new government regarded cinema, like the print media, as a tool that would embody and spread the proper message of the socialist revolution. For this reason cinema gained instant importance, but its form was limited by the party's notions of what cinematic styles and contents would properly disseminate the socialist political message necessary to complete and sustain the people's revolution. To further these purposes, all artistic production was subsumed within a comprehensive program that defined permissible styles, narratives, characterizations, and dialogue according to ideological dictates of a socialist policy devoted to the "interests of the working class," as part of a "progressive culture" furthering the "construction of socialism." The government formed committees of Romanian intellectuals such as George Călinescu and Mihail Sadoveanu to establish the parameters of a new Romanian socialist culture that would determine the aesthetic and political guidelines for all art (Cretzianu, 129).

Part of the problem with this programmatization was that it too quickly attempted to impose upon the nascent Romanian film industry ideas that controverted the almost Boulevardesque film aesthetic that had been developed before the war. Instead of working well with the skills of the few directors such as Mihail and Georgescu trained in the French tradition, it demanded instant and quite artificial change to socialist realism. The second problem was a lack of appropriate material; the Romanian habit of adaptation required a literature or film tradition that could be used in cinema. Until a new Romanian socialist literature was developed, the only sources for films would be either socialist reinterpretations of events from Romanian history or the adaptation of recent, simplistic doctrinarian literature. A third problem was that the precepts of socialist realism were imported from the Soviet Union, toward which the Romanians had exercised a dislike since Russia had dispossessed them of Bessarabia. The response to cultural programs was, thus, slowed.

The final problem, which could be more easily solved, was Romania's almost total lack of film production facilities. The new government responded to this obstacle by augmenting the national base already established in the National Tourist Office. To increase production, they built Bucureşti Studios at Buftea outside of Bucharest (referred to as either Bucureşti or Buftea Studios). Envisioned as a film city containing everything from sound stages to stables, Buftea Studios took seven years—from 1950 to 1957—to complete. Buftea, as the primary site for feature film production, then took its place in the array of specialized facilities along with Alexandru Sahia Studios devoted to the making of short subjects, and Animafilm Studios, the site for animation. Filmmaking would henceforward be a group process, planned in relation to resources and the needs of socialism. The problem of personnel was solved by establishing the film section of the I. L. Caragiale Institute of Theatrical Art (IATC) in Bucharest.

The first moves towards a socialist Romanian cinema were made, ironically, by old hands. In the final years of the war and in the period immediately after, Georgescu continued to make his comedies, co-writing and directing *Visul Unei Nopti de Iarna* (*Dream of a Winter's Eve*), 1945, and Jean Mihail, the pre-war director of adaptations, turned to documentary, directing *Poporul român în luptă pentru democraţie* (*The Romanian People in the Fight for Democracy*), 1946. It was the pre-war documentarist, Paul Călinescu, however, who directed the first post-war fiction film, *Răsună valea* (*The Valley Resounds*), 1949, produced under the auspices of the nationalized film industry. Typical of the rather simple "them" (capitalist, old-style Romanian, bourgeois) versus "us" (Romanian socialist workers) formula that would come to dominate the Romanian film industry, *The Valley Resounds* illustrates the victory of the workers over the interests of capitalist imperialists. Combining a theatrical style left over from pre-war cinema with the new vocabulary of socialist-realism and produced in an environment of zealous political scrutiny, *The Valley Resounds* establishes the confused, somewhat hackneyed norm for the Romanian post-war film (Liehm and Liehm, 140).

The emerging Romanian cinema did develop within set sub-genres that were the logical product of a film industry run by political prescription. Because Romania was still largely rural, narratives appropriate to the needs of that large working class took the struggles of rural society as its subject. The setting for socialist allegories, these rural or "village" films contained predictable casts of characters, from the sturdy peasant people's hero who lived out in small scale the desirable virtues of the socialist individual to the base, sloppy, retrograde capitalist. The conflict between the hero, who was selflessly concerned with the weal of all, and the capitalist, who stood selfishly in the way of progress, personified the struggle of the people to overcome the remaining injustices of those not yet convinced of the rightness of the socialist system (Liehm and Liehm, 142). One of the most famous of these "rural" films was *Mitrea Cocor,* 1952, based on the novel by Mihail Sadoveanu, one of the most prominent new socialist writers, and directed by Victor Iliu who specialized in this genre. Iliu had paired with veteran Jean Georgescu to direct *In sat la noi* (*In Our Village*), another rural comedy the previous year and went on to direct another, *Moara cu noroc* (*Mill of Good Luck*), 1955, based on the novel by Ion Slavici. Veteran Paul Călinescu also contributed to this genre with the 1954 film, *Desfăşurarea* (*Development [(In a Village)]*).

Instead of relying on literary sources, director Dinu Negreanu used the material of the socialist struggle itself, employing cinema to illustrate the continuing battle of the working people to overcome oppressive class prejudice and the interference of foreign imperialistic interests. One of the few Moscow-trained Romanian directors, Negreanu established a socialist struggle sub-genre, making a series of films that demonstrated the victory of oppressed people over those who resisted or who actively opposed the new socialist order. Beginning in 1952 with *Viaţa învinge* (*Life Prevails*), Negreanu directed a two-part epic of Romanian socialist struggle, *Nepoţii gornistului* (*The Bugler's Grandsons*), 1953, covering the period between World War I and the 1930s, and part two, *Răsare soarele* (*The Sun Rises*), 1954, covering the period after World War II. He went on to direct several more films of the genre, including *Alarmă în munţi* (*Alarm in the Mountains*), 1955, and *Pasărea furtunii* (*Stormy Bird*), 1956. Despite his adherence to the most orthodox socialist precepts, Negreanu later emigrated to the United States.

As long as films represented the new aesthetic, they could be drawn from any source. Veteran Jean Mihail, who had begun his post-war career with a documentary, continued to show his versatility with a socialist-struggle film, *Bragada lui Ionut* (*The Ionutz Brigade*), 1954, followed in 1956 by *Rîpa dracului* (*The Devil's Abyss*), another of the same genre. Jean Georgescu continued his fascination with Caragiale's comedies, adapting three to film in 1952: *Arendaşul roman* (*Romanian Farmer*); *Lanţul slabiciunilor* (*Chain of Weakness*); and *Vizita* (*The Visit*). Georgescu's comic talent also enabled him to develop the first Romanian socialist comedy, *Directorul nostru* (*Our Director*), 1955, a Romanian adaptation of the popular socialist formula of poking fun at bureaucracy through the persona of an abusive director who meets his downfall.

THE NEW GENERATION, 1955-1970

Jean Georgescu continued to develop his comic style, escaping finally the strict dictates of the Zhdanovian socialist realists, but still preferring adaptations, particularly the works of Caragiale. In 1957 he directed *Doua Lozuri* (*Two Lottery Tickets*); in 1962 a retrospective of Romanian film, *Lanterna cu amintiri* (*Lantern of Memories*); and in 1964, the collection of Caragiale stories, *Mofturi 1900* (*Potpourri 1900*). His final film was the 1968 *Pantoful Cenusaresei* (*Cinderella's Shoes*). Though veterans such as Georgescu and Victor Iliu, who directed *Comoara din Vadul Vechi* (*The Treasure of Vadu Vechi*) in 1964, continued to work, they were joined by a wave of new directors, less adherent to the rigid dictates applied to the emerging cinema of post-war Romania, but still conforming to the basic formulas of socialist struggle set in a socialist realist frame.

A fully operational feature film studio and an extended period of domestic stability allowed the Romanian film industry to expand, making more films per year (39 features and shorts by 1970) with improved technology, including color and wide screen. Even so, the IATC's production of graduates so exceeded the facilities and resources available for filmmaking that some of its film programs had to be suspended between 1957 and 1963. The Communist Party's strict hold over cultural matters continued to limit originality in filmmaking, though the first steps of a liberalization appeared in Premier Chivu Stoica's desire to reopen cultural links with France and other nations of Europe and South America. But this temporary opening was deleted by purges of intellectuals, who were suspected of sympathizing with the Hungarian revolution of 1956 (Liehm and Liehm, 252). In the early 1960s Romania's cultural reliance on the Soviet Union faded, replaced by a more urgent sense of Romanian nationalism and a desire to consolidate the works of Romanian artists wherever they might be. While this resulted in a broader range of works to be adapted and a slightly freer stylistic rein, Romanian cinema stayed on the Party's somewhat single-minded course, opening up only in its willingness to engage in international co-productions, and becoming more liberal about which Romanian authors' works might be cinematically adapted.

The first signs of any slight liberalization came in 1955 with Romania's first color film, *Nufărul roşu* (*The Red Water Lily*), directed by Gheorghe Tobias, and with the screening of Iulian Mihu and Manole Marcus's lyrical *La mere* (*Pinching Apples*), their graduation film from IATC. *Pinching Apples*'s more poetic, consciously aesthetic style deviated from the strict socialist realist mandate that had governed both rural comedies and socialist struggle films. While their experimentalism gained them notoriety, it also tended to make film opportunities less available to them, though they continued to make some of the more innovative films of the period, including *Viaţa nu iartă* (*Life Will Not Forgive*), 1958, based on the work of writer Alexandru Sahia. Marcus also tried his hand at comedy, directing the mediocre *Nu vreau să mă însor* (*I Don't Want to Get Married*), 1960, and returned to more serious fare, the 1964 film *Cartierul veseliei* (*The District of Gaiety*), and the 1966 *Zodia fecioarei* (*Virgo*). Mihu had even less access to production, directing only *Procesul alb* (*White Trial*), 1965, in the first ten years after graduation.

More conformist graduates of the IATC were prolific, continuing the Romanian tradition of films illustrating the socialist struggle and developing, in the new wave of Romanian nationalism, a new sub-genre: the historical epic, which enjoyed its heyday in the decade between 1960 and 1970. Graduate directors such as Mircea Drăgan, Dinu-Constantin Cocea, and Gheorghe Vitanidis joined with Moscow-trained Lucian Bratu, renowned theater director Liviu Ciulei, and the versatile and prolific Sergiu Nicolaescu to tap Romanian history as a new source for spectacular historical dramas that illustrated the battle of the Romanian oppressed and the victories of Romanian champions of the people in a distinctly nationalistic vein. Importation of wide screen technology and the full operation of the studios at Buftea provided materials for large-scale costume dramas such as Bratu's *Tudor,* 1963, an extremely expensive rendition of the 1821 Romanian revolt against the Turks, focusing on the Romanian leader, Tudor, who is depicted as a precursor to the generous, socially minded hero of the socialist struggle.

Mircea Drăgan was perhaps the most orthodox of the new directors, developing the socialist struggle film in both epic and socially responsible directions. After a film debut co-directing *Dincolo de brazi (Beyond the Fir Trees)* with Mihai Iacob in 1956, Drăgan was the first to use wide screen technology in his 1960 film *Setea (Thirst),* adapted from a novel by Titus Popovici, who also wrote the film's screenplay. Concerned with social inequities, Drăgan next made *Lupeni 29,* 1962, based on the miners' strike in 1929, and its sequel *Golgota (Golgotha),* 1967, about six of the miners' widows. Returning in 1968 to the work of Titus Popovici, he directed, in cooperation with CCC Filmkunst, *The Column,* a film about the ancient beginnings of the Romanian people.

In keeping with Drăgan's discovery of the value of recent history, Liviu Ciulei also made epic films set in twentieth-century scenes of struggle. His first solo film, *Erupţia (Eruption),* 1957, was set in oilfields and his next, *Valurile Dunării (The Danube Waves),* 1959, treated the dilemma of a World War II navigator who betrays the Nazis in favor of Communist fighters. A graduate of both the Faculty of Architecture and the Conservatory of Dramatic Arts, Ciulei began his film career as an actor, then assisted Victor Iliu in *In sat la noi (In Our Village).* His most famous film, *Pădurea Spînzuraţilor (The Forest of the Hanged),* 1965, was set in World War I, narrating the plight of a Romanian soldier from Hungarian Transylvania forced to fight against his own countrymen. The film's sensitively executed cinematography won the Romanian film industry's prize of excellence and Ciulei won the prize for best direction at the 1966 Cannes Festival.

Drăgan's orthodox creativity and Ciulei's dramatic sensibility established an aesthetic of socially responsible but sometimes overstated bravado. Their versions of history contrasted more current social problems against the more epic treatments of Romanian history from such directors as Gheorghe Vitanidis, Dinu Cocea, and Sergiu Nicolaescu. Vitanidis co-directed several Romanian co-productions with France stimulated by Romania's brief mid–1950s spurt of liberalization, including the 1958 *Ciulinii Băraganului (The Thistles of the Baragan).* Working with Louis Daquin on a script adapted from a novel by expatriate proletarian Romanian novelist Panait Istrati, *The Thistles of the Baragan* commemorates the fiftieth anniversary of the 1907 peasant uprising. The way that this same topic was taken up again eight years later by director Mircea Mureşan in *Răscoala (Flaming [Blazing] Winter),* 1966, shows the slow but gradual development of a more individualized Romanian cinema, as Mureşan focuses more on issues of individual destiny rather than on epic forces.

Despite the strain of more subdued films made in the 1960s by such directors as Ciulei, Mureşan, Andrei Blaier, and Lucian Pintilie, Cocea and Nicolaescu were responsible for even more swashbuckling epic films. Cocea made a series of films based on the exploits of the Haiduks or the Outlaws, including *Haiducii (The Haiduks)*, 1965; *Rape of the Maidens*, 1968; *Razbunarea haiducilor (Return [Revenge] of the Haiduks [Outlaws])*, 1968; and *Haiducii lui Saptecai (The Haiduks of Captain Anghel)*, 1970. Written by Eugene Barbu, this series of adventure films followed a Robin Hood plot of "good" outlaws resisting the "bad" forces of corrupt tyrants. Nicolaescu, a jack of all trades who worked himself up to director by serving in almost every other capacity in film production, entered the epic arena with *Dacii (The Warriors [The Dacians])*, 1966, following the history of the Dacians, considered the forefathers of modern Romanians. Nicolaescu also directed Oscar-nominated *Mihai Viteazul (Last Crusade [Michael the Brave])*, 1971, which focused on another chapter of Romanian history, this time the story of sixteenth-century King Michael, who attempted to unite a divided Romanian people. Nicolaescu was also a premier adapter, filming the works of James Fenimore Cooper in the series of films *Aventuri in Ontario (Adventures in Ontario)*, 1968; *Ultimul Mohican (The Last of the Mohicans)*, 1968; and *Vînătorul de cerbi (The Deerslayer)*, 1969.

This escapist epic trend was countered by more thoughtful films directed by young graduates of IATC. Mircea Mureşan began his career with *Partea de ta vină (Your Share of the Responsibility [You Are Guilty Too])*, a 1962 exploration of the complex problems facing the leader of the 1907 peasant revolt. Focusing more on the individual than on the group, Mureşan's *Răscoala (Flaming [Blazing] Winter)* continued his interest in the plight of individuals in historical crises, beginning a career that would explore such dilemmas. And while history, even recent history, came to form merely a backdrop for the same old "them" versus "us" plot as was reflected in a series of 1960s anti-fascist films—Francisc Munteanu's *Cerul n-are gratii (Sky Without Bars)*, 1962, and *Tunelul (Tunnel)*, 1966 (the latter, perhaps predictably a Romanian-Soviet co-production); Manole Marcus' *Cartierul veseliei (The District of Gaiety)*, 1964; and Iulian Mihu's *Procesul alb (White Trial)*, 1965—other filmmakers began to focus on some of the frustration of individuals struggling in a system that did not always work. Virgil Calotescu, director of *Camera Alba (White Ward)*, 1965, also made *Subteranul (Underground)*, 1967; and Andrei Blaier *Dimineţile uhui băiat cuminte (The Mornings of a Sensible Youth)*, 1966, focused on the problems of disenchanted youth.

Perhaps the most innovative and individual director to emerge in the 1960s was Lucian Pintilie. Like Ciulei, Pintilie was a veteran of the theater and brought to the screen his understanding of the subtleties of personal motivation and dramatic proportion. His first film, *Duminică la ora 6 (Sunday at Six)*, 1965, still centers on recent history—the resistance in World War II— but his treatment of the conflict is original and responsive to the interactions of individuals. His second film, *Reconstituirra (Reconstruction)*, made in 1969 but not released until 1970, tells the story of two men, whose overtly meta-cinematic reconstruction of a tavern fight results in the death of one of them (Liehm and Liehm, 354). The shift toward the sensitive, lyrical, the individual, and even toward dark humor that began with Marcus arrives in 1969 in both Pintilie's *Reconstruction* and Gheorghe Vitanidis' *O femeie pentru un anotimp (A Woman for One Season)*, a film that focuses on the personal emotions of a doctor (Liehm and Liehm, 355).

Though the Romanian cinema of the 1960s did not seem to make much headway toward developing a substantial vision or unique aesthetic, it had succeeded in enlarging its scope, varying its earlier formulas, becoming more subtle in its treatment of history and socialist themes, and with the emergence of filmmakers like Pintilie, promised to provide more innovative and personal films. Even women began to enter the filmmaking force. Malvina Urşianu directed *Gioconda fara suris (The Unsmiling Giaconda [Giaconda Without That Smile])* in 1968, a film focusing on a woman's experience, and Elisabeta Bostan began making short films for children. Perhaps the most important aspect of Romanian cinema of this period, however, was animation, brilliantly developed by Ion Popescu-Gopo. Already established in Romania's early cinema, Romania's importance in the world of animation is attested not only by Popescu-Gopo's original, non-Disney approach to animation but also by the fact that the annual International Festival of Animated Film is held in Romania. The internationally renowned Popescu-Gopo, who established the first animation studio in Romania in 1950, became known for his "little-man" series, making such films as *Scurtă istorie (A Short History)*, 1957; *Sapte arte (The Seven Arts)*, 1958; *Homo Sapiens*, 1960; *S a furat o bombă (Stolen Bomb)*, 1961; *Allo! Allo! (Hello! Hello!)*, 1962; *Pasi spre lună (Steps to the Moon)*, 1963; and *Harap Alb (The White Moor)*, 1965.

GENERATION '70

By 1970, a second generation of directors was graduated from IATC. Schooled now by Romanian mentors such as Mircea Drăgan, Professor of Direction at IATC, Manole Marcus, and Gheorghe Vitanidis, these new directors inherited what there was of a Romanian film tradition, beginning in the early '70s with the best of the old and the new. Working within an established tradition of Romanian film with a corps of trained actors such as Amza Pellea, Ilarion Ciobanu, George Constantin, Margareta Pîslaru, Silvia Popovici, and Dan Nuţu, and expert cinematographers such as Nicu Stan, Alexandru Intorsureanu, and Iosef Demian, the most recent IATC graduates could concentrate on the artistic challenge presented by the confluence of cinema and socialist ideology. In addition, they gained the benefit of the new decentralized production system instituted in 1972, when the production of feature films, previously the function of a central committee, was divided among five autonomous companies who would continue to use the three production facilities available. Not only was this intended to increase film production, but ultimately to make film production in Romania financially self-supporting. Both the number of features produced and viewers did increase in the 1970s, films climbing from an average of fifteen per year to an average of twenty-five and the number of admissions paid mounting to 40 million.

No longer as strongly influenced by Soviet aesthetics, these new directors were much freer to pursue the promising directions that had just begun to appear in Romanian cinema in the late 1960s. While young directors such as Mureşan, Blaier, Marcus, and Urşianu continued to develop their skills, and the more practiced hands Drăgan and Nicolaescu continued to produce popular hits, filmmakers of the newest generation—Mircea Veroiu, Dan Piţa, Alexandru Tatos, Constantin Vaeni, Doru Năstase, Serban Creangă, and Dinu Tănase—began more experimental approaches that would further define and enlarge Romanian cinema.

The beginning of the seventies was marked by Manole Marcus' two-part film debate on power, government, and truth, *Puterea si adevarul (The Power and The Truth)*, 1972. Though the film was a biography of Premier Nicolae Ceaucescu, as in his graduation film, Marcus, with veteran screenwriter Titus Popovici, set out the artistic conflict of the times: the choice between a blind operation of power or a more sensitive acknowledgment of the pragmatic truth of socialist existence. Marcus' political inquiry set the tone for other examinations of human experience, from the more individualistic strain of works by filmmakers Malvina Urşianu, Iulian Mihu, and Alexandru Tatos to the aesthetic experiments of Mircea Veroiu and Dan Piţa. As Marcus' films illustrate, however, despite the more obvious inquiry permitted, the socialist program of Romania still held reign over the content and style of cinema, even after Ceaucescu declared an end to censorship in 1977.

The mainstream of Romanian cinema in the first half of the 1970s was still dominated by the prolific actor/director Sergiu Nicolaescu and the versatile Marcus, who both continued to make popular action films and historical epics. While Marcus was making *The Power and the Truth,* Nicolaescu was developing his series of successful mystery and gangster films, including *Cu mîinile curate (With Clean Hands),* 1972; *Ultimul Cartus (The Last Bullet),* 1973; and *Un Comisar Acuză (A Police Inspector Accuses),* 1973, as well as the historical dramas *Mihai Viteazul (Last Crusade [Michael the Brave]),* 1971, and its 1975 sequel, *Nemuritorii (The Immortals),* and the more psychological dramas, *Moartea hui Ipu (Ipu's Death),* 1972, and *Zile Fierbinţi (Hot Days),* 1975, with a script by Francisc Munteanu. Marcus, ever the experimenter, began the decade with *Canarul si viscolul (The Canary and the Storm),* 1970, a film organized around visual relations, but returned to the stock Romanian sub-genre, directing *Capcana (Single-Handed),* 1973, a gangster film, and *Actorul si salbaticii (The Player and the Savages),* 1974. Other historical subjects were contributed by Gheorghe Vitanidis with *Dimitrie Cantemir,* 1973, the biography of a king, and *Ciprian Porumbescu (The Ballad),* 1973, the biography of a Romanian composer, and by Mircea Drăgan with *Fratii Jderi (The Captain Martens Brothers),* 1973.

Mircea Mureşan continued the strain of anti-fascist resistance films with the 1974 film *Portile Alabastre ale Orasului* (*The Blue Gates of the City*), and George Saizescu directed the comedy *Saturday Night Dance*.

While the standard genres thrived, the influence of younger directors was felt in the emergence of more poetical films focused on personal and interpersonal conflict that shifted from the socialist "hero" of old to a fresher, more dynamic portrait of individual struggle. Malvina Urşianu, who had begun to probe the quality of life and relationships in a socialist society, directed *Serata* (*The Party*), 1971, and *Trecătoarele iubiri* (*Transient Loves*), 1974. New directors Radu Gabrea and Serban Creangă made sensitive films in the same vein, Gabrea directing *Prea mic pentru un război atît de mare* (*Too Small for Such a Big War*), a 1970 television film, and *Dincolo de nisipuri* (*Beyond the Sands*), 1973, the story of a resistance fighter's search for the murderer of his father. Creangă made *Proprietarii* (*The Owners*), 1973, which explores the conflict between old and young.

Perhaps the most influential new force in the Romanian cinema of the 1970s was the emergence of two new innovative directors, Mircea Veroiu and Dan Piţa, who would come to dominate Romanian cinema of the late 1970s and 1980s. Veroiu and Piţa emerged in a joint project, *Nuntă de Pietră* (*Stone Wedding*), in 1973. Composed of two separate stories, one directed by each, *Stone Wedding* treats peasant life in the Carpathian Mountains. Both segments are visually compelling and expertly filmed by cinematographer Iosef Demian; in them Veroiu and Piţa introduce two versions of the more elliptical, visually dominant style that would help bring Romanian cinema into a more aesthetic realm. *Stone Wedding* was auspiciously successful, receiving mention at Cannes and awards for direction, cinematography, and the performance of Leopoldina Balanuta.

Launching a veritable Romanian new wave, Veroiu and Piţa continued to make films both together and independently. Having begun as opportunistic documentarists filming the floods in 1970 in *Apa ca un bivol negru* (*Water As a Black Buffalo*), 1970, Veroiu and Piţa continued their collaboration on another two-part film, *Duhul aurului* (*The Spirit of Gold*), 1974. By themselves, both Veroiu and Piţa made substantial contributions to Romanian cinema from almost the beginning of their careers, experimenting in different genre. Veroiu directed *Sapte Zile* (*Seven Days*), 1973, a thriller again heavily dependent on visual impressions, and the science fiction film *Hyperion*, 1975. With *Dincolo de pod* (*The Other Side of the Bridge*), 1975, a Romeo-Juliet plot set in a Transylvanian village, Veroiu established the combination of visual beauty and psychological plot that would shape his next few films. Dan Piţa, the writer of the two, began his film career working with Victor Iliu, filming shorter films, *Paradisul* (*Paradise*), 1967; *Dupăamiază obişnuită* (*Common Afternoon*), 1968; and *Viaţa in roz* (*Life in Pink*), 1969. After the two joint ventures with Veroiu, Piţa directed *Filip cel Bun* (*Phillip the Kind*), 1974, the contemporary portrait of a young man's struggle for moral values.

Pița and Veroiu's more visually oriented cinema tipped the balance for the next decade toward more complex, less predictable psychological investigations into the problems of ordinary people even within the well-used genres of historical drama and literary adaptation so prevalent in Romanian film. Dan Pița combines them all in *Tănase Scatiu* (1976), adapted from the work of Duiliu Zamfirescu, tracing via individuals, the late-nineteenth century conflict between aristocracy and bourgeoisie. Veteran Sergiu Nicolaescu contributes his own adaptation, *Osinda (The Punishment)*, 1977, also a return to more psychological fare. Throughout the next ten years, the familiar genres of literary adaptation, historical dramas, thrillers, and comedies would be joined by the growing interest in visual style and personal statement, as well as Dan Pița's incursions into the Romanian Western. The by-now well-established newcomers Veroiu and Pița were joined by Urșianu, Munteanu, Mărgineau, Calotescu, and Vaeni, veterans Nicolaescu, Vitanidis, Mihu, Bostan, and Saizescu, and newcomers Alexandru Tatos and Mircea Daneliuc as Romanian cinema rounded out the old formulas with more complex visions filmed in more "experimental" visual styles.

Literary adaptations still dominated the field in the late 1970s and 1980s with contributions from all three generations of working filmmakers. Gheorghe Vitanidis contributed a piercing political analysis based on a contemporary novel by Dinu Sararu, *Clipa (The Moment)*, 1979. Newcomer Alexa Visarion, a stage director, made *Inainte de tăcere (Ahead of the Silence)*, 1979, based on a story by Caragiale. Cinematographer Iosef Demian directed *O Lacrimă de Fată (A Girl's Tears)*, 1980, after the novel by Petre Salcudeanu, which combines the police thriller with a portrait of a rural community. Stere Gulea's 1981 *The Castle in the Carpathians* adapted a Jules Verne novel, and cameraman Nicolae Mărgineanu made the biography of a Romanian artist, *Stefan Luchian* (1981). In 1984, Constantin Vaeni adapted Martin Preda's novel *The Intruder* in *Impossibilia iubire (Impossible Love)*, 1984.

Two powerful historical epics continued the strong presence of historical drama in Romanian filmmaking. Director Doru Nastase made the imminently Romanian film *Vlad Tepeș (Vlad the Impaler: The True Life of Dracula)*, 1979, the history of that most Romanian figure, which focuses on history rather than on the gruesome. Malvina Urșianu, known for her sensitive intellectual portrayals of contemporary problems, offered her own analysis of power via the sixteenth-century figure King Lapusneanu in *Intoarcerea Lui Vodă Lăpusneanu (The Return of King Lapusneanu)*, 1979. Even Dan Pița made his contribution to the historical genre by way of two films set in the American West: *Profetul, aurul si ardele nii (The Prophet, Gold and the Transylvanians)*, 1978, and *Oil, the Baby, and the Transylvanians*, 1981. Pița's comic/historical westerns joined other comedies of the years between 1975 and 1990, including Nicolaescu's *Uncle Marin, the Multimillionaire*, 1979; George Saizescu's *Santaj (Blackmail)*, 1981; and *Secretual lui Bachus (The Secret of Bacchus)*, 1984, and Manole Marcus's *Mitică Popescu*, 1984.

During this period two other popular Romanian genre—animations and children's films—also thrived. Ion Popescu-Gopo continued to produce animated features, winning first prize at the Chicago Children's Festival for *Maria Marabela*, 1984. Elisabeta Bostan, known for her children's films, *Veronica*, 1972, and *Veronica se Întoarce* (*Veronica Comes Back*, 1973), made the spectacular musical *Ma-Ma* in 1978, co-produced with France and the USSR. In 1981, Bostan turned to more serious fare in *Saltimbancii* (*The Clowns*).

While Nicolaescu continued making comedies and thrillers, including the excellent *The Revenge*, 1978, other newer filmmakers such as Francisc Munteanu, Cristiana Nicolae, and veteran Iulian Mihu began making films concerned with everyday life in Romania, Munteanu with *Un petec de cer* (*A Piece of Sky*), 1984, and Nicolae, an emerging woman filmmaker, with the prize-winning *De dragul tau Anca* (*For Your Sake, Anca*), 1984. Mihu, whose sparse output represents his thoughtful care, directed *Lumina Palida a Durerii* (*The Pale Light of Sorrow*), 1980, a poetic film about peasant life on the eve of World War II. A logical step in the shift from sweeping sociological dramas to the conflicts of individuals within history, portraits of everyday life made the Romanian cinema more personal, subtle, and dependent upon the quality of the camera work rather than the filming of spectacular scenes. The trend toward more visually inspired and thoughtful films continued with Mircea Veroiu and two newcomers, Alexandru Tatos and Mircea Daneliuc. Veroiu continued his work with visual form in the 1978 film *Intre oglinzi paralele* (*Between Opposite Mirrors*), tracing the story of two students in pre-World War I Romania. In *Semnul sarpelui* (*In the Sign of the Serpent*), 1981, he combined his interest in the image with the human portrait of a Romanian village during the final years of World War II. His two 1982 films, *Asteptind un tren* (*Waiting for a Train*) and *Sfirsitul nopti* (*The End of Night*), are both action films, the first set at the end of the war, the second, a television movie treating contemporary Romania. *Să mori rănit din dragoste de viaţă* (*To Die from Love of Life*), a 1983 film, again traces two men, this time in the 1930s as does *Adela*, 1984.

The cinematic exploration of interpersonal relations was also the subject matter for the humorous Alexandru Tatos and the more ironical Mircea Daneliuc. Tatos, who like Liviu Ciulei and Lucian Pintilie, came to cinema from the theater, produced a similar spirit of analytical investigation and attention to detail in his first film, *Mere Rosii* (*Red Apples*), 1978, about a young rural surgeon. After directing *Rătăcire* (*The Wandering*), 1978, he made two other films about the plight of professionals in rural backwaters, *Casa dintre cîmpuri* (*The House in the Fields*), 1980, and *Duios Anastasia trecea* (*Gently Passed Anastasia*), 1980. In 1984, Tatos directed *Fructe de padure* (*Forest Fruit*), the portrait of a seduced country girl.

While Tatos brings a gentle humor to his visions of Romanian life, Mircea Daneliuc brings irony. His first film, *Opera prima, Cursa* (*The Long Drive*), 1975, looks closely at two truck drivers and a female hitchhiker. His second film, the thriller *Ediţie speciala* (*Special Issue*), 1978, and his third, the romance *Probă de microfon* (*Microphone Testing*), 1980, took commonplace film stories and rendered them in exciting and fresh ways. His subtle portrait of Romanians in *Croaziera (The Cruise)*, 1981, and the combination of dream, fantasy, and insight in the 1984 *Glissando* make Daneliuc a master of the emerging genre of human interest films.

THE FUTURE

After 1985, Romanian cinema continues to produce new directors and features from practiced veterans. The events of 1989–1990 promise continued change in Romanian cinema, which is poised to continue its development of the delicate portrayal of Romanian life in a more international frame. The existence of a strong, financially self-supporting system of film production and the excellent facilities of the film center at Buftea give Romania a good beginning in a potential world market. Sustained by old hands like Sergiu Nicolaescu, who directed *The Z Day, Kiuleandra,* and *The Last Assault* in 1986; Dan Piţa, who continues to make innovative films like *Concurs (Orientering),* 1984; *Dreptate in Lanturi (Chained Justice),* 1984; and *Paso Doble* (1985); Malvina Urşianu with *Pe Malul Stîng al dunarii Albastre (On the Left Bank of the Blue Danube),* 1984, and *O lumină la etajul X (A Light on the Tenth Floor),* 1984; and Alexandru Tatos with *Sequences,* Romanian cinema keeps producing and developing new directors such as Cristiana Nicolae *(Fourth Fence along the Wharf),* 1986; Dinu Tănase *(Radio Romania Keeps Broadcasting),* 1986; and Serban Creangă *(A Spare Moment),* 1986. While the imperative to illustrate ideological truths may disappear with a new form of government, the skills gained by Romanian filmmakers who had to negotiate style, content, and ideology can only be used to the advantage of a growing Romanian film industry.

BIBLIOGRAPHY

Cantacuzino, Ion. *Momente din trecutul filmului romanesc.* Bucharest: Editura Meridiane, 1965.
Cernat, Manuela. *A Concise History of the Romanian Film.* Bucharest: Editura Stiintifica si Enciclopedica, 1982.
Bawden, Liz-Anne, ed. *The Oxford Companion to Film.* New York: Oxford University Press, 1976.
Bergan, Ronald, and Robyn Karney, eds. *The Holt Foreign Film Guide.* New York: Henry Holt, 1988.
Boussinot, Roger, ed. *L'Encyclopédie du cinéma.* Paris: Bordas, 1989.
Catalogue of Romanian Short Films. Bucharest: Romania Film, 1975.
Catalogue of Romanian Animation Films. Bucharest: Romania Film, 1975.
Cowie, Peter, ed. *International Film Guide.* London: Tantivy, 1970–1989. Entries on Romania by Manuela Cernat.
Cretizianu, Alexandre, ed. *Captive Romania.* New York: Praeger, 1956.
"Eastern Europe—Rumania." *Variety,* Wednesday, July 1, 1987, 109–110.
Ellis, Jack. *A History of Film.* Englewood Cliffs, N.J.: Prentice-Hall, 1979.
Fischer, Mary Ellen. *Nicolae Ceausescu.* Boulder, Colo.: Lynne Rienner, 1989.

Floyd, David. *Rumania*. New York: Praeger, 1965.
Hibbin, Nina. *Eastern Europe: An Illustrated Guide*. New York: A. S. Barnes, 1969.
Katz, Ephraim, ed. *The Film Encyclopedia*. New York: Crowell, 1979.
Liehm, Mira, and Antonin Liehm. *The Most Important Art: East European Film After 1945*. Berkeley: University of California Press, 1977.
Lyon, Christopher, ed. *The International Directory of Films and Filmmakers: Vol. II, Directors/Filmmakers*. Chicago: MacMillan, 1984.
Magill, Frank, ed. *Magill's Survey of Cinema, Foreign Language Films*. Englewood Cliffs, N.J.: Salem Press, 1985.
Manvell, Roger, ed. *International Encyclopedia of Film*. New York: Crown, 1972.
Popescu-Gopo, Ion. *All About Films*. Bucharest: Meridiane Publishing House, 1963.
Ratiu, Ion. *Contemporary Romania*. Richmond, England: Foreign Affairs Publishing, 1957.
Sadoul, Georges. *Dictionary of Film Makers*. Berkeley: University of California Press, 1972.
Slide, Anthony, ed. *The International Film Industry: A Historical Dictionary*. New York: Greenwood, 1989.
Stoil, Michael Jon. *Cinema Beyond the Danube: The Camera and Politics*. Metuchen, N.J.: Scarecrow, 1974.
Whyte, Alistair. *New Cinema in Eastern Europe*. London: Dutton, 1971.

BIOGRAPHICAL SKETCHES

BLAIER, ANDREI (1933–   ). A graduate of the Bucharest film school (IATC), Blaier is interested in the problems of youth and the frustrations of individuals in an imperfect system. Beginning with short films, Blaier directed several insignificant features, *Era prietenul meu (He Was My Friend)*, 1961, and *Casa neterminata (The Unfinished House)*, 1964, before his more successful 1966 film *Diminețile unui băiat cuminte (The Mornings of a Sensible Youth)*.* Continuing to make films in a more psychological vein, he directed *Then Came the Legend*,* 1968; *Illustrate cu flori de cimp (Maps Colored with Wildflowers)*,* 1974; *Prin cenusa imperiulul (On the Ashes of an Empire)*; *Padurea pierduta (The Lost Forest)*; *Trepte spre cer (Steps Toward the Sky)*,* 1977; *Urgia (Calamity)*,* 1977; *Totul despre fotbal (All About Football)*,* 1978; *Intunerical alb (The White Night)*,* 1983; *Fapt divers (Diverse Facts)*,* 1984; *Rideti ca-n viota (Then Laugh, That's Life!)*,* 1984; and *Bătălia din umbra (Battle in the Shadows)*,* 1987.

BOSTAN, ELISABETA (1931–   ). Known primarily for her films about childhood, featuring the character of a little boy, Naica, Bostan is a graduate of the IATC. Her feature films include *The Kid*, 1962; *Recollections from Childhood*, 1964; *Youth Without Old Age*,* 1968; *Veronica*,* 1972; *Veronica se întoarce (Veronica Comes Back)*,* 1973; the musical extravaganza *Ma-Ma*,* 1978; *Rock and roll's/woolf*, 1979; and *Saltimbancii (The Clowns)*,* 1981.

BRATU, LUCIAN (1924–   ). Born in Bucharest, Bratu became a student of painting in the Fine Arts school in Bucharest and went to Moscow to study cinema. In the first half of his career as a director, he specialized in historical feature films, focusing on Tudor Vladimirescu, a nineteenth-century hero. Later films became more thoughtful, concentrating on the problems of youth. Feature films include *Secretul cifrului (The Secret Code)*,* 1959; the spectacular *Tudor*,* 1964; *Saratul (The Kiss)*,* 1965; *Un film cu o fata fermeca-toare (A Charming Girl)*,* 1966; and *Mireasa din tren (The Bride from the Train)*,* 1980.

CĂLINESCU, PAUL (1907–   ). One of the pioneers of Romanian cinema, Călinescu began to make documentary films in 1934 and won a prize at the Venice Festival in 1938 for his documentary on Transylvania, *Țara Moților* (*The Country of Motzi*). He also directed the first post-war Romanian feature film, *Răsună valea* (*The Valley Resounds*),* 1949. Other films include *Bucharest,** 1936; *Desfășurarea* (*Development [In a Village]*),* 1954; *Pe răspunderea* (*On My Responsibility*),* 1956; *Porto Franco,** 1961; and *Titanic-vals* (*Titanic Waltz*),* 1964.

CIULEI, LIVIU (1923–   ). An actor and director, Ciulei graduated from both the Faculty of Architecture and the Conservatory of Dramatic Arts. A successful theatrical designer, Ciulei made his film debut as an actor in *In sat la noi* (*In Our Village*),* 1951, and assisted Victor Iliu in *Mitrea Cocor,** 1952. An influential director known for his ability to create psychological drama, Ciulei directed *Erupția* (*Eruption*),* 1957; *Valurile Dunării* (*The Danube Waves*),* 1958; and *Pădurea spînzuraților* (*The Forest of the Hanged*),* 1965, for which he won an award at Cannes for Best Direction.

COCEA, DINU-CONSTANTIN (1929–   ). Graduating from IATC in 1953, Cocea served as an assistant director until 1962. He became famous for his series of Outlaw films, directing *Haiducii* (*The Haiduks*),* 1965; *Rape of the Maidens,** 1968; *Răzbunarea haiducilor* (*Return [Revenge] of the Haiduks [Outlaws]*),* 1968; *Haiducii lui Saptecai* (*The Haiduks of Captain Anghel*),* 1970; and a more topical film, *Stejar, extrema urgenta* (*Oak Tree, Top Emergency*),* 1974.

DANELIUC, MIRCEA (1943–   ). After earning a Master's degree in French literature from Bucharest University, Daneliuc graduated from the IATC. Considered an "intellectual" director, Daneliuc rapidly gained stature in the Romanian film industry in the late 1970s. Features include *Opera prima, Cursa* (*The Long Drive*),* 1975; *Ediție speciala* (*Special Issue*),* 1978; *Probă de microfon* (*Microphone Testing*),* 1980; *Croaziera* (*The Cruise*),* 1981; and *Glissando,** 1984.

DRĂGAN, MIRCEA (1932–   ). Director of spectacular historical epics, Drăgan was a critic before he became a film director. After he graduated from the IATC in 1955, he quickly became a proficient filmmaker and teacher who brought contemporary history and issues of social responsibility into Romanian film. Drăgan served as professor of Film Direction and head of the Direction Department at the IATC as well as director of the National Film Center. His films include *Dincolo de brazi* (*Beyond the Fir Trees*),* 1956; *Setea* (*Thirst*),* 1960; *Lupeni 29,** 1962; *Neamul Soimarestilor* (*The Soimaresti Family*),* 1964; *Golgota* (*Golgotha*),* 1967; *Columna* (*The Column*),* 1968; *Explosia* (*The Explosion*),* 1973; *Cuibul slamandelor* (*The Knot of the Salamander*); *Aurel Vlaicu;*

Le Bras d'Aphrodite (*The Arms of Aphrodite*), 1978; and *Le Rallye* (*The Rally*), 1984.

GEORGESCU, JEAN (1904–   ). Beginning his career as a stage actor in Romania, Georgescu acted in films in the early twenties. After making *Milionar pentru o zi* (*Millionaire for a Day*)* in Romania in 1924, he moved to Paris, where he made films through the late 1920s and 1930s, directing *L'Heureuse adventure et les compagnons de Saint Hubert* (*The Happy Adventure and Pals of Saint Hubert*). Returning to Romania at the beginning of World War II, Georgescu directed *O noapte furtunosa* (*Stormy Night*)* in 1942; *Visul unei nopti de iarna* (*Dream of a Winter's Eve*),* 1945; and the documentaries *Petrolul* in 1949 and *Pădurile* (*The Forests*) in 1950. One of the three pioneering directors who formed the Romanian national cinema, Georgescu co-directed (with Victor Iliu) *In sat la noi* (*In Our Village*),* 1951, and, in 1952, a series of one-act comedies by I. L. Caragiale: *Lanţul slăbiciunilor* (*Chain of Weakness*),* *Vizita* (*The Visit*),* and *Arendaşul Roman* (*Romanian Farmer*).* He also directed the socialist comedy *Directorul nostru* (*Our Director*),* 1955; *Două Lozuri* (*Two Lottery Tickets*),* 1957; *Mofturi 1900* (*Potpourri 1900*),* 1964; the retrospective, *Lanterna cu amintiri* (*Lantern of Memories*),* 1962; and *Pantoful Cenusaresei* (*Cinderella's Shoes*),* 1968. Georgescu twice received the State Prize for his filmmaking.

ILIU, VICTOR (1912–1968). Director of "village dramas," Iliu graduated from the business academy before directing his first film, the documentary *1848* (1949), made in collaboration with Jean Mihail. After making another documentary, *Scrisoarea lui Ion Marin catre scintea* (*Letter from Ion Marin for the "Scinteia"*), Iliu worked with another film pioneer, Jean Georgescu, co-directing *In sat la noi* (*In Our Village*),* 1951. Continuing to make village dramas, Iliu directed *Mitrea Cocor* (1952),* *O scrisoare pierduta* (*A Lost Letter*),* 1953; *Moara cu noroc* (*Mill of Good Luck*),* 1955; and *Comoara din Vadul Vechi* (*The Treasure of Vadu Vechi*),* 1964.

MARCUS, MANOLE (1928–   ). Marcus's 1955 graduation film from IATC, *La mere* (*Pinching Apples*) caused a stir with its experimental style. He became a lecturer in the IATC Directors section and continued to make stirring and often innovative films, including *Viaţa nu iartă* (*Life Will Not Forgive*),* 1958, co-directed with Iulian Mihu, his co-director on *Pinching Apples,** 1955; *Nu vreau să mă însor* (*I Don't Want to Get Married*),* 1960; *Strazile au amintiri* (*Streets Have Memories*),* 1961; *Cartierul veseliei* (*The District of Gaiety*),* 1964; *Zodia fecioarei* (*Virgo*),* 1966; *Canarul si viscolul* (*The Canary and the Storm*),* 1970; *Puterea si adevarul* (*The Power and The Truth*),* 1972; *Capcana* (*Single-Handed*),* 1973; *Actorul si salbaticii* (*The Player and the Savages*),* 1974; *Mitică Popescu,** 1984; *Conspiratia* (*Conspiracy*); *Departe de Tipperary* (*Far from Tipperary*); and *Cianura si picatura de ploaie* (*Cyanide and Drops of Rain*).

MIHAIL, JEAN (1896–1963). One of the co-founders of the nationalized film industry, Mihail directed pre-war adaptations of literature, *Pagat (Sin)*,* 1924; *Manasse*,* 1925; and *Lia*,* 1927, before turning to more topical fare: *Poporul român în luptă pentru democraţie (The Romanian People in the Fight for Democracy)*,* 1946; *Bragada lui Ionut (The Ionutz Brigade)*,* 1954; and *Rîpa dracului (The Devil's Abyss)*,* 1956.

MIHU, IULIAN (1926–). A director who graduated from IATC in 1955, Mihu co-directed his innovative graduation film, *La mere (Pinching Apples)*,* with Manole Marcus. Both directors gained a reputation for challenging the aesthetic norms of the time, though Mihu's career did not advance as rapidly as Marcus', as Mihu made only one solo film in the first ten years after graduation. As he gradually gained skill and insight, his films became more interesting and notable. Features include *Viaţa nu iartă (Life Will Not Forgive)*,* 1958, co-directed with Marcus; *Procesul alb (White Trial)*,* 1965; *Felix and Otilia*,* 1972 and the critically successful *Lumina palida a durerii (The Pale Light of Sorrow)*,* 1980.

MUNTEANU, FRANCISC (1924–). Munteanu began as a writer, producing the scripts for such films as *Valurile Dunării (The Danube Waves)*,* 1959, and Muresan's *Partea de ta vină (Your Share of the Responsibility [You Are Guilty Too])*,* 1962. Beginning with the anti-fascist resistance films *Soldati fara uniforma (Soldiers Without Uniform)*,* 1960; *Lada cu zestre (The Trunk and the Trousseau)*,* 1961; *Cerul n-are gratii (Sky Without Bars)*,* 1962; and *Tunelul (Tunnel)*,* 1966, a Soviet-Romanian co-production, Munteanu continued to both write and direct films, writing the screenplay for Sergiu Nicolaescu's 1975 film, *Zile Fierbinţi (Hot Days)*,* and directing *La virsta dragostei (At the Age of Love)*,* 1963; *La patru pasi de infinit (Four Steps to the Infinite)*,* 1964; *Beyond the Railway Gate*, 1965; *The Sky Begins on the Third Floor*, 1967; *Sainte Thérèse et le diable (Saint Teresa and the Devil)*, 1979; *Melodie, Melodie* (1980); and *Un petec de cer (A Piece of Sky)*,* 1984.

MUREŞAN, MIRCEA (1928–). Graduating from the IATC in 1956, Muresan began his career as an actor and became an assistant director to Victor Iliu. A lecturer in the Direction faculty at the IATC, Muresan directed shorts and feature films, including *Partea de ta vină (Your Share of the Responsibility [You Are Guilty Too])*,* 1962; *Răscoala (Flaming [Blazing] Winter)*,* 1966; *Asediul (Siege)*,* 1971; *Bariera (Barrier)*,* 1972; and *Portile Alabastre ale Orasului (The Blue Gates of the City)*,* 1974.

NEGREANU, DINU (1919–). As chief director of both Bucharest National Theater and Buftea Studios, Moscow-trained Negreanu made films focused on common peoples' battles for social justice, making five films in the early years of post-war Romanian national cinema, including *Viaţa învinge (Life Prevails)*,*

1952; *Nepoţii gornistului (The Bugler's Grandsons)*,* 1953; *Răsare soarele (The Sun Rises)*,* 1954; *Alarmă în munţi (Alarm in the Mountains)*,* 1955; and *Pasărea furtunii (Stormy Bird)*,* 1956. In the 1960s he emigrated to the United States.

NICOLAESCU, SERGIU (1930–   ). Born in Tirgu-Jiu, Nicolaescu went to schools to become a naval officer, sculptor, mathematician, athlete, and parachutist. He worked during the fifties at the Bucharest "Alexandru Sahia" Documentary Studio, where he shot underwater films, serving as an engineer, cameraman, scriptwriter, and director of short films. Tremendously prolific, Nicolaescu directed historical epics, literary adaptations, police thrillers, and psychological dramas and acted in many of them. Features include *Dacii (The Warriors [The Dacians])*,* 1966; *Aventuri in Ontario (Adventures in Ontario)*,* 1968; *Ultimul Mohican (The Last of the Mohicans)*,* 1968; *Vînătorul de cerbi (The Deerslayer)*,* 1969; *Mihai Viteazul (Last Crusade [Michael the Brave])*,* 1971; *Moartea hui Ipu (Ipu's Death)*,* 1972; *Cu mîinile curate (With Clean Hands)*,* 1972; *Ultimul Cartus (The Last Bullet [The Last Cartridge])*,* 1973; *Un Comisar Acuză (A Police Inspector Accuses)*,* 1973; *Nemuritorii (The Immortals)*,* 1975; *Zile Fierbinţi (Hot Days)*,* 1975; *Osinda (The Punishment)*,* 1977; *The Revenge,* 1978; *Uncle Marin, the Multimillionaire,* 1979; *The Z Day,* 1986; *The Last Assault,* 1986; and *Kiuleandra,* 1986.

PINTILIE, LUCIAN (1933–   ). Originally a theatrical director, Pintilie made a few very influential films. Beginning with television drama, Pintilie directed Shaw's *Ceasar and Cleopatra*, Frisch's *Biederman and the Firebug*, and Gorki's *Children of the Sun* before directing the films *Duminică la ora 6 (Sunday at Six)*,* 1965, and the interesting *Reconstituirra (Reconstruction)*,* 1970. Pintilie returned to the theater and ultimately emigrated.

PIŢA, DAN (1938–   ). Born in Dorohoi in Moldavia, Piţa first graduated from a Bucharest medical school and worked as a medical assistant for ten years before beginning a career in film. A pupil of Victor Iliu at the IATC, Piţa's student films include *Paradisul (Paradise)*, 1967; *Dupăamiază obişnuita (Common Afternoon)*, 1968; and *Viaţa in roz (Life in Pink)*, 1969. With Mircea Veroiu, he directed *Nuntă de pietră (Stone Wedding)*,* 1973, and *Duhul aurului (Lust for Gold)*,* 1974, both films introducing a more visual and elliptical style. His solo features include *Filip cel Bun (Philip the Kind)*,* 1974; *Tănase Scatiu (Summer Tale)*,* 1976; *August in flacari (August in Flames)* for Romanian television; the westerns *Profetul, aurul si ardele nii (The Prophet, Gold and the Transylvanians,* 1978, and *Oil, the Baby, and the Transylvanians,* 1981; *Concurs (Orientering,)* 1984; *Dreptate în Lanturi (Chained Justice)*,* 1984; and *Paso Doble,* 1985.

POPESCU-GOPO, ION (1923–   ). World-famous animator Popescu-Gopo formed the acclaimed Romanian animation industry. Eschewing the strictly figurative Disneylike aesthetic that governed cartoons, Popescu-Gopo developed the grotesque but gentle character, the "little man," who starred in a series of "histories," including *Scurtă istorie (A Short History),* 1957; *Sapte arte (The Seven Arts),* 1958; *Homo Sapiens,* 1960; and *Allo! Allo! (Hello, Hello!),* 1962. Popescu-Gopo directed a number of other features, including the live action films *S a furat o bombă (Stolen Bomb),* 1961; *Paşi spre lună (Steps to the Moon),* 1963; *Harap Alb (The White Moor),* 1965; and more little man cartoons, including *Pilule 1 (Pill 1),* 1966; *Pilule 2 (Pill 2),* 1967; *Sancta Simplicitas,* 1968; *Eu + Eu = Eu (Me + Me = Me,)* 1969; *Sarutari (Good Kisses),* 1970; *Clepsidra,* 1972; *1, 2, 3,* 1975; *Infinit (Infinity,)* 1977; *Ecce Homo,* 1978; *Trei mere (Three Apples),* 1979; *Si totusi si misca (And She Turns Anyway),* 1980; *Orgolii (Pride),* 1982; *Tu (You),* 1983; *Vmor sportif (Sports Humor),* 1984; a collection of his own cartoons, *Quo vadis, homo sapiens,* 1983; and *Galax,* 1984.

POPOVICI, TITUS (1930–   ). Novelist and prolific screenwriter, Popovici has worked with the best Romanian filmmakers, including Victor Iliu in *Moara cu noroc (Mill of Good Luck),* 1955; Liviu Ciulei and Francisc Munteanu in *Valurile Dunării (The Danube Waves),* 1959; Mircea Drăgan in *Setea (Thirst),* 1960, and *Columna (The Column),* 1968; Mihai Iacob in *Strainul (Stranger),* 1963; Ciulei again in *Pădurea spînzuraţilor (The Forest of the Hanged),* 1965; Nicolaescu in *Moartea hui Ipu (Ipu's Death),* 1972, and *Cu mîinile curate (With Clean Hands),* 1972; and *Ultimul Cartus (The Last Bullet [The Last Cartridge]),* 1973; Manole Marcus in *Capcana (Single-Handed),* 1973, Dan Piţa in *Oil, the Baby, and the Transylvanians,* 1981; and George Saizescu in *Secretual lui Bachus (The Secret of Bacchus),* 1984.

SAIZESCU, GEORGE (1932–   ). Mainly known as a director of comedies, Saizescu won a state scholarship to the IATC for his own film, *The Adventure of the Good Soldier Schweik.* He acted in several films and directed *The Saturday Night Dance,* 1968; *Santaj (Blackmail),* 1981; and *Secretual lui Bachus (The Secret of Bacchus),* 1984.

TATOS, ALEXANDRU. Trained in the theater, Tatos emerged in the late 1970s as a sensitive, humorous filmmaker attuned to the plights of individuals. He directed *Mere Rosii (Red Apples),* 1978; *Rătăcire (The Wandering),* 1978; *Casa dintre cîmpuri (The House in the Fields),* 1980; *Duios Anastasia trecea (Gently Passed Anastasia),* 1980; *Fructe de padure (Forest Fruit),* 1984; and *Sequences,* 1986.

URŞIANU, MALVINA (1927–   ). Educated in both law and music, Urşianu became assistant to veteran Jean Georgescu. Departing from his comic style in her own films, Urşianu sensitively treats existential dilemmas and the personal conflicts arising in a socialist community, usually performing many of the film's key tasks—directing, writing, even art direction. Her films include *Gioconda fara suris* (*The Unsmiling Gioconda [Giaconda Without That Smile]*),* 1968; *Serata* (*The Party*),* 1971; *Trecătoarele iubiri* (*Transient Loves [These Fleeting Loves]*),* 1974; *Intoarcerea lui vodă Lăpusneanu* (*The Return of King Lapusneanu*),* 1979; *O lumină la etajul X* (*A Light on the Tenth Floor*),* 1984; and *Pe Malul Stîng al dunarii Albastre* (*On the Left Bank of the Blue Danube*),* 1984.

VAENI, CONSTANTIN (1942–). Graduating from the school of documentary, Vaeni became a specialist in anti-fascist resistance and historical films. His first film, *Zidul* (*The Wall*),* 1974, traced the psychological effects of solitude on an imprisoned anti-Nazi fighter. Other films include *Stefan cel mare* (*Stephen the Great*); *Buzduganul cu Trei Peceti* (*Buzduganul of the Three Rings*),* 1978; *Vacances Tragiques,** 1979; and *Impossibilia iubire* (*Impossible Love*),* 1984.

VEROIU, MIRCEA (1941–). Born in Tirgu-Jiu, Veroiu went to sports school and worked as a physical education teacher until he began at the IATC in 1965. Student films include *Intr-o dimineata* (*One Morning*), *Preludiu*, and *Cercul* (*The Circle*). With Dan Piţa, he directed *Apa ca un bivol negru* (*Water As a Black Buffalo*),* 1970; *Nuntă de pietră* (*Stone Wedding*),* 1973; and *Duhul aurului* (*Lust for Gold*),* 1974, films that influenced the Romanian film industry with their attention to the image and their adoption of a more elliptical style. He also directed *Sapte Zile* (*Seven Days*),* 1973; *Hyperion,** 1975; *Dincolo de Pod* (*Beyond the Bridge*),* 1975; *Intre oglinzi paralele* (*Between Opposite Mirrors*),* 1978; *Minia* (*Chronicle of the Barefoot Emperors*),* 1978; *Semnul sarpelui* (*In the Sign of the Serpent*),* 1981; *Asteptind un tren* (*Waiting for a Train*),* 1982; *Sfirsitul nopti* (*The End of Night*),* 1982; *Să mori rănit din dragoste de viaţă* (*To Die from Love of Life*),* 1983; and *Adela,** 1984.

VITANIDIS, GHEORGHE (1929–). Director and film theoretician, Vitanidis graduated from the IATC in 1953 and has been a lecturer there ever since. Beginning with newsreels and shorts at Alexandru Sahia Studios while a student, Vitanidis represented Romania in three international co-productions, including *The Broken Citadel* with Marc Maurette, 1956; *Ciulinii Bărăganului* (*The Thistles of the Baragan*),* 1958, with Louis Daquin, and *Fêtes galantes,** 1965, with René Clair. He also directed the successful *O femeie pentru un anotimp* (*A Woman for a Season*),* 1968; *Ciprian Porumbescu* (*The Ballad*),* 1973; *Dimitrie Cantemir,** 1973; and *Clipa* (*The Moment*),*1979.

SELECTED FILMOGRAPHY

1911

Fatal Love. d. Grigore Brezeanu. First fiction film in Romania.

1912

The War for Independence. d. Grigore Brezeanu.

1924

Pagat (Sin). d. Mihail;* au. I. L. Caragiale.
Milionar pentru o zi (Millionaire for a Day). d. Georgescu.*

1925

Manasse. d. Mihail;* au. Ronetti-Roman; with Romald Bulfinschi.

1927

Lia. d. Mihail.*

1930

Ecaterina Teodoroiu. Producer: Ion Niculescu Bruna.

1936

Bucharest. d. Călinescu.*

1938

Tara Moliţor (The Country of Motzi). d. Călinescu.* Honored at Venice film festival.

1942

O noapte furtunosa (Stormy Night). d. Georgescu;* au. I. L. Caragiale; with Radu Beligan, Al Giugaru, G. Ciprian, & Florica Demion.

1945

Visul unei nopti de iarna (Dream of a Winter's Eve). d. Georgescu;* sw. Georgescu and T. Musatescu; with G. Demetru, M. Filotti, Misu Fotino, Radu Baligan, & S. Dendrino.

1946

Pădurea îndrăgostiților (The Forest of Lovers). d. Cornel Dimitrescu. Privately produced comedy.
Poporul român în luptă pentru democrație (The Romanian People in the Fight for Democracy). d. Mihail.* Documentary.

1947

Două lumi si o dragoste (Two Worlds and One Love). d. Viktor Gertler. Romanian-Hungarian private co-production.

1949

Răsună valea (The Valley Resounds). d. Călinescu.*

1951

In sat la noi (In Our Village). d. Iliu* and Georgescu.*

1952

Arendașul roman (Romanian Farmer). d. Georgescu;* au. I. L. Caragiale; with C. Ramadan, G. Vasiliu Birlic, Radu Beligan, & Marcel Angheslescu.
Lanțul slăbiciunilor (Chain of Weakness). d. Georgescu;* au. I. L. Caragiale; with C. Ramadan, G. Vasiliu Birlic, Radu Beligan, & Marcel Angheslescu.
Mitrea Cocor. d. Iliu;* au. Mihail Sadoveanu.
Viața învinge (Life Prevails). d. Negreanu.*
Vizita (The Visit). d. Georgescu;* au. I. L. Caragiale; with C. Ramadan, G. Vasiliu Birlic, Radu Beligan, & Marcel Angheslescu.

1953

Nepoții gornistului (The Bugler's Grandsons). d. Negreanu.*
O scrisoare pierduta (A Lost Letter). d. Iliu;* with A. Giugaru, C. Antoniu, M. Anghelescu, & G. Birlic.

1954

Bragada lui Ionut (*The Ionutz Brigade*). d. Mihail.*
Desfășurarea (*Development [In a Village]*). d. Călinescu.*
Răsare soarele (*The Sun Rises*). d. Negreanu.*

1955

Alarmă în munti (*Alarm in the Mountains*). d. Negreanu.*
Directorul nostru (*Our Director*). d. Georgescu;* with Al Giugaru, G. Vasiliu Birlic, C. Ramadan, Radu Beligan, & Angela Ciaru.
La mere (*Pinching Apples*). d. Mihu* and Marcus;* au. Chekhov. Graduation film from IATC.
Moara cu noroc (*Mill of Good Luck*). d. Iliu;* au. Ion Slavici; sw. Titus Popovici; with Geo Barton & O. Codrescu.
Nufărul roșu (*The Red Water Lily*). d. Gheorghe Tobias. First Romanian color film.

1956

Dincolo de brazi (*Beyond the Fir Trees*). d. Drăgan* & Mihai Iacob.
Pasărea furtunii (*Stormy Bird*). d. Negreanu.*
Pe răspunderea (*On My Responsibility*). d. Călinescu.*
Rîpa dracului (*The Devil's Abyss*). d. Mihail.*

1957

Două Lozuri (*Two Lottery Tickets*). d. Georgescu.*
Erupția (*Eruption*). d. Ciulei.*
Scurtă istorie (*A Short History*). d. Popescu-Gopo.* Animation.

1958

Alo? ați greșit numărul (*Hello? Wrong Number*). d. Andrei Călărasu.
Ciulinii Bărăganului (*The Thistles of the Baragan [Baragan Thistles]*). d. Louis Daquin and Vitanidis;* c. André Dumaître; with Nuta Chirlea, Ana Vladescu, & Florin Piersic.
Sapte arte (*The Seven Arts*). d. Popescu-Gopo.* Animation.
Viața nu iartă (*Life Will Not Forgive*). d. Mihu* and Marcus.*

1959

Secretul cifrului (*The Secret Code*). d. Bratu.*
Valurile Dunării (*The Danube Waves*). d. Ciulei;* sw. Popovici* and Munteanu.*

1960

Darclée. d. Mihai Iacob.
Homo Sapiens. d. Popescu-Gopo.* Animation.
Nu vreau să mă însor (*I Don't Want to Get Married*). d. Marcus.*

ROMANIA

Setea (Thirst). d. Drăgan;* au. & sw. Popovici.*
Soldati fara uniforma (Soldiers Without Uniform). d. Munteanu.*

1961

Lada cu zestre (The Trunk and the Trousseau). d. Munteanu.*
Porto-Franco. d. Călinescu;* au. Jean Bart.
S a furat o bombă (Stolen Bomb). d. Popescu-Gopo.*
Strazile au amintiri (Streets Have Memories). d. Marcus;* sw. Dimos Rendis & Ioan Grigorescu.

1962

Allo! Allo! (Hello, Hello!). d. Popescu-Gopo.* Animation.
Cerul n-are gratii (Sky Without Bars). d. Munteanu.*
Lanterna cu amintiri (Lantern of Memories). d. Georgescu.*
Lupeni 29. d. Drăgan;* sw. Dragan, N. Tic, & Eugen Mandric.
Partea de ta vină (Your Share of the Responsibility [You Are Guilty Too]). d. Mureşan.*

1963

Codin. d. Henri Colpi; au. Panait Istrati.
La virsta dragostei (At the Age of Love). d. Munteanu.*
Paşi spre lună (Steps to the Moon). d. Popescu-Gopo;* with Radu Beligan & G. Birlic.
Strainul (Stranger). d. Mihai Iacob; au. Popovici.*

1964

Cartierul veseliei (The District of Gaiety). d. Marcus;* sw. L. Grigorescu.
Comoara din Vadul Vechi (The Treasure of Vadu Vechi). d. Iliu.*
La patru pasi de infinit (Four Steps to the Infinite). d. Munteanu.*
Mofturi 1900 (Potpourri 1900). d. Georgescu;* au. I. L. Caragiale.
Neamul Soimarestilor (The Soimaresti Family). d. Drăgan;* au. Mihail Sadoveanu.
Titanic-vals (Titanic Waltz). d. Călinescu;* with Birlic.
Tudor. d. Bratu;* sw. Mihnea Gheorghiu.

1965

Camera alba (White Ward). d. Virgil Calotescu.
Duminică la ora 6 (Sunday at Six). d. Pintilie;* sw. Ion Mihaileanu; c. Sergiu Huzum.
Fêtes galantes. d. Vitanidis* & René Clair. Co-produced with France.
Haiducii (The Haiduks). d. Cocea;* sw. Eugene Barbu.
Harap Alb (The White Moor). d. Popescu-Gopo;* with Florin Piersie & Cristea Avram.
Pădurea spînzuraţilor (The Forest of the Hanged). d. Ciulei;* sw. Popovici;* c. Ovidiu Gologan. Won Cannes award for best direction, 1966 and the prize of excellency for cinematography.
Procesul alb (White Trial). d. Mihu;* sw. Eugene Barbu.
Saratul (The Kiss). d. Bartu.*

1966

Dimineţile unui băiat cuminte (*The Mornings of a Sensible Youth*). d. Blaier.*
Meandre (*Meanders*). d. Mircea Saucan.
Răscoala (*Flaming Winter*). d. Mureşan;* au. Liviu Rebreanu.
Dacii (*The Warriors* [*The Dacians*]). d. Nicolaescu;* c. Costache Ciubotaru; with Amza Pellea, Marie José Nat, & Pierre Brice. Bucuresti Studios and Franco-London Film.
Tunelul (*Tunnel*). d. Munteanu.* Romanian-Soviet co-production.
Un film cu o fata fermeca-toare (*A Charming Girl*). d. Bratu;* sw. Radu Cosasu.
Zodia fecioarei (*Virgo*). d. Marcus;* sw. Mihnea Gheorghiu.

1967

Golgota (*Golgotha*). d. Drăgan.*
Subteranul (*Underground*). d. Virgil Calotescu.

1968

The Ages of Man. d. Alecu Croitoru; sw. Croitoru; c. Gheorghe Cristea & Mircea Mladin; with Eugenia Bosinceanu & Carmen Lucia Rusu.
A Ballad for Mariuca. d. Constantin Neagu & Titel Constantinescu; sw. Calin Gruia; c. Viorel Todan; with Brindusa Hudescu & G. Popa Mija.
Aventuri in Ontario (*Adventures in Ontario*). d. Nicolaescu.*
Black Saturday. d. Virgil Calotescu; sw. Alecu Ivanm-Ghilia; c. Constantin Ionescu-Tonciu; with Stefan Ciobotarasu, & Ioana Dragan.
Columna (*The Column*). d. Drăgan;* p. Bucaresti Studies with CCC Filmkunst; sw. Popovici;* c. Nicu Stan; with Richard Johnson & Antonella Lualdi.
Gioconda fara suris (*The Unsmiling Gioconda* [*Giaconda Without That Smile*]). d. sw. Urşianu;* c. Ion Anton; with Silvia Popovici & Ion Marinescu.
O femeie pentru un anotimp (*A Woman for a Season*). d. Vitanidis;* sw. Nicolae Breban; c. Aurel Kostrachievici; with Irina Petrescu & Iurie Darie.
Pantoful Cenusaresei (*Cinderella's Shoes*). d. Georgescu;* sw. Georgescu & Alexandru Culescu; c. Costache Ciubotaru; with Ioana Pavelescu & Dorin Varga.
Rape of the Maidens. d. Cocea;* sw. Eugen Barbu, Mihai Opris, & D. Cocea; c. George Voicu; with Emanoil Petrut & Marga Barbu.
Răzbunarea haiducilor (*Return* [*Revenge*] *of the Haiduks* [*Outlaws*]). d. Cocea;* sw. Eugen Barbu; c. George Voicu; with Emanoil Petrut & Marga Barbu.
Shots in the Stave. d. Cezar Grigoriu; sw. Grigoriu; c. Alexandru Intorsureanu; with Maragareta Pislaru, & Mihai Berechet.
The Saturday Night Dance. d. Saizascu;* sw. D. R. Popescu and G. Saizascu; c. George Cornea; with Sebatian Papaiani, Mariella Petrescu, & Ana Szeles.
Then Came the Legend. d. Blaier;* sw. Constantin Stoiciu; c. Nicu Stan; with Margareta Pogonat & Ilarionn Ciobanu.
Ultimul Mohican (*The Last of the Mohicans*). d. Nicolaescu,* Jean Dreville, & Pierre Gaspard-Huit; au. James Fenimore Cooper.
Youth Without Age. d. Bostan;* sw. Bostan; c. Iulius Druckmann; with Miha Paladescu, Emaoil Petrut, & Ana Szeles

ROMANIA 337

1969

Vînătorul de cerbi (The Deerslayer). d. Nicolaescu,* Jean Dreville, & Pierre Gaspard-Huit; au. James Fenimore Cooper.

1970

Apa ca un bivol negru (Water As a Black Buffalo). d. Veroiu* and Pįta.*
Canarul si viscolul (The Canary and the Storm). d. Marcus;* sw. Ioan Grigorescu.
Haiducii lui Saptecai (The Haiduks of Captain Anghel). d. Cocea;* sw. Eugene Barbu.
Prea mic pentru un război atît de mare (Too Small for Such a Big War). d. Radu Gabrea.
Reconstituirra (Reconstruction). d. Pintilie;* sw. Horia Patarscu; c. Sergiu Huzum; with George Constantin & Vladimir Gaitan.

1971

Animale bolnave (Sick Animals). d. Nicolae Breban.
Asediul (Siege). d. Muresan.*
Mihai Viteazul (Last Cruşade [Michael the Brave]). d. Nicolaescu.* Nominated for Oscar. Co-production with West.
Serata (The Party). d. Urşianu.*

1972

Bariera (Barrier). d. Mureşan.*
Because They Are in Love. d. Mihai Iacob; sw. Ion Omescu & Iacob; with Emeric Schäffer & Illinca Tomoroveanu.
Cu mîinile curate (With Clean Hands). d. Nicolaescu;* sw. Popovici* & Petre Salvudeanu; with Nicolaescu & Ilarion Ciobanu.
Felix and Otilia. d. Mihu;* sw. Ioan Grigorescu; c. Alexandru Intorsureanu; with Radu Boruzescu & Julieta Szönyi.
Love Begins on Friday. d. Virgil Calotescu.
Moartea hui Ipu (Ipu's Death). d. Nicolaescu;* sw. Popovici;* c. Alexandru David; with Amza Pellea, Christian Sofron, & Ion Besoiu.
One Hundred Bullets. d. Mircea Succan.
Puterea si adevarul (The Power and The Truth), two-part work. d. Marcus;* with Mircea Albulescu, Amza Pellea, & Ion Besoiu. Biography of N. Ceaucescu.
Veronica. d. Bostan.*

1973

Capcana (Single-Handed). d. Marcus;* sw. Popovici;* c. Nicu Stan; with Ilarion Ciobanu & Mariana Mihut.
Ciprian Porumbescu (The Ballad). d. Vitanidis;* sw. Vitanidis; c. Ovidiu Gologan; with Vlad Radescu & Alexandru Repan.
Dimitrie Cantemir. d. Vitanidis;* sw. Mihnea Gheorghiu; c. Ovidiu Gologan; with Iurie Darie & Alexandru Repan.
Dincolo de nisipuri (Beyond the Sands). d. Radu Gabrea; sw. Fănus Neagu; c. Dinu Tănase; with Dan Nuţu & Georg Constantin.

Explosia (*The Explosion*). d. Drăgan.*
Fratii Jderi (*The Captain Martens Brothers*). d. Drăgan;* sw. Profira Sadoveanu & Constantin Mitru; c. Nicolae Margineanu & Mircea Mladin; with Gheorghe Cozorici & Sebastion Papaiani.
Nuntă de pietră (*Stone Wedding*). d. Veroiu* and Piţa;* au. Ion Agarbiceanu; c. Iosef Demian; with Leopoldina Bălănuţă & Radu Boruzescu. Two episodes, each directed by one director.
Proprietarii (*The Owners*). d. Serban Creangă; sw. Mihai Creanga & Serban Creanga; c. Ion Marinescu; with George Constantin, Stefan Iordache, & Amza Pellea.
Sapte Zile (*Seven Days*). d. Veroiu;* c. Calin Ghibu.
The Prodigal Father. d. Adrian Petringenaru; sw. Eugen Barbu; c. Viorel Todan; with Toma Caragiu, & Leopoldina Balanuta.
Ultimul Cartus (*The Last Bullet* [*The Last Cartridge*]). d. Nicolaescu;* sw. Popovici* & Petre Salcudeanu; c. Sandu David; with Ilarion Ciobanu, Nicolaescu, & George Constantin.
Veronica se Întoarce (*Veronica Comes Back*). d. Bostan;* sw. Bostan, & Vasilica Istrate; c. Iulius Druckmann; with Lulu Mihaescu & Margareta Pîslaru.
Un Comisar Acuză (*A Police Inspector Accuses*). d. Nicolaescu;* sw. Nicolaescu & Vintila Corbul; c. Sandu David; with Amza Pellea, Gheorghe Dinica, & Nicolaescu.

1974

Actorul si salbaticii (*The Player and the Savages*). d. Marcus;* with Toma Caragiu & Mircea Diaconu.
Duhul aurului (*The Spirit of Gold*). d. Veroiu* and Piţa.* Special Jury prize at Cannes.
Filip cel Bun (*Phillip the Kind*). d. Piţa;* sw. Constantin Stoiciu; c. Florin Mihailescu; with Ileana Popovici, & Mircea Diaconu.
Illustrate cu flori de cimp (*Maps Colored with Wildflowers*). d. Blaier.*
Portile Alabastre ale Orasului (*The Blue Gates of the City*). d. Mureşan;* sw. Marin Preda; c. Viorel Todan; with Romeo Pop & Dan Nutu.
Stejar, extrema urgenta (*Oak Tree, Top Emergency*). d. Cocea;* sw. Horia Lovinescu & Mihai Opris; c. Ion Marinescu; with Constantin Diplan & Ion Caramitru.
Trecătoarele iubiri (*Transient Loves* [*These Fleeting Loves*]). d. & sw. Urşianu;* c. Sandu Intorsureanu & G. Fischer; with George Mottoi, Silvia Popovici, & Gina Patrichi.
Zidul (*The Wall*). d. Vaeni.*

1975

Dincolo de pod (*The Other Side of the Bridge*). d. Veroiu;* au. Ion Slavici; c. Călin Ghibu; with Irina Petrescu.
Hyperion. d. Veroiu;* sw. Mihnea Gheorghiu; c. Călin Ghibu; with Adela Marculescu & Emmeric Schaffer.
Nemuritorii (*The Immortals*). d. Nicolaescu.*
Opera prima, Cursa (*The Long Drive*). d. Daneliuc.*
Zile Fierbinţi (*Hot Days*). d. Nicolaescu;* sw. Francisc Munteanu; c. Nicolae Girardi; with Nicolaescu & Vladimir Gaitan.

1976

Tănase Scatiu (Summer Tale). d. Piţa;* sw. Mihnea Gheorghiu; c. Nicolae Margineanu; with Victor Rebengiuc & Eliza Petrachescu.

1977

Osinda (The Punishment). d. Nicolaescu;* sw. Anusavan Salamanian & Nicolaescu; au. Victor Ion Popa; c. Alexandru David; with Amza Pellea, Ioana Paveslescu, & Nicolaescu.
Trepte spre cer (Steps Toward the Sky). d. Blaier.*
Urgia (Calamity). d. Blaier.*

1978

Acţiunea autobuzul (The Bus Action). d. Virgil Calotescu.
Buzduganul cu Trei Peceti. d. Vaeni;* sw. Eugen Mandric; c. Iosef Demian; with Victor Rebengiuc & Toma Caragiu.
Dr. Poenaru. d. Dinu Tanase.
Ediţie speciala (Special Issue). d. Daneliuc.*
Iarba verde de acasa (The Green Grass of Home). d. Stere Gulea.
Intre oglinzi paralele (Between Opposite Mirrors). d. Veroiu;* c. Călin Ghibu.
Ma-Ma. d. Bostan;* sw. Vasilica Istrate; c. Kostea Petricenko; with George Mihaita, Florian Pittis, & Lulu Mihăescu. Co-produced with France and USSR.
Mere Rosii (Red Apples). d. Tatos;* sw. Ion Baiesu; c. Florin Mihăilescu; with Mircea Diaconu & Carmen Galin.
Minia (Chronicle of the Barefoot Emperors); d. Veroiu;* sw. Alecu Ivan Ghilia.
Povestea Dragostei (The Story of Love). d. Ion Popescu; sw. Popescu; c. Grigore Ionescu & Stefan Horvath; with Eugenia Popovici & Mircea Bogdan.
Profetul, aurul si ardele nii (The Prophet, Gold and the Transylvanians). d. Piţa.*
Rătăcire (The Wandering). d. Tatos.*
Septembrie (September). d. Timotei Ursu.
The Revenge. d. Nicolaescu;* sw. Vintila Corbu & Mircea Burada.
Totul despre fotbal (All About Football). d. Blaier.*

1979

Clipa (The Moment). d. Vitanidis;* au. Dinu Săraru.
Inainte de tăcere (Ahead of the Silence). d. Alexa Visarion; au. Caragiale.
Intoarcerea Lui Vodă Lăpusneanu (The Return of King Lăpusneanu). d. & sw. Urşianu;* c. A. Intorsureanu & G. Fisher; with George Mottoi Silvia Popovici.
Omul în loden (The Man in the Overcoat). d. Nicolae Margineanu.
Rug si flacără (The Stake and the Flame). d. Adrian Petringenaru.
Uncle Marin, the Multimillionaire. d. Nicolaescu;* with Amza Pellea.
Vacances Tragiques. d. Vaeni;* au. Mihail Sadoveanu.
Vlad Tepes (Vlad the Impaler: The True Life of Dracula). d. Doru Nastase; with Stefan Sileanu.

1980

Casa dintre cîmpuri (The House in the Fields). d. Tatos.*
Duios Anastasia trecea (Gently Passed Anastasia). d. Tatos;* sw. D. R. Popescu.
Lumina Palida a Durerii (The Pale Light of Sorrow). d. Mihu;* sw. George Macovescu; c. Gabor Tarko; with Liliana Tudor, Violeta Andrei, & Florina Luican.
Mireasa din tren (The Bride from the Train). d. Bratu;* sw. D. R. Popescu.
Nodul gordian (The Gordian Knot). d. Zoltan Szilaghyi. Animation.
O Lacrimă de Fată (A Girl's Tears). d. Iosef Demian; sw. Petre Salcudeanu; c. Constantin Chelba; with Dorel Visan & Luiza Orosz.
Probă de microfon (Microphone Testing). d. Daneliuc.*
Stop Cadru la Masa (Freeze Frame at Table). d. Ada Pistiner; sw. Stefan Iures; c. Anghel Decca; with Aleksandr Kaliaghin & Anda Calugareanu.

1981

Croaziera (The Cruise). d. Daneliuc;* sw. Daneliuc; c. Gabor Tarko; with Tora Vasilescu & Nicolae Albani.
Invingătorul (The Winner). d. Tudor Mărăscu; sw. Dumitru Furdui; c. Valentin Ducaru; with Marian Culiniac & Tora Vasilescu.
Oil, the Baby, and the Transylvanians. d. Piţa;* sw. Popovici.*
Saltimbancii (The Clowns). d. Bostan;* sw. Vailica Istrate; c. Ion Marinescu & Nicolae Girardi; with Carmen Galin & Octavian Cotescu.
Santaj (Blackmail). d. Saizescu;* sw. Rodica Ojoc Brasoveanu & Saizescu; c. Nicolai Girardi; with Ileana Ionescu & Sebastian Papaiani.
Semnul sarpelui (In the Sign of the Serpent). d. Veroiu.*
Stefan Luchian. d. Nicolae Mărgineanu; sw. Mărgineanu & Iosif Naghiu; c. Calin Ghibu; with Ion Caramitru & Goerge Constantin.
The Castle in the Carpathians. d. Stere Gulea; au. Jules Verne.

1982

Asteptind un tren (Waiting for a Train). d. Veroiu.*
Sfirsitul nopti (The End of Night). d. Veroiu.*

1983

Intunerical Alb (The White Night). d. Blaier.*
Să mori rănit din dragoste de viaţă (To Die from Love of Life). d. Veroiu;* sw. Anghle Mora; c. Doru Mitran; with Claudiu Bleont & Gheorghe Visu.

1984

Adela. d. Veroiu.*
Concurs (Orientering). d. Piţa.*
De dragul tău Anca (For Your Sake, Anca). d. Cristiana Nicolae.
Dreptate în Lanturi (Chained Justice). d. Piţa;* sw. Mihai Stoian; c. Vlad Paunescu; with Ovidiu Iuliu Moldovan & Claudiu Bleont.
Fapt divers (Diverse Facts). d. Blaier.*

Fructe de padure (Forest Fruit). d. Tatos;* sw. Dumitru Popescu; c. Florin Mihăilescu; with Manuela Boboc & Mihaela Mihut.
Galax. d. Popescu-Gopo.*
Glissando. d. & sw. Daneliuc;* au. Cezar Petrescu; c. Călin Ghibu; with Stefan Iordache & Tora Vasilescu.
Impossibilia iubire (Impossible Love). d. Vaeni;* au. Marin Preda; with Serban Ionescu.
Intoarcerea din iad (Return from Hell). d. Nicolae Margineanu; au. Agîrbiceanu; with Maria Ploaie, Remus Margineanu, & Constantin Brinzea.
Lovind o pasăre de prada (To Kill a Bird of Prey). d. Iosef Demian.
Mitică Popescu. d. Marcus;* c. Alexandru Intorsureanu.
O lumină la etajul X (A Light on the Tenth Floor). d. Urşianu;* with Irina Petrescu.
Pe Malul Stîng al dunarii Albastre (On the Left Bank of the Blue Danube). d. & sw. Urşianu;* c. Vasile Vivi Drăgon; with Gina Patrichi & Gheorghe Dinica.
Rideti ca-n viota (Then Laugh, That's Life!). d. Blaier.*
Secretual lui Bachus (The Secret of Bacchus). d. Saizescu;* sw. Popovici.*
Un petec de cer (A Piece of Sky). d. Munteanu.*
Vreau să stiu de ce am aripi (I Want to Know Why I Have Wings). d. Nicu Stan.

1985

Confessions of Love. d. Nicolae Corjos; sw. Nicolae Sovu.
Paso Doble. d. Piţa.*

1986

A Spare Moment. d. Serban Creangă; with Stefan Iordache.
Califar's Mill. d. Serban Marinescu; au. Gala Galaction.
Fourth Fence along the Wharf. d. Cristiana Nicolae; sw. Cristache Nicolae.
Kiuleandra. d. Nicolaescu;* au. Liviu Rebreanu.
Radio Romania Keeps Broadcasting. d. Dinu Tănase.
Sequences. d. Tatos.*
The Last Assault. d. Nicolaescu.*
The Z Day. d. Nicolaescu.*

1987

Bătălia din umbra (Battle in the Shadows). d. Blaier.*
Liceenii (The Graduates). d. Nicolae Corjos; sw. Nicolae Sovu.
Pădureanca (The Forest Maiden). d. Nicolae Mărgineanu; au. Ion Slavici; c. Doru Mitran.
Recital in grădina cu pitici (Violin Solo in the Elves' Garden). d. Cristiana Nicolae.
Un oaspete la cină (A Guest at Dinner). d. Mihai Constantinescu; sw. Ioan Bucheru.

8

Bruce R. S. Litte

BULGARIA

Unlike Soviet, Polish, Czech, and Hungarian film, Bulgarian film is very little known in the United States and Western Europe. Apart from screenings at film festivals and in the largest cities, Bulgarian films are not available to film students, to say nothing of average viewers; nor have they become available on video. They have not even been much written about in scholarly or popular film literature. Bulgarian directors have not achieved the worldwide recognition of a Wajda or a Zanussi, of a Forman, or of a Szabó. Despite being often ignored in its remote corner of southeast Europe (though the monumental changes sweeping all Eastern Europe have drawn Bulgaria onto the front pages in 1989), in the past forty years Bulgaria has developed a considerable film industry, one that deserves to be better known in the West for its revelations about a little-known culture, with centuries of Turkish and Greek influence underlying this, until recently, most quiescent of Eastern Block nations, for its modest but undeniable contribution to the cinema of Eastern Europe, and for the intrinsic artistic merits of a number of its contributions. While many of the social and political forces acting upon cinema have been the same as those affecting other nations of Eastern Europe, the unique position of Bulgaria at the corner, close to the bridge between Asia and Europe, of Europe has provided Bulgarian filmmakers with artistic styles and thematic material rather different from that available to their counterparts in the other Socialist Block countries. What follows in this chapter is an account, drawn from the limited recent scholarship and reviews, of this neglected film culture.

Bulgarian cinema for years was permitted only modest creative freedom (the imperatives of official Marxist political doctrines), was firmly tied to both historical and social realities (the imperatives of official social realism, the poverty, the isolation, the Soviet hegemony), and was dominated by the national literary revival of the past century (the nationalistic imperatives of culture formation—nationalistic imperatives that antedated socialism by more than half a century). Only slowly, with a burst of creative energy in the late 1950s and a more sustained flow during the 1970s, has it developed a more visual, cinematic, poetic cinema, free of stark politically motivated simplifications.

This "poetic cinema" has been distinctively shaped by the natural bent of Bulgarian filmmakers for the literary and the theatrical. Ronald Holloway, one of the two foremost Bulgarian film scholars writing in English, has shown that throughout much of the history of Bulgarian cinema "theatrical narrative dominates over visual expression." Visual expression has stemmed from the icon, rather than from "Western painting tempered by the Renaissance" (*Bulgarian Cinema*, 17).

A significant feature film industry developed late in Bulgaria because of a combination of cultural isolation, poverty, political instability, and domestic repression. It is not that rudimentary filmmaking appeared so much later here than elsewhere in Eastern or even Western Europe (newsreels and short documentaries were being shot and produced in the earliest years of the century; Sofia saw its first movie theater in 1908, its first film journal in 1913, its first film in 1915). Rather, in a small, poor, backward, overwhelmingly agrarian country that was only beginning to shape its national and cultural identity, Bulgaria lacked the technology, the capital, and the market to support commercial cinema. The first native feature films (destroyed in a 1944 air raid on Sophia) were made by Vassil Gendov during World War I, when the supply of French imports dried up—especially the Max Linder comedies that stimulated the nineteen-year-old Gendov to make *Balgaran e Galant* (*The Bulgarian is Gallant*). Gendov, the "moving spirit" of early Bulgarian cinema (Bawden, 96), made eleven feature films between 1915 and 1937. While Gendov's films are no longer available to any viewer, even a Bulgarian, the films of another pioneer are. Boris Grezhov was the most significant pre-war filmmaker, making seven feature films between 1923 and 1947 (the eighteen films of these two directors account for a significant proportion of the fifty-five feature films produced prior to the nationalization of the film industry in 1948). Of Grezhov's films, one has been called a masterpiece, *Sled Poshara W Russia* (*After the Fire over Russia*), 1929. This work was "rediscovered" when it was shown at a Lausanne, Switzerland, film symposium in 1979. Holloway describes it as an account of White Russians who immigrated to Bulgaria to work in the mines and finds it "remarkable for its restrained acting and psychological realism, as well as its rather controversial subject matter in the wake of the 1917 Revolution" (77).

Commercial production restarted after the war, and eight more feature films appeared before the nationalization of the film industry in 1948. That the film industry was not nationalized until two years after the installation of the People's Republic in 1946, and the first film not made until four years later, suggests the "peripheral nature" of Bulgarian cinema at this time (Liehm and Liehm, 133), as well as its technical impoverishment. In fact, the first film produced by the Bulgarian State Film Industry, *Kalin Orelat* (*Kalin the Eagle*), 1950, was begun as a private venture directed by Orlin Vassilev, a director who had made some not insignificant pre-war films, especially *Strahil Voyvoda* (*Strahil the Voyvoda*),

1938. While the earlier work was based on a popular romantic novel, and the later work yoked old-fashioned patriotic themes to the new doctrines of social realism, both films dealt with the standard Bulgarian theme of Turkish oppression (not surprisingly, since the Turks had ruled the Bulgarians for five hundred years, from 1396 to 1878). Old nationalistic themes worked well in the new political climate. If economic factors were the source of the chief restrictions on pre-war Bulgarian filmmakers, then political limitations were the source of the primary restraints for post-war filmmakers, even more than the initial paucity of technical facilities (which should not be discounted, for the reborn industry had to start with very few cameras, primitive sound equipment and laboratories, very few theaters, and restricted film personnel) (Holloway, *Bulgarian Cinema,* 82). During the early post-war years, until the mid–1950s, the very small nationalized film industry was locked in the grip of the Bulgarian version of Stalinism, the era of the personality cult, when historical, anti-fascist, and socio-political themes dominated the cinema, as indeed they dominated all cultural life.

The Soviet domination of all facets of Bulgarian life did much to strangle cultural life, but paradoxically it also made cultural life possible, at least in the cinema, for it was through the assistance of Soviet filmmakers, with Soviet technical equipment and advisers, and with the training of young native directors in Moscow, that Bulgaria even developed any real film culture at all. (It was not until the 1970s that many natively trained filmmakers began to appear.) The assistance was considerable, but the price was heavy in terms of expected artistic conformity. Young Bulgarians interested in studying in Moscow "were carefully screened for political reliability . . . were given large doses of ideological indoctrination. . . . Consequently, the productions of the three Balkan states [Rumania and Albania, as well as Bulgaria] are the most orthodox in their socialist realist style" (Stoil, 104). In the early post-war years, a "Russification campaign" dominated the socialist countries, the object of which "was to convince the peoples of the occupied areas that Russian culture, science, political aspirations and friendship were superior to anything the West had to offer" (Stoil, 104).

The success of this campaign may be seen in the next film, *Trevoga (Alarm)*, 1951, directed by Zahari Zhandov, a work that truly reflected the new era in Bulgaria. Though it was a simplistic and schematic story of the 1944 Resistance movement, telling of a father, an old royal army officer, torn between two sons, one a fascist officer, the other a Communist, it was notable for containing contributions of two artists who would feature prominently in the next decades: Angel Wagenstein and Rangel Vulchanov. In 1954 Zhandov and Wagenstein collaborated on *Septemvriytsi (Septembrists)*. This film, made shortly after the death of Stalin, is less doctrinaire than *Alarm*. Holloway notes its "warm, human portraits," seeing it as representing a "new trend" in Bulgarian cinema, a film in which historical accuracy (the events surrounding the 1923 anti-military uprising) overshadows ideology (*Bulgarian Cinema,* 147).

Nevertheless, retreat from the rigorous excesses of Stalinism came much more slowly and fitfully in Bulgaria than elsewhere in Eastern Europe: "The Bulgarian film industry was among the last in Eastern Europe to take advantage of the political and cultural thaw that followed Stalin's death'' (Liehm and Liehm, 138).

The mid–1950s marked the beginning of a specialized contribution of Bulgarian cinema that has won it its greatest international recognition—animation. This genre, by its technical nature, by its artificiality, was able to respond more quickly to post-Stalinist opportunities than feature films. It is to Todor Dinov to whom much of the credit goes, for this one-time newspaper caricaturist virtually founded this genre with *Junak Marko*) in 1953 (released, 1955). He broke with the Disney models of animation dominant at the Moscow Soyuzmultfilm Studio, which used ''stereotyped anthropomorphic characters'' (Holloway, 84), basing characters on human figures inspired by national folklore, songs, and dances. *Brave Marko* was followed by *Kinostarchel* (*Kino Prickles*), 1955; *Malkoto Antsche* (*Little Annie*), 1958; and many others. By the 1960s the ''Bulgarian School of Animation,'' with its emphasis on ''folk tales and philosophical fables'' became ''the talk of the short film and animation festivals of Europe.'' This genre was developed even further in the 1970s by Donyo Donev, ''who made the folkloric parable into a finely honed expression of philosophical truth focusing on the foibles of mankind.'' Films like *De Facto,* 1973; *Musikalnoto Darwo* (*The Musical Tree*), 1976; and *Causa Perduta* (*Lost Cause*), 1977, ''literally charmed and amazed audiences at international film festivals'' and ''belong in the annals of the best of world animation for their moral acerbity and intellectual wit'' (Holloway, ''Bulgaria,'' 246).

Feature film production began to pick up by 1956, a year of modest but short-lived political and cultural thaw, when eight films were produced, a then all-time record by Bulgarian standards (the figures for preceding years are dismal: 1950: 1; 1952: 2; 1953: 1; 1954: 4; 1955: 2). In film and in literature, ''the unified note of enthusiasm disappeared . . . to be replaced by the dissonance of disillusionment, attempts at criticism, and reflections on the path that Bulgaria had taken''—explorations of national identity and authenticity (Liehm and Liehm, 234). The mid–1950s saw the beginnings of the ''poetic cinema''—a movement characterized by an emphasis on the visual rather than the verbal (and verbal oversimplification and schematization). The movement may be illustrated by seven films made in the late 1950s and early 1960s, a new, distinctively Bulgarian style, roots of which may be seen in the 1954 collaboration of Borislav Sharaliev and Hristo Ganev, *Pessen sa Choveka* (*Song of Man*), a tribute to the humanitarian poet Nikola Vaptsarov, who died before a fascist firing squad in 1942.

Unfortunately, the weather had hardly begun to warm up before it started cooling off. As early as 1957, the new national leader, Todor Zhivkov, was officially condemning ''all spontaneous development in literature and art'' as ''alien to our Party and our Marxism-Leninism'' (quoted in Liehm and Liehm, 234–235). But it took a few years for the chill to reach the isolated film industry. Of the seven films completed in 1957, two are culturally significant: both had been officially approved the previous year, but while one became a landmark of Bulgarian and Eastern European film, the other was never officially released. The casualty of state censorship, containing a critical look at the personality cult, was *Partizani: Zhivotat si Teche Tiho* (*Partisans: Life Flows Quietly By*), a film directed by Binka Zhelyazkova from a script by her husband, Hristo Ganev, artists who would figure prominently in the later development of Bulgarian cinema. But Rangel Vulchanov's film *Na Malkiya Ostrov* (*On a Small Island*), released 1958, escaped censorship, though not criticism, for being pessimistic, existential, and Freudian (Liehm and Liehm, 235). In his debut film, Vulchanov worked with a script by poet Valeri Petrov—now recognized as Bulgaria's national poet—that focused on four imprisoned victims of the military dictatorship that followed the 1923 uprising. Dimo Kolarov photographed it utilizing "the rawness of reality without the artificiality of the studio (Liehm and Liehm, 235). The film departs widely from the norms of socialist realism, being a national fable or parable with tragic and epic dimensions, and showing Vulchanov's familiarity with developments in international cinema.

Vulchanov, Petrov, and Kolarov cooperated on two more films, *Parvi Urok* (*The First Lesson*), 1960, and *Slantseto i Syankata* (*Sun and Shadow*), 1962. This pair, along with *On a Small Island,* forms a trilogy epitomizing "poetic cinema" (Holloway, *Bulgarian Cinema,* 85). *The First Lesson* is a tragic love story set in the wartime resistance, a "film of pure poetic and philosophical vision"; *Sun and Shadow,* about young love struggling to grow under the threat of nuclear disaster, is less a narrative than "a lyrical abstract avant-garde poem" (Holloway, *Bulgarian Cinema,* 86) and was attacked for its "abstract humanism" (Liehm and Liehm, 236). It was one of the first films to get many showings outside Bulgaria.

Quite a number of Bulgarian films, especially in the earlier post-war years, were co-productions, made with the more advanced technical resources of other Eastern Block countries, especially the Soviet Union and East Germany. One of the major products of the "poetic cinema" was made through the collaboration of the German Konrad Wolf and the Bulgarian Angel Wagenstein (both former students at the Moscow Film Academy). The result, entitled *Zdezdi/Sterne* (*Stars*), 1959, is an extraordinary, compassionate love story of a German soldier and a Jewish girl who is being transported to Auschwitz (Holloway, *Bulgarian Cinema,* 150). Anti-Nazi (anti-fascist) themes had been and would continue to be a mainstay of all socialist cinema, but *Stars,* unlike the conventional treatments, "personalizes its evaluation of Nazism" (Bawden, 97).

The last two examples of "poetic cinema" are pinnacles of "expressionistic and symbolic language" (Liehm and Liehm, 238). *A Byahme Mladi* (*We Were Young*), 1961, a collaboration of Binka Zhelyazkova and Hristo Ganev, is a tragic love story set in war-torn Sofia, a film that "concentrated primarily on capturing the atmosphere of the recent war years and succeeded admirably" (Holloway, *Bulgarian Cinema,* 151). *Smurt Nyama* (*There Is No Death*), 1963, directed by Hristo Piskov and Irina Aktasheva, a film which became widely known throughout Eastern Europe, sets a story of "work, love, and everyday heroism" on a large construction project. It has been praised for its unprecedentedly honest realism, "the first time that Bulgarian film depicted workers made of flesh and blood, people full of doubts, anxieties, and weaknesses, who spend hours of solitude over a glass of cheap liquor, with few illusions about themselves and others" (Liehm and Liehm, 238).

The poetic realism of these films has been compared with Italian neo-realism, with the pre-war films of Marcel Carné, with the Polish School of Andrzej Wajda and Andrzej Munk, with the Soviet films of Mikhail Kalatozov, and with the Hungarian films of Zoltan Fábri. None of them were typical of their respective national film cultures of the time, but they were all ground-breaking reactions to socialist realism and they all attracted official critical displeasure.

Throughout the mid 1960s Vulchanov continued making significant films, but because of the growing cultural chill, he started living and working abroad. Two of his "black" films, *ciné noir,* "confirmed his . . . status as one of the leading psychological directors working in East Europe" (Holloway, *Bulgarian Cinema,* 88). *Inspektorat i Noshta (The Inspector and the Night),* 1963, made with the gifted young writer Bogomil Raynor, was a psychological thriller; *Valchitsata (The She-Wolf/The Wolverine),* 1965, focused on young people in a reformatory.

As restrictions on artistic expression increased during the mid–1960s, both established and rising directors became increasingly frustrated and less productive. Vladimir Yanchev's *Neveroyatna Istoriya (An Incredible Tale),* a fairly mild attempt at satirical comedy, completed in 1962, met substantial official resistance and was not released until the end of 1964. Binka Zhelyazkova made an absurdist comedy in 1966, *Privarzaniyat Balon (The Attached Balloon),* saw it delayed for a year, released briefly, and then withdrawn (though a decade later it was turned into a stage production). Petrov turned from film scripts to theater and Shakespeare translation; Ganev turned to documentaries; Wagenstein left Bulgaria.

Paradoxically, as artistic freedom decreased and the number of artistically important films decreased, the technical resources that filmmakers had at their disposal increased. Liehm and Liehm note that during the 1960s Sophia's studios were becoming adequately equipped and were producing about ten feature films annually. But most of these films "catered to popular taste and offered simple-minded entertainment, and all of them were limited to the domestic market" (240–241).

Yet there were exceptions to the decline in quality. High marks for three of the decade's more accomplished films go to Vulo Radev, an experienced cameraman, who made his directing debut in 1964 with *Kradetsut na Praskovi (The Peach Thief).* Its refinement and subtlety won it admiration internationally, Radev being the first Bulgarian director to win international acclaim. Liehm and Liehm see it as "a chamber piece . . . made in the style of the then popular realistic psychological literature. Its reserved, restrained, and lyrical visual and spoken language was the film's most distinguishing quality" (242). But it takes a most unusual political position. Starting with a story of a small-town love triangle set during World War I involving an elderly Bulgarian officer, his young wife, and an imprisoned Serbian officer, the director unexpectedly shows sympathies with the Serbian rather than the Bulgarian officer in their relationship with the young wife. The love between traditional enemies is depicted as "something positive, although doomed, against the background of war, which maims, brutalizes, and destroys" (Whyte, 148). Whyte further describes it as "an extremely moving film distinguished by its beautifully composed shots and its skillful evocation of period atmosphere" (148). Given the endemic ethnic hostilities between the Bulgarians and the Serbians, this stance showed considerable cultural emancipation. Two years later, in 1966, Radev made his nation's first wide-screen historical epic, *Tsar i General (The King and the General)*. The film was quite as stylish but politically more constrained than its predecessor, a portrayal of the World War II conflict between King Boris III, who favored an alliance with Germany, and General Zaymov, who desired alignment with the Soviet Union.

Radev followed these two films with *Nay Dalgata Nosht (The Longest Night)*, 1963, another war story that once again displays unexpected political sympathies. The protagonist of this World War II film is a British pilot who, hunted by the Gestapo and the Bulgarian police, is hiding on a train. It "shows the initial fears and hesitations of the passengers, but gradually a feeling of solidarity grows up between them until these ordinary people are willing to endanger themselves in order to save the fugitive." Despite somewhat stereotyped characters and conventional heroics, both keeping the film from attaining the real subtlety of *The Peach Thief*, the film indicates the development of a major career (Whyte 148).

Even in these repressive years, when it was still considered an achievement by many filmmakers to escape the governmental pressure to produce political works, a few ventured into such themes. In 1967 one film, *Otkolnenie (Detour/Sidetrack)*, which Whyte finds reminiscent of Alain Resnais (153), deals openly with the Stalinist mistakes. A veteran of the Sophia theater, Grisha Ostrovski, and an experienced cameraman, Todor Stoyanov (*The Peach Thief*), tell the story of an unexpected encounter of an engineer and an archaeologist, lovers seventeen years before, who recall the past (the war and the Stalinist era) that had disrupted their lives and destroyed their relationship (Holloway, *Bulgarian Cinema*, 94). They realize that they had mistakenly viewed love as a distraction, or detour, from the serious business of life, political engagement. Another film, *Byalata Staya (The White Room)*, 1968, directed by Metodi Andonov, attempts a demystification of the personality cult by telling of an independent-thinking scientist whose failure to adjust his research to official dogmas leads to his death in a state hospital, "a balance sheet of bitterness, injustice, and wasted life: the hero dies at the moment when his life's work, a book, is finally approved for publication" (Liehm and Liehm, 342).

The end of the decade saw the production of one of the greatest accomplishments of all Bulgarian cinema. Todor Dinov, that accomplished animationist, joined directional forces with Hristo Hristov (a young stage director fresh from the Moscow Film School) to make *Ikonostatin,* 1969. The film is a loose adaptation of a famous Bulgarian historical novel about Bulgarian desires to break free of the Ottoman Empire, an "epic on a religious theme" (Holloway, *Bulgarian Cinema,* 96). It has been called "one of the high points of European cinema of the late sixties. . . . a work with a beautiful multidimensional structure, a work full of intimations and silences, with a vague, merely outlined plot and a wealth of fantasy, unfolding in grandly conceived cinemascope" (Liehm and Liehm, 343–344). The theme is free artistic expression, a story of a nineteenth-century woodcarver creating an iconostasis ("an Eastern Orthodox carved wooden screen decorated with icons dividing the sanctuary from the nave"— Johnson 1447) amidst the "apathy, hatred, backwardness, and prejudice" of the benighted countryside (Liehm and Liehm, 344).

This film, like a number of others of this period, owed much of its innovation to the "daring use of dramatic metaphor and . . . a loose narrative structure that blended dreams, memories, and reality" (Liehm and Liehm, 344). This strength can be seen in the personal, metaphorical titles of these films: *The Peach Thief, The Attached Balloon, Iconostasis, The Goat Horn*—about which there is nothing grandiose or ideological—none of the heavy-handed, heroically inspirational titles of social realist films.

The success of *Iconostasis* in the late 1960s marks the beginning of a second relaxation in official cultural policies, a time when a leading literary editorial could get away with asking "official critics to stop treating artists the way 'governesses treat mentally retarded children.' " (Liehm and Liehm, 337). When, in 1971, Pavel Pissarev became general director of Bulgarian cinema, injunction turned to change as he encouraged filmmakers to participate in state film production. He supported the founding of a Film Academy in 1973, encouraged the creation of three independent film units in 1973, supplemented by a fourth in 1978 (Holloway, *Bulgarian Cinema,* 100).

The red-letter year was 1972. Metodi Andonov completed *Koziyat Rog (The Goat Horn),* a major work that further indicated that "a new style of Bulgarian cinema had burst upon the scene," a style that was rejuvinating an industry that "had been in the doldrums for more than a decade (Holloway, "Bulgaria," 233). Andonov's film gathered critical acclaim and three million Bulgarian viewers for this inspired tragedy, the story of which comes from Bulgarian folk roots, from tales of resistance and revenge during the Ottoman empire. Hristo Hristov, working with Yordan Radichkov, completed *Posledno Lyato (The Last Summer),* which faced careful official scrutiny before being released in 1974 (Hristov having made himself officially unpopular for his screenplay for *The Attached Balloon*) and quickly became a milestone in Bulgarian cinema. It tells of "a villager who refused to abandon his home (and traditional way of life), although a newly constructed dam will shortly submerge the area under water," developing the story in "stream-of-consciousness passages, surrealistic fantasies, and monologues set against visual juxtapositions" (Holloway, *Bulgarian Cinema,* 103)—

techniques at far remove from myths of state-led progress that had been dominant not many years before.

Of course, films of the late 1960s and early 1970s still employed anti-fascist themes, but at least they offered some new twists and drew on increased technological resources. One example is Zako Kheskia's *Zarevo nad Drava* (*Dawn over the Drava*), 1973, the first Bulgarian superspectacular to work with a relatively contemporary (World War II) theme (resistance to the Germans), rather than epic themes drawn from the heroic past (resistance to the Turks). But "the most ostentatious displays of the technical capabilities of Bulgarian cinema" (Liehm and Liehm, 345) were *Shibil,* 1968, directed by Zakhari Zhandov, and named for a legendary Bulgarian outlaw fighting the Turks and Peter Vassilev's *Knyazut* (*The Prince*), 1970, about a fourteenth-century ruler regaining lost territory from the Mongols and Byzantines.

While directors like Hristov and Radichkov expanded the subject matter of Bulgarian film by drawing on folk traditions, Georgi Stoyanov moved away from traditional subject matter altogether by making Bulgaria's first science fiction film, *Treta Sled Slantseto* (*The Third Planet in the Solar System*), 1972. This omnibus film consists of three separate stories that "focus on the past, present, and future in an H. G. Wells time-machine atmosphere, each story containing a subtle twist of irony at the end" (Holloway, *Bulgarian Cinema,* 103). It was a novelty, strong in invention but seriously in need of a Bulgarian Spielberg to heighten dreary special effects.

In the early 1970s attitudes toward history began changing, becoming less moralistic, less preachy. Filmmakers started more effectively utilizing visual composition, eschewing "bathetic dialogue and stilted scripts" (Liehm and Liehm, 346). Yet the literary orientation of Bulgarian cinema remained strong, as it displayed fewer examples of *films d'auteur* than elsewhere in Eastern Europe. By 1973 some notably innovative productions began coming from younger filmmakers: Ivan Terziev, Eduard Zakhariev, and Georgi Djulgerov. First, Terziev began a series of honest, realistic films on workers and their jobs with *Mazhe Bez Rabota* (*Men Without Work*), a study of the social views of laid-off road construction workers. Then Zahariev made an absurdly satirical comedy, a milestone in Bulgarian cinema, *Prebroyavane Na Divite Zaytsi* (*The Hare Census*), a piece that involves villagers having their fun with a government official who arrives to determine the number of local rabbits. Finally, Djulgerov threw out old formulas for war films with the beautifully lyric *I Doyde Denyat* (*And The Day Came*), treating young resistance fighters in non-heroic terms, though not denying their pain, sacrifice, and courage.

By the early 1970s several older directors were returning to the screen. After her difficulties with *The Attached Balloon* in the late 1960s and after some years of silence, Zhelyazkova fared better with *Poslednata Duma* (*The Last Word*), 1973, a coolly rational but humane study of six women prisoners, all former resistance fighters who have the power to save themselves by betraying the others. Vulchanov returned from Czechoslovakia, where he had made *Ezop* (*Aesop*) and *Sance* (*Chance*) in 1968 and 1969. Named an Honored Artist of the Bulgarian People's Republic, he did no more than make a musical in the Czech style, *Byagstvo V Ropotamo* (*Escape to Ropotamo*), 1973, about a leading Bulgarian popular singer, Lili Ivanova, a work memorable only for being the first Bulgarian musical. Hristo Piskov and Irina Aktasheva returned in 1972 to make *Kato Pesen* (*Like a Song*), a rather indifferent autobiographical evocation of revolutionary youth.

Valeri Petrov, as well as Hristo Ganev, disappeared from Bulgarian film life, punished by expulsion from the Union of Writers and the Communist Party in 1971 for refusing to go along with the official condemnation of Alexander Solzhenitsyn (Liehm and Liehm, 340). Petrov's final script, directed by Borislav Sharaliev, had appeared in 1966 as *Ritsar Bez Bronya* (*Knight Without Armor*), a story dealing with the ethics of emotional relationships, "a view of social ills through the eyes of a small boy, a depiction of the discrepancies between truth and lies, words and deeds" (Liehm and Liehm, 341).

Directors increasingly turned to contemporary subjects in the early and mid– 1970s—education, conflicts of rural and urban values, and the moral emptiness of the rising professional class. Among the noteworthy films on ethical topics were Sharaliev's *Sbogom, Pryatelya* (*So Long, Friends*), 1970, an exploration of the educational theme of old-fashioned teachers and outdated teaching techniques facing discontented students moving toward adulthood. In 1974 Hristo Hristov's mildly sentimental *Darvo Bez Koren* (*A Tree Without Roots*) explored the alienation of an old rural man from urban life. An excellent collaboration of Georgi Mishev and Lyudmil Kirkov, *Selyaninat s Koleloto* (*Peasant on a Bicycle*), covered the same theme in a human and comic sketch of a peasant who cycles to an abandoned village, having failed to adjust to urban life. Assen Shopov's *Vechni Vremena* (*Eternal Times*) tells of a forester clinging to his village as the rest of the inhabitants slowly slip away. A more ambitious film, and a box office success at home and abroad, was Eduard Zahariev's *Vilna Zona* (*Villa Zone*), based on a script by Georgi Mishev, a "sardonic and unrelentingly critical" satire on urban life, on the rising governmental functionaries "who elbow aside anyone and anything standing in the way of status in the new suburban community" (Holloway, *Bulgarian Cinema*, 108). Kirkov and Mishev made a sequel to their 1972 film *A Boy Becomes a Man*, entitled *Ne Si Otivay* (*Don't Go Away*). The idealistic student of the earlier film has become a teacher, only to find that his values set him at odds with the administrators. Rangel Vulchanov's *Sledovatelyat I Gorata* (*The Inspector and the Forest*) was a sequel to *The Inspector and the Night* of 1963. In this detective story that probes contemporary moral values, a country girl is pushed into murder after having been victimized by a pimp and a blackmailer.

The actor-cartoonist Ivan Andonov and Lyudmil Staikov expanded their careers, the former collaborating with Georgi Mishev to make *Samodivsko Horo* (*Fairy Dance*), 1976, a work whose "satire on the art world and the related provincial consumer mentality was fresh, and reflected a sophisticated scene in the bohemian quarters of the country" (Holloway, *Bulgarian Cinema*, 109). The latter worked with a script by Angel Wagenstein to make *Dopalnenie Kam Zakona Za Zashtito Na Darzhavata* (*Amendment to the Defense-of-State Act*), 1976, a film reconstructing the 1925 bombing of Sophia's Saint Nedelya Cathedral, a shocking terrorist act that disrupted a state funeral and led to a military dictatorship.

Hristo Hristov and Georgi Stoyanov both made highly successful, innovative films in 1976, the former making the tour de force *Tsiklopat* (*Cyclops*). This was a new development in Bulgarian cinema, for Hristov not only scripted and directed it but also designed the sets, thus coming up with the first truly *auteur* film in a collectivistic industry, a fragmented story of flashback and fantasies in the mind of a U-boat commander on a mysterious cruise. For the latter, *Shturets v Uhoto* (*A Cricket in the Ear*), Stoyanov devised an inspired satire about two Beckett-like hitchhikers who encounter a wide variety of social types (Holloway, *Bulgarian Cinema*, 111).

By the late 1970s Bulgarian cinema, Ivan Stoyanovich argues, was coming of age, achieving both high artistic achievement and widespread international recognition, with animated films, documentaries, as well as feature films winning prizes at international festivals (*IFG*, 1977, 93). Bulgaria, although still firmly under the control of Todor Zhivkov (as it had been since the mid–1950s and would be until late 1989), experienced less of the unrest brewing in other Eastern European countries. Since 1965 Zhivkov had permitted a relaxation of cultural control, allowing increased publication of Western writers like T. S. Eliot, dissidents like Solzhenitsyn, and native Bulgarian authors—and this relaxation won him, for a time, the "sympathy of most of the intelligentsia" (Crampton, 184). Through crafty and clever political manipulation he kept to minimum the political unrest bubbling in Czechoslovakia, Poland, and Hungary, partially through exercise of repressive controls but also partially through "a shift in economic priorities and . . . a more sensitive approach to the public by party officials." In the late 1970s he made sure that shops were filled and consumer goods were relatively abundant, that political corruption was kept in check, and the Party's image was kept clean. In contrast to Poland, Bulgaria was not desperately hard-pressed financially, the Bulgarians did not have "the alternative focus on loyalty or national identity" that the Church provided for the Poles, "and the traditional Bulgarian response to a political system which was not liked was apathy and withdrawal rather than opposition and confrontation" (Compton, 188).

One might go so far as to trace the flowering of Bulgarian cinema in the late 1970s and early 1980s to the rise of Luidmila Zhivkova from her role as deputy chair of the Committee for Art and Culture in 1971, to its chairwoman in 1976, when she also gained responsibility for the radio, television, and the press, to chairwoman of the politburo Commission on Science, Culture and Art. Despite a career development that smacks of blatant nepotism (she was, after all, Zhivkov's daughter), Zhivkova had a positive effect on Bulgarian culture. She was both a cosmopolitan (having been a graduate student at Oxford) and a cultural nationalist, who emphasized Bulgaria's separate cultural identity and achievement. But she also had unexpectedly unorthodox interests in "mysticism and non-materialistic ideas, "e.g. Buddism" (Compton, 189). Her early death in 1981 of a cerebral hemorrhage, without having reached forty, was a blow to Bulgarian cinema, as well as to the entire national culture and most Bulgarians (Compton, 201).

In 1977 and 1978 Georgi Djulgerov, Eduard Zahariev, Binka Zhelyazkova, Rangel Vulchanov, Ivan Andonov, Lyudmil Kirkov, Georgi Stoyanov, and Ivan Nichev all made noteworthy films. Djulgerov's *Avantazh (Advantage)* won the best director prize at the Berlin Film Festival. Telling the story of a famous con artist in the Stalinist era, "its loose, improvisational style ... offered a great deal of information on past East European and Bulgarian political history ... tell[ing] more about Bulgaria's past than any film made in the country" (Holloway, *Bulgarian Cinema,* 113). Georgi Stoyanov, who had been trained in Paris and who worked with a script by Vassil Akyov, turned to the wartime resistance to tell in *Panteley* an absurdist story of "an unwilling Resistance fighter drawn into the conflict for having lost his identity papers," a story that suggests Beckett and Pinter (Holloway, *Bulgarian Cinema,* 113). Nichev and Wagenstein turned to turn-of-the-century Bulgaria for *Zvezdi V Kossite, Salzi v Ochite (Stars in Her Hair, Tears in Her Eyes)*, a nostalgic piece about a traveling theater group, the founding of a national theater tradition, and the founding of a national identity. Zahariev and Nikolai Haitov turned to folk traditions in the award-winning *Muzhki Vremena (Manly Times)* to produce a story of a kidnapped young woman falling in love with her kidnapper during a mountain journey.

The years 1977–1978 also marked the return of two productive collaborations from the previous decade: Zhelyazkova once again joined talents with Ganev to make *Basseynat (The Swimming Pool)* and Vulchanov revived an old collaboration with Petrov to make *S Lyubov i Nezhnost (With Love and Tenderness)*. In the first film, the pool motif is used to take the memories of an elderly revolutionary activist, whose moral integrity has been challenged, back to the period of the personality cult. In keeping with the new openness in Bulgarian culture, Holloway notes, Zhelyazkova's film treated the personality cult "in a frankly open and morally consequential manner" ("Bulgaria," 236). Djulgerov's *Trampa (Swap)* treats a similar theme, the protagonist here being an eminent writer whose memory is drawn back to his co-opted days as a young journalist. In the second, Vulchanov and Petrov produce a "human comedy" about a "sculptor and his acquaintances at a Black Sea exile" (Holloway, *Bulgarian Cinema,* 182). These films illustrate what Holloway sees as a social theme characteristic of the late 1970s, "Guilt and corruption in the professional fields and among the well-to-do" ("Bulgaria," 238).

Social dislocation is another facet of this social theme. Lyudmil Kirkov used a script by Georgi Mishev to make *Matriarhat (Matriarchate),* 1977, a social satire examining the matriarchy of collective farms and villages resulting from the departure of the men, who have left to work in factories: the plight of "an emerging industrial country breaking with a rural and pastoral past" (Holloway, *Bulgarian Cinema*, 117). In *Pokriv (The Roof)*, 1978, Ivan Andonov examined the conflict between the public and the private sectors, the construction of private homes with pilfered public building materials, in a tragicomedy about "a wheeler-dealer, his dream-house, and a spitfire he falls in love with on his rounds to collect materials for the roof over his head" (Holloway, *Bulgarian Cinema*, 182). This film was praised not merely for its honest social observations but also for its "brittle love story" and "its fluid narrative style" (Holloway, *Bulgarian Cinema*, 117).

Zhivkova, in her final years, did much to prepare for the greatest celebration of Bulgarian history, the 1,300th anniversary of the Bulgarian nation, observed in 1981. Preparations for this gala event had been long in the making; starting in the late 1970s the nation's artistic energies were intent upon gaining international attention for a heritage and a culture. The energies contributed to some of the finest films yet made—even before the festive year began. After a lapse of fifteen years Vulchanov was able to film his major screenplay from the mid–1960s—*Lachenite Obouvki na Neznainiya (The Unknown Soldier's Patent Leather Shoes)*, an "endearing ... lyrical poem on a fading peasant culture and the irretrievable past," a "poem" Vulchanov set at the turn of the century, using an entirely non-professional cast. This film opened the 1979 London Film Festival and then won a Grand Prix at New Dehli in 1981. Holloway considers it "one of the highest achievements in Bulgarian film history" (*Bulgarian Cinema*, 117). Also in 1979 Hristov won a first prize at the Moscow Film Festival for *Barierata (Barrier)*, an imaginative fantasy about a composer at a mid-life crisis who meets an ethereal woman who teaches him to fly, though flight leads to his death. "The superbly lensed flying scenes are Chagall-like and earned photographer Atanas Tasses recognition as one of the country's top cinema talents" (Holloway, *Bulgarian Cinema*, 117).

Four significant films looked at social corruption. Nichev's *Bumerang (Boomerang)*, 1979, examined an overly ambitious young journalist who recognized few moral limits in his desire to rise in his profession. Kirkov's *Kratko Sluntse (Short Sun/A Ray of Sunlight)*, 1979, is "a strong critical film of social conscience" (Holloway, *Bulgarian Cinema*, 185) about a university student on a well-digging crew at a Sophia villa who digs up bones of old freedom fighters from the twenties. The property owner, to stop the potentially damaging news of this uncovered past, doesn't hesitate to arrange an accidental death. Andonov's *Chereshova Gradina (The Cherry Orchard)*, 1979, depicts the conflict between an honest forester and a dishonest cooperative farm manager over the preservation of an orchard. This was a restatement of a popular Bulgarian theme of the day, a representative of the old agrarian order pitted against and destroyed by a member of the new managerial class. This conflict reappears in Hristov's *Kamionat (The Truck)*, 1980, an exceptional psychological film, a version of Clouzot's *Wages of*

Fear, a highly metaphorical account of Bulgaria's movement from an agarian to an industrialized nation, a film in which "the social microcosm is packed with motifs, symbols, and images from Hristov's prior masterful portraits of a society in the throes of change" (Holloway, *Bulgarian Cinema,* 122).

The greatly touted 1,300th anniversary celebration brought a crop of superspectacles in 1981. Zahari Zhandov's *Boyanskiyat Maistor (Master of Boyana)* paid grand tribute to the nation's cultural and religious past by offering a fictionalized biography of the painter who created the magnificent frescoes at Boyana Church (near Sofia) in 1259, works that antedated the creations of Cimabue and Giotto by two generations. Zhelyazkova's *Golyamoto Noshtno Kupane (The Big Night Bathe),* a parable on national traditions, was the Cannes entry of 1981. Of particular significance was Georgi Djulgerov's *Mera Spored Mera (Measure for Measure),* a three-part epic chronicle of an uprising in Macedonia in 1903, the story based on documents and eyewitness accounts of the overthrow of Turkish occupation—"One of the most significant achievements in Bulgarian film history" (Holloway, *Bulgarian Cinema,* 125). But the great blockbuster of the crop was Staikov's six-hour *Khan Asparukh.* With its cast of thousands, its elaborate costumes and massive scenes, this nationalistic extravaganza compares well, Holloway tells us, with Hollywood extravaganzas (Holloway, *Bulgarian Cinema,* 133, 194). Its three parts cover the Central Asian origins of the Bulgars (originally a Turkic, not a Slavic people), their migration to the western shores of the Black Sea, and the founding of Bulgaria in the seventh century by their leader, Khan Asparukh. Surprisingly, perhaps, the film did not ignore their conflicts with the indigenous Slavic people, with whom, however, they eventually assimilated. Its native success, not surprisingly, was enormous: it was seen by some eleven million people, rather more than the total population of the country. Stoyanovich suggests that this could be a world record in per capita attendance (*IGF,* 1983, 84). A shortened English version, made by Warner Brothers, appeared in early 1984.

For several years following the Bulgarian *annus mirabilis,* several more fine films appeared, a continuation of the great nationalistic momentum. The year 1983 saw the first two (of three) parts of Georgi Stoyanov's *Konstantin Filosof (Constantine the Philosopher),* the story of the two saints and brothers, Cyril (Constantine) and Methodius, who created the Cyrillic alphabet and whose missionary work led to the conversion of the Bulgarian people. A year later Borislav Sharaliev's *Boris Purvi (Boris the First)* continued the story of this conversion, showing how Boris, through his conversion in 864 and his adherence to Constantinople rather than Rome, did much to determine the path of Bulgaria's future development.

Smaller films on contemporary topics did not disappear amidst historical glorifications. Dimiter Petrov's *Kouche v Chekmedzhe (A Dog in the Drawer),* 1982, tells of the attachment of three young boys to a stray dog. Hristo Piskov's *Lavina (Avalanche),* 1982, offers a metaphorical treatment of an avalanche that shows how the individual must triumph over self-interest (Holloway, 194). A more ambitious film was Ivan Andonov's *Byala Magiya* (*White Magic*), 1982, a philosophical parable set in the Bulgarian countryside in the 1920s and 1930s. Stoyanovich says that "a wide variety of national characters are seen in a melee of tragi-comic fairground elation—perhaps a final desperate indulgence in the face of the impending, but as yet unperceived threat, of the violence of the Twenties and Thirties" (*IFG*, 1983, 86).

Political subjects were not neglected, some rising far above ideological hackwork. One of the more ambitious undertakings was *Predouprezhdeniyeto* (*The Warning*), 1982, a co-production of Bulgaria, East Germany, and the USSR, in which the Bulgarian contribution was the largest, even though the director, Juan Antonio Bardem, was Spanish. It is a historical epic about the Bulgarian Communist and international workers' leader Georgi Dimitrov and his role in the Leipzig trial of 1933, where he was accused of planning the Reichstag fire, and where he won a moral victory over facism (Stoyanovich, *IFG*, 1983, 86).

Another major film of considerable artistic significance, *Hotel Tsentral* (*Hotel Central*), 1983, dealt with the same period. Vesselin Branev wrote and directed a film set during the 1934 coup d'état that overthrew the parliamentary democracy, such as it was, and established a dictatorship. It tells of a hotel maid in a small town who is forced into prostitution, an innocent girl victimized by corrupt local political figures. It won international recognition as a 1983 entry in the Venice film festival.

Also winning international recognition in the same year, at Munich and Montreal, was Vulchanov's *Posledni Zhelania* (*Last Wishes*). According to Stoyanovich, it "occupies a special place among recent Bulgarian films . . . a bizarre grotesque featuring a bunch of half-real, half-phantasmal characters" (*IFG*, 1984, 83) set during World War I. It is a bitter satire of "royal families congregat[ing] on a battlefield during a truce to continue their family spats in an absurd setting . . . contrast[ing] royal amusements with the harsh realities of war and killing" (Holloway, *Bulgarian Cinema*, 199).

Observers of Bulgarian cinema have noted the recent return of drought following the fruitful crop of the very early 1980s. Holloway speculates on the possibile causes, suggesting five contributing factors: (1) the premature death of Liudmila Zhivkova (whom he refers to as Luidmila Shivkova—merely a difference in transliteration); (2) the fact that Nikolai Nenov, film minister from 1980 to 1986, did little to encourage "sociocritical and sociopolitical films"; (3) the resignation of Hristov as head of the Union of Bulgarian Filmmakers in 1983 (and both he and his successor, Georgi Stoyanov, were having trouble getting their films released); (4) the enormous expense of the celebratory spectacles (this small nation's cinematic binge), which reduced financial resources; (5) the retirement of internationally recognized directors like Georgi Djulgerov, which left a creative gap (Holloway, *Bulgarian Cinema*, 243). While major directors like Hristov, Zahariev, and Vulchanov remained active, they were, however, producing artistically less ambitious, thematically more conventional films.

Ivan Stoyanovich sees hope in administrative changes: in the appointment of director Lyudmil Staikov as chairman of the Bulgarian Cinematography Corporation and in the establishment of five artistically and financially independent production units, directed by highly respected directors: Borislav Sharaliev, Ivanka Grubcheva, Ivan Andonov, Lyudil Kirkov, and Zacco Heskia (*IFG*, 1988, 125). Holloway sees hope in a coming generation of natively trained filmmakers, who, since the foundation of the Sofia Film and Theater Academy (VITIS) in 1973—where Vulchanov, Hristov, and Djulgerov have been teaching—will rejuvenate the industry. One new talent is that of Kiran Kolarov, who has made three noteworthy films: *Slouzhebno Polozheniye—Ordinarests* (*Status—Orderly*), 1978; *Vuzdushniyat chovek* (*The Airman*), 1980; and *Delo No. 205/1913* (*Case No. 205/1913*), 1984. This last film is a tribute to Bulgaria's admired turn-of-the-century revolutionary poet, Peyo Yavorov, an examination of the troubled relationship of the poet with his wife, her suicide in 1914 leading to his. Through imaginative use of historical documents, Kolarov captured the period of the development of Bulgarian literature (Stoyanovich, *IFG*, 1984, 82). Another belongs to Nikolai Volev, whose *All For Love*, 1986, "is a sharply critical film directed against spiritual and material corruption" (Stoyanovich, IFG, 1988, 125). While new talent is appearing, established masters are still active. Vulchanov has recently made *Where Are You Going?*, 1986, which "seeks to prove on a plane of paradoxical absurdity that the flight from boredom and inanity disguised as academic routine only leads to a different kind of inanity" (Stoyanovich, IFG, 1988, 125). Zahariev's *My Darling, My Darling* "examines the seemingly healthy but inwardly devastated social cell of the family." Films that have either appeared in the past year or two or are about to appear are Staikov's *Time of Parting,* Dyulgerov's *Acadamus,* a musical resembling *Pygmalion,* and Vulchanov's *Third Round,* a coming-of-age story about university life.

One cannot begin to predict the changes the democratization movement will bring to Bulgarian cinema. The disappearance of remaining Communist ideological constraints may further the cinematographic exploration of national identity, without, one may hope, an exacerbation of xenophobic tendencies, especially anti-Turkish prejudices. The constraints under which Bulgarian filmmakers have been operating have been considerable. Liehm and Liehm have concluded, with considerable justice, that Bulgarian cinema has not been rooted as deeply in a highly articulated cultural and national identity as Polish, Hungarian, and Czechoslovakian cinema; that less thematic continuity is observable: "A glance at its development shows a certain degree of randomness and heterogeniousness; that in the midst of the mediocre, and often less than mediocre, something extraordinary would crop up now and again, but the artist responsible for it rarely remained at the top." Despite the cinemagraphic talent and increased technological resources, "the provincial attitudes and values of the overall cultural atmosphere . . . kept giving renewed support to the convention of schematism and the mechanism of auto-censorship" (347). The talent has been there, and it has given rise to a small library of expressive, provocative films. In view of the political repression of more than forty years, the achievements, however uneven, may be considered remarkable, and could become more so if external and auto-censorship continue to disappear. A year or two ago, even before the fall of Zhivkov, Ivan Stoyanovich was predicting that the "future...looks brighter than the present" (*IFG*, 1988, 127). Today this brighter future looks closer than ever. Western film students might even have increased opportunities to see the output of a small group of filmmakers that has produced an uneven but sometimes impressive contribution to contemporary cinema.

BIBLIOGRAPHY

Bawden, Liz-Anne. *Oxford Companion to Film*. New York: Oxford University Press, 1976.
Compton, R. J. *A Short History of Modern Bulgaria*. Cambridge: Cambridge University Press, 1987.
Cowie, Peter, ed. *International Film Guide*. 1963–1988. London: Tantivy, published annually.
Holloway, Ronald. "Bulgaria: The Cinema of Poetics." *Post New Wave Cinema in the Soviet Union and Eastern Europe*. Edited by Daniel J. Goulding. Bloomington: Indiana University Press, 1988.
———. *The Bulgarian Cinema*. Rutherford, N.J.: Fairleigh Dickinson University Press, 1986.
Johnson, William. Review of *Ikonstasut (Iconostasis)*, by Todor Dinov and Bristo Hristov. *Magill's Survey of Cinema*, 1446–1449.
Liehm, Mira, and Antonin J. Liehm. *The Most Important Art: Soviet and East European Film After 1945*. Berkeley: University of California Press, 1977.
MacDermott, Mercia. *A History of Bulgaria: 1393–1885*. London: Allen and Unwin, 1962.
Manvill, Roger. *New Cinema in Europe*. New York: Dutton, 1966.
Stoil, Michael Jon. *Cinema Beyond the Danube*. Metuchen, N.J.: Scarecrow, 1974.
Stoyanovich, Ivan. "Bulgaria." Annually in *International Film Guide*. Edited by Peter Cowie, 1965–1988.
White, Alistair. *New Cinema in Eastern Europe*. New York: Dutton, 1971.

BIOGRAPHICAL SKETCHES

ANDONOV, IVAN (1934–), actor, animator, director. As a popular film and stage actor, Andonov is especially admired for his role in Rangel Vulchanov's *Na Malkiya Ostrov* (*On a Small Island*), 1958;* he made notable and prize-winning animated films in the 1960s; he directed and starred in *Trudna Lyubov* (*A Difficult Love*), 1974; he successfully directed *Samodivski Horo* (*Fairy Dance*), 1976,* and *Chereshova Gradina* (*The Cherry Orchard*), 1979.*

ANDONOV, METODI (1932–1974), theater and film director. A graduate of the Sofia Academy of Dramatic Art, Andonov made significant contributions to Bulgarian cinema before his premature death, most notably *Koziyat Rog* (*The Goat Horn*), 1972,* among the greatest Bulgarian box office hits. He also made two successful detective films from scripts by Bogomil Rainov, *Nyama Nishto Pohubavo ot Loshoto Vreme* (*There's Nothing Finer Than Bad Weather*), 1971, and *Goliamata Skuka* (*The Great Boredom*), 1973.

BOROZANOV, BORIS (1897–), director. After making commercial films during the war, Borozanov made an old-fashioned nationalistic epic, *Kalin Orelat* (*Kalin the Eagle*), 1950,* the first film from the Bulgarian nationalized film industry.

DAKOVSKI, DAKO (1919–1962), director. One of the first of many graduates of the Moscow Film School, Dakovski contributed to the birth of the Bulgarian national film industry, beginning with an adaptation of Ivan Vazov's classic national novel *Pod Igoto* (*Under the Yoke*), 1952,* and continuing with a series of films about contemporary issues, especially those involving peasant life: *Nespokoen Pat* (*The Troubled Road*), 1955,* and *Taynata Vecherya Na Sedmatsite* (*The Secret Supper of the Sedmaks*), 1957.*

DINOV, TODOR (1919–), animationist, director. Celebrated as the father of Bulgarian animation, Dinov has also worked as co-director (with Hristo Hristov) on the masterly *Iconostasis*, 1969.* On his own, he has made *Barouten Boukvar* (*Gunpowder*), 1969, and *Lamyata* (*The Dragon*), 1974, a medieval fairy tale.

DJULGEROV, GEORGI (1943–), director, film teacher. Trained in Moscow, Djulgerov remade his diploma film upon returning home, changing the location from Armenia to the Bulgarian mountains and the title to *Ispit* (*The Test*), 1971: it appeared as part of a two-part feature film *Sharen Svyat* (*Colorful World*), 1971.* These were followed by a lost generation-resistance movement film, *I Doyde Denyat* (*And the Day Came*), 1973;* a film about a Stalinist con-artist, *Avantazh* (*Advantage*), 1977;* another study of the personality cult, *Trampa* (*Swap*), 1978;* and most significant of all, *Mera Spored Mera* (*Measure for Measure*), 1981.*

GANEV, HRISTO (1924–), director. A 1950 graduate of the Moscow Film School, he has collaborated extensively with his wife Binka Zhelyazkova, wrote the script for Borislav Sharaliev's *Pessen Sa Choveka* (*Song of Man*), 1954,* and contributed (with Angel Wagenstein*) to Sharaliev's comedy *Dve Pobedi* (*Two Victories*), 1956. He has also written and directed major documentary films.

GREZHOV, BORIS (1899–1967), director. The first significant Bulgarian filmmaker, trained in Berlin between 1917 and 1921, Grezhov made seven feature films between 1923 and 1947, the most notable being *Sled Poshara W Russia* (*After the Fire over Russia*), 1929.

HAITOV, NIKOLAI (1919–), storyteller, dramatist, scriptwriter. From shepherd and forester, to story writer in the mid–1950s, to dramatist in the 1960s, to screenwriter in the 1970s, Haitov has had an unusually varied career. He worked on scripts for Djulgerov's *Ispit* (*The Test*), 1971;* Milen Nikolov's *Gola Suvest* (*Naked Conscience,*) 1970, these two short films being combined to form Nikolov's full-length *Sharen Svyat* (*Colorful World*), 1971;* and most notably on the original screenplay for Metodi Andonov's very successful *Koziyat Rog* (*The Goat Horn*), 1972.* He has also written the screenplays for Eduard Zahariev's *Muzhki Vremena* (*Manly Times*), 1977,* and Ivan Andonov's *Chereshova Gradina* (*The Cherry Orchard*), 1979.* His story "Darvo Bez Koren" ("A Tree without Roots") provides the basis for Hristov's 1974 film of the same title.

HRISTOV, HRISTO (1926–), director. Besides having been president of the Union of Bulgarian Filmmakers for 10 years and a film teacher, Hristov has made two of the milestones of Bulgarian cinema: *Iconostasis*, 1969,* with Todor Dinov, and *Posledno Lyato* (*The Last Summer*), 1974.* His other films include *Nakovalnya Ili Chuk* (*Hammer or Anvil*), 1972;* *Darvo Bez Koren* (*A Tree without*

Roots), 1974;* *Tsiklopat (Cyclops)*, 1976;* *Barierata* (Barrier), 1979;* *Edna Zhena Na Trideset I Tri (A Woman at Thirty-three)*, 1982;* and *Subessednik Po Zhelanie (Question Time)*, 1984.

ILINCHEV, KIRIL (1921–), director. Trained at the FAMU film school in Prague, Ilinchev graduated in 1951 and returned to Bulgaria to direct numerous theatrical films, including *Golemanov,* 1958, a popular satirical play.

KIRKOV, LYUDMIL (1933–), director. A graduate of both the Sofia Academy of Dramatic Arts and the Moscow Film School, Kirkov began making strong films in the early 1970s, including collaborations with Georgi Mishev: *Momcheto Si Otiva (A Boy Becomes a Man)*, 1972; *Selyaninat S Koleloto (Peasant on a Bicycle)*, 1974;* *Ne Si Otivay (Don't Go Away)*, 1976; and *Matriarhat (Matriarchate)*, 1977*—and with Stanislav Stratiev: *Kratko Sluntse (Short Sun)*, 1979;* *Orkestur Bez Ime (A Nameless Band)*, 1982;* and *Ravnovessie (Balance)*, 1983.* He has served as artistic manager of the Subremenik (Contemporary) film unit.

KORABOV, NIKOLA (1926–), director. A 1952 graduate of the Moscow Film School (VGIK), Korabov has made both historical epics: *Tutyun (Tobacco)*, 1962,* and *Ivan Kondarev,* 1974; contemporary films: *Vula (Permission of Marry)*, 1965, and *Orissia (Destiny)*, 1983; and documentary films: *Nikolai Ghiaurov—50,* 1980.

MISHEV, GEORGI (1935–), scriptwriter. Beginning as a journalist and writer of children's literature, and moving into films in the late 1960s, Mishev has produced a major series of significant satirical films, working with three leading directors: Eduard Zahariev on *Ako Ne Ide Vlak (If The Train Doesn't Arrive)*, 1967;* *Prebroyavane Na Divite Zaytsi (The Hare Census)*, 1973;* and *Vilna Zona (Villa Zone)*, 1975;* Lyudmil Kirkov on *Momcheto Si Otiva (A Boy Becomes a Man)*, 1972; *Selyaninat S Koleloto (Peasant on a Bicycle),* 1974;* *Ni Si Otivay (Don't Go Away),* 1976; and *Matriarhat (Matriarchate,)* 1977;* and Ivan Andonov on *Samodivski Horo (Fairy Dance)*, 1976,* and *Dami Kanyat (Ladies' Choice)*, 1980.

PETROV, VALERI (1920–), poet and scriptwriter. Trained as a physician, recognized as a major national poet, nationally acclaimed as a translator of Shakespeare into Bulgarian, Petrov began writing filmscripts in the late 1950s with a script for Rangel Vulchanov's seminal *Na Malkiya Ostrov (On a Small Island),* 1958,* which was followed by scripts for the same director's *Parvi Urok (First Lesson),* 1960,* and *Slantseto i Syankata (Sun and Shadow),* 1962.* Besides making distinguished contributions to children's films, he has more recently collaborated with Vulchanov on *S Lyubov i Nezhnost (With Love and Tenderness),* 1978.*

PISKOV, HRISTO (1927–), director. A graduate of the Moscow Film School (VGIK), Piskov was assistant director of Lev Arnstam's *Urok Na Istoriyata (History Lesson)*, 1957.* He has co-directed films with his wife, the Soviet actress Irina Aktasheva: *Bednata Ulitsa (Poor Man's Street)*, 1960,* and *Ponedelnik Sutrin (Monday Morning)*, 1966.*

RADEV, VULO (1923–), director, scriptwriter. Trained at the Moscow Film School, Radev began as a cameraman, making his directing and scriptwriting debut with the major international success *Kradetsat Na Praskovi (The Peach Thief)*, 1964.* Other significant films include *Tsar I General (Tsar and General)*, 1966;* *Nay-Dalgata Nosht (The Longest Night)*, 1967;* and *Chernite Angeli (Black Angels)*, 1970.* He is closely associated with the films of poetic realism of Rangel Vulchanov and Binka Zhelyazkova.

RADICHKOV, YORDAN (1929–), writer, dramatist. As a highly productive author, often compared to Gogol, Radichkov has had many of his stories and plays adapted as films: by Binka Zhelyazkova, *Privarzaniyat Balon (The Attached Balloon)*, 1967;* by Hristo Hristov in *Posledno Lyato (The Last Summer)*, 1974;* by Krikor Azarian in *Vsichki I Nikoy (Everybody and Nobody)*, 1978.

SHARALIEV, BORISLAV (1922–), director. An early postwar graduate of the Moscow Film School, Sharaliev collaborated with Hristo Ganev on *Pessen Sa Choveka (Song of Man)*, 1954,* made some children's and youth films, and, notably, the celebratory epic (with script by Angel Wagenstein*) *Boris Purvi (Boris the First)*, 1984.*

STAIKOV, LYUDMIL (1937–), television, stage, film director. Graduating in theater in 1962 from the Sofia Academy, Staikov turned to film in the 1970s, making his feature film debut in *Obich (Affection)*, 1972,* continuing successfully with *Dopalnenie Kam Zakona Za Zashtito Na Darzhavata (Amendment to the Defense-of-State Act)*, 1976,* and *Iluziya (Illusion)*, 1980.* His greatest achievement has been his mammouth historical epic *Khan Asparukh*, 1981.* He is artistic manager of the Mladost ("Youth") film unit.

STOYANOV, GEORGI (1939–), director. Beginning as a mechanical engineering student, Stoyanov, instead of staying in the Eastern Bloc, went to Paris, getting his degree from IDHEC in 1964. After making documentaries and shorts, he made his feature film debut with *Sluchayat Penleve (The Painleve Case)*, 1968.* He has made films in a diversity of styles—grotesque, lyrical, science fiction, and historical epic. With scriptwriter Vassil Akyov he made *Ptitsi Hratki (Birds and Greyhounds)*, 1969,* and *Panteley*, 1978.* More recently he has made a super-spectacle celebrating the 1300th anniversary of the Bulgarian nation, *Konstantin Filosof (Constantine the Philosopher)*, 1983.* He has played an active role in Bulgarian film culture, having served as president of the Union of Bulgarian Filmmakers since 1982.

STOYANOV, TODOR (1930–   ), cinematographer, director. Stoyanov has worked as co-director with Grisha Ostrovski on the significant *Otklonenie (Sidetrack)*, 1967,* and on the more conventional *Mazhe V Komandirovka (Men on a Business Trip)*, 1969; on his own he has made a detective-spy film, *Stranen Dvuboy (Strange Duel)*, 1971.

TERZIEV, IVAN (1934–   ), director. Graduating from the Sofia Academy in 1958 with training in acting, and studying directing at the Moscow Film School, Terziev made several adventurous films in the 1970s, including *Mazhe Bez Rabota (Men Without Work)*, 1973,* and *Silna Voda (Strong Water)*, 1975.*

VULCHANOV, RANGEL (1927–   ), director. Bulgaria's pre-eminent director, Vulchanov is unusual among his generation for not having been trained abroad. As a student he acted in Zhandov's *Trevoga (Alarm)*, 1951.* He directed the watershed film *Na Malkiya Ostrov (On a Small Island)*, 1958,* his first feature film, which brought him and his nation's cinema international recognition. This has been followed by a range of varied and artistically accomplished films, including *Parvi Urok (First Lesson)*, 1960;* *Slantseto i Syankata (Sun and Shadow)*, 1962;* *Inspektorat I Noshta (The Inspector and the Night)*, 1963;* *Valchitsata (The She-Wolf/Wolverine)*, 1965;* *Sledovatelyat I Gorata (The Inspector and the Forest)*, 1975;* *S Lyubov I Nezhnost (With Love and Tenderness)*, 1978;* *Lachenite Obouvki Na Neznainiya (The Unknown's Soldier's Patent Leather Shoes)*, 1979;* and *Posledni Zhelania (Last Wishes)*, 1983.* He has also made films in Czechoslovakia, including the Bulgarian-Czech co-production (with Angel Wagenstein) of *Ezop (Aesop)*, 1970; *Face Behind the Mask,* 1970; and *Chance,* 1970.

WAGENSTEIN, ANGEL (1922–   ), scriptwriter. A prolific filmwriter, Wagenstein has been active through the entire period of post-war Bulgarian cinema, beginning with an adaptation of a play by Orlin Vassilev's for Zahari Zhandov's film *Trevoga (Alarm)*, 1951,* and further collaborating with Zhandov on *Septemvriytsi (Septembrists)*, 1954.* Work with East German director Konrad Wolf on *Zdezdi (Sterna/Stars)*, 1959,* brought international recognition. More recently he has worked with Wolf on a film about the painter Goya, *Goya,* 1971, and on an adaptation of Saint-Exupery's *The Little Prince,* 1966, for East German Television. Other major scripts include those for Ivan Nichev's *Zvezdi V Kossite, Salzi V Ochite (Stars in Her Hair, Tears in Her Eyes)*, 1977;* for Lyudmil Staikov's *Dopalnenie Kam Zakona Za Zashtito Na Darzhavata (Amendment to the Defense-of-State Act)*, 1976;* and for Vulchanov's Czech co-production, *Ezop (Aesop)*, 1970.

YAKIMOV, YAKIM (1925–), director. A student of the Łodz Film School in Poland, Yakimov has focused on youth problems and the generation gap, especially in *Nespokoen Dom (Troubled Home)*, 1965.*

YANKOV, YANKO (1924–), director. A 1952 graduate of the Moscow Film School, Yankov made the first post-war Bulgarian comedy, *Tova Se Sluchi Na Ulizata (It Happened on the Streets)*, 1956;* the controversial *Godini Za Lyubov (Years of Love)*, 1957;* and *Priznanie (Confession)*, 1969.

ZAHARIEV, EDUARD (1938–), director. After graduating from the Budapest Film School in 1961 and then making a series of significant documentaries, Zahariev demonstrated remarkable talents in the controversial *Ako Ne Ide Vlak— Moreto (If the Train Doesn't Arrive—the Sea)*, 1967;* *Prebroyavane Na Divite Zaytsi (The Hare Census)*, 1973;* *Vilna Zona (Villa Zone)*, 1975,* these last two films winning international recognition and prizes (at Locarno and Karlovy Vary, respectively). More recently he has made *Muzhki Vremena (Manly Times)*, 1977,* starring his wife Marianna Dimitrova, and *Pochti Lyubova Istoria (Almost a Love Story)*, 1980.*

ZHANDOV, ZAHARI (1911–), director. Beginning as a documentary filmmaker before the war, and now recognized as the father of modern Bulgarian cinema, Zhandov initiated the true beginning of the state film industry with *Trevoga (Alarm)*, 1951.* On this film, and on *Septemvriytsi (Septembrists)*, 1954,* he collaborated with Angel Wagenstein. His finest work, however, came in 1981: *Boyanskiyat Maistor (Master of Boyanna)*.*

ZHELYAZKOVA, BINKA (1923–), director. A graduate of the Academy of Dramatic Art in Sofia, Zhelyazkova has been one of the great forces in Bulgarian cinema. Often working in tandem with her scriptwriter husband, Hristo Ganev, she has continued to push open the doors of Bulgarian artistic freedom with films like *A Byahme Mlady (We Were Young)*, 1961;* *Privarzaniyat Balon (The Attached Balloon)*, 1967;* *Poslednata Duma (The Last Word)*, 1973;* *Basseynat (The Swimming Pool)*, 1977;* *Golyamoto Noshtno Kupane (The Big Night Bathe)*, 1980.*

SELECTED FILMOGRAPHY

1950

Kalin Orelat (Kalin the Eagle). d. Boris Borozanov;* sw. Orlin Vassilev; c. Vassil Holiolchev; with Ivan Dimov, Petya Lambrinova, Boris Ganchev, Stefan Petrov, & Konstantin Kissimov. 93 m.

1951

Trevoga (Alarm). d. Zahari Zhandov; sw. Orlin Vassilev, & Angel Wagenstein;* c. Emil Rashev & Zahari Zhandov; with Stefan Savov, Nadya Stanislavska, Gancho Ganchev, Karolina Gancheva, & Rangel Vulchanov.* 119 m.
Utro Nad Rodinata (Dawn over the Homeland). d. Anton Marinovich & Stefan Surchadjiev; sw. Kamen Kalchev; c. Boncho Karastoyanov & Konstantin Yanakiev; with Lyubomir Kabalchiev, Ivan Stefanov, Zheni Bozhinova, & Apostol Karamitev. 88 m.

1952

Pod Igoto (Under the Yoke). d. Dako Dakovski; sw. Pavel Spassov & Georgi Kransov (from the famous novel by Ivan Vazov, Bulgarian national poet); c. Boncho Karastoyanov; with Miroslav Mindov, Lily Popivanova, Petko Karlukovski, Vassil Kirkov, & Nikola Popov. 123 m.

1954

Pessen Sa Choveka (Song of Man). d. Borislav Sharaliev;* sw. Hristo Ganev;* c. Emil Rashev; with Dinko Dinev, Stefan Karalambov, Ivan Bratanov, Ivan Tonev, & Nikolina Kelova. 115 m.
Septemvriytsi (Septembrists). d. Zahari Zhandov; sw. Angel Wagenstein;* c. Vassil Holiolchev; with Asparukh Temelkov, Boris Ganchev, Lyuboslav Stefanov, Ivan Bratanov, & Ani Damyanova. 123 m.

1955

Geroite Na Schipka (The Heroes at Shipka Pass). d. Sergei Vassilev; w. A. Perevenzev; c. Mihail Kyrilov; with Ivan Pereversev, Victor Samoilov, Zheni Bozhinova, & Katya Chukova. Co-production with USSR. 138 m.

Nespokoen Pat (The Troubled Road). d. Dako Dakovski; sw. Stoyan Daskalov; c. Emil Rashev; with Ivan Vratanov, Tsvetana Nikolova, Stefan Savov, & Georgi Georgiev-Gets. 116 m.

1956

Dimitrovgradisi (People of Dimitrovgrad). d. Nikola Korabov & Ducho Mundrov; sw. Buryan Enchev; c. Valo Radev; with Georgi Kaloyanchev, Matia Russalieva, Ivan Dimov, Boris Chirkov, & Ina Makarova. 112 m.

Rebro Adamovo (Adam's Rib). d. Anton Marinovich; sw. Angel Wagenstein;[*] c. Emil Rashev; with Emilia Radeva, Georgi Popov, Lyubomir Kabakchiev, & Nikola Popov. 98 m.

Sledite Ostavat (The Traces Remain). d. Peter Vassilev; sw. Pavel Vezhinov (from his novella "Incident of a Quiet Street"); c. Boncho Karastoyanov; with Krassimir Medarov, Vera Drzhostinova, Stefan Danailov, & Georgi Naumov. 100 m.

Tochka Parva (Item One). d. Boyan Danovski; sw. Valeri Petrov; c. Vassil Holiolchev & Dimo Kolarov; with Romyana Chokoyska, Vesselin Boyadjiev, Stefan Dimitrov, & Zheni Bozhinova. 80 m.

Tova Se Sluchi Na Ulizata (It Happened on the Streets). d. Yanko Yankov;[*] sw. Pavel Yezhinov; c. Georgi Karayordanov; with Apostol Karamitev, Petya Lambrinova, Zheni Bozhinova, Stefan Paychev, Lyubomir Sharlandjiev, & Andrei Chaprazov. 87 m.

1957

Godini Za Lyubov (Years of Love). d. Yanko Yankov;[*] s. Vesselin Hanchev; c. Dimo Kolarov; with Apostol Karamitev, Ginka Stancheva, & Stefan Peychev. 96 m.

Taynata Vecherya Na Sedmatsite (The Secret Supper of the Sedmaks). d. Dako Dakovski; sw. Stoyan Daskalov; c. Emil Rashev; with Ivan Bratanov, Nikola Boychev, & Dimiter Boynozov. 99 m.

Urok Na Istoriyata (History Lesson). d. & sw. Lev Arnstam; c. Alexander Shelenkov & Yolanda Chen-Yu-Lan; with Stefan Savov, Tsvetana Arnaudova, Ivan Tonev, & Georg Yudin. Co-production with USSR. 91 m.

Zemya (Land). d. Zahari Zhandov; sw. Vesselin Hanchev (from novel of Elin Pelin); c. Boncho Karastoyanov; with Bogomil Simeonov, Ginka Stancheva, Slavbka Slavova, & Stefan Petrov. 102 m.

1958

Geratsite (The Gerak Family). d. Anton Marinovich; sw. Hristo Santov (from the novel of Elin Pelin); c. Trendafil Zahariev; with Georgi Stamatov, Angelina Sarova, Ivan Dimov, & Gancho Ganchev. 96 m.

Na Malkiya Ostrov (On a Small Island). d. Rangel Vulchanov;[*] sw. Valeri Petrov; c.

Dimo Kolarov; with Ivan Kondov, Stefan Peychev, Konstantin Kotsev, Ivan Andonov, & Naycho Petrov. 98 m.

Partizani/Zhivotat Si Teche Tiho (Partisans/Life Flows Quietly By). d. Binka Zhelyazkova;* & Hristo Ganev;* sw. Hristo Ganev; c. Vassil Holiolchev; with Bogomil Simeonov, Georgi Georgiev-Gets, Emilia Radeva, Ivan Bratanov, Dimiter Boyunozov, Ivanka Dimitrova, Ivan Kondov, Lyubomir Dimitrov, Nikola Dadov, Kunka Baeva, & Adriana Andreyeva. Restricted release. 106 m.

1959

V Navecherieto (On the Eve). d. & sw. Vladimir Petrov* (from a Turgenev story); c. Vulo Radev;* m. Aram Khachaturian; with Lyubomir Kabalchiev, Irina Milpolskaya, Boris Livanov, & Olga Androvskaya. Co-production with USSR. 88 m.

Zdezdi (Sterne/Stars). d. Konrad Wolf; sw. Angel Wagenstein;* c. Werner Bergmann; with Sasha Krusharska, Jurgen Frohriep, Erich Klen, Steran Peychev, Georgi Naumov, & Hannjo Hasse. Co-production with DDR. 103 m.

1960

Bednata Ulitsa (Poor Man's Street), d. Hristo Piskov;* with Peter Donev; c. Georgi Alurkov & Todor Stoyanov; with Kosta Tsonev, Valentin Russetski, Nikolina Genova, & Lily Eneva. 95 m.

Parvi Urok (First Lesson). d. Rangel Vulchanov;* sw. Valeri Petrov;* c. Dimo Kolarov; with Kornelia Bozhanova, Georgi Naumkov, Georgi Georgiev-Gets, Georgi Kaloyanchev, & Konstantin Kotsev. 98m.

1961

A Byahme Mladi (We Were Young). d. Binka Zhelyazkova;* c. Hristo Ganev;* c. Vassil Holiolchev; with Rumyana Karabelova, Dimiter Bouynozov, & Lyudmila Cheshmedjieva. 115 m.

Stramnata Pateka (The Steep Path). d. Yanko Yankov;* sw. Emil Manov & Kosta Strandjiev; c. Emil Rashev; with Lyubomir Kabakchiev, Georgi Georgiev-Gets, Zvetko Kikolov, & Ivan Brantanov. 100 m.

1962

Pleneno Yato (Captured Squadron). d. Ducho Mundrov; sw. Emil Manov; c. Georgi Alurkov; with Peter Slabakov, Kiril Kovachev, Dimiter Buynozov, & Stefan Iliev. 90 m.

Slantseto i Syankata (Sun and Shadow). c. Rangel Vulchanov;* sw. Valeri Petrov;* c. Dimo Kolarov; with Anna Prucnal & Georgi Naumov. 73 m.

Tyutyyn (Tobacco). d. Nikola Korabov; sw. Dimiter Dimov & Nikola Korabov (from Dimov's novel); c. Vulvo Radev;* with Nevena Kokanova, Yordan Matev, Wolfgang Langhoff, & Peter Slabokov. 150 m.

1963

Kapitanat (The Captain). d. Dimiter Petrov; sw. Atanas Pavlov; c. Trendafil Zahariev; with Rayko Bodurov & Yanush Alurkov. 80 m.

BULGARIA 369

Smart Nyama (There Is No Death). d. Hristo Piskov* & Irina Aktasheva; sw. Todor Monov (from his novel); c. Podor Stoyyanov; with Peter Slabakov, Grigor Vachov, Djoko Rossich, Valentin Russetski, & Medy Dimitrova. 93 m.
Inspektorat I Noshta (The Inspector and the Night). d. Rangel Vulchanov;* Bogomil Rainov; c. Dimo Kolarov; with Georgi Kaloyanchev, Nevena Kokanova, Dimiter Panov, & Leo Konforti. 96 m.

1964

Neprimirimite (The Intransigents). d. & sw. Yanko Yankov;* c. Trendafil Zahariev; with Ivan Raev, Dusica Zegarac, Banko Bankov, Yordan Matev. 84 m.
Kradetsat Na Praskovi (The Peach Thief). d. & sw. Vulo Radev* (from story by Emilian Stanev); c. Todor Stoyanov;* with Nevena Kohanova, Rade Markovic, Mihail Mihailov, Vassil Vachev, Naum Shopov. 103 m.
Verigata (The Chain). d. Lyubomir Sharlandjiev; sw. Angel Wagenstein;* c. Emil Wagenstein;* with Vassil Popiliev, Ivan Bratanov, Leo Konforti, & Grigor Vachkov. 91 m.

1965

Nespokoen Dom (Troubled Home). d. Yakim Yakimov;* sw. Pavel Vezhinov (from his own story); c. Emil Wagenstein; with Ivan Kondov, Emilia Radeva, Elena Rainova, & Milen Penev. 91 m.
Valchitsata (The She-Wolf/Wolverine). d. Rangel Vulchanov;* sw. Chain Oliver; c. Dimo Kolarov; with Ilka Safirova, Georgi Kaloyanchev, Naum Shopov, & Krassimira Apostolova. 87 m.

1966

Goreshto Pladne (Torrid Noon). d. Zako Heskia; s. Yordan Radichkov (from his own story); c. Todor Stoyanov;* with Peter Slabakov, Plamak Nakov, Kamil Kyuchukov, & Lachezar Yankov. 88 m.
Ponedelnik Sutrin (Monday Morning). d. Hristo Piskov;* sw. Nikolai Tiholov; c. Dimo Kolarov; with Pepa Nikolova, Assen Kissimov, Peter Slabokov, Kiril Gospodinov, Stefan Danilov, Russi Chanev & Plamen Donchev. 103 m.
Ritsar Bez Bronya (Knight without Armor). d. Borislaw Sharaliev;* sw. Valeri Petrov;* Atanas Tassev; with Oleg Kovachev, Apostol Karamitev, Psvyatko Nikolov, & Maria Russalieva. 85 m.
Tsar I General (Tsar and General). d. Vulo Radev.* sw. Lyuben Stanev; c. Borislav Punchev; with Peter Slabakov, Naum Shopov, Stoycho Mazgalov, & Georgi Cherkelov. 79 m.

1967

Ako Ne Ide Vlak—Moreto (If the Train Doesn't Arrive—The Sea). I. *Ako Ne Ide Wlak.* d. Eduard Zahariev;* sw. Georgi Mischev; c. Boris Yanakiev; with Andrei Avramov, Naum Shopov, Kiril Yanev, Ilka Safirova, & Georgi Georgiev-Gets. 37 m. II. *Moreto.* d. Peter Donev; sw. Georgi Branev; c. Boris Yanakiev. 71 m.
Malchalivite Pateki (Quiet Paths). d. Vladislav Ikonomov; sw. Lyubomir Levchev; c.

Krum Krumov; with Georgi Cherkelov, Mihail Mihailov, & Evstati Stratev. 81 m.
Nay-Dalgata Nosht (The Longest Night). d. Vulo Radev;* sw. Esselin Branev; c. Broislaw Punchev; with Georgi Kaloyanchev, Nevena Kohanova, Ivan Bratanov, Georgi Georgiev-Gets, Victor Rebenchuk & Russi Chanev. 100 m.
Otklonenie (Sidetrack). d. Grisha Ostrovski & Todor Stoyanov;* sw. Blaga Dimitrova (from her own story); c. Todor Stoyanov; with Nevena Kokanova, Ivan Andonov, Stefan Iliev, & Katya Pashaleva.
Privarzaniyat Balon (The Attached Balloon). d. Binka Zhelyazkova;* sw. Rordan Badichkov (from his own story); c. Emil Wagenstein; with Georgi Kaloyanchev, Ivan Bratanov, Georgi Georgiev-Gets, Georgi Partsalev, Konstantin Kotsev, & Lyuben Dimitrov. 98 m.
Byalata Staya (The White Room). d. Metodi Andonov; sw. Bogomil Rainov (from his own novel); c. Dimo Kolarov; with Apostol Karamitev, Dorothea Toncheva, Elena Rainova, Konstantin Kotsev, & Ilka Azrfirova. 85 m.
Nebeto Na Veleka (The Sky over the Veleka). d. Eduard Zahariev;* sw. Diko Fuchedjiev; c. Ivan Tsonev; with Georgi Georgiev-Gets, Todor Shtonev, Mihail Mihailov, & Georgi Kaloyanchev. Restricted release. 101 m.
Prokirorat (The Prosecutor). d. Lyubomir Sharlandjiev; sw. Budimir Metalnikov (based on novel by Georgi Djagarov); c. Borislav Punchev; with Georgi Georgi-Gets, Yordan Matevf, Olga Kicheva, Stefan Peychev, & Dorothea Toncheva. Restricted release. 101 m.
Shibil. d. & sw. Zahari Zhandov & Magda Petkanova (based on novel by Yordan Yovkov); c. Ivailo Trenchev; with Peter Slabakov, Dorothea Toncheva, Ivan Bratanov, Dimitrina Savova, Stoycho Mazgalov. 100 m.
Sluchayat Penleve (The Painleve Case). d. Georgi Stoyanov; sw. Svoboda Buchvarova & Peter Nesnakomov; c. Victor Chichov & Violetta Yovcheva; with Naum Shjopov, Konstantin Kotsev, Stoyan Gadev, Vassil Vachev, Stefan Mavrodiev, Emilia Radeva, & Tatyana Lolova. 83 m.

1969

Ikonostasat (Iconostasis). d. & sw. Todor Dinov* & Hristo Hristov (from Dimiter Talev's novel *The Iron Candlestick*); c. Atanas Tassev; with Dimiter Tashev, Emilia Radeva, Violetta Gindeva, Nikolai Ouzunov, Ani Spassova, & Stoyan Gudev. 100 m.
Ptitsi Hratki (Birds and Greyhounds). d. Georgi Stoyanov;* sw. Vassil Akyov; c. Victor Chichov; with Kiril Gospodinov, Stefan Mavrodiev, Kosta Karageorgiev, Dimiter Kokanov, & Peter Slabakov. 82 m.

1970

Chernite Angeli (Black Angels). d. & sw. Vulo Radev* (from Mitka Grubcheva's memoirs, *In the Name of the People*); c. Atanas Tassev; with Stefan Danilov, Dorothea Toncheva, Violetta Gindeva, & Dobrinka Stankova. 137 m.
Sbogom, Priyateli (Farewell, Friends!). d. Borislav Sharaliev;* sw. Atanas Tsevev; c. Atanas Tassev; with Vladimir Smirnov, Mladen Mladenov, Nikolai Binev, & Violetta Pavlova. 100 m.

1971

Ptitsi Dolitat Pri Nas (Birds Are Flying Our Way). d. Zahari Zhandov; sw. Peter Slavinski; c. Ivan Bossev; with Borislav Ivanov, Victor Banchenko, Nikolina Genova, Yordan Mitov, & Nelly Topalova. 82 m.

Sharen Svyat (Colorful World). I. "Gola Suvest" ("Naked Conscience"). d. Milen Nikolovl; sw. Nikolai Haitov;* c. Brum Krumov; with Konstantin Kotsev, Georgi Georgiev-Gets, Zhelcho Mandadjiev, Naum Shopov, Domna Ganeva, Georgi Chajarkelov, & Ivan Kondor. II. "Izpit" ("The Test"). d. Georgi Djulgerov;* sw. Nikola Haitov;* c. Radoslav Spassov; with Philip Trifonov, Vulcho Kamareshev, Nikola Todev, Peter Slavov, Srefan Mavrodiev, Evtim Kirilov, & Snezhina Balabanova. 106 m.

Trimata Ot Zapasa (Three Reserve Officers). d. Zako Heskia; sw. Pavel Vezhinov; c. Hristo Vulchanov; with Georgi Partsalev, Kikola Anastassov, & Kiril Gospodinov. 93 m.

1972

Koziyat Rog (The Goat Horn). d. Metodi Andonov; sw. Nikolai Haitov;* c. Dimo Kolarov; with Anton Gorchev, Katya Paskaleva, Kliment Denchev, Todor Kolev, & Milen Penev. 103 m.

Nakovalnya Ili Chuk (Hammer or Anvil). d. Hristo Hristov; sw. Lyuben Stanev, Ivan Radev, & Wolfgang Ebeling; c. Atanas Tassev; with Stefan Setsov, Hannjo Hasse, Martin Florchinger, Frank Oberman, & Michaela Kreisler. Co-production with GDR and USSR. 160 m.

Obich (Affection). d. Lyudmil Staikov;* sw. Alexander Karasimeonov; c. Boris Yanakiev; with Violetta Doneva; Nevena Kokanova, Ivan Kondov, & Nikolai Binev. 91 m.

1973

I Doyde Denyat (And the Day Came). d. Georgi Djulgerov;* sw. Vassil Akyov; c. Radoslav Spassov; with Plamen Mazlarov, Elena Mirchovska, Panteley Panteleyev, & Kliment Mihailov. 86 m.

Kato Pesen (Like a Song). d. Irina Aktasheva & Hristo Piskov;* c. Yatsek Todorov; with Filip Trifonov, Irina Rossich, & Vassil Mihailov. 97 m.

Mazhe Bez Rabota (Men Without Work). d. Ivan Terziev; sw. Nikolai Nikoforov; c. Rumen Georgiev; with Stefan Peychev, Anton Karastoyanov, & Katya Paskaleva. 74 m.

Poslednata Duma (The Last Word). d. & sw. Binka Zhelyazkova;* c. Boris Yanakiev; with Emilia Radeva, Tsvetana Maneva, Bela Tsonevga, Dorothea Toncheva, & Aneta Petrovska. 188 m.

Prebroyavane Na Divite Zaytsi (The Hare Census). d. Eduard Zahariev;* sw. Georgi Mishev; c. Venets Dimitrov; with Itzhyak Fintsi, Nikola Todev, & Filip Trifonov. 69 m.

1974

Darvo Bez Koren (A Tree Without Roots). d. Hristo Hristov;* sw. Hristov & Panteley Panteleyev (from two Nikolai Haitov stories); c. Atanas Tassev; with Nikola Dadov, Nevena Kokanova, & Marin Yanev. 83 m.

Ivan Kondarev. d. Nikola Korabov; sw. Korabov & Nikola Ticholov; c. Emil Wagenstein; with Anton Gorchev, Katya Paskaleva, Ivan Andonov, Todor Kolev, Stefan Danailov, & Vassil Popiliev. 169 m.

Posledno Lyato (The Last Summer). d. Hristo Hristov; sw. Yordan Radichkov; c. Tsvetan Chobanski; with Grigor Vachkov, Bogdan Spassov, Dimiter Ikonomov, & Vesko Sehirov. 86 m.

Selyaninat S Koleloto (Peasant on a Bicycle). d. Lyudmil Kirkov; sw. Georgi Mishev; c. Georgi Russinov; with Georgi Georgiev-Gets, Diana Chelebieva, & Georgi Russev. 102 m.

1975

Nedelnite Machove (Sunday Marches). d. Todor Andreikov; sw. Anton Kafeschiev; c. Ivan Tsonev & Stoyan Slachkin; with Konstantin Kiriyakov, Kornelia Petkova, & Ivo Russev. 91 m.

Silna Voda (Strong Water). d. Ivan Terziev; sw. Boyan Parazov; c. Plamen Wagenstein; with Ivan Grigorov, Kiril Kavadarkov, & Meglena Terzieva. 84 m.

Sledovatelyat I Gorata (The Inspector and the Forest). d. & sw. Rangel Vulchanov;* c. Victor Chichov; with Sonya Boshkova, Lyudomir Buchvarov, & Alexander Pritup. 100 m.

Vechni Vremena (Eternal Times). d. Assen Shopov; sw. Vassil Popov; c. Ivailo Trenchev; with Peter Slabakov, Grigor Vachkov, Konstantin Kotsev, & Nikola Todev. 93 m.

Vilna Zona (Villa Zone). d. Eduard Zahariev;* sw. Georgi Mishev;* c. Radoslav Spassov; with Katya Paskaleva, Itzhak Fintsi, Naum Shopov, & Evstati Stratev. 79 m.

1976

Dopalnenie Kam Zakona Za Zashtito Na Darzhavata (Amendment to the Defense-of-State Act). d. Lyudmil Staikov;* with Angel Wagenstein;* c. Boris Yanakiev; with Stefan Getsov, Violetta Doneva, Ivan Kondov, Stefan Danialov, Georgi Cherkelov, & Naum Shopov. 157 m.

Samodivski Horo (Fairy Dance). d. Ivan Andonov;* sw. Georgi Mishev;* c. Radoslav Spassov; with Pavel Poppandov, Marianna Dimitrova, Peter Slabakov, & Katya Chukova. 85 m.

Spomen Za Bliznachkata (Memory of the Twin Sister). d. Lyubomir Sharlandjiev; sw. Konstantin Pavlov; c. Tsancho Tsanchev; with Nevena Kokanova, Nikola Todev, Grigor Vachkov, & Emilia Radeva. 137 m.

Tsiklopat (Cyclops). d. & sw. Hristo Hristov; c. Venets Dimitrov; with Mihail Mutaffov, Nevena Kokanova, & Penka Tsizelkova. 95 m.

1977

Avantazh (Advantage). d. Georgi Djulgerov;* sw. Djulgerov & Russi Chanev; c. Radoslav Spassov; with Russi Chanev, Maria Statulova, Plamena Getova; Radosveta Vasisleva, Plamen Donchef, & Velyo Goranov. 137 m.

Basseynat (The Swimming Pool). d. Binka Zhelyazkova;* sw. Hristo Ganev;* c. Ivailo Trenchev; with Yanina Kasheva, Kosta Tsonev, Kliment Denchev, Tsvetana Maneva, & Peter Slabakov. 145 m.

Muzhki Vremena (*Manly Times*). d. Eduard Zahariev;* sw. Nikolai Haitov;* c. Radoslav Spassov; with Grigor Vachkov, Marianna Dimitrova, Kilola Todev, Trayan Yankov, Georgi Georgiev-Gets, Velko Kunev, & Teofil Badelov. 125 m.

Zvezdi V Kossite, Salzi V Ochite (*Stars in Her Hair, Tears in Her Eyes*). d. Ivan Nichev; sw. Angel Wagenstein;* c. Tsvetan Chobanski; with Katya Paskaleva, Peter Slabakov, Tatyana Lolova, Nikolai Binev, Ivan Dervishev, Leda Tasseva, Antoni Genov, Ivan Tsvetarski, & Nikolai Nachkov. 110 m.

1978

Panteley. d. Georgi Stoyanov;* sw. Vassil Akyov; c. Radoslav Spassov; with Pavel Poppandov, Dobrinka Stankova, Velko Kunev, Nikola Anastassov, & Nikolai Nikolaev. 101 m.

Pokriv (*The Roof*). d. Ivan Andonov;* sw. Kuncho Atanassov; c. Victor Chichov; with Peter Slabakov, Pepa Nikolova, Katya Paskaleva, Velko Lunev, Maria Statulova, & Nadya Todorova. 98 m.

Slouzhebno Polozheniye—Ordinarets (*Status—Orderly*). d. & sw. Kiran Kolarov; c. Radoslav Spassov; with Elefteri Elefterov, Tsvetana Mameva, Peter Despotov, & Vulcho Kamarashev. 80 m.

S Lyubov I Nezhnost (*With Love and Tenderness*). d. Rangel Vulchanov;* sw. Valeri Petrov;* c. Dimko Minov; with Alexander Djakov, Tsvetana Eneva, Gergana Gerassimova, Yossif Surchadjiev, & Teodor Yurukov, 85 m.

Trampa (*Swap*). d. Georgi Djulgerov;* sw. Vladimir Ganev & Djulgerov; c. Radoslav Spassov. 89 m.

1979

Barierata (*Barrier*). d. Hristo Hristov; sw. Pavel Vezhinov; c. Atanas Tassev; with Innokenti Smoktunovsky, Vany Tsvetkova, & Maria Dimcheva. 111 m.

Bumerang (*Boomeranq*). d. Ivan Nichev; sw. Svoboda Buchvarova, Nichev, & Jenny Radeva; c. Victor Chichov; with Lyuben Chatalov, Yavor Spassov, Nikolai Binev, & Katya Paskaleva. 110 m.

Chereshova Gradina (*The Cherry Orchard*). d. Ivan Andonov;* sw. Nikolai Haitov;* c. Plamen Wagenstein; with Peter Slabakov, Nikola Todev, Maria Statulova, Stoyan Gudev, & Ani Petrova. 86 m.

Lachenite Obouvki Na Neznainiya Voin (*The Unknown Soldier's Patent Leather Shoes*). d. & sw. Rangel Vulchanov;* c. Radoslav Spassov; with Borislav Tsankov, Slavka Ankova, Ivan Soychkov, Emilia Marinska, & Nikolai Velichkov. 109 m.

1980

Golyamoto Noshtno Kupane (*The Big Night*). d. Binka Zhelyazkova;* sw. Hristo Ganev;* c. Plamen Wagenstein; with Malgorzanta Braunek, Yuazas Budraitis, Ventsislav Bozhinov, Yanina Kasheva, Nikolai Sotirov, Tanya Shahova, Ilya Karaivanov, Lyuben Chatalov, & Ivan Kondov. 152 m.

Iluziya (*Illusion*). d. Lyudmil Staikov;* sw. Konstantin Pavlov; c. Boris Yanakiev; with Russi Chanev, Lyuben Chatalov, Suzanna Kocurikova, & Peter Slabakov. 110 m.

Kamionat (*The Truck*). d. & sw. Hristo Hristov; c. Atanas Tassev; with Djoko Rossich,

Stefan Dimitrov, Vesselin Vulkov, Lilyana Kovachera, Grigor Vachkov, & Zhivka Peneva. 107 m.
Pochti Lyubovna Istoria (Almost a Love Story). d. Eduard Zahariev;* sw. Zahariev, Georgi Danailov, & Georgi Mishev; c. Georgi Nikolov; with Marianna Dimitrova, Yavor Spassov, & Grigor Vachkov. 85 m.

1981

Boyanskivat Maistor (Master of Boyanna). d. Zahari Zhandov; sw. Zhandov & Evgeni Konstantinov; c. Emil Wagenstein; with Peter Despotov, Emil Markov, Atanas Bozhinov, Yordan Spirov, Boyka Velkova, & Lyubomir Dimitrov. 106 m.
Khan Asparukh. d. Lyudmil Staikov;* sw. Vera Mutafchieva; c. Boris Yanakiev; with Stoyko Peyev, Antoni Genov, Vanya Tsvetkova, Marie Syur, Yossif Surchadjiev, & Peter Slabakov. In three parts, 338 m.
Massovo Choudo (Mass Miracle). d. Ivan Pavlov; sw. Konstantin Pavlov; c. Plamen Hinkov; with Dimiter Ganev, Georgi Sreganov, Konstantin Dimchev, Ruth Spassova, & Minka Minkov. 74 m.
Mera Spored Mera (Measure for Measure). d. Georgi Djulgerov;* sw. Djulgerov & Russi Chanev; c. Radoslav Spassov; with Russi Chanev, Stefan Mavrodiev, Grigor Vachkov, Katya Ivanova, Tsvetana Maneva, & Rumena Trifonova. In three parts, 288 m.

1982

Byala Magiya (White Magic). d. Ivan Andonov;* sw. Konstantin Pavlov; c. Victor Chichov; with Pater Slabakov, Georgi Kaloyanchev, Kunka Baeva, Ilka Zafirova, Plamena Getova, Velko Kunev, & Ivan Grigorov. 97 m.
Chassa Duzhd (24 Hours of Rain). d. Vladislav Ikonomov; sw. Ikonomov & Nikola Tiholov (from Yordan Yavkov's story "The Private Teacher"); c. Kum Krumov; with Stefan Mavrodiev, Stefan Danailov, Eva Dzikulska, Kiril Varjuyski, & Velyo Goranov. 86. m.
Edna Zhena Na Trideset I Tri (A Woman at Thirty-Three). d. Hristo Hristov; sw. Boyan Popazov; c. Atanas Tassev; with Liliana Kovacheva, Bogdan Glishev, Vesselin Vulkov, Gergana Burdarova, & Pavel Spassov. 102 m.
Kouche v Chekmedzhe (A Dog in the Drawer). d. Dimiter Petrov; sw. Rada Moskova; c. Atanbas Tassev; with Zhivok Garvonov, Maria Statulova, Ruzha Delcheva, Pavel Poppandov, Annetta Sotirova, Ivan Yanchev, Vesselin Prahov, Emil Dimitrov, & Martin Stoyanov. 95 m.
Lavina (Avalanche). d. & sw. Irna Aktasheva, & Hristov Piskov; c. Tsvetan Chobanski; with Ivan Ivanov, Vanya Tsvetkova, Lyuben Chatalov, Filip Trifonov, & Pavel Poppandov. 153 m.
Orkestur Bez Ime (A Nameless Band). d. Lyudmil Kirkov; sw. Stanislav Stratiev; c. Victor Chichov; with Velko Kunev, Pavel Popandov, Georgi Mamalev, Filip Trifonov, Maria Kavardjikova, & Katerina Evro. 115 m.
Predouprezhdeniyeto (The Warning). d. Juan Antonio Bardem; sw. Lyuben Stanev; c. Plamen Wagenstein; with Peter Gyurov, Nevena Kokanova, Boria Lukanov, Assen Dimitrov, Gavril Tsonkov, Doromir Manev, & Alexander Lilov. 180 m.

BULGARIA

1983

Hotel Tsentral (*Hotel Central*). d. & sw. Vesselin Branev (from a pair of stories by Konstantin Konstantinov); c. Yatsek Todorov; with Irene Krivoshieva, Reneta Dralcheva, Boryana Puncheva, Zhivko Garvanov, & Anton Radichev. 105 m.

Konstantin Filosof (*Constantine the Philosopher*). d. Georgi Stoyanov;* sw. Nikola Russev; c. Hristo Totev; with Russi Chanev, Konstantin Tsanev, Naum Shopov, Itzhak Fintsi, Dobrinka Stankova, Elly Skorcheva, Velko Kunev, Rashko Mladenov, Nevena Kokanova, & Itomir Saruivanov. In two parts, 240 m.

Posledni Zhelania (*Last Wishes*). d. Rangel Vulchanov;* sw. Marianna Basheva & Vulchanov; c. Radoslav Spassov; with Stefan Mavrodiev, Antonia Zhekova, Diana Sofronieva, Georgi Mamalev, Lyubomir Ouzunov, Emile Dyurov, & Aleko Minchev. 102 m.

Ravnovessie (*Balance*). d. Lyudmil Kirkov;* sw. Stanislav Stratiev; c. Dimko Minaov; with Pavel Poppandov, Plamena Getova, Georgi Georgiev-Gets, Katerina Evro, Konstantin Kotsev, Lychezar Stoyanov, Vanya Tsvetkova, & Stefan Danailov. 140 m.

1984

Boris Purvi (*Boris the First*). d. Borislav Sharaliev;* sw. Angel Wagenstein;* c. Venets Dimitrov; with Stefan Canailov, Antoni Genov, Ventsislav Kissyov, Kosta Tsonev, Aneta Petrovska, Boris Lukanov, Stoyan Stoev, Plamen Donchev, Peter Petrov, & Ivan Ivanov. Epic in two parts; 240 m.

Chernite Lebedi (*The Black Swans*). d. & sw. Ivan Nichev; c. Richard Lenchevski; with Diana Rainova, Dorothea Toncheva, Zornitsa Popova, Todor Kolev, & Donka Shishmanova. 106 m.

Delo No. 205/1913 (*Case No. 205/1913*). d. Kiran Kolarov; sw. Kolarov & Ivan Dechev (from Nikola Gayderov's *The Drama of Yavorov's Life*); c. Radoslav Spassov; with Yavor Milushev, Katya Ivanova, Bogdan Glishev, Stoyan Stoev, Plamen Sirakov, Boris Lukanov, Martin Penchev, & Vulcho Kamarsahev. 158 m.

Subessednik Po Zhelanie (*Question Time*). d. Hristo Hristov;* sw. Hristov & Vladimir Ganev; c. Atanas Tassev; with Vassil Milailov, Lilyana Kovacheva, Ivan Kondov, Vassil Popiliev, Zhana Karayordanova, & Vulcho Karmarashev. 97 m.

681 A.D./The Glory of Khan: Edited English version of *Khan Asparukh.* Warner Brothers. 95 m.

1985

Denyat Na Vladetelite (*The Day of the Rulers*). d. Vladislav Ikonomov; sw. Ikonomov & Nikola Tiholov; c. Krum Krumov; with Vassil Mihailov, Lyuben Chatalov, Georgi Georgiev-Gets, Velyo Foranov, Stefan Mavrodiev, Vulcho Kamarashev, Pavel Pappandov, & Stoycho Mazgalov.

Herakteristika (*Reference*). d. Hristo Hristov; sw. Alexander Tomov; c. Atanas Tasev; with Ivailo Geraskov, Georgeta Nikolova, Atanas Atanassov, Liliana Kovacheva, Vassil Mihailov, Itzak Fintsi, & Georgi Kaloyanchev.

Skupi Moi, Skupa Moya (*My Darling, My Darling*). d. Eduard Zahariev;* sw. Zahariev,

& Plamen Maslarov; c. Stefan Trifonov; with Marianna Dimitrova, Plamen Sirakov, Ivan Donve, Anton Radichev, Itzak Fintsi, Stoyan Stoev, & Ana Guncheva.
Smurtta Mozhe Da Pochaka (*Death Can Wait Awhile*). d. Evgeni Mihailov; sw. Alexander Tomov; c. Elly Mihailova; with Todor Kolev, Momchil Karamitev, Dilyana Hadjikyankova, Ilya Karaivanov, Ginda Stanchev, & Nikolai Nachkov.

APPENDIX

A Chronology of Major Historical, Cultural and Film Events in the Soviet Union and Eastern Europe, 1890–1990

1890s   Bulgaria moves towards forming a stable nation-state under Prime Minister Stambolov throughout the decade.

　　　　First film showing in Romania, Bucharest—1896.

　　　　First films shown in the Velence Cafe, Budapest, Hungary—1896.

　　　　Jan Križenecký produces and shows first film strips made in Prague, Czechoslovakia—1898.

　　　　Founding of first Hungarian film company, The Projectograph—1898.

1900s   Macedonian revolt in Bulgaria—1903.

　　　　Revolutionary uprising in Poland—1905.

　　　　Alexander Drankov founds first Russian film company—1908.

　　　　Antonín Pech founds first Czech production company, Kinofa—1908.

　　　　Bulgarian independence officially proclaimed—1908.

　　　　First Bulgarian movie theater opens in Sofia—1908.

1910s   First permanent Polish cinemas established—1910.

　　　　First Romanian fiction film, *Fatal Love,* by Grigore Brezeanu—1911.

　　　　Czech filmmaker Max Urban and his actress wife Andula Sedlacková found the Fotokinema company, which quickly becomes ASUM, the name being constructed from their initials—1911–1912.

　　　　Establishment of first film studio, Hunnia (Miklós Faludi, director) and publication of first film weekly, *Pesti Mozi (Pest Cinema)*, edited by Sandor Korda, in Hungary—1912.

　　　　Release of the first Hungarian fiction film, *Ma és holnap (Today and Tomorrow)*, probably directed by Mihály Kertész (Michael Curtiz)—October 14, 1912.

First Balkan War (Bulgaria, Serbia, Greece defeat Turkey)—1912–1913.

Second Balkan War (Bulgaria against Serbia and Greece)—1913.

Czechoslovakia's Alois Jalovec founds Illusionfilm—1913.

Bulgaria's 1st film journal—1913.

Bulgaria's alliance with the Central Powers—1914.

First Bulgarian film, Vassil Gendov's *Balgaran e Galant (The Bulgarian is Galant)*—1915.

Lucernafilm founded in Czechoslovakia, but quickly absorbed during post-war expansion mergers—1916–1917.

February revolution topples Russian monarchy, bringing provisional government of Alexander Kerensky to power; October Bolshevik revolution brings Communists to power, inaugurating the Soviet Union—1917.

Collapse of war effort; abdication of Ferdinand; proclamation of Republic of Bulgaria under King Boris; independence of Poland, Hungary, and Czechoslovakia following break-up of Habsburg Empire—1918.

Weteb Company begins operations in Czechoslovakia, with Vaclav Binovec as chief director—1918.

Lenin signs first and second decrees for nationalizing the cinema and gives support to young avant-garde directors; founding of Moscow State Film Institute—1919.

First nationalization of Hungarian film industry under short-lived Republic of Councils—April–August 1919.

1920s   Dziga Vertov travels Russian countryside gathering newsreel footage for *Kino-Eye;* Lev Kuleshov film workshop develops theories of montage—1919–1922.

With no party gaining a majority, Czechoslovakia is continuously ruled by coalitions—1920s to 1930s.

Polish-Soviet War ("Miracle on the Vistula")—1920.

Establishment of key Polish cultural journal, *Skamander*—Warsaw, 1920.

AB Vinohrady Studios open in Czechoslovakia—1920.

Lack of scripts and film stock produces directorial freedom in Soviet Union—early 1920s.

Growth of Poland's commercial film industry—early 1920s.

Bulgaria gains leftist agrarian government under Stamboliski, major economic and agararian reforms result—1920.

Czech Communist Party founded—1921.

End of Russian Civil War, Bolshevik's solidify power—1921.

Lenin tells Cultural Affairs Minister Lunacharsky, "To us, film, of all forms of art, is the most important"—February 1922.

Record thirty-four films produced in Czechoslovakia—1922. But the total sinks to seven in 1924.

First successful Bulgarian film, Gendov's *Bay Genyu*—1922.

Creation of Lenin's first five-year economic plan—1923.

Fall of Bulgaria's Stamboliski in September revolt—1923.

Democratic Alliance controls Bulgaria—1923–1931.

Poland's Władysław Reymont wins the Nobel Prize for literature—1924.

Poland's Karol Irzykowski publishes *Dziesiata Muza (The Tenth Muse)*—1924.

Release of Sergei Eisenstein's *Bronenosets Potemkin (The Battleship Potemkin)* in the Soviet Union—1925.

Kavalirka Studios opens, mostly due to the efforts of Karal Lamač. It produces some of the finest Czech silents—1925.

Release of Vsevelod Pudovkin's *Mat (Mother)* in the Soviet Union—1926.

The May Coup in Poland—Jozef Piłsudski takes over the government—1926.

Josef Stalin comes to power in the Soviet Union. Believes all aspects of society should be directed towards Communist Party goals. Top education officials ban several films and charge Sovkino with pandering to public tastes—1927.

Poland's Alexander Ford makes his first documentaries—late 1920s.

Release of Vertov's masterpiece *Chelovek s ruzh'em (The Man With the Movie Camera)* in the Soviet Union—1928.

First All-Soviet Union Party Conference on cinema questions declares art films must be able to be appreciated by the masses—1928.

Creation of Main Administration on Affairs of Art and Literature in the Soviet Union—1928–1929.

Soviet Association for Revolutionary Film holds frequent meetings to enforce the Party line—1928–1932.

The Devětsil avant-garde group produces heavy influence on artistic development of Czech film—late 1920s to early 1930s.

Gustav Machatý produces *Erotikon,* featuring Ita Rina in the first Czech nude scene—1929.

Collapse of Hungarian film industry under the Miklos Horthy regime—1929.

Release of Boris Grezhov's *Sled Poshara W Russia (After the Fire Over Russia)* in Bulgaria—1929.

1930s   All-Soviet Union Photo-Cinema Corporation, "Soyuzkino," founded—1930.

Boris Shumyatski takes over leadership of Soviet film administration with the goal of increasing production—1930.

Release of Alexander Dovzhenko's last great film, *Zemlya (Earth)* in the Soviet Union—1930.

Poland's START (Society for the Devotees of Artistic Film) established—1930.

First Romanian sound film, *Ecaterina Teodoroiu,* by Ion Brună—1930.

Soviets begin production of sound films, theaters, and equipment—1931.

Revival of Hungarian film industry with the introduction of sound; establishment of the rigid Film Industry Fund—1931.

Poland's Ford begins making feature films—early 1930s.

The coming of sound in Soviet cinema forces the writing of detailed scenarios and makes ideological control through censorship practical. Purges install reliable Party men throughout the government—1930s.

The Union of Film and Photography Workers replaces the Association for Revolutionary Film in the Soviet Union. All subsequent meetings are controlled by Party officials with more power given to studio executives and the national film administration—1932.

Release of Pal Fejős' *Tavaszi zápor* (*Spring Shower/Marie*), the first Hungarian artistic success abroad—1932.

Soviet Cinema Administration absorbed into General Administration of the Cinema and Photo Industry, directly subordinated to the Council of People's Commissariats of the USSR—1933.

With Kavalirka Studios destroyed by fire, the Barrandov complex takes over from AB Vinohrady—1933.

Řeka (*The River*) gains an honorable mention at the Venice film festival and establishes Josef Rovenský as head of the "lyrical" style of Czech film—1933.

Czech production of Gustav Machatý's *Extase* (*Ecstasy*), featuring the famous Hedy Lamarr nude scene—1933.

Maxim Gorky and Andrei A. Zhdanov proclaim the doctrine of socialist realism at the inaugural Congress of Writers Union Meeting—1934.

Military coup and movement towards fascism in Bulgaria—1934.

King Boris' personal rule of Bulgaria—1934–1939.

Hostavar and Radlice Studios open in 1935 and 1937 respectively.

Establishment of Romanian National Cinematograph Office, 1936.

After two years work, Sergei Eisenstein is forced to stop production of *Bezhin Meadow* and make a public confession of his errors on the project. The only print of the film is destroyed—1937.

Shumyatsky removed from head of Soviet film administration for failing to meet production goals and "political blindness"—1938.

Stalin allows more free expression as part of effort to rally the country against foreign threats. Liberalized attitudes dominate until the end of the war—1938.

Release of Orlin Vassilev's *Strahil the Voyvoda* in Bulgaria—1938.

Significant Yiddish films produced in Poland—late 1930s.

German occupation of Czechoslovakia and commandeering of its film studios—March 1939–1945.

German-Soviet Pact of Nonaggression—August 1939.

German invasion of Poland—September 1, 1939.

Soviet invasion of Poland—September 17, 1939.

1940s   Bulgarian involvement with Axis powers—1940.

Auschwitz inaugurated—1940.

Destruction of Polish film industry—early 1940s.

Bulgarian entry into war—against Britain and France, but not the Soviet Union—1941.

German governor of Czechoslovakia, Reinhard Heydrich, is assassinated. The Nazis respond with mass killings and destruction of Lidice and Lezaky, shocking the world—1942.

István Szőts's *Emberek a havason* (*People in the Alps*) wins first international prize for a Hungarian film, best debut film at the Venice film festival—1942.

Warsaw ghetto uprising—1943.

Czesław Miłosz writes his great, long poem, "Swiat" ("The World"), 1944.

Establishment of Polish Committee of National Liberation in Lublin (beginning of Soviet administration)—July 22, 1944.

Warsaw Uprising—August–September 1944.

Bulgaria withdraws from the war and is occupied by the Soviet Union—1944.

Yalta Conference—1945.

Declaration of Peace—May 9, 1945.

Completion of Soviet "liberation" of Hungary—1945.

Establishment of the Budapest Theater Academy (later Theater and Film Academy) in Hungary under the leadership of Béla Balázs—1945.

Czech President-in-exile Eduard Beneš returns to Czechoslovakia with his cabinet, closely following the Russian troops. He orders nationalization of the film industry later that year. Also, the founding of the Czech film school, FAMU—1945.

Founding of Filmactif and production of *Augenzeuge* (Eyewitness) newsreels in East Berlin—1945.

Bulgaria moves towards forming a People's Republic—1946.

Polish film industry nationalized; Film Polski established under direction of Alexander Ford—1946.

DEFA (Deutsche Film Aktiengesellschaft), East Germany's only film production company, founded—May 1946.

First East German feature film, *Die Mörder sind unter uns* (*The Murderers Are Among Us*), produced in Berlin by DEFA—1946.

Stalin condemns Part II of Eisenstein's *Ivan the Terrible* trilogy and burns all the work on Part III. Eisenstein's health declines, leading to his death—1946–1948.

Soviet production and attendance decline. Artists and audiences resist restrictive guidelines—1946–1952.

Czech director Karel Steklý's *Siréna* (*The Strike*) wins the Grand Prize at the Venice film festival. Slovak cinema begins. Jiří Trnka initiates the strong tradition of Czech puppet films—1947.

Polish Communists come to power in post-war "elections"—1947.

Hungary restored to its 1938 borders—1947.

First issue of *Kultura* published in Paris—1947.

Beginning of stricter production controls in East Germany signaled by the removal of Soviet cultural adviser Sergei Tulpanov, a member of the liberal Leningrad group, from his post—1947.

Communist Party gains power in Czechoslovakia, forcing the abdication of Eduard Beneš—1948.

Communist nationalization of Hungarian film industry—March 21, 1948.

Romanian cinema nationalized under new socialist government—1948.

Nationalization of Bulgarian film industry—1948.

Approximate date of Andrei Zhdanov's death, probably a victim of Stalin—1949.

Consolidation of monolithic Communist power in Hungary; dissolution of opposition parties—1949.

Formal separation of East and West Germany; Sepp Schwab, adherent of strict ideological compliance, takes over as chief of DEFA; East German directors Arthur Rabenalt, Gerhard Lamprecht, and Erich Engel leave for the West; production of *Unser täglich Brot* (*Our Daily Bread*), by Slatan Dudow, an influential "rubble film"—1949.

First graduates from FAMU (Czech Film School)—1949–1950.

First Romanian color film, *Nufărul rosu,* by Gheorghe Tobias—1949.

1950s   Stalin calls for fewer and better films. Scripts now have to pass twenty-eight checkpoints, causing annual production in the Soviet Union to drop to five films. Anti-American themes dominate—1950.

Czechoslovakia's Central Committee, Minister of Information and Public Culture, and Chairman of State Film Dramaturgy set strict Stalinist guidelines for film. Directors respond by turning to safe biographical and historical subjects for the next six years—1950.

Vulko Chervenkov takes power in Bulgaria; Stalinism and socialist realist artistic philosophies become dominant throughout the Soviet Union and Eastern Europe—1950–1956.

Congress of Wisla imposes cultural Stalinism in Poland—1950.

Release of Vassilev's *Kalin the Eagle,* first film of the Bulgarian State Film Industry—1950.

Milosz publishes *The Captive Mind* in France—1951.

East German State Committee for Cinematography established; Sepp Schwab replaced as head of DEFA—1952.

Josef Stalin dies, producing a struggle for power among several Soviet leaders, including Nikita Khrushchev—1953.

Imre Nagy replaces Mátyás Rákosi as Hungarian Prime Minister; anti-Stalinist reform movement begins—July 1953.

East German workers' strike leads to a purge of leadership and a brief loosening of ideological controls on filmmaking—1953.

East German State Committee for Cinematography dissolved—1954.

Brief cultural thaw and increased film production in Soviet Union and Eastern Europe during late 1950s and early 1960s.

Worker bread riots and political return of Poland's Gomulka—late 1950s.

Andrzej Wajda's "Polish Trilogy," central works of "The Polish School" film era—1955–1961.

Matayas Rákosi temporarily recaptures complete power to stop Hungarian reform movement—April 1955.

Release of *La mere* (*Pinching Apples*), challenging graduation film by Romanian directors Manole Marcus and Iulian Mihu—1955.

Khrushchev exposes Stalin's atrocities at the start of the 20th Congress of the Communist Party, leading to a relaxation of artistic guidelines throughout the Soviet Bloc and Khrushchev's assumption of power—1956.

Student demonstrations begin the Hungarian Revolution—October 23, 1956.

Soviet Army occupies Hungary, crushing the Revolution; Janos Kádár regime installed—November 4, 1956.

Culmination of attacks on intellectuals in East Germany stimulated by events following Stalin's death result in re-imposition of tighter ideological controls over film production—1956.

Release of Todor Dinov's animated *Junak Marko* (*Brave Marko*) in Bulgaria—1956.

Rise of Bulgaria's Todor Zhivkov—1956.

Mikhail Kalatozov's *Letyat zhuravli* (*The Cranes Are Flying*) gains international recognition and returns Soviet film to world prominence—1957.

Release of Rangel Vulchanov's *Na Malkiya Ostroy* (*On a Small Island*) in Bulgaria—1957.

Forcing of Boris Pasternak's refusal of the Nobel Prize for literature indicates continued uncertainties for Soviet artists—1958.

Kadar's government officially accepts "temporary" presence of Soviet troops in Hungary—May 27, 1958.

Creation of the Béla Balázs Studio in Hungary, firmly established by 1958–1961

Release of *Ciulinii Bărăganului* (*Baragan Thistles*), a Romanian-French co-production directed by Louis Daquin and Gheorghe Vitanidis—1958.

Release of Grigori Chukrai's *Ballada o soldate* (*Ballad of a Soldier*) in the Soviet Union—1959.

11th Czech Communist Party Congress at Banska Bystrica condemns "revisionism" and singles out specific films for criticism—1959.

Sterne (*Stars*), directed by East Germany's Konrad Wolf and co-produced with Bulgaria, wins Cannes Jury prize—1959.

1960s Flowering of Bulgarian School of Animation—1960s.

Decentralization of Polish film industry into several units—1960.

Jerzy Grotowski founds his Laboratory Theater—1960.

Erection of Berlin Wall; relative isolation of East Germany marks beginning of slight relaxation of ideological controls and beginning of production cooperation with the West—1961.

Death of Polish director Andrej Munk—1961.

Increased constraints on artistic expression in Poland, decline in film quality and originality—early 1960s.

Soviet filmmaker Andrei Tarkovski gains international recognition for *Ivanovo detstvo* (*Ivan's Childhood*)—1962.

The Czech New Wave, whose triumphs include Academy Awards as Best Foreign Film for Jan Kadár and Elmar Klos' *Obchod na korse* (*Shop on Main Street*), 1965, and Jiří Menzel's *Ostře sledované vlaky* (*Closely Watched Trains*), 1967. Its emergence is assisted by the twelfth Communist Party Congress, which relaxes the Banska Bystrica restrictions and calls for promoting new figures in the arts—1962–1969.

Stalinist attacks on Khrushchev force a return to drabness in Soviet film—1963.

Soviet refusal to grant author Alexander Sozhenitsyn the Lenin Prize—1963.

Jaromil Jires's *Krik* (*The Cry*), Věra Chytilová's *O něčem jénem* (*About Something Else*), and Miloš Forman's *Konkurs* (*Competition*) firmly establish the Czech New Wave—1963.

Soviet film industry headed by Puritanical Party idealist Alexei Romanov, who strongly opposes several films that are later successful—1963–1973.

Khrushchev forced from power by a Stalinist coalition including Leonid Brezhnev—1964.

Soviet director Grigori Kozintsev's masterful *Hamlet* shows an intellectual's fate in a corrupt society—1964.

Sergei Parajanov's *Teni zabytykh predkov* (*Shadows of Forgotten Ancestors*) resurrects the value of folklore and local artistic traditions in Soviet film—1964.

Release of Radev's *Praskovi* (*The Peach Thief*) in Bulgaria—1964.

Bulgaria sees major relaxation of cultural controls, more translations of Western authors, and more opportunities for native authors—early 1960s.

In September, first Soviet writers are jailed since Khrushchev's 1956 speech, signaling an end to artistic freedoms. In October the Central Committee informs the First Congress of the Union of Film Workers that artists are expected to follow an ideological line—1965.

Romanian Liviu Ciulei wins Cannes Best Direction Prize for *Pădurea Spînzuraţilor* (*The Forest of the Hanged*)—1965.

Release of *Szegénylegények* (*The Round-Up*) introduces unique style of Hungarian director Miklós Jancsó and begins his remarkable international career—1965.

Bulgaria's Zhivkov fully consolidates power—1965.

Rise of historical film spectaculars in Poland—mid-1960s.

Filmmakers attempt to use fables, allegories, and parables, but government crushes scripts that deviate too much from official guidelines, especially after the invasion of Czechoslovakia in 1968. Still, Soviet and East European film had now advanced too far to permanently retreat—1965–1969.

Brezhnev solidifies power in the Soviet Union—1966.

Eleventh Plenary session of the SED (Sozialistische Einheitspartei Deutschlands), the governing party of East Germany, reasserts an insistence on ideological conformity resulting in the banning of a number of films produced in 1965–1966, including Kurt Maetzig's *Kaninchen bin ich* (*The Rabbit is Me*), 1965–1966.

Alexander Dubček replaces the Stalinist Antonín Novotný as Czech President, initiating the "Prague Spring"—December 1967.

Hungarian Ferenc Kósa's *Tizezer nap* (*Ten Thousand Suns*) receives award for best direction at the Cannes Film Festival—1967.

Ich war neunzehn (*I Was Nineteen*), by East Germany's Wolf, released—1967.

Soviet invasion of Czechoslovakia, with participation of Polish troops. Many filmmakers either flee or simply decide not to return—August 1968.

Political crisis in Poland and disruption and reorganization of the film industry—1968.

Relaxation of ideological purity in East Germany permits some experimenting with form in film—1968.

1970s   Riots after attempted food price hikes in Poland; soldiers fire at the workers—1970.

Reorganization of Czechoslovak State Film. Five production groups in Prague abolished—1970.

Hungarian István Gaál's *Magasiskola* (*The Falcons*) receives the Jury's Prize at the Cannes Festival—1970.

A truly autonomous film culture emerges in the Soviet Union. The government responds with more centralization and political repression of nationalist heresies. A huge film bureaucracy grows, including many levels, with the elite having special privileges. Everyone becomes cautious, no new styles or trends develop, and film takes a low place in intellectual life. Both public and creative filmworkers act hostile to artistic directors such as Tarkovski and Otar Ioseliani—1970s.

Polish film units again reorganized and given greater autonomy; production stabilizes—1971.

Poland's Edward Gierek comes to power—1971.

Hungarian actresses Lili Darvas and Mari Torócski receive Special Prizes at Cannes Festival for their performances in Károly Makk's *Szerelem* (*Love*)—1971.

Honecker replaces Ulbricht as East German leader—1971.

Chief of Soviet film production Fillipp Ermash reasserts pedagogic priorities.

Driven by love of power and the Hollywood model, he keeps actors' salaries down and profits up—1972.

Hungarian Miklós Jancsó's *Még kér a nép* (*Red Psalm*) awarded for best direction at Cannes Festival—1972.

Romanian film production split into five independent companies—1972.

Release of acclaimed Romanian film *Nuntă de Pietră* (*Stone Wedding*), directed by Mircea Veroiu and Dan Pița—1973.

Soviet director Parajanov arrested on fabricated charges unrelated to filmmaking—1974.

Jakob der Lügner (*Jacob the Liar*), by East Germany's Frank Beyer, nominated for Best Foreign Film Oscar—1974.

Romanians Veroiu and Pița win Special Jury Prize at Cannes for *Duhul aurului* (*The Spirit of Gold*)—1974.

Lotte in Weimar, directed by East Germany's Egon Günther, becomes first East-West German co-production—1975.

Jiří Menzel and Věra Chytilová return to work in Czechoslovakia—1975–1976.

Committee for the Defense of Workers established in Poland—1976.

Czech dissidents, including Vaclav Havel, form Charter 77—1977.

Hungarian Márta Mészáros' *Kilenc hónap* (*Nine Months*) wins FIPRESCI Prize at Cannes Festival—1977.

Romanian dictator Nikolai Ceaucescu declares an end to censorship—1977.

Poland's "Cinema of Moral Concern"—late 1970s.

Rise of Bulgaria's Liudmila Zhivkova, Zhivkov's daughter, to great power in all cultural affairs, promoted national cultural identity—late 1970s.

Hungarian Pál Gábor's *Angi Vera* wins FIPRESCI Prize at Cannes Festival—1979.

Critically acclaimed *Solo Sunny*, directed by East Germany's Wolf and Kohlhaase, released—1979.

Bulgaria gains improved relations and emigration agreements with Turkey, lasting until the mid–1980s.

1980s Bulgaria produces extensive contacts with Third World—late 1970s to early 1980s.

Soviet director Vladimir Menshov's *Moskva slezam ne verit* (*Moscow Does Not Believe in Tears*) wins an Academy Award for Best Foreign Film—1980.

Czesław Miłosz wins Nobel Prize for literature—1980.

Poland's Independent Writers' Union established (to be dissolved after martial law)—1980.

Birth of Solidarity in Poland—August 1980.

Martial law declared in Poland—December, 1981. Disruption of film production shortly after.

Hungarian István Szabó's *Mephisto* receives the award for best screenplay as well as a FIPRESCI Prize at the Cannes Festival—1981.

1,300th anniversary of the founding of the first Bulgarian state—1981.

Death of Bulgarian cultural authority Zhivkova—1981.

Emigration of many Polish artists—early 1980s.

Increased cultural restrictions and lethargy in Bulgaria—early 1980s.

Leonid Brezhnev dies. Yuri Andropov assumes position of General Secretary of the Soviet Union—1982.

Soviet director Parajanov again arrested—1982.

Hungarian István Szabó's *Mephisto* wins the American Academy Award as Best Foreign Film of the Year; British Film Critics bestow a similar recognition; Péter Gothár's *Megáll za idő* (*Time Stands Still*) wins the Youth Prize at the Cannes Festival where Karoly Makk's *Egymásra nézve* (*Another Way*) receives Best Actress Award (Jadwiga Jankowska-Cieślak)—1982.

Andropov dies. Constantin Chernenko assumes power in the Soviet Union—1984–1985.

Hungarian Márta Mészáros' *Napló gyermekeimnek* (*Diary for My Children*) wins Grand Prix at Cannes Festival—1984.

Chernenko dies. Mikhail S. Gorbachev assumes power, initiating liberal cultural policy of *glasnost*—1985.

Slow regeneration of Polish film industry—mid-1980s.

Soviet director Tarkovski dies in exile—1986.

Liberal Soviet director Elem Klimov wins surprise election to head of Soviet Filmmakers' Union—1986.

Jiří Menzel's *Vésničko má, středisková* (*My Sweet Little Village*) nominated for an Academy Award as Best Foreign Film—1986.

Tengiz Abuladzie's *Pokaianie* (*Repentance*) and Alexander Askoldov's *Komissar* (*The Commissar*) given international release after years of restrictions. Several other previously banned Soviet films are also released—1987.

Bony a Klid (*Big Money*) and *Proč?* (*Why?*) by Czech filmmakers Vít Olmer and Karel Smyczek, respectively, are the sensations of the Karlovy Vary Film Festival—1988.

Vassili Pitchul's *Malinkaiya Vera* (*Little Vera*) becomes leading Soviet attempt to gain international commercial success—1989.

Several Soviet directors and documentary films tour the United States as part of the Glasnost Film Festival—1989.

Berlin Wall dismantled—1989.

Poland's first post-war independent film produced—1989.

Communist rule overthrown in Czechoslovakia; playwright Vaclav Havel assumes the presidency—1989.

Hungarian Ildikó Enyedi's *Az én XX. századom* (*My 20th Century*) wins "Golden Camera" for Best Debut at Cannes Festival—1989.

Cooling of Bulgaria's relations with the Soviet Union in the Gorbachev era.

Abrupt decline of Communist Party and rise of democratization throughout Eastern Europe—1989–1990.

1990s   Emergence of Soviet Khazikhstan New Wave.

Reunification of Germany.

SUBJECT INDEX

Abrahmson, Kyell Albin, 93
Abuladze, Tengiz, 22, 23, 33
Academy of the Arts of the GDR, 295
Academy Award, 22, 142, 143, 149, 156, 159, 162, 192, 218, 243, 251, 288, 290, 317
Aćimović-Godina, Karpo, 200
Aczel, Gyorgy, xii
Afric, Vjekoslav, 188, 213
Agit-trains (SU), 3, 39, 41, 46
Aktasheva, Irina, 347, 352, 363
Akyov, Vassil, 354, 363
Alexander I, of Serbia, 186
Alexandrov, Grigori, 33, 36, 38, 295
All the Bright Young Men and Women, 165
Althoff Studios (EGr), 275
Amirkulov, Ardak, 24
Amov, Aleksander, 20
Andonov, Ivan, 354, 355, 357, 358, 360, 361, 362
Andonov, Metodi, 349, 350, 352, 360, 361
Andor, Tamás, 260
Andrássy, Countess Katinka, 245
Andrejew, Piotr, 95
Andrzejewski, Jerzy, 70, 72–73, 95
"Aneks" Film Unit (Po), 87
Animafilm Studios (Ro), 310, 313
Animation Film Studio (EGr), 277

Antczak, Jerzy, 87, 95, 96, 98
Anton, Karel, 134, 163
Antonioni, Michelangelo, 138, 236
Apparatus Works (EGr), 277
Aprimov, Serik, 24
Arnheim, Rudolf, 230
Arnstam, Lev, 363
Art of the Cinema, The, 40
Art Council of the Committee for Cinema Affairs (SU), 33
Asanova, Dinara, 21
Askoldov, Aleksander, 20, 23
Austro-Hungarian Empire, 186, 230, 235
Avala Film Studio (Yu), 188
Averbakh, M., 35

Babac, Marko, 195
Babaja, Ante, 193, 199, 209, 213
Bacsó, Peter, 245–46, 260, 267
Baierl, Helmut, 286
Bajcsy-Zsilinszky, Endre, 241
Bajon, Filip, 95, 96, 109
Bajor, Michał, 95–96
Balanuta, Leopoldina, 320
Balázs, Béla, 230, 232, 233, 260–61
Balco, Vladimir, 150
Baletić, Branko, 208, 213
Balint, Andras, 250, 261
Balk, Teodor, 189
Balkan Wars, 309

Bán, Frigyes, 232, 264
Banovich, Tamas, 235
Bánsági, Ildikó, 261
Banska Bystrica Conference (Cz), 140, 146
Bara, Margit, 235, 261
Baranov, Alexander, 24
Baránski, Andrzej, 91, 96, 98
Barbelian, Nicolae, 311
Barbu, Eugene, 317
Bardem, Juan Antonio, 357
Barlog, Boleslaw, 276, 279
Barnet, Boris, 14, 33–34, 38, 40, 44
Barrandov Studio (Cz), 135, 146
Barthel, Kurt, 284
Básti, Juli, 260
Batalov, Alexei, 17, 34
Batalov, Nikolai B., 34
Bauer, Branko, 191, 192, 200, 213
Bauer, Evgeni, 3, 4, 34, 39
Becker, Jaques, 213
Beckett, Samuel, 354
Béla Balázs Studio (Hu), 235–36, 249, 252, 253, 254, 255, 261, 262, 263, 264, 265, 266
Belgrade Academy of Dramatic Arts, 213, 215, 216, 217
Benes, Eduard, 135, 136
Bereményi, Géza, 256, 261
Bergman, Ingmar, 236
Bergmann, Werner, 286
Berković, Zvonimir, 199, 209
Berliner Zeitung, 295
Beyer, Frank, 282, 283, 284, 288, 290
Biederman and the Firebug, 329
Binczycki, Jerzy, 96
"Black Cat, The," 210
Blaier, Andrei, 316, 317, 319, 325
Blum, Victor, 291
Bobrowski, Johannes, 287
Bočan, Hynek, 145, 154, 159, 161
Bódy, Gábor, 261
Bohdziewicz, Antoni, 69, 72, 73, 96, 107
Bolshevik Party, 2, 3, 4, 6, 7, 8, 14
Bolshevik Revolution, 2, 4, 7, 8, 21, 39, 231, 238, 282, 344
Bonaparte, Napoleon, 92

Bondarchuk, Sergei, 34
Bonnet, Horst, 288
Borges, Jorge Luis, 208
Boris III, of Bulgaria, 349
Borowczyk, Walerian, 96, 109
Borozanov, Boris, 360
Bosna Film Studio (Yu), 193, 200
Bossak, Jerzy, 86
Bostan, Elisabeta, 318, 321, 322, 325
Braginsky, Emil, 43
Brandauer, Klaus-Maria, 251
Brandys, Kazimierz, 70, 83, 96
Branev, Vesselin, 357
Bratny, Roman, 78
Bratu, Lucian, 315, 316, 325
Brauer, Jürgen, 286, 288
Braunek, Malgorzata, 96
Brecht, Bertolt, 260, 275, 290, 291
Brejchova, Jana, 154
Brešan, Ivo, 202
Brezeanu, Grigore, 311, 377
Brezhnev, Leonid, 20, 24, 25
Bryll, Ernest, 87
Brynych, Zbyněk, 138, 141, 144, 154, 155, 161
Bucaresti (Buftea) Studios (Ro), 310, 313, 316, 323, 328
Bucharest "Alexander Sahia" Documentary Studio, 329, 331
Bucharest National Theater, 328
Buchner, Georg, 278
Buczkowski, Leonard, 69, 71, 72, 73, 74, 96–97, 100, 102, 108
Budapest Academy of Theater and Film Art, 236, 248, 253, 257, 260, 261, 262, 263, 264, 265, 266, 267
"Budapest Documentary School," 255, 256, 261, 266
Budapest Film School, 365
Budapest Film Studio, 236
Bulajić, Veljko, 191, 192, 213
Bulgakov, Mikhail, 197
Bulgarian Cinematography Corporation, 358
Bulgarian Film Academy, 350
Bulgarian State Film Industry, 344
Bulgarian Union of Writers, 352
Buñuel, Luis, 233

Burek, Zlatko, 193
Burian, E. F., 154
Burian, Vlasta, 134, 155
Burton, Richard, 202
Bykov, Rolan, 17, 23, 34–35
Byrylska, Barbara, 97

Čalić, Zoran, 210
Călinescu, Paul, 311, 312, 313, 314, 326
Calotescu, Virgil, 317, 321
Cannes Film Festival, 22, 90, 136, 204, 208, 209, 240, 241, 243, 247, 248, 251, 252, 253, 254, 255, 256, 282, 295, 316, 320, 326
Čáp, Frantisek, 136, 157, 165, 191
Čapek, Karel, 134, 155
Caragiale, I. L., 311, 314, 321, 327
Carmen Sylvia Theater (Ro), 310
Carne, Marcel, 348
Carol I, of Romania, 310
Carow, Heiner, 283, 286, 290
Ceasar and Cleopatra, 329
Ceausescu, Nicolae, 246, 319
Cekalski, Evgeniusz, 93, 109
Čengić, Bato, 193, 200, 209, 214
Central Committee (of the Communist Party-SU), 12, 20
Central Office of Cinematography (Po), 78
Chabrol, Claude, 215
Chaplin, Charles, 11, 132
Chardynin, Petr, 41
Chekhov, Anton, 17, 21, 38
Cherkasov, Nikolai, 35
Chiaureli, Mikhail, 14, 35
Children of the Sun, 329
Chkheidze, Revaz, 33
Chmielewski, Tadeusz, 87
Chukhrai, Grigori, 18, 35, 40
Churikova, Inna, 41
Chytilová, Věra, 141, 143, 144, 145, 149–50, 161, 162, 165
Cikán, Miroslav, 165
Cinema Arts Workshop (SU), 5
Cinema of Moral Concern (Po), 89, 90, 91, 105
Ciobanu, Ilarion, 318

Ciulei, Liviu, 315, 316, 317, 322, 326, 330
Clair, Rene, 82, 331
Clouzot, Henri-Georges, 355
Cocea, Dinu-Constantin, 315, 316, 326
Commission on Science, Culture, and Art (Bu), 353
Committee of Cinematography, Council of Peoples' Commissars (Cabinet) of the USSR, 11
Communist Party, 1, 2, 6, 10, 11, 12, 13, 15, 17, 20, 37, 42, 72, 86, 137, 195, 196, 201, 229, 231, 232, 233, 234, 235, 240, 257, 276, 315, 353
Connery, Sean, 39
Conservatory of Dramatic Arts (Ro), 316
Constantin, George, 318
Cooper, James Fenimore, 317
Cortazar, Julio, 208
Corvin Film Studio (Hu), 230
Ćosić, Dobrica, 192
Craef, Roland, 286
Creangă, Serban, 319, 320, 323
Cserhalmi, György, 261
Cukor, George, 42
Čuřik, Jan, 155
Curtiz, Michael. *See* Kertész, Mihály
Cybulski, Zbigniew, 77, 83, 90, 97, 105
Cyril, Saint (Constantine), 356
Czech Spring, 86
Czechoslovak Film Society, 135
Czechoslovak Writers' Congress (1967), 145
Czinkóczi, Zsuzsa, 247, 248, 260
Czyzewska, Elizbieta, 97

Dakovski, Dako, 360
Dalkowska, Ewa, 98
Danelia, Georgi, 21, 35
Daneliuc, Mircea, 321, 322, 323, 326
Daniel, František, 131
Daquin, Louis, 316, 331
Dárday, István, 255–56, 261
Darvas, Iván, 235, 262
Darvas, Lili, 243
Dassin, Jules, 215
de Broca, Philippe, 215
Degl, Emanuel, 155

Degl, Karel, 131, 135, 155, 158
Demian, Iosef, 318, 320, 321
Deppe, Hans, 280
Der Geist des Films (Spirit of Film), 260
Deren, Maya, 156
Déry, Tibor, 242
De Sica, Vittorio, 233
Destin, Emmy, 147
Deutsche Film Aktiengesellschaft (DEFA), 276, 277, 278, 279, 280, 281, 282, 283, 285, 286, 288, 290, 291, 292, 294
DEFA-Aussenhandel (Exporting Agency), 277
DEFA-Kopierwerke (Printing Works), 277
DEFA Studio for Popular Science Films, 277, 290
Devětsil Group (Cz), 132, 133, 162
Devils of Loudon, The, 84
Dewey, Langdon, 130, 134, 155
Dialóg Film Studio (Hu), 236, 260, 264
Dimitrescu, Cornel, 312
Dimitrov, Georgi, 357
Dimitrova, Marianna, 365
Dinov, Todor, 346, 349, 361
Disneyland, 102
Distribution Division (Polish film), 78
Djulgerov, Georgi, 351, 354, 356, 357, 358, 361
Dmochowski, Mariusz, 98
"Dom" Film Unit (Po), 87
Domarádzki, Jerzy, 98, 99
Donev, Donyo, 346
Donskoi, Mark Semyonovich, 35–36, 37, 46
Đorđević, Puriša, 193, 196, 198, 202, 209, 214
Dostoevsky, Fyodor, 43
Dovniković, Borivoj, 193
Dovzhenko, Alexander, 2, 7, 8, 9, 10, 13, 16, 20, 36, 42
Drăgan, Mircea, 315, 316, 318, 319, 326–27
Drahota, Andrea, 260
Drankov, Alexander, 3, 36, 39
Drašković, Boro, 200, 209
Drha, Vladimír, 150

Dubcek, Alexander, 129, 145, 146
Dudow, Slatan, 275, 278, 279, 280, 281, 282, 286, 290–91
Duga Film Studio (Yu), 192, 215
Dunaevski, Isaak, 36
Dunav Film Studio (Yu), 193
Dvořák, Antonin, 147
Dygat, Stanisław, 70, 78, 83, 98, 102
Dymna, Anna, 98
Dzigan, Efim, 14
Dziki, Waldemas, 102

Early Works (Marx), 198
East Berlin School of Drama, 293
Economic Division (of Polish film), 78
Eisenstein, Sergei, xi, 2, 4, 7–9, 11, 13, 15, 16, 33, 35, 36, 40, 46, 275, 290
Ekk, Nikolai, 14, 34
Eliot, T. S., 353
Elley, Derek, 82, 83, 84
Engel, Erich, 275, 279, 283, 291
Enyedi, Ildikó, 256
Eperjes, Károly, 260
Erdöss, Pál, 256
Ermash, Filipp, 24, 36–37
Ermler, Friedrich Markovich, 14, 37, 46
Ermolev, Osip, 37

Fábri, Zoltán, 234–35, 261, 262, 264, 348,
Factory of Eccentric Actors (FEKS) Group (SU), 37, 39, 46
Fairbanks, Douglas, 11
Falk, Feliks, 89, 91–92, 96, 98, 99, 108
Federation of Film Discussion Clubs (Po), 78
Federation of Hungarian Film and Television Artists, 262
Fehér, Imre, 235
Fejós, Pál, 232, 262
Fencl, Antonin, 135, 155
Feuchtwanger, Lion, 287
Fiedler, E. W., 281
Filac, Vilko, 203, 207, 208
Filipski, Ryszard, 87
Film, 132
Film (journal-Yu), 187, 189
Film Authors' Studio (FAS) (Yu), 193

SUBJECT INDEX

Film City (Filmski grad-Yu), 187
Film Faculty of the Academy of the Performing Arts (FAMU) (Cz), 131, 133, 136, 203, 207, 214, 215, 216, 217, 218, 362
Film Fund (Po), 78
Film Industry Fund (Hu), 231
Film Polski, 71
Film Repertory Councils (Po), 78
Film School at Potsdam (EGr), 277, 292, 293, 294
Filmactiv Group (EGr), 275, 292
Filmmakers' Union (SU), 24, 39, 40
Finci, Eli, 189
First Congress of Film Workers (SU), 20
First Congress of Soviet Writers, xii, 12
Fisher, William, 257
Flidr, Zdenek, 150
Ford, Aleksander, 69, 70, 71, 72, 73, 84, 86, 97, 98–99, 100, 103, 107, 108
Forman, Miloš, xi, xiii, 81, 129, 132, 136, 137, 139, 140, 141, 142, 143, 154, 156, 160, 163, 164, 165, 167, 343
Fotokinema Company (Cz), 167
Frank, Herz, 22
Freitag, Manfred, 286
Frič, Martin, 132, 134, 136, 137, 155, 156, 162, 165, 167, 168
Frisch, Max (Rudolph), 329
Fronczewski, Piotr, 99
Fuksiewicz, Jacek, 70, 79, 82, 83
Fundamentals of Film Directing, 40

Gaál, István, 252–53, 255, 262, 264, 266, 267
Gábor, Pál, 236, 253, 262, 263, 267
Gabrea, Radu, 320
Gabreu, Paul, 320
Gabrilovic, Evgeni, 43
Gale, Jože, 191
Ganev, Hristo, 346, 347, 348, 352, 354, 361, 363, 365
Gardin, Vladimir, 37
Gárdos, Péter, 256
Gašparović, Zdenko, 210
Der Geist des Films (Spirit of film), 260

Gendov, Vassil, 344
Georgescu, Jean, 311, 312, 313, 314, 327, 330
Gerasimov, Sergei Appolinarievich, 37, 38, 295
German, Alexei, 20, 21, 35, 37–38
Gertler, Viktor, 312
Geschonneck, Erwin, 286
Gierek, Edward, 87
Gilić, Vlatko, 214
Glasnost, 23, 25, 26, 43
Godard, Jean-Luc, 85, 200, 215, 249
Godina, Karpo, 209, 214
Goethe, Johann Wolfgang von, 249, 286, 287
Gogoberidze, Lana, 21, 38
Gogol, Nikolai, 17, 249, 363
Golan, Menachem, 92
Gombrowicz, Witold, 80, 81
Gomulka, Władysław, 77, 81, 87, 91
Goncharov, Ivan, 21
Good Soldier Svejk, The, 129
Gorbachev, Mikhail S., 23, 25, 146, 150
Gorki, Maxim, 329
Goskino (State Committee for Cinematography-SU), 20, 24, 36, 39
Gothár, Péter, 255, 256, 261, 262
Gottschalk, Joachim, 278
Green, Joseph, 71
Grezhov, Boris, 344, 361
Grgić, Zlatko, 193
Griffith, D. W., 5, 133, 162
Grlic, Rajko, 203, 204, 205, 206, 214
Grubcheva, Ivanka, 358
Gründgens, Gustav, 252
Gruza, Jerzy, 106
Gubenko, Nikolai, 22
Gulea, Steve, 321
Gunther, Egon, 284, 285, 286, 287, 291
Gurchenko, Ludmila, 38
Gyöngyössy, Imre, 254, 262, 263

Haas, Hugo, 131, 133, 134, 155, 156, 157
Habbema, Cox, 286
Hackenschmied (Hammid), Alexander, 156
Hadžić, Fadil, 192, 214–15

Haitov, Nikolai, 354, 361
Hames, Peter, 132, 133, 138, 139, 143, 144, 145, 147, 148
Hammid, Alexander. *See* Hackenschmied, Alexander
Hanák, Dušan, 148, 156
Hanžeković, Fedor, 191
Hapsburg Empire, 229, 251
Haraszti, Miklos, xii–xiii, 11
Has, Wojciech, 71, 75, 82, 83, 84, 87, 96, 97, 98, 99, 100, 101, 103, 104, 105, 107, 109
Hašek, Jaroslav, 129, 157
Havel, Václav, 129, 164
Heifitz, Iosef, 17, 34, 35, 38
Helge, Ladislav, 138, 140, 157
Hellberg, Martin, 279, 280, 281, 282, 291–92
Heller, Otto, 131, 157
Hernadi, Gyula, 232, 263
Herz, Juraj, 145, 148, 157, 161
Heskia, Zacco, 358
Heymann, Karl Heinz, 286, 288
Heynowski, Walter, 285
Higher School of Film (Po), 71
Hitchcock, Alfred, 74, 134, 163
Hitel (journal-Hu), 258 n.2
Hitler, Adolf, 14, 232, 241, 290
Hladnik, Boštjan, 193, 194, 195, 199, 209, 215
Hoffman, E. T. A., 287
Hoffman, Jerzy, 84, 87, 96, 97, 98, 99, 100, 101, 103, 104, 105, 107, 109, 110
Hoffman, Jutta, 286
Holland, Agnieszka, 89, 91, 92, 95, 98, 99, 105, 108
Holloway, Ronald, 344, 354, 355, 357, 358
Holoubek, Gustavo, 98, 99–100, 110
Honzl, Jindřich, 133
Hoppe, Rolf, 286
Horthy, Admiral Miklós, 229, 246, 260
Horton, Andrew, 25, 26, 204
Houston, Penelope, 241
Hrabal, Bohumil, 145, 147, 157
Hristov, Hristo, 349, 350, 351, 352, 353, 355, 356, 357, 358, 360–61, 363

Hrušinský, Rudolf, 157–58
Hubáček, Miroslav, 137
Hübner, Zygmunt, 100
Hungarian National Theater, 262, 265, 267
Hungarian Republic of Councils, 231, 239, 260
Hungarian Revolution (1956), 232–33, 255, 256, 280, 315
Hungarian Socialist Workers' Party, 235
Hungarofilm, 256, 257 n.1, 260
Hunnia Film Studio (Hu), 230, 236
Huppert, Isabelle, 247
Husák, Gustav, 146
Huszárik, Zoltan, 253–54, 255, 263, 266
Huxley, Aldous, 84

Iacob, Mihai, 316, 330
Idziak, Slawomir, 100
I. L. Caragiale Institute of Theatrical Art (IATC) (Ro), 310, 313, 315, 317, 318, 325, 326, 327, 328, 329, 330, 331
Ilenko, Yuri, 22, 38–39
Ilinchev, Kiril, 362
Ilinski, Igor, 38, 42
Iliu, Victor, 313, 314, 316, 320, 326, 327, 328, 329, 330
Illik, Josef, 158
Iluzjion Film Unit (Po), 78, 87
Innemann, Svatopluk, 131, 134, 135, 156, 158
Inspector General, The, 249
Institute of Theatrical Studies (Berlin), 290
International Federation of Film Art Academies, 265
International Film Critics Union, 104
Intorsureanu, Alexandru, 318
Intruder, The, 321
Iorda, Marin, 311
Irzykowski, Karol, 70, 71
Istrati, Panait, 316
Ivanda, Branko, 209
Ivanov, Alexander, 45
Ivanova, Lili, 352
Ivans, Joris, 295
Iwaszkiewicz, Jaroslaw, 70

SUBJECT INDEX

Jadran Film Studio, 193
Jahoda, Miecyzsław, 100, 108
Jakim, Ladislav, 142
Jakšić-Fando, Milorad, 200
Jakubisko, Juraj, 145, 148, 158
Jakubowska, Wanda, 69, 72, 73, 98, 100, 104, 107, 109
Jancsó, Miklós, 236–42, 246, 257, 261, 263, 264
Jancsó, Miklós (Nyika), Jr., 249, 263
Janda, Krystyna, 92, 100
Janković, Stole, 191, 192, 215
Jankowska-Cieślak, Jadwiga, 243, 260
Jannings, Emil, 164
Jára Cimrman Theatre (Cz), 166
Jasny, Vojtech, 81, 137, 138, 145, 146, 158, 159, 161
Jeles, András, 256
Ježek, Jaroslav, 132
Jires, Jaromil, 132, 141, 145, 148, 155, 158–59, 160, 161, 162, 163
John, Radek, 159
Jovanović, Soja, 191
Jung-Alsen, Kurt, 281, 284
Junghans, Karl, 135, 159
Jurácek, Pavel, 164
Jutriša, Vladimir, 193

Kabay, Barna, 254, 262
Kacer, John, 159
Kachyňa, Karel, 137, 145, 148, 154, 158, 159, 161, 164, 165
Kadár, Jan, 136, 139, 140, 145, 159
Kádár, János, 229, 234, 235, 249
"Kadr" Film Unit (Po), 78, 87
Kafka, Franz, 83, 129
Kalatozov, Mikhail, 17–18, 39, 46, 348
Kalik, Mikhail, 20
"Kamera" Film Unit (Po), 78, 86
Kamshalov, Alexander, 24
Karanović, Srđan, 203, 204, 205, 214, 215
Károlyi, Count Mihaly, 231, 244
Karpikov, Abai, 24
Kawalerowicz, Jerzy, 71, 72, 74, 75, 81, 84, 87, 91, 97, 100, 102, 103, 104, 105, 106, 108, 109, 110, 214
Kazakhstan "New Wave," 24

Keaton, Buster, 11, 132
Kedzierski, Pawel, 98, 99
Kende, János, 263
Kepler, Johannes, 287
Kerensky, Alexander, 9
Kertesz, Mihály (Michael Curtiz), 230
Kerumpuh (journal-Yu), 214
Kézdi-Kovács, Zsolt, 254, 261, 263
Khanzhonkov, Alexander, 39
Kheskia, Zako, 351
Khokhlova, Alexandra, 40
Kholodnaia, Vera, 39
Khrushchev, Nikita, 13, 17, 20, 138, 140, 234
Kiesler (Lemarr), Hedy, 130, 133, 162
Kieślowski, Krzysztof, 87, 89, 92, 96, 100, 101, 105, 108
Kijowski, Janusz, 89, 101
Kilibaev, Bakhyt, 24
Kinema, 132
Kino-Eye, 46
Kinofa Studio (Cz), 163
Kirkov, Lyndmil, 352, 354, 355, 358, 362
Kirsten, Ralf, 285, 287
Klaren, Georg, 276, 279
Klein, Dušan, 147
Klein, Gerhard, 281, 282, 292
Klimov, Elem, 21, 24, 39, 44
Klopčič, Matjaž, 193, 199, 200, 209, 215
Klos, Elmar, 136, 139, 140, 145, 158, 159
Klosiński, Edward, 101
Kluba, Henryk, 85, 86, 101, 105
Kobiela, Bogumil, 101
Kohlhasse, Wolfgang, 286, 288
Kolár, Jan, 135, 159–60, 163
Kolar, Slavko, 191, 193
Kolarov, Dion, 347
Kolarov, Kiran, 358
Koliba Studio (Bratislava, Cz), 146
Kolker, Robert, 25, 26
Koltai, Lajos, 252, 263
Komarov, Sergei, 38
Komorowska, Maja, 88, 89, 101
Kondratiuk, Tadeusz, 96

Konwicki, Tadeusz, 70, 75, 81, 84, 87, 91, 97, 98, 100, 102, 103, 108
Korabov, Nikola, 362
Korda, Alexander. *See* Korda, Sándor
Korda, Sándor (Alexander Korda), 230
Korda, Vincent, 230
Korda, Zoltan, 230
Kósa, Ferenc, 254, 255, 264, 266
Kossuth, Francis, 231, 237
Kostelac, Nikola, 193
Kovač, Mirko, 206
Kovačević, Dušan, 207, 209, 215
Kovács, András, 244–45, 261, 264
Kovács, Kati, 260
Kowalski, Władysław, 102
Kozintsev, Grigori Mikhailovich, 11, 17, 35, 39–40, 44, 45, 46
"Krakow" Film Unit (Po), 87
Krejčík, Jiří, 136, 138, 147, 154, 160, 163
Kresadlova, Vera, 160
Kristl, Vladimir, 193
Kriuckov, Nikolai, 40
Křízenecký, Jan, 130, 134, 160
Krolikiewicz, Grzegorz, 87, 88, 102
Krössner, Renate, 288
Krška, Václav, 136, 138, 139, 158, 160, 165
Krumbachová, Ester, 160–61
Ktorov, Anatoli, 42
Kubat, Eduard, 280
Kučera, Jaroslav, 161
Kudeříková, Maruška, 148
Kuhn, Siegfried, 285, 286, 287, 292
Kuleshov, Lev, 5, 33, 34, 39, 40, 42, 44
Kulijanov, Lev, 24, 40
Kun, Béla, 231, 260
Kundera, Milan, 145, 159, 161
Kunert, Joachim, 281, 283, 284, 292
Kusík, Karel, 145
Kusturica, Emir, 207, 208, 215
Kutz, Kazimierz, 80, 81, 87, 97, 102, 103, 105

Lamac, Karel, 157, 160, 163
Lamarr, Hedy. *See* Kiesler, Hedy
Lambrinova, Petya
Lamprecht, Gerhard, 275, 277, 279, 293
Lang, Fritz, 294
Lapicki, Andrezej, 98, 102–3
Laskowski, Jan, 102
Látal, Stanislav, 150
Latinovits, Zoltan, 264
Laurel and Hardy, 132, 168
Lawton, Anna, 24
Le Chanois, Jean-Paul, 281
Legoshin, Vladimir, 14
Lenartowicz, Stanisław, 80, 97, 100, 102, 103
Lenfilm Studios (SU), 44
Lenin, Vladimir, xi, 3, 4, 5, 6, 124, 287
Lenin Train, The, 3
Lesiewicz, Witold, 79
Leszczynski, 105
Levaco, Ron, 40
Levitski, Alexander Andreevich, 40–41
Leyda, Jay, xi
Liehm, Antonin J. and Mira, 136, 150, 231, 236, 288, 348, 358
Linder, Max, 344
Lipman, Jerzy, 74, 87, 103
Lipsky, Oldrich, 145, 148, 154, 161, 166
Little Prince, The, 364
Ljubljana Academy of Dramatic Arts (Yu), 214, 215
Llosa, Mario Vargas, 208
Łodz Film School (Po), 86, 101, 365
Łomnicki, Tadeusz, 103
Lopushansky, Konstantin, 35
Losey, Joseph, 105
Lubitsch, Ernst, 81
Lucernafilm Studios (Cz), 157
Luderer, Wolfgang, 285
Lugosi, Béla, 231
Lukács, György, 234
Lukaszewicz, Olgierd, 103
Lumière brothers, 310
Lumière Film Co. (Fr), 2
Lustig, Arnost, 141, 144, 161
Luther, Igor, 158

Mach, Josef, 284
Machatý, Gustav, 130, 131, 132, 133, 135, 156, 162, 165
Machulski, Julian, 91, 103
Madaras, Jozsef, 264

SUBJECT INDEX

Maetzig, Kurt, 275, 276, 278, 279, 280, 281, 282, 283, 284, 285, 286, 287, 292–93, 295
Mafilm Production Co. (Hu), 236, 257
Main Board of Film (EGr), 277, 285
Majewski, Janus, 85, 86, 96, 98, 103, 104, 109, 110
Makarova, Tamara, 38
Makavejev, Dušan, 193, 196, 197, 201, 209, 215–16
Makk, Károly, 242–44, 260, 261, 264
Malenkov, Georgi, 17, 234
Mann, Heinrich, 279
Mann, Klaus, 252
Mann, Thomas, 287
Manvell, Roger, 69, 78
Marcel, Martin, 45
Marcus, Manole, 315, 317, 318, 319, 320, 321, 327, 328, 330
Marcuse, Herbert, 12
Mărgineau, Nicolae, 321
Máriássy, Félix, 235, 236, 263, 264–65
Máriássy, Judit, 235
Marinović, Miloslav, 204
Marković, Goran, 203, 205, 214, 216
Marks, Aleksandar, 193, 210
Marquez, Gabriel Garcia, 208
Marshall, Herbert, 7, 12, 13
Martinkova, Pavla, 143
Marušić, Joško, 210
Marx, Karl, 2, 198
Máša, Antonín, 145
Mast, Gerald, 2
Mastroianni, Marcello, 26, 41, 266
Matavulj, Simo, 191
Matyjaszkiewicz, Stefan, 104
Maurette, Marc, 331
Mayakovsky, Vladimir, 11
Medvedkin, Alexander I., 7, 14, 41
Melies, Georges, 3
Menshov, Vladimir, 22
Menšik, Vladimír, 147
Menu, Paul, 311
Menzel, Jiří, 130, 132, 139, 141, 143, 144, 147, 149, 157, 158, 160, 162, 165, 166, 167
Mészáros, Márta, 246–49, 257, 258 n.2, 260, 261, 263, 264, 265, 266, 267

Methodius, Saint, 356
Meyer, Otto, 280
Meyerhold, Vsevolod, 3, 11, 43
Michałek, Bolesław, 73, 76, 77, 79, 80, 81, 86, 87, 104
Michiewicz, Adam, 86
Mihail, Jean, 311, 312, 313, 314, 327, 328
Mihić, Gordan, 208, 216
Mihu, Iulian, 315, 317, 319, 321, 322, 328
Mikhalkov, Nikita, 21, 26, 38, 41
Mikhalkov-Konchalovski, Andrei, 17, 21, 22, 38, 41, 45
Milošović, Mića, 210
Milošović, Slobodan, 202, 203
Miłosz, Czesław, 91, 95
Mimica, Vatroslav, 192, 193, 198, 199, 206, 209, 216
Ministry of Culture (Hu), 236
Ministry of Culture and Art (Po), 78
Mishev, Georgi, 352, 354, 362
Mitrović, Živorad (Žika), 191, 200
Mladost ("Youth") Film Unit (Bu), 363
Mokep Production Co., 257
Monori, Lili, 247, 265
Monty Python, 81
Morgernstern, Janusz, 81, 87, 95, 97, 100, 102, 104, 105, 106, 110
Moscow Art Theater, 34, 71
Moscow Dramatic Arts Institute, 43
Moscow State Institute of Cinematography (VGIK), 33, 41, 42, 43, 46, 265, 295, 350, 360, 361, 362, 363, 364, 465
Mosfilm Studios, 33, 43
Moskalyk, Antonin, 161
Mozhukhin, Ivan, 37, 41
Müller, Hans, 281
Munich Conference (1938), 135
Munk, Andrez, 79, 80, 85, 97, 98, 101, 103, 104, 105, 106, 107, 108, 109, 348
Munteanu, Francisc, 317, 319, 321, 322, 328, 330
Mureşan, Mircea, 316, 317, 319, 320, 328
Mussolini, Benito, 206, 232

Nagy, Imre, 234
Nakhapetov, Rodion, 45
Nanović, Vojislav, 188
Narliev, Khodzhikuli, 22
Nasfetex, Janusz, 97
Năstase, Doru, 319, 321
National Cinematographe Office (Ro), 310, 311
Naumov, Vladimir, 20
Nazi Party, 275
Negreanu, Dinu, 314, 328–29
Negulesco, Jean, 311
Němec, Jan, 138, 141, 144, 161, 162, 163, 165
Nenov, Nikolai, 357
Nestler, Jochen, 286
Neumann, Claus, 286
Newerly, Igor, 74
Nezval, Vitezslav, 132, 133, 159, 162
Nichev, Ivan, 354, 355, 364
Nicolae, Cristiana, 322, 323
Nicolaescu, Sergiu, 315, 316, 317, 319, 321, 322, 323, 328, 329, 330
Nikolić, Božidar, 207, 209, 216
Nikolov, Milen, 361
Nordisk Film Co. (Den), 2
Norwid, Cyprian, 77
Nóti, Károlyi, 232
Novaković, Radoš, 189, 191, 192, 216
Novotný, Antonín, 131, 145, 155
Nowak, Leopold, 92
Nowicki, Jan, 104, 247, 260
Nugmanov, Rashid, 24
Nuremberg Trials, 280
"Nurt" Film Unit (Po), 87
Nuţu, Dan, 318

Objectiv Film Studio (Hu), 236
Oblomov, 21
Oehme, Roland, 286
Ogorodnikov, Valeri, 24
Okeev, Tolomush, 22
"Oko" Film Unit (Po), 87, 97
Olbrychski, Daniel, 92, 105
Olivier, Lawrence, 131, 157
Olmer, Vít, 150, 159, 162
Ondráková, Anny, 134, 155, 157
Ondricek, Miroslav, 162

Ophuls, Max, 131
Orlova, Liubov, 33
Ostrovski, Grisha, 349, 364
Otsep, Fyodor, 33, 38
Oz, Frank, 148

Pabst, G. W. (Georg Wilhelm), 260, 294
Pajkic, Nebojsa, 207
Pal, George, 166
Palmer, Lili, 286
Panfilov, Gleb, 20, 21, 22, 41–42
"Panorama" Film Unit (Po), 87
Papić, Krsto, 193, 199, 201, 209, 216–17
Papoušek, Jaroslav, 142, 145, 160, 163
Papp, Veronika, 260
Parajanov, Sergei, 19–20, 22, 38, 39, 42
Páral, Vladimir, 148, 159
Paskaljevic, Goran, 203, 204, 214, 217
Passendorfer, Jerzy, 71, 80, 87, 98, 100, 102, 103, 105, 108, 110
Passer, Ivan, 81, 142, 145, 149, 160, 163
Pathé Film Co. (Fr), 2
Paul, David, xi, xii, 250
Pavlović, Živojin (Žika), 193, 195, 196, 197, 202, 205, 209, 217
Peasant Party (Hu), 233
Pech, Antonin, 163
Pellea, Amza, 318
Perestiani, Ivan, 34
Perestroika, 43
"Perspektywa" Film Unit (Po), 87
Petelska, Ewa, 105, 106
Petelski, Czeslaw, 73, 87, 105
Petrescu, Aurel, 311
Petrie, Graham, 233, 237, 240, 242, 243, 250, 254, 257 n.1
Petrov, Dimiter, 356
Petrov, Valeri, 347, 348, 352, 354, 362
Petrović, Aleksandar, 193, 194, 195, 196, 197, 200, 201, 209, 217
Petrycki, Jacek, 105
Pichul, Vasili, 24
Pick, Lupu, 311
Picon, Molly, 71
Pieczka, Franciszek, 105
Pinter, Harold, 354

Pinter, Tomislav, 200
Pintilie, Lucian, 316, 317, 318, 322, 329
Piscator, Erwin, 275, 293
Piskov, Hristo, 347, 352, 356, 363
Pislaru, Margareta, 318
Pissarev, Pavel, 350
Piţa, Dan, 319, 320, 321, 323, 329, 330, 331
Piwowski, Marek, 88
Platonov, 21
Plicka, Karel, 156, 163
"Po Prostu" Film Unit (Po), 96
Podnieks, Iuris, 24
Poe, Edgar Allan, 210
Pogačić, Vladimir, 189, 191, 192, 217
Pohl, Arthur, 281
Polański, Roman, 85, 101, 103, 105
Poledňak, Alois, 146
Poleska-Petelska, Ewa, 73
Polish Film Critics Union, 104
Polish Film School, 86, 103, 104, 109
Polish Filmmakers' Association, 97, 104
Politburo (SU), 36
Polony, Anna, 260
Polsný, Viktor, 159
Popescu-Gopo, Ion, 318, 322, 329
Popov, Alexei, 11
Popov, Stole, 208, 217
Popović, Jovan, 189
Popović, Miča, 195, 198
Popovic, Nikola, 188
Popovici, Silvia, 318
Popovici, Titus, 316, 319, 330
Poręba, Bohdan, 87
Potocki, Count Jan, 83
Potsdam Free German Youth, 293
Pragafilm (Cz), 157
Prague Spring, 146
Praxis (journal-Yu), 200
Preda, Martin, 321
Prochazka, Jan, 159, 164
Production Division (of Polish film), 78
"Profil" Film Unit (Po), 87
Progress (Distribution Co.-EGr), 277
Proletkino (Proletarian Cinema-SU), 39
"Proprostu" Film Unit (Po), 78
Protazanov, Yakov Alexandrovich, 3–4, 34, 37, 38, 41, 42

Provisional Government (Rus), 4, 6, 9
Prus, Boleslaw, 70, 83, 84
Pryl, Karel, 146
"Pryzmał Film Unit (Po), 87
Pszoniak, Wojciech, 92, 106
Pudovkin, Vsevolod, 2, 7, 8, 9, 11, 13, 16, 34, 42
Pyriev, Ivan, 36, 43

Radev, Vulo, 348–49, 363
Radichkov, Yordan, 350, 351, 363
Radivojević, Miloš, 209, 217
Radok, Alfred, 136, 160, 164
Radványi, Géza, 233, 264, 265
Radziwilowicz, Jerzy, 106
Raizman, Yuli, 43
Rajk, László, 233
Rakonjac, Kokan, 193, 195, 196, 198
Rákosi, Mátyás, 234, 242, 245
Rauković, Aleksandar, 196
Raynor, Bogomil, 348, 360
Rebanalt, Arthur, 279
Redl, Alfred, 252
Reicher, Emanuel, 290
Reinhardt, Max, 275, 291, 293
Reisch, Günther, 283, 287, 288, 293
Reisz, Karel, 214
Renoir, Jean, 82
Resnais, Alain, 349
Révai, József, 234
Reymont, Stanislaw, 70
Riazanov, Eldar, 20, 38, 41, 43, 45
Riefenstahl, Leni, 14, 260
Rina, Ita, 133, 134
Robar-Dorin, Filip, 209
Rodchenko, Alexander, 46
Romania Film (production co.), 310
Romm, Mikhail Ilich, 11, 14, 43, 45
"Rondo" Film Unit (Po), 87
Room, Abram, 16, 34, 43–44, 213
Rosselini, Roberto, 233
Rouleau, Raymond, 281
Rovenský, Josef, 131, 134, 155, 164, 165
Różewicz, Stanisław, 78, 87, 99, 100, 106, 110
Rózsa, Śandor, 237, 238
Rücker, Günther, 286, 293

Rudziutak, Y. A., 11
Russell, Ken, 84
Russian Association of Proletarian Writers (RAPP), 11
Russian Civil War, 21, 39, 46, 238
Russian Revolution (1905), 8
Ruttkai, Éva, 265
Rybkowski, Jan, 72, 73, 96, 97, 98, 100, 102, 106, 107, 108, 109, 110
"Rytm" Film Unit (Po), 78
Rzeszewski, Henryk, 108

Sabinsky, Cheslav, 39
Sadoveanu, Mihail, 312, 313
Sahia, Alexandru, 315
Saint-Exupery, Antoine, 364
Saizescu, George, 320, 321, 330
Salcudeanu, Petre, 321
Sándor, Pál, 254, 255, 265–66
Sára, Sándor, 236, 254, 255, 262, 266
Sararu, Dinu, 321
Sass, Barbara, 91, 97, 102
Satie, Erik, 210
Savchenko, Igor, 42
Schamoni, Peter, 287
Schlesinger, John, 214
Schlóndorff, Volker, 100, 105
Schmeling, Max, 134, 162
Schmidt, Jan, 145, 154, 164
Schorm, Evald, 141, 144, 150, 154, 155, 159, 164–65
Schulz, Bruno, 70, 83
Schwab, Sepp, 279
Scibor-Rylski, Aleksander, 74, 87, 97, 107
Scnitzer, Luda and Jean, 45
Seemann, Horst, 286, 287, 293
Seifert, Jaroslav, 129
Semafor Theatre (Cz), 142, 157, 160, 165
Sennett, Mack, 41
Seweryn, Andrzej, 107
Shakhnazarov, Karen, 24
Shamshiev, Bolotbek, 22
Sharaliev, Borislav, 346, 352, 356, 358, 361, 363
Shaw, George Bernard, 329
Shepitko, Larisa, 20, 44

Shklovski, Victor Borisovich, 11, 44
Shopov, Assen, 352
Shostakovich, Dmitri, 44
Shub, Esther, 44
Shukshin, Vasili, 20, 22, 44
Shumiatsky, Boris, 45
Sidran, Abdulah, 207, 208
Sienkiewicz, Henryk, 70, 84, 99, 107, 108
Sight and Sound (journal-Br), 241, 257
Šijan, Slobodan, 207, 217–18
"Silesia" Film Unit (Po), 87
Simjanović, Zoran, 204, 205
Simon, Günther, 286
Siodmak, Robert, 215
Skolimowski, Jerzy, 85, 86, 95, 97, 103, 104, 107, 110
Skupa, Josef, 166
Škvorecký, Josef, 129, 132, 134, 136, 144, 150, 164, 165
Słaska, Aleksandra, 107
Slavici, Ion, 314
Šlechta, Josef, 131
Ślesicki, Wladyslaw, 107–8
Šlitr, Jiří, 133, 165
Slowacki, Juliusz, 77
Smallholders' Party (Hu), 233
Smoktunovski, Innokenti, 45
Smoljak, Ladislav, 147, 148, 150, 161, 165, 166
Smyczek, Karel, 150, 159
Sobanski, Oskar, 87
Social Democratic Party (Hu), 233
Socialistische Einheitspartei Deutschlands (SED) (EGr), 276, 284
Society of the Devotees of Artistic Film (START) (Po), 70, 71, 72, 100
Sofia Academy of Dramatic Art, 360, 362, 363, 364, 365
Sofia Film and Theater Academy (VITIS), 358
Sofr, Jaromir, 165
Sokurov, Alexsander, 24, 25, 45
Solan, Peter, 141
Solidarity Movement, 86, 90, 248
Solovyov, Sergei, 24
Solzhenitsyn, Alexander, 352, 353
Somló, Tamás, 266

SUBJECT INDEX

Soukup, Jaroslav, 150
Soviet Film (journal), xiii
Soyuzkino (State Directorate for the Cinema and Photography Industry-SU), 45
Sozialistische Einheitspartei Deutschlands (SED) (EGr), 276, 284
Spanish Civil War, 284
Šrámek, Fráňa, 138, 160
Sremac, Steven, 191
Staatstheater (EGr), 290
Stahnke, Günther, 284
Staikov, Lyudmil, 352, 354, 363, 364
Stalich, Jan, 131, 158, 165
Stalin, Josef, xii, 1, 7, 8, 11, 12, 13, 14, 15, 16, 17, 18, 22, 35, 40, 42, 136, 197, 199, 208, 233, 235, 248, 280
Štalter, Pavao, 193, 210
Stan, Nicu, 318
Stanislavsky, Konstantin, 71, 233, 265
Stanković, Bora, 189
Starewicz (Starevich), Wladyslaw, 3, 166
Starski, Ludwik, 73, 108
"Start" Film Unit (Po), 78
State Film Archives (EGr), 277
Staudte, Wolfgang, 275, 276, 277, 279, 282, 288, 293–94
Stawinski, Jerzy Stefan, 78, 87, 108
Steklý, Karel, 136
Stephan, Bernard, 287
Stevenin, Jean-François, 92
Štiglic, France, 189, 191, 192, 218
Stoica, Chivu, 315
Stojanović, Dušan, 194, 196
Stojanović, Lazar, 201
Stoyanov, Georgi, 351, 353, 354, 356, 357
Stoyanov, Todor, 349, 364
Stoyanovich, Ivan, 353, 356, 357, 359
Stranka, Erwin, 287, 288
Stratiev, Stanislav, 362
Strecha, Jiří, 150
Střelecká, Lenka, 150
"Studio" Film Unit (Po), 78, 86
Studio for Synchronization (EGr), 277
Stuhr, Jerzy, 108
Subremenik ("Contemporary") Film Unit (Bu), 362
Suchý, Jiří, 133, 165

Švankmajer, Jan, 145, 150, 165
Svěrák, Zdeněk, 147, 148, 161, 165, 166
Svoboda, Jiří, 150, 154, 166
"Syrena" Film Unit (Po), 78
Szabó, István, xi, 100, 236, 246, 249–52, 255, 257, 261, 264, 266, 343
Szapotowska, Grazyna, 243, 260
Székely, István (Steve Székely), 231–32
Székely, Steve. *See* Székely, István
Szirtes, Ádám, 266
Szöts, István, 232–33, 264, 266
Szulkin, Piotr, 108, 109

Talankin, Igor, 35
Tănase, Dinu, 319, 323
Tarkovski, Andrei, 18–19, 25, 41, 45
Társulás Studio (Hu), 256, 261
Tasses, Atanas, 355
Tatos, Alexandru, 319, 321, 322, 323, 330
Terziev, Ivan, 351, 364
Thälmann, Ernst, 287
Theodorescu, Constantin, 310
Theory of the Film: Character and Growth of a New Art (Film—Werden und Wesen einer neue Kunst), 261
Thorndike, Andrew, 278, 280, 281, 282, 283, 285, 293, 294
Thorndike, Annelie, 283, 285, 293, 294
Threepenny Opera, 275, 291
Tiege, Karel, 132
Tille, Václav, 132
Timár, Péter, 256
Tisse, Eduard, 40, 46
Tito, Josip Broz, 186, 187, 188, 199, 202, 208
Tobias, Gheorghe, 315
Toeplitz, Jerzy, 86
Tolstoi, Leo, 3, 37, 133
"Tor" Film Unit (Po), 78, 87, 96
Törócsik, Mari, 243, 267
Trauberg, Leonid, 11, 39, 40, 44, 46
Trauffaut, Françious, 249
Treaty of Trianon, 229
"Tree Without Roots, A," ("Darvo Bez Koren"), 361
Tregubovich, Viktor, 38
Třeštíková, Helena, 150

Tretiakov, Sergei, 10
Trnka, Jiří, 137, 139, 166
Troška, Zdeněk, 150
Tulpanov, Colonel, 276, 278
Turaj, Frank, 73, 79, 80, 81, 86, 87
20th Congress of the Soviet Communist Party, 17
Tyszkiewicz, Beata, 108

Udvaros, Dorottya, 260
Ugrešić, Dubravka, 206
Uher, Štefan, 141, 148, 166–67
Ulbricht, Walter, 282, 283
Union of Bulgarian Filmmakers, 361, 364
Union of Czechoslovak Film and Television Artists, 146
Urban, Max, 167
Urşianu, Malvina, 318, 319, 320, 321, 323, 330–31
Urusevski, Sergei, 46

Vaculik, Ludvik, 145
Vaeni, Constantin, 319, 321, 331
Vančura, Vladislav, 132, 135, 158, 167
Vaptsarov, Nikola, 346
Varkonyi, Zoltán, 242, 262, 264, 266
Vasiliev, Georgi and Sergei, 15
Vassilev, Orlin, 344
Vassilev, Peter, 351, 364
Vavpotić, Rudi, 200
Vávra, Otakar, 133–34, 135, 136, 137, 145, 148, 149, 158, 161, 164, 167
Vávrova, Yvonee, 150
Vazov, Ivan, 360
Veiczi, Janos, 283
Verhoeven, Paul, 279
Verne, Jules, 321
Veroiu, Mircea, 319, 320, 321, 322, 329, 331
Vertov, Dziga (pseud. for Denis Arkadievich Kaufman), 3, 4, 5–6, 7, 12, 13, 46
Vích, Václav, 131, 133, 158
Vihanová, Drahomíra, 150
Visarion, Alexa, 321
Viskovsky, Vyacheslav, 39

Vitanidis, Gheorghe, 315, 316, 318, 319, 321, 331
Vláčil, František, 132, 141, 145, 147, 148, 150, 155, 159, 167
Vladimirescu, Tudor, 325
Vodopivec, Frano, 200
Vogel, Amos, 24
Vogel, Frank, 284, 285, 287
Voit, Mieczyslaw, 108
Volev, Nikolai, 358
von Arnim, Bettina, 288
von Stroheim, Erich, 133, 162
von Wagenheim, Gustav, 280, 281
Voskovec, Jiri (George), 132, 133, 155, 167–68
Vučo, Aleksandar, 187
Vukotić, Dušan, 192, 218
Vulchanov, Rangel, 345, 347, 348, 352, 354, 355, 357, 358, 360, 362, 363, 364

Wachowiak, Jutta, 286
Wagenstein, Angel, 345, 347, 348, 353, 354, 361, 363, 364, 365
Wajda, Andrzej, 74, 75, 76, 77, 79, 80, 81, 84, 85, 87, 88, 89, 90, 91, 92, 95–110, 214, 249, 344, 348
Warneke, Lothar, 286, 287, 294
Waszynski, Michael, 71
Weimar Republic, 279
Weiss, Jiří, 136, 137, 138, 145, 154, 168
Weiss, Ulrich, 286
Wells, H. G., 351
Werich, Jan, 132, 133, 155, 167–68
Weteb Co. (Cz), 157
Whyte, Alistair, 349
Wilhelmi, Roman, 109
Winnicka, Lucyna, 74, 109
Wohl, Stanislaw, 78, 109
Wojcik, Jerzy, 109–10
Wolf, Christa, 284
Wolf, Friedrich, 275, 276, 280, 281, 295
Wolf, Konrad, 281, 282, 283, 284, 285, 286, 287, 288, 295, 347, 364
Workshop for Experimental Film (SU), 14
World War I, 42, 46, 186, 131, 230,

235, 245, 285, 309, 314, 316, 322, 344, 349, 357
World War II, 14, 18, 21, 33, 37, 39, 69, 71, 98, 135–36, 145, 147, 166, 186, 189, 206, 213, 232, 236, 244, 247, 263, 275, 282, 284, 285, 291, 293, 294, 309, 310, 311, 314, 316, 317, 322, 327, 349, 351
Wyspianski, Stanislaw, 70, 77, 90

"X" Film Unit, 87, 91, 104
Xantus, János, 256

Yakimov, Yakim, 365
Yanchev, Vladimir, 348
Yankov, Yanko, 365
Yavorov, Peyo, 358
Yesenin, Sergei, 46
Young Filmmakers Workshop (Po), 71
Yugoslav National War of Liberation, 186, 188, 191, 192, 198
Yutkevich, Sergei, 11, 17, 33, 35, 37, 39, 46

Zábransky, Miloš, 150
Zafranovic, Lordan, 203, 206, 214, 218
Zagreb Academy of Theater and Film Arts, 213
Zagreb Film Studio (Yu), 192, 193, 215, 216
Zalar, Živko, 203, 205
Zalkariev, Eduard, 351, 352, 354, 357, 358, 361, 362, 365
Zaluski, 104

Zamfirescu, Duiliu, 321
Zanussi, Krzstof, 87, 88, 91, 92, 98, 99, 100, 101, 102, 104, 110, 343
Zaoral, Zdeněk, 150
Zaorski, Janusz, 87, 89, 91, 96, 98, 99, 100, 105, 110
Zapasiewicz, Zbigniew, 110
Zarkhi, Alexander, 35, 38
Zarzycki, Jerzy, 71, 72, 95, 100, 102
Zavattini, Cesare, 192, 213
Zawadzka, Magdalena, 110
Zaymov, General, 349
Zebrowski, Edward, 95, 96, 98, 99, 100, 102, 106, 110
Zeman, Karel, 137, 139
Zeromski, Stefan, 70, 84, 85
Zhandov, Zahari, 345, 351, 356, 364, 365
Zhdanov, Andrei A., xii, 12, 13, 16, 188, 233
Zheliabuzhsky, Yuri, 38
Zhelyazkova, Binka, 347, 348, 351, 354, 361, 363, 365
Zhivkov, Todor, 346, 353, 359
Zhivkova, Luidmila, 353–54, 355, 357
Žilnik, Želmir, 193, 198, 209, 218
Žižic, Bogdan, 218
"Zodiak" Film Unit (Po), 87
Zolnay, Pál, 267
Zschoche, Hermann, 286, 287
Zsombolyai, Janos, 267
Zuławski, Andrzej, 88–89, 96, 110
Zweig, Arnold, 287
Zygadto, Tomasz, 91, 111

FILM INDEX

Abatises (Zasieki) (Po), 126
About Something Else (O něčem jiném) (Cz), 141, 143, 155, 165, 175
Absentee, The (A rejtözködö) (Hu), 263
Acadamus (Bu), 358
Accused, The (Obžalovaníý) (Cz), 159
Adam's Rib (Rebro Adamovo) (Bu), 367
Adela (Ro), 322, 331, 340
Adela Hasn't Had Supper Yet/Dinner for Adele/Nick Carter in Prague (Adela ještě nevečeřla) (Cz), 148, 161, 180
Adelheid (Cz), 145, 159, 167, 178
Admiral Nakhimov (SU), 55
Adoption (Örökbefogadás) (Hu), 246–47, 263, 265, 271
Adrift (Hrst vody) (Cz), 159, 178
Advantage (Avantazh) (Bu), 354, 361, 372
Adventure in Mariensztat (Przygoda na Mariensztacie) (Po), 97, 108, 114
Adventure of the Good Soldier Schweik, The, (Ro), 330
Adventures in Ontario (Aventuri in Ontario) (Ro), 317, 329, 336
Adventures of a Dentist (Pokhozhdenin zubnogo vracha) (SU), 59
Adventures of Oktyabrina (Pokhozdenia Oktyabriny) (SU), 49
Adventures of Till Ulenspiegel, The (Die Abenteuer des Till Ulenspiegel) (EGr), 299
Aventures of Werner Holt, The (Die Abenteuer des Werner Holt) (EGr), 284, 292, 301
Aelita (SU) 34, 38, 42, 48–49
Aerograd (SU), 36, 52
Aesop (Ezop) (Bu), 352, 364
Affection (Obich) (Bu), 363, 371
Afonia (SU) 21, 35
After the Fire Over Russia (Sled Poshara W Russia) (Bu), 344, 361
An Afternoon Affair (Szeretök) (Hu), 264
Age of Daydreaming, The (Álmodozások kora) (Hu), 249, 250, 252, 261, 266, 269
Ages of Man, The (Ro), 336
Agitki (SU) 3, 7, 37
Agnus Dei (Égi bárány) (Hu), 240
Agony (SU). *See* Rasputin
Ahead of the Silence (Inainte de tăcere) (Ro), 321, 339
Aimless Walk (Bezůčelná procházka) (Cz), 156
Airman, The (Vuzdshniyat chovek) (Bu), 358
Airship (Das Luftschiff) (EGr), 286, 306
Alarm, The (Nabut) (SU), 34, 48
Alarm (Trevoga) (Bu), 345, 364, 365, 366
Alarm in the Circus (Alarm im Zirkus) (EGr), 281, 292, 298

Alarm in the Mountains (Alarmá in munţi) (Ro), 314, 329, 334
Alexander Nevsky (SU), 13, 15, 35, 36, 53
All About Football (Totul despre fotbal) (Ro), 325, 339
All For Love (Bu), 358
All Soul's Eve (Zaduszki) (Po), 81, 102, 108, 117
All Those Good Countrymen (Všichni dobří rodaci) (Cz), 146, 147, 158, 161, 178
Allegro Barbaro (Hu). *See* Hungarian Rhapsody
Almost a Love Story (Pochti Lyubova Istoria) (Bu), 365, 374
Alois Won the Sweepstakes (Alois vyhral na los) (Cz), 169
Alone (Odna) (SU), 40
Alone (Sam) (Yu), 192, 217, 219
Alone (Samac) (40), 193
Amadeus (Am), 155
Ambush, The (Zaseda) (Zu), 197, 205, 217, 222
Amendment to the Defense-of-State Act (Dopalnenie kam Zakona Za Zashtito Na Darzhavata) (Bu), 353, 363, 364, 372
American Fragment (HU). *See* American Torso
American Torso/American Fragment (Amerikai anzix) (Hu), 261, 271
Anatomy of Love, The (Anatomia Mitowści) (Po), 97, 104, 122
And Give My Love to the Swallows (A pozdravuji vlaštovky) (Cz), 148, 155, 159, 179
And She Turns Anyway (Si Totusi si misca) (Ro), 330
And the Day Came (I Doyde Denyat) (Bu), 351, 361, 371
And the Silence Will Follow (Potem Nastapi cisza) (Po), 105, 110, 120
And What If It's Love? (A esli, eto liubov?) (SU), 43
And Your Love Too (Une deine Liebe auch) (EGr), 284, 300
Andrei Rublev (SU), 19, 45, 58

The Angel's Bite (Ujed Andela (Yu), 206
Angi Vera (Hu), 253, 262, 263, 271
Anna/Mother and Daughter (Anna) (Hu), 260, 263, 265, 272
Anna Karenina (SU), 59
Annunciation, The (Angyali üdvözlet) (Hu), 256, 272
Another Way (Egymásra nézve (Hu), 243, 260, 264, 272
Answer to Violence (Zamach) (Po), 103, 105, 108, 116
Anthony's Chance (Antonyho šance) (Cz), 162, 181
Antiquities (Antyki) (Po), 124
Anton the Magician (Anton der Zauberer) (EGr), 288, 293, 305
Apachen (EGr), 303
Apachen, Pt. 2 (Ulzana) (EGr), 305
Appeal, The (Molba) (SU), 33
Apple Game, The (Hra o jablko) (Cz), 149, 155, 179
Apprehension (EGr), 286, 287, 295, 306
Archangel Gabriel and Mother Goose, The (Archandél Gabriel a pani Husa) (Cz), 166
Archives Testify, The series (EGr), 283, 294, 299
Aria for an Athlete (Aria dla Atlety), (Po), 95, 109, 124
Arms of Aphrodite, The (Le Bras d'Aphrodite) (Ro), 327
Arsenal (SU), 9, 10, 36, 51
Ascent, The (Voskhoshdenie) (SU), 44, 62
Ashes (Popioty) (Po), 84, 85, 89, 103, 104, 105, 107, 108, 109, 110, 119
Ashes and Diamonds (Popiot i Diament) (Po), 75, 76, 77, 95, 97, 101, 109, 116
Assa (SU), 65
Assauge My Sorrow (Utoli pechali) (SU), 25
Assya (SU), 61
Asta my Angel (Asta meiu Engelchen) (EGr), 286, 306
Asya's Happiness (Asino schaste) (SU), 41, 58–59

Asylum, The (Azyl) (Po), 124
At Home Among Strangers, Stranger at Home (Svoi sredi chuzhikh, chuzhoi sredi svoikh) (SU), 21, 41
At 6 p.m. After the War (V schest chasov vechera posle voiny) (SU), 43
At the Age of Love (La virsta dragostei) (Ro), 328, 335
At the Close of the Night (SU), 45, 67
At the Photographer's (Kod fotografa) (Yu), 193
At the Terminal Station (Tam na konečné) (Cz), 159, 173
Atlantic Story, The (Opowieść Alantycka) (Po), 100, 109, 114
Attached Balloon, The (Privarzaniyat Balon) (Bu), 348, 350, 365, 370
Attendance Compulsory (Erscheinen Pflict) (EGr), 306
Auf der Sonnenseite (EGr), 300
Augenzeuge (Eyewitness) Newsreels (EGr), 275–76, 277, 292
August in Flames (August in flacari) (Ro), 329
Aurel Vlaicu (Ro), 326
Autumn Marathon (Osennii marafon) (SU), 21, 35, 62
Avalanche (Lavina) (Bu), 356, 374
Awakening (Probuzení) (Cz), 138, 154, 160, 174
Awakening of the Rats (Budjenje pacova) (Yu), 196, 217, 221
Axe of Wandsbek, The (Das Beil von Wandsbek) (EGr), 291, 297

Bagful of Fleas, A (Pytel blech) (Cz), 155, 175
Baker's Emporer, The (Pe kařův císař) (Cz), 132, 137, 156, 165, 168, 173
Balance (Ravnovessie) (Bu), 362, 375
Balint Fabian Meets God (Fabian Balint talakozasa istennel) (Hu), 262
Balkan Express (Balkan ekspres) (Yu), 208
Balkan Spy, The (Balkanski špijun) (Yu), 209, 215, 216, 226
Ballad, The (Ciprian Porumbescu) (Ro), 319, 331, 337

Ballad for Mariuca, A (Ro), 336
Ballad of a Soldier (Ballada o soldate) (SU), 18, 35, 40, 57
Ballad of a Trumpet and a Cloud (Balada o trobenti in oblaku) (Yu), 218
Baltic Deputy (Deputat Baltiki) (SU), 35, 38, 53
Banana Skin Waltz (Banánhéjkeringö) (Hu), 245, 260, 273
Banquet for Achilles, A (Bankett fur Achilles) (EGr), 304
Baritone, The (Baryton) (Po), 91, 98, 99, 110, 127
Barrier (Bariera) (Po), 85, 103, 104, 107, 120
Barrier (Bariera) (Ro), 328, 337
Barrier (Barierata) (Bu), 355, 362, 373
Bartered Bride, The (Prdaná nevěsta) (Cz), 167, 169
Batalion (Cz), 170
Bath, The (Bania) (SU), 57
Battle in the Shadows (Bătălia din umbra) (Ro), 325, 341
Battle of Stalingrad, The (Stalingradskaya bitva) (SU), 14
Battle on the River (Bitka na Neretvi) (Yu), 213
Battleship Potemkin (Bronenosets 'Potyomkin') (SU), 4, 7–8, 36, 49
Bayaya (Cz), 166
Beach Guard in Winter (Čuvar plaže u zimskom periodu) (Yu), 203, 217, 223
Beacon (Leuchtfeuer) (EGr), 282, 294, 298
Beads of the Same Rosary (Paciorki Jedrego Różańca) (Po), 102
Bear, The (Miś) (Po), 125
Bear Ye One Another's Burdens (EGr), 295, 307
Beater, The (Naganiacz) (Po), 119
Beautiful Leukanida (SU), 3
Beauti-i-ful Acrobat (Akrobat schö-ö-ön) (EGr), 293
Beaver Coat (Der Beberpelz) (EGr), 279, 291, 297
Because They Are In Love (Ro), 337
Bed and Sofa (Tretia meshchanskaia) (SU), 34, 43, 50

Beethoven—Days from a Life (Beethoven—Tago aus einem Leben) (EGr), 287, 293, 305
Before Graduation (Před maturitou) (Cz), 132, 167, 171
Behind the Wall (Za Sciana), 101
Belorussian Station (Belorussky vokzal) (SU), 59
Beloved Woman of Mechanic Gavrilov, The (Liubimaia zhenshchina mekhanika Gavrilova) (SU), 63–64
Benderath Incident, The (EGr), 283, 298
Benthin Family, The (Familíe Benthin) (EGr), 280, 291, 292, 297
Berlin Romance (Eine Berliner Romanze) (EGr), 282, 292, 298
Berlin, Schoenhauser Corner (Berlin, Ecke Schoenhauser) (EGr), 282, 292, 299
Berlin Under Construction (Berlin im Aufbau) (EGr), 296
Best Years, The (Die besten Jahre) (EGr), 293, 301
Between Opposite Mirrors (Intre oglinzi paralele) (Ro), 322, 331, 339
Between the Wars (Miedzy wojnami) (Po), 96
Beyond the Bridge (Dincolo de Pod) (Ro), 331
Beyond the Fir Trees (Dincolo de brazi) (Ro), 316, 326, 334
Beyond the Railway Gate (Ro), 328
Beyond the Sands (Dincolo de nisipuri) (Ro), 320, 337
Bezhin Meadow (SU), 13
Bicycle Thieves (It), 233
Big and Small (Veliki i mali) (Yu), 192, 217, 219
Big Beat, The (Mocne Uderzenie) (Po), 110
Big Family (Bolshaya semya) (SU), 34
Big Money (Bony a klid) (Cz), 150, 159, 162, 182
Big Night, The (Bathe) (Golyamoto Noshtno Kupane) (Bu), 356, 365, 373
Big Run, The (Wielki Bieg) (Po), 127
Binding Sentiments (Holdudvar) (Hu), 265

Birch Tree (Breza) (Yu), 199, 213, 221
Birchwood (Brzezina) (Po), 90, 103, 105, 109, 121
Birds and Greyhounds (Ptitsi Hratki) (Bu), 370
Birds Are Flying Our Way (Ptitsi Dolitat Pri Nas) (Bu), 371
Birds, Orphans, and Fools (Vtáčkovia, siroty a blázni) (Cz), 158, 178
Birth of Menyhert Simon, The (Simon Menyhért születése) (Hu), 242, 264, 266, 267
Black Angels (Chernite Angeli) (Bu), 363, 370
Black Monk, The (SU), 24
Black Peter/Peter and Paula (Černý Peter) (Cz), 129, 141, 142, 156, 163, 175
Black Rose Stands for Sadness—Red Rose Stands for Love (Chomaya rosa—emblema bechali, belaya rosa—emblema lyubvi) (SU), 66
Black Sail, The (Cherni parus) (SU), 46, 51
Black Saturday (Ro), 336
Black Swans, The (Chernite Lebedi) (Bu), 375
Black Zwieback (Schwarzer Zwieback) (EGr), 303
Blackmail (Br), 134
Blackmail (Santaj) (Ro), 330, 340
Blindfold (Bekötött szemmel) (Hu), 244, 264, 270
Blue Cross, The (Błękitny Krzyż) (Po), 104, 114
Blue Gates of the City, The (Portile Alabastre ale Orasului) (Ro), 320, 328, 338
Blue Mountains, or An Improbable Story (Golubye gory, ili Nepravdopodobnaia is toriia) (SU), 64
Bluebeard the Knight (Ritter Blaubart) (EGr), 304
Blum Affair, The (Affäre Blum) (EGr), 279, 291, 296
Boarding House for Bachelors (Penzion pro svobodné pány) (Cz), 160
Bodensee (Jezioro Bodeńskie) (Po), 91, 127

Body Scent (Zadah tela) (Yu), 209, 217, 225
Boomerang (Bumerang) (Bu), 355, 373
Border Street (Ulica Graniczna) (Po), 72, 98, 108, 112
Boring Afternoon, A (Fádní odpoledne) (Cz), 163, 176
Boris Godunov (SU), 47
Boris the First (Boris Purvi) (Bu), 356, 363, 375
Born to Win (Am), 163
Boundary, The (Granica) (Po), 106, 107, 124,
Bow of Queen Dorothy, The (Cz), 154
Boy Becomes a Man, A (Momcheto Si Otiva) (Bu), 353, 362
Boys of Paul Street, The (A Pál utcai fiúk) (Hu), 262
Boxer and the Death (Cz), 141
Brave Marko (Junak Marko) (Bu), 346
Brave Seven, The (Semero smelykh) (SU), 37
Bravo Maestro (Yu), 205, 214, 224
Breakdown (Kvar) (Yu), 217, 224
Bride from the Train, The (Mireasa din tren) (Ro), 325, 340
Bright Fields (Jasne łany) (Po), 73, 109, 112
Broken Citadel, The (Ro), 331
Brothers Karamazov, The (Bratya Karamazovy) (SU), 43
Bucahrest (Ro), 311, 326, 332
Bueduganul of the Three Rings (Buzduganul cu Trei Peceti) (Ro), 331, 339
Bugler's Grandsons, The (Nepoţii gornistului) (Ro), 314, 329, 333
Build a House, Plant a Tree (Postav dom, zasaď strom) (Cz), 148, 180
Builder of the Cathedral, The (Stravitel chrámu) (Cz), 131, 135, 155, 169
Bulgarian is Gallant, The (Balgaran e Galant) (Bu), 344
Burglar, The (Vzomshchik) (SU), 24
Bus Action, The (Actiunea autobuzul) (Ro), 339
Bus Leaves at 6:20 (Autobus Odjezdza) (Po), 106, 113
By Accident (Przypadek), (Po), 100, 101

By Mandate of Hogler (Der Auftrag Höglers) (EGr), 280, 297
By the Lake (U ozera) (SU), 60
By the Law (Po zakonu) (SU), 5, 40, 44, 49
Bye-Bye Red Riding Hood (Piroska ēs a tarkas) (Hu), 249, 263, 265, 273–74

Calamity (Kalamita) (Cz), 149, 155, 180
Calamity (Urgia) (Ro), 325, 339
Califer's Mill (Ro), 341
Camera Buff (Amator) (Po), 101, 105, 124
Cameraman's Revenge, The (SU), 3
Camouflage (Barwy Ochronne) (Po), 88, 98, 101, 110, 122
Canal (Kanal) (Po), 75, 76, 79, 108, 114
Canary and the Storm, The (Canarul si viscolul) (Ro), 319, 327, 337
Cantata (Oldás és kötés) (Hu), 236, 263, 264, 266, 269
Capricious Summer (Rozmarné léto) (Cz), 132, 143, 158, 162, 165, 167, 177
Captain, The (Kapitanat) (Bu), 368
Captain Lesi (Kapetan Leši) (Yu), 191
Captain Martens Brothers, The (Fratii Jderi) (Ro), 319, 338
Captain of Cologne, The (Der Hauptmann von Köln) (EGr), 282, 291, 298
Captains Do Not Leave the Ship (Kapitäne bleiben an Bord) (EGr), 282, 292, 299
Captured Squadron (Pleneno yato) (Bu), 368
Career, The (Kariera) (Po), 114
Careful, a Turtle! (Vnimanie, cherepakha) (SU), 34
Carnival Night (Karnavlnaia noch) (SU), 38, 43
Casablanca (Am), 230
Case for the New Hangman, The (Pripad pro zaćiňajićiho kata) (Cz), 179
Case No. 205/1913 (Delo No. 205/1913) (Bu), 358, 375
Cassandra Cat (Až prijdé kocour) (Cz), 158, 161, 174

Castle in the Carpathians, The (Ro), 321, 340
Catapult (Katapult) (Cz), 148, 159
Cathy (Katka) (Cz), 136
Catsplay (Macskajáték) (Hu), 243, 264, 267
Ceiling, The (Strop) (Cz), 155, 165, 174
Chain, The (Verigata) (Bu), 369
Chain of Weakness (Lanțul slabiciunilor) (Ro), 314, 327, 333
Chained Justice (Dreptate in Lanturi) (Ro), 323, 329, 340
Chalk Sketches (Szkice Weglem) (Po), 115
Chance (Sance) (Bu), 352, 364
Chance, The (Szansa) (Po), 89, 98, 108, 125
Chapaev (SU), 15, 52
Charming Girl, A (Un film cu o fata fermeca-toare) (Ro), 325, 336
Check Point (SU). *See* Trial on the Road
Checkered Bedspread/Life in the Ticking, The (Buntkarierten) (EGr), 278, 292, 296
Cheese Beer or the Stolen Battle (Käsebier oder die gesthlene Schlact) (EGr), 303
Cherry Orchard (Chereshova Gradina) (Bu), 355, 360, 361, 373
Chess Fever (Shakhmatnaia goriachka) (SU), 42, 49
Child of the Big City (Ditia bolshovo goroda) (SU), 34, 47
Childhood (EGr), 292, 307
Childhood of Gorki (Detstvo Gorkovo) (SU), 35, 53
Childhood Scenes from Provincial Life (Sceny Dzieciece z Zycia Prowincji) (Po), 91, 110, 127
Chord of Death (Akord smrti) (Cz), 160, 169
Chronicle of Amorous Accidents, A (Kronika Wypadków Mitosnych) (Po), 101, 102, 103, 109, 127
Chronicle of the Barefoot Emperors (Minia) (Ro), 331, 339
Cigarette-Girl from Mosselprom (Papirosnitsa ot Mosselproma) (SU), 38

Cinderella's Shoes (Pantoful Cenusaresei) (Ro), 314, 327, 336
Circle, The (Cercul) (Ro), 331
Circus (Tsirk), 33
Circus Maximus (Hu), 233
City, The (Grad) (Yu), 195
City in Ferment (Uzaureli grad) (Yu), 192
Claqueur, The (Klakier) (Po), 96, 126
Clean Up the Light of Common Sense (Putzt das Licht der Vernunet) (EGr), 287, 305
Clear Sky (Chistoe nebo) (SU), 35, 57
Clepsidra (Ro), 330
Clinch, The (Klincz) (Po), 95, 124
Cloak, The (Shinel, 1926) (SU), 40, 50
Closely Watched Trains (Ostře sledované vlaky) (Cz), 143, 145, 149, 157, 162, 177
Clothes Make the Man (Šaty dělají člověka) (Cz), 167
Clouds Will Role Away, The (Není stále zamračeno) (Cz), 137
Clowns, The (Saltimbancii) (Ro), 322, 325, 340
Club of the Big Deed, The (S.V.D.) (SU), 40, 50
Clue of the Falcon (Spur des Falken) (EGr), 302
Coach to Vienna, The (Kočár do Vídne) (Cz), 158, 159, 161, 164, 177
Cobwebs and Pilgrims (Cz), 150
Coca Cola Kid, The (Aus), 209, 216
Cockeyed Luck (Zezowate Szczęście) (Po), 79, 101, 104, 106, 108, 117
Code, The (Szyfry) (Po), 83, 97, 99, 100, 120
Codin (Ro), 335
Cold Days (Hildeg napok) (Hu), 244, 262, 264, 266, 269
Cold Heart, The (Das kalte herz) (EGr), 279, 297
Cold Summer of '53, The (SU), 25, 66
Colonel Redl (Redl Ezredes/Oberst Redl) (Hu), 251, 252, 264, 266, 272
Colonel Wołodyjowski (Pan Wołodyjowski) (Po), 84, 97, 98, 99, 101, 103, 104, 107, 110, 121

Colorful World (Sharen Svyat) (Bu), 361, 371
Colors of Struggle (Barwy Walki) (Po), 105
Colors of the Pomegranate, The (Tsvety granata) (SU), 19, 42, 59
Column, The (Ro), 316, 326, 330, 336
Come and See (Idi i smotri) (SU), 22, 39, 64–65
Commissar (Komissar) (SU), 23, 65
Common Afternoon (Dupăamiază obişnuita) (Ro), 329
Common Room, The (Wspólny Pokój) (Po), 82, 99, 117
Commotion (Perepolokh) (SU), 21, 38, 61
Communist, The (Kommunist) (SU), 43, 56
Community, A (Gromada) (Po), 113
Competition (Konkurs) (Cz), 139, 141, 142, 156, 160, 165, 175
Composer Glinka, The (Kompozitor Glinka) (SU), 33
Concert at the End of the Summer (Koncert na konci léta) (Cz), 147
Concrete Pastures (Pásla kone na betóne) (Cz), 148, 166, 180
Condemned Village, The (Das veruvteilti Dorf) (EGr), 280, 292, 297
Conductor, The (Dyrygent) (Po), 100, 107, 109, 125
Confession (SU), 24
Confession (Priznanie) (Bu), 365
Confessions of Love (Ro), 341
Confidence (Bizalom) (Hu), 251, 261, 263, 266, 271
Confrontation, The (Fényes szelek) (Hu), 239–40, 261, 264, 266, 270
Conscience (Svědomí) (Cz), 136, 160, 172
Conspiracy (Conspiratia) (Ro), 327
Constant Factor, The (Constans) (Po), 88, 110, 125
Constantine the Philosopher (Konstantin Filosof) (Bu), 356, 363, 375
Contract, The (Kontrakt) (Po), 88, 100, 102, 103, 110, 125

Contribution, The (Kontrybucja) (Po), 121
Corporal's Gun, The (EGr), 301
Cossacks of the Kuban (Kubanskiye kazaki) (SU), 36
Council of the Gods (EGr). *See* Divine Councils
Counterplan (Vstrechnyi) (SU), 14, 37, 46, 52
Countess Cosel, The (Hrabina Cosel) (Po), 95, 98, 121
Country of Motzi, The (Tara Moliţor) (Ro), 311, 326, 332
Courage for Every Day (Každý den odvahu) (Cz), 144, 154, 155, 159, 164, 175
Courier, The (Kurier) (SU), 24, 65
Cranes Are Flying, The (Letiat zhuravli) (SU), 17–18, 39, 46, 56
Craziness of Love (Verwirrung der Liebe) (EGr), 282, 291, 300
Crazy Years (Lude godine) (Yu), 210
Cremator of Corpses, The (Spalovač mrtvol) (Cz), 157, 178
Cricket in the Ear, A (Shturets V Uhoto) (Bu), 353
Crime and Punishment (Prestuplenie i nakaznie) (SU), 40, 60
Crime in the Girl's School (Zločin v dívčí škole) (Cz), 160, 162
Crime in the Nightclub (Zločin v šantánu) (Cz), 143, 165
Criminal and a Maid, A (Zbrodniarz i Panna) (Po), 97
Criminal Who Stole His Crime, The (Zbrodniarz Który Ukradt Zbrodnie) (Po), 86, 104, 121
Cross of Valor (Krzy z Walecznych) (Po), 80, 102, 116
Crows (Vrane) (Yu), 222
Crucial Years (Kristove roky) (Cz), 158, 177
Crucible, The (Die Hexen von Salem) (EGr), 281, 299
Cruise, The (Craziera) (Ro), 323, 326, 340
Cruise, The (Rejs) RO), 88, 92
Cry, The (Křik) (Cz), 141, 158, 161, 175

Cry and Cry Again (Kiáltás és kiáltás) (Hu), 263
Crystal Structure, The (Struktura Krysztalu) (Po), 88, 104, 105, 110, 121
Csontvary (Hu), 263
Current (Sodrasban) (Hu), 252, 255, 262, 264, 266, 269
Cutter's Way (Am), 163
Cutting it Short (Postřižiny) (Cz), 147, 157, 162, 180
Cyanide and Drops of Rain (Cianura si picatura de ploaie) (Ro), 327
Cybernetic Grandma (Kybernetická babička) (Cz), 166
"Cyclist's Story, The" ("Nowela Kolaska") (Po), 103
Cyclops (Tsiklopat) (Bu), 362, 372
Czech Year, The (Špalíček) (Cz), 166

Dacians, The (Ro). See The Warriors
Daimler-Benz Limousine, The (Limuzyna Daimler-Benz) (Po), 95, 96, 126
Daisies (Sedmikrásky) (Cz), 143, 155, 161, 177
Dalmation Chronicle (Dalmatinska kronika) (Yu), 206
Dance in the Rain (Ples v dežju (Yu), 194, 199, 215, 220
Dance Leader, The (Wodzirej) (Po), 89, 98, 108, 124
Dancing on Water/Hey Babu Riba (Bal na vodi) (Yu), 226
Dangerous Load (Die gefährliche Fracht) EGr), 281, 298
Daniel Takes a Train (Szerencsés Dániel) (Hu), 255, 265, 272
Danton (Fr), 91, 104, 106, 109, 126
Danube Waves, The (Valurile Dunarii) (Ro), 316, 326, 328, 330, 334
Darclee (Ro), 334
Dark Eyes (SU/It), 26, 41
Dark Glasses (Po), 92
Dawn, The (L'Aube) (Fr), 241
Dawn over the Drava (Zarevo nad Drava) (Bu), 351
Dawn Over the Homeland (Utro Nad Rodinata) (Bu), 366

Day Is Longer Than the Night, The (Den' dlinnee nochi) (SU), 38, 64
Day Lasts More Than a Hundred Years, The (SU), 25
Day of Happiness (SU), 34
Day of the Rulers, The (Denyat Na Vladetelite) (Bu), 375
Day the Trees Will Bloom, The (Cz), 158, 160
Days (Dani) (Yu), 195, 217, 220
Days of Betrayal (Dny zrady) (Cz), 147
Days of the Eclipse (SU), 45
Days on Earth are Flowing By (Zomaljski dani teku) (Yu), 203, 224
Dead Landscape (Holt vidék) (Hu), 252, 253, 262, 267, 270
Dead Stay Young, The (Die Toten bleiben jung) (EGr), 292, 301
Dear, Dearest, Beloved, Only . . . (Milyi, dorogoi, liubimyi, edistvennyi . . .) (SU), 64
Death Bay (Buhkta smerti) (SU), 44, 49
Death Can Wait Awhile (Smurtta Mozhe Da Pochaka) (Bu), 376
Death is Called "Engelchen" (Smrť sa volá Engelchen) (Cz), 159, 175
Death of Mr. Balthazar (Smrt pána Baltazára) (Cz), 176
Death of the President (Smierc Prezydenta (Po), 104, 125
Death Ray, The (Luch smerti) (SU), 40, 41, 49
Debut (Nachalo) (SU), 21, 42, 59
Debutante (Debiutantka), The (Po), 97, 103, 106, 125
Decalogue (Po), 92, 101
Deep End (Br), 86
Deep in the Heart (Po), 92
Deerslayer, The (Vinătorul de cerbi) (Ro), 317, 329, 337
DeFacto (Bu), 346
Defeat of Japan (SU), 38
Defense Counsel Sedov (Zashchitnik Sedov) (SU), 67
Deja vu (Već videno) (Yu), 205, 216, 227
Deluge, The (Potop) (Po), 84, 96, 99, 105, 107, 109, 110, 123

FILM INDEX

Demetrie Cantemir (Ro), 319, 331, 337
Demon, The (Ashik kerib) (SU), 19, 42, 66
Deport of the Dead (Baza Ludzi Umarlych) (Po), 105
Description of a Summer (Beschreibung eines Sommers) (EGr), 300
Deserter (Dezertir) (SU), 13, 52
Deserter and the Nomads, The (Zbehovia a pútnici) (Cz), 158, 178
Desire (Touha) (Cz), 138, 158, 174
Desolate King of Brandenburg, The (Der Wüstenkönig von Brandenburg) (EGr), 304
Destiny (Orissia) (Bu), 362
Destiny of a Man (Sudba cheloveka) (SU), 34, 57
Detour/Sidetrack (Otklonenie) (Bu), 349, 364, 370
Development [In a Village] (Desfăşurarea) (Ro), 314, 326, 334
Devil, The (Diabex) (Po), 89, 110
Devils, The (Br), 84
Devil's Abyss, The (Ripa dracului) (Ro), 314, 328, 334
Devil's Trap, The (Ďáblová past) (Cz), 174
Devil's Wheel, The (Chertovo koleso) (SU), 39–40, 49
Diamonds of the Night (Démanty noci) (Cz), 144, 161, 162, 175
Diary for My Children (Napló gyermekeimnek) (Hu), 248, 263, 265, 272
Diary for My Father and Mother (Napló apámnak, anyámnak) (Hu), 248–49, 261, 263, 265, 267, 274
Diary for My Loves (Napló szerelmeimnek) (Hu), 248, 263, 265, 273
Diary Trilogy, The (Hu), 247, 249, 267
A Difficult Love (Trudna Lyubov) (Bu), 360
Difficult to Get Engaged (Schwierig sich zu verloben) (EGr), 286, 306
Dimensions of Dialogue (Možnosti dialogu) (Cz), 166, 180
Dinner for Adele (Cz). *See* Adele Hasn't Had Supper Yet

Direction: Berlin (Kierunek Berlin) (Po), 105
Disciples, The (A tanítvanyok) (Hu), 261, 273
Disco Story (Cz), 150
Dissolved and Let Out (Rozpustený a vypustený) (Cz), 166
District of Gaiety, The (Cartierul veseliei) (Ro), 315, 317, 327, 335
Dita Saxová (Cz), 161
Diverse Facts (Fapt divers) (Ro), 325, 340
Divided Sky, The (Der Geteilte Himmel) (EGr), 284, 295, 301
Divine Councils (Rat der Götter) (EGr), 280, 292, 297
Divine Emma, The (Božská Ema) (Cz), 147, 160, 163
Do I Love You? (SU), 37
Do You Remember Dolly Bell? (Sjećas li se Dolly Bell) (Yu), 207, 215, 225
Dr. Med Sommer II (EGr), 285, 294, 302
Dr. Poenaru (Ro), 339
A Dog in the Drawer (Kouche v Chekmedzhe) (Bu), 356, 374
Dog Who Loved Trees, The (Pas koji je voleo vozove) (Yu), 203
Dog's Night Song, The (Kuty éji dala) (Hu), 261, 272
Doll, The (Lalka) (Po), 83, 98, 99, 101, 103, 104, 107, 120
Doll With Millions, The (Kukla s millionami) (SU), 38
Don Quixote (SU), 17, 35, 40, 56
Don Sancho (Cz), 178
Donbass Symphony, The (SU). *See* Enthusiasm
Don't Cheat, Darling (Nicht Scummeln, Liebling!) (EGr), 304
Don't Dream Annette (Träum nicht, Annette), (EGr), 296
Don't Forget My Traudel (Vergesst mir meine Traudel nicht) (EGr), 282, 292, 299
Don't Go Away (Ne Si Otivay) (Bu), 352, 362
Don't Grieve! (Ne goriui!) (SU), 59–60

Don't Lean Out the Window (Ne naginji se van) (Yu), 218
Don't Turn Round, My Son (Ne okreći se, sine) (Yu), 192, 213
Door in the Wall, A (Drzwi w Murze) (Po), 123
Down to Earth (Spravca skanzenu) (Cz), 183
Down to the Cellar (Do sklepa) (Cz), 166, 181
Dragon, The (Lamyata) (Bu), 361
Dragonfly and the Ant, The (SU), 3
Dream (San) (Yu), 198, 214, 221
Dream of a Winter's Eve (Visul Unei Nopti de Iarna) (Ro), 313, 327, 333
Dreambook for Our Time, A (Sennik wspolczesnyl) (Po), 102
Duped till Doomsday (Bertrogen bis zum Jüngsten) (EGr), 284, 299
Dybukk (Po), 71

Ear, The (Ucho) (Cz), 159, 164
Early Works (Rani radori) (Yu), 198, 218, 222
Earth (Zemlia) (SU), 36, 51
Earth is Singing, The (Zem spieva) (Cz) 156, 163, 171
Easy Money (Legkie dengi) (SU), 63
Ecaterina Teodoroiu (Ro), 332
Ecce Homo (Ro), 330
Ecce Homo Homolka (Cz), 160, 178
Echelon of Dr. M (Ešalon Doktora M) (Yu), 191
Echo, The (Echo) (Po), 119
Ecstasy (Extase) (Cz), 130, 131, 133, 162, 163, 171
Egg, The (Jaje) (Yu), 193
Eighth Day of the Week, The (Ósmy Dzień Tygodnia—Der achte Wochentag) (Po), 97, 99, 103, 126
Elective Affinities (Wahlver wandtschaften) (EGr), 286, 287, 292, 304
El Dorado/The Midas Touch (Eldorádo) (Hu), 256, 261, 273
Elektreia (Szerelmem, Elektra) (Hu), 240, 264, 267, 271

Elixer of the Devil (Die Eliziere des Teufels) (EGr), 287, 304
Embryos (Embriok) (Hu), 267
Emilia Galotti (EGr), 282, 292, 299
Emperor and the Golem, The (Cz), 173
Emperor's Baker, The (Ciśařův pekář) (Cz), 132, 137, 156, 165, 168, 173
Emperor's Nightingale, The (Cisařův slavík) (Cz), 166
Empire Gone With a Sneeze, The (Az eltüsszentett birodalom) (Hu), 235
Enchanted Stations, The (Zaklęte Rewiry—Dvoi Svět Hotelu Pacifik) (Po), 109, 123
Encounters (Spotkania) (Po), 103, 115
End of a Priest (Farářův konec) (Cz), 144, 146, 154, 164, 165, 178
End of August at the Hotel Ozone, The (Koneč srpna hotelu Ozón) (Cz), 164, 176–77
End of Civilization, The (O-bi, O-ba, Koniec Cywilizacji) (Po), 108, 127
End of Night, The (Sfirsital nopti) (Ro), 322, 331, 340
End of Old Times, The (Konec starých časvu) (Cz), 183
End of Our World, The (Koniec Naszego Świata) (Po), 119
End of St. Petersburg, The (Konets Sankt-Peterburga) (SU), 50
End of the Lonely Farm Berhof (Zánik samoty Berhof) (Cz), 166, 180
Enemy, The (Neprijatelj) (Yu), 196
Enthusiasm/The Donbass Symphony (Entuziazm) (SU), 4, 13, 46, 51
Eolomea (EGr), 302
Epitaph for Barbara Radziwill, The (Epitafum dla Barbary Radzwittowny) (Po), 86, 104, 126
Ernst Thalmann—Leader of His Class (Ernst Thalmann—Führer seiner Klasse) (EGr), 281, 287, 292, 298
Ernst Thalmann, Son of His Class (Ernst Thalmann—Sohn seiner Klasse) (EGr), 281, 287, 292, 298
Eroica (Po), 79, 98, 101, 103, 104, 108, 109, 110, 115

Erotikon (Cz), 131, 132, 133, 156, 162, 169
Ersatz (Surogat) (Yu), 193, 218
Eruption (Eruptia) (Ro), 316, 326, 334
Escape to Ropotamo (Byagstov V Ropotamo) (Bu), 352
Ete and Ali (EGr), 307
Eternal Times (Vechni Uremena) (Bu), 352, 372
Europe Danced the Waltz (Europa tančila valčík) (Cz), 183
Eve of Ivan Kupala Day, The [Halloween Night] (Vecher nakanune Ivana Kupaly) (SU), 38–39
Eve Wants to Sleep (Ewa Chce Spać) (Po), 81, 97, 115
Evening Bells (Večernja zvona) (Yu), 206, 218, 227
Event, The (Dogadaj) (Yu), 199
Everybody and Nobody (Vsichki I Nikoy) (Bu), 363
Everything for Sale (Wszystko na Sprzedaz) (Po), 90, 97, 101, 103, 105, 108, 109, 120
Examination, The (Die Prüfung) (EGr), 280, 294, 297
Excuse me—Are You Watching Football? (Verzeihung, sehen sie Fussball?) (EGr), 307
Excuse Me, Do They Beat You Up Here? (Przepraszam Czy Tu Bija?) (Po), 88, 123
Exhibition Sausage Vendor, The (Vystavni' parkar a lepič plakátů) (Cz), 130, 167, 169
"Existence Circle, The" ("Krg Isthienia") (Po), 118
Exploring the Marches of Brandenburg (EGr), 306
Explosion, The (Explosia) (Ro), 326, 338
Extraordinary Adventures of Mr. West in the Land of The Bolsheviks, The (Neobychainye prikliucheniya Mistera Vesta v stranye bolshevikov) (SU), 5, 33, 40, 41, 48

Face Behind the Mask (Bu), 364
Face to Face (Licem u lice) (Yu), 213, 220
Faded Writing, The (Setřele písmo) (Cz), 170
Fairy Dance (Samodvsko Horo) (Bu), 352–53, 360, 362, 372
Falcons, The (Magasiskola) (Hu), 252, 262, 270
Fall of Berlin, The Pts. I and II (Padenie Berlina) (SU), 35
Fall of Italy, The (Pad Italije) (Yu), 206, 225
Fall of the House of Usher (Zánik domu Usheru) (Cz), 166, 180
Fall of the Romanov Dynasty (Padenie dinastii Romanovykh) (SU), 44, 50
Fallow Land (A magyar ugarou) (Hu), 264, 270
Family Life (Zycie Rodzinne) (Po), 88, 92, 104, 110, 122
Famous Duels (Divoká srdce) (Cz), 183
Fanatics, The (Megszállottak) (Hu), 264
Far from Tipperary (Departe de Tipperary) (Ro), 327
Farewell (Abschied) (EGr), 285, 291, 302
Farewell (Proshchanie) (SU), 39, 44, 63
Farewell, Friends! (Sbogom, Priyateli) (Bu), 370
Farewell, Till Tomorrow (Do Widzenia, Do Jutra) (Po), 97, 104, 106, 116
Farewells (Pozegnania) (Po), 83, 98, 99, 100, 101, 116
Fariaho (EGr), 306
Fatal Error (Tödlicher Irrtum) (EGr), 302
Fatal Love (Ro), 311, 332, 377
Fatal Shot (Fejloves) (Hu), 260
Fates of Women (EGr). See Women's Destiny
Father (Apa) (Hu), 249–50, 255, 261, 264, 266, 269
Father Cira and Father Spira (Pop Čira i pop Spira) (Yu), 191
Father Sergius (Otets Sergii, 1918) (SU), 3–4, 41, 42, 48
Father Sergius (Otets Sergii, 1978) (SU), 62
Father Vojtech (Páter Vojtěch) (Cz), 170
Felix and Otilia (Ro), 328, 337
Ferocious One, The (Liutyi) (SU), 60

Ferydurke (Po), 80
Fetes galantes (Ro/Fr), 331, 335
Fetish, The (Fetysz) (Po), 127
Fever, A (Gorczka) (Po), 89, 99, 125
Fiancée, The (Die Verlobte) (EGr), 286, 293, 306
Fiddler on the Roof (Am), 71
Fidlovačka (Cz), 131, 171
Field Marshall, The (C. ak. polni marsalek) (Cz), 170
Fiery Summer (Ohnive leto) (Cz), 172
Fifth Horseman is Fear, The (A pátý jezdec je strach) (Cz), 154, 161, 175
Fifth Seal, The (Az ötödik pecsét) (Hu), 262, 264
Fighting Film Albums (SU), 33
Fireman's Ball, The (Hoří, má panenko!) (Cz), 142, 146, 156, 177
First Day, The (Pervyi den') (SU), 56
First Day of Freedom, The (Pierwszy Dzień Wolnosci) (Po), 97, 99, 103, 108, 119
First Days (Pierwsze Dni) (Po), 106
First Echelon, The (Pervyi eshelon) (Su), 56
First Lesson, The (Parvi Urok) (Bu), 347, 362, 364, 368
First Spaceship on Venus (EGr/Po), 282, 292, 299
First Take-Off, The (Pierwszy Start) (Po), 73, 96–97, 108, 112–13
First Teacher, The (Pervyi uchitel) (SU), 41, 58
Fisheye (Riblje oko) (Yu), 210
Five Boys from Barska Street (Piątka z Ulicy Barskiej) (Po), 74, 98, 103, 107, 113
Five Cartridges (Fünf Patronenhülsen) (EGr), 284, 290, 300
Five Evenings (Piat' vecherov) (SU), 21, 38, 41, 62
Five Girls to Deal With (Pět holek na krku) (Cz), 144, 155, 164, 177
Flag at Krivoy Rog, The (Die Fahne von Krivoy Rog) (EGr), 285, 293, 301
Flaming [Blazing] Winter (Răscoala) (Ro), 316, 317, 328, 336
Flat, The (Byt) (Cz), 166

Fledermaus Squadron (Geschwader Fledermaus) (EGr), 283, 291, 299
Flight, The (Die Flucht) (EGr), 305
Flight of a Dead Bird, The (Let mrtve ptice) (Yu), 202, 223
Flowers of Reverie (Szirmak, viragok, koszoruk) (Hu), 261, 272
Flying High (Ledim na konari a je me dobre) (Cz), 158, 183
Follow Me, Mob! (Mir nach, Canaillen!) (EGr), 285, 301
For the Red Banner (Za krasnoye znamia) (SU), 48
For Your Sake, Anca (De dragul tau Anca) (Ro), 322, 340
Forbidden Songs (Po), 71, 72, 74, 96–97, 102, 108, 112
Forefather's Eve (Dziady) (Po), 86
Forest Fruit (Fructe de padure) (Ro), 322, 330, 341
Forest Maiden, The (Pădureanca) (Ro), 341
Forest of Lovers, The (Pădurea indrago stitilor) (Ro), 312, 333
Forest of the Hanged, The (Padurea spînzurailor) (Ro), 316, 326, 330, 335
Forests, The (Pădurile) (Ro), 327
A Forgotten Tune for the Flutes (SU), 43, 66
Forty-First, The (Sorok pervyi–1927) (SU), 42, 50
Forty-First, The (Sorok pervyi–1956) (SU), 40, 56
Fountain, The (SU), 24
Four Steps to the Infinite (La patru pasi de infinit) (Ro), 328, 335
Fourth Fence along the Wharf (Ro), 323, 341
Fragment of an Empire (Oblomok imperil) (SU), 14, 37
Freckles and Ghosts (Pehavý max a strašidlá) (Cz), 182, 183
Free City (Wolne Miasto) (Po), 80
Free Land (Freies Land) (EGr), 296
Freedom is Paradise (SU), 25
Freeze Frame at Table (Stop Cadru la Masa) (Ro), 340

FILM INDEX 417

Friendship Wins (Fruendschaft Siegt) (EGr), 280, 294, 297
From Hamburg to Stralsund (Von Hamburg bis Stralsand), (EGr), 278, 294, 297
From Our Times (Aus unseren Tagen) (EGr), 294
From Saturday to Sunday (Ze soboty na neděli) (Cz), 132, 133, 156, 162, 171
From the Life of a Good-for-nothing (Aus dem Leben eines Taugenichts) (EGr), 303–04
Frozen Bridge, The (Die vereiste Brucke) (EGr), 304
Frozen Lightening (Die gofrorenen Blitze) (EGr), 301
Full Ahead (Cata Naprzód) (Po), 103, 120
Funny Man, The (Směšný pán) (Cz), 159, 164, 178

Ga, Ga, Glory to Heroes (Ga, Ga Chawła Bohaterom) (Po), 108, 127
Galax (Ro), 330, 341
Gambler, The (Igrok) (SU), 34, 60
Game, A (Gra), (Po), 121
Garage (Garazh) (SU), 20, 43
Garden, The (Záhrada) (Cz), 166, 178
Geese of Batzow, The (Die Gänze von Batzow) (EGr), 307
A Gem of Free Conscience (Klejnot Wolnego Sumienia) (Po), 102, 126
General Line, The (SU). See Old and New
Generation (Pokolenie) (Po), 75, 76, 97, 103, 106, 109, 114
Genesis (Po), 92
Gentlemen, I Have Killed Einstein (Cz), 154, 161
Gently Passed Anastasia (Duios Anastasia trecea) (Ro), 322, 330, 340
Geometrickou radou (Cz), 182
Gerak Family, The (Geratsite) (Bu), 367
German Story, The (EGr). See You and Other Comrades
Ghost That Never Returns, The (Prividenie, kotoroe ne vozvrashchaetsia) (SU), 44

Giaconda Without That Smile (Ro). See The Unsmiling Giaconda
Girl (Devojka) (Yu), 196, 198, 214, 220
Girl, The (Eltávozott nap) (Hu), 246, 264, 265, 266, 270
Girl, The Christine (Das Mädchen Christine) (EGr), 279, 297
Girl No. 217 (Chelovek No. 217) (SU), 54
Girl of Good Family, A (Dziewczyna Z Dobrego Domu) (Po), 117
Girl on the Diving Board (EGr), 293, 301
Girl With a Hatbox (Devuska s korobkoi) (SU), 33
Girl Without an Address (Devushka bez adresa) (SU), 43
Girls from Nowolipki Street, The Apple Tree of Paradise (Dziewczęta z Nowolipek, Rajska Jabłon) (Po), 106, 127
Girl's Tears, A (O Lacrimă de Fată) (Ro), 321, 340
Giuseppe in Warsaw (Giuseppe w Warszawie) (Po), 97, 119
Glass of Beer, A (Egy pikoló világos) (Hu), 265
Gleiwitz Case, The (Der Fall Gleiwitz) (EGr), 292, 293, 300
Glissando (Ro), 323, 326, 341
Glory of Khan, The (Bu). See Khan Asparukh
Goat Horn, The (Koziyat Rog) (Bu), 350, 360, 361, 371
God's Finger (Palec Boży) (Po), 122
Gold (Zloto) (Po), 97, 99, 102, 104, 118
Golden Heart, The (Zlaté srdéčko) (Cz), 135, 155, 169
Golden Rennet, The (Zlatá reneta) (Cz), 176
Golem (Po), 108, 125
Golemanov (Bu), 362
Golgotha (Golgota) (Ro), 316, 326, 336
Good Kisses (Sarutari) (Ro), 330
Good Pal, A (Kamarad do deště) (Cz), 182
Good Soldier Svejk, The (Cz), 157
Gordian Knot, The (Nodul gordian) (Ro), 340

Gorki Trilogy, The (SU), 35
Goya (Goya) (Bu), 364
Goya (EGr), 287, 302
Graduates, The (Liceenii) (Ro), 341
Grandfather Automobile (Dědeček automobil) (Cz), 136, 160, 164, 173
Grandma, Iliko, Illarion, and Me (Ya, babushka, Iliko i Illarion) (SU), 33
Great Boredom, The (Goliamata Shuka) (Bu), 360
Great Citizen, A Pts. I and II (Veliki grazhdanin) (SU), 14, 37, 53, 54
Great Comforter (Velikii uteshitel) (SU), 52
Great Road, The (Veliki put) (SU), 44, 50
Great Seclusion, The (Velká samota) (Cz), 139, 157, 174
Great Turning Point, The (Veliki perelom) (SU), 37, 55
Green Grass of Home, The (Iarba verde de acasa) (Ro), 339
Green Years, The (Zoldár) (Hu), 262, 269
Grey Seagull (Sinji galeb) (Yu), 191
Gritta of the Castle of Rats (Gritta vom Rattenschloss) (EGr), 288, 307
Grown Up, as from Today (Ab heute erwachsen) (EGr), 307
Guard, The (Karaul) (SU), 66
Guardian Angel (Andeo čuvar) (Yu), 204, 217, 227
Guest at Dinner, A (Un oaspete la cină) (Ro), 341
Guild of the Kutna Hora Maidens (Cech panen Kutnohorských) (Cz), 134, 172
Gunpowder (Barouten Boukvar) (Bu), 361
Guns and Sorrell (Karbid und Sauerampfer) (EGr), 284, 290, 300

Hack, The (Pismak) (Po), 99, 100, 127
Haiduks, The (Haiducii) (Ro), 317, 326, 335
Haiduks of Captain Anghel, The (Haiducii lui Saptecai) (Ro), 317, 326, 337
Half Time (Polocas rozpadu) (Cz), 159
Hamlet (SU), 17, 40, 44, 45

Hammer Against Witches (Kladivo na čarodějnice) (Cz), 134, 158, 161, 167, 179
Hammer or Anvil (Nakovalnka Ili Chuk) (Bu), 361, 371
Hand, The (Ruka) (Cz), 166
Handcuffs (Lisice) (Yu), 199, 217, 222
Hands Up! (Ręce Do Gory) (Po), 86, 107, 127
Hans Rockle and the Devil (Hans Röckle und der Teufel) (EGr), 305
Hanussen (Hu/WGr), 251, 252, 261, 264, 266, 273
Happiness (SU), 14
Happy Adventure and Pals of Saint Hubert, The (L'Heureuse adventure it les compagnous de Saint Hubert) (Fr), 327
Happy New Year 1949 (Srećna nova '49) (Yu), 208, 217, 227
Hare Census, The (Prebroyavane Na Divite Zaytsi) (Bu), 351, 362, 365, 371
He Was My Friend (Eva prietenul meu) (Ro), 325
Heart of a Mother (Serdtse materi) (SU), 36
Heat (Zroi) (SU), 44
Heave Ho! (Hej rup!) (Cz), 132, 133, 156, 157, 168, 171
Heaven and Hell (Pielko i Niebo) (Po), 120
Heir to Genghis-Khan/Storm Over Asia, The (Potomok Chengis-khann) (SU), 9–10, 42, 51
Heiresses, The (Örökség) (Hu/Fr), 247–48, 258 n.2, 265, 272
Hello, Hello! (Allo! Allo!) (Ro), 318, 330, 335
Hello, Pointed-Beard or the Last Performance of Yeggs King (Hallo, Szpicbrodka, Czyli Ostatni Wystep Krola Kasiarzy) (Po), 108
Hello? Wrong Number (Alo? aţi greşit numărul) (Po), 334
Heritage, The (Dediščina) (Yu), 209, 226
Hero of the Year (Bohater roku) (Po), 91, 127
Heroes at Shipka Pass, The (Geroite Na Shipka) (Bu), 367

Hey Babu Riba (Yu). *See* Dancing on Water
Hey, Maestro! (SU), 66
Hic sunt Leones [Scars of the Past] (Zde jsou lvi) (Cz), 138, 160, 174
Higher Principle, The (Vyšši princíp) (Cz), 138, 160, 171
His Call (Ego prizyv) (SU), 42
History Lesson (Urok Na Istoriyata) (Bu), 363, 367
History of the Civil War (Istoriia grazhdanskoi voiny) (SU), 48
Hitler-Youth Shlomo (Po), 92
Holiday in Britain (Jutalomutazás) (Hu), 255, 261, 263, 271
Holiday on Sylt (Urlaub auf Sylt) (EGr), 283, 293, 294, 299
Holiday of St. Jorgen, The (Prazdnik svyatogo Iorgena) (SU), 42
Home in the Wilderness, A (Dom na Pustkowiu) (Po), 73, 107, 109, 112
Homo Sapiens (Ro), 318, 330, 334
Honor and Glory (Čést a sláva) (Cz), 154
Hop Pickers, The (Starci na chmelu) (Cz), 175–76
Hopelessly Lost (Sovsem propavshii) (SU), 60
Horizon (Horizont) (Hu), 253, 262, 264, 267, 270
Horn (Klakson) (Yu), 196, 198
Horoscope (Horoskop) (Yu), 200, 222
Hospital of the Transfigurtion (Szpital Przemieniena) (Po), 98, 100, 102, 110, 125
Hot Days (Zile Fierbinţi) (Ro), 319, 328, 329, 338
Hotel Central (Hotel Tsentral) (Bu), 357, 375
Hotel for Strangers (Hotel pro cizince) (Cz), 176
Hours of Hope (Godziny Nadziei) (Po), 106, 114
House at the Terminus (Tam na konečné) (Cz), 139
House for Two, A (Cz), 150
House I Live In, The (Dom, v kotorom ya zhivu) (SU), 40, 56

House in the Fields, The (Casa dintre cîmpuri) (Ro), 322, 330, 340
House in the Snow-Drifts (Dom v sugrobakh) (SU), 37
House in the Suburbs, A (Dam na předměsti) (Cz), 165, 171
House No. 42 (Kaca br. 42) (Yu), 210
House of Joy, The (Dům radosti) (Cz), 176
House of the Dead, The (Mërtvyi dom) (SU), 52
House on the River (Haus am Fluss) (EGr), 286, 307
House on Trubnaya Square, The (Dom na Trubroi) (SU), 34, 44
How Does One Feed an Ass? (Wie fuettert man einem Esel?) (EGr), 305
How far from Here, How Near (Jak Daleko Stad, Jad Blisko) (Po), 100, 102, 103, 122
How I Was Systematically Destroyed by an Idiot (Kako sam sistematski uništer od idiota) (Yu), 218
How the Berlin Worker Lives (Wie der Berliner Arbeiter wohnt) (EGr), 291
How the Steel Was Tempered (Kak zakalya las stal) (SU), 35, 54
How to be Loved (Jak Być Kochana) (Po), 83, 96, 97, 99, 104, 118
How to Do a Film Report (Ro), 311
How to Do a Radio Report (Ro), 311
How to Marry a Millionaire (Am), 311
Hundred Soldiers and Two Girls, A (Sto soldat i dve devushki) (SU), 67
Hungarian Rhapsody-Allegro Barbaro (Magyar rapszódia-Allegro Barbaro) (Hu), 241, 263
Hungarians, The (Magyarok) (Hu), 262
Hunger-Hunger-Hunger (Golod-golod-golod) (SU), 37, 48
Hunting Flies (Polowanie na Muchy) (Po), 90, 96, 105, 109
Hyperion (Ro), 320, 331, 338

I am Cuba (Ya Kuba) (SU), 39, 46, 58
I Don't Want to Get Married (Nu vreau să mă însor) (Ro), 315, 327, 334

I Even Met Happy Gypsies (Shapljači perja) (Yu), 197, 217, 221–22
I Love, You Love (Ja milujem, ty miluješ) (Cz), 156–57, 180
I Survived My Death (Prezil jsem svou smrt) (Cz), 138, 158
I Walk About Moscow (Ya shagayu po Moskve) (SU), 35
I Want to Know Why I Have Wings (Vreau să stiu de ce am aripi) (Ro), 341
I Was Caught By the Night (Zastihla mě noc) (Cz), 157, 180
I Was Nineteen (Ich war nuenzehn) (EGr), 285, 295, 301
Iconostasis (Ikonostasat) (Bu), 350, 361, 370
Identification Marks: None (Po), 85, 97, 107, 119
Idiot, The (SU), 43
Idiots May Apply (Hülyeség nem akadály) (Hu), 256
Idol, The (Idol) (Po), 98, 127
IF I Had a Gun (Keby som mal pusku) (Cz), 148, 167, 179
If the Train Doesn't Arrive . . . the Sea (Ako Ne Ide Vlak . . . Moreto) (Bu), 362, 365, 369
If There Were No Music (Kdyby ty muziky nebyly) (Cz), 156
If We Meet Again (Jesli Sie Odnajdzierny) (Po), 126
Illumination (Iluminacja) (Po), 88, 92, 101, 110
Illusion (Iluziya) (Bu), 363, 373
I'm Jumping Over Puddles Again (Už zase skáču pres kaluže) (Cz), 159, 179
I'm Twenty [or, Lenin's Sentries] (Mne dvadtsat let) (SU), 58
Immortal Youth (Besmrtna mladost) (Yu), 188
Immortals, The (Nemuritorii) (Ro), 319, 329, 338
Impossible Love (Impossibilia iubre) (Ro), 321, 331, 341
Imposters (Podvonići) (Cz), 176
Impure Blood (Necista krv) (Yu), 189

In Broad Daylight (W Biały Dzień) (Po), 95–96, 102, 110, 125
In Midsummer (W Srodku Lata) (Po), 98, 123
In Our Village (In sat la noi) (Ro), 313, 316, 326, 327, 333
In Spite of Everything (Naperekor vsemu) (SU), 39
In Spite of It All (Trotz Alledam) (EGr), 293, 303
In the Big City (SU), 35
In the Desert and in a Wilderness (W Pustyni i w Puszczy) (Po), 107, 122
In the Field of Tension (Im Sparnungsfeld) (EGr), 285, 292, 302
In the Mountains of Yugoslavia (U planinoma Jugoslavije) (SU), 213
In the Name of the Fatherland (Vo imia rodiny) (SU), 54
In the Name of the People (Bu),
In the Name of the People (U ime naroda) (Yu), 216, 227
In the Penalty Zone (V trestnem území) (Cz), 137
In the Sign of the Serpent (Semnul sarpelui) (Ro), 322, 331, 340
Incomplete Eclipse (Neuplene zatmeni) (Cz), 159
Incorrigible Barbara (Unverbesserliche Barbara) (EGr), 286–87, 294, 305
Incredible Tale, An (Neveroyatna Istoriya) (Bu), 348
Index, The (Indeke) (Po), 101, 125
Infinity (Infinit) (Ro), 330
Inheritance, The (Dediščina) (Yu), 215
Inn, The (Austeria) (Po), 91, 101, 102, 105, 126
Innocence Unprotected (Nevinost bez zaštite) (Yu), 197, 216, 222
Innocent Sorcerers (Niewinni Czarodzieje) (Po), 85, 95, 97, 103, 106, 107, 109, 116–17
Inspector and the Forest, The (Sledovatelyat I Gorata) (Bu), 352, 364, 372
Inspector and the Night, The (Inspektorat i Noshta) (Bu), 348, 352, 364, 369
Inspector General, The (Revizor) (Cz), 134

Interrogation of the Witnesses (EGr), 307
Intergirl (SU), 25
Intimate Lighting (Intimní osvětlení) (Cz), 160, 163, 176
Intolerance (Am), 5
The Intransigents (Neprimirimite) (Bu), 369
Intrigue and Love (Kabale und Liebe) (EGr), 282, 292, 299
Invasion (Nashestvie), 16, 44, 54
Invention for Destruction (Vynález zkázy) (Cz), 174
Invincible Love (Königskinder) (EGr), 283–84, 290, 300
Invitation to Dance (Zaproszenie do Tanca) (Po), 100, 127
Ionitz Brigade, The (Bragada lui Ionut) (Ro), 314, 328, 334
Ipu's Death (Moartea hui Ipu) (Ro), 319, 329, 330, 337
Iron Heel, The (Zheleznaya piata) (SU), 37
Irony of Fate, or Have a Good Sauna (Ironia sud'by, ili s legkim parom) (SU), 20, 43
Is It Easy to be Young? (Legdo li byt' molodym?) (SU), 24
Isabel on the Stairs (Isabel auf der treppe) (EGr), 307
Island of Swans (Insel der Schwäne) (EGr), 307
Issa Valley (Dolina Issy) (Po), 91, 98, 102, 103, 125–26
It Happened in Berlin (EGr), 283, 292, 299
It Happened on the Streets (Toua Se Sluchi Na Ulizata) (Bu), 365, 366
It Is an Old Story (Es ist eine alte Geschichte) (EGr), 282, 294, 303
It Rains on My Village (Biće skoro propast sveta) (Yu), 197, 217, 222
Item One (Tochka Parva) (Bu), 367
It's Only Rock 'n Roll (To Tylko Rock) (Po), 127
Ivan (SU), 36, 51
Ivan Kondarev (Bu), 362, 372
Ivan the Terrible, Pt. I (Ivan Grozny) (SU), 13, 15, 35, 36, 54

Ivan the Terrible, Pt. II (Ivan Grozny) (SU), 13, 16, 35, 36, 55
Ivan the Terrible, Pt. III (Ivan Grozny) (SU), 16
Ivan's Childhood (Ivanovo detstvo) (SU), 18–19, 58

Jabberwocky (Cz), 166
Jacob the Liar (Jakob der Lügner) (EGr), 288, 290, 304
Jánošík (Cz), 132, 171
Janus's Head (Januskopf) (EGr), 286, 293, 302
Jaws of Life, The (U raljama života) (Yu), 205, 206, 214, 226
Jazz Comedy (Veselye rebiata) (SU), 33, 36
Jazzman (My iz dzhaza) (SU), 64
Jealousy (Cz), 162
Jealousy and Medicine (Zazdrosc i Medycyna) (Po), 86, 98, 123
Jester and the Queen, The (Šašek a králouna) (Cz), 149, 155, 182
Jesus Christ's Horoscope (Jézus Krisztus horoszkópia) (Hu), 241–42, 261, 263, 273
Joachim, Put It in the Machine (Jáchyme, hod ho do stroje) (Cz), 161, 166
Job's Revolt (Jób lázadása) (Hu), 254, 262, 272
Johnny Belinda (Am), 311
Joke, The (Žert) (Cz), 155, 158, 160, 161
Josef Kilian (Cz), 155, 164, 175
Journey to the Primeval Time (Cesta do pravěku) (Cz), 173
Journeys with Jacob (Utazás Jakabbal) (Hu), 253, 261, 262, 263, 270
Jowita (Po), 97, 104, 126
Judge of Salamea, The (Richter von Zalamea) (EGr), 282, 292, 298
Judgment (Í télet) (Hu), 264, 266
Julia Lives (Julia lebt) (EGr), 284, 300
Just a Little Whistle (Jen si tak trochu pisknout) (Cz), 159
Just Don't Think I'm Crying (Denk bloss nicht, ich heule) (EGr), 284, 301

Just Like America (Tiszta Amerika) (Hu), 261, 262, 273
Just Like at Home (Olyan, mint otthon) (Hu), 263, 265, 271

Kaiser's Lackey/The Underdog/The Submissive, The (Der Untertan) (EGr), 279, 294, 297
Kaja, I'll Kill You (Kaja, ubit ću te), (Yu), 199, 206, 216, 221
Kalin the Eagle (Kalin Orelat) (Bu), 344, 360, 366
Kardiogram, A (Kardiogram) (Po), 122
Karl and Anna (EGr), 307
Karla (EGr), 301
Kathe Kollwitz—Pictures of a Life (EGr), 307
Katka's Reinette Apples (Katka—bumazhnyi ranet) (SU), 37, 49
Kekec (Yu), 191
Kerosene Lamps (Petrolejove lampy) (Cz), 179
Keys, The (Die Schlüssel) (EGr), 291, 304
Khan Asparukh (Bu), 356, 363, 374, 375
Kid, The (Ro), 325
Kidnapped (Únos) (Cz), 173
Kidnapping of Banker Fux, The (Únos bankéře Fuxe) (Cz), 163, 170
The Killing of the Aunt (Zabicie Ciotki) (Po), 102, 127
Kindergarten (Detsii sad) (SU), 64
Kinfolk (Rodnia) (SU), 21, 41, 63
King and the General, The (Tsar i General) (Bu), 349
King Lear (Korol Lir) (SU), 17, 40, 44, 60
King Mat I (Krol Macius I) (Po), 109, 115
King of Paris, The (Korol Parizha) (SU), 34, 47
Kino-Eye (Kino-Glaz) (SU), 5, 49
Kino pravda (SU), 46, 48
Kino Prickles (Kinostarchel) (Bu), 346
Kiss, The (Sarutul) (Ro), 325, 335
Kiuleandra (Ro), 323, 329, 341
Knife in the Water (Nóż w Wodzie) (Po), 85, 103, 106, 107, 118

Knight, A (Rycerz) (Po), 125
Knight Without Armor (Ritsar Bez Bronya) (Bu), 352, 369
Knot of the Salamander, The (Cuibul slamandelor) (Ro), 326
Komsomolsk (SU), 53
Konopielka (Po), 126
Korczak (Po), 92
Kozara (Yu), 213, 220
Krakatit (Cz), 134
Kreutzer Sonata, The (Kreitzerova sonata) (SU), 41
Kreutzer Sonata, The (Kreutzerova sonáta) (Cz), 133, 162, 170
Kühle Wampe (EGr), 275, 278, 291
Kung Fu (Po), 101, 125

Lace (Kruzheva) (SU), 50
Ladies Choice (Dami Kanyet) (Bu), 362
Lady Doctors (Arztinnen) (EGr), 287, 293, 306
Lady With the Little Dog, The (SU), 17, 34, 38, 57
Lady With the Small Foot, The (Dáma s malou nožkou) (Cz), 163, 169
Lame Devil, The (Kulhavý ďábel) (Cz), 157
Land, The (Zemia) (Po), 115
Land (Zemya) (Bu), 367
Land of the Miraculous Rabbis, The (Hu/WGr). *See* That Ye Inherit
Land of Miracles (Délibábok országa) (Hu), 249
Landscape After Battle (Krajobraz po Bitwie) (Po), 90, 96, 105, 109, 122
Lanfieri Colony, The (Kolonie Lanfieri) (Cz), 164
Lannekin Wedding, The (EGr), 290, 300
Lantern of Memories (Lanterna cu amintiri) (Ro), 314, 327, 335
Last Assault, The (Ro), 323, 329, 341
Last Bullet, The /The Last Cartridge (Ultimul Cartus) (Ro), 319, 329, 330, 338
Last Cartridge, The (Ro). *See* The Last Bullet
Last Chance, The (Harmadik nekifutás) (Hu), 245, 260, 264, 270

Last Crusade (Ro). *See* Michael the Brave
Last Day of Summer, The (Ostatni Dzień Lata) (Po), 81, 102, 115
Last Days (Ostatnie Dni) (Po), 105
Last Night, The (Posledniaia noch) (SU), 43
Last of the Mohicans, The (Ultimul Mohican) (Ro), 317, 329, 336
Last Stage, The (Ostatni Etap) (Po), 72, 100, 107, 112
Last Summer, The (Posledno Lyato) (Bu), 350, 361, 363, 372
Last Wishes (Posledni Zhelania) (Bu), 357, 364, 375
Last Word, The (Poslednata Duma) (Bu), 351, 365, 371
Late Passers-by, The (Spóźieni Przechodnie) (Po), 95, 98, 118
Laughing and Crying (Pláčo a smích) (Cz), 130, 160, 169
Laughing Man, The (Der lachende Mann) (EGr), 301
Leave It to Me (Nechte to na mně) (Cz), 132, 156
Legend About the Death and Resurrection of Two Young Men (Mezteler vagy) (Hu), 262
Legend of Paul and Paula, The (Die Legende von Paul und Paula) (EGr), 286, 290, 303
Legend of the Surami Fortress, The (Legenda o Suramskoi kreposti) (SU), 19, 42, 65
Lemonade Joe (Limonádový Joe) (Cz), 161, 175
Lenin in 1918 (Lenin v 1918) (SU), 53
Lenin in October (Lenin v Oktiabre) (SU), 14, 43, 53
Lenin in Poland (Lenin v Polshe) (SU), 46, 58
Leninist Film-truth (Leniniskaia kinopravda) (SU), 46, 49
Leonardo's Diary (Leonarduv deník) (Cz), 166, 179
Les Misérables (Die Elenden) (EGr), 281, 299
Lesson of Dead Language, A (Lekcja Martwego Jezyka) (Po), 86, 103, 104, 124
Let It Be Known to All Your Loves (Oznamuje so láskám vašim) (Cz), 182
Let the Nightmare Fly (Niech Cie Odleci Mara) (Po), 96, 126
Letter from Ion Marin for the "Scinteia" (Scrisoarea lui Ion Marin catre scintea) (Ro), 327
Letter That Wasn't Sent, The (Neotpravlennoye pismo) (SU), 46, 57
Letters From a Dead Man (Pis'ma mertvogo cheloveka) (SU), 35
Levin's Mill (Levin's Mühle) (EGr), 287, 293, 306
Lia (Ro), 311, 328, 332
Liane (EGr), 287, 307
Liberation of Prague (Osvobození Prahy) (Cz), 147
Life Begins (Das Leben beginnt) (EGr), 290, 299
Life for a Life, A (Zhizn za Zhizn) (SU), 34, 47
Life in Death (Zhizn v smerti) (SU), 34, 47
Life in Germany (Tito in Deutschland) (EGr), 294, 301
Life in Pink (Viaţa in roz) (Ro), 320, 329
Life in the Ticking (EGr). *See* The Checkered Bedspread
Life is at the End (Cz), 150
Life is Beautiful (Život je lep) (Yu), 209, 214, 226
Life of Matthew, The (Zywot Mateusza) (Po), 105, 121
Life Once Again (Zycie Raz Jeszcze) (Po), 81, 104, 110, 128
Life Prevails (Viaţa învinge) (Ro), 314, 328, 333
Life Was the Stake (Hra o život) (Cz), 168
Life Will Not Forgive (Viata nu iarta) (Ro), 315, 327, 328, 334
Life with Uwe (Leben mit Uwe) (EGr), 287, 294, 304
Light on the Tenth Floor, A (O lumină la etajul X) (Ro), 323, 331, 341
Like a Song (Kato Pesen) (Bu), 352, 371

Like Poison (Jako jed) (Cz), 162, 181
Liliomfi (Hu), 242, 262, 264, 265
Lily in Love (Jatszani kell) (Hu/Am), 243, 260, 264, 272
Limited Sky (Mniejsze Niebo) (Po), 125
Line, The (Linia) (Po), 123
Lissy (EGr), 282, 299
Little and Big Happiness (Das kleine und das grosse Glück) (EGr), 281, 292, 298
Little Annie (Malkoto Antsche) (Bu), 346
Little Girl, The (O děvčicu) (Cz), 135
Little Magician and the Bad Mark, The (Der kleine Zauberer und die grosse Fünf) (EGr), 288, 305
Little Mook (Die Geschichte vom kleinen Muck) (EGr), 282, 288, 294, 298
Little Shop of Horrors, The (Am), 148
Little Soldiers (Mali vojnici) (Yu), 200, 214, 221
Little Story, A (Mala Kronika) (Yu), 193
Little Vera (Malenkaia Vera) (SU), 24, 25, 66
Living Corpse, The (Zhivoi trup) (SU), 33, 39
Living Like the Rest of Us (Živeti kao sav normalan svet) (Yu), 209, 217
Loaf of Bread, A (Sousto) (Cz), 161, 162
Local Romance, A (Žižkovská romance) (Cz), 138, 154, 155, 174
Lodger, The (Sublokator) (Po), 86, 104, 110, 120
Lokis (Po), 122
Lone White Sail (SU), 14, 52–53
Lonely Woman, The (Kobuta Samotna) (Po), 89, 99, 127
Long Drive, The (Opera prima, Curse) (Ro), 322, 326, 338
Long Journey, The (Daleká cesta) (Cz), 136, 164, 172
Long Live the Republic (Af žije republika) (Cz), 159, 164, 165, 176
Longest Night, The (Nay-Dalgata Nosht) (Bu), 349, 363, 370
Look Out for Cars (Beregis avtomobilia) (SU), 43, 45
Lorenz v. Lorenz (EGr), 292, 299
Los Olvidados (Sp), 233

Lost Cause (Causa Perduta) (Bu), 346
Lost Feelings (Zagubione Uczucia) (Po), 95, 115
Lost Forest, The (Padurea pierduta) (Ro), 325
Lost Letter, A (O scrisoare pierduta) (Ro), 327, 333
Lotna (Po), 90, 103, 116
Lot's Wife (Lot's Weib) (EGr), 284, 286, 291, 301
Lotte in Weimar (EGr/WGr), 286, 287, 291, 305
Lottery Swede, The (EGr), 283, 292, 299
Loud and Soft is Love (Laut und leise ist die Liebe) (EGr), 303
Love (Ljubav) (Yu), 214
Love (Szerelem) (Hu), 242–43, 262, 264, 267, 270
Love Affair or the Tragedy of a Switchboard Operator (Ljubavni slučaj ili tragedija službenice PTT) (Yu), 197, 216, 221
Love at 16 (Liebe mit 16) (EGr), 305
Love Begins on Friday (Ro), 337
Love Film (Szerelmesfilm) (Hu), 250, 261, 266, 270
Love in Germany, A (Milosc w Niemczech) (WGr), 91, 99
Loves of a Blonde (Lásky jedné plavovlásky) (Cz), 142, 147, 149, 156, 176
Lupeni 29 (Ro), 316, 326, 335
Lust for Gold (Duhul aurulai) (Ro), 329, 331
Lutzower (EGr), 303
Lynx, The (Rys) (Po), 126

Magdana's Donkey (Lurdzha Madany) (SU), 33, 56
Magic Lantern (Laterna Magica) (Cz), 164
Magical Hat, The (Divotvorný klobouk) (Cz), 164
Maibowle (EGr), 283, 293, 299
Maids of Wilko, The (Panny z Wilka-Les Demoiselles de Wilko) (Po), 101, 103, 105, 109, 124
Ma-Ma (Ro/Fr/SU), 322, 325, 339
Mamel (Po), 71

Man from the Oak Forest (Covek iz hrastove šume) (Yu), 195, 198
Man From the Restaurant, The (Chelovek iz retorana) (SU), 42
Man in the Overcoat, The (Omul în loden) (Ro), 339
Man is Not a Bird (Čovek nije tica) (Yu), 196, 197, 216, 220
Man of Iron (Człowiek z Zelazza) (Po), 90, 100, 101, 106, 107, 109, 125, 249
Man of Marble (Człowiek z Marmuru) (Po), 90, 100, 101, 106, 107, 109, 124, 249
Man on the Track, The (Człowiek na Torze) (Po), 79, 104, 108, 114
Man Who Came After the Grandmother, The (Der Mann, der nach der oma kam) (EGr), 303
Man With a Movie Camera (Chelovek s kinoapparatom) (SU), 6, 46, 51
Man With the Gun, The (Chelovek s ruzhem) (SU), 35, 46
Manasse (Ro), 311, 328, 332
Manifesto (Am/Yu), 209, 216
Manly Times (Muzhki Vremena) (Bu), 354, 361, 365, 373
Manner of Behaving, A (Sposob Bycia) (Po), 96, 107, 120
Man's Lonely Voice, A (Odinokii golos cheloveka) (SU), 45, 65
Manuscript Found in Saragossa, The (Rękopis Znaleziony w Saragossie) (Po), 83, 97, 99, 100, 101, 105, 119–20
Manxman (Br), 134
Maps Colored with Wildflowers (Illustate cu flori de cimp) (Ro), 325, 338
Marathon Runner, The (Maratonci trče posčasni krug) (Yu), 218
Marecek, Pass Me a Pen (Mařečku, podejtě mi péro) (Cz), 161, 166
Maria Marabela (Ro), 322
Marie (Hu). *See* Spring Shower
Marketa Lazarova (Cz), 132, 145, 162, 177
Marriage in the Shadow (Ehe im Schatten) (EGr), 278, 292, 296
Marriage of Figaro, The (Figaros Hochzeit) (EGr), 279, 297

Martyrs of Love (Mučedniči lásky) (Cz), 144, 161, 162, 163, 177
Maryša (Cz), 164, 171
Mashenka (SU), 43
Mass Miracle (Massovo Choudo) (Bu), 376
Master and Margaret, The (Majstor i Margarita) (Yu), 197, 207, 217, 223
Master of Boyana (Boyanski yat Maistor) (Bu), 356, 365, 374
Master of One's Own Body (Svoga tela gospodar), (Yu), 191
Mathew Passions, The (Muke po mati) (Yu), 206
Matriachate (Matriarhat) (Bu), 354–55, 362
Matter to Settle, A (Sprawa do Załatwienia) (Po), 73, 113
Maxim Trilogy (SU), 40, 44
May I Call You Petrushka? (EGr), 288, 306
May I Have the Floor (Proshu slova) (SU), 21, 42, 61
May Story, The (Pohádka máje) (Cz), 170
Mayakovsky Laughs (Mayakovsky smeetsia) (SU), 61
Mazepa (Po), 110
Mazurka Danced at Dawn, The (Biały Mazur) (Po), 98, 100, 104, 124
Me + Me = Me (Eu + Eu = Eu) (Ro), 330
Meanders (Meandre) (Ro), 336
Measure for Measure (Mera Spored Mera) (Bu), 356, 361, 374
Mechanics of the Brain (Meekhanikha golovnovo mozga) (SU), 49
Medicine for Love, A (Lekarstwo na Miłosc) (Po), 103
Meeting in the Cafe, The "Tale" (Społkanie w "Bajce") (Po), 118
Meeting on the Atlantic, A (Społkanie na Atlantyku) (Po), 104
Meeting With Shadows, A (Schuzka se stíny) (Cz), 154, 166
Melodie, Melodie (Ro), 328
Melody Haunts My Memory, The (Yu). *See* You Only Love Once

Member of the Government (Chlen pravitelstva) (SU), 38
Memory of the Twin Sister (Spomen Za Bliznchkata) (Bu), 372
Men Offside (Muži v offsidu) (Cz), 134, 156, 171
Men on a Business Trip (Mazhe U Komandirovka) (Bu), 364
Men Without Beards (Männer ohne Bart) (EGr), 303
Men Without Wings (Muži bez křídel) (Cz), 136, 165, 172
Men Without Work (Mazhe Bez Rabota) (Bu), 351, 364, 371
Mephisto (Hu/WGr), xi, xiii, 100, 251–52, 261, 264, 266, 272
Merry-Go-Round (Körhintu), 234, 262, 266, 267, 268
Merrymaker from Holy-Cross Mountains, The (Sovrizdral Swietokrzyski) (Po), 101
Meshes of the Afternoon (Am), 156
Message of Times Past and Future, A (Masseba) (Cz), 183
Michael the Brave/Last Crusade (Mihai Viteazul) (Ro), 317, 319, 329, 337
Michurin (SU), 36, 55
Microphone Testing (Probă de microfon) (Ro), 322, 326, 340
Midas Touch, The (Hu). *See* El Dorado
Midsummer Night's Dream, A (Sen noci svatojanské) (Cz), 166
Migrations (Yu/Fr), 209
Mill of Good Luck (Moara cu noroc) (Ro), 314, 327, 330, 334
Millennial Bee, The (Tisićročná v čela) (Cz), 148, 158, 181
Millions on an Island (Milijuni na otoku) (Yu), 191
Mimino (SU), 21, 35, 61
Minin and Pozharski (Minin i Pozharski) (SU), 42
Mirror (Zerkalo) (SU), 19, 45, 60–61
Miss Arizona (Hu/It), 266
Miss Butterfly (Fräulein Schmetterling) (EGr), 284, 301
Miss Mend (SU), 38
Miss Stone (Mis Ston) (Yu), 191

Mr. Edgar's Last Trick (Poslední trik pána Edgara a pána Schwarzwalda) (Cz), 166
Mitică Popescu (Ro), 321, 327, 341
Mitrea Cocor (Ro), 313, 326, 333
Moment, The (Clipa), 321, 331, 339
Monday Morning (Ponedelnik Sutrin) (Bu), 363, 369
Monday or Tuesday (Ponedeljak ili utorak) (Yu), 199
Monk Brne's Pupil (Bakonja Fra Brne) (Yu), 191
Montenegro (Br/Swed), 209, 216
Moon Over the River (Měsíc nad řekou) (Cz), 138, 139, 160, 173
Moonlighting (Br), 86, 107
Morgiana (Cz), 161, 179
Morning (Jutro) (Yu), 198, 214, 221
Mornings of a Sensible Youth, The (Diminetile unul băiat cuminte) (Ro), 317, 325, 336
Moscow Does Not Believe in Tears (Moskva slezam ne verit) (SU), 22, 37, 63
Most Beautiful Age, The (Nejkrásnější věk) (Cz), 160, 163, 178
Moth, A (Cma) (Po), 91, 110
Mother, The (Mat–1926) (SU), 9, 34, 42, 49
Mother (Mat–1956) (SU), 36
Mother and Daughter (Hu). *See* Anna
Mother Joan of the Angels (Matka Joanna od Aniotów) (Po), 81, 84, 101, 102, 105, 108, 109, 110, 117
Mother of the Krol Family (Matka Królów) (Po), 91, 96, 105, 110, 127
Mother's Devotion, A (Vernost materi) (SU), 36
Moving Sands (Ruchome Piaski) (Po), 107
Mrs. Dery, Where Are You? (Deryné, hol van?) (Hu), 267
Much Ado About Nothing (Cz), 167
Mum, I'm Alive (Mama, ich lebe) (EGr), 295, 305
Murder of Mr. Devil, The (Cz), 161
Murderer Leaves Traces (Morderca Zostawia Slad) (Po), 97

FILM INDEX

Murderers Are Among Us, The (Die Mörder sind unter uns) (EGr), 277, 294, 296
Music from Mars (Hudba z marsu) (Cz), 159, 173
Musical Tree, The (Musikalnoto Darwo) (Bu), 346
My Childhood (Aus meiner Kindheit) (EGr), 287, 304
My Darling, My Darling (Skupi moi, Skupa, moya) (Bu), 358, 375
My Dear Fellow! (Dorogoi moi chelovek!) (SU), 56
My Dear Robinson (Mein lieber Robinson) (EGr), 303
My Father's House (Otchii dom) (SU), 57
My Friend Ivan Lapshin (Moi drug Ivan Lapshin) (SU), 21, 38, 65
My Friend Sybille (EGr), 285, 301
My Old Man (Mój Stary) (Po), 118
My Sweet Little Village (Vesničko má středisková) (Cz), 130, 139, 147, 149, 158, 162, 166, 181
My 20th Century (Az én XX századom) (Hu), 256, 273
My Uncle's Legacy (Život sa stricem) (Yu), 209, 217, 227
My Universities (Moi univesitety) (SU), 35
My Way Home (Igy jöttem) (Hu), 236–37, 263, 264, 266, 269

Nadezhda (SU), 36
Naked Among Wolves (Nackt unter Wölfen) (EGr), 284, 290, 300
Naked Conscience (Gola Suvest) (Bu), 361
Naked Man on the Athletic Field, The (Der nackte Mann auf dem Sportplatz) (EGr), 295, 304
Nameless Band, A (Orkestur Bez Ime) (Bu), 362, 374
Napoleon et l'Europe (Po), 92
National Category up to 785 cm (Nacionalwa klasa do 785 cm)(Yu), 205, 224
Needle, The (SU), 25
Nest, The (Gniazdo) (Po), 123

Nest of Gentry, A (Dvorianskoye gnezdo) (SU), 41, 59
Network (Netzwerk) (EGr), 285, 302
New Babylon (Novyi Vavilon) (SU), 40, 44, 51
New Fighters Will Arise (Vstanou noví bojvníći) (Cz), 137, 168, 172
New Year's Punch (Silvesterpunsch) (EGr), 293, 300
Nice Neighbor, The (A kedves szomszéd) (Hu), 263
Nick Carter in Prague (Cz). See Adela Hasn't Had Supper Yet
Night Moth, The (Noční motýl) (Cz), 157, 172
Night of Remembrance, A (Celuloza) (Po), 74, 100, 113
Night of the Bride, The (Noc nevesty) (Cz), 154, 158, 159, 164
Night Train (Pociga) (Po), 116
Nightmares (Zmory) (Po), 125
Nights and Days (Noce i Dnie) (Po), 95, 96, 98, 123
Nikodem Dyzma (Po), 108
Nikolai Ghiaurov—50 (Bu), 362
Nikolai Stavrogin (SU), 41
Nine Days in a Year (Deviat dnei odnogo goda) (SU), 43, 45, 57
Nine Months (Kilenc hónap) (Hu), 247, 258 n.2, 263, 265, 271
Ninth Circle, The (Deveti krug) (Yu), 192, 218, 220
No Ford in the Fire (V ogne broda net) (SU), 21, 42, 59
No One Calling (Nikt Nie Wola) (Po), 81, 117
No Place for Love (Kein Platz für Liebe) (EGr), 280, 297
Nobody Shall Be Laughing (Nikdo se nebude smát) (Cz), 154, 159, 161, 176
Noon (Podne) (Yu), 198, 214, 222
Noose, The (Pętla) (Po), 82, 99, 100, 115
Nostalgia (SU), 19, 45
No. 8, Seller Street (EGr), 292, 300
Number Eleven (Odinnadtsatyi) (SU), 46, 50

Nuremburg Epilogue, The (Epilog Norymberski) (Po), 95

Oak Tree, Top Emergency (Stejar, extrema urgenta) (Ro), 326, 338
Obsession (Opetanie) (Po), 103, 122
Obsession (Opsesija) (Yu), 210
Obsession (Vasen) (Cz), 166
Occupation in 26 Pictures (Okupacija u 26 slika) (Yu), 206, 218, 224
Oceans Are Calling, The (Die Meere rufen) (EGr), 280, 297
October (SU), 4, 9, 11, 36, 50
Office Romance, An (Sluzhebnyi romans) (SU), 20, 62
Oh, Bloody Life (Te rongyos elet) (Hu), 260
Oil, the Baby, and the Transylvanians (Ro), 329, 330, 340
O.K. (EGr), 301
Old and New/The General Line (Staroe i novoe) (SU), 9, 36, 51
Old Czech Legends (Stare pověsti české) (Cz), 166
Old Love, An (Ein alte Liebe) (EGr), 283, 290, 299
Old Men Alone (Vychyo, starichyo) (SU), 67
"Old Professor, The" ("Stary Professor") (Po), 95
Old Walls, The (Starye steny) (SU), 38
Ole Henry (EGr), 307
On a Small Island (Na Malkiya Ostrov) (Bu), 347, 360, 362, 364, 367–68
On My Responsibility (Pe răspunderea) (Ro), 326, 334
On Saturday Evening (Sabotom uveče) (Yu), 192, 217, 219
On the Ashes of an Empire (Prin cenusa imperiulúl) (Ro), 325
On the Corner of Brzeka and Capri Streets (Rog Brzeskiej i Capri) (Po), 125
On the Eve (V Navecherieto) (Bu), 368
On the Left Bank of the Blue Danube (Pe Malul Stîng al dunarii Albastre) (Ro), 323, 331, 341

On the Move (Utkozben) (Hu), 260, 265, 271
On the Red Front (Na krasnom fronte) (SU), 40, 48
On the Silver Globe (Na Srebynym Globie) (Po), 89, 110
On the Sunny Side (Na sluneční straně) (Cz), 167
On the Way to Lenin (Unter wegs zu Lenin) (EGr), 287, 293, 302
On Their Own Ground (Yu), 189
On Wings of Paper (Na papirnatih avionih) (Yu), 200, 215, 221
Once is Nonce (Einmal ist Keinmal) (EGr), 281, 295, 298
One Flew Over the Cuckoo's Nest (Am), 156
One Hundred Bullets (Ro), 337
One More Day (Dan vise) (Yu), 214
One Morning (Intr-o dimineata) (Ro), 331
1, 2, 3 (Ro), 330
Open City (It), 233
Open Town (Wolne Miasto) (Po), 99, 106, 116
Opening Tomorrow (Jutro Premiera) (Po), 117–18
Opera Europa (Hu/Br), 252
Operation "Brutus" (Akcja "Brutus") (Po), 100, 105, 122
Operation Teutonic Sword (Unternehmen Teutonenschwert) (EGr), 283, 293, 294, 299
Oratorio for Prague (Cz), 144, 162
Ordinary Fascism (Obyknovennyi fashizm) (SU), 43, 58
Orfeus in the Underworld (Orpheus in der Unterwelt) (EGr), 288, 304
Organ, The (Organ) (Cz), 167
Organist of St. Vit, The [Vitus] (Varhaník u Sv. Víta) (Cz), 156, 162, 170
Orientering (Concurs) (Ro), 323, 329, 340
Orphans, The (Podranki) (SU), 22–23
Ossuary, The (Kostnice) (Cz), 179
Otar's Widow (Otarova vdova) (SU), 35
Othello (SU), 17, 46, 56

ABOUT THE CONTRIBUTORS

DANIEL J. GOULDING, Professor of Film Studies and Theater Arts at Oberlin College, has lectured and published widely on film and related subjects. His book *Liberated Cinema: The Yugoslav Experience* (Indiana University Press, 1985) received the first "Close-up" award from the Yugoslav Film Institute for "outstanding scholarship and promoting the value of Yugoslav film art internationally." His most recent book, for which he was editor and contributor, is *Post New Wave Cinema in the Soviet Union and Eastern Europe* (Indiana University Press, 1989). Scheduled for publication early in 1993 is his latest book *Five Filmmakers: Challenging the Boundaries* (Indiana University Press).

BRUCE R. S. LITTE, Associate Professor of English at Northwest Missouri State University, has published and taught primarily in literature while also building a film studies program and successful film series at his home school.

JUDITH ROOF teaches film and feminist critical studies at the University of Delaware. She is co-editor of *Feminism and Psychoanalysis* and author of *A Lure of Knowledge: Lesbian Sexuality and Theory* as well as essays on Beckett, Pinter, Duras, Freud, Lacan, and film.

TOMASZ WARCHOŁ, a native of Poland, is an Assistant Professor in the English Department of Georgia Southern University in Statesboro where he teaches writing, world literature, and film. His publications include essays on Miloš Forman for *The New Orleans Review,* on Polish cinema for *Sight and Sound,* and on early and contemporary American fiction for the Ball State University *Forum* and Beacham Publishing.

THOMAS J. SLATER, Assistant Professor of Film and Literature at Indiana University of Pennsylvania, has previously published *Miloš Forman: A Bio-Bibliography* (Greenwood Press, 1987), a two-part interview with Forman, an essay on the adaptation of *One Flew Over the Cuckoo's Nest,* and essays on the teaching of Vietnam documentaries and film's impact on language.

White Ward (Camera Alba) (Ro), 317, 335
White Wolves (Weisse Wölfe) (EGr), 302
Who Looks For Gold? (Kdo hledá zlaté dno?) (Cz), 162
Whoever Loves His Wife (Wer seine Frau lieb hat) (EGr), 281, 298
Whooping Cough (Szamárköhögés) (Hu), 256, 267, 273
Whore's Holiday (Praznik kurvi) (Yu), 206, 227
Who's That Singing Over There? (Ko to tamo peva) (Yu), 207, 215, 218, 224
Why? (Proc?) (Cz), 150, 159, 182
Widowhood of Karolina Žašler, The (Vdovstvo Karoline Žašler) (Yu), 223
Wilhelm Pieck—The Life of Our President (Wilhelm Pieck—das Leben unseres Präsidenten) (EGr), 280, 294, 297
Wind in My Pocket (Vitr v kapse) (Cz), 180-81
Wings (Krylia) (SU), 44, 59
Winner, The (Invingatŏrul) (Ro), 340
Winter Dusk (Zimowy Zmierzch) (Po), 102, 103, 115
Winter Wind (Hu). See Sirocco
With Clean Hands (Cu miinile curate) (Ro), 319, 329, 330, 337
With Love and Tenderness (S Lyubov i Nezhnost) (Bu), 354, 362, 364, 373
Without (Bez) (Yu), 217
Without Anesthesia (Bez Znieczulenia) (Po), 90, 99, 100, 101, 106, 108, 109, 124
Without Dowry (Bespridannitsa) (SU), 53
Without End (Bez Kónca) (Po), 96, 101, 105, 126
Without Love (Bez Miłości) (Po), 102, 106, 125
Without Witnesses (Bez svidotelei) (SU), 41, 63
Witness, The (A tanu) (Hu), 245, 260, 265
Wolf Trap (Vlčí jáma) (Cz), 138, 168, 174

Wolf's Cabin (Vlčí bouda) (Cz), 149, 155, 181-82
The Wolverine (BU). See The She-Wolf
Wolz—The Life and Work of a German Anarchist (Wolz—Leben und Verklarung eines deutschen Anarchisten) (EGr), 287, 293, 305
Woman and the Stranger, The (Die Frau und der Fremde) (EGr), 307
Woman at Thirty-three, A (Edna Zhena Na Trideset I Tri) (Bu), 374
Woman for One Season, A (O femeie pentru un anotimp) (Ro), 318, 331, 336
Woman in a Hat, The (Kobieta w Kapeluscu) (Po), 106
Woman Who Invented Love, The (Zhenshchina, kotoraya izobrela liubov) (SU), 39
Women (Hu). See The Two of Them
Women's Destiny (Frauenschicksale) (EGr), 280, 286, 291, 297
Woodpeckers Don't Get Headaches (Ne bolit golova u diatla) (SU), 21, 60
World Belongs to Us, The (Svět patřínám) (Cz), 132, 133, 156, 168
World Knows Nothing, The (Svet nic nevi) (Cz), 182
World Snack Bar, The (Automat svět) (Cz), 176
Worries (Trápení) (Cz), 158, 159, 164
Wozzeck (EGr), 278-79, 296

Yankee Doodle Dandy (Am), 230
Year of the Quiet Sun, The (Rok Spokojnego Słonca) (Po), 92, 98, 100, 110, 127
Years of Love (Godini za Lyubov) (Bu), 365, 367
Years of Struggle (Po). See Soldier of Victory
Yesterday Indeed (Naprawdę Wczoraj) (Po), 106, 108, 119
Yiddle with his Fiddle (Yidl Mitn Fidl) (Po), 71
You (Te) (Hu), 249, 266
You (Tu), (Ro), 330
You and I (Ty i ya) (SU), 44

FILM INDEX

Vow, The (Kliatva) (SU), 14, 35, 55
Vyborg Side, The (Vyborgskaia storona) (SU), 40

WR: Mysteries of the Organism (WR: Mysterije organizma) (Yu), 197, 209, 216, 223
Wages of Fear (Bu), 355–56
Waiting for a Train (Asteptind un tren) (Ro), 322, 331, 340
Walkover (Walkower) (Po), 85, 107, 120
Wall, The (Mur) (Po), 96
Wall, The (Zidul) (Ro), 331, 338
Wandering (Bloudení) (Cz), 176
Wandering, The (Rătăcire) (Ro), 322, 330, 339
War and Peace (Voina i mir) (SU), 34, 59
War for Independence (Ro), 311, 332
War of the Worlds—The Next Century (Wojna Światów—Nastepne Stulecie) (Po), 108, 109
Ward No. 9 (A 9-es kórterem) (Hu), 242, 264
Waranty for One Year (Bürgschaft für ein Jahr) (EGr), 287, 306
Warning, The (Predouprezhdeniyet) (Bu), 374
Warriors, The-The Dacians (Dacii) (Ro), 317, 329, 336
Warsaw Priemiere (Warszawska Premiera) (Po), 73, 106, 113
Water As a Black Buffalo (Apa ca un bivol negru) (Ro), 320, 331, 337
Waterloo (SU), 34
Way of Youth, The (Droga Mlodych) (Po), 70
Way Up, The (Der Weg nach oben) (EGr), 294, 297
We Are Alone in the World (Po), 81
We Are From Kronstadt (My iz Kronstadta) (SU), 14, 53
We Eat the Fruit of the Tree of Paradise (Ovoce stromů rajských jíme) (Cz), 143, 161, 178
We Were Young (A Byahme Mladi) (Bu), 347, 365, 368

Wedding, The (Wesele) (Po), 77, 103, 109, 123
Wedding in the Coral Sea (Cz), 135
Wedding-Night in the Rain (Hochzeits Nacht im Regen) (EGr), 302
Week in the Quiet House (Týden v tichém domě) (Cz), 160, 172
Welcome! (Dobro pozhalovat) (SU), 39, 58
Westerplatte (Po), 106, 110, 121
When Father Was Away on Business (Otac na službenom putu) (Yu), 207, 208, 215, 226
When I am Pale and Dead (Kad badem mrtav i beo) (Yu), 197, 217, 221
When Joseph Returns (Ha megjön József) (Hu), 254, 263, 265, 271
When the Strings Weep (Když struny lkají) (Cz), 171
When You Grow Up, Dear Adam (Wenn du gross bist, lieber Adam) (EGr), 291, 301
Where Are You Going? (Bu), 358
Where is the General? (Gdzie Jest Generał?) (Po), 97, 119
Where to Find Nophelet (SU), 25
Whichever Way the Ball Bounces (Kud Puklo da puklo) (Yu), 205
White Bird with a Black Spot (Be lain ptitsa s chernoi otmetinoi) (SU), 38
White Dove, The (Holubice) (Cz), 141, 167, 174
White Eagle, The (Belyi orel) (SU), 42, 50
White Magic (Byala Magiya) (Bu), 357, 374
White Moor, The (Harap Alb) (Ro), 318, 330, 335
White Night, The (Intunerical alb) (Ro), 325, 340
White Nights (Am), 107
White Nights (Belye nochi) (SU), 43
White Plague, The (Bílá nemoc) (Cz), 131, 134, 156, 157, 171
White Room, The (Byalata Staya) (Bu), 349, 370
White Trial (Procesul alb) (Ro), 315, 317, 328, 335

Uncle Marin, the Multimillionaire (Ro), 321, 329, 339
Uncle Vanya (Diadia Vania) (SU), 17, 41, 45, 60
Undefeatable, The (Die Unbesiegbaren) (EGr), 281, 298
Under the Pear Tree (Unterm Birnbaum) (EGr), 305
Under the Phrygian Star (Pod Gwiazdą Frygijska) (Po), 74, 100, 109, 113–14
Under the Yoke (Pod Igoto) (Bu), 360, 366
Underdog, The (EGr). *See* The Kaiser's Lackey
Underground (Subteranul), (Ro), 317, 336
Unfaithful Marijka, The (Marijka nevěrnice) (Cz), 167
Unfinished House, The (Casa neterminata) (Ro), 325
Unfinished Piece for Player Piano (Neokonchennaia p'esa dlia mekhanicheskogo pianino) (SU), 21, 41, 61
Unfinished Sentence, The (141 perc a befejezetlen mondatbol) (Hu), 262
Unfinished Story (Neokonchennaya povest) (SU), 56
Unforgettable Year 1919, The (Nezabyvaemyi 1919 god) (SU), 55
Uninteresting Story, An (Nieciekawa Historia) (Po), 99–100, 126
Unknown Soldier's Patent Leather Shoes, The (Lachenite Obouvki na Nezhainiya) (Bu), 355, 364, 373
Unsmiling Giaconda, The/Giaconda Without That Smile (Gioconda fara suris) (Ro), 318, 331, 336
Upthrown Stone, The (Feddobott kö) (Hu), 255, 266, 270

Vabank (Po), 91, 103, 126
Vabank II (Po), 91, 103, 126
Vacancies Tragiques (Ro), 331, 339
Valentina (SU), 62–63
Valerie and Her Week of Wonders (Valérie a týden divů) (Cz), 132, 155, 158, 161, 162, 178
Valley of the Bees (Údoli včel) (Cz), 145, 159, 167, 177
Valley of the Seven Moons, The (EGr), 301
Valley Resounds, The (Răsună valea) (Ro), 313, 326, 333
Value of Man, The (SU), 35
Variola Vera (Yu), 205, 216, 225
Vasili and Vasilisa (Vasilii i Vasilisa) (SU), 63
Vassa (SU), 42, 64
Velvet Revolution, The (Cz), 150
Verdict of Lake Balaton, The (Ítél a Balaton) (Hu), 232
Veronica (Ro), 322, 325, 337
Veronica Comes Back (Veronica se intoarce) (Ro), 322, 325, 338
Very Late Afternoon of a Faun, The (Faunovo příliš pozdní odpoledne) (Cz), 149, 155, 161, 181
Very Moral Night, A (Egy erkölcsös ejszaka) (Hu), 261, 264
Vesna (Yu), 191
Victory (Po). *See* Soldier of Victory
Victory (Pobeda) (SU), 53
Villa Zone (Vilna Zona) (Bu), 352, 362, 365, 372
Village Mill, The (Gromada) (Po), 74
Village on the Frontier (Ves v pohraničí) (Cz), 160, 172
Village Performance of Hamlet, A (Predstava Hamleta u selu Mrduša Donja) (Yu), 201, 223
Violin Solo in the Elves' Garden (Recital in grădina cu pitici) (Ro), 341
Virginity (Panenství) (Cz), 164
Virgo (Zodia fecioarei) (Ro), 315, 327, 336
Visit, The (Vizita) (Ro), 314, 327, 333
Visit to the Scene of the Crime—1901, The (Wizja Lokalna—1901) (Po), 95, 110, 125
Vlad the Impaler: The True Life of Dracula (Vlad Tepes) (Ro), 321, 339
Voice from the Next World, A (Glos z Tamtego Świata) (Po), 106, 117
Voices (Głosy) (Po), 101, 126
Volga-Volga (SU), 33, 38

Toughs, The (Delije) (Yu), 198
Town Will Die Tonite, A (Dziś W Nocy Umrze Miasto) (Po), 102, 106, 108, 117
Traces Remain, The (Sledite Ostavat) (Bu), 367
Track of Stones (Spur der Steine) (EGr), 284, 290, 301
Tractor Drivers (Traktoristy), (SU), 36
Train, The (Pociag) (Po), 97
Train Station for Two (Vokzal dlia dvoikh) (SU), 38, 41, 43, 64
Train Stopped, The (Ostanovilsia poezd) (SU), 63
Train to Heaven Station, The (Vlak do stanice nebe) (Cz), 158
Train Without a Time Schedule (Vlak bez voznog reda) (Yu), 192, 213, 219
Traitor (Izdajnik) (Yu), 198
Traitor (Predateol) (SU), 49–50
Transient Loves/These Fleeting Loves (Tre că toarele iubiri) (Ro), 320, 331, 338
Transport From Paradise (Transport z ráje) (Cz), 141, 144, 154, 175
Treasure (Skarb) (Po), 72, 108
Treasure of Vadu Vechi, The (Comoara din Vadul Vechi) (Ro), 314, 327, 335
Tree Without Roots, A (Darvo Bez Koren) (Bu), 352, 361–62, 371
Trial on the Road (Proverka na dorogakh) (SU), 21, 34–35, 37–38, 65
Tricks of Deceptive Love (Lásky hry šálivé) (Cz), 160
Trip to Sundevit, The (Die Reise nach Sundevit) (EGr), 290, 301
Trip to Wisbaden, A (Puteshestraviye v Visbaden) (SU), 66–67
Trotter's Gait, The (Beg inokhodtsa) (SU), 46
Troubled Home (Nespokoen Dom) (Bu), 365, 369
Troubled Road, The (Nespokoen Pat) (Bu), 360, 367
Trout, The (La Truite), 105
Truck, The (Kamionat) (Bu), 355–56, 373
True End of the War, The (Prawdziwy Koniec Wielkiej Wojny) (Po), 74, 100–101, 103, 109, 115
True Friends (Vernye druzia) (SU), 56
Trunk and the Trousseau, The (Lada cu zestre) (Ro), 328, 335
Tsar and Carpenter (Zar und Zimmerman) (EGr), 281, 298
Tsar and General (Tsar I General) (Bu), 363, 369
Tudor (Ro), 316, 325, 335
Tunnel (Tunelul) (Ro/SU), 317, 328, 336
Turksib (SU), 51
Turning Point, The (Der Auftenhalt) (EGr), 290, 306
Turning Point, The (Povorot) (SU), 62
Turnover (Krugovorot) (SU), 65
Twenty Days Without War (Dvadtsat' dnei bez voiny) (SU), 21, 38, 61
Twenty Hours (Húsz óra) (Hu), 262, 266
25 Fireman Street (Tüzoltó utca 25) (Hu), 250–51, 255, 261, 266, 270
24 Hours of Rain (Chassa Du zhd) (Bu), 374
26 Days in the Life of Dostoevsky (26 dnei v zhizni Dostoevskogo) (SU), 63
Two (Dvoje) (Yu), 194, 217, 220
Two Brigades (Dwie Brygady) (Po), 73
Two Grownups and a Child (Dvoye i Odna) (SU), 66
Two Half-Times in Hell (Két félidö a pokolban) (Hu), 262
Two Lottery Tickets (Doua Lozuri) (Ro), 314, 327, 334
Two Men and a Wardrobe (Dwaj Ludzie z Szafa) (Po), 101, 106
Two Mothers (Zwei Mütter) (EGr), 282, 290, 299
Two of Them/Women, The (Ök ketten) (Hu), 247, 258 n.2, 265, 271
Two Victories (Dve Pobedi) (Bu), 361
Two Worlds and One Love (Doua lumi si o dragoste) (Ro/Hu), 312,
Two Worlds and One Love (Doua lumi si o dragoste) (Ro/Hu), 312, 333
Tyrant's Heart, The (A zsarnok szíve) (Hu), 241

Uncertain Season (Nejistá sezóna) (Cz), 182

(Nyama Nishto Pohubavo ot Loshoto Vreme) (Bu), 360
These Fleeting Loves (Ro). *See* Transient Loves
They Called Him Amigo (Sie nannten ihn amigo) (EGr), 283, 290, 300
Third Blow, The (Tretty udar) (SU), 14
Third One, The (Der Dritte) (EGr), 286, 291, 303
Third Part of the Night, The (Trzecia Część Nocy) (Po), 89, 96, 110, 122
Third Planet in the Solar System (Treta Sled Slantseto) (Bu), 351
Third Round (Bu), 358
Third Wish, The (Třetí přání) (Cz), 139, 140, 174
Thirst (Setea) (Ro), 316, 326, 330, 335
Thirteen, The (Trinadstsat) (SU), 43
13th October, The (Der 13. Oktober) (EGr), 278, 294, 297
This Love Must Die (Trzeba Zabić Te Miłość) (Po), 104
This People Must Live (Živjeće ovaj narod) (Yu), 188
Thistles of Baragan, The (Ciulinii Bărăganului) (Ro/Fr), 316, 331, 334
Those Over Forty Today (Die heute über vierzig sind) (EGr), 284, 300
Those Wonderful Movie Cranks (Báječní muzú s klikou) (Cz), 162
Three (Tri) (Yu), 196, 197, 217, 220–21
Three Apples (Tre mere) (Ro), 330
Three Million Case, The (Protsess o trekh millionakh) (SU), 38, 50
Three Reserve Officers (Trimata Ot Zapasa) (Bu), 371
Three Songs of Lenin (Tri pesni o Lenine) (SU), 13, 46, 52
Three Starts (Trzy Starty) (Po), 103, 114
Three Stories (Trzy Powiesci) (Po), 73, 106
322 (Cz), 156
Three's Happiness (Za sreću je potrebno troje) (Yu), 205, 227
Throatful of Strawberries, A (Jagode u grlu) (Yu), 204, 215, 226
Through and Through (Na Wylot) (Po), 89, 122

Through Mountains—Through Valleys (Cz), 156, 163
Tight Spot, The (Tesna koža) (Yu), 210
'Til Death Do Us Part (Bis dass der Tod euch scheidet) (EGr), 290, 307
Til Eulenspiegel (SU), 61
Till Eulenspiegel (EGr), 305
Time (Ido van) (Hu), 262
Time for Life, The (Zeit zumleben) (EGr), 293, 302
Time of Desires (Vremia zhelanii) (SU), 43
Time of Parting (Bu), 358
Time of the Gypsies (Dom za vešanje) (Yu), 207, 208, 215, 216, 227–28
Time of the Storks (Zeit der Störche) (EGr), 292, 302
Time Stands Still (Megáll az idö) (Hu), 256, 262, 264, 272
"Time Unites or Divides, The" ("Czas przybliza, czas oddala") (Po), 118
Tin Drum, The (WGr), 100, 105
Titania, Titania (Hu), 246, 260, 273
Titanic Waltz (Titanic-vals) (Ro), 326, 335
To Die from Love of Life (Să mori rărit din dragoste de viaţă) (Ro), 322, 331, 340
To Kill a Bird of Prey (Lovind o pasăre de prada) (Ro), 341
Tobacco (Tutyun) (Bu), 362, 368
Today and Tomorrow (Ma és holnap) (Hu), 230
Tonka, Tart of the Gallows (Tonka šibenice) (Cz), 134, 164, 171
Too Skinny for Love? (Für Liebe noch zu mager?) (EGr), 304
Too Small for Such a Big War (Prea mic pentru un razboi atit de mare) (Ro), 320, 337
Top Dog (Po), 91
Top Secret (Streng geheim) (EGr), 300
Torrid Noon (Goreshto Pladne) (Bu), 369
Tortured Imagination (Muka obraznosti) (Cz), 183
Toth Family, The (Isten hozta, örnagy úr) (Hu), 262
Tough Kids (Patsany) (SU), 64

Sun Is Far Away, The (Daleko je sunce) (Yu), 192
Sun Rises, The (Răsare soarele) (Ro), 314, 329, 334
Sun Rises Once a Day, The (Słonce Wschodzi Raz na Dzien) (Po), 86, 101, 105, 122
Sun Seekers, The (Die Sonnensucher) (EGr), 283, 295, 299
Sunday at Six (Duminică la ora 6) (Ro), 317, 329, 335
Sunday Marches (Nedelnite Machove) (Bu), 372
Sunday of Justice (Niedziela Sprwiedliwości) (Po), 120
Sunday Romance, A (Bakaruhaban) (Hu), 235, 261, 262, 266, 269
Sunday II (Nedelja II) (Yu), 206
Sunshine in a Net (Slnko v sieti) (Cz), 141, 166, 175
Superfluous (Prekobrojna) (Yu), 213
Superior Toys—Made in the USA (Feine Spielwaren—Made in USA) (EGr), 302
Suvorov (SU), 42, 54
Suzanne and the Magic Ring (Susanne und der Zauberring) (EGr), 304
Svejk (Cz–192(7?)), 133
Svejk (Cz–1955), 166
Swan Lake: The Zone (SU/Ukraine/Swed/Can), 26
Swan Song (Labedzi Spiew) (Po), 95
Swap (Trampa) (Bu), 354, 361, 373
Sweet Movie (Can/Fr/WGr), 209, 216
Swelling Melodies (Rauschende Melodien) (EGr), 281, 298
Swimming Pool, The (Basseynat) (Bu), 354, 365, 372

Tailor from Torzhok, The (Zakroischchik iz Tozhka) (SU), 38
Taiwan Canasta (Tajvanska kanasta) (Yu), 205, 226
Take Care When You Kiss (Hut ab, wenn du küsst) (EGr), 302
Take Off, The (Vzlet) (SU), 63
Taken for a Ride (Bockshorn) (EGr), 290, 306

Taras Shevchenko (SU), 55
"Teacher, The" ("Nouczycielka") (Po), 118
Teacher of Oriental Languages (Učitel orientálních jazyků) (Cz), 169
Teacher, Teacher (Majstori, majstori) (Yu), 205
Technique and Rite (La tecnic ed il rito) (It), 240
Teddy'd Like a Smoke (Teddy by kouřil) (Cz), 169
Telegram (Telegramma) (SU), 34
Ten Thousand Suns (Tizezer nap) (Hu), 254–55, 264, 266, 269
Tenth Muse, The (Dziesiąta Muza) (Po), 70
Test, The (Ispit) (Bu), 361
Test Shots (Zdjcia Próbne) (Po), 98, 99, 124
Teutonic Knights (Krzy zacy) (Po), 84, 99, 100, 107, 108, 116
That Ye Inherit/The Land of the Miraculous Rabbis (Add tudtul fiadnak) (Hu/WGr), 254
That's Life (Takový je život) (Cz), 159, 170
Their Ordinary Days (Ich Dzień Powszedni) (Po), 97, 118
Theme (Tema) (SU), 21, 42
Then Came the Legend (Ro), 325, 336
Then Laugh, That's Life (Rideti ca-n viota) (Ro), 325, 341
There Is No Death (Smurt Nyama) (Bu), 347–48
There Was an Old Man and an Old Woman (Zhili byli starik so starukhoi) (SU), 35, 40
There Was Jazz (Był Jazz) (Po), 89, 96, 98, 126–27
There Won't Be Any More Divorces (Rozwodów Nie Bedzie) (Po), 119
There's a Bagful of Fleas at the Ceiling (U stropu je pytel blech) (Cz), 155, 175
There's a Certain Fellow (Zhivet takoi paren) (SU), 44, 58
There's Nothing Finer Than Bad Weather

Stars (Sterne/Zdezdi) (EGr/Bu), 281, 282, 295, 300, 347, 364, 368
Stars in Her Hair, Tears in Her Eyes (Zvezdi V Kossite, Salzi V Ochite) (Bu), 354, 364
Start (Anlauf) (EGr), 286, 291, 302
Status—Orderly (Slouzhebno Polozheniye—Ordinarests) (Bu), 358, 373
Steamroller and the Violin, The (Katok i skripka) (SU), 45, 57
Steep Path, The (Stramnata Pateka) (Bu), 368
Stefan Luchian (Ro), 321, 340
Stenka Razin (SU), 36, 47
Step by Step (EGr), 300
Stephen the Great (Stefan cel mare) (Ro), 331
Steppe, The (Step) (SU), 61–62
Steps to the Moon (Pasi spre lună) (Ro), 318, 330, 335
Steps Toward the Sky (Trepte spre cer) (Ro), 325, 339
Still Lacking a Good Title (Za sada bez dobrog naslova) (Yu), 204, 227
Stolen Bomb (S a furat o bombă) (Ro), 318, 330, 335
Stolen Frontier (Uloupená hranice) (Cz), 136, 168
Stone Wedding (Nuntă de Pietră) (Ro), 320, 329, 331, 338
Stories About Lenin (Rasskazy o Lenine) (SU), 57
Stories of that Night (EGr), 301
Storm Over Asia (SU). *See* The Heir to Genghis-Khan
Stormy Bird (Pasărea furtunii) (Ro), 314, 329, 334
Stormy Night (O Noapte Furtunosa) (Ro), 311, 327, 333
Story in Red, A (Opowieść w Czerwieni) (Po), 123
Story of a Factory (Yu), 189
Story of a Girl (Povest ob odroi devushke) (SU), 35
Story of a Young Couple (Roman einer Ehe) (EGr), 280, 292, 297
Story of Love, The (Povesta Dragostei) (Ro), 339

Story of Sin, The (Oziege Grzechu) (Po), 96, 109, 123
Strahil the Voyvoda (Strahil Voyvoda) (Bu), 344–45
Strange Adventure of Herr Fridolin B., The (Die seltsamen Abenteuer des (Herrn) Fridolin B.) (EGr), 279, 294, 296
Strange Duel (Stranen Dvuboy) (Bu), 364
Strange Love Affair, A (Eine sonderbare Liebe) (EGr), 295, 306
Strange People (Strannye liudi) (SU), 22, 44
Strange Woman, A (Strannaia zhenshchina) (SU), 43, 62
Stranger (Strainul) (Ro), 330, 335
Strangler vs. Strangler (Davitelj protiv davitelja) (Yu), 207, 218, 226
Straw Bells (SU), 39
Street Legion, The (Legion Vlicy) (Po), 71, 98
Streets Have Memories (Strazile au amintiri) (Ro), 327, 335
Stride, Soviet! (Shagai, Soviet!) (SU), 46, 50
Strike, The (Siréna) (Cz), 136, 172
Strike (Stachka) (SU), 8–9, 36, 49
Strong Man (Silnyi chelovek) (SU), 3
Strong Water (Silna Voda) (Bu), 364, 372
Stronger Than the Night (Stärker als die Nacht) (EGr), 281, 291, 298
Stud Farm, The (A ménesgazda) (Hu), 244, 263, 264, 271
Submissive, The (EGr). *See* The Kaiser's Lackey
Suburban Legend (Külvárosi legenda) (Hu), 235, 265, 267, 269
Such is Life (Cz), 135
Summer of White Roses, The (Yu/Br), 206
Summer Tale (Tănase Scatiu) (Ro), 321, 329, 339
A Summer to Remember (Serezha) (SU), 35, 57
Summons for the Queen (Cz), 146
Sun and Shadow (Slantseto i Syankata) (Bu), 347, 362, 364, 368

FILM INDEX

Sindbad (Szindbád) (Hu), 253–54, 255, 261, 263, 264, 265, 266, 270
Sing Your Song, Poet (Poi pesniu, poet) (SU), 46
Single-Handed (Capcana) (Ro), 319, 327, 330, 337
Sirocco/Winter Wind (Sirokkó) (Hu), 240
681 A.D. (Bu). *See* Khan Asparukh
Sixth of the World, A (Shestaia chast mira) (SU), 50
Sketches in Charcoal (Szkice Weglem) (Po), 107
Skid (Smyk) (Cz), 138, 174
Skinny and Others (Chudy i Inni) (Po), 86, 101, 120
Sky Begins on the Third Floor, The (Ro), 328
Soldiers Without Uniform (Soldati fara uniforma) (Ro), 328, 335
Solemn Heartlessness (Skorbnoe beschuvstvie) (SU), 45, 65
Soliaris (SU), 19, 45, 60
Solo Sailor, The (EGr), 287, 307
Solo Sunny (EGr), 288, 295, 306
Solvay Dossier, The (Geheimakten Solvay) (EGr), 280, 292, 297
Solovetsky Power (SU), 24
Some Days in the Life of I. I. Oblomov (Neskolko dnei iz zhizni I.I. Oblomova) (SU), 21, 41, 63
Some Interviews on Personal Matters (Neskolko interviu po lichnym voprosam) (SU), 21, 38, 62
Somersault, The (Salto) (Po), 97, 102–3, 120
Something In-Between (Nešto izmedu) (Yu), 204, 215, 225
Somewhere in Berlin (Irgendwo in Berlin) (EGr), 277, 296
Somewhere in Europe (Valahol Európában) (Hu), 233, 242, 261, 265, 268
Son, The (Syn), 67
Song About Happiness (Pesnia o schaste) (SU), 37
Song of Gold, The (Zpěvzlata) (Cz), 163, 170
Song of Man (Pessen sa Choveka) (Bu), 346, 361, 366

Song of the Cornfields (Ének a búzamezökröl) (Hu), 232, 261, 266
Song of the Prairie (Arie prérie) (Cz), 166
Song of Triumphant Love (Pesn torzhestvuyushchei liubvi) (SU), 39, 47
Sonnenbrucks (EGr), 297
Sons of the Great Bear (Die Sohne der grossen Bärin) (EGr), 284, 301
Sorrows of Young Werther, The (Die Leiden des jungen Werthers) (EGr), 286, 287, 291, 305
Sound Eroticism (Egészséges erótika) (Hu), 256, 273
Souvenir of Cellulose (Po), 74
Spare Moment, A (Ro), 323, 341
Special Education (Specijalno vaspitanje) (Yu), 205, 216, 224
Special Issue (Editie speciala) (Ro), 322, 326, 339
Special Peculiarities: None (EGr), 281, 292
Special Treatment (Poseban tretman) (Yu), 203–4, 225
Speech for the Defense (Slovo dlia zashchity) (SU), 61
Spell of the River, The (Reka caruje) (Cz), 160
Spiral (Spirala) (Po), 88, 101–2, 104, 110, 124
Spirit of Gold, The (Dahul aurului) (Ro), 320, 338
Spiritual Retreats (Rekolekcje) (Po), 124
Sports Humor (Vmor sportif) (Ro), 330
Spring Needs Time (Der Frühling braucht zeit) (EGr), 284, 301
Spring Shower/Marie (Tavaszi zápor) (Hu), 232, 262, 268
Spring Symphony (Frühlingssinfonie) (EGr), 287, 306
Springtime in Budapest (Budapesti tavasz) (Hu), 265
Staff, The (Personel) (Po), 101
Stake and the Flame, The (Rug si flacără) (Ro), 339
Stalker (SU), 19, 45, 62
Star Called Wormwood, A (Hvězda zvaná pelynek) (Cz), 156

Shadows of Forgotten Ancestors (Teni zabytkh predkov) (SU), 19–20, 38, 42, 58
Shadows Over Islands (Schatten uber Inseln) (EGr), 280, 297
Shame (Stud) (Cz), 157
Shchors (SU), 13, 16, 36, 54
She Defends Her Country (Ona zashchishchaet rodinu) (SU), 54
Sheep and Mammoths (Ovni in mamuti) (Yu), 209, 226
She-Wolf, The/The Wolverine (Valchitsata) (Bu), 348, 364, 369
Sheriff Teddy (EGr), 290, 299
She's a Leper (Tredowsata) (Po), 98
Shibil (Bu), 351, 370
Sidetrack (Bu). *See* Detour
Ship, The (Korabl) (SU), 65–66
Shop Crumbs (Pe chki lavochki) (SU), 44
Shop on Main Street, The (Obchod na korse) (Cz), 145, 159
Short History, A (Scurtă istorie) (Ro), 318, 330, 334
Short Sun/A Ray of Sunlight (Kratko Sluntse) (Bu), 355, 362
Shots in the Stave (Ro), 336
Shout, The (Br), 86
... Shucks, I'm Grown Up (... verdammt, ich bin erwachsen) (EGr), 304
Shy People (Am), 41
Siberiade, The (SU). *See* Sibiriana
Sky over the Veleka, The (Nebeto Na Veleka) (Bu), 370
Sky Without Bars (Cerul n-are gratii) (Ro), 317, 328, 335
Skylarks on a String (Skřivánci na niti) (Cz), 143, 144, 150, 157, 160, 162, 178
Slave of Love, A (Raba liubvi) (SU), 21, 41, 61
Slavica (Yu), 188, 213, 219
Small Train Robbery, The (Mala pljačka) (Yu), 226
Smell of a Dog's Coat (Zapach Psiej Siersci) (Po), 109
Smoke on the Potato Fields (Dym bramborove nate) (Cz), 148, 167, 179
Snatchers (Stiazhateli) (SU), 41

Snowball Reaction (Kopytem sein, kopytem tam) (Cz), 182
Snowdrop Festival, The (Slávnosti sněženek) (Cz), 147, 157, 162, 181
So Long As I Live (Solange Leber in mir ist) (EGr), 293, 301
So Long, Friends (Sbogom, Pryatelya) (Bu), 352
So Many Dreams (EGr), 307
Soap Bubbles (Seifenblasen) (EGr), 290–91
Social Games (Društvena igra) (Yu), 204
Sofka (Yu), 189, 192, 219
Soil under Your Feet, The (Talpalatnyi föld) (Hu), 232, 242, 264, 266
Soimaresti Family, The (Neamul Soimarestilor) (Ro), 326, 335
Soldier of Victory (Zolnierz zwyciestwa); Pt. I: Years of Struggle (Lata walki); Pt. 2: Victory (Zwyciestwa) (Po), 73, 109, 113
Soldiers, The (Soldaty) (SU), 45
Sibiriana/The Siberiade (Sibiriada) (SU), 21, 38, 41, 62
Sick Animals (Animale bolnave) (Ro), 337
Sick White Elephant, The (Nemocný bílý sion) (Cz), 183
Sidetrack (Bu). *See* Detour
Siege (Asediul) (Ro), 328, 337
Siegfrid (Zygfryd) (Po), 128
Sign of the Crab, The (Znamení Raka) (Cz), 157
Signals (Sygnaty) (Po), 116
Silence (Milczenie) (Po), 97, 118
Silence and Cry (Csend és kiáltás) (Hu), 239, 263, 264, 267, 269
Silent Barricade (Němá barikáda) (Cz), 136
Silent Joy (Tichá radosť) (Cz), 148, 156, 181
Silent Night (Wśród Nocnej Ciszy) (Po), 124
Silvery Wind (Stříbrný vítr) (Cz), 138, 139, 160, 173
Simple Case, A (Prostoi sluchai) (SU), 2, 13, 42, 52
Sin (Pagat) (Ro), 311, 328, 332

FILM INDEX

St. Johan's Rapids, The (Svatojanské proudy) (Cz), 134
Saint Teresa and the Devil (Sainte Thérèse et le diable) (Ro), 328
St. Wenceslas (Svatý Václav) (Cz), 135, 160, 170
Salt for Svanetia (Sol Svanetii) (SU), 39
Salt of the Black Earth (Sól Ziemi Czarnej) (Po), 87, 102, 103, 122
Salvation, The (Ocalenie) (Po), 99, 110, 122
Samson (Po), 90, 96, 102, 110
Sanatorium Under the Sign of the Hourglass, The (Santorium pod Klepsydra (Po), 83, 99, 104, 110, 122
Sancta Simplicitas (Ro), 330
Sand Castle (Pešćeni grad) (Yu), 195, 199, 215, 220
Satiemania (Yu), 210
Saturday Night Dance (Ro), 320, 330, 336
Scalpel, Please (Skalpel, prosiń) (Cz), 166, 181
Scar, A (Blizna) (Po), 101, 105, 108, 123
Scarecrow (Chuchelo) (SU), 23, 34, 64
Scenes from the Life of Shock Workers (Slike iz života udarnika) (Yu), 200, 214, 223
Scent of Wild Flowers, The (Miris poljskog cveća) (Yu), 204, 215, 223–24
School for Fathers (Skola otců) (Cz), 138–39, 157, 173
Scrawny and Others (Chudy i Inni) (Po), 105
Scream, The (Kryzk) (Po), 91, 106, 126
Season of Monsters (Szörnyek évadja) (Hu), 241, 261, 263, 264, 273
Seclusion Near a Forest (Na samotě u lesa) (Cz), 147, 162, 165, 166, 179
Second Life of Friedrich Wilhelm Georg Platow, The (Das zweite Leben des Friedrich Wilhelm Georg Platow) (EGr), 286, 292, 303
Second Rib, The (Dwa żebra Adama) (Po), 119
Second Track, The (EGr), 300

Secret, A (Sekret) (Po), 122
Secret Code, The (Secrtul cifralui) (Ro), 325, 334
Secret of Bacchus, The (Secretual lui Bachus) (Ro), 321, 330, 341
Secret Supper of the Sedmaks, The (Taynata Vecherya Na Sematsite) (Bu), 360, 367
See You in Hell, Fellows (Cz), 158
Semmelweis—Savior of Mothers (Semmelweis—Retter der Mütter) (EGr), 279, 297
Sensitive Spot (Cz), 150, 182
Senta Goes Astray (Senta auf Abwegen) (EGr), 282–83, 292, 300
Separation, The (Rozstanie) (Po), 99, 102, 104, 117
September (Septembrie) (Ro), 339
September Love (Septemberliebe) (EGr), 283, 292, 300
September Nights (Zářijové noci) (Cz), 138, 158, 173
Septembrists, The (Septemvriytsi) (Bu), 345, 364, 365, 366
Sequences (Ro), 323, 330, 341
Sergeant Kelan (Ogniomistrz Kalen) (Po), 105
Seven Arts, The (Sapte arte) (Ro), 318, 330, 334
Seven Days (Sapte Zile) (Ro), 320, 331, 338
Seven from the Rhine (Seben vom Rhein) (EGr), 281, 294, 298
Seventh Day, Eighth Night (Den sedmý, osmá noc) (Cz), 144, 164
Seventh Year (Das siebente Jahre) (EGr), 285, 302
Severe Young Man, A (Strogii yunosha) (SU), 44
Sex Mission (Seksmisja) (Po), 91, 103, 108, 126
Shades of Ferns, The (Stín kpradiny) (Cz), 148, 167
Shadow (Cien) (Po), 74, 103, 114
Shadow Line, The (Smuga Cienia) (Po), 100, 106, 110, 123
Shadows of a Hot Summer (Stíny horkého léta) (Cz), 148, 167

Restricted Key, The (Kliuch bez prava peredachi) (SU), 21, 61
Return, The (Povratak) (Yu), 196
Return, The (Powrot) (Po), 102, 105
Return from Hell (Intoarcerea din iad) (Ro), 341
Return of King Lăpusneanu, The (Intoareerea Lui Vodă Lăpusneanu) (Ro), 321, 331, 339
Return of Maxim, The (Vozvrashchenie Maksima) (SU), 40, 53
Return [Revenge] of the Haiduks [Outlaws] (Razbunarea hiaducilor) (Ro), 316, 326, 336
Return of the Prodigal Son (Návrat ztraceného syna) (Cz), 144, 154, 159, 164, 177
Return of Vasily Bortnikov, The (Vozvrashchenie Vasili Bortnikova) (SU), 13, 42, 55
Revenge, The (Ro), 322, 329, 339
Revolutionary Year, 1848, The (Revoluční rok 1848) (Cz), 158, 160, 165
Revolutionist, The (Revolutsioner) (SU), 34, 48
Rich Bride, The (Bogataya nevesta) (SU), 36
Richard III (Br), 157
Riddance (Szabad lélegzet) (Hu), 265
Ripe Cherries (Reife Kirschen) (EGr), 286, 293, 303
River, The (Řeka) (Cz), 131, 164, 165, 171
Road to Life, The/A Pass to Life (Putëvka v zhizn) (SU), 14–15, 34, 51
Robinson Warszawski (Po), 72–73, 95
Rock and roll's/woolf (Ro), 325
Role of My Family in the World Revolution, The (Uloga moje porodice u svetskoj revoluciji) (Yu), 200, 214
Romance (Cz), 176
Romance for Flugelhorn (Romance pro křídlovka) (Cz), 134, 167
Romanian Farmer (Arendaşul roman) (Ro), 314, 327, 333
Romanian People in the Fight for Democracy, The (Poporul roman in luptă pentru democraţie) (Ro), 313, 328, 333

Romanticism (Romantika) (Hu), 254, 263, 264, 266, 270
Rome Wants Another Caesar (Roma rivuole Cesare) (It), 240
Romeo, Juliet, and the Darkness (Romeo, Júlie, a tma) (Cz), 138, 174
Rondo (Yu), 199, 221
Roof, The (Pokriu) (Bu), 355, 373
Room Overlooking the Sea, The (Pokój z Widokiem na Morze) (Po), 89, 99, 110, 124
Rose-Tinted Dreams (Ružové sny) (Cz), 148, 156, 179–80
Rosina the Foundling (Rozina sebranec) (Cz), 172
Rotation (EGr), 279, 297
Round-Up (Razzia) (EGr), 296
Round-Up, The (Szegénylegények) (Hu), 236, 237–38, 263, 264, 266, 268
"Rubble films" (Trümmerfilme) (EGr), 277, 294
Ruined Shopkeeper, The (U sněděného krámu) (Cz), 134
Run, Waiter, Run (Vrchní, prchni) (Cz), 166, 180
Runaway Train (Am), 41
Russia of Nikolai II and Lev Tolstoy, The (Rossiia Nikolaia II i Lev Tolstoi) (SU), 44
Russian Miracle, The (Das Russische Wunder) (EGr), 293, 294, 300
Russian Question, The (Russkii vopros) (SU), 55
Russians Are Coming, The (EGr), 290, 302
Rust (Rdza) (Po), 124
Ruthless Romance, A (Zhestoki romans) (SU), 41, 43, 64

S.V.D. (SU). *See* The Club of the Big Deed
Sabine Kleist, 7 (Sabine Kleist, 7 Jahre) (EGr), 306
Sabra (Po), 71
Sacrifice, The (Fr/Swed), 19, 45
Sailors' Song (Das Lied der Matrosen) (EGr), 282, 283, 292, 293, 299

FILM INDEX

(Pometej s otoka Viševice) (Yu), 198, 220
Promotion, The (Awans) (Po), 123
Promised Land, The (Ziemia Obiecana) (Po), 106, 107, 109
Prophet, Gold and the Transylvanians, The (Proteful, aurul si ardele nii) (Ro), 321, 329, 339
Prosecutor, The (Prokirorat) (Bu), 370
Provincial Actors (Aktorzy prowincjonalni) (Po), 89, 98, 99, 105, 108, 124
Provincial Woman, A (Kobieta z Prowincji) (Po), 91, 96, 98, 127
Pugowitza (EGr), 306
Punch and Judy (Radvičkárna) (Cz), 166, 177
Punishment, The (Osinda) (Ro), 321, 329, 339
Puzzle (Rebus) (Po), 110, 124
Pyramid for Me, A (Eine Pyramide für mich) (EGr), 305

Quack, The (Znachor) (Po), 96, 98, 126
Quarterly Balance-Taking, The (Bilano Kwartalny) (Po), 88, 98, 99, 100, 101, 123
Que Viva Mexico! (SU), 33, 36
Queen of Spades (Pickovaya dama) (SU), 3, 41
Question Time (Subessednik Po Zhelanie) (Bu), 375
Quiet Don, The, Pts. I, II, and III (Tikhi Don) (SU), 37, 56
Quiet Paths (Malchalivite Pateki) (Bu), 369–70
Quiet Week at Home, A (Tichý týden u dome) (Cz), 166, 178
Quo vadis, homo sapiens (Ro), 330

Rabbit Case, The (Causa králik) (Cz), 159, 180
Rabbit Is Me, The (Das Kaninchen bin ich) (EGr), 284, 293, 301
Rabid (Wściekły) (Po), 125
Radio Romania Keeps Broadcasting (Ro), 323, 341
Radopolje (Yu), 215

Raft of Medusa (Splav meduze) (Yu), 209, 214, 225
Rainbow, The (Raduga) (SU), 36
Raindrops, Waters, Warriors (Kapi, vode, ratnici) (Yu), 195
Rally, The (Le Rallye) (Ro), 327
Rape of the Maidens (Ro), 316, 326, 336
Rasputin (Agoniia) (SU), 21, 39, 64
Ray of Sunlight, A (Bu). *See* Short Sun
Recollections from Childhood (Ro), 325
Reconstruction (Reconstituirra) (Ro), 317, 318, 329, 337
Recovery (Genesung) (EGr), 282, 295, 298
Red and Gold (Czerwone i Zlote) (Po), 121
Red and the White, The (Csillagosok, katonák) (Hu), 238–39, 263, 269
Red Apples (Mere Rosii) (Ro), 322, 330, 339
Red Boogie (Rdeči boogie) (Yu), 209
Red Countess, The (A vörös grófnö) (Hu), 244–45, 264, 273
Red Guelder Rose, The (Kalina krasnaia) (SU), 22
Red Horse, The (Crveni konj) (Yu), 208, 217
Red Imps (Krasnye diavolata) (SU), 48
Red Psalm (Még kér a nép) (Hu), 240–41, 261, 263, 264, 270
Red Snowball Bush, The (Kalina krasnaya) (SU), 44
Red Tent, The (Krasnaia palatka) (SU), 39
Red Water Lily, The (Nufăul rosu) (Ro), 315, 334
Red Wheat, The (Rdeče klasje) (Yu), 197, 222
Reference (Herakteristika) (Bu), 375
Reiterate the Warning (Cz), 132
Rendezvous at the Mill (Dostavenićko ve mlynici) (Cz), 130, 160, 169
Repentance (Pokaianie) (SU), 23, 33, 66
Report on the Party and the Guests (Oslávnosti a hostech) (Cz), 144, 146, 161, 162, 165, 177
Reportage 1957 (EGr), 299
Requiem (Hu), 262

FILM INDEX   429

Other People's Children (Chuzhie deti),
   33
Other Person, The (A másik ember)
   (Hu), 264
Other Side of the Bridge, The (Dincolo
   de pod) (Ro), 320, 338
Other Woman, The (SU), 43
Our Daily Bread (Unser täglich Brot)
   (EGr), 278, 291, 297
Our Director (Directorul nostru) (Ro),
   314, 327, 334
Our Short Life (Unser Kurzes Leben)
   (EGr), 294–95, 306
Out in the World (V liudiakh) (SU), 35
Out of Love (Cz), 150
Outbreak (Kitörés) (Hu), 245, 260, 270
Outskirts (Okraina) (SU), 14, 34, 40
Overcoat, The (Shinel–1959) (SU), 17,
   34
Owners, The (Proprietarii) (Ro), 320,
   338
Oxygen (Oksigen) (Yu), 200, 215

Pacifista, La (It), 240
Painlevé Case, The (Sluchayat Penleve)
   (Bu), 363, 370
Palaces and Huts (Schlösser und Katen)
   (EGr), 282, 292, 299
Pale Light of Sorrow, The (Lumina Pìida
   a Durerii) (Ro), 322, 328, 340
Palm Sunday (Virágvasárnap) (Hu), 262
Panteley (Bu), 363, 373
Pants of the Knight from Bredow, The
   (Die Hosen des Ritters von Bredow)
   (EGr), 304
Parade of Planets (Parad planet) (SU), 64
Paradise (Paradisul) (Ro), 320, 329
"Paris" ("Paryz") (Po), 118
Parisian Cobbler (Parizhski sapozhnik)
   (SU), 37, 51
Partisan Stories (Partizanske priče) (Yu),
   192, 215
Partisans: Life Flows Quietly By (Parti-
   zani: Zhivotat si Teche Tiho) (Bu),
   347, 368
Partita for a Wooden Instrument (Partita
   na Instrument Drewniany) (Po), 100,
   110, 123

Party, The (Serata) (Ro), 320, 331, 337
Paso Doble (Ro), 323, 329, 341
Pass to Life, A (SU). *See* Road to Life
Passenger, The (Pasażerka) (Po), 79, 80,
   97, 104, 107, 118
Passion, A (Pasja) (Po), 98, 124
Pavle Pavlović (Yu), 202
Peace of Mind (Spokój) (Po), 101
Peach Thief, The (Kradetsat na Praskovi)
   (Bu), 348–49, 350, 363, 369
Pearl in the Crown, The (Perła w Ko-
   ronie) (Po), 88, 102, 103, 105, 122
Pearls at the Bottom (Perličky na dně)
   (Cz), 145, 157, 161, 176
Peasant On a Bicycle (Seyaninat S Ko-
   woto (Bu), 372
Peasants (Chłopi) (Po), 122
Peasants (Krestiane) (SU), 52
Penal Servitude (Katorga) (SU), 43
Penguin (Pingwin) (Po), 119
Pent-up (Zazidani) (Yu), 198
People From the Alps (Emberek ahava-
   son) (Hu), 232, 266, 268
People of Dimitrovgrad (Dimitrogradisi)
   (Bu), 367
People of the Metro (Lidé z metra) (Cz),
   155
People of the Vistula (Ludzie Wisły)
   (Po), 71
People on a Train (Ludzie z Pociągu)
   (Po), 81, 102, 117
People With Wings (Leute mit Flügeln)
   (EGr), 295, 300
Perinbaba (Cz), 158
Permission to Marry (Vula) (Bu), 362
Personal Diary of a Sinner, Written in
   His Own Hand (Osobisty Pamietnik
   Grzesznika, Przez Niego Samego Spi-
   sany) (Po), 88, 99, 127
Peter and Paula (Cz). *See* Black Peter
Peter the Great (Petr Pervyi) (SU), 53–54
Petrija's Wreath (Petrijin venac) (Yu),
   204, 215, 224–25
Petroiul (Ro), 327
Pharoah, The (Faraon) (Po), 81, 84, 97,
   101, 102, 109, 110, 120
Peasant Tomorrow (Holnap lesz fácán)
   (Hu), 255, 266, 271

FILM INDEX

Philipp the Kind (Filip cel Bun) (Ro), 320, 329, 338
Photography (Fotográfia) (Hu), 267, 270
Picture of Dorian Gray, The (Portret Doriana Greya) (SU), 3, 40, 47
Piece of Sky, A (Un petec de cer) (Ro), 328, 341
Pilate and Others—A Film for Good Friday (Pilatus und Andere—Ein Film für Karfreitag) (WGr), 106
Pilgrimage to the Virgin (Procesi k panence) (Cz), 138
Pill 1 (Pilule 1) (Ro), 330
Pill 2 (Pilule 2) (Ro), 330
Pills for Aurelia (Pigułki Dla Aurelii) (Po), 80, 103, 115–16
Pilots in Pajamas (Piloten im Pyjama) (EGr), 302
Pinching Apples (La mère) (Ro), 315, 327, 328, 334
Pipes (Dýmky) (Cz), 161
Pirosmani (SU), 60
Pit, the Pendulum, and Hope, The (Kyvadlo, jáma a nadĕje) (Cz), 166, 180
Plague, The (Zaraza) (Po), 122
Plan of Great Works (Plan velikikh rabot) (SU), 44
Plastic Jesus (Plastični Isus) (Yu), 201
Player and the Savages, The (Actorul si salbaticii) (Ro), 319, 327, 338
Pliumbum, or A Dangerous Game (Pliumbum, ili Opasnaia igra) (SU), 65
Plum Juice (Sok od šljiva) (Yu), 208
Poacher's Ward, The (Pytlákova schovanka) (Cz), 136
Polan Hotel and its Guests, The (Hotel Polan und seine Gäste) (EGr), 293, 306
Polaniecki Family, The (Rodzina Polanieckich) (Po), 107
Police Inspector Accuses, A (Un Comisar Acuză) (Ro), 319, 329, 338
Polish Complex, The (Kompleks Polski) (Po), 102
Polish Manchester's Pulse (Tętno Polskiego Manchesteru) (Po), 70
Polish Sketch-Book (Album Polski) (Po), 97, 106, 107, 121
Poor Man's Street (Bednata Ulitsa) (Bu), 363, 368
Porto Franco (Ro), 326, 335
Postcard from a Trip, A (Po), 102
Potpourri 1900 (Mofturi 1900) (Ro), 314, 327, 335
Powder and Gasoline (Pudr a benzin) (Cz), 133, 168, 171
Power (Moc) (Yu), 214
Power and the Truth, The (Puterea si adevarul) (Ro), 319, 327, 337
Prague Adamites, The (Pražští Adamité) (Cz), 135
Prague Castle (Na Pražském hradě) (Cz), 156
Prayer (Molba) (SU), 59
Prefab Story (Panelstory) (Cz), 149, 155, 180
Preludiu (Ro), 331
Present Indicative (Jelenidő) (Hu), 260
Priceless Day, A (Ajándék ez a nap) (Hu), 256, 262, 264, 271
Pride (Orgolii) (Ro), 330
Prince, The (Knyazat) (Bu), 351
Prince Behind the Seven Seas, The (Der Prinz hinter den sieben Meeren) (EGr), 307
Princess, The (Adj király katonát!) (Hu), 256, 264, 272
Prishvin's Paper Eyes (Bumazhniya glaza Prishvina) (SU), 66
Private Hurricane (Soukromá vichřice) (Cz), 154, 177
Private Life (Chastnaia zhizn) (SU), 43, 63
Private Vices, Public Virtues (Vizi privati, pubbliche virtù) (Hu), 241, 263, 271
Prizes and Distinctions (Nagrody i Odznaczenia) (Po), 123
Prodigal Father, The (Ro), 338
Professor Hannibal (Hannibál tanár úr) (Hu), 234, 262, 268
Professor Mamlock (EGr), 295, 300
Prolonged Time (Prodloužený čas) (Cz), 159
Prometheus from the Island of Vishevica

You and Other Comrades/The German Story (Du und mancher Kamerad) (EGr), 283, 293, 294, 298
You Are Guilty Too (Ro). *See* Your Share of the Responsibility
You Are Mine, A German Diary (Du bist mein, ein Deutsches Tagesbuch) (EGr), 294, 302
You Only Love Once/The Melody Haunts My Memory (Samo jednom se ljubi) (Yu), 205, 214, 225
Young Chopin, The (Młodość Chopina) (Po), 73, 98, 107, 113
Young Girls, Crazy Guys (Blázni a děvčátka) (Cz), 183
Young Man and the White Whale (Mladý muž a bíla velryba) (Cz), 148, 159
Young Woman of 1914, A (Junge Frau von 1914) (EGr), 286, 287, 291, 302
Your Acquaintance (Vasha znakomaia) (SU), 50

Your Contemporary (Tvoi sovremennik) (SU), 43
Your Money or Your Life (Peniźe nebo život) (Cz), 133, 168, 171
Your Share of the Responsibility/You Are Guilty Too (Partea de ta vina) (Ro), 317, 328, 335
Your Son and Brother (Vash syn i brat) (SU), 44
Your Unknown Brother (EGr), 306, 307
Youth of Maxim, The (Yunost Maksima) (SU), 40, 52
Youth Without Old Age (Ro), 325, 336

Z Day, The (Ro), 323, 329, 341
Zernik Affair, The (Leichensache Zernik) (EGr), 292, 302
Zero City (Gorod zero) (SU), 66
Zillie and Me (Zille und ich) (EGr), 288, 307
Zvenigora (SU), 9, 10, 36, 51